Expert F#

■ ■ ■

Don Syme, Adam Granicz, and
Antonio Cisternino

Apress®

Expert F#

Copyright © 2007 by Don Syme, Adam Granicz, and Antonio Cisternino

ISBN-13: 978-1-59059-850-4

ISBN-10: 1-59059-850-4

eISBN-13: 978-1-4302-0285-1

Printed and bound in the United States of America 9 8 7 6 5 4 3 2

Trademarked names may appear in this book. Rather than use a trademark symbol with every occurrence of a trademarked name, we use the names only in an editorial fashion and to the benefit of the trademark owner, with no intention of infringement of the trademark.

Lead Editors: Jim Huddleston, Jonathan Hassell
Technical Reviewer: Tomáš Petrícek
Editorial Board: Steve Anglin, Ewan Buckingham, Tony Campbell, Gary Cornell, Jonathan Gennick, Jason Gilmore, Kevin Goff, Jonathan Hassell, Matthew Moodie, Joseph Ottinger, Jeffrey Pepper, Ben Renow-Clarke, Dominic Shakeshaft, Matt Wade, Tom Welsh
Project Manager: Sofia Marchant
Copy Editor: Kim Wimpsett
Associate Production Director: Kari Brooks-Copony
Production Editor: Ellie Fountain
Compositor: Susan Glinert
Proofreader: April Eddy
Indexer: Present Day Indexing
Artist: Kinetic Publishing Services, LLC
Cover Designer: Kurt Krames
Manufacturing Director: Tom Debolski

Distributed to the book trade worldwide by Springer-Verlag New York, Inc., 233 Spring Street, 6th Floor, New York, NY 10013. Phone 1-800-SPRINGER, fax 201-348-4505, e-mail orders-ny@springer-sbm.com, or visit http://www.springeronline.com.

For information on translations, please contact Apress directly at 2855 Telegraph Avenue, Suite 600, Berkeley, CA 94705. Phone 510-549-5930, fax 510-549-5939, e-mail info@apress.com, or visit http://www.apress.com.

The information in this book is distributed on an "as is" basis, without warranty. Although every precaution has been taken in the preparation of this work, neither the author(s) nor Apress shall have any liability to any person or entity with respect to any loss or damage caused or alleged to be caused directly or indirectly by the information contained in this work.

The source code for this book is available to readers at http://www.expert-fsharp.com.

*This book is dedicated to the memory of James Huddleston,
the editor at Apress who initiated this book project and encouraged
the authors with his insights, loyalty, enthusiasm, and humor.
Jim passed away in February 2007, an enormous loss
to his family, Apress, and the authors.*

Contents at a Glance

Contents

■CHAPTER 4　Introducing Imperative Programming 69

■CHAPTER 12 Working with Symbolic Representations 317

■CHAPTER 13 Reactive, Asynchronous, and Concurrent Programming 355

Foreword

According to Wikipedia, "Scientists include theoreticians who mainly develop new models to explain existing data and experimentalists who mainly test models by making measurements—though in practice the division between these activities is not clear-cut, and many scientists perform both." The domain-specific language that many scientists use to define their models is mathematics, and since the early days of computing science, the holy grail has been to close the semantic gap between scientific models and executable code as much as possible. It is becoming increasingly clear that all scientists are practicing applied mathematics, and some scientists, such as theoretical physicists, are behaviorally indistinguishable from pure mathematicians. The more we can make programming look like mathematics, the more helpful we make it to scientists and engineers.

John Backus wrote the design for the "IBM Mathematical Formula Translating System," which later became the language FORTAN, in the early 1950s. Still today, FORTRAN is popular within the scientific community for writing efficient numeric computations. The second oldest programming language, Lisp, was invented by John McCarthy in 1958. Like FORTRAN, Lisp was also inspired by mathematics, in this case by Alonzo Church's lambda calculus. Today, Lisp is still popular in the scientific community for writing high-level symbolic computations.

Interestingly, despite their common roots in mathematics, one can consider FORTRAN as the mother of all imperative and object-oriented languages and Lisp as the mother of all declarative languages. Their differences can be accounted to point of view: FORTRAN starts close to the machine with numbers and moves upward toward the mathematics, adding layers of abstraction where possible. Lisp starts with the mathematics with symbols and grows downward to the machine, peeling off layers of abstraction when necessary. But just as the previous quote remarks that the division between theoretical and experimental scientists is not clear-cut, in practice many programming problems require both imperative and declarative aspects.

Functional programming today is a close-kept secret amongst researchers, hackers, and elite programmers at banks and financial institutions, chip designers, graphic artists, and architects. As the grandchildren of Lisp, functional programming languages allow developers to write concise programs that are extremely close to the mathematical models they develop to understand the universe, the human genome, the pricing of options, the location of oil, the serving of advertisements on web pages, or the writing of fault-tolerant distributed systems. However, to the uninformed developer, functional programming seems a cruel and unnatural act, effete mumbo jumbo. The academic and mathematical origins of functional programming plays up in scary big words such as *type inference, structural types, closures, currying, continuations, principal types, monads, inference, impredicative higher-ranked types*, and so on. Even worse, most pure functional languages today are not well integrated with mainstream professional tools and IDEs, libraries, and frameworks.

Imperative programming today is the tool of choice for scientific programmers who simulate fluid dynamics, chemical reactions, mechanical models, and commercial software developers who write operating systems, enterprise applications, and shrink-wrapped software such as word processors, spreadsheets, games, media players, and so on. Imperative languages typically have great tool support, debuggers, profilers, refactoring editors, unit test frameworks, and so on, and large standard numeric libraries that have been perfected over decades by domain experts. As grandchildren of FORTRAN, they focus on machine operations first and build abstractions upward. Compared to functional languages, their syntax is unnecessarily verbose, and they lack modern features emerging from the mathematics of computing itself, such as closures, type inference, anonymous and structural types, and pattern matching. These features are essential for the kind of compositional development that makes functional programming so powerful.

F# is unique amongst both imperative and declarative languages in that it is the golden middle road where these two extremes converge. F# takes the best features of both paradigms and tastefully combines them in a highly productive and elegant language that both scientists and developers identify with. F# makes programmers better mathematicians and mathematicians better programmers.

Erik Meijer

About the Authors

DON SYME is the main designer of F# and has been a functional programmer since 1989. Since joining Microsoft Research in 1998, he has been a seminal contributor to a wide variety of leading-edge projects, including generics in C# and the .NET Common Language Runtime. He received a Ph.D. from the University of Cambridge Computer Laboratory in 1999.

ADAM GRANICZ is the founder of IntelliFactory, a consultancy firm providing F# expertise. He has done research on extensible functional compilers, formal environments, and domain-specific languages. Adam has consulted for EPAM Systems, the leading software outsourcing company in CE Europe, and he is an industry domain expert in gambling, airline and travel package distribution, reverse logistics, and insurance/health care. He has a M.Sc. from the California Institute of Technology.

ANTONIO CISTERNINO is assistant professor in the Computer Science Department of the University of Pisa. His primary research is on meta-programming and domain-specific languages on virtual-machine-based execution environments. He has been active in the .NET community since 2001, and he recently developed annotated C#, an extension of C#, and Robotics4.NET, a framework for programming robots with .NET. Antonio has a Ph.D. in computer science from the University of Pisa.

About the Technical Reviewer

TOMÁŠ PETRÍCEK is a graduate student of Charles University in Prague. Tomas is active in the .NET community, and he has been Microsoft MVP since 2004, awarded for his technical articles and presentations. Recently, he spent three months as an intern at Microsoft Research working with the F# team, and he also developed the F# WebTools project. His articles about F# and various other topics can be found at his website at `http://tomasp.net`.

Acknowledgments

We would like to thank Jonathan Hassell, our editor, and Sofia Marchant, our project manager, for their guidance and flexible schedules to keep us on track for publication. Likewise, we thank Tomáš Petrícek, the primary technical reviewer, whose comments were invaluable in ensuring that the book is a comprehensive and reliable source of information. We also thank Chris Barwick, our original technical reviewer, and Dominic Cooney and Joel Pobar, who both helped with planning the early structure of the book. Any remaining mistakes are of course our own responsibility.

The various drafts of the chapters were read and commented on by many people, and the book has benefited greatly from their input. In particular, we would like to thank Ashley Feniello whose meticulous reviews have proved invaluable and uncovered numerous errors and inconsistencies, as well as John Bates, Nikolaj Bjorner, Laurent Le Brun, Richard Black, Chris Brumme, Jason Bock, Dominic Cooney, Can Erten, Thore Graepel, György Gyurica, Jon Hagen, Jon Harrop, Andrew Herbert, Ralf Herbrich, Jason Hogg, Anders Janmyr, Paulo Janotti, Pouya Larjani, Julien Laugel, James Margetson, Richard Mortier, Enrique Nell, Gregory Neverov, Ravi Pandya, Robert Pickering, Darren Platt, Joel Pobar, Andy Ray, Mark Shields, Guido Scatena, Mark Staples, Phil Trelford, Dave Waterworth, Dave Wecker, and Onno Zoeter, to name but a few.

We also thank Microsoft Research, without which neither F# nor this book would have been possible, and we are very grateful for the help and support given to F# by other language designers, including Anders Hejlsberg, Xavier Leroy, Simon Marlow, Erik Meijer, Malcom Newey, Martin Odersky, Simon Peyton Jones, Mads Torgersen, and Phil Wadler.

Finally, we thank our families and loved ones for their long-suffering patience. It would have been impossible to complete this book without their unceasing support.

CHAPTER 1

Introduction

F# is a typed functional programming language for the .NET Framework. It combines the succinctness, expressivity, and compositionality of typed functional programming with the runtime support, libraries, interoperability, tools, and object model of .NET. Our aim in this book is to help you become an expert in using F# and the .NET Framework.

Functional programming has long inspired researchers, students, and programmers alike with its simplicity and expressive power. Applied functional programming is booming: a new generation of typed functional languages is reaching maturity; some functional language constructs have been integrated into languages such as C#, Python, and Visual Basic; and there is now a substantial pool of expertise in the pragmatic application of functional programming techniques. There is also strong evidence that functional programming offers significant productivity gains in important application areas such as data access, financial modeling, statistical analysis, machine learning, software verification, and bio-informatics. More recently, functional programming is part of the rise of declarative programming models, especially in the data query, concurrent, reactive, and parallel programming domains.

F# differs from many functional languages in that it embraces imperative and object-oriented (OO) programming. It also provides a missing link between compiled and dynamic languages, combining the idioms and programming styles typical of dynamic languages with the performance and robustness of a compiled language. The F# designers have adopted a design philosophy that allows you to take the best and most productive aspects of these paradigms and combine them while still placing primary emphasis on functional programming techniques. This book will help you understand the power that F# offers through this combination.

F# and .NET offer an approach to computing that will continue to surprise and delight, and mastering functional programming techniques will help you become a better programmer regardless of the language you use. There has been no better time to learn functional programming, and F# offers the best route to learn and apply functional programming on the .NET platform.

The lead designer of the F# language, Don Syme, is one of the authors of this book. This book benefits from his authority on F# and .NET and from all the authors' years of experience with F# and other programming languages.

The Genesis of F#

F# began in 2002 when Don Syme and others at Microsoft Research decided to ensure that the "ML" approach to pragmatic but theoretically-based language design found a high-quality expression for the .NET platform. The project was closely associated with the design and implementation of Generics for the .NET Common Language Runtime. The first major pre-release of F# was in 2005.

F# shares a core language with the programming language OCaml, and in some ways it can be considered an "OCaml for .NET." F# would not exist without OCaml, which in turn comes from the ML family of programming languages, which dates back to 1974. F# also draws from Haskell, particularly with regard to two advanced language features called *sequence expressions* and *workflows*. There are still strong connections between the designers of these languages and overlap in their user communities. The rationale for the design decisions taken during the development of F# is documented on the F# project website.

Despite the similarities to OCaml and Haskell, programming with F# is really quite different. In particular, the F# approach to type inference, OO programming, and dynamic language techniques is substantially different from all other mainstream functional languages. Programming in F# tends to be more object-oriented than in other functional languages. Programming also tends to be more flexible. F# embraces .NET techniques such as dynamic loading, dynamic typing, and reflection, and it adds techniques such as expression quotation and active patterns. We cover these topics in this book and use them in many application areas.

F# also owes a lot to the designers of .NET, whose vision of language interoperability between C++, Visual Basic, and "the language that eventually became C#" is still rocking the computer industry today. Today F# draws much from the broader community around the Common Language Infrastructure (CLI). This standard is implemented by the Microsoft .NET Framework, Mono, and Microsoft's client-side execution environment Silverlight. F# is able to leverage libraries and techniques developed by Microsoft, the broader .NET community, and the highly active open source community centered around Mono. These include hundreds of important libraries and major implementation stacks such as language-integrated queries using Microsoft's LINQ.

About This Book

This book is structured in two halves: Chapters 2 to 10 deal with the F# language and basic techniques and libraries associated with the .NET Framework. Chapters 11 to 19 deal with applied techniques ranging from building applications through to software engineering and design issues.

Throughout this book we address both *programming constructs* and *programming techniques*. Our approach is driven by examples: we show code, and then we explain it. Frequently we give reference material describing the constructs used in the code and related constructs you might use in similar programming tasks. We've found that an example-driven approach helps bring out the essence of a language and how the language constructs work together. You can find a complete syntax guide in the appendix, and we encourage you to reference this while reading the book.

Chapter 2, *Getting Started with F# and .NET*, begins by introducing F# Interactive, a tool you can use to interactively evaluate F# expressions and declarations and that we encourage you to use while reading this book. In this chapter you will use F# Interactive to explore some basic F# and .NET constructs, and we introduce many concepts that are described in more detail in later chapters.

Chapter 3, *Introducing Functional Programming*, focuses on the basic constructs of typed functional programming, including arithmetic and string primitives, type inference, tuples, lists, options, function values, aggregate operators, recursive functions, function pipelines, function compositions, pattern matching, sequences, and some simple examples of type definitions.

Chapter 4, *Introducing Imperative Programming*, introduces the basic constructs used for imperative programming in F#. Although the use of imperative programming is often minimized with F#, it is used heavily in some programming tasks such as scripting. You will learn about loops, arrays, mutability mutable records, locals and reference cells, the imperative .NET collections, exceptions, and the basics of .NET I/O.

Chapter 5, *Mastering Types and Generics*, covers types in more depth, especially the more advanced topics of generic type variables and subtyping. You will learn techniques you can use to make your code generic and how to understand and clarify type error messages reported by the F# compiler.

Chapter 6, *Working with Objects and Modules*, introduces object-oriented programming in F#. You will learn how to define concrete object types to implement data structures, how to use object-oriented notational devices such as method overloading with your F# types, and how to create objects with mutable state. You will then learn how to define object interface types and a range of techniques to implement objects, including object expressions, constructor functions, delegation, and implementation inheritance.

Chapter 7, *Encapsulating and Packaging Your Code*, shows the techniques you can use to hide implementation details and package code fragments together into .NET assemblies. You will also learn how to use the F# command-line compiler tools and how to build libraries that can be shared across multiple projects. Finally, we cover some of the techniques you can use to build installers and deploy F# applications.

Chapter 8, *Mastering F#: Common Techniques*, looks at a number of important coding patterns in F#, including how to customize the hashing and comparison semantics of new type definitions, how to precompute and cache intermediary results, and how to create lazy values. You'll also learn how to clean up resources using the .NET idioms for disposing of objects, how to avoid stack overflows through the use of tail calls, and how to subscribe to .NET events and publish new .NET-compatible events from F# code.

Chapter 9, *Introducing Language-Oriented Programming*, looks at what is effectively a fourth programming paradigm supported by F#: the manipulation of structured data and language fragments using a variety of concrete and abstract representations. In this chapter you'll learn how to use XML as a concrete language format, how to convert XML to typed abstract syntax representations, how to design and work with abstract syntax representations, and how to use F# active patterns to hide representations. You will also learn three advanced features of F# programming: F# computation expressions (also called *workflows*), F# reflection, and F# quotations. These are used in later chapters, particularly Chapters 13 and 15.

Chapter 10, *Using the F# and .NET Libraries*, gives an overview of the libraries most frequently used with F#, including the .NET Framework and the extra libraries added by F#.

Chapters 11 to 19 deal with applied topics in F# programming. Chapter 11, *Working with Windows Forms and Controls*, shows how to design and build graphical user interface applications using F# and the .NET Windows Forms library. We also show how to design new controls using standard object-oriented design patterns and how to script applications using the controls offered by the .NET libraries directly.

Chapter 12, *Working with Symbolic Representations*, applies some of the techniques from Chapter 9 and Chapter 11 in two case studies. The first is symbolic expression differentiation and rendering, an extended version of a commonly used case study in symbolic programming. The second is verifying circuits with propositional logic, where you will learn how to use symbolic techniques to represent digital circuits, specify properties of these circuits, and verify these properties using binary decision diagrams (BDDs).

Chapter 13, *Reactive, Asynchronous, and Concurrent Programming*, shows how you can use F# for programs that have multiple logical threads of execution and that react to inputs and messages. You will first learn how to construct basic background tasks that support progress reporting and cancellation. You will then learn how to use F# asynchronous workflows to build scalable, massively concurrent reactive programs that make good use of the .NET thread pool and other .NET concurrency-related resources. This chapter concentrates on message-passing techniques that avoid or minimize the use of shared memory. However, you will also learn the fundamentals of concurrent programming with shared memory using .NET.

Chapter 14, *Building Web Applications*, shows how to use F# with ASP.NET to write server-side scripts that respond to web requests. You will learn how to serve web page content using ASP.NET controls. We also describe how open source projects such as the F# Web Toolkit let you write both parts of Ajax-style client/server applications in F#.

Chapter 15, *Working with Data*, looks at several dimensions of querying and accessing data from F#. You'll first learn how functional programming relates to querying in-memory data structures, especially via the LINQ paradigm supported by .NET and F#. You'll then look at how to use F# in conjunction with relational databases, particularly through the use of the ADO.NET and LINQ-to-SQL technologies that are part of the .NET Framework.

Chapter 16, *Lexing and Parsing*, shows how to deal with additional concrete language formats beyond those already discussed in Chapter 9. In particular, you will learn how to use the F# tools for generating lexers and parsers from declarative specifications and how to use combinator techniques to build declarative specifications of binary format readers.

Chapter 17, *Interoperating with C and COM*, shows how to use F# and .NET to interoperate with software that exports a native API. You will learn more about the .NET Common Language Runtime itself, how memory management works, and how to use the .NET Platform Invoke mechanisms from F#.

Chapter 18, *Debugging and Testing F# Programs*, shows the primary tools and techniques you can use to eliminate bugs from your F# programs. You will learn how to use the .NET and Visual Studio debugging tools with F#, how to use F# Interactive for exploratory development and testing, and how to use the NUnit testing framework with F# code.

Chapter 19, *Designing F# Libraries*, gives our advice on methodology and design issues for writing libraries in F#. You will learn how to write "vanilla" .NET libraries that make relatively little use of F# constructs at their boundaries in order to appear as natural as possible to other .NET programmers. We will then cover functional programming design methodology and how to combine it with the object-oriented design techniques specified by the standard .NET Framework design guidelines.

The appendix, *F# Brief Language Guide*, gives a compact guide to all key F# language constructs and the key operators used in F# programming.

Because of space limitations, we have only partially addressed some important aspects of programming with F#. It is easy to access hundreds of other libraries with F# that are not covered in this book, including Managed DirectX, Windows Presentation Foundation (WPF), Windows Communication Foundation (WCF), Windows Workflow Foundation (WWF), Irrlicht, the Mono Unix bindings, the Firebird.NET database bindings, several advanced SQL Server APIs, and mathematical libraries such as Extreme Optimization and NMath. There are also hundreds of open-source projects related to .NET programming, some with a specific focus on F#. F# can also be used with alternative implementations of the CLI such as Mono and Silverlight, topics we address only tangentially in this book. Quotation meta-programming is described only briefly in Chapter 9, and some topics in functional programming such as the design and implementation of applicative data structures are not covered at all. Also, some software engineering issues such as performance tuning are largely omitted. Many of these topics are addressed in more detail in *Foundations of F#* by Robert Pickering, also published by Apress.

Who This Book Is For

We assume you have some programming knowledge and experience. If you don't have experience with F# already, you'll still be familiar with many of the ideas it uses. However, you may also encounter some new and challenging ideas. For example, if you've been taught that object-oriented (OO) design and programming are the only ways to think about software, then programming in F# may be a reeducation. F# fully supports OO development, but F# programming combines elements of both functional and OO design. OO patterns such as implementation inheritance play a less prominent role than you may have previously experienced. Chapter 6 covers many of these topics in depth.

The following notes will help you set a path through this book depending on your background:

C++, C#, Java, and Visual Basic: If you've programmed in a typed OO language, you may find functional programming, type inference, and F# type parameters take a while to get used to. However, you'll soon see how to use these to make you a more productive programmer. Be sure to read Chapters 2, 3, 5, and 6 carefully.

Python, Scheme, Ruby, and dynamically typed languages: F# is statically typed and type-safe. As a result, F# development environments can discover many errors while you program, and the F# compiler can more aggressively optimize your code. If you've primarily programmed in an untyped language such as Python, Scheme, or Ruby, you may think that static types are inflexible and wordy. However, F# static types are relatively nonintrusive, and you'll find the language strikes a balance between expressivity and type safety. You'll also see how type inference lets you recover succinctness despite working in a statically typed language.

Be sure to read Chapters 2 to 6 carefully, paying particular attention to the ways in which types are used and defined.

Typed functional languages: If you are familiar with Haskell, OCaml, or Standard ML, you will find the core of F# readily familiar, with some syntactic differences. However, F# embraces .NET, including the .NET object model, and it may take you a while to learn how to use objects effectively and how to use the .NET libraries themselves. This is best done by learning how F# approaches OO programming in Chapters 6 to 8 and then exploring the applied .NET programming material in Chapters 10 to 19, referring to earlier chapters where necessary. Haskell programmers will also need to learn the F# approach to imperative programming, described in Chapter 4, since many .NET libraries require a degree of imperative coding to create, configure, connect, and dispose of objects.

We strongly encourage you to use this book in conjunction with a development environment that supports F# directly, such as Visual Studio 2005 or Visual Studio 2008. In particular, the interactive type inference in the F# Visual Studio environment is exceptionally helpful for understanding F# code: with a simple mouse movement you can examine the inferred types of the sample programs. These types play a key role in understanding the behavior of the code.

■**Note** You can download and install F# from `http://research.microsoft.com/fsharp`. Your primary source for information on the aspects of F# explored in this book is `http://www.expert-fsharp.com`, and you can download all the code samples used in this book from `http://www.expert-fsharp.com/CodeSamples`. As with all books, it is inevitable that minor errors may have crept into the text. Adjustments may also be needed to make the best use of versions of F# beyond version 1.9.2, which was used for this book. An active errata and list of updates will be published at `http://www.expert-fsharp.com/Updates`.

CHAPTER 2

∎∎∎

Getting Started with F# and .NET

In this chapter, we cover some simple interactive programming with F# and .NET. By now you should have downloaded and installed a version of the F# distribution as described in Chapter 1. In the sections that follow, we use F# Interactive, a tool you can use to execute fragments of F# code interactively and a convenient way to explore the language. Along the way, you'll see examples of the most important F# language constructs and many important libraries.

Creating Your First F# Program

Listing 2-1 shows your first complete F# program. You may not follow it all at first glance, but we explain it piece by piece after the listing.

Listing 2-1. *Analyzing a String for Duplicate Words*

```
#light
/// Analyze a string for duplicate words
let wordCount text =
    let words = String.split [' '] text
    let wordSet = Set.of_list words
    let nWords = words.Length
    let nDups  = words.Length - wordSet.Count
    (nWords,nDups)

let showWordCount text =
    let nWords,nDups = wordCount text
    printfn "--> %d words in the text" nWords
    printfn "--> %d duplicate words" nDups
```

You can paste this program into F# Interactive, which you can start either by using the command line, by running fsi.exe from the F# distribution, or by using an interactive environment such as Visual Studio. If running from the command line, remember to enter ; ; to terminate the interactive entry:

```
C:\Users\dsyme\Desktop> fsi.exe
MSR F# Interactive, (c) Microsoft Corporation, All Rights Reserved

NOTE: See 'fsi --help' for flags
NOTE:
NOTE: Commands: #r <string>;;     reference (dynamically load) the given DLL.
NOTE:            #I <string>;;     add the given search path for referenced DLLs.

NOTE:            #use <string>;;   accept input from the given file.
NOTE:            #load <string> ...<string>;;
NOTE:                              load the given file(s) as a single unit.
NOTE:            #quit;;           exit.
NOTE:
NOTE: Visit the F# website at http://research.microsoft.com/fsharp.
NOTE: Bug reports to fsbugs@microsoft.com. Enjoy!

> <paste in the earlier program here> ;;
val wordCount : string -> int * int
val showWordCount : string -> unit
```

Here F# Interactive has reported the type of the functions wordCount and showWordCount (you'll learn more about types in a moment). The keyword val stands for *value*; in F# programming, functions are just values, a topic we return to in Chapter 3. Also, sometimes F# Interactive will show a little more information than we show in this book (such as some internal details of the generated values); if you're trying out these code snippets, then you can just ignore that additional information. For now let's just use the wordCount function interactively:

```
> let (nWords,nDups) = wordCount "All the king's horses and all the king's men";;
val nWords : int
val nDups  : int

> nWords;;
val it : int = 9

> nDups;;
val it : int = 2

> nWords - nDups;;
val it : int = 7
```

This code shows the results of executing the function wordCount and binding its two results to the names nWords and nDups, respectively. You can examine the values by just entering each as a single expression, which assigns the result to a value called it and displays the value.

Examining the values shows that the given text contains nine words: two duplicates and seven words that occur only once. showWordCount prints the results instead of returning them as a value:

```
> showWordCount "Couldn't put Humpty together again";;
--> 5 words in the text
--> 0 duplicate words
```

From the output you can more or less see what the code does. Now that you've done that, we'll go through the program in detail.

■**Tip** You can start F# Interactive in Visual Studio by selecting Tools ➤ Add-in Manager and then selecting F# Interactive for Visual Studio in the Add-in Manager dialog box. A tool window will then appear, and you can send text to F# Interactive by selecting the text and pressing Alt+Return.

Turning On the Lightweight Syntax Option

The first line of the file simply turns on the F# lightweight syntax option. This option is assumed throughout this book; in other words, you should have #light at the head of all your source files:

```
#light
```

This option allows you to write code that looks and feels simpler by omitting recurring F# tokens such as in, done, ; (semicolon), ;; (double semicolon), begin, and end. The option instructs the F# compiler and F# Interactive to use the indentation of F# code to determine where constructs start and finish. The indentation rules are very intuitive, and we discuss them in the Appendix, which is a guide to the F# syntax. Listing 2-2 shows a fully qualified version of the first function.

Listing 2-2. *A Version of the wordCount Function That Doesn't Use the #light Syntax Option*

```
/// Analyze a string for duplicate words
let wordCount text =
    let words = String.split [' '] text in
    let wordSet = Set.of_list words in
    let nWords = words.Length in
    let nDups  = words.Length - wordSet.Count in
    (nWords,nDups)
```

Double semicolons (;;) are still required to terminate entries to F# Interactive even when using the #light syntax option. However, if you're using an interactive development environment such as Visual Studio, then the environment typically adds this automatically when code is selected and executed. We show the double semicolons in the interactive code snippets used this book, though not in the larger samples.

■Tip We recommend that you use four-space indentation for F# code. Tab characters cannot be used in #light code, and the F# tools will give an error if they are encountered. In Visual Studio, selecting Tools ➤ Options reveals an Options tab for controlling the options used by F# Interactive at start-up; for example, you can use --light to turn on the lightweight syntax option automatically on start-up.

Documenting Code Using XMLDocs

The first real line of the program in Listing 2-1 is not code but a comment:

```
/// Analyze a string for duplicate words
```

Comments are either lines starting with // or blocks enclosed by (* and *). Comment lines beginning with three slashes (///) are XMLDoc comments and can, if necessary, include extra XML tags and markup. The comments from a program can be collected into a single .xml file and processed with additional tools or can be converted immediately to HTML by the F# command-line compiler (fsc.exe). We cover using the F# command-line compiler in more detail in Chapter 7.

■Tip The F# command-line compiler (fsc.exe) options for generating HTML documentation are --generate-html and --html-output-directory. To generate an XMLDoc file, use -doc.

Understanding Scope and Using "let"

The next two lines of the program in Listing 2-1 introduce the start of the definition of the function wordCount and define the local value words, both using the keyword let:

```
let wordCount text =
    let words = ...
```

let is the single most important keyword you'll use in F# programming: it is used to define data, computed values, functions, and procedures. The left of a let binding is often a simple identifier but can also be a pattern. (See the "Using Tuples" section for some simple examples.) It can also be a function name followed by a list of argument names, as in the case of wordCount, which takes one argument: text. The right of a let binding (after the =) is an expression.

Local values such as words and wordCount can't be accessed outside their *scope*. In the case of variables defined using let, the scope of the value is the entire expression that follows the definition, though not the definition itself. Here are two examples of invalid definitions that try to access variables outside their scope. As you can see, let definitions follow a sequential, top-down order, which helps ensure that programs are well-formed and free from many bugs related to uninitialized values:

```
let badDefinition1 =
    let words = String.split text
                          ^^^^  error: text is not defined
    let text = "We three kings"
    words.Length

let badDefinition2 = badDefinition2+1
                     ^^^^^^^^^^^^^^  error: badDefinition2 is not defined
```

Sometimes it is convenient to write `let` definitions on a single line, even when using the `#light` syntax option. You can do this by separating the expression that follows a definition from the definition itself using `in`. For example:

```
let powerOfFour n =
    let nSquared = n * n in nSquared * nSquared
```

Here's an example use of the function:

```
> powerOfFour 3;;
val it : int = 81
```

Indeed, `let pat = expr1 in expr2` is the true primitive construct in the language, where *pat* stands for *pattern* and *expr1* and *expr2* stand for *expressions*. The `#light` syntax option simply provides a veneer that lets you optionally omit the `in` if *expr2* is column-aligned with the `let` keyword on a subsequent line, and a preprocessing stage inserts the `in` token for you.

Within function definitions, values can be *outscoped* by declaring another value of the same name. For example, the following function computes (n*n*n*n)+2:

```
let powerOfFourPlusTwo n =
    let n = n * n
    let n = n * n
    let n = n + 2
    n
```

This code is equivalent to the following:

```
let powerOfFourPlusTwo n =
    let n1 = n * n
    let n2 = n1 * n1
    let n3 = n2 + 2
    n3
```

Outscoping a value doesn't change the original value; it just means the name of the value is no longer accessible from the current scope.

Because let bindings are just one kind of expression, you can use them in a nested fashion. For example:

```
let powerOfFourPlusTwoTimesSix n =
    let n3 =
        let n1 = n * n
        let n2 = n1 * n1
        n2 + 2
    let n4 = n3 * 6
    n4
```

In the previous example, n1 and n2 are values defined locally by let bindings within the expression that defines n3. These local values are not available for use outside their scope. For example, the following code gives an error:

```
let invalidFunction n =
    let n3 =
        let n1 = n + n
        let n2 = n1 * n1
        n1 * n2
    let n4 = n1 + n2 + n3      // Error! n3 is in scope, but n1 and n2 are not!
    n4
```

Local scoping is used for many purposes in F# programming, especially to hide implementation details that you don't want revealed outside your functions or other objects. We cover this topic in more detail in Chapter 7.

VALUES AND IMMUTABILITY

In other languages, a local *value* is called a local *variable*. However, in F# you can't change the immediate value of locals after they've been initialized, unless the local is explicitly marked as mutable, a topic we return to in Chapter 4. For this reason, F# programmers and the language specification tend to prefer the term *value* to *variable*.

As you'll see in Chapter 4, data indirectly referenced by a local value can still be mutable even if the local value is not; for example, a local value that is a handle to a hash table cannot be changed to refer to a different table, but the contents of the table itself can be changed by invoking operations that add and remove elements from the table. However, many values and data structures in F# programming are *completely immutable*; in other words, neither the local value nor its contents can be changed through external mutation. These are usually just called *immutable values*. For example, all basic .NET types such as integers, strings, and System.DateTime values are immutable, and the F# library defines a range of immutable data structures such as Set and Map, based on binary trees.

Immutable values bring many advantages. At first it might seem strange to define values you can't change. However, knowing a value is immutable means you rarely need to think about the *object identity* of these values—you can pass them to routines and know they won't be mutated. You can also pass them between multiple threads without worrying about unsafe concurrent access to the values, discussed in Chapter 14. You can find out more about programming with immutable data structures at http://www.expert-fsharp.com/Topics/FunctionalDataStructures.

Understanding Types

F# is a typed language, so it's reasonable to ask what the *type* of wordCount is, and indeed F# Interactive has shown it already:

```
val wordCount : string -> int * int
```

This indicates that wordCount takes one argument of type string and returns int * int, which is F#'s way of saying "a pair of integers." The keyword val stands for *value*, and the symbol -> represents a function. No explicit type has been given in the program for wordCount or its argument text, because the full type for wordCount has been "inferred" from its definition. We discuss type inference further in the "What Is Type Inference?" sidebar and in more detail in later chapters.

Types are significant in both F# and .NET programming more generally for reasons that range from performance to coding productivity and interoperability. Types are used to help structure libraries, to guide the programmer through the complexity of an API and to place constraints on code to ensure it can be implemented efficiently. However, unlike many other typed languages, the type system of F# is both simple and powerful because it uses orthogonal, composable constructs such as tuples and functions to form succinct and descriptive types. Furthermore, type inference means you almost never have to write types in your program, though doing so can be useful. Table 2-1 shows some of the most important type constructors. We discuss all these types in more detail in Chapter 3 and Chapter 4.

Table 2-1. *Some Important Types, Type Constructors, and Their Corresponding Values*

Family of Types	Examples	Description
int	int	32-bit integers. For example: -3, 0, 127.
type option	int option, option<int>	A value of the given type or the special value None. For example: Some 3, Some "3", None.
type list	int list, list<int>	An immutable linked list of values of the given type. All elements of the list must have the same type. For example: [ ], [3;2;1].
type1 -> *type2*	int -> string	A function type, representing a value that will accept values of the first type and compute results of the second type. For example: (fun x -> x+1).
type1 * ... * *typeN*	int * string	A tuple type, such as a pair, triple, or larger combination of types. For example: (1,"3"), (3,2,1).
type []	int[]	An array type, indicating a flat, fixed-size mutable collection of values of type *type*.
unit	unit	A type containing a single value (), akin to void in many imperative languages.
'a, 'b	'a, 'b, 'Key, 'Value	A variable type, used in generic code.

Some type constructors such as list and option are *generic*, which means they can be used to form a range of types by instantiating the generic variables, such as int list, string list, int list list, and so on. Instantiations of generic types can be written using either prefix notation (such as int list) or postfix notation (such as list<int>). Variable types such as 'a are placeholders for any type. We discuss generics and variable types in more detail in Chapter 3 and Chapter 5.

WHAT IS TYPE INFERENCE?

Type inference works by analyzing your code to collect constraints. These are collected over the scope of particular parts of your program, such as each file for the F# command-line compiler and each chunk entered in F# Interactive. These constraints must be consistent, thus ensuring your program is well-typed, and you'll get a type error if not. Constraints are collected from top to bottom, left to right, and outside in, which is important because long identifier lookups, method overloading, and some other elements of the language are resolved using the normalized form of the constraint information available at the place where each construct is used.

Type inference also *automatically generalizes* your code, which means that when your code is reusable and generic in certain obvious ways, then it will be given a suitable generic type without you needing to write the generic type down. Automatic generalization is the key to succinct but reusable typed programming. We discuss automatic generalization in Chapter 5.

Calling Functions

Functions are at the heart of most F# programming, and it's not surprising that the first thing you do is call a library function, in this case, String.split:

```
let wordCount text =
    let words = String.split [' '] text
```

The function String.split takes two arguments. F# Interactive reveals the type of String.split as follows:

```
> String.split;;
val it: char list -> string -> string list
```

To understand this type, let's first investigate String.split by running F# Interactive:

```
> String.split [' '] "hello world";;
val it : string list = [ "hello"; "world" ]

> String.split ['a';'e';'i';'o';'u'] "hello world";;
val it : string list = [ "h"; "ll"; " w"; "rld" ]
```

You can see that String.split breaks the given text into words using the given characters as delimiters. The first argument is the list of delimiters, and the second is the string to split.

String.split takes two arguments, but the arguments are given in a style where the arguments come sequentially after the function name, separated by spaces. This is quite common in F# coding and is mostly a stylistic choice, but it also means functions can be *partially applied* to fewer arguments, leaving a residue function, which is a useful technique you'll look at more closely in Chapter 3.

In the earlier code, you can also see examples of the following:

- Literal characters such as ' 'and 'a'

- Literal strings such as "hello world"

- Literal lists of characters such as ['a';'e';'i';'o';'u']

- Literal lists of strings such as the returned value ["hello"; "world"]

We cover literals and lists in detail in Chapter 3. Lists are an important data structure in F#, and you'll see many examples of their use in this book.

WHAT IS "STRING" IN "STRING.SPLIT"?

The name String references the F# module Microsoft.FSharp.Core.String in the F# library. This contains a set of simple operations associated with values of the string type. It is common for types to have a separate module that contains associated operations. All modules under the Microsoft.FSharp namespaces Core, Collections, Text, and Control can be referenced by simple one-word prefixes, such as String.split and open String. Other modules under these namespaces include List, Option, and Array.

Since String is a standard .NET type, you can also use functions provided by the .NET Framework runtime located under System.String and other important namespaces such as System.Text. RegularExpresions. Throughout this book, we use both the .NET Framework library and the F# additions extensively. We give an overview of the most commonly used .NET and F# libraries in Chapter 10.

Using Data Structures

The next portion of the code is as follows:

```
let wordCount text =
    let words = String.split [' '] text
    let wordSet = Set.of_list words
```

This gives you your first taste of using data structures from F# code, and the last of these lines lies at the heart of the computation performed by wordCount. It uses the function Set.of_list from the F# library to convert the given words to a concrete data structure that is, in effect, much like the mathematical notion of a set, though internally it is implemented using a data structure based on trees. You can see the results of converting data to a set by using F# Interactive:

```
> Set.of_list ["b";"a";"b";"b";"c" ];;
val it : Set<string> = set [ "a"; "b"; "c" ]

> Set.to_list (Set.of_list ["abc"; "ABC"]);;
val it : string list = [ "ABC"; "abc" ]
```

Here you can see several things:

- F# Interactive prints the contents of structured values such as lists and sets.

- Duplicate elements are removed by the conversion.

- The elements in the set are ordered.

- The default ordering on strings used by sets is case sensitive.

Using Properties and the Dot-Notation

The next two lines of the wordCount function compute the result we're after—the number of duplicate words. This is done by using two properties, Length and Count, of the values you've computed:

```
let nWords = words.Length
let nDups = words.Length - wordSet.Count
```

F# performs resolution on property names at compile time (or interactively when using F# Interactive, where there is no distinction between compile time and run time). This is done using compile-time knowledge of the type of the expression on the left of the dot—in this case, words and wordSet. Sometimes a type annotation is required in your code in order to resolve the potential ambiguity among possible property names. For example, the following code uses a type annotation to note that inp refers to a list. This allows the F# type system to infer that Length refers to a property associated with values of the list type:

```
let length (inp : 'a list) = inp.Length
```

Here the 'a indicates that the length function is generic; that is, it can be used with any type of list. We cover generic code in more detail in Chapter 3 and Chapter 5. Type annotations can be useful documentation and, when needed, should generally be added at the point where a variable is declared.

As you can see from the use of the dot-notation, F# is both a functional language and an object-oriented language. In particular, properties are a kind of *member*, a general term used for any functionality associated with a type or value. Members referenced by prefixing a type name are called *static members*, and members associated with a particular value of a type are called *instance members*; in other words, instance members are accessed through an object on the left of the dot. We discuss the distinction between values, properties, and methods later in this chapter, and we discuss members in full in Chapter 6.

Sometimes explicitly named functions play the role of members. For example, we could have written the earlier code as follows:

```
let nWords = List.length words
let nDups = List.length words - Set.size wordSet
```

You will see both styles in F# code. Some F# libraries don't use members at all or use them only sparingly. However, judiciously using members and properties can greatly reduce the need for trivial get/set functions in libraries, can make client code much more readable, and can allow programmers who use environments such as Visual Studio to easily and intuitively explore the primary features of libraries they write.

If your code does not contain enough type annotations to resolve the dot-notation, you will see an error such as the following:

```
> let length inp = inp.Length;;

  let length inp = inp.Length;;
  ----------------^^^

stdin(1,17): error: Lookup on object of indeterminate type. A type annotation may
be needed prior to this program point to constrain the type of the object. This
may allow the lookup to be resolved.
```

You can resolve this simply by adding a type annotation as shown earlier.

Using Tuples

The final part of the wordCount function returns the results nWords and nDups as a *tuple*.

```
let nWords = words.Length
let nDups  = words.Length - wordSet.Size
(nWords,nDups)
```

Tuples are the simplest but perhaps most useful of all F# data structures. A tuple expression is simply a number of expressions grouped together to form a new expression:

```
let site1 = ("www.cnn.com",10)
let site2 = ("news.bbc.com",5)
let site3 = ("www.msnbc.com",4)
let sites = (site1,site2,site3)
```

Here the inferred types of site1 and sites are as follows:

```
val site1 : string * int
val sites : (string * int) * (string * int) * (string * int)
```

Tuples can be decomposed into their constituent components in two ways. For pairs—that is, tuples with two elements—you can explicitly call the functions fst and snd, which, as their abbreviated names imply, extract the first and second parts of the pair:

```
> fst site1
val it : string = "www.cnn.com"

> let relevance = snd site1
val relevance : int

> relevance;;
val it : int = 10
```

The functions fst and snd are defined in the F# library and are always available for use by F# programs—here are their simple definitions:

```
let fst (a,b) = a
let snd (a,b) = b
```

More commonly tuples are decomposed using *patterns*, as in the following code:

```
let url,relevance = site1
let site1,site2,site3 = sites
```

In this case, the names in the tuples on the left of the definitions are bound to the respective elements of the tuple value on the right, so again url gets the value "www.cnn.com" and relevance gets the value 10.

Tuple values are typed, and strictly speaking there are an arbitrary number of families of tuple types, one for pairs holding two values, one for triples holding three values, and so on. This means if you try to use a triple where a pair is expected, then you'll get a type-checking error before your code is run:

```
> let a,b = (1,2,3);;
error: this pattern matches values of type 'int * int' but is here used
with values of type 'int * int * int'. The tuples have different lengths.
```

Tuples are often used to return multiple values from functions, as in the wordCount example earlier. They are also often used for multiple arguments to functions, and frequently the tupled output of one function becomes the tupled input of another function. Here is an example that shows a different way of writing the showWordCount function defined and used earlier:

```
let showResults (nWords,nDups) =
    printfn "--> %d words in the text" nWords
    printfn "--> %d duplicate words" nDups
let showWordCount text = showResults (wordCount text)
```

The function showResults accepts a pair as input, decomposed into nWords and nDups, matching the results of wordCount.

> **VALUES AND OBJECTS**
>
> In F# everything is a *value*. In some other languages everything is an *object*. In practice, you can use the words largely interchangeably, though F# programmers tend to reserve *object* for special kinds of values:
>
> - Values whose observable properties change as the program executes, usually through the explicit mutation of underlying in-memory data or through external state changes
>
> - Values that refer to data or state that reveal an identity, such as a unique integer stamp or the underlying .NET object identity, where that identity may differ from otherwise identical values
>
> - Values that can be queried to reveal additional functionality, through the use of casts, conversions, and interfaces
>
> F# thus supports objects, but not all values are referred to as objects. We discuss identity and mutation further in Chapter 4.

Using Imperative Code

The showWordCount and showResults functions defined in the previous section output the results using a library function called printfn:

```
printfn "--> %d words in the text" nWords
printfn "--> %d duplicate words" nDups
```

For those familiar with OCaml, C and C++ printfn will look familiar as a variant of printf—printfn also adds a newline character at the end of printing. Here the pattern %d is a placeholder for an integer, and the rest of the text is output verbatim to the console. F# also supports related functions such as printf, sprintf, and fprintf, which are discussed further in Chapter 4. Unlike C/C++, printf is a type-safe text formatter, where the F# compiler checks that the subsequent arguments match the requirements of the placeholders. There are also other ways to format text with F#. For example, you could have used the .NET libraries directly:

```
System.Console.WriteLine("--> {0} words in the text", box(nWords))
System.Console.WriteLine("--> {0} duplicate words", box(nDups))
```

Here {0} acts as the placeholder, though no checks are made that the arguments match the placeholder before the code is run. The use of printfn also shows how you can use sequential expressions to cause effects in the outside world.

As with let ... in ... expressions, it is sometimes convenient to write sequential code on a single line. You can do this by separating two expressions by a semicolon (;), and again this is the primitive construct of the language. The first expression is evaluated (usually for its side effects), its result is discarded, and the overall expression evaluates to the result of the second. Here is a simpler example of this construct:

```
let two = (printfn "Hello World"; 1+1)
let four = two + two
```

When executed, this code will print Hello World precisely once, when the right side of the definition of two is executed. F# does not have statements as such: the fragment (printfn "Hello World"; 1+1) is an expression, but when evaluated, the first part of the expression causes a side effect, and its result is discarded. It is also often convenient to use parentheses to delimit sequential code. The code from the script could in theory be parenthesized with a semicolon added to make the primitive constructs involved more apparent:

```
(printfn "--> %d words in the text" nWords;
 printfn "--> %d duplicate words" nDups)
```

■**Note** The token ; is used to write sequential code within expressions, and ; ; is used to terminate interactions with the F# Interactive session. Semicolons are optional when the #light syntax option is used and the individual fragments of your sequential code are placed on separate lines beginning at the same column position.

Using .NET Libraries from F#

The true value of F# lies not just in what you can do inside the language but in what you can connect to outside the language. For example, F# does not come with a GUI library. Instead, F# is connected to .NET and via .NET to most of the significant programming technologies available on major computing platforms. To emphasize this, our second sample uses two of the powerful libraries that come with the .NET Framework: System.Net and System.Windows.Forms. The full sample is in Listing 2-3 and is a script for use with F# Interactive.

Listing 2-3. *Using the .NET Framework Windows Forms and Networking Libraries from F#*

```
open System.Windows.Forms

let form = new Form(Visible=true,TopMost=true,Text="Welcome to F#")

let textB = new RichTextBox(Dock=DockStyle.Fill, Text="Here is some initial text")
form.Controls.Add(textB)

open System.IO
open System.Net

/// Get the contents of the URL via a web request
let http(url: string) =
    let req = System.Net.WebRequest.Create(url)
    let resp = req.GetResponse()
    let stream = resp.GetResponseStream()
    let reader = new StreamReader(stream)
    let html = reader.ReadToEnd()
    resp.Close()
    html
```

```
let google = http("http://www.google.com")
textB.Text <- http("http://news.bbc.co.uk")
```

This example uses several important .NET libraries and will help you to explore some interesting F# language constructs. We walk you through this listing in the following sections.

Using open to Access Namespaces and Modules

The first thing you see in the sample is the use of open to access functionality from the namespace System.Windows.Forms:

```
open System.Windows.Forms
```

We discuss namespaces in more detail in Chapter 7. The earlier declaration simply means you can access any content under this path without quoting the long path. If it had not used open, you would have to write the following, which is obviously a little verbose:

```
let form = new System.Windows.Forms.Form(Visible=true,TopMost=true,
                                          Text="Welcome to F#")
```

You can also use open to access the contents of an F# module such as Microsoft.FSharp.Core.String without using long paths. We discuss modules in more detail in Chapter 7.

MORE ABOUT OPEN

Using open is an easy way to access the contents of namespaces and modules. However, there are some subtleties. For example, open doesn't actually load or reference a library—instead, it reveals functionality from already-loaded libraries. Libraries themselves are loaded by referring to a particular DLL using #r in a script or -r as a command-line option. Libraries and namespaces are orthogonal concepts: multiple libraries can contribute functionality to the same namespace, and each library can contribute functionality to multiple namespaces. Often one particular library contributes most of the functionality in a particular namespace. For example, most of the functionality in the System.Windows.Forms namespace comes from a library called System.Windows.Forms.dll. As it happens, this library is automatically referenced by F#, which is why you haven't needed an explicit reference to the library so far. You can place your code in a namespace by using a namespace declaration at the top of your file, discussed further in Chapter 7.

In an earlier example, you saw that String in String.split referenced a value in the module Microsoft.FSharp.Core.String. By default, all F# code is interpreted with an implicit open of the following namespaces and modules:

- Microsoft.FSharp.Core: Contains modules such as String, Int32, Int64, and Option and contains types such as 'a option and 'a ref

- Microsoft.FSharp.Core.Operators: Contains values such as +, -, *, box, unbox, using, and lock

- Microsoft.FSharp.Collections: Contains modules such as List, Seq, HashSet, Map, and Set and contains types such as 'a list

- `Microsoft.FSharp.Control`: Contains modules such as `Lazy`, `Async`, and `IEvent` and contains types such as `'a lazy` and `IEvent<'a>`

- `Microsoft.FSharp.Text`: Contains modules such as `Printf`

If two namespaces have types, subnamespaces, and/or modules with identical names, then when you open these, you can access the contents of both using the same shortened paths. For example, the namespace `System` contains a type `String`, and the namespace `Microsoft.FSharp.Core` contains a module `String`. In this case, long identifier lookups such as `String.split` search the values and members under both of these, preferring the most recently opened if there is an ambiguity.

Finally, if you ever have name collisions, you can define your own short aliases for modules and types, such as by using `module MyString = My.Modules.String` and `type SysString = System.String`.

Using new and Setting Properties

The next lines of the sample script use the keyword `new` to create a top-level window (called a *form*) and set it to be visible. If you run this code in F# Interactive, you will see a top-level window appear with the title text *Welcome to F#*.

```
let form = new Form(Visible=true,TopMost=true,Text="Welcome to F#")
```

Here, `new` is shorthand for calling a function associated with the type `System.Windows.Forms.Form` that constructs a value of the given type—these functions are called *constructors*. Not all F# and .NET types use constructors; you will also see values being constructed using names such as `Create` or via one or more functions in a related module such as `String.create` or `Array.init`. You'll see examples of each throughout this book.

A form is an *object*; that is, its properties change during the course of execution, and it is a handle that mediates access to external resources (the display device, mouse, and so on). Sophisticated objects such as forms often need to be configured, either by passing in configuration parameters at construction or by adjusting properties from their default values after construction. The arguments `Visible=true`, `TopMost=true`, and `Text="Welcome to F#"` set the initial values for three properties of the form. The labels `Visible`, `TopMost`, and `Text` must correspond to either named arguments of the constructor being called or properties on the return result of the operation. In this case, all three are object properties, and the arguments indicate initial values for the object properties.

Most properties on graphical objects can be adjusted dynamically. You set the value of a property dynamically using the notation `obj.Property <- value`. For example, you could also have constructed the form object as follows:

```
open System.Windows.Forms
let form = new Form()
form.Visible <- true
form.TopMost <- true
form.Text <- "Welcome to F#"
```

Likewise, you can watch the title of the form change by running the following code in F# Interactive:

```
form.Text <- "Programming is Fun!"
```

Setting properties dynamically is frequently to configure objects, such as forms, that support many potential configuration parameters that evolve over time.

The object created here was bound to the name form. Binding this value to a new name doesn't create a new form; rather, two different handles now refer to the same object (they are said to *alias* the same object). For example, the following code sets the title of the same form, despite it being accessed via a different name:

```
let form2 = form
form2.Text <- "F# Forms are Fun"
```

VALUES, METHODS, AND PROPERTIES

Here are the differences between values, methods, and properties:

- *Simple values*: Functions, parameters, and top-level items defined using let or pattern matching. Examples: form, text, wordCount.

- *Methods*: Function values associated with types. Interfaces, classes, and record and union types can all have associated methods. Methods can be overloaded (see Chapter 6) and must be applied immediately to their arguments. Examples: System.Net.WebRequest.Create and resp.GetResponseStream.

- *Properties*: A shorthand for invoking method members that read or write underlying data. Interfaces, classes, and record and union types can all have associated properties. Examples: System.DateTime.Now and form.TopMost.

- *Indexer properties*: A property can take arguments, in which case it is an *indexer property*. Indexer properties named Item can be accessed using the .[_] syntax. Examples: vector.[3] and matrix.[3,4].

The next part of the sample creates a new RichTextBox control and stores it in a variable called textB. A control is typically an object with a visible representation, or more generally, an object that reacts to operating system events related to the windowing system. A form is one such control, but there are many others. A RichTextBox control is one that can contain formatted text, much like a word processor.

```
let textB = new RichTextBox(Dock= DockStyle.Fill)
form.Controls.Add(textB)
```

Fetching a Web Page

The second half of Listing 2-3 uses the System.Net library to define a function http to read HTML web pages. You can investigate the operation of the implementation of the function by entering the following lines into F# Interactive:

```
> open System;;
> open System.IO;;
> open System.Net;;

> let req = WebRequest.Create("http://www.microsoft.com");;
val req : WebRequest

> let resp = req.GetResponse();;
val resp : WebResponse

> let stream = resp.GetResponseStream();;
val stream : Stream

> let reader = new StreamReader(stream);;
val reader : StreamReader

> let html = reader.ReadToEnd();;
val html : string

> textB.Text <- html;;
```

The final line will set the contents of the text box form to the HTML contents of the Microsoft home page. Let's take a look at this code line by line.

The first line of the code creates a WebRequest object using the static method Create, a member of the type System.Net.WebRequest. The result of this operation is an object that acts as a handle to a running request to fetch a web page—you could, for example, abandon the request or check to see whether the request has completed. The second line calls the instance method GetResponse. The remaining lines of the sample get a stream of data from the response to the request using resp.GetResponseStream(), make an object to read this stream using new StreamReader(stream), and read the full text from this stream. We cover .NET I/O in more detail in Chapter 4, but for now you can test by experimentation in F# Interactive that these actions do indeed fetch the HTML contents of a web page. The inferred type for http that wraps up this sequence as a function is as follows:

```
val http : string -> string
```

Note *Static members* are items qualified by a concrete type or module. Examples include System.String.Compare, System.DateTime.Now, List.map, and String.split. *Instance members* are methods, properties, and values qualified by an expression. Examples include form.Visible, resp.GetResponseStream(), and cell.contents.

XML HELP IN VISUAL STUDIO

In a rich editor such as Visual Studio 2005, you can easily find out more about the functionality of .NET libraries by hovering your mouse over the identifiers in your source code. For example, if you hover over Dock in textB.Dock, you'll see the XML help shown here:

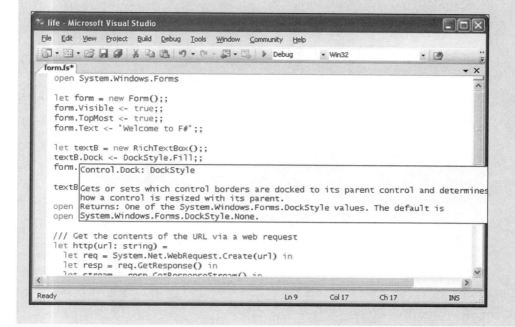

Summary

In this chapter, you took a look at some simple interactive programming with F# and .NET. Along the way, you met many of the constructs you'll use in your day-to-day F# programming. In the next chapter, you'll take a closer look at these and other constructs that are used to perform compositional and succinct functional programming in F#.

■**Note** In Chapter 3 you'll use some of the functions you defined in this chapter, so if you're using F# Interactive, you might want to leave your session open as you proceed.

CHAPTER 3

∎∎∎

Introducing Functional Programming

F# is effective and productive primarily because it is built on the tried and tested constructs of functional programming. In this chapter, we cover the core building blocks of functional programming with F#, including simple types and function values, pattern matching, lists, options, and sequences, as well as how to declare some of your own simple types. We cover imperative programming, generics, and object-oriented programming in Chapters 4 through 6.

Getting Started with F# Arithmetic

We first cover the most common base types of data manipulated in F# code, beginning with the basics of F# arithmetic.

Basic Literals

Table 3-1 lists the basic numeric types used in F# code and their corresponding literal forms. We've also listed the non-numeric types bool and unit.

Table 3-1. *Basic Types and Literals*

Type	Description	Sample Literals	.NET Name
bool	True/false values	true, false	System.Boolean
byte	8-bit unsigned integers	0uy, 19uy, 0xFFuy	System.Byte
sbyte	8-bit signed integers	0y, 19y, 0xFFy	System.SByte
int16	16-bit signed integers	0s, 19s, 0x0800s	System.Int16
uint16	16-bit unsigned integers	0us, 19us, 0x0800us	System.UInt16
int, int32	32-bit signed integers	0, 19, 0x0800, 0b0001	System.Int32
uint32	32-bit unsigned integers	0u, 19u, 0x0800u	System.UInt32
int64	64-bit signed integers	0L, 19L, 0x0800L	System.Int64

Table 3-1. *Basic Types and Literals (Continued)*

Type	Description	Sample Literals	.NET Name
uint64	64-bit unsigned integers	0UL, 19UL, 0x0800UL	System.UInt64
nativeint	Machine-sized signed integers	0n, 19n, 0x0800n	System.IntPtr
unativeint	Machine-sized unsigned integers	0un, 19un, 0x0800un	System.UIntPtr
single, float32	32-bit IEEE floating-point	0.0f, 19.7f, 1.3e4f	System.Single
double, float	64-bit IEEE floating-point	0.0, 19.7, 1.3e4	System.Double
decimal	High-precision decimal values	0M, 19M, 19.03M	System.Decimal
bigint	Arbitrarily large integers	0I, 19I	Math.BigInt
bignum	Arbitrary-precision rationals	0N, 19N	Math.BigNum
unit	The type with only one value	()	Core.Unit

Arithmetic Operators

Table 3-2 lists the most commonly used arithmetic operators. These are overloaded to work with all the numeric types listed in Table 3-1.

Table 3-2. *Arithmetic Operators and Examples*

Operator	Description	Sample Use on int	Sample Use on float
+	Unchecked addition	1 + 2	1.0 + 2.0
-	Unchecked subtraction	12 - 5	12.3 - 5.4
*	Unchecked multiplication	2 * 3	2.4 * 3.9
/	Division	5 / 2	5.0 / 2.0
%	Modulus	5 % 2	5.4 % 2.0
-	Unary negation	-(5+2)	-(5.4+2.4)

The behavior of these and other operators can be extended for user-defined types, a topic we cover in Chapter 6. In F#, addition, subtraction, and multiplication over integers are unchecked; that is, if overflow or underflow occurs beyond the representable range, then wraparound occurs. For example, 2147483647 is the largest representable 32-bit integer of the int type:

```
> 2147483647+1;;
val it : int = -2147483648
```

Checked versions of arithmetic operators that raise System.OverflowException exceptions can be accessed by opening the Microsoft.FSharp.Core.Operators.Checked module. If avoiding overflow is a priority, then using the decimal, bigint, and bignum types is recommended. Division by zero raises a System.DivideByZeroException exception, except in the case of floating-point numbers where it returns one of the special floating point numbers Infinity or -Infinity. Operator overloading interacts with type inference—if a use of an overloaded operator is not otherwise constrained to work on a particular type, then F# will assume it works on 32-bit integers. To constrain a use of an operator to a particular type, you must give a type annotation that has the effect of telling the compiler the type on the left of the two arguments to the binary operator. For example, in the absence of additional type information, the following function is assumed to work with integers:

```
> let squareAndAdd a b = a * a + b;;
val squareAndAdd: int -> int -> int
```

A single type annotation on a is sufficient to indicate that a * a is an operation on float values, and thus returns a float value, and that a * a + b is also an operation on float:

```
> let squareAndAdd (a:float) b = a * a + b;;
val squareAndAdd: float -> float -> float
```

If you want, you can also give full type annotations for the arguments and return type of a function:

```
> let squareAndAdd (a:float) (b:float) : float = a * a + b;;
val squareAndAdd: float -> float -> float
```

Bitwise Operations

All the integer types listed in Table 3-1 support bitwise manipulations on their underlying representations. Table 3-3 shows the bitwise manipulation operators.

Table 3-3. *Bitwise Arithmetic Operators and Examples*

Operator	Description	Sample Use	Result
&&&	Bitwise "and"	0x65 &&& 0x0F	0x05
|||	Bitwise "or"	0x65 ||| 0x18	0x7D
ööö	Bitwise "exclusive or"	0x65 ööö 0x0F	0x6A
~~	Bitwise negation	~~~0x65	0xFFFFFF9a
<<<	Left shift	0x01 <<< 3	0x08
>>>	Right shift (arithmetic if signed)	0x65 >>> 3	0x0C

The following sample shows how to use these operators to encode 32-bit integers into 1, 2, or 5 bytes, represented by returning a list of integers. Integers in the range 0 to 127 return a list of length 1:

```
let encode (n: int32) =
    if   (n >= 0    && n <= 0x7F)   then [ n ]
    elif (n >= 0x80 && n <= 0x3FFF) then [ (0x80 ||| (n >>> 8)) &&& 0xFF;
                                           (n &&& 0xFF) ]
    else [ 0xC0; ((n >>> 24) &&& 0xFF);
                 ((n >>> 16) &&& 0xFF);
                 ((n >>> 8)  &&& 0xFF);
                 (n          &&& 0xFF) ]
```

Here's an example of the function in action:

```
encode 32;;
val it : int32 list = [32]

> encode 320;;
val it : int32 list = [129; 64]

> encode 32000;;
val it : int32 list = [192; 0; 0; 125; 0]
```

Arithmetic Conversions

Numeric types are not implicitly converted—conversions between different numeric types must be made explicitly. You do this by using overloaded conversion operators. These work in the same way as overloaded infix operators such as + and *. Table 3-4 shows the primary conversion operators.

Table 3-4. *Overloaded Arithmetic Conversions and Examples*

Operator	Description	Sample Use	Result
sbyte	Convert/truncate to sbyte	sbyte (-17)	-17y
byte	Convert/truncate to byte	byte 255	255uy
int16	Convert/truncate to int16	int16 0	0s
uint16	Convert/truncate to uint16	uint16 65535	65535us
int/int32	Convert/truncate to int32	int 17.8	17
uint32	Convert/truncate to uint32	uint32 12	12u
int64	Convert/truncate to int64	int64 (-100.4)	-100L
uint64	Convert/truncate to uint64	uint64 1	1UL
float32	Convert to float32/single	float32 65	65.0f
float	Convert to float/double	float 65	65.0

These conversions are all unchecked in the sense that they will not raise exceptions. Again, the Microsoft.FSharp.Core.Operators.Checked module has corresponding definitions of these operators. An alternative is to use the .NET static methods contained in the type System.Convert, such as System.Convert.ToDouble( ). These do perform checking, which means they raise an exception if the source number can't be represented within the numeric range of the target type. As with many .NET constructs, uses of System.Convert methods may require type annotations to resolve overloading, discussed further in Chapter 5 and Chapter 6.

Arithmetic Comparisons

When used with numeric values, the binary comparison operators =, <>, <, <=, >, >=, min, and max perform comparisons according to the natural ordering for each particular numeric type. You can also use these operators on other data types, such as to compare lists of integers, and you can customize their behavior for new types you define. We discuss generic comparison in detail in Chapter 5, and we discuss customizing generic comparison in Chapter 8.

When used with floating-point values, these operators implement the IEEE semantics for NaN (Not a Number) values. For example, (NaN = NaN) is false, as is (NaN <= NaN) and (NaN < NaN).

Overloaded Math Functions

The module Microsoft.FSharp.Core.Operators includes the definition of a number of useful overloaded math operators. These are shown in Table 3-5 and are overloaded either on a suitable range of integer types or on the basic floating-point types.

Table 3-5. *Overloaded Math Functions and Examples*

Function	Description	Sample Use	Result
abs	Absolute value of signed numeric types	abs (-10.0f)	10.0f
cos, sin, tan	Trigonometric functions	cos 0.0	1.0
cosh, sinh, tanh	Hyperbolic trigonometric functions	cosh 1.0	1.543080635
acos, asin, atan, atan2	Inverse trigonometric functions	acos 1.0	0.0
ceil, floor	Round up, round down	ceil 1.001	2.0
truncate	Round toward zero	truncate 8.9	8.0
exp, log, log10	Exponent, logarithm, base-10 logarithm	exp 1.0	2.718281828
(**)	Power	2.0 ** 4.0	16.0

Introducing Simple Strings

The F# type string is an abbreviation for .NET type System.String and represents a sequence of Unicode UTF-16 characters. In the following sections, we briefly introduce strings and the most useful functions for formatting them.

Working with String Literals and Primitives

Table 3-6 shows the different forms for writing string literals.

Table 3-6. *String and Character Literals*

Example	Kind	Type
`"Humpty Dumpty"`	String	`string`
`"c:\\Program Files"`	String	`string`
`@"c:\Program Files"`	Verbatim string	`string`
`"xyZy3d2"B`	Literal byte array	`byte[]`
`'c'`	Character	`char`

Table 3-7 shows the escape characters that you can use in strings and characters.

Table 3-7. *Escape Characters in Nonverbatim Strings*

Escape	Character	ASCII/Unicode Value	Examples
\n	New line	10	`"\n"`
\r	Carriage return	13	`"\r"`
\t	Tab	9	`"\t"`
\b	Backspace	8	
NNN	Trigraph	NNN	`"\032"` *(space)*
\u*NNNN*	Unicode character	NNNN	`"\u00a9"` (©)
\U*NNNNNNNN*	Long Unicode character	NNNN NNNN	`"\U00002260"` (≠)

As shown in Table 3-6, a literal form is also available for arrays of bytes: the characters are interpreted as ASCII characters, and non-ASCII characters can be embedded by escape codes. This can be useful when working with binary protocols:

```
> "MAGIC"B;;
val it : byte [] = [|77uy; 65uy; 71uy; 73uy; 67uy|]
```

Verbatim string literals are particularly useful for file and path names that contain the backslash character (\):

```
> let dir  = @"c:\Program Files";;
val dir : string
```

You can also use multiline string literals:

```
> let s = "All the kings horses
- and all the kings men";;
val s : string
```

The operator .[] is used to access the elements of a string, and the property .Length retrieves its length:

```
> let s = "Couldn't put Humpty";;
val s : string

> s.Length;;
val it : int = 19

> s.[13];;
val it : char = 'H'
```

Strings are immutable; that is, a string value cannot be modified once built. For example, the Substring method on the string type doesn't modify the original string but returns a new string representing the result. As mentioned in Chapter 2, immutability is a key concept for many F# values, and you'll encounter it at many places in this book. If you attempt to mutate a string, you will get an error like the one shown here:

```
> let s = "Couldn't put Humpty";;
val s : string = "Couldn't put Humpty"

> s.[13] <- 'h';;

  s.[13] <- 'h';;
  ^^
stdin(75,0): error: FS0001: Type error in the use of the overloaded operator
'set_Item'. The type 'string' does not support any operators named 'set_Item'
```

Building Strings

The simplest way to build strings is via concatenation using the + operator:

```
> "Couldn't put Humpty" + " " + "together again";;
val it : string = "Couldn't put Humpty together again"
```

You can also build strings using objects of the .NET type System.Text.StringBuilder. These objects are mutable buffers that you can use to accumulate and modify text, and they are more efficient than repeated uses of the + operator. Here's an example:

```
> let buf = new System.Text.StringBuilder();;
val buf : System.Text.StringBuilder

> buf.Append("Humpty Dumpty");;

> buf.Append(" sat on the wall");;

> buf.ToString();;
val it : string = "Humpty Dumpty sat on the wall"
```

■**Note** For compatibility with OCaml, the ^ operator can also be used for string concatenation, though it is generally used only when cross-compiling code with OCaml.

Working with Lists and Options

Some of the foundational data structures of F# coding are tuples, lists, and options. In the following sections, we discuss these and some related topics by example.

Using F# Lists

F# lists are a common data structure used in functional programming. You saw some examples of concrete lists when using the results of the String.split function in Chapter 2. Table 3-8 shows the primitive constructs for building lists.

Table 3-8. *Some List-Related Language Constructs and Operators*

Operator/Expression	Description	Examples
[]	The empty list	[]
expr :: expr	"Cons" an element with a list	1 :: [2; 3]
[expr; ...; expr]	A list value	[1; 2; 3]
[expr .. expr]	A range of integers	[1 .. 99]
[for x in list -> expr]	A generated list (see end of chapter)	[for x in 1..99 -> x * x]
expr @ expr	Concatenates two lists	[1; 2] @ [3]

Here are some basic list values:

```
let oddPrimes = [3; 5; 7; 11]
let morePrimes = [13; 17]
let primes = 2 :: (oddPrimes @ morePrimes)
```

The value and type of primes are as follows:

```
val primes : int list = [2; 3; 5; 7; 11; 13; 17]
```

It is important to note that lists are immutable: the "cons" :: and "append" @ operations do not modify the original lists; instead, they create new lists. You can see this in the following interactive session:

```
> let people = [ "Adam"; "Dominic"; "James" ];;
val people : string list

> people;;
val it : string list = [ "Adam"; "Dominic"; "James" ]

> "Chris" :: people;;
val it : string list = [ "Chris"; "Adam"; "Dominic"; "James" ]

> people;;
val it : string list = [ "Adam"; "Dominic"; "James" ]
```

Note that people has not been changed by the construction of a new list using the "cons" operator. That is, lists and tuples are unchangeable, immutable values. F# lists are represented in memory as linked lists, and each F# list value is a "cons" cell containing a value plus a pointer to the next chain in the list, or else it is a special "nil" object. When you create a new list using the :: operator, then the tail of the new list will point to the old list, which ensures that the inner memory associated with lists is often reused as part of multiple list values. You can decompose lists from the head downward by using *pattern matching*. You saw some simple examples of pattern matching on tuples in Chapter 2, and we'll look at pattern matching in more detail in "Getting Started with Pattern Matching" later in this chapter. Here is an example of using pattern matching with lists:

```
let printFirst primes =
    match primes with
    | h :: t -> printfn "The first prime in the list is %d" h
    | [] -> printfn "No primes found in the list"
```

```
> printFirst oddPrimes;;
The first prime in the list is 3
val it : unit = ()
```

The first line after the match is a pattern-matching rule that matches the input primes against the pattern h :: t. If primes is a nonempty list, then the match will be successful, and the first printfn will be executed with h bound to the head of the list and t to its tail. The second line considers the case where primes is an empty list. Note that the :: and [] symbols can be used both to build up lists in expressions and to decompose them in pattern matching. The F# library also includes a module List that contains some useful functions related to programming with lists. You'll be seeing many of these functions in the next section and throughout this book. Table 3-9 shows some of these.

F# lists are not appropriate for all circumstances; for example, very large data structures should probably be represented using arrays or other data structures or even managed by an external tool such as a relational database. We discuss a number of immutable data structures in the "Some Common Immutable Data Structures" sidebar.

Table 3-9. *Some Sample Functions in the List Module*

Function	Type	Description
List.length	: 'a list -> int	Returns the length of the list.
List.hd	: 'a list -> 'a	Returns the first element of a nonempty list.
List.tl	: 'a list -> 'a list	Returns all the elements of a nonempty list except the first.
List.init	: int -> (int -> 'a) -> 'a list	Returns a new list of length given by the first parameter and elements generated by the second function parameter.
List.append	: 'a list -> 'a list -> 'a list	Returns a new list containing the elements of the first list followed by the elements of the second list.
List.filter	: ('a -> bool) -> 'a list -> 'a list	Returns a new list containing only those elements of the original list where the function returns true.
List.map	: ('a -> 'b) -> 'a list -> 'b list	Returns a new list where the function has been applied to each element of the list.
List.iter	: ('a -> unit) -> 'a list -> unit	Executes the given function for each element of the list.
List.unzip	: ('a * 'b) list -> 'a list * 'b list	Returns two new lists containing the first and second elements of the pairs in the input list.
List.zip	: 'a list -> 'b list -> ('a * 'b) list	Returns a new list containing the elements of the two input lists combined pairwise. The input lists must be the same length; otherwise, an exception is raised.
List.to_array	: 'a list -> 'a[]	Converts the list to an array.
List.of_array	: 'a[] -> 'a list	Converts the array to a list.

Here are examples of how to use some of the functions from Table 3-9. The last two examples use *function values*, which we cover in more detail in "Introducing Function Values" later in this chapter.

```
> List.hd [5; 4; 3];;
val it : int = 5

> List.tl [5; 4; 3];;
val it : int list = [ 4; 3 ]

> List.map (fun x -> x*x) [1; 2; 3];;
val it : int list = [ 1; 4; 9 ]

> List.filter (fun x -> x % 3 = 0) [2; 3; 5; 7; 9];;
val it : int list = [ 3; 9 ]
```

SOME COMMON IMMUTABLE DATA STRUCTURES

Data structures are generally divided between *mutable* and *immutable*, a distinction touched upon in Chapter 2 and covered in more detail in Chapter 4. Immutable data structures are sometimes called *persistent* or simply *functional*. Here are some of the immutable data structures commonly used with F#:

- *Tuple values and option values*: These are immutable and are basic workhorses of F# programming.

- *Immutable linked lists of type* `'a list`: These are cheap to access from the left end. They are inefficient for random access lookup because the list must be traversed from the left for each lookup, that is, random access lookup is O(n) where n is the number of elements in the collection. The full name of this type is `Microsoft.FSharp.Collections.List<'a>`.

- *Immutable sets based on balanced trees*: We show some example uses of immutable sets in Chapter 2, and an implementation is provided via the type `Set<'a>` in the F# library namespace `Microsoft.FSharp.Collections`. These are cheap to add, access, and union, with O(log(n)) access times, where n is the number of elements in the collection. Because the type is immutable, internal nodes can be shared between different sets.

- *Immutable maps based on balanced trees*: These are similar to immutable sets but associate keys with values (that is, they are immutable dictionaries). One implementation of these is provided via the F# library type `Map<'key,'value>` in `Microsoft.FSharp.Collections`. As with sets, these have O(log(n)) access times.

We cover imperative programming and mutable data structures in Chapter 4.

Using F# Option Values

Like lists and tuples, option values are simple constructs frequently used as the workhorses in F# coding. An option is simply either a value Some(v) or the absence of a value None. For example, options are useful for returning the value of a search where you might or might not have a result. You shall see in "Defining Discriminated Unions" that the option type is defined in the F# library as follows:

```
type 'a option =
  | None
  | Some of 'a
```

The following is a data structure that uses options to represent the (optional) parents of some well-known characters:

```
> let people = [ ("Adam", None);
                 ("Eve" , None);
                 ("Cain", Some("Adam","Eve"));
                 ("Abel", Some("Adam","Eve")) ];;
val people : (string * (string *string) option) list
```

Pattern matching is frequently used to examine option values:

```
> let showParents (name,parents) =
      match parents with
      | Some(dad,mum) -> printfn "%s has father %s, mother %s" name dad mum
      | None          -> printfn "%s has no parents!" name;;
val showParents : (string * (string * string) option) -> unit

> showParents ("Adam",None);;
Adam has no parents
val it : unit = ()
```

The F# library also includes a module Option that contains some useful functions for programming with options. Table 3-10 shows some of these. Although it is easy to code these by hand using pattern matching, it can also be useful to learn and rely on the standard definitions.

Table 3-10. *Some Sample Functions in the Option Module*

Function	Type	Description
Option.get	: 'a option -> 'a	Returns the value of a Some option.
Option.is_some	: 'a option -> bool	Returns true for a Some option.
Option.map	: ('a -> 'b) -> 'a option -> 'b option	Given None, returns None. Given Some(x), returns Some(f x), where f is the given function.
Option.iter	: ('a -> unit) -> 'a option -> unit	Applies the given function to the value of a Some option; otherwise, does nothing.

Using Option Values for Control

You can use option values for both data and control; they're often used to represent the success or failure of a computation. This can be useful when catching an exception, as shown in the following sample (this sample uses the function http from Chapter 2):

```
let fetch url =
    try Some(http(url))
    with :? System.Net.WebException -> None
```

We describe exceptions in more detail in Chapter 4—what matters here is that if a network error occurs during the HTTP request, then the exception will be caught, and the result of the fetch function will be the value None. Successful web page requests will return a Some value. Option values can then be discriminated and decomposed using pattern matching, as shown here:

```
> match (fetch "http://www.nature.com") with
  | Some(text) -> printfn "text = %s" text
  | None -> printfn "**** no web page found";;
text = <HTML> ... </HTML>  (note: the HTML is shown here if connected to the web)
val it : unit = ()
```

Working with Conditionals: && and ||

A basic control construct in F# programming is if/then/elif/else. Here's an example:

```
let round x =
    if x >= 100 then 100
    elif x < 0 then 0
    else x
```

Conditionals are really shorthand for pattern matching; for example, the previous code could have been written like this:

```
let round x =
    match x with
    | _ when x >= 100 -> 100
    | _ when x < 0    -> 0
    | _               -> x
```

Conditionals are always guarded by a Boolean-valued expression. You can build them using && and || (the "and" and "or" operators) as well as any library functions that return Boolean values:

```
let round2 (x,y) =
    if x >= 100 || y >= 100 then 100,100
    elif x < 0 || y < 0 then 0,0
    else x,y
```

The operators && and || have the usual "shortcut" behavior in that the second argument of && is evaluated only if the first evaluates to true, and likewise, the second argument of || is evaluated only if the first evaluates to false.

■**Note** If you don't use the #light lightweight syntax option, then when you combine conditionals with imperative code, you will sometimes need to use parentheses, as in (. . .), or begin/end to delimit the regions covered by each branch of the conditional, for example, if x > 100 then (...). If you use the #light syntax option, then these are optional, as long as the branches are correctly indented from the if, elif, and else tokens of the construct.

Defining Recursive Functions

One of the fundamental building blocks of computation in F# is recursion. The following code shows a simple well-known recursive function:

```
> let rec factorial n = if n <= 1 then 1 else n * factorial (n-1);;
val factorial : int -> int

> factorial 5;;
val it : int = 120
```

This example shows that a recursive function is simply one that can call itself as part of its own definition. Recursive functions are introduced by let rec. Functions are not recursive by default, since it is wise to isolate recursive functions to help you control the complexity of your algorithms and keep your code maintainable. It may help to visualize the execution of factorial 5 in the following way (though note that in reality F# executes the function using efficient native code):

```
factorial 5
= 5 * factorial 4
= 5 * (4 * factorial 3)
= 5 * (4 * (3 * factorial 2))
= 5 * (4 * (3 * (2 * factorial 1 )))
= 5 * (4 * (3 * (2 * 1)))
= 5 * (4 * (3 * 2))
= 5 * (4 * 6)
= 5 * 24
= 120
```

As with all calls, the execution of the currently executing instance of the function is suspended while a recursive call is made.

Many of the operators you have encountered so far can be coded as recursive functions. For example, the following is one possible implementation of List.length:

```
let rec length l =
    match l with
    | [] -> 0
    | h :: t -> 1 + length t
```

Likewise, many functions such as List.map are implemented using recursive functions.

Recursion is sometimes used as a means of programming particular patterns of control. This is usually used in contexts where functions have deliberate side effects. For example, the following code repeatedly fetches the HTML for a particular web page, printing each time it is fetched:

```
let rec repeatFetch url n =
    if n > 0 then
        let html = http url
        printfn "fetched <<< %s >>> on iteration %d" html n
        repeatFetch url (n-1)
```

Recursion is powerful but not always the ideal way to encode either data manipulations or control constructs, at least if other techniques are readily available. For example, the previous program could be implemented using a for loop, as explained in Chapter 4, which would be clearer. Likewise, explicit recursion should typically be avoided if an operator is available that captures the pattern of recursion being used. For example, many explicit loops and recursive functions can be replaced by uses of functions such as List.map and Array.map.

A typical error with recursion is to forget to decrement a variable at the recursive call. For example, the author incorrectly entered the following nonterminating function when writing this chapter:

```
let rec badFactorial n = if n <= 0 then 1 else n * badFactorial n
```

You should always check your recursive calls to ensure that the function is tending toward termination, that is, that the arguments are approaching the base case. This is called *well-founded recursion.*

You can define multiple recursive functions simultaneously by separating the definitions with and. These are called *mutually recursive functions.* For example:

```
let rec even n = (n = 0u) || odd(n-1u)
and     odd n = (n <> 0u) && even(n-1u)
```

This gives the following types:

```
val even : uint32 -> bool
val odd : uint32 -> bool
```

Of course, a more efficient, nonrecursive implementation of these is available!

```
let even (n:uint32) = (n % 2u) = 0u
let odd  (n:uint32) = (n % 2u) = 1u
```

You must sometimes take care with recursive functions to ensure that they are *tail recursive*, or else the computation stack of your program may be exhausted by large inputs. This is particularly important for library functions or functions that operate over large data structures with very large numbers of recursive calls. Indeed, the implementation of length shown previously is not tail recursive. We discuss tail recursion in depth in Chapter 8.

Introducing Function Values

In this section, we cover the foundational building block of F# functional programming: function values. We begin with a simple and well-known example: using function values to transform one list into another.

One of the primary uses of F# lists is as a general-purpose concrete data structure for storing ordered lists input and ordered results. Input lists are often transformed to output lists using "aggregate" operations that transform, select, filter, and categorize elements of the list according to a range of criteria. These aggregate operations provide an excellent introduction to how to use function values. Let's take a closer look at this in the following code sample, which continues from the definition of http in Listing 2-2 in Chapter 2:

```
> let sites = [ "http://www.live.com";
                "http://www.google.com" ];;
val sites : string list

> let fetch url = (url, http url);;
val fetch : string -> string * string

> List.map fetch sites;;
val it : (string * string) list
= [ ("http://www.live.com", "<html>...</html>");
    ("http://www.google.com", "<html>...</html>"); ]
```

The first interaction defines sites as a literal list of URLs, and the second defines the function fetch. The third calls the aggregate operation List.map. This accepts the function value fetch as the first argument and the list sites as the second argument. The function applies fetch to each element of the list and collects the results in a new list.

Types are one useful way to help learn what a function does. Here's the type of List.map:

```
> List.map;;
val it: ('a -> 'b) -> 'a list -> 'b list
```

This says List.map accepts a function value as the first argument and a list as the second argument, and it returns a list as the result. The function argument can have any type 'a -> 'b, and the elements of the input list must have a corresponding type 'a. The symbols 'a and 'b are called *type parameters*, and functions that accept type parameters are called *generic*. We discuss type parameters in detail in Chapter 5.

■**Tip** You can often deduce the behavior of a function from its type, especially if its type involves type parameters. For example, look at the type of List.map. Using type parameters, you can observe that the type 'a list of the input list is related to the type 'a accepted by the function passed as the first parameter. Similarly, the type 'b returned by this function is related to the type 'b list of the value returned by List.map. From this it is reasonable to conclude that List.map will call the function parameter for items in the list and construct its result using the values returned.

Using Anonymous Function Values

Function values are so common in F# programming that it is convenient to define them without giving them names. Here is a simple example:

```
> let primes = [2; 3; 5; 7];;
val primes : int list

> let primeCubes = List.map (fun n -> n * n * n) primes;;
val primeCubes: int list

> primeCubes;;
val it : int list = [8; 27; 125; 343]
```

The definition of primeCubes uses the *anonymous function value* (fun n -> n * n * n). These are similar to function definitions but are unnamed and appear as an expression rather than as a let declaration. fun is a keyword meaning "function," n represents the argument to the function, and n * n * n is the result of the function. The overall type of the anonymous function expression is int -> int. You could use this technique to avoid defining the intermediary function fetch in the earlier sample:

```
let resultsOfFetch = List.map (fun url -> (url, http url)) sites
```

You will see anonymous functions throughout this book. Here is another example:

```
> List.map (fun (_,p) -> String.length p) resultsOfFetch;;
val it : int list = [3932; 2827 ]
```

Here you see two things:

- The argument of the anonymous function is a tuple pattern. Using a tuple pattern automatically extracts the second element from each tuple and gives it the name p within the body of the anonymous function.

- Part of the tuple pattern is a wildcard pattern, indicated by an underscore. This indicates you don't care what the first part of the tuple is; you're interested only in extracting the length from the second part of the pair.

Computing with Aggregate Operators

Functions such as List.map are called *aggregate operators*, and they are powerful constructs, especially when combined with the other features of F#. Here is a longer example that uses the aggregate operators List.filter and List.map to count the number of URL links in an HTML page and then collects stats on a group of pages (this sample uses the function http defined in Chapter 2):

```
let delimiters = [ ' '; '\n'; '\t'; '<'; '>'; '=' ]
let getWords s = String.split delimiters s
let getStats site =
    let url = "http://" + site
    let html = http url
    let hwords = html |> getWords
    let hrefs = html |> getWords |> List.filter (fun s -> s = "href")
    (site,html.Length, hwords.Length, hrefs.Length)
```

Here we use the function getStats with three web pages:

```
> let sites = [ "www.live.com";"www.google.com";"search.yahoo.com" ];;
val sites : string list

> sites |> List.map getStats;;
val it : (string * int * int * int) list
  = [("www.live.com", 7728, 1156, 10);
     ("www.google.com", 2685, 496, 14);
     ("search.yahoo.com", 10715, 1771, 38)]
```

The function getStats computes the length of the HTML for the given website, the number of words in the text of that HTML, and the approximate number of links on that page.

The previous code sample extensively uses the |> operator to *pipeline* operations, discussed in the "Pipelining with |>" sidebar. The F# library design ensures that a common, consistent set of aggregate operations is defined for each structured type. Table 3-11 shows how the same design patterns occur for the map abstraction.

Table 3-11. *A Recurring Aggregate Operator Design Pattern from the F# Library*

Operator	Type
List.map	: ('a -> 'b) -> 'a list -> 'b list
Array.map	: ('a -> 'b) -> 'a[] -> 'b[]
Option.map	: ('a -> 'b) -> 'a option -> 'b option
Seq.map	: ('a -> 'b) -> #seq<'a> -> seq<'b>

Frequently, types will also define methods such as `Map` that provide a slightly more succinct way of transforming data. For example, we could have written `sites |> List.map getStats` like so:

```
sites.Map(getStats)
```

Both styles are used in F# programming, depending on the methods and properties that are available for a particular data type.

PIPELINING WITH |>

The `|>` "forward pipe" operator is perhaps the most important operator in F# programming. Its definition is deceptively simple:

```
let (|>) x f = f x
```

Here is how to use the operator to compute the cubes of three numbers:

```
[1;2;3] |> List.map (fun x -> x * x * x)
```

This produces `[1;8;27]`, just as if you had written this:

```
List.map (fun x -> x * x * x) [1;2;3]
```

In a sense, `|>` is just "function application in reverse." However, using `|>` has distinct advantages:

- *Clarity*: When used in conjunction with operators such as `List.map`, the `|>` operator allows you to perform the data transformations and iterations in a forward-chaining, pipelined style.

- *Type inference*: Using the `|>` operator allows type information to be flowed from input objects to the functions manipulating those objects. F# uses information collected from type inference to resolve some language constructs such as property accesses and method overloading. This relies on information being propagated left to right through the text of a program. In particular, typing information to the right of a position is not taken into account when resolving property access and overloads.

For completeness, here is the type of the operator:

```
val (|>) : 'a -> ('a -> 'b) -> 'b
```

Composing Functions with >>

You saw earlier how to use the `|>` "forward pipe" operator to pipe values through a number of functions. This was a small example of the process of *computing with functions*, an essential and powerful programming technique in F#. In this section, we cover ways to compute new function values from existing ones using compositional techniques. First let's take a look at function composition. For example, consider the following code:

```
let google = http "http://www.google.com"
google |> getWords |> List.filter (fun s -> s = "href") |> List.length
```

You can rewrite this code using function composition as follows:

```
let countLinks = getWords >> List.filter (fun s -> s = "href") >> List.length
google |> countLinks
```

Let's take a look at this more closely. We have defined countLinks as the composition of three function values using the >> "forward composition" operator. This operator is defined in the F# library as follows:

```
let (>>) f g x = g(f(x))
```

You can see from the definition that f >> g gives a function value that first applies f to the x and then applies g. Here is the type of >>:

```
val (>>) : ('a -> 'b) -> ('b -> 'c) -> ('a -> 'c)
```

Note that >> is typically applied to only two arguments—those on either side of the binary operator, here named f and g. The final argument x is typically supplied at a later point. F# is good at optimizing basic constructions of pipelines and composition sequences from functions—for example, the function countLinks shown earlier will become a single function calling the three functions in the pipeline in sequence. This means sequences of compositions can be used with relatively low overhead.

Building Functions with Partial Application

Composing functions is just one way to compute interesting new functions. Another useful way is by using *partial application*. Here's an example:

```
let shift (dx,dy) (px,py) = (px + dx, py + dy)
let shiftRight = shift (1,0)
let shiftUp    = shift (0,1)
let shiftLeft  = shift (-1,0)
let shiftDown  = shift (0,-1)
```

The last four functions have been defined by calling shift with only one argument, in each case leaving a residue function that expects an additional argument. F# Interactive will report the types as follows:

```
val shift : int * int -> int * int -> int * int
val shiftRight : int * int -> int * int
val shiftLeft  : int * int -> int * int
val shiftUp    : int * int -> int * int
val shiftDown  : int * int -> int * int
```

Here is an example of how to use shiftRight and how to apply shift to new arguments (2,2):

```
> shiftRight (10,10);;
val it : int * int = (11,10)

> List.map (shift (2,2)) [ (0,0); (1,0); (1,1); (0,1) ];;
val it : int * int list = [ (2,2); (3,2); (3,3); (2,3) ]
```

In the second example, the function shift takes two pairs as arguments. We bind the first parameter to (2, 2). The result of this partial application is a function that takes one remaining tuple parameter and returns the value shifted by two units in each direction. This resulting function can now be used in conjunction with List.map.

Using Local Functions

Partial application is one way in which functions can be "computed," rather than simply defined. This technique becomes very powerful when combined with additional local definitions. Here's a simple and practical example, representing an idiom common in graphics programming:

```
open System.Drawing;;
let remap (r1: Rectangle) (r2: Rectangle) =
    let scalex = float r2.Width / float r1.Width
    let scaley = float r2.Height / float r1.Height
    let mapx x = r2.Left + truncate (float (x - r1.Left) * scalex)
    let mapy y = r2.Top + truncate (float (y - r1.Top) * scaley)
    let mapp (p: Point) = Point(mapx p.X, mapy p.Y)
    mapp
```

The function remap computes a new function value mapp that maps points in one rectangle to points in another. F# Interactive will report the type as follows:

```
val remap : Rectangle -> Rectangle -> (Point -> Point)
```

The type Rectangle is defined in the .NET library System.Drawing.dll and represents rectangles specified by integer coordinates. The computations on the interior of the transformation are performed in floating point to improve precision. You can use this as follows:

```
> let mapp = remap (Rectangle(100,100,100,100)) (Rectangle(50,50,200,200));;
val mapp : Point -> Point

> mapp (Point(100,100));;
val it : Point = X=50,Y=50

> mapp (Point(150,150));;
val it : Point = X=150,Y=150
```

```
> mapp (Point(200,200));;
val it : Point = X=250,Y=250
```

The intermediate values `scalex` and `scaley` are computed only once. This is despite that we've called the resulting function `mapp` three times. It may be helpful to think of `mapp` as a function object being generated by the `remap` function.

In the previous sample, `mapx`, `mapy`, and `mapp` are *local functions*, that is, functions defined locally as part of the implementation of `remap`. Local functions can be context dependent; in other words, they can be defined in terms of any values and parameters that happen to be in scope. Here `mapx` is defined in terms of `scalex`, `scaley`, `r1`, and `r2`.

■**Note** Local and partially applied functions are, if necessary, implemented by taking the *closure* of the variables they depend upon and storing them away until needed. In optimized F# code, the F# compiler often avoids this and instead passes extra arguments to the function implementations. Closure is a powerful technique that we use frequently in this book. It is often used in conjunction with functions, as in this chapter, but is also used with object expressions, sequence expressions, and class definitions.

Using Functions As Abstract Values

The function `remap` from the previous section generates values of type `Point -> Point`. You can think of this type as a way of representing "the family of transformations for the type `Point`." Many useful concepts can be modeled using function types and values. For example:

- The type `unit -> unit` is frequently used to model "actions," that is, operations that run and perform some unspecified side effect. For example, consider the expression `(fun () -> printfn "Hello World")`.

- Types of the form *type* `->` *type* `->` `int` are frequently used to model "comparison functions" over the type *type*. You will also see *type* `*` *type* `->` `int` used for this purpose, where a tuple is accepted as the first argument. In both cases, a negative result indicates "less than," zero indicates "equals," and a positive result indicates "greater than." Many collection types will accept such a value as a configuration parameter. For example, consider the F# `compare` function, which performs generic comparison on values (see Chapter 5).

- Types of the form *type* `->` `unit` are frequently used to model *callbacks*. Callbacks are often run in response to a system event, such as when a user clicks a user interface element. In this case, the parameter sent to the handler will have some specific type, such as `System.Windows.Forms.MouseEventArgs`.

- Types of the form `unit` `->` *type* are frequently used to model *delayed computations*, which are values that will, when required, produce a value of type *type*. For example, a threading library can accept such a function value and execute it on a different thread, eventually producing a value of type *type*. Delayed computations are related to lazy computations and sequence expressions, discussed in "Using Sequence Expressions."

- Types of the form *type* -> unit are frequently used to model *sinks*, which are values that will, when required, consume a value of type *type*. For example, a logging API might use a sink to consume values and write them to a log file.

- Types of the form $type_1$ -> $type_2$ are frequently used to model *transformers*, which are functions that transform each element of a collection. You will see this pattern in the map operator for many common collection types.

- Types of the form $type_1$ -> $type_2$ -> $type_2$ are frequently used to model *visitor accumulating functions*, which are functions that visit each element of a collection (type $type_1$) and accumulate a result (type $type_2$). For example, a visitor function that accumulates integers into a set of integers would have type int -> Set<int> -> Set<int>.

■**Note** The power of function types to model many different concepts is part of the enduring appeal of functional programming. Indeed, this is one of the refreshing features F# brings to object-oriented programming: many simple abstractions are modeled in very simple ways and often have simple implementations through orthogonal, unified constructs such as anonymous function values and function compositions.

Iterating with Aggregate Operators

It is common to use data to drive control, and indeed in functional programming the distinction between data and control is often blurred: function values can be used as data, and data can influence control flow. One example is using a function such as List.iter to iterate over a list. Let's take a simple example:

```
let sites = [ "http://www.live.com";
              "http://www.google.com";
              "http://search.yahoo.com" ]
sites |> List.iter (fun site -> printfn "%s, length = %d" site (http site).Length)
```

List.iter simply calls the given function (here an anonymous function) for each element in the input list. Here is its type:

```
val iter: ('a -> unit) -> 'a list -> unit
```

Many additional aggregate iteration techniques are defined in the F# and .NET libraries, particularly by using values of type seq<*type*>, discussed in "Getting Started with Sequences" later in this chapter.

Abstracting Control with Functions

As a second example of how you can abstract control using functions, let's consider the common pattern of timing the execution of an operation (measured in wall-clock time). First let's explore how to use System.DateTime.Now to get the wall-clock time:

```
> open System;;
> let start = DateTime.Now;;
val start : DateTime

> http "http://www.newscientist.com";;
val it : string = "<html>...</html>"

> let finish = DateTime.Now;;
val finish : DateTime

> let elapsed = finish - start;;
val elapsed : TimeSpan

> elapsed;;
val it : TimeSpan = 00:00:01.9799671
```

Note the type `TimeSpan` has been inferred from the use of the overloaded operator in the expression `finish - start`. We discuss overloaded operators in depth in Chapter 6. You can now wrap up this technique as a function `time` that acts as a new control operator:

```
open System
let time f =
    let start = DateTime.Now
    let res = f()
    let finish = DateTime.Now
    (res, finish - start)
```

This function runs the input function `f` but takes the time on either side of the call. It then returns both the result of the function and the elapsed time. The inferred type is as follows:

```
val time : (unit -> 'a) -> 'a * TimeSpan
```

Here `'a` is a *type variable* that stands for "any" type, and thus the function can be used to time functions that return any kind of result. Note that F# has automatically inferred a generic type for the function, a technique called *automatic generalization* that lies at the heart of F# programming. We discuss automatic generalization in detail in Chapter 5. Here is an example of using the `time` function, which again reuses the `http` function defined in Chapter 2:

```
> time (fun () -> http "http://www.newscientist.com");;
val it : string * TimeSpan = ...   (The HTML text and time will be shown here)
```

Using .NET Methods As First-Class Functions

You can use existing .NET methods as first-class functions. For example:

```
> open System.IO;;
> [@"C:\Program Files"; @"C:\Windows"] |> List.map Directory.GetDirectories;;

val it : string [] list =
  [ [|"C:\\Program Files\\Adobe"; "C:\\Program Files\\Apoint";
      "C:\\Program Files\\CA"; "C:\\Program Files\\CE Remote Tools"; ...]; ... ]
```

Sometimes you will need to add extra type information to indicate which "overload" of the method is required. We discuss method overloading in more detail in Chapter 6. For example, the following causes an error:

```
> open System;;
> let f = Console.WriteLine;;

C:\misc\test.ml(11,8): error: FS0041: The method WriteLine is overloaded.
Possible matches are shown below. Resolve the overloading by adding further
type annotations to the arguments.

Possible overload: 'Console.WriteLine(bool value) : unit'.

Possible overload: 'Console.WriteLine(char value) : unit'.
...
```

However, the following succeeds:

```
> let f = (Console.WriteLine : string -> unit);;
val f : string -> unit
```

Getting Started with Pattern Matching

One important tool in F# programming is *pattern matching*, a general construct that combines decomposition and control. In the previous sections, you got a taste of how you can use pattern matching with tuple, list, and option values. However, you can also use pattern matching in many other situations. You'll see many other examples of pattern matching in this book, but let's start with some simple pattern matching over strings and integers. As you've already seen, pattern matches on explicit values are introduced using the match ... with ... construct:

```
let urlFilter url agent =
    match (url,agent) with
    | "http://www.control.org", 99 -> true
    | "http://www.kaos.org"   , _ -> false
    | _, 86 -> true
    | _ -> false
```

The inferred type of the function is as follows:

```
val urlFilter: string -> int -> bool
```

The expression (url,agent) after the keyword match is a tuple of type (string*int). Each rule of the match is introduced with a | followed by a pattern, then ->, and then a result expression. When executed, the patterns of the rules are used one by one, and the first successful pattern match determines which result expression is used. In the previous example, the first pattern will match if url and agent are "http://www.control.org" and 99, respectively. The next will match if url is "http://www.kaos.org". The third pattern will match if agent is 86. The last three rules all use *wildcard* patterns represented by the underscore character; these match all inputs.

The overall conditions under which urlFilter returns true can be read off simply by reading through the pattern match: agent 99 can access "http://www.control.org", no one can access "http://www.kaos.org", and, excluding the latter, agent 86 can access anything.

Patterns are a rich and powerful technique for simultaneous data analysis and decomposition. Table 3-12 summarizes all the ways to form patterns in F#; many of these involve building up patterns from other patterns. The sections that follow look at some of these constructs, and we cover active patterns in Chapter 9.

Table 3-12. *Different Ways to Form Patterns*

General Form	Kind	Example
(pat, ... ,pat)	Tuple pattern	(1,2,("3",x))
[pat; ... ;pat]	List pattern	[x;y;z]
[| pat; ...; pat |]	Array pattern	[| "cmd"; arg1; arg2 |]
{ id=pat; ...; id=pat }	Record pattern	{ X=1; Y=2 }
Tag(pat, ... ,pat)	Tagged union or active pattern	Point(x,y)
pat | pat	"Or" pattern	[x] | ["X";x]
pat & pat	"And" pattern	[p] & [Point(x,y)]
pat as id	Named pattern	[x] as inp
id	Variable pattern	x
_	Wildcard pattern	_
Any literal	Constant pattern	36, "36", 27L, System.DayOfWeek.Monday
:? type	Type test pattern	:? string
null	Null test pattern	null

Matching on Structured Values

Pattern matching can be used to decompose structured values. Here is an example where we match nested tuple values:

```
let highLow a b =
    match (a,b) with
    | ("lo", lo), ("hi", hi) -> (lo,hi)
    | ("hi", hi), ("lo", lo) -> (lo,hi)
    | _ -> failwith "expected a both a high and low value";;
```

The match examines two pairs and looks at the strings in the first element of each, returning the associated values:

```
> highLow ("hi",300) ("lo",100);;
val it : int * int = (100,300)
```

The first rule matches if the first parts of the input pairs are the strings "lo" and "hi", respectively. It then returns a pair made from the respective second parts of the tuples. The second rule is the mirror of this in case the values appeared in reverse order.

The final cases of both of the previous examples use wildcard patterns to cover remaining cases. This makes the patterns *exhaustive*. Frequently, no wildcard is needed to ensure this, because for many input types F# is able to determine whether the given set of rules is sufficient to cover all possibilities for the given shape of data. However, if a match is not exhaustive, a warning is given:

```
> let urlFilter3 url agent =
      match url,agent with
      | "http://www.control.org", 86 -> true
      | "http://www.kaos.org", _ -> false;;

  match url,agent with
  ^^^^^^^^^^^^^^^^^^^

warning: Incomplete pattern match.
```

In these cases, it may be necessary to add an extra exception-throwing clause to indicate to the F# compiler that the given inputs are not expected:

```
let urlFilter4 url agent =
    match url,agent with
    | "http://www.control.org", 86 -> true
    | "http://www.kaos.org", _ -> false
    | _ -> failwith "unexpected input"
```

Nonexhaustive matches are automatically augmented by a default case where a MatchFailureException is thrown. We discuss exceptions in Chapter 4.

F# is frequently able to determine whether pattern-matching rules are redundant, such as if a rule can never be selected because previous rules subsume all such cases. In this case, a warning is given. For example:

```
> let urlFilter2 url agent =
    match url,agent with
    | "http://www.control.org", _ -> true
    | "http://www.control.org", 86 -> true
    | _ -> false;;

    | "http://www.control.org", 86 -> true
    ^^^^^^^^^^^^^^^^^^^^^^^^^^^^^^^^^^^^^^^^^
warning: This rule will never be matched.
```

Tip Use wildcard patterns with care. F# can often determine whether a match is exhaustive, and the use of wildcard patterns effectively disables this analysis for any particular pattern match. Sometimes it is better to write out the extra cases of a match as explicit patterns, because you can then adjust your code when new kinds of input data are introduced.

Guarding Rules and Combining Patterns

Individual rules of a match can be guarded by a condition that is executed if the pattern itself succeeds. Here is a simple use of this mechanism to record the three clauses of computing the sign of an integer:

```
let sign x =
    match x with
    | _ when x < 0 -> -1
    | _ when x > 0 ->  1
    | _ -> 0
```

Two patterns can be combined to represent two possible paths for matching:

```
let getValue a =
    match a with
    | (("lo" | "low") ,v) -> v
    | ("hi",v) | ("high",v) -> v
    | _ -> failwith "expected a both a high and low value";;
```

Here the pattern ("lo" | "low") matches either string. The pattern ("hi",v) | ("high",v) plays essentially the same role by matching pairs values where the left of the pair is "hi" or "high" and by binding the value v on either side of the pattern.

■**Note** Individual patterns cannot bind the same variables twice. For example, a pattern (x,x) is not permitted, though (x,y) when x = y is permitted. Furthermore, each side of an "or" pattern must bind the same set of variables, and these variables must have the same types.

Getting Started with Sequences

Many programming tasks require the iteration, aggregation, and transformation of data streamed from various sources. One important and general way to code these tasks is in terms of values of the .NET type System.Collections.Generic.IEnumerable<*type*>, which is typically abbreviated to seq<*type*> in F# code. A seq<*type*> is simply a value that can be *iterated*, producing results of type *type* on demand. Sequences are used to wrap collections, computations, and data streams and are frequently used to represent the results of database queries. In the following sections, we present some simple examples of working with seq<*type*> values.

Using Range Expressions

You can generate simple sequences using *range expressions*. For integer ranges, these take the form of seq {n .. m} for the integer expressions n and m.

```
> seq {0 .. 2};;
val it : seq<int> = seq [ 0; 1; 2; ]
```

You can also specify range expressions using other numeric types such as double and single:

```
> seq {-100.0 .. 100.0};;
val it : seq<double> = seq [ -100.0; -99.0; -98.0; ... ]
```

By default F# Interactive shows the value of a sequence only to a limited depth. Indeed, seq<'a> values are *lazy* in the sense that they compute and return the successive elements on demand. This means you can create sequences representing very large ranges, and the elements of the sequence are computed only if they are required by a subsequent computation. In the next example, we don't actually create a concrete data structure containing one trillion elements but rather a sequence value that has the *potential* to yield this number of elements on demand. The default printing performed by F# Interactive forces this computation up to depth 4:

```
> seq {1I .. 1000000000000I};;
val it : seq<bigint> = seq [ 0I; 1I; 2I; 3I; ... ]
```

The default increment for range expressions is always 1. A different increment can be used via range expressions of the form seq { n .. skip .. m }:

```
> seq { 1 .. 2 .. 5 };;
val it : seq<int> = seq [ 1; 3; 5 ]

> seq { 1 .. -2 .. -5 };;
val it : seq<int> = seq [ 1; -1; -3; -5 ]
```

If the skip causes the final element to be overshot, then the final element is not included in the result:

```
> seq { 0 .. 2 .. 5 };;
val it : seq<int> = seq [ 0; 2; 4 ]
```

The (..) and (.. ..) operators are overloaded operators in the same sense as (+) and (-), which means their behavior can be altered for user-defined types. We discuss this in more detail in Chapter 6.

Iterating a Sequence

Sequences can be iterated using the for ... in ... do construct, as well as the Seq.iter aggregate operator discussed in the next section. Here is a simple example of the first:

```
> let range = seq {0 .. 2 .. 6};;
val range : seq<int>

> for i in range do
      printfn "i = %d" i;;
i = 0
i = 2
i = 4
i = 6
```

This construct forces the iteration of the entire seq so must be used with care when working with sequences that may yield a large number of elements.

Transforming Sequences with Aggregate Operators

Any value of type seq<type> can be iterated and transformed using functions in the Microsoft.FSharp.Collections.Seq module. For example:

```
> let range = seq {0 .. 10};;
val range : seq<int>

> range |> Seq.map (fun i -> (i,i*i));;
val it : seq<int * int> = seq [ (0, 0); (1, 1); (2, 4); (3, 9) ... ]
```

Table 3-13 shows some important functions in this library module. The following operators necessarily evaluate all the elements of the input seq immediately:

- Seq.iter: This iterates all elements, applying a function to each one.

- Seq.to_list: This iterates all elements, building a new list.

- Seq.to_array: This iterates all elements, building a new array.

Most of the other operators in the Seq module return one or more seq<*type*> values and force the computation of elements in any input seq<*type*> values only on demand.

Table 3-13. *Some Important Functions and Aggregate Operators from the Seq Module*

Operator	Type
Seq.append	: #seq<'a> -> #seq<'a> -> seq<'a>
Seq.concat	: #seq< #seq<'a> > -> seq<'a>
Seq.choose	: ('a -> 'b option) -> #seq<'a> -> seq<'b>
Seq.delay	: (unit -> #seq<'a>) -> seq<'a>
Seq.empty	seq<'a>
Seq.iter	: ('a -> unit) -> #seq<'a> -> unit
Seq.filter	: ('a -> bool) -> #seq<'a> -> seq<'a>
Seq.map	: ('a -> 'b) -> #seq<'a> -> seq<'b>
Seq.singleton	: 'a -> seq<'a>
Seq.truncate	: int -> #seq<'a> -> seq<'a>
Seq.to_list	: #seq<'a> -> 'a list
Seq.of_list	: 'a list -> seq<'a>
Seq.to_array	: #seq<'a> -> 'a[]
Seq.of_array	: 'a[] -> seq<'a>

Which Types Can Be Used As Sequences?

Table 3-13 includes types prefixed with #, such as #seq<'a>. This simply means the function will accept any type that is compatible with (that is, is a subtype of) seq<'a>. We explain the notions of subtyping and compatibility in more detail in Chapter 5, but to OO programmers the concept will be familiar, because it is the same as that used by other .NET languages such as C#, which itself is close to that used by Java. In practice, you can easily discover which types are compatible with which by using F# Interactive and tools such as Visual Studio, because when you hover over a type name, the compatible types are shown as well. You can also refer to the online documentation for the F# libraries and the .NET Framework, easily searched by using the major search engines.

Here are some of the types compatible with seq<'a>:

- *Array types*: For example, int[] is compatible with seq<int>.

- *F# list types*: For example, int list is compatible with seq<int>.

- *All other F# and .NET collection types*: For example, System.Collections.Generic.
  SortedList<string> is compatible with seq<string>.

The following types are not directly type compatible with seq<'a> but can readily be converted into sequences when needed:

- Some .NET types are compatible with a somewhat deprecated nongeneric .NET 1.0 construct called System.Collections.IEnumerable (note the absence of any generic parameter) but are not actually compatible with the newer .NET construct System.Collections.Generic.IEnumerable<*type*>, called seq<*type*> in F# code.

- Some .NET types such as System.Text.RegularExpressions.MatchCollection support only a GetEnumerator method and can't be used directly as values of type seq<*type*>. However, these can be converted into sequences by using them in conjunction with either the sequence expression syntax mentioned earlier, such as seq{ for x in matchCollection -> x } or for x in matchCollection do ....

Expressions of the form for *pat* in *seq* are described in the section "Using Sequence Expressions" and in Chapter 4.

Using Lazy Sequences from External Sources

Sequences are frequently used to represent the process of streaming data from an external source, such as from a database query or from a computer's file system. For example, the following recursive function constructs a seq<string> that represents the process of recursively reading the names of all the files under a given path. The return types of Directory.GetFiles and Directory.GetDirectories are string[], and as noted earlier, this type is always compatible with seq<string>.

```
open System.IO
let rec allFiles dir =
    Seq.append
        (dir |> Directory.GetFiles)
        (dir |> Directory.GetDirectories |> Seq.map allFiles |> Seq.concat)
```

This gives the following type:

```
val allFiles : string -> seq<string>
```

Here is an example of the function being used on one of our machines:

```
> allFiles @"c:\WINDOWS\system32";;
val it : seq<string> =
      = seq ["c:\\WINDOWS\\system32\\$winnt$.inf";
            "c:\\WINDOWS\\system32\\12520437.cpx";
            "c:\\WINDOWS\\system32\\12520850.cpx";
            "c:\\WINDOWS\\system32\\6to4svc.dll"; ...]
```

The allFiles function is interesting partly because it shows many aspects of F# working seamlessly together:

- *Functions are values*: The function allFiles is recursive and is used as a first-class function value within its own definition.

- *Pipelining*: The pipelining operator |> provides a natural way to present the transformations applied to each subdirectory name.

- *Type inference*: Type inference computes all types in the obvious way, without any type annotations.

- *NET interoperability*: The System.IO.Directory operations provide intuitive primitives, which can then be incorporated in powerful ways using succinct F# programs.

- *Laziness where needed*: The function Seq.map applies the argument function lazily (on demand), which means subdirectories will not be read until really required.

One subtlety with programming with on-demand or lazy values such as sequences is that side effects such as reading and writing from an external store should not in general happen until the lazy sequence value is actually consumed. For example, the previous allFiles function reads the top-level directory C:\ as soon as allFiles is applied to its argument. This may not be appropriate if the contents of C:\ are changing. You can delay the computation of the sequence by using the library function Seq.delay or by using a sequence expression, covered in the next section, where delays are inserted automatically by the F# compiler.

Using Sequence Expressions

Aggregate operators are a powerful way of working with seq<type> values. However, F# also provides a convenient and compact syntax called *sequence expressions* for specifying sequence values that could be built using operations such as choose, map, filter, and concat. Sequence expressions can also be used to specify the shapes of lists and arrays. It is valuable to learn how to use sequence expressions:

- They are a compact way of specifying interesting data and generative processes.

- They are used to specify database queries when using data access layers such as Microsoft's Language Integrated Queries (LINQ). See Chapter 15 for examples of using sequence expressions in this way.

- They are one particular use of *workflows,* a more general concept that has several uses in F# programming. We discuss workflows in Chapter 9, and we show how to use them for asynchronous and parallel programming in Chapter 13.

Creating Sequence Expressions Using for

The simplest form of a sequence expression is seq { for *value* in *expr* .. *expr* -> *expr* }. Here -> should be read as "yield." This is simply a shorthand way of writing Seq.map over a range expression. For example, you can generate an enumeration of numbers and their squares as follows:

```
> let squares = seq { for i in 0 .. 10 -> (i,i*i) };;
val squares : seq<int * int>

> squares;;
val it : seq<int * int> = [ (0,0); (1,1); (2,4); (3,9); ... ]
```

The more complete form of this construct is seq{ for *pattern* in *seq* -> *expression* }. The pattern allows you to decompose the values yielded by the input enumerable. For example, you can consume the elements of squares using the pattern (i,isquared):

```
> seq { for (i,isquared) in squares -> (i,isquared,i*isquared) };;
val it : seq<int * int * int> = [ (0,0,0); (1,1,1); (2,4,8); (3,9,27); ... ]
```

The input *seq* can be a seq<*type*> or any type supporting a GetEnumerator method. (The latter is supported because some important types from the .NET libraries support this method without directly supporting the seq interface.) The following is an example where the input is a list of options. If the pattern fails to match the element of the enumerable, it is skipped, and no result is yielded for that element:

```
> seq { for Some(nm) in [ Some("James"); None; Some("John") ] -> nm.Length };;
val it : seq<int> = [ 5; 4 ]
```

Enriching Sequence Expressions with Additional Clauses

A sequence expression generally always begins with for ... in ..., but you can use additional constructs. For example:

- *A secondary iteration:* for *pattern* in *seq* do *seq-expr*

- *A filter:* if *expression* then *seq-expr*

- *A conditional:* if *expression* then *seq-expr* else *seq-expr*

- *A* let *binding:* let *pattern* = *expression* in *seq-expr*

- *A final yield:* -> *expression* or yield *expression*

- *A final yield of another sequence:* ->> *expression* or yield! *expression*

Secondary iterations generate additional sequences, all of which are collected and concatenated together. Filters allow you to skip elements that do not satisfy a given predicate. To see both of these in action, the following computes a checkerboard set of coordinates of a rectangular grid:

```
let checkerboardCoordinates n =
    seq { for row in 1 .. n do
             for col in 1 .. n do
                 if (row+col) % 2 = 0 then
                     yield (row,col) }
```

```
> checkerboardCoordinates 3;;
val it : seq<(int * int)> = seq [(1, 1); (1, 3); (2, 2); (3, 1); ...]
```

Using `let` clauses in sequence expressions allows you to compute intermediary results. For example, the following code gets the creation time and last-access time for each file in a directory:

```
let fileInfo dir =
    seq { for file in Directory.GetFiles(dir) do
             let creationTime = File.GetCreationTime(file)
             let lastAccessTime = File.GetLastAccessTime(file)
             yield (file,creationTime,lastAccessTime) }
```

In the previous examples, each step of the iteration produces zero or one result. The final yield of a sequence expression can also be another sequence, signified through the use of the ->> symbol or the yield! keyword. You generally use -> and ->> in compact sequence expressions that don't contain let, if, and other more advanced constructs. The following sample shows how to redefine the allFiles function from the previous section using a sequence expression. Note that multiple generators can be included in one sequence expression; the results are implicitly collated together using Seq.append.

```
let rec allFiles dir =
    seq { for file in Directory.GetFiles(dir) -> file
          for subdir in Directory.GetDirectories dir ->> (allFiles subdir) }
```

■**Note** When using the #light syntax option, the do and in tokens can be omitted when immediately followed by a -> or ->> or when part of a sequence of for or let bindings.

Enriching Sequence Expressions to Specify Lists and Arrays

You can also use range and sequence expressions to build list and array values. The syntax is identical except the surrounding braces are replaced by the usual [ ] for lists and [| |] for arrays. We discuss arrays in more detail in Chapter 4.

```
> [ 1 .. 4 ];;
val it: int list = [ 1; 2; 3; 4 ]

> [ for i in 0 .. 3 -> (i,i*i) ];;
val it : (int * int) list = [ (0,0); (1,1); (2,4); (3,9) ]

> [| for i in 0 .. 3 -> (i,i*i) |];;
val it : (int * int) [] = [ (0,0); (1,1); (2,4); (3,9) ]
```

Caution F# lists and arrays are finite data structures built immediately rather than on demand, so you must take care that the length of the sequence is suitable. For example, [1I .. 1000000000I] will attempt to build a list that is one billion elements long.

Exploring Some Simple Type Definitions

F# is a typed language, and it is often necessary for the programmer to declare new "shapes" of types via type definitions and type abbreviations. In this chapter, we cover only some of the simpler type definitions that are useful and succinct workhorses for functional programming. F# also lets you define a range of sophisticated type definitions related to object-oriented programming, which we discuss in Chapter 6. However, these are often not required in basic functional programming.

Defining Type Abbreviations

Type abbreviations are the simplest type definitions:

```
type index = int
type flags = int64
type results = string * TimeSpan * int * int
```

It is common to use lowercase names for type abbreviations, but it's certainly not compulsory. Type abbreviations can be generic:

```
type StringMap<'a> = Microsoft.FSharp.Collections.Map<string,'a>
type Projections<'a,'b> = ('a -> 'b) * ('b -> 'a)
```

Type abbreviations are not "concrete," because they simply alias an existing type. Type abbreviations are expanded during the process of compiling F# code to the format shared between multiple .NET languages. The difference can, for example, be detected by other .NET languages, and because of this, a number of restrictions apply to type abbreviations. For example, you cannot augment type abbreviations with additional members, as can be done for concrete types such as records, discriminated unions, and classes. In addition, you cannot truly hide a type abbreviation using a signature or private declaration (see Chapter 7).

Defining Records

The simplest concrete type definitions are records. Here's our first example:

```
type Person =
    { Name: string;
      DateOfBirth: System.DateTime; }
```

You can construct record values simply by using the record labels:

```
> { Name = "Bill"; DateOfBirth = new System.DateTime(1962,09,02) };;
val it : Person = { Name="Bill"; DateOfBirth = 09/02/1962 }
```

You can also construct record values by using the following more explicit syntax, which names the type should there be a conflict between labels amongst multiple records:

```
> { new Person
    with Name = "Anna"
    and  DateOfBirth = new System.DateTime(1968,07,23) };;
val it : Person = { Name="Anna"; DateOfBirth = 23/07/1968 }
```

Record values are often used to return results from functions:

```
type PageStats =
    { Site: string;
      Time: System.TimeSpan;
      Length: int;
      NumWords: int;
      NumHRefs: int }
```

This technique works well when returning a large number of heterogeneous results:

```
let stats site =
    let url = "http://" + site
    let html,t = time (fun () -> http url)
    let hwords = html |> getWords
    let hrefs = hWords |> List.filter (fun s -> s = "href")
    { Site=site; Time=t; Length=html.Length;
      NumWords=hwords.Length; NumHRefs=hrefs.Length }
```

Here is the type of stats:

```
val stats : string -> PageStats
```

Here is how F# Interactive shows the results of applying the function:

```
> stats "www.live.com";;
val it : PageStats = { Site="www.live.com"; Time=0.872623628;
                        Length=7728, NumWords=1156; NumHRefs=10; }
```

Handling Non-unique Record Field Names

Records labels need not be unique amongst multiple record types. Here is an example:

```
type Person =
    { Name: string;
      DateOfBirth: System.DateTime; }

type Company =
    { Name: string;
      Address: string; }
```

When record names are non-unique, constructions of record values may need to use object expressions in order to indicate the name of the record type, thus disambiguating the construction. For example, consider the following type definitions:

```
type Dot = { X: int; Y: int }
type Point = { X: float; Y: float }
```

On lookup, record labels are accessed using the "." notation in the same way as properties. One slight difference is that in the absence of further qualifying information, the type of the object being accessed is inferred from the record label. This is based on that latest set of record labels in scope from record definitions and uses of open. For example, given the previous definitions, you have the following:

```
> let coords1 (p:Point) = (p.X,p.Y);;
val coords1 : Point -> float * float

> let coords2 (d:Dot) = (d.X,d.Y);;
val coords2 : Dot -> int * int

> let dist p = sqrt (p.X * p.X + p.Y * p.Y);; // use of X and Y implies type "Point"
val dist : Point -> float
```

The accesses to the labels X and Y in the first two definitions have been resolved using the type information provided by the type annotations. The accesses in the third definition have been resolved using the default interpretation of record field labels in the absence of any other qualifying information.

Cloning Records

Records support a convenient syntax to clone all the values in the record, creating a new value, with some values replaced. Here is a simple example:

```
type Point3D = { X: float; Y: float; Z: float }
let p1 = { X=3.0; Y=4.0; Z=5.0 }
```

```
> let p2 = { p1 with Y=0.0; Z=0.0 };;
val p2 : Point3D
```

The definition of p2 is identical to this:

```
let p2 = { X=p1.X; Y=0.0; Z=0.0 }
```

This expression form does not mutate the values of a record, even if the fields of the original record are mutable.

Defining Discriminated Unions

The second kind of concrete type definition we look at in this section is a discriminated union. Here is a very simple example:

```
type Route = int
type Make = string
type Model = string
type Transport =
    | Car of Make * Model
    | Bicycle
    | Bus of Route
```

Each alternative of a discriminated union is called a *discriminator*. You can build values simply by using the discriminator much as if it were a function:

```
> let nick = Car("BMW","360");;
val nick : Transport

> let don = [ Bicycle; Bus 8 ];;
val don  : Transport list

> let james = [ Car ("Ford","Fiesta"); Bicycle ];;
val james  : Transport list
```

You can also use discriminators in pattern matching:

```
let averageSpeed (tr: Transport) =
    match tr with
    | Car _ -> 35
    | Bicycle -> 16
    | Bus _ -> 24
```

Several of the types you've already met are defined as discriminated unions. For example, the 'a option type is defined as follows:

```
type 'a option =
    | None
    | Some of 'a
```

Discriminated unions can include recursive references (the same is true of records and other type definitions). This is frequently used when representing structured languages via discriminated unions, a topic covered in depth in Chapter 9:

```
type Proposition =
    | True
    | And of Proposition * Proposition
    | Or of Proposition * Proposition
    | Not of Proposition
```

Recursive functions can be used to traverse such a type. For example:

```
let rec eval (p: Proposition) =
    match p with
    | True -> true
    | And(p1,p2) -> eval p1 && eval p2
    | Or (p1,p2) -> eval p1 || eval p2
    | Not(p1) -> not (eval p1)
```

Indeed, the F# type of immutable lists is defined in this way:

```
type 'a list =
    | ([])
    | (::) of 'a * 'a list
```

A broad range of tree-like data structures are conveniently represented as discriminated unions. For example:

```
type Tree<'a> =
    | Tree of 'a * Tree<'a> * Tree<'a>
    | Tip of 'a
```

You can use recursive functions to compute properties of trees:

```
let rec size tree =
    match tree with
    | Tree(_,l,r) -> 1 + size l + size r
    | Tip _ -> 1
```

Here is the inferred type of size:

```
val size : Tree<'a> -> int
```

Here is an example of a constructed tree term and the use of the size function:

```
> let small = Tree("1",Tree("2",Tip("a"),Tip("b")),Tip("c"));;
val small : Tree<string>

> small;;
val it : Tree<string> = Tree ("1",Tree ("2",Tip("a"),Tip("b")),Tip("c"))

> size small;;
val it : int = 5
```

We discuss symbolic manipulation based on trees in detail in Chapters 8, 9, and 12.

■**Note** Discriminated unions are a powerful and important construct and are useful when modeling a finite, sealed set of choices. This makes them a perfect fit for many constructs that arise in applications and symbolic analysis libraries. They are, by design, nonextensible: subsequent modules cannot add new cases to a discriminated union. This is deliberate: you get strong and useful guarantees by placing a limit on the range of possible values for a type. Extensible types can be defined through the use of records of functions and object interface types, discussed in Chapter 5 and Chapter 6.

Using Discriminated Unions As Records

Discriminated union types with only one data tag are an effective way to implement record-like types:

```
type Point3D = Vector3D of float * float * float
let origin = Vector3D(0.,0.,0.)
let unitX  = Vector3D(1.,0.,0.)
let unitY  = Vector3D(0.,1.,0.)
let unitZ  = Vector3D(0.,0.,1.)
```

These are particularly effective because they can be decomposed using succinct patterns in the same way as tuple arguments:

```
let length (Vector3D(dx,dy,dz)) = sqrt(dx*dx+dy*dy+dz*dz)
```

This technique is most useful for record-like values where there is some natural order on the constituent elements of the value (as shown earlier) or where the elements have different types.

Defining Multiple Types Simultaneously

Multiple types can be declared together to give a mutually recursive collection of types, including record types, discriminated unions, and abbreviations. The type definitions must be separated by the keyword and:

```
type node =
    { Name : string;
      Links : link list }
and link =
    | Dangling
    | Link of node
```

Summary

F# is a multiparadigm language, and in this chapter you looked at the core language constructs used for functional programming. In the next chapter, you'll look at how to use F# for imperative programming, that is, how to use mutable state, raise and handle exceptions, and perform I/O.

CHAPTER 4

■ ■ ■

Introducing Imperative Programming

In Chapter 3 you saw some of the simple but powerful data types and language constructs that make up F# functional programming. The functional programming paradigm is strongly associated with "programming without side effects," called *pure* functional programming. In this paradigm, programs compute the result of a mathematical expression and do not cause any side effects, except perhaps reporting the result of the computation. The formulae used in spreadsheets are often pure, as is the core of functional programming languages such as Haskell. F# is not, however, a "pure" functional language; for example, you can write programs that mutate data, perform I/O communications, start threads, and raise exceptions. Furthermore, the F# type system doesn't enforce a strict distinction between expressions that perform these actions and expressions that don't.

Programming with side effects is called *imperative* programming. In this chapter, we look more closely at a number of constructs related to imperative programming. We describe how to use loops, mutable data, arrays, and some common input/output techniques.

If your primary programming experience has been with an imperative language such as C, C#, or Java, you will initially find yourself using imperative constructs fairly frequently in F#. However, over time F# programmers generally learn how to perform many routine programming tasks within the side-effect-free subset of the language. F# programmers tend to use side effects in the following situations:

- When scripting and prototyping using F# Interactive

- When working with .NET library components that use side effects heavily, such as GUI libraries and I/O libraries

- When initializing complex data structures

- When using inherently imperative, efficient data structures such as hash tables and hash sets

- When locally optimizing routines in a way that improves on the performance of the functional version of the routine

- When working with very large data structures or in scenarios where the allocation of data structures must be minimized for performance reasons

Some F# programmers don't use any imperative techniques at all except as part of the external wrapper for their programs. Adopting this form of "pure" functional programming for a time is an excellent way to hone your functional programming techniques.

Tip Programming with fewer side effects is attractive for many reasons. For example, eliminating unnecessary side effects nearly always reduces the complexity of your code, so it leads to fewer bugs. Another thing experienced functional programmers appreciate is that the programmer or compiler can easily adjust the order in which expressions are computed. A lack of side effects also helps you *reason* about your code: it is easier to visually check when two programs are equivalent, and it is easier to make quite radical adjustments to your code without introducing new, subtle bugs. Programs that are free from side effects can often be computed on demand where necessary, often by making very small, local changes to your code to introduce the use of delayed data structures. Finally, side effects such as mutation are difficult to use when data is accessed concurrently from multiple threads, as you'll see in Chapter 14.

Imperative Looping and Iterating

Three looping constructs are available to help make writing iterative code with side effects simple:

- *Simple* for *loops*: for var = start-expr to end-expr do expr done

- *Simple* while *loops*: while expr do expr done

- *Sequence loops*: for pattern in expr do expr done

All three constructs are for writing imperative programs, indicated partly by the fact that in all cases the body of the loop must have a return type of unit. Note that unit is the F# type that corresponds to void in imperative languages such as C, and it has the single value (). We now cover these three constructs in more detail.

Note The done token is optional when using the #light lightweight syntax option (the body of the loop must be indented on a new line).

Simple for loops

Simple for loops are the most efficient way to iterate over integer ranges. This is illustrated here by a replacement implementation of the repeatFetch function from Chapter 2:

```
let repeatFetch url n =
    for i = 1 to n do
        let html = http url
        printf "fetched <<< %s >>>\n" html
    printf "Done!\n"
```

This loop is executed for successive values of i over the given range, including both start and end indexes.

Simple while loops

The second looping construct is a while loop, which repeats until a given guard is false. For example, here is a way to keep your computer busy until the weekend:

```
open System

let loopUntilSaturday() =
    while (DateTime.Now.DayOfWeek <> DayOfWeek.Saturday) do
        printf "Still working!\n"

    printf "Saturday at last!\n"
```

When executing this code in F# Interactive, you can interrupt its execution by using Ctrl+C.

More Iteration Loops Over Sequences

As discussed in Chapter 3, any values compatible with the type seq<*type*> can be iterated using the for *pattern* in *seq* do ... construct. The input *seq* may be an F# list value, any seq<*type*>, or a value of any type supporting a GetEnumerator method. Here are some simple examples:

```
> for (b,pj) in [ ("Banana 1",true); ("Banana 2",false) ] do
      if pj then printfn "%s is in pyjamas today!" b;;
Banana 1 is in pyjamas today!
```

The following is an example where we iterate the results of a regular expression match. The type returned by the .NET method System.Text.RegularExpressions.Regex.Matches is a MatchCollection, which for reasons known best to the .NET designers doesn't directly support the seq<Match> interface. It does, however, support a GetEnumerator method that permits iteration over each individual result of the operation, each of which is of type Match, and the F# compiler inserts the conversions necessary to view the collection as a seq<Match> and perform the iteration. You'll learn more about using the .NET Regular Expression library in Chapter 10.

```
> open System.Text.RegularExpressions;;
> for m in (Regex.Matches("All the Pretty Horses","[a-zA-Z]+")) do
      printf "res = %s\n" m.Value;;
res = All
res = the
res = Pretty
res = Horses
```

Using Mutable Records

The simplest mutable data structures in F# are mutable records. In Chapter 3 you saw some simple examples of immutable records. A record is mutable if one or more of its fields is labeled `mutable`. This means that record fields can be updated using the <- operator, that is, the same syntax used to set a property. Mutable fields are usually used for records that implement the internal state of objects, discussed in Chapter 6 and Chapter 7.

For example, the following code defines a record used to count the number of times an event occurs and the number of times that the event satisfies a particular criterion:

```
type DiscreteEventCounter =
    { mutable Total: int;
      mutable Positive: int;
      Name : string }

let recordEvent (s: DiscreteEventCounter) isPositive =
    s.Total <- s.Total+1
    if isPositive then s.Positive <- s.Positive+1

let reportStatus (s: DiscreteEventCounter) =
    printfn "We have %d %s out of %d" s.Positive s.Name s.Total

let newCounter nm =
    { Total = 0;
      Positive = 0;
      Name = nm }
```

We can use this type as follows (this sample uses the `http` function from Chapter 2):

```
let longPageCounter = newCounter "long page(s)"

let fetch url =
    let page = http url
    recordEvent longPageCounter (page.Length > 10000)
    page
```

Every call to the function `fetch` mutates the mutable record fields in the global variable `longPageCounter`. For example:

```
> fetch "http://www.smh.com.au" |> ignore;;
val it : unit = ()

> fetch "http://www.theage.com.au"  |> ignore;;
val it : unit = ()

> reportStatus longPageCounter;;
We have 1 long page(s) out of 2
val it : unit = ()
```

Record types can also support members (for example, properties and methods) and give implicit implementations of interfaces, discussed in Chapter 6. Practically speaking, this means you can use them as one way to implement object-oriented abstractions.

Mutable Reference Cells

One particularly useful mutable record is the general-purpose type of mutable reference cells, or *ref* cells for short. These often play much the same role as pointers in other imperative programming languages. You can see how to use mutable reference cells in the following example:

```
> let cell1 = ref 1;;
val cell1 : int ref

> cell1;;
val it : int ref = { contents = 1 }

> !cell1;;
val it : int = 1

> cell1 := 3;;
val it : unit = ()

> cell1;;
val it : int ref = { contents = 3 }

> !cell1;;
val it : int = 3
```

The key type is 'a ref, and its main operators are ref, !, and :=. The types of these operators are as follows:

```
val ref  : 'a -> 'a ref
val (:=) : 'a ref -> 'a -> unit
val (!)  : 'a ref -> 'a
```

These allocate a reference cell, read the cell, and mutate the cell, respectively. The operation cell1 := 3 is the key one; after this operation, the value returned by evaluating the expression !cell1 is changed. You can also use either the contents field or the Value property to access the value of a reference cell.

Both the 'a ref type and its operations are defined in the F# library as a simple record data structure with a single mutable field:

```
type 'a ref = { mutable contents: 'a }
let (!) r = r.contents
let (:=) r v = r.contents <- v
let ref v = { contents = v }
```

The type `'a ref` is actually a synonym for a type `Microsoft.FSharp.Core.Ref<'a>` defined in this way.

WHICH DATA STRUCTURES ARE MUTABLE?

It is useful to know which data structures are mutable and which are not. If a data structure can be mutated, then this will typically be evident in the types of the operations you can perform on that structure. For example, if a data structure `Table<'Key,'Value>` has an operation like the following, then in practice you can be sure that updates to the data structure modify the data structure itself:

```
val add : Table<'Key,'Value> -> 'Key -> 'Value -> unit
```

That is, the updates to the data structure are *destructive*, and no value is returned from the operation; the result is the type `unit`, which is akin to `void` in C and many other languages. Likewise, the following member indicates the data structure is almost certainly mutable:

```
member Add : 'Key * 'Value -> unit
```

In both cases, the presence of `unit` as a return type is a sure sign that an operation performs some imperative side effects. In contrast, operations on immutable data structures typically return a new instance of the data structure when an operation such as `add` is performed. For example:

```
val add : 'Key -> 'Value -> Table<'Key,'Value> -> Table<'Key,'Value>
```

Or for example:

```
member Add : 'Key * 'Value -> Table<'Key,'Value>
```

As discussed in Chapter 3, immutable data structures are also called *functional* or *persistent*. The latter name is used because the original table is not modified when adding an element. Well-crafted persistent data structures don't duplicate the actual memory used to store the data structure every time an addition is made; instead, internal nodes can be shared between the old and new data structures. Example persistent data structures in the F# library are F# lists, options, tuples, and the types `Microsoft.FSharp.Collections.Map<'Key,'Value>` and `Microsoft.FSharp.Collections.Set<'Key>`. Most data structures in the .NET libraries are not persistent, though if you are careful, you can use them as persistent data structures by accessing them in "read-only" mode and copying them where necessary.

Avoiding Aliasing

Like all mutable data structures, two mutable record values or two values of type `'a ref` may refer to the same reference cell—this is called *aliasing*. Aliasing of immutable data structures is not a problem; no client consuming or inspecting the data values can detect that the values have been aliased. However, aliasing of mutable data can lead to problems in understanding code. In general, it is good practice to ensure that no two values currently in scope directly alias the same mutable data structures. The following example continues that from earlier and shows how an update to `cell1` can affect the value returned by `!cell2`:

```
> let cell2 = cell1;;
val cell2 : int ref

> !cell2;;
val it : int = 3

> cell1 := 7;;
val it : unit = ()

> !cell2;;
val it : int 7
```

Hiding Mutable Data

Mutable data is often hidden behind an *encapsulation boundary*. We'll look at encapsulation in more detail in Chapter 7, but one easy way to do this is to make data private to a function. For example, the following shows how to hide a mutable reference within the inner closure of values referenced by a function value:

```
let generateStamp =
    let count = ref 0
    (fun () -> count := !count + 1; !count)
```

```
val generateStamp: unit -> int
```

The line let count = ref 0 is executed once, when the generateStamp function is defined. Here is an example of the use of this function:

```
> generateStamp();;
val it : int = 1

> generateStamp();;
val it : int = 2
```

This is a powerful technique for hiding and encapsulating mutable state without resorting to writing new type and class definitions. It is good programming practice in polished code to ensure that all related items of mutable state are collected under some named data structure or other entity such as a function.

UNDERSTANDING MUTATION AND IDENTITY

F# encourages the use of objects whose logical identity (if any) is based purely on the characteristics (for example, fields and properties) of the object. For example, the identity of a pair of integers (1,2) is determined by the two integers themselves; two tuple values both containing these two integers are for practical purposes identical. This is because tuples are immutable and support structural equality, hashing, and comparison, discussed further in Chapter 5 and Chapter 8.

Mutable reference cells are different; they can reveal their identities through aliasing and mutation. However, not all mutable values necessarily reveal their identity through mutation. For example, sometimes mutation is used just to "bootstrap" a value into its initial configuration, such as when connecting the nodes of a graph. These are relatively benign uses of mutation.

Ultimately you can detect whether two mutable values are the same object by using the function System. Object.ReferenceEquals. You can also use this function on immutable values to detect whether two values are represented by the physically same value. However, in this circumstance, the results returned by the function may change according to the optimization settings you apply to your F# code.

Using Mutable Locals

You saw in the previous section that mutable references must be explicitly dereferenced. F# also supports mutable locals that are *implicitly* dereferenced. These must either be top-level definitions or be a local variable in a function.

```
> let mutable cell1 = 1;;
val mutable cell1 : int

> cell1;;
val it : int = 1

> cell1 <- 3;;
val it : unit = ()

> cell1;;
val it : int = 3
```

The following shows how to use a mutable local:

```
let sum n m =
    let mutable res = 0
    for i = n to m do
        res <- res + i
    res
```

```
> sum 3 6;;
val it : int = 18
```

In the release of F# at the time of writing, there are strong restrictions on the use of mutable locals. In particular, unlike mutable references, mutable locals are guaranteed to be stack-allocated values, which is important in some situations because the .NET garbage collector won't move stack values. As a result, mutable locals may not be used at all in any inner lambda expressions or other closure constructs, with the exception of top-level mutable values, which can be used anywhere, and mutable fields of records and objects, which are associated with the heap allocated objects themselves. You'll learn more about mutable object types in Chapter 6. There has been discussion amongst the F# designers about lifting these restrictions; until that is done, reference cells and types containing mutable fields can be used to make the existence of heap-allocated imperative state obvious.

Working with Arrays

Mutable arrays are a key data structure used as a building block in many high-performance computing scenarios. The following example illustrates how to use a one-dimensional array of double values:

```
> let arr = [| 1.0; 1.0; 1.0 |];;
val arr : float[]

> arr.[1];;
val it : float = 1.0

> arr.[1] <- 3.0;;
val it : unit = ()

> arr;;
val it : float[] = [| 1.0; 3.0; 1.0 |]
```

F# array values are usually manipulated using functions from the Array module, whose full path is Microsoft.FSharp.Collections.Array, but that can be accessed with the short name Array. Arrays are created either by using the creation functions in that module (such as Array. init, Array.create, and Array.zero_create) or by using sequence expressions, as discussed in Chapter 3. Some useful methods are also contained in the System.Array class. Table 4-1 shows some common functions from the Array module.

F# arrays can be very large, up to the memory limitations of the machine (a 3GB limit applies on 32-bit systems). For example, the following creates an array of 100 million elements (of total size approximately 400MB for a 32-bit machine):

```
> let (r : int[]) = Array.zero_create 100000000;;
val r : int array
```

The following attempt to create an array more than 4GB in size causes an
OutOfMemoryException on one of our machines:

```
> let (r : int[]) = Array.zero_create 1000000000;;
System.OutOfMemoryException: Exception of type 'System.OutOfMemoryException'
was thrown.
```

Table 4-1. *Some Important Functions and Aggregate Operators from the Array Module*

Operator	Type	Explanation
Array.append	: 'a[] -> 'a[] -> 'a[]	Returns a new array containing elements of the first array followed by elements of the second array
Array.sub	: 'a[] -> int -> int -> 'a[]	Returns a new array containing a portion of elements of the input array
Array.copy	: 'a[] -> 'a[]	Returns a copy of the input array
Array.iter	: ('a -> unit) -> 'a[] -> unit	Applies a function to all elements of the input array
Array.filter	: ('a -> bool) -> 'a[] -> 'a[]	Returns a new array containing a selection of elements of the input array
Array.length	: 'a[] -> int	Returns the length of the input array
Array.map	: ('a -> 'b) -> 'a[] -> 'b[]	Returns a new array containing the results of applying the function to each element of the input array
Array.fold_left	: ('a -> 'b -> 'a) -> 'a -> 'b[] -> 'a	Accumulates left to right over the input array
Array.fold_right	: ('a -> 'b -> 'b) -> 'a[] -> 'b -> 'b	Accumulates right to left over the input array

■Note Arrays of *value types* (such as int, single, double, int64) are stored *flat*, so only one object is allocated for the entire array. Arrays of other types are stored as an array of object references. Primitive types such as integers and floating-point numbers are all value types, and many other .NET types are also value types. The .NET documentation indicates whether each type is a value type or not. Often the word *struct* is used for *value types*. You can also define new struct types directly in F# code, discussed in Chapter 6. All other types in F# are reference types, such as all record, tuple, discriminated union, and class and interface values.

Generating and Slicing Arrays

In Chapter 3, you saw in passing that you can use sequence expressions as a way to generate interesting array values. For example:

```
> let arr = [| for i in 0 .. 5 -> (i,i*i) |];;
val arr : (int*int)[]

> arr;;
val it : (int*int)[] = [|(0, 0); (1, 1); (2, 4); (3, 9); (4, 16); (5, 25)|]
```

You can also use a convenient syntax for extracting subarrays from existing arrays; this is called *slice notation*. A slice expression for a single-dimensional array has the form *arr.[start..finish]* where one of start and finish may optionally be omitted, and index zero or the index of the last element of the array is assumed instead. For example:

```
> let arr = [| for i in 0 .. 5 -> (i,i*i) |]
val arr : (int*int)[]

> arr;;
val it : (int*int)[] = [|(0, 0); (1, 1); (2, 4); (3, 9); (4, 16); (5, 25)|]

> arr.[1..3];;
val it : (int*int)[] = [| (1, 1); (2, 4); (3, 9); |]

> arr.[..2];;
val it : (int*int)[] = [| (0, 0); (1, 1); (2, 4); |]

> arr.[3..];;
val it : (int*int)[] = [| (3, 9); (4, 16); (5, 25) |]
```

We use slicing syntax extensively in the example "Verifying Circuits with Propositional Logic" in Chapter 12. You can also use slicing syntax with strings and several other F# types such as vectors and matrices, and the operator can be overloaded to work with your own type definitions. The F# library definitions of vectors and matrices can be used as a guide.

> ■**Note** Slices on arrays generate fresh arrays. Sometimes it can be more efficient to use other techniques, such as to access the array via an accessor function or object that performs one or more internal index adjustments before looking up the underlying array. If you add support for the slicing operators to your own types, you can choose whether they return copies of data structures or an accessor object.

Two-Dimensional Arrays

Like other .NET languages, F# directly supports two-dimensional array values that are stored flat, that is, where an array of dimensions (N, M) is stored using a contiguous array of N * M elements. The types for these values are written using [,], such as in int[,] and double[,], and these types also support slicing syntax. Values of these types are created and manipulated using the values in the Array2 module. Likewise, there is a module for manipulating three-dimensional array values whose types are written int[, ,]. You can also use the code in those modules as a template for defining code to manipulate arrays of higher dimension.

Introducing the Imperative .NET Collections

The .NET Framework comes equipped with an excellent set of imperative collections under the namespace System.Collections.Generic. You have seen some of these already. In the following sections, we'll take a look at some simple uses of these collections.

Using Resizeable Arrays

As mentioned in Chapter 3, the .NET Framework comes with a type System.Collections.Generic.List<'a>, which, although named List, is better described as a *resizeable array*. The F# library includes the following type abbreviation for this purpose:

```
type ResizeArray<'a> = System.Collections.Generic.List<'a>
```

Here is a simple example of using this data structure:

```
> let names = new ResizeArray<string>();;
val names : ResizeArray<string>

> for name in ["Claire"; "Sophie"; "Jane"] do
      names.Add(name);;
val it : unit = ()

> names.Count;;
val it : int = 3

> names.[0];;
val it : string = "Claire"
```

```
> names.[1];;
val it : string = "Sophie"

> names.[2];;
val it : string = "Jane"
```

Resizable arrays use an underlying array for storage and support constant-time random-access lookup. This makes a resizable array more efficient than an F# list in many situations, which supports efficient access only from the head (left) of the list. You can find the full set of members supported by this type in the .NET documentation. Commonly used properties and members include Add, Count, ConvertAll, Insert, BinarySearch, and ToArray. A module ResizeArray is included in the F# library that provides operations over this type in the style of the other F# collections.

Like other .NET collections, values of type ResizeArray<'a> support the seq<'a> interface. There is also an overload of the new constructor for this collection type that lets you specify initial values via a seq<'a>. This means you can create and consume instances of this collection type using sequence expressions:

```
> let squares = new ResizeArray<int>(seq { for i in 0 .. 100 -> i*i });;
val squares : ResizeArray<int> = [0; 1; 4; 9; ...]

> for x in squares do
      printfn "square: %d" x;;
square: 0
square: 1
square: 4
square: 9
...
```

Using Dictionaries

The type System.Collections.Generic.Dictionary<'key,'value> is an efficient hash table structure that is excellent for storing associations between values. The use of this collection from F# code requires a little care, because it must be able to correctly hash the key type. For simple key types such as integers, strings, and tuples, the default hashing behavior is adequate. Here is a simple example:

```
> open System.Collections.Generic;;

> let capitals = new Dictionary<string, string>();;
val capitals : Dictionary <string, string>

> capitals.["USA"] <- "Washington";;
val it : unit = ()
```

```
> capitals.["Bangladesh"] <- "Dhaka";;
val it : unit = ()

> capitals.ContainsKey("USA");;
val it : bool : true

> capitals.ContainsKey("Australia");;
val it : bool : false

> capitals.Keys;;
val it : KeyCollection<string,string> = seq["USA"; "Bangladesh"]

> capitals.["USA"];;
val it : string = "Washington"
```

Dictionaries are compatible with the type seq<KeyValuePair<'key,'value>>, where
KeyValuePair is a type from the System.Collections.Generic namespace and simply supports
the properties Key and Value. (From the F# perspective, we may have expected this type to be
seq<('key * 'value)>, but tuples are not available in the .NET collection library design.) Armed
with this knowledge, we can now use iteration to perform an operation for each element of the
collection:

```
> for kvp in capitals do
      printf "%s has capital %s\n" kvp.Key kvp.Value;;
USA has capital Washington
Bangladesh has capital Dhaka
val it : unit = ()
```

Using Dictionary's TryGetValue

The Dictionary method TryGetValue is of special interest, because its use from F# is a little
nonstandard. This method takes an input value of type 'Key and looks it up in the table. It
returns a bool indicating whether the lookup succeeded: true if the given key is in the dictionary and false otherwise. The value itself is returned via a .NET idiom called an *out parameter*.
From F# code there are actually three ways to use .NET methods that rely on out parameters:

- You may use a local mutable in combination with the address-of operator &.

- You may use a reference cell.

- You may simply not give a parameter, and the result is returned as part of a tuple.

Here's how you do it using a mutable local:

```
open System.Collections.Generic
```

```
let lookupName nm (dict : Dictionary<string,string>) =
    let mutable res = ""
    let foundIt = dict.TryGetValue(nm, &res)
    if foundIt then res
    else failwithf "Didn't find %s" nm
```

At the time of this writing, the previous code gives a warning in F# since the use of the address-of operator & may lead to "unverifiable" or even invalid .NET code. The use of a reference cell can be cleaner. For example:

```
> let res = ref "";;
val res: string ref

> capitals.TryGetValue("Australia", res);;
val it: bool = false

> capitals.TryGetValue("USA", res);;
val it: bool = true

> res;;
val it: string ref = { contents = "Washington" }
```

Finally, here is the technique where you simply don't pass the final parameter, and instead the result is returned as part of a tuple:

```
> capitals.TryGetValue("Australia");;
val it: bool * string = (false, null)

> capitals.TryGetValue("USA");;
val it: bool * string = (true, "Washington")
```

Note the value returned in the second element of the tuple may be null if the lookup failed when this technique is used. null values are discussed in the section "Working with null Values" at the end of this chapter.

Using Dictionaries with Compound Keys

You can use dictionaries with compound keys such as tuple keys of type (int * int). If necessary, you can specify the hash function used for these values when creating the instance of the dictionary. The default is to use *generic* hashing, also called *structural* hashing, a topic covered in more detail in Chapter 8. If you want to indicate this explicitly, you do so by specifying Microsoft.FSharp.Collections.HashIdentity.Structural when creating the collection instance. In some cases, this can also lead to performance improvements because the F# compiler often generates a hashing function appropriate for the compound type.

Here is an example where we use a dictionary with a compound key type to represent sparse maps:

```
> open System.Collections.Generic;;
> open Microsoft.FSharp.Collections;;

> let sparseMap = new Dictionary<(int * int), float>();;
val sparseMap : Dictionary <string, string list>

> sparseMap.[(0,2)] <- 4.0;;
val it : unit = ()

> sparseMap.[(1021,1847)] <- 9.0;;
val it : unit = ()

> sparseMap.Keys;;
val it : Dictionary.KeyCollection<(int * int),float>  = seq [(0,2); (1021; 1847) ]
```

Some Other Mutable Data Structures

Some of the other important mutable data structures in the F# and .NET libraries are as follows:

System.Collections.Generic.SortedList<'key,'value>: A collection of sorted values. Searches are done by a binary search. The underlying data structure is a single array.

System.Collections.Generic.SortedDictionary<'key,'value>: A collection of key/value pairs sorted by the key, rather than hashed. Searches are done by a binary chop. The underlying data structure is a single array.

System.Collections.Generic.Stack<'a>: A variable-sized last-in/first-out (LIFO) collection.

System.Collections.Generic.Queue<'a>: A variable-sized first-in/first-out (FIFO) collection.

System.Text.StringBuilder: A mutable structure for building string values.

Microsoft.FSharp.Collections.HashSet<'key>: A hash table structure holding only keys and no values. From .NET 3.5, a HashSet<'a> type is available in the System.Collections. Generic namespace.

Exceptions and Controlling Them

When a routine encounters a problem, it may respond in several ways, such as by recovering internally, emitting a warning, returning a marker value or incomplete result, or throwing an exception. The following code indicates how an exception can be thrown by some of the code we have already been using:

```
> let req = System.Net.WebRequest.Create("not a URL");;
System.UriFormatException: Invalid URI: The format of the URI could not be
determined.
```

Similarly, the GetResponse method also used in the http function may raise a System.Net.WebException exception. The exceptions that may be raised by routines are typically recorded in the documentation for those routines. Exception values may also be raised explicitly by F# code:

```
> (raise (System.InvalidOperationException("not today thank you")) : int);;
System.InvalidOperationException: not today thank you
```

In F#, exceptions are commonly raised using the F# failwith function:

```
> if false then 3 else failwith "hit the wall";;
Microsoft.FSharp.Core.FailureException: hit the wall
```

The types of some of the common functions used to raise exceptions are shown here:

```
val failwith  : string -> 'a
val raise: #exn -> 'a
val failwithf  : StringFormat<'a,'b> -> 'a
val invalid_arg  : string -> 'a
```

Note that the return types of all these are generic type variables, meaning that the functions never return "normally" and instead return by raising an exception. This means they can be used to form an expression of any particular type and indeed can be handy when you're drafting your code. For example, in the following program we've left part of the program incomplete:

```
if (System.DateTime.Now > failwith "not yet decided") then
    printfn "youÕve run out of time!"
```

Table 4-2 shows some of the common exceptions that are raised by failwith and other operations.

Table 4-2. *Common Categories of Exceptions and F# Functions That Raise Them*

Exception Type	F# Abbreviation	Description	Example
FailureException	Failure	General failure	failwith "fail"
InvalidArgumentException	Invalid_arg	Bad input	invalid_arg "x"
EndOfStreamException	End_of_file	End of input reached	raise End_of_file
DivideByZeroException		Integer divide by 0	1 / 0
NullReferenceException		Unexpected null	(null : string).Length

Catching Exceptions

You can catch exceptions using the try ... with ... language construct and :? type-test patterns, which filter any exception value caught by the with clause. For example:

```
> try
      raise (System.InvalidOperationException ("it's just not my day"))
  with
      | :? System.InvalidOperationException -> printfn "caught!";;
caught!
```

We cover these patterns more closely in Chapter 5. The following code sample shows how to use try ... with ... to catch two kinds of exceptions that may arise from the operations that make up the http method, in both cases returning the empty string "" as the incomplete result. Note that try ... with ... is just an expression, and it may return a result in both branches:

```
open System.IO

let http(url: string) =
    try
        let req = System.Net.WebRequest.Create(url)
        let resp = req.GetResponse()
        let stream = resp.GetResponseStream()
        let reader = new StreamReader(stream)
        let html = reader.ReadToEnd()
        html
    with
        | :? System.UriFormatException -> ""
        | :? System.Net.WebException -> ""
```

When an exception is thrown, a value is created that records information about the exception. It is this value that is being matched against the earlier type-test patterns. This value may also be bound directly and manipulated in the with clause of the try ... with constructs. For example, all exception values support the Message property:

```
> try
      raise (new System.InvalidOperationException ("invalid operation"))
  with
      | err -> printfn "oops, msg = '%s'" err.Message;;
oops, msg = 'invalid operation'
```

Using try . . . finally

Exceptions may also be processed using the try ... finally ... construct. This guarantees to run the finally clause both when an exception is thrown and when the expression evaluates normally. This allows the programmer to ensure that resources are disposed after the completion of an operation. For example, we can ensure that the web response from the previous example is closed as follows:

```
let httpViaTryFinally(url: string) =
    let req = System.Net.WebRequest.Create(url)
    let resp = req.GetResponse()
    try
        let stream = resp.GetResponseStream()
        let reader = new StreamReader(stream)
        let html = reader.ReadToEnd()
        html
    finally
        resp.Close()
```

In practice, you can use a shorter form to close and dispose of resources, simply by using a use binding instead of a let binding. This closes the response at the end of the scope of the resp variable, a technique is discussed in full in Chapter 8. Here is how the previous function looks using this form:

```
let httpViaUseBinding(url: string) =
    let req = System.Net.WebRequest.Create(url)
    use resp = req.GetResponse()
    let stream = resp.GetResponseStream()
    let reader = new StreamReader(stream)
    let html = reader.ReadToEnd()
    html
```

Defining New Exception Types

F# lets you define new kinds of exception objects that carry data in a conveniently accessible form. For example, here is a declaration of a new class of exceptions and a function that wraps http with a filter that catches particular cases:

```
exception BlockedURL of string

let http2 url =
    if url = "http://www.kaos.org"
    then raise(BlockedURL(url))
    else http url
```

The information from F# exception values can be extracted, again using pattern matching:

```
> try
    raise(BlockedURL("http://www.kaos.org"))
  with
    | BlockedURL(url) -> printf "blocked! url = '%s'\n" url;;
blocked! url = 'http://www.kaos.org'
```

Exception values are always subtypes of the F# type exn, an abbreviation for the .NET type System.Exception. The declaration exception BlockedURL of string is actually shorthand for defining a new F# class type BlockedURLException that is a subtype of System.Exception. Exception types can also be defined explicitly by defining new object types. You'll look more closely at object types and subtyping in Chapters 5 and 6.

Table 4-3 summarizes the exception-related language and library constructs.

Table 4-3. *Exception-Related Language and Library Constructs*

Example Code	Kind	Notes
raise *expr*	F# library function	Raises the given exception
failwith *expr*	F# library function	Raises the FailureException exception
try *expr* with *rules*	F# expression	Catches expressions matching the pattern rules
try *expr* finally *expr*	F# expression	Executes the finally expression both when the computation is successful and when an exception is raised
| :? ArgumentException ->	F# pattern rule	A rule matching the given .NET exception type
| :? ArgumentException as e ->	F# pattern rule	A rule matching the given .NET exception type and naming it as its stronger type
| Failure(msg) -> *expr*	F# pattern rule	A rule matching the given data-carrying F# exception
| exn -> *expr*	F# pattern rule	A rule matching any exception, binding the name exn to the exception object value
| exn when *expr* -> *expr*	F# pattern rule	A rule matching the exception under the given condition, binding the name exn to the exception object value

Having an Effect: Basic I/O

Imperative programming and input/output are closely related topics. In the following sections, we show some very simple I/O techniques using F# and .NET libraries.

Very Simple I/O: Reading and Writing Files

The .NET types System.IO.File and System.IO.Directory contain a number of simple functions to make working with files easy. For example, here's an easy way to output lines of text to a file:

```
> open System.IO;;

> File.WriteAllLines("test.txt", [| "This is a test file.";
                                     "It is easy to read." |]);;
val it : unit = ()
```

Many simple file-processing tasks require reading all the lines of a file. You can do this by reading all the lines in one action as an array using System.IO.File.ReadAllLines:

```
> open System.IO;;

> File.ReadAllLines("test.txt");;
val it : string [] = [| "This is a test file.";  "It is easy to read." |]
```

If necessary, the entire file can be read as a single string using System.IO.File.ReadAllText:

```
> File.ReadAllText("test.txt");;
val it : string = "This is a test file.\r\nIt is easy to read\r\n"
```

You can also use the results of System.IO.File.ReadAllLines as part of a list or sequence defined using a sequence expression:

```
> [ for line in File.ReadAllLines("test.txt") do
      let words = line.Split [| ' ' |]
      if words.Length > 3 && words.[2] = "easy" then
          yield line ];;
val it : seq<string> = [| "It is easy to read." |]
```

.NET I/O via Streams

The .NET namespace System.IO contains the primary .NET types for reading/writing bytes and text to/from data sources. The primary output constructs in this namespace are as follows:

System.IO.BinaryWriter: Writes primitive data types as binary values. Create using new BinaryWriter(stream). You can create output streams using File.Create(filename).

System.IO.StreamWriter: Writes textual strings and characters to a stream. The text is encoded according to a particular Unicode encoding. Create by using new StreamWriter(stream) and its variants or by using File.CreateText(filename).

System.IO.StringWriter: Writes textual strings to a StringBuilder, which eventually can be used to generate a string.

Here is a simple example of using `System.IO.File.CreateText` to create `StreamWriter` and write two strings:

```
> let outp = File.CreateText("playlist.txt");;
val outp : StreamWriter

> outp.WriteLine("Enchanted");;
val it : unit = ()

> outp.WriteLine("Put your records on");;
val it : unit = ()

> outp.Close();
```

These are the primary input constructs in the `System.IO` namespace:

`System.IO.BinaryReader`: Reads primitive data types as binary values. When reading the binary data as a string, it interprets the bytes according to a particular Unicode encoding. Create using `new BinaryReader(stream)`.

`System.IO.StreamReader`: Reads a stream as textual strings and characters. The bytes are decoded to strings according to a particular Unicode encoding. Create by using `new StreamReader(stream)` and its variants or by using `File.OpenText(filename)`.

`System.IO.StringReader`: Reads a string as textual strings and characters.

Here is a simple example of using `System.IO.File.OpenText` to create a `StreamReader` and read two strings:

```
> let inp = File.OpenText("playlist.txt");;
val inp : StreamReader

> inp.ReadLine();;
val it : string = "Enchanted"

> inp.ReadLine();;
val it : string = "Put your records on"

> inp.Close();;
val it : unit = ()
```

■**Tip** Whenever you create objects such as a `StreamReader` that have `Close` or `Dispose` operations or that implement the `IDisposable` interface, you should consider how you will eventually close or otherwise dispose of the resource. We discuss this later in this chapter and in Chapter 8.

Some Other I/O-Related Types

The System.IO namespace contains a number of other types, all of which are useful for some corner cases of advanced I/O but that you won't need to use from day to day. For example, you will see the following abstractions when browsing the .NET documentation:

System.IO.TextReader: Reads textual strings and characters from an unspecified source. This is the common functionality implemented by the StreamReader and StringReader types and the System.Console.In object. The latter is used to access the stdin input.

System.IO.TextWriter: Writes textual strings and characters to an unspecified output. This is the common functionality implemented by the StreamWriter and StringWriter types and the System.Console.Out and System.Console.Error objects. The latter are used to access the stdout and stderr output streams.

System.IO.Stream: Provides a generic view of a sequence of bytes.

Some functions that are generic over different kinds of output streams make use of these; for example, the formatting function twprintf discussed in section "Using printf and Friends" writes to any System.IO.TextWriter.

Using System.Console

Some simple input/output routines are provided in the System.Console class. For example:

```
> System.Console.WriteLine("Hello World");;
Hello World

> System.Console.ReadLine();;
<enter "I'm still here" here>
val it : string = "I'm still here"
```

The System.Console.Out object can also be used as a TextWriter.

Using printf and Friends

Throughout this book we have been using the printfn function, which is one way to print strings from F# values. This is a powerful, extensible technique for type-safe formatting. A related function called sprintf builds strings:

```
> sprintf "Name: %s, Age: %d" "Anna" 3;;
val it : string = "Name: Anna, Age: 3"
```

The format strings accepted by printf and sprintf are recognized and parsed by the F# compiler, and their use is statically type checked to ensure the arguments given for the formatting holes are consistent with the formatting directives. For example, if you use an integer where a string is expected, you will see a type error:

```
> sprintf "Name: %s, Age: %d" 3 10;;
----------------------------^
error: FS0001: This expression has type int but is here used with type string
```

Several printf-style formatting functions are provided in the Microsoft.FSharp.Text.
Printf module. Table 4-4 shows the most important of these.

Table 4-4. *Formatting Functions in the printf Module*

Function(s)	Outputs via Type	Outputs via Object	Example
printf(n)[a]	TextWriter	Console.Out	printf "Result: %d" res
eprintf(n)	TextWriter	Console.Error	eprintf "Result: %d" res
twprintf(n)	#TextWriter	Any TextWriter	twprintf stderr "Error: %d" res
sprintf	string	Generates strings	sprintf "Error: %d" res
bprintf(n)	StringBuilder	Any StringBuilder	bprintf buf "Error: %d" res

[a] *The functions with a suffix n add a new line to the generated text.*

Table 4-5 shows the basic formatting codes for printf-style formatting.

Table 4-5. *Formatting Codes for printf-style String and Output Formatting*

Code	Type Accepted	Notes
%b	bool	Prints true or false
%s	string	Prints the string
%d, %x, %X, %o, %u	int/int32	Decimal/hex/octal format for any integer types
%e, %E, %f, %g	float	Floating-point formats
%M	decimal	See .NET documentation
%A	Any type	Uses structured formatting, discussed in section "Generic Structural Formatting" and in Chapter 5
%O	Any type	Uses Object.ToString()
%a	Any type	Takes two arguments; one is a formatting function, and one is the value to format
%t	Function	Runs the function given as an argument

Any value can be formatted using a %O or %A pattern; these are extremely useful when prototyping or examining data. %O converts the object to a string using the Object.ToString() function supported by all values. For example:

```
> System.DateTime.Now.ToString();;
val it : string = "28/06/20.. 17:14:07 PM"

> sprintf "It is now %O" System.DateTime.Now;;
val it : string = "It is now 28/06/20... 17:14:09"
```

Note The format strings used with `printf` are scanned by the F# compiler during type checking, which means the use of the formats are type-safe; if you forget arguments, a warning will be given, and if your arguments are the wrong type, an error will be given. The format strings may also include the usual range of specifiers for padding and alignment used by languages such as C, as well as some other interesting specifiers for computed widths and precisions. You can find the full details in the F# library documentation for the `Printf` module.

Generic Structural Formatting

`Object.ToString()` is a somewhat undirected way of formatting data. Structural types such as tuples, lists, records, discriminated unions, collections, arrays, and matrices are often poorly formatted by this technique. The %A pattern uses the F# library functions `any_to_string` and `output_any` that use .NET reflection to format any F# value as a string based on the structure of the value. For example:

```
> any_to_string (1,2);;
val it : string = "(1, 2)"

> any_to_string [1;2;3];;
val it : string = "[1; 2; 3]"

> printf "The result is %A\n" [1;2;3];;
"The result is [1; 2; 3]"
```

Generic structural formatting can be extended to work with any user-defined data types, a topic covered on the F# website. Another extremely useful aspect of the `printf` formatting functions is their extensibility using %a patterns, which accept both a formatting function and a value to format. This is covered in detail in the F# library documentation for the `Microsoft.FSharp.Text.Printf` module.

Cleaning Up with IDisposable, use, and using

Many constructs in the `System.IO` namespace need to be closed after use, partly because they hold on to operating system resources such as file handles. This issue can be ignored when prototyping code in F# Interactive. However, as we touched on earlier in this chapter, in more polished code you should use language constructs such as use *var* = *expr* to ensure the resource is closed at the end of the lexical scope where a stream object is active. For example:

```
let myWriteStringToFile () =
    use outp = File.CreateText(@"playlist.txt")
    outp.WriteLine("Enchanted")
    outp.WriteLine("Put your records on")
```

This is equivalent to the following:

```
let myWriteStringToFile () =
    using (File.CreateText(@"playlist.txt")) (fun outp ->
        outp.WriteLine("Enchanted")
        outp.WriteLine("Put your records on"))
```

where the function using has the following definition in the F# library:

```
let using (ie : #System.IDisposable) f =
    try f(ie)
    finally ie.Dispose()
```

use and using ensure that the underlying stream is closed deterministically and the operating system resources are reclaimed when the lexical scope is exited. This happens regardless of whether the scope is exited because of normal termination or because of an exception. We cover the language construct use, the operator using, and related issues in more detail in Chapter 8.

Note If you do not use using or otherwise explicitly close the stream, then the stream will be closed when the stream object is "finalized" by the .NET garbage collector. However, it is generally bad practice to rely on finalization to clean up resources in this way, since finalization is not guaranteed to happen in a deterministic, timely fashion.

Working with null Values

The keyword null is used in imperative programming languages as a special, distinguished value of a type that represents an uninitialized value or some other kind of special condition. In general, null is not used in conjunction with types defined in F# code, though it is common to simulate null with a value of the option type. For example:

```
> let parents = [("Adam",None); ("Cain",Some("Adam","Eve"))];;
val parents : (string * (string * string) option) list
```

However, reference types defined in other .NET languages do support null, and when using .NET APIs, you may have to explicitly pass null values to the API and also, where appropriate, test return values for null. The .NET Framework documentation specifies when null may be returned from an API. It is recommended that you test for this condition using null pattern tests. For example:

```
match System.Environment.GetEnvironmentVariable("PATH") with
| null -> printf "the environment variable PATH is not defined\n"
| res -> printf "the environment variable PATH is set to %s\n" res
```

The following is a function that incorporates a pattern type test and a null-value test:

```
let switchOnType (a:obj) =
    match a with
    | null                   -> printf "null!"
    | :? System.Exception as e -> printf "An exception: %s!" e.Message
    | :? System.Int32 as i   -> printf "An integer: %d!" i
    | :? System.DateTime as d -> printf "A date/time: %O!" d
    | _                      -> printf "Some other kind of object\n"
```

There are other important sources of null values. For example, the "semisafe" function Array.zero_create creates an array whose values are initially null or, in the case of value types, an array each of whose entries is the zero bit pattern. This function is included with F# primarily because there is really no other alternative technique to initialize and create the array values used as building blocks of larger, more sophisticated data structures such as queues and hash tables. Of course, this function must be used with care, and in general you should hide the array behind an encapsulation boundary and be sure the values of the array are not referenced before they are initialized.

■**Note** Although F# generally enables you to code in a "null-free" style, F# is not totally immune from the potential existence of null values: they can come from the .NET APIs, and it is also possible to use Array. zero_create and other "backdoor" techniques to generate null values for F# types. If necessary, APIs can check for this condition by first converting F# values to the obj type by calling box and then testing for null (see the F# Informal Language Specification for full details). However, in practice, this is not required by the vast majority of F# programs, and for most purposes, the existence of null values can be ignored.

Some Advice: Functional Programming with Side Effects

F# stems from a tradition in programming languages where the emphasis has been on declarative and functional approaches to programming where state is made explicit, largely by passing extra parameters. Many F# programmers use functional programming techniques first before turning to their imperative alternatives, and we encourage you to do the same, for all the reasons listed at the start of this chapter.

However, F# also integrates imperative and functional programming together in a powerful way, and indeed F# is actually an extremely succinct imperative programming language! Furthermore, in some cases, no good functional techniques exist to solve a problem, or those that do are too experimental for production use. This means in practice using imperative constructs and libraries is common in F#: for example, many of the examples you saw in Chapter 2 and Chapter 3 used side effects to report their results or to create GUI components.

Regardless of this, we still encourage you to "think functionally," even about your imperative programming. In particular, it is always helpful to be aware of the potential side effects of your overall program and the particular characteristics of those side effects. The following sections describe five ways to help tame and reduce the use of side effects in your programs.

Consider Replacing Mutable Locals and Loops with Recursion

When imperative programmers begin to use F#, they frequently use mutable local variables or reference cells heavily as they translate code fragments from their favorite imperative language into F#. The resulting code often looks very bad. Over time, they learn to avoid many uses of mutable locals. For example, consider the following (naive) implementation of factorization, transliterated from C code:

```
let factorizeImperative n =
    let mutable primefactor1 = 1
    let mutable primefactor2 = n
    let mutable i = 2
    let mutable fin = false
    while (i < n && not fin) do
        if (n % i = 0) then
            primefactor1 <- i
            primefactor2 <- n / i
            fin <- true
        i <- i + 1

    if (primefactor1 = 1) then None
    else Some (primefactor1, primefactor2)
```

This code can be replaced by the following use of an inner recursive function:

```
let factorizeRecursive n =
    let rec find i =
        if i >= n then None
        elif (n % i = 0) then Some(i,n / i)
        else find (i+1)
    find 2
```

The second code is not only shorter, but it also uses no mutation, which makes it easier to reuse and maintain. It is also easy to see that the loop terminates (i is increasing toward n) and to see the two exit conditions for the function (i >= n and n % i = 0). Note that the state i has become an explicit parameter.

Separate Pure Computation from Side-Effecting Computations

Where possible, separate out as much of your computation as possible using side-effect-free functional programming. For example, sprinkling printf expressions throughout your code may make for a good debugging technique but, if not used wisely, can lead to code that is difficult to understand and inherently imperative.

Separating Mutable Data Structures

A common technique of object-oriented programming is to ensure that mutable data structures are private, nonescaping, and, where possible, fully *separated*, which means there is no chance that distinct pieces of code can access each other's internal state in undesirable ways. Fully separated state can even be used inside the implementation of what, to the outside world, appears to be a purely functional piece of code.

For example, where necessary, you can use side effects on private data structures allocated at the start of an algorithm and then discard these data structures before returning a result; the overall result is then effectively a side-effect-free function. One example of separation from the F# library is the library's implementation of List.map, which uses mutation internally, but the writes occur on an internal, separated data structure that no other code can access. Thus, as far as callers are concerned, List.map is pure and functional. The following is a second example, where we divide a sequence of inputs into equivalence classes (the F# library function Seq.groupBy does a similar thing):

```
open System.Collections.Generic

let divideIntoEquivalenceClasses keyf seq =

    // The dictionary to hold the equivalence classes
    let dict = new Dictionary<'key,ResizeArray<'a>>()

    // Build the groupings
    seq |> Seq.iter (fun v ->
        let key = keyf v
        let ok,prev = dict.TryGetValue(key)
        if ok then prev.Add(v)
        else let prev = new ResizeArray<'a>()
             dict.[key] <- prev
             prev.Add(v))

    // Return the sequence-of-sequences. Don't reveal the
    // internal collections: just reveal them as sequences
    dict |> Seq.map (fun group -> group.Key, Seq.readonly group.Value)
```

This uses the Dictionary and ResizeArray mutable data structures internally, but these mutable data structures are not revealed externally. The inferred type of the overall function is as follows:

```
val divideIntoEquivalenceClasses : ('a -> 'key) -> #seq<'a> -> seq<'key * seq<'a>>
```

Here is an example use:

```
> divideIntoEquivalenceClasses (fun n -> n % 3) [ 0 .. 10 ];;

val it : seq<int * seq<int>>
= seq [(0, seq [0; 3; 6; 9]); (1, seq [1; 4; 7; 10]); (2, seq [2; 5; 8])]
```

Not All Side Effects Are Equal

It is often helpful to use the "weakest" set of side effects necessary to achieve your programming task and at least be aware when you are using "strong" side effects:

- *Weak side effects* are ones that are effectively benign given the assumptions you are making about your application. For example, writing to a log file is very useful and is essentially benign (if the log file cannot grow arbitrarily large and crash your machine!). Similarly, reading data from a stable, unchanging file store on a local disk is effectively treating the disk as an extension of read-only memory, so reading these files is a weak form of side effect that will not be difficult to incorporate into your programs.

- *Strong side effects* have a much more corrosive effect on the correctness and operational properties of your program. For example, blocking network I/O is a relatively strong side effect by any measure. Performing blocking network I/O in the middle of a library routine can have the effect of destroying the responsiveness of a GUI application, at least if the routine is invoked by the GUI thread of an application. Any constructs that perform synchronization between threads are also a major source of strong side effects.

Whether a particular side effect is stronger or weaker depends very much on your application and whether the consequences of the side effect are sufficiently isolated and separated from other entities. Strong side effects can and should be used freely in the outer shell of an application or when scripting with F# Interactive; otherwise, not much can be achieved.

When writing larger pieces of code, you should write your application and libraries in such a way that most of your code either doesn't use strong side effects or at least makes it obvious when these side effects are being used. Threads and concurrency are commonly used to mediate problems associated with strong side effects; we cover these issues in more depth in Chapter 14.

Avoid Combining Imperative Programming and Laziness

It is generally thought to be bad style to combine delayed computations (that is, laziness) and side effects. This is not entirely true; for example, it is reasonable to set up a read from a file system as a lazy computation using sequences. However, it is relatively easy to make mistakes in this sort of programming. For example, consider the following code:

```
open System.IO
let reader1, reader2 =
    let reader = new StreamReader(File.OpenRead("test.txt"))
    let firstReader() = reader.ReadLine()
    let secondReader() = reader.ReadLine()
```

```
    // Note: we close the stream reader here!
    // But we are returning function values which use the reader
    // This is very bad!
    reader.Close()
    firstReader, secondReader

// Note: stream reader is now closed! The next line will fail!
let firstLine = reader1()
let secondLine = reader2()
firstLine, secondLine
```

This code is wrong because the StreamReader object reader is used after the point indicated by the comment. The returned function values are then called, and they will try to read from the "captured" variable reader. Function values are just one example of *delayed computations*: other examples are lazy values, sequences, and any objects that perform computations on demand. Be careful not to build delayed objects such as reader that represent handles to transient, disposable resources unless those objects are used in a way that respects the lifetime of that resource.

The previous code can be corrected to avoid using laziness in combination with a transient resource. For example:

```
open System.IO
let line1, line2 =
    let reader = new StreamReader(File.OpenRead("test.txt"))
    let firstLine = reader.ReadLine()
    let secondLine = reader.ReadLine()
    reader.Close()
    firstLine, secondLine
```

Another technique is to use language and/or library constructs that tie the lifetime of an object to some larger object. For example, we might want to read from a file to generate a delayed sequence. The Seq.generate_using function is useful for opening disposable resources and using them to generate results:

```
let reader =
    Seq.generate_using
        (fun () -> new StreamReader(File.OpenRead("test.txt")))
        (fun reader -> if reader.EndOfStream then None else Some(reader.ReadLine()))
```

You can also simply use a use binding within a sequence expression, which augments the sequence object with the code needed to clean up the resource when iteration is finished or terminates, a technique discussed further in Chapter 8 and shown by example here:

```
let reader =
    seq { use reader = new StreamReader(File.OpenRead("test.txt"))
          while not reader.EndOfStream do
              yield reader.ReadLine() }
```

The general lesson here is to try to keep your core application pure and use both delayed computations (laziness) and imperative programming (side effects) where appropriate but to be careful about using them together.

Summary

In this chapter, you learned how you do imperative programming in F#, from some of the basic mutable data structures such as reference cells to working with side effects such as exceptions and I/O. You also looked at some general principles for avoiding the need for imperative programming and isolating your uses of side effects. In the next chapter, we return to some of the building blocks of both functional and imperative programming in F#, with a deeper look at types, type inference, and generics.

CHAPTER 5

■ ■ ■

Mastering Types and Generics

F# constructs such as lists, tuples, and function values are all *generic*, which means they can be instantiated at multiple different types. For example, int list, string list, and (int * int) list are all instantiations of the generic family of F# list types. Likewise, int -> int and string -> int are both instantiations of the generic family of F# function types. The F# library and the .NET Framework have many other generic types and operations in addition to these.

Closely related to generics is the notion of *subtyping*. Generics and subtyping combine to allow you to write code that is generic over families of types. In this chapter, we cover .NET and F# types in general and generics and subtyping in particular. We show how F# uses *automatic generalization* to automatically infer generic types for your code, and we cover some of the basic generic functions you will find in the F# libraries such as generic comparison, hashing, and binary serialization.

Understanding Generic Type Variables

Generic constructs are always represented through the use of *type variables*, which in F# syntax are written 'a, 'b, 'k, 'key, 'K, and so on. For example, the definition of the list type in the F# library begins like this:

```
type 'a list = ...
```

You can write declarations of type variables in prefix position as shown previously or in postfix position; in other words, the previous declaration could just as well have been like this:

```
type list<'a> = ...
```

Values can also be generic. A typical generic value is List.map, whose type is as follows:

```
val map : ('a -> 'b) -> 'a list -> 'b list
```

Each time you name a generic type or value, the F# type system must infer instantiations for the type variables involved. For example, in Chapter 3 we used List.map fetch over an input list, where fetch had the following type:

```
val fetch : string -> string * string
```

In this case, the type variable 'a in the signature of List.map is instantiated to string, and the type variable 'b is instantiated to string * string, giving a return type of (string * string) list.

Generic values and functions such as List.map are common in F# programming; in fact, they're so common that we usually don't even write the declarations of the type variables in the types of these values. However, sometimes the declaration point of these variables is made explicit in output from tools and the F# compiler. For example, you may see this:

```
val map<'a,'b> : ('a -> 'b) -> 'a list -> 'b list
```

Frequently, type variables have an implicit scope, governed by the rules of automatic generalization discussed in the section "Writing Generic Functions." This means you can introduce type variables simply by writing them as part of the type annotations of a function:

```
let rec map (f : 'a -> 'b) (l : 'a list) =
    match l with
    | h :: t -> f h :: map f t
    | [] -> []
```

If you want, you can also write the type parameters explicitly on a declaration. You will typically have to use each type variable at least once in a type annotation in order to relate the type parameters to the actual code:

```
let rec map<'a,'b> (f : 'a -> 'b) (l : 'a list) =
    match l with
    | h :: t -> f h :: map f t
    | [] -> []
```

Writing Generic Functions

A key feature of F# is the automatic generalization of code. The combination of automatic generalization and type inference makes many programs simpler, more succinct, and more general. It also greatly enhances code reuse. Languages without automatic generalization force programmers to compute and explicitly write down the most general type of their functions, and often this is so tedious that programmers do not take the time to abstract common patterns of data manipulation and control.

For example, type parameters are automatically introduced when writing simple functions that are independent of some of their arguments:

```
let getFirst (a,b,c) = a
```

The inferred type of getFirst is reported as follows:

```
val getFirst: 'a * 'b * 'c -> 'a
```

Here getFirst has been *automatically inferred to be generic.* The function is generic in three type variables, where the result type is the first element of the input tuple type. Automatic generalization is applied when a let or member definition doesn't fully constrain the types of inputs or outputs. You can tell automatic generalization has been applied by the presence of type variables in an inferred type and ultimately by the fact you can reuse a construct at multiple types.

Automatic generalization is particularly useful when taking functions as inputs. For example, the following takes two functions as input and applies them to each side of a tuple:

```
let mapPair f g (x,y) = (f x, g y)
```

The generalized, inferred type is as follows:

```
val mapPair : ('a -> 'b) -> ('c -> 'd) -> ('a * 'c) -> ('b * 'd)
```

Understanding Some Important Generic Functions

The F# and .NET libraries include definitions for some important generic functions. You saw a number of these in action in earlier chapters. It is important to have a working knowledge of these building blocks, because often your code will automatically become generic when you use these primitives.

Generic Comparison

The first primitives are all related to *generic comparison*, also often called *structural comparison*. Every time you use operators such as <, >, <=, >=, =, <>, compare, min, and max in F# code, you are using generic comparison. All of these operators are located in the Microsoft.FSharp.Core. Operators module, which is opened by default in all F# code. Some important data structures also use generic comparison internally; for example, you may also be using generic comparison when you use F# collection types such as Microsoft.FSharp.Collections.Set and Microsoft. FSharp.Collections.Map. This is discussed in the documentation for these types. The type signatures of the basic generic comparison operators are shown here:

```
val compare : 'a -> 'a -> int
val (=) : 'a -> 'a -> bool
val (<) : 'a -> 'a -> bool
val (<=) : 'a -> 'a -> bool
val (>) : 'a -> 'a -> bool
val (>=) : 'a -> 'a -> bool
val (min) : 'a -> 'a -> 'a
val (max) : 'a -> 'a -> 'a
```

All of these routines are implemented in terms of compare, which returns 0 if the arguments are equal and returns –1 and 1 for less than and greater than, respectively.

On ordinary simple types such as integers, generic comparison works by invoking the default .NET behavior for these types, giving the natural ordering for these types. For strings, culture-neutral "ordinal" comparison is used, which means the local "culture" settings on your machine won't affect string comparison (see System.Globalization for more information on local settings). Most other .NET base types implement the System.IComparable interface, such as System.DateTime values, and generic comparison uses these implementations where necessary.

You can also use the comparison operators on most structured types. For example, you can use them on F# tuple values, where a lexicographic left-to-right comparison is used:

```
> ("abc","def") < ("abc","xyz");;
val it : bool = true

> compare (10,30) (10,20);;
val it : int = 1
```

Likewise, you can use generic comparison with list and array values:

```
> compare [10;30] [10;20];;
val it : int = 1

> compare [| 10;30 |] [| 10;20 |];;
val it : int = 1

> compare [| 10;20 |] [| 10;30 |];;
val it : int = -1
```

For the most part, generic comparison is implemented efficiently—code is autogenerated for each type definition where possible "fast path" comparison techniques are used. For example, the generated code will use primitive IL/native instructions for integer comparisons. This means that in practice structural comparison is typically fast when used with appropriately sized keys. However, you should consider the following before using generic comparison over complex new data types:

- Generic comparison may raise runtime exceptions when used on inappropriate types. It can be used safely with .NET numeric types, F# tuple, list and option types, F# record and discriminated union types, and types implementing the System.IComparable interface. It is not safe to use on types such as function types.

- You should consider customizing the behavior of generic comparison for new types you define, at least whenever those types will be used as keys in a data structure. You can do this by implementing the System.IComparable interface, covered in Chapter 8.

- Collections built using generic comparison are efficient over small key terms. However, performance issues will arise if generic comparison is used repeatedly over large structured terms. In high-performance situations, you should be careful to use small keys and, where necessary, use custom comparison functions. Most collections based on generic comparison allow you to specify a custom comparer when constructing instances of the type.

■**Tip** You can customize the behavior of generic comparison for new types that you define by implementing the System.IComparable interface for those types. We cover this in Chapter 8.

Generic Hashing

An important partner of generic comparison is *generic hashing*. The primary primitive function used to invoke generic hashing is hash, again located in the Microsoft.FSharp.Operators module. The type signature is as follows:

```
val hash : 'a -> int
```

When used with simple structural types, the function returns an integer that gives a stable hash of the input value:

```
> hash 100;;
val it : int = 100

> hash "abc";;
val it : int = 536991770

> hash (100,"abc");;
val it : int = 1073983640
```

Generic hashing is implemented in a similar way to generic comparison, although it uses a "node count" limitation to help ensure that large structured values are not hashed in their entirety but instead have a hash code computed from only part of the value. Like generic comparison, generic hashing should generally be used only with base types such as integers and structural types built using records and discriminated unions. Generic hashing can be customized for new types by either overriding the GetHashCode method or implementing the Microsoft.FSharp.Core.IStructuralHash interface, covered in Chapter 8.

Generic Pretty-Printing

Some useful generic functions are those that do generic formatting of values. The simplest ways to access this functionality are the %A specifiers in printf format strings and the any_to_string function:

```
val any_to_string : 'a -> string
```

Here is a simple example:

```
> any_to_string (Some(100,[1.0;2.0;3.1415])));;
val it : string = "Some (100, [1.0; 2.0; 3.1415])"

> sprintf "result = %A" ([1], [true]);;
val it : string = "result = ([1], [true])"
```

These functions use .NET and F# reflection to walk the structure of values to build a formatted representation of the value. Structural types such as lists and tuples are formatted using the syntax of F# source code. Unrecognized values are formatted by calling the .NET ToString() method for these values. We discuss F# and .NET reflection in more depth toward the end of Chapter 9.

Generic Boxing and Unboxing

Two useful generic functions convert any F# data to and from the "universal" type System.Object (the F# type obj):

```
val box   : 'a -> obj
val unbox : obj -> 'a
```

Here are some simple examples of these functions in action:

```
> box 1;;
val it : obj = 1

> box "abc";;
val it : obj = "abc"

> let sobj = box "abc";;
val sobj : obj = "abc"

> (unbox<string> sobj);;
val it : string = "abc"

> (unbox sobj : string);;
val it : string = "abc"
```

Note that using unbox generally requires you to specify the target type, given either as an explicit type parameter unbox<string> or as a type constraint (unbox sobj : string)—these forms are equivalent. A runtime check is performed on unboxing to ensure that the object can be safely converted to the target type. That is, values of type obj carry dynamic type information, and attempting to unbox a value at an incompatible type will raise an error:

```
> (unbox sobj : int);;
System.InvalidCastException: Specified cast is not valid.
   at <StartupCode>.FSI_0014._main()
stopped due to error
```

Boxing is important partly because many .NET libraries provide generic operations through functions that accept arguments of type obj. You will see an example in the next section. Furthermore, some .NET APIs are dynamically typed, and almost all parameters are of type obj.

Generic Binary Serialization via the .NET Libraries

The .NET libraries provide an implementation of generic binary serialization that is useful as a "quick and easy" way of saving computed values to disk and sending values over the network. We use this as an example to show how building-block generic operations can be defined using functionality in the .NET libraries combined with box and unbox. We first define functions with the following signatures:

```
val writeValue   : #System.IO.Stream -> 'a -> obj
val readValue    : #System.IO.Stream -> 'a
```

The function writeValue takes an arbitrary value and writes a binary representation of its underlying object graph to the given I/O stream. The function readValue reverses this process, in much the same way that unbox reverses the process performed by box. Here are the implementations of the functions in terms of the .NET binary serializer located in the namespace System.Runtime.Serialization.Formatters.Binary:

```
open System.IO
open System.Runtime.Serialization.Formatters.Binary

let writeValue outputStream (x: 'a) =
    let formatter = new BinaryFormatter()
    formatter.Serialize(outputStream,box x)

let readValue inputStream =
    let formatter = new BinaryFormatter()
    let res = formatter.Deserialize(inputStream)
    unbox x
```

Note that box and unbox are used in the implementation, because the Serialize and Deserialize functions accept and return a value of type obj. Here is an example of how to use the functions to write a value of type Microsoft.FSharp.Collections.Map<string,string> to a FileStream and read it back in again:

```
open System.IO
let addresses = Map.of_list [ "Jeff", "123 Main Street, Redmond, WA 98052";
                              "Fred", "987 Pine Road, Phila., PA 19116";
                              "Mary", "PO Box 112233, Palo Alto, CA 94301" ]
```

```
let fsOut = new FileStream("Data.dat", FileMode.Create)
writeValue fsOut addresses
fsOut.Close()
let fsIn = new FileStream("Data.dat", FileMode.Open)
let res : Map<string,string> = readValue fsIn
fsIn.Close()
```

The final result of this code when executed interactively is as follows:

```
val it : Map<string,string>
       = seq
           [[Fred, 987 Pine Road, Phila., PA 19116]
             {Key = "Fred";
              Value = "987 Pine Road, Phila., PA 19116";};
            [Jeff, 123 Main Street, Redmond, WA 98052]
             {Key = "Jeff";
              Value = "123 Main Street, Redmond, WA 98052";};
            [Mary, PO Box 112233, Palo Alto, CA 94301]
             {Key = "Mary";
              Value = "PO Box 112233, Palo Alto, CA 94301";}]
```

Note that values of type Map<string,string> are printed interactively as sequences of key/value pairs. Also, a type annotation was required when reading the data back in using readValue, and a runtime type error will result if the types of the objects reconstructed from the binary data don't match this type annotation.

Making Things Generic

In the following sections, we discuss how to make existing code more generic (that is, reusable) and how to systematically represent the abstract parameters of generic algorithms.

Generic Algorithms Through Explicit Arguments

A common pattern in F# programming is to accept function parameters in order to make an algorithm abstract and reusable. A simple sample is the following generic implementation of Euclid's algorithm for finding the highest-common-factor (HCF) of two numbers:

```
let rec hcf a b =
    if   a=0 then b
    elif a<b then hcf a (b-a)
    else hcf (a-b) b
```

The type of this function is as follows:

```
val hcf : int -> int -> int
```

For example:

```
> hcf 18 12;;
val it : int = 6

> hcf 33 24;;
val it : int = 3
```

However, this algorithm is not generic, since as written it works only over integers. In particular, although the operator (-) is by default overloaded in F#, each use of the operator must be associated with at most one type decided at compile time. We discuss this restriction in more detail in the section "Understanding Generic Overloaded Operators." In addition, the constant 0 is an integer and is not overloaded.

Despite this, this algorithm can be easily generalized to work over any type. To achieve this, you must provide an explicit zero, a subtraction function, and an ordering. Here's one way to do this:

```
let hcfGeneric (zero,sub,lessThan) =
    let rec hcf a b =
        if   a=zero then b
        elif lessThan a b then hcf a (sub b a)
        else hcf (sub a b) b
    hcf
```

The inferred, generic type of this function is as follows:

```
val hcfGeneric : 'a * ('a -> 'a -> 'a) * ('a -> 'a -> bool) -> ('a -> 'a -> 'a)
```

Here the numeric type being manipulated has type 'a in the inferred type, and the result is a computed function. This uses techniques for computing functions similar to those discussed in Chapter 3. Here are some examples of using this generic function:

```
let hcfInt    = hcfGeneric (0, (-),(<))
let hcfInt64  = hcfGeneric (0L,(-),(<))
let hcfBigInt = hcfGeneric (0I,(-),(<))
```

Note that when we instantiate the generic function for the particular cases, we are drawing on particular instances of the default overloaded operator (-). We can check that the code is executing correctly as follows:

```
> hcfInt 18 12;;
val it : int = 6
```

```
> hcfBigInt 181028711616223238303957I 123902817829309283048023903I;;
val it : bigint = 33224I
```

Generic Algorithms Through Abstract Object Types

The generic implementation from the previous section took three related parameters for zero, comparison, and subtraction. It is common practice to package related operations together. One way to do this is to use a concrete record type containing function values:

```
type Numeric<'a> =
    { Zero: 'a;
      Subtract: ('a -> 'a -> 'a);
      LessThan: ('a -> 'a -> bool); }

let intOps    = { Zero=0 ; Subtract=(-); LessThan=(<) }
let bigintOps = { Zero=0I; Subtract=(-); LessThan=(<) }
let int64Ops  = { Zero=0L; Subtract=(-); LessThan=(<) }

let hcfGeneric (ops : Numeric<'a>) =
    let rec hcf a b =
        if a= ops.Zero then b
        elif ops.LessThan a b then hcf a (ops.Subtract b a)
        else hcf (ops.Subtract a b) b
    hcf

let hcfInt    = hcfGeneric intOps
let hcfBigInt = hcfGeneric bigintOps
```

The inferred types are as follows:

```
val hcfGeneric : Numeric<'a> -> ('a -> 'a -> 'a)
val hcfInt : (int -> int -> int)
val hcfBigInt : (bigint -> bigint -> bigint)
```

Here are some examples of the functions in action:

```
> hcfInt 18 12;;
val it : int = 6
```

```
> hcfBigInt 181028711616223238303957I 123902817829309283048023903I;;
val it : bigint = 33224I
```

Record types such as `Numeric<'a>` are often called *dictionaries of operations* and are similar to vtables from object-oriented programming and the compiled form of type classes from Haskell. As you have seen, dictionaries such as these can be represented in different ways according to your tastes, using tuples or records. For larger frameworks, a carefully constructed classification of *object interface types* is often used in place of records. We discuss object interface types in more detail in Chapter 6, and the F# namespace `Microsoft.FSharp.Math.Classifications` contains a number of numerical classification types. Here is an interface type definition that plays the same role as the record in the previous example:

```
type INumeric<'a> =
    abstract Zero : 'a
    abstract Subtract: 'a * 'a -> 'a
    abstract LessThan: 'a * 'a -> bool
```

You can implement and use abstract object types in a similar way to record values:

```
let intOps =
    { new INumeric<int> with
        member ops.Zero = 0
        member ops.Subtract(x,y) = x - y
        member ops.LessThan(x,y) = x < y }
```

```
val intOps : INumeric<int>
```

The code for Euclid's algorithm using abstract object types is essentially the same as for the code based on record types:

```
let hcfGeneric (ops : INumeric<'a>) =
    let rec hcf a b =
        if a= ops.Zero then b
        elif ops.LessThan(a,b) then hcf a (ops.Subtract(b,a))
        else hcf (ops.Subtract(a,b)) b
    hcf
```

GENERIC ALGORITHMS AND FUNCTION PARAMETERS

One of the remarkable features of functional programming with F# is that generic programming is practical even when the types involved are not explicitly related. For example, the previous generic algorithm shows how reusable code can be written without resorting to relating the types involved through an inheritance hierarchy: the generic algorithm works over any type, if an appropriate set of operations is provided to manipulate values of that type. This is a form of *explicit factoring by functions*. Object-oriented programming typically uses *implicit factoring by hierarchy*, since the library designer decides the relationships that hold between various types and these are fixed in stone.

Type inference in F# makes explicit factoring by functions convenient. Given the simplicity and flexibility of this approach, it is a useful way to write applications and to prototype frameworks. However, factoring by hierarchy still plays a role in F# programming. For example, all F# values can be implicitly converted to and from the type `System.Object`, something that is extremely useful when interoperating with many libraries. It would obviously be inconvenient to have to pass around functions to marshal (box/unbox) types to `System.Object` and back. Similarly, many F# values can be implicitly converted to the `IDisposable` interface. Hierarchical factoring requires careful design choices, and in general we recommend you use explicit factoring first, moving toward implicit factoring only when a design pattern is truly universal and repeats itself many times, as is the case with the `IDisposable` idiom. The .NET and F# libraries contain definitions of many of the implicit factors you'll need to use in practice, such as `IDisposable` and `IEnumerable`.

Some functional languages such as Haskell allow you to implicitly pass dictionaries of operations through an extension to type inference known as *type classes*. At the time of writing, this is not supported by F#. However, the designers of F# have stated that they expect a future version of the language to support this. Either way, explicitly passing dictionaries of operations is common in all functional programming and important technique to master.

Understanding .NET Types

For the most part, programming in F# involves using types in a "simple" way: each type has some values, and types are related by using explicit functions to map from one type to another. However, in reality, types in F# are more sophisticated than this simple story implies. First, F# types are really .NET types, and .NET makes some distinctions between different kinds of types that are occasionally important, such as between value types and reference types. Furthermore, .NET and F# support hierarchical relationships between types through *subtyping*. In the following sections, we first cover .NET types from the F# perspective, and then we cover subtyping.

Reference Types and Value Types

The .NET documentation and other .NET languages often describe types as either *reference types* or *value types*. We can use `System.String` and `System.DateTime` as a typical example of each. First note that both of these types are *immutable*. That is, given a value of type `System.String`, you cannot modify the contents of the string; the same is true for `System.DateTime`. This is by far the most important fact you need to know about these types: for immutable types the reference/value type distinction is relatively unimportant. However, it is still useful to know the following:

Representation: Values of type `System.String` are single pointers into the garbage-collected heap where the actual data for the string resides. Two `System.String` values may point to the same data. In contrast, values of type `System.DateTime` are somewhat larger blobs of integer data (64-bits of data in this case), and no data lives on the garbage-collected heap. The full data for the value is copied as needed.

Boxing: All .NET types can be marshaled to and from the .NET type `System.Object` (the F# type `obj`) by using F# functions such as `box` and `unbox`. All reference types are trivially marshaled to this type without any change of representation or identity, so for reference types, `box` is a no-op. Boxing a value type involves a heap allocation, resulting in a new object. Often this object is immediately discarded after the operation on the `obj` type has been performed.

If a value can be mutated, then the distinction between value types and reference types is more serious. Fortunately, essentially all mutable values in the .NET libraries are reference types, which means mutation actually mutates the heap-allocated data referred to by the reference.

Other Flavors of .NET Types

The .NET type system makes some additional distinctions between types that are occasionally significant for F# programming. We briefly summarize these here:

Delegate types: Delegate types such as `System.Windows.Forms.MouseEventHandler` are a form of "named" function type supported by all .NET languages. They tend not to be as convenient to use as F# function types, since they do not support compositional operations such as pipelining and forward composition. However, .NET APIs use delegates extensively. To create a delegate value, you name the delegate type and pass it a function value accepting the same arguments as expected by the delegate type, such as `MouseEventHandler(fun sender args -> printf "click!\n")`.

Attribute types: Types derived from the `System.Attribute` class are used to add metadata to source code declarations and typically end in the suffix `Attribute`. You can access these attributes via .NET and F# reflection. You can add attributes to F# declarations using the `[<...>]` syntax. For example, the `System.ObsoleteAttribute` marks functions as obsolete, and the F# compiler will produce a warning if the function is used:

```
[<System.Obsolete("Don't use this one")>]
let oldFunction() = printf "obsolete!\n"
```

Exception types: Types derived from the `System.Exception` class are used to represent raised exceptions. We discussed exceptions in detail in Chapter 4.

Enum types: .NET enum types are simple integer-like value types associated with a particular name. They are typically used for specifying flags to APIs; for example, `FileMode` in the `System.IO` namespace is an enum type with values such as `FileMode.Open` and `FileMode.Create`. .NET enum types are easy to use from F# and can be combined using bitwise AND, OR, and XOR operations using the `&&&`, `|||`, and `^^^` operators. Most commonly, the `|||` operator is used to combine multiple flags. On occasion you may have to mask an attribute value using `&&&` and compare the result to `Enum.of_int(0)`. You'll see how to define .NET-compatible enum types in F# at the end of Chapter 6.

Understanding Subtyping

Simple types are related in simple ways; for example, values of the type `int` are distinct from values of the type `float`, and values of one record type are distinct from values of another. This approach to types is powerful and often sufficient, partly because type inference and function values make it easy to write generic code. However, .NET and F# also support hierarchical relationships between types through *subtyping*. Subtyping is a key concept of object-oriented programming, and we discuss it in more detail in Chapter 6. In addition, you can use subtyping in conjunction with pure functional programming, because it offers one technique to make algorithms generic over a restricted family of types.

In the following sections, we explain how these constructs appear to the F# programmer and the role they play in F# programming. Subtyping in F# is the same as that used by the .NET Framework, so if you are familiar with another .NET language, you'll already know how things work.

Casting Up Statically

You can explore how subtyping works by using F# Interactive. First let's look at how some of the F# types you've already seen relate to the type obj:

```
> let xobj = (1 :> obj);;
val xobj : obj = 1

> let sobj = ("abc" :> obj);;
val sobj : obj = "abc"
```

Here you are simply investigating the subtyping relationship through the use of the built-in coercion (or *upcast*) operator, which is :>. This operator converts a value to any of its super-types in precisely the same way as the box function.

The previous code indicates the subtyping between ordinary types and the type obj. Subtyping occurs between other kinds of types as well (we discuss the various kinds of type definitions such as records, discriminated unions, classes, and interfaces in Chapter 3 and Chapter 6):

- All types are subtypes of System.Object (called obj in F#).

- Record and discriminated union types are subtypes of the interface types they implement.

- Interfaces types are subtypes of the other interfaces they extend.

- Class types are subtypes of both the interfaces they implement and the classes they extend.

- Array types are subtypes of the .NET type System.Array.

- Value types (types such as int32 that are abbreviations of .NET value types) are subtypes of the .NET type System.ValueType. Likewise, .NET enumeration types are subtypes of System.Enum.

Casting Down Dynamically

Values that may have subtypes carry a *runtime type*, and you can use runtime type tests to query the type of an object and convert it to one of the subtypes. You can do this in three main ways: the unbox operation, downcasts, and pattern type tests. We've already explained the unbox function. As with most object-oriented languages, the upcasts performed through subtyping are reversible through the use of downcasts, in other words, by using the :?> operator. You can see this through the following examples:

```
> let boxedObject = box "abc";;
val boxedObject : obj

> let downcastString = (boxedObject :?> string);;
val downcastString  : string = "abc"
```

Downcasts are checked at runtime and are safe because all values of the obj type are implicitly annotated with the runtime type of the value. The operator :?> will raise an exception if the object is not of a suitable type:

```
> let xobj = box 1;;
val xobj : obj = 1

> let x = (xobj :?> string);;
error: InvalidCastException raised at or near stdin:(2,0)
```

Performing Type Tests via Pattern Matching

A more convenient way of performing dynamic types tests is by using *type-test patterns*, in particular the :? pattern construct, which you encountered in Chapter 4 in the context of catching various .NET exception types. Here is an example where we use a pattern type test to query the dynamic type of a value of type obj:

```
let checkObject (x: obj) =
  match x with
  | :? string -> printfn "The object is a string"
  | :? int    -> printfn "The object is an integer"
  | _         -> printfn "The input is something else"
```

```
> checkObject (box "abc")
The input is a string
val it : unit = ()
```

Such a pattern may also bind the matched value at its more specific type:

```
let reportObject (x: obj) =
  match x with
  | :? string as s -> printfn "The input is the string '%s'" s
  | :? int as d    -> printfn "The input is the integer '%d'" d
  | _              -> printfn "the input is something else"
```

```
> reportObject (box 17)
The input is the integer '17'
val it : unit = ()
```

Using Flexible # Types

F# functions can be declared to accept parameters that are any subtype of a particular type by using type annotations of the form #*type*, where *type* is some type that supports subtyping. This is particularly common when working with .NET libraries that use subtyping heavily. For example:

```
> open System.Windows.Forms
> let setTextOfControl (c : #Control) (s:string) = c.Text <- s;;
val setTextOfControl: #Control -> string -> unit
```

This notation is called a *flexible type constraint* and is shorthand for a generic function and a "constraint" on the type variable, and we could equally have written this:

```
> open System.Windows.Forms;;

> let setTextOfControl (c : 'a when 'a :> Control) (s:string) = c.Text <- s;;
val setTextOfControl: #Control -> string -> unit
```

Automatic generalization lifts the constraints implicit in types of the form #*type* to the nearest enclosing function or member definition.

Flexible type constraints occur frequently when working with sequence values. For example, consider the following two functions from the F# library:

```
module Seq =
    ...
    val append : #seq<'a> -> #seq<'a> -> seq<'a>
    val concat : #seq<#seq<'a>> -> seq<'a>
    ...
```

You can read the first signature of append as "Seq.append accepts two arguments, each of which must be compatible with the type seq<'a>, and it produces a seq<'a>." In practice, this means you can use Seq.append to append two F# lists, or an F# list and an F# array, or an F# sequence and an F# list, or two F# arrays, and so on. This is shown by the following calls, all of which result in a seq<int> yielding values 1 through 6:

```
Seq.append [1;2;3] [4;5;6]
Seq.append [| 1;2;3 |] [4;5;6]
Seq.append (seq { for x in 1 .. 3 -> x }) [4;5;6]
Seq.append [| 1;2;3 |] [| 4;5;6 |]
```

However, the element types of the two collections must be the same: the flexibility applies to the collection type rather than the element type. You can see a similarly advanced use of flexible types in the type signature for the function Seq.concat. You can use this function with a list of lists, or a list of arrays, or an array of lists, and so forth. For example:

```
Seq.concat [ [1;2;3]; [4;5;6] ]
Seq.concat [ [| 1;2;3 |]; [| 4;5;6 |] ]
```

Knowing When Upcasts Are Applied Automatically

Most object-oriented languages automatically apply upcasts whenever a function or method is called or wherever a value is used. F# takes a different approach on this matter: on the whole, upcasts are applied only when a function or member signature indicates that it may be used in a flexible way.

In practice, this means you sometimes have to add explicit upcasts to your code to "throw away" information. For example, if each branch of an `if ... then ... else ...` construct returns different types, then you will need to upcast the results of one or both of the branches, as shown by the type error given for the following code that returns `Console.In` (a `TextReader`) from one branch and the results of `File.OpenText` (a `StreamReader`) from the other branch:

```
open System
open System.IO
let textReader =
    if DateTime.Today.DayOfWeek = DayOfWeek.Monday
    then Console.In
    else File.OpenText("input.txt")
```

The error reported is as follows:

```
> ...(enter the text above)...;;

    else File.OpenText("input.txt")
         ^^^^^^^^^^^^^^^^^^^^^^^^^^^
 error: FS0001: This expression has type
        StreamReader
but is here used with type
        TextReader
stopped due to error
```

`StreamReader` is a subtype of `TextReader`, so the code can be corrected by "throwing away" the information that the returned type is a `StreamReader`:

```
let textReader =
    if DateTime.Today.DayOfWeek = DayOfWeek.Monday
    then Console.In
    else (File.OpenText("input.txt") :> TextReader)
```

Upcasts are applied automatically in the following situations:

- When calling functions with flexible parameter types such as `#TextReader`.

- When passing arguments to members associated with .NET and F# objects and types.

- When accessing members using the "dot" notation. For example, given a value of type `StreamReader`, all the members associated with `TextReader` can also be accessed without needing to apply an upcast.

Troubleshooting Type Inference Problems

In the following sections, we cover some of the techniques you can use to understand the type inference process and to debug problems when inferred types are not as expected.

Using a Visual Editing Environment

The best and most important technique to debug and understand type inference is to use a visual editing environment for F# such as Visual Studio that performs interactive type checking as you are writing your code. These tools display errors interactively and show inferred types as you move the mouse pointer over identifiers.

Note At the time of writing, the F# distribution comes with the component `FSharp.Compiler.dll` that can be used to add interactive type checking and IntelliSense-like features to other editors.

Using Type Annotations

Type inference in F# works through a process of type constraint *propagation*. As a programmer, you can add further type constraints to your code in several ways. For example, you can do the following:

- Add a rigid type constraint using the : notation, such as `let t : float = 5.0`.

- Add a flexible type constraint using the # notation, such as `let setTextOfControl (c : #Control) (s:string) = c.Text <- s`.

- Apply a function that accepts only a particular type of argument, such as `let f x = String.length x`. Here the use of `String.length` generates a constraint on the type of x.

Adding and removing type annotations from your code is the standard technique to troubleshoot type inference problems. For example, the following code does not type check:

```
> let transformData inp =
    inp |> Seq.map (fun (x,y) -> (x,y.Length)) ;;

inp |> Seq.map (fun (x,y) -> (x,y.Length))
--------------------------------^^^^^^^^

stdin(11,36): error: Lookup on object of indeterminate type. A type annotation
may be needed prior to this program point to constrain the type of the object.
This may allow the lookup to be resolved.
```

You can easily solve this problem simply by adding a type annotation, such as to y:

```
let transformData inp =
    inp |> Seq.map (fun (x,y:string) -> (x,y.Length))
```

You can also use type annotations to discover why code is not as generic as you think it should be. For example, the following code has a mistake, and the F# type checker says the code is less generic than expected:

```
let printSecondElements (inp : #seq<'a * int>) =
    inp
    |> Seq.iter (fun (x,y) -> printfn "y = %d" x)
```

```
> ... enter the code above ...

    |> Seq.iter (fun (x,y) -> printfn "y = %d" x)
-------------------------------------^^^^^^^^^

stdin(21,38): warning: FS0064: This construct causes code to be less generic than
indicated by the type annotations. The type variable 'a has been constrained to
the type 'int'.
```

The mistake here is that we are printing the variable x instead of y, but it's not always so easy to spot what has caused this kind of problem. One way to track down this problem is to temporarily change the generic type parameter to some arbitrary, unrelated type, After all, if code is generic, then you should be able to use *any* type, and by changing the type variable to an unrelated type, you can track down where the inconsistency has first arisen. For example, let's change 'a to the type PingPong:

```
type PingPong = Ping | Pong
```

```
let printSecondElements (inp : #seq<PingPong * int>) =
    inp
    |> Seq.iter (fun (x,y) -> printfn "y = %d" x)
```

You now get a different and in many ways more informative error message, localized to the first place that the value x marked with type PingPong is used in an unexpected way:

```
> ... enter the code above ...

    |> Seq.iter (fun (x,y) -> printfn "y = %d" x)
-------------------------------------------------^

stdin(27,47): error: FS0001: The type 'PingPong' is not compatible with any of
the types byte,int16,int32,int64,sbyte,uint16,uint32,uint64,nativeint,unativeint,
arising from the use of a printf-style format string
```

Understanding the Value Restriction

F# sometimes requires a little help before a definition is automatically generalized. In particular, only function definitions and simple immutable data expressions are automatically generalized;

this is called the *value restriction*. For example, the following definition does not result in a generic type and gives an error:

```
> let empties = Array.create 100 [];;
------^^^^^^
error: FS0030: Value restriction. Type inference has inferred the signature
       val empties : '_a list []
but its definition is not a simple data constant. Either define 'empties' as a
simple data expression, make it a function, or add a type constraint to
instantiate the type parameters.
```

The code attempts to create an array of empty lists. Here the error message indicates that type inference has given empties the type '_a list []. The underscore (_) indicates that the type variable 'a is *ungeneralized*, that is, that this code is not fully generic. This is because it would make no sense to give empties the truly generic type 'a list [], because this would imply that we've created an array of lists somehow suitable for use with any type 'a. In reality, any particular array should have one specific type, such as int list [] or string list [], but not both. (If it were usable with both types, then we could store an integer list in the array and fetch it out as a string list!)

The value restriction ensures that declarations don't result in this kind of confusion; automatic generalization is not applied to declarations unless they are functions or simple, immutable data constructs. One way to think of this is that you can create concrete objects only once the type inference problem is sufficiently constrained so that every concrete object created at the top level of your program has a ground type, in other words, a type that doesn't contain any ungeneralized type variables.

The value restriction doesn't apply to simple immutable data constants or function definitions. For example, the following declarations are all automatically generalized, giving the generic types shown:

```
let emptyList = []
let initialLists = ([],[2])
let listOfEmptyLists = [[];[]]
let makeArray () = Array.create 100 []
```

```
val emptyList : 'a list
val initialLists : ('a list * int list)
val listOfEmptyLists : 'a list list
val makeArray : unit -> 'a list []
```

Working Around the Value Restriction

The value restriction crops up with mild regularity in F# coding, particularly when using F# Interactive, where the scope of type inference is at the granularity of each entry sent to the tool rather than an entire file, and hence there are fewer constraints placed on these code fragments. You can work around the value restriction in several ways, depending on what you are trying to do.

Technique 1: Constrain Values to be Nongeneric

The first technique applies when you make a definition such as empties shown earlier but when you really meant to create one value. Recall that this definition was problematic because it's not clear what type of array is being created:

```
let empties = Array.create 100 []
```

If you really meant to create one value with a specific type, then simply use an explicit type annotation:

```
let empties : int list [] = Array.create 100 []
```

The value is then not generic, and the value restriction doesn't apply.

Technique 2: Ensure Generic Functions Have Explicit Arguments

The next technique applies when you are defining generic functions. In this case, make sure you define these with explicit arguments. For example, take a look at the following definition of a function value:

```
let mapFirst = List.map fst
```

You might expect this to be a generic function with type ('a * 'b) list -> 'a list. However, this is not quite what happens: type variables are automatically generalized at true "syntactic" function definitions, that is, function definitions with *explicit* arguments. The function mapFirst has *implicit* arguments. Fortunately, it is easy to work around this simply by making the arguments explicit:

```
let mapFirst inp = List.map fst inp
```

This function now has the following type:

```
val mapFirst : ('a * 'b) list -> 'a list
```

When there is only one argument, our favorite way of writing the extra arguments is as follows:

```
let mapFirst inp = inp |> List.map (fun (x,y) -> x)
```

The same problem arises when you try to define functions by composition. For example:

```
let printFstElements = List.map fst >> List.iter (printf "res = %d")
```

Once again the arguments here are implicit, which causes problems. This definition will not be automatically generalized since this is not a syntactic function. Again, just make the arguments explicit:

```
let printFstElements inp = inp |> List.map fst |> List.iter (printf "res = %d")
```

Technique 3: Add Dummy Arguments to Generic Functions When Necessary

Let's take a look at this definition once again:

```
let empties = Array.create 100 []
```

It's possible that you really did intend to define a function that generates arrays of different types on demand. In this case, just add a dummy argument:

```
let empties () = Array.create 100 []
let intEmpties : int list [] = empties()
let stringEmpties : string list [] = empties()
```

The dummy argument ensures that `empties` is a function with generic arguments and can be automatically generalized.

Technique 4: Add Explicit Type Arguments When Necessary

There is one final technique used to make a value generic. This one is used rarely but is very useful when it is required. It is normally used when you are defining values that are generic but that are neither functions nor simple data expressions. For example, let's define a sequence of 100 empty lists:

```
let emptyLists = Seq.init_finite 100 (fun _ -> [])
```

The expression on the right is not a function or simple data expression (it is a function application), so the value restriction applies. One solution is to add an extra dummy argument, as in the previous section. However, if you are designing a library, then this can seem very artificial. Instead, you can use the following declaration form to make `emptyLists` generic:

```
let emptyLists<'a> : seq<'a list> = Seq.init_finite 100 (fun _ -> [])
```

You can now use `emptyLists` as a *type function* to generate values of different types. For example:

```
> Seq.length emptyLists;;
val it : int = 100

> emptyLists<int>;;
val it : seq<int list> = seq [[]; []; []; []; ...]

> emptyLists<string>;;
val it : seq<string list> = seq [[]; []; []; []; ...]
```

Some values and functions in the F# library are defined in this way, including `typeof<'a>`, `Seq.empty`, and `Set.empty`. We cover `typeof` in Chapter 9.

Understanding Generic Overloaded Operators

There is one further important way in which code does not automatically become generic in F#: when you use overloaded operators such as +, -, *, and /, or overloaded conversion functions such as float and int64. For example, the following is *not* a generic function:

```
let twice x = (x + x)
```

In the absence of further information, the type of this function is as follows:

```
val twice : int -> int
```

This is because the overloaded operator + defaults to operating on integers. If you add type annotations or further type constraints, you can force the function to operate on any particular type supporting the overloaded + operator:

```
let twiceFloat (x:float) = x + x
```

```
val twiceFloat : float -> float
```

The information that resolves a use of an overloaded operator can come after the use of the operator:

```
let threeTimes x = (x + x + x)

let sixTimesInt64 (x:int64) = threeTimes x + threeTimes x
```

```
val threeTimes : int64 -> int64
val sixTimesInt64 : int64 -> int64
```

Note how the constraint in the definition of sixTimesInt64 is the only mention of int64 and has affected the type of threeTimes. The technical explanation is that overloaded operators such as + give rise to *floating* constraints, which can be resolved later in the type inference scope.

Summary

F# is a typed language, and F# programmers often use types in sophisticated ways. In this chapter, you learned about the foundations of types, focusing on how types are used in functional programming and on generics and subtyping in particular. In the next chapter, we cover the related topics of object-oriented and modular programming in F#.

■ ■ ■

CHAPTER 6

Working with Objects and Modules

Chapters 2 through 5 dealt with the basic constructs of F# functional and imperative programming, and by now we trust you are familiar with the foundational concepts and techniques of practical, small-scale F# programming. In this chapter, we cover language constructs related to *object-oriented (OO) programming*. We assume some familiarity with the basic concepts of OO programming, though you may notice that our discussion of objects deliberately de-emphasizes techniques such as implementation inheritance.

The first part of this chapter focuses on OO programming with concrete types. We then introduce the notion of object interface types and show some simple techniques to implement them. We then cover more advanced techniques to implement objects using function parameters, delegation, and implementation inheritance. Finally, we cover the related topics of modules (which are simple containers of functions and values) and extensions (in other words, how to add ad hoc dot-notation to existing modules and types). We cover the topic of encapsulation in Chapter 7.

Getting Started with Objects and Members

One of the most important activities of object-oriented programming is defining *concrete types* equipped with the dot-notation. A concrete type has *fixed* behavior, that is, uses the same member implementations for each concrete value of the type.

You have already met many important concrete types, such as integers, lists, strings, and records (introduced in Chapter 3). It is easy to add object-oriented members to concrete types. Listing 6-1 shows an example.

Listing 6-1. *A Vector2D Type with Object-Oriented Members*

```
type Vector2D =
    { DX: float; DY: float }
    member v.Length = sqrt(v.DX * v.DX + v.DY * v.DY)
    member v.Scale(k) = { DX=k*v.DX; DY=k*v.DY }
    member v.ShiftX(x) = { v with DX=v.DX+x }
    member v.ShiftY(y) = { v with DY=v.DY+y }
    member v.ShiftXY(x,y) = { DX=v.DX+x; DY=v.DY+y }
```

```
static member Zero = { DX=0.0; DY=0.0 }
static member ConstX(dx) = { DX=dx; DY=0.0 }
static member ConstY(dy) = { DX=0.0; DY=dy }
```

You can use the properties and methods of this type as follows:

```
> let v = {DX = 3.0; DY=4.0 };;
val v : Vector2D

> v.Length;;
val it : float = 5.0

> v.Scale(2.0).Length;;
val it : float = 10.0

> Vector2D.ConstX(3.0);;
val it : Vector2D = {DX = 3.0; DY = 0.0}
```

As usual, it is useful to look at inferred types to understand a type definition. Here are the inferred types for the Vector2D type definition of Listing 6-1.

```
type Vector2D =
    { DX: float; DY: float }
    member Length : float
    member Scale : k:float -> Vector2D
    member ShiftX : x:float -> Vector2D
    member ShiftY : y:float -> Vector2D
    member ShiftXY : x:float * y:float -> Vector2D
    static member Zero : Vector2D
    static member ConstX : dx:float -> Vector2D
    static member ConstY : dy:float -> Vector2D
```

You can see that the Vector2D type contains the following:

- A collection of record fields

- One instance property (Length)

- Four instance methods (Scale, ShiftX, ShiftY, ShiftXY)

- One static property (Zero)

- Two static methods (ConstX, ConstY)

Let's take a look at the implementation of the Length property:

```
member v.Length = sqrt(v.DX * v.DX + v.DY * v.DY)
```

Here the identifier v stands for the Vector2D value on which the property is being defined. In many other languages, this is called this or self, but in F# you can name this parameter as you see fit. The implementation of a property such as Length is executed each time the property is invoked; in other words, properties are syntactic sugar for method calls. For example, let's repeat the earlier type definition with an additional property that adds a side effect:

```
member v.LengthWithSideEffect =
    printfn "Computing!"
    sqrt(v.DX * v.DX + v.DY * v.DY)
```

Each time you use this property, you see the side effect:

```
> let x = {DX = 3.0; DY=4.0 };;
val x : Vector2D

> x.LengthWithSideEffect;;
Computing!
val it : float = 5.0

> x.LengthWithSideEffect;;
Computing!
val it : float = 5.0
```

The method members for a type look similar to the properties but also take arguments. For example, let's take a look at the implementation of the ShiftX method member:

```
member v.ShiftX(x) = { v with DX=v.DX+x }
```

Here the object is v, and the argument is dx. The return result clones the input record value and adjusts the DX field to be v.DX+dx. Cloning records is described in Chapter 3. The ShiftXY method member takes two arguments:

```
member v.ShiftXY(x,y) = { DX=v.DX+x; DY=v.DY+y }
```

Like functions, method members can take arguments in either tupled or iterated form. For example, you could have defined ShiftXY as follows:

```
member v.ShiftXY x y = { DX=v.DX+x; DY=v.DY+y }
```

However, it is conventional for methods to take their arguments in tupled form. This is partly because OO programming is strongly associated with the design patterns and guidelines of the .NET Framework, and using tupled arguments ensures that the members appear in a form that is most natural when used from other .NET languages. We discuss this issue in more depth in Chapter 19.

Discriminated unions are also a form of concrete type. In this case, the shape of the data associated with a value is drawn from a finite, fixed set of choices. Discriminated unions can also be given members. For example:

```
type Tree<'a> =
    | Tree of 'a * Tree<'a> * Tree<'a>
    | Tip of 'a
    member t.Size =
        match t with
        | Tree(_,l,r) -> 1 + l.Size + r.Size
        | Tip _ -> 1
```

SHOULD I USE MEMBERS OR FUNCTIONS?

F# lets you define both members associated with types and objects via the dot-notation and static functions that can perform essentially the same operations. For example, the length of a string s can be computed by both the s.Length property and the `String.length` function. Given the choice, which should you use in your code? Although there is no fixed answer to this, here are some general rules:

- Use members (methods and properties) where they already exist, unless you have other good reasons not to do so. It is better to use s.Length than `String.length`, simply because it is shorter, even if it occasionally requires using an additional type annotation. Likewise, it is reasonable to use a method such as `dict.Map(f)`. That is, embrace the dot-notation, but use it tastefully.

- When designing a framework or library, define members for the intrinsic, essential properties and operations associated with a type.

- When designing a framework or library, define additional functionality in new modules or by using extension members. We cover extension members in the "Extending Existing Types and Modules" section later in this chapter.

- Sometimes there is duplication in functionality between the dot-notation members and the values in associated modules. This is intended and should just be accepted as part of the mixed OO/functional nature of F#.

Using Constructed Classes

Record types are symmetric: the values used to *construct* an object are the same as those *stored* in the object, which are a subset of those *published* by the object. This symmetry makes record types succinct and clear, and it helps give them other properties; for example, the F# compiler automatically derives generic equality, comparison, and hashing routines for these types.

However, more advanced object-oriented programming often needs to break these symmetries. For example, let's say you want to precompute and store the length of a vector in each vector value. It is clear you don't want everyone who creates a vector to have to perform this computation for you. Instead, you precompute the length as part of the construction sequence for the type. You can't do this using a record, except by using a helper function, so it is convenient to switch to a more general notation for *constructed class types*. Listing 6-2 shows the Vector2D example using a constructed class type.

Listing 6-2. *A Vector2D Type with Length Precomputation via a Constructed Class Type*

```
type Vector2D(dx: float, dy: float) =
    let len = sqrt(dx * dx + dy * dy)
    member v.DX = dx
    member v.DY = dy
    member v.Length = len
    member v.Scale(k)  = Vector2D(k*dx,  k*dy)
    member v.ShiftX(x) = Vector2D(dx=dx+x, dy=dy)
    member v.ShiftY(y) = Vector2D(dx=dx, dy=dy+y)
    member v.ShiftXY(x,y) = Vector2D(dx=dx+x, dy=dy+y)
    static member Zero = Vector2D(dx=0.0, dy=0.0)
    static member OneX = Vector2D(dx=1.0, dy=0.0)
    static member OneY = Vector2D(dx=0.0, dy=1.0)
```

You can now use this type as follows:

```
> let v = Vector2D(3.0, 4.0);;
val v : Vector2D

> v.Length;;
val it : float = 5.0

> v.Scale(2.0).Length;;
val it : float = 10.0
```

Once again it is helpful to look at the inferred type signature for the Vector2D type definition of Listing 6-2:

```
type Vector2D =
    new : dx:float * dy:float -> Vector2D
    member DX : float
    member DY : float
    member Length : float
    member Scale : k:float -> Vector2D
    member ShiftX : x:float -> Vector2D
    member ShiftY : y:float -> Vector2D
    member ShiftXY : x:float * y:float -> Vector2D
    static member Zero : Vector2D
    static member ConstX : dx:float -> Vector2D
    static member ConstY : dy:float -> Vector2D
```

The signature of the type is almost the same as that for Listing 6-1. The primary difference is in the construction syntax. Let's take a look at what's going on here. The first line says we're defining a type Vector2D with a *construction sequence,* where constructions take two arguments, dx

and dy. The variables dx and dy are in scope throughout the nonstatic members of the type definition. The second line is part of the computation performed each time an object of this type is
constructed.

```
let len = sqrt(dx * dx + dy * dy)
```

Like the input values, the len value is in scope throughout the rest of the nonstatic members of
the type. The next three lines publish both the input values and the computed length as properties:

```
member v.DX = dx
member v.DY = dy
member v.Length = len
```

The remaining lines implement the same methods and static properties as the original
record type. The Scale method creates its result by calling the constructor for the type using the
expression Vector2D(k*dx, k*dy). In this expression, arguments are specified by position.

Constructed class types always have the following form, where elements in brackets are
optional and * indicates the element may appear zero or more times:

```
type TypeName optional-type-arguments arguments [ as ident ] =
    [ inherit type { as base} ]
    [ let-binding | let-rec bindings ] *
    [ do-statement ] *
    [ abstract-binding | member-binding | interface-implementation ] *
```

We cover inheritance, abstract bindings, and interface implementations in later sections.

The Vector2D in Listing 6-2 uses a construction sequence. Construction sequences can
enforce object invariants. For example, the following defines a vector type that checks that its
length is close to 1.0 and refuses to construct an instance of the value if not:

```
type UnitVector2D(dx,dy) =
    let tolerance = 0.000001
    let length = sqrt(dx * dx + dy * dy)
    do if abs(length - 1.0) >= tolerance then failwith "not a unit vector";
    member v.DX = dx
    member v.DY = dy
    new() = UnitVector2D (1.0,0.0)
```

This example shows something else: sometimes it is convenient for a class to have multiple
constructors. You do this by adding extra *explicit constructors* using a member named new.
These must ultimately construct an instance of the object via the primary constructor. The
inferred signature for this type contains two constructors:

```
type UnitVector2D =
    new : unit -> UnitVector2D
    new : dx:float * dy:float -> UnitVector2D
    member DX : float
    member DY : float
```

This represents a form of method overloading, covered in more detail in the "Adding Method Overloading" section later in this chapter.

Adding Further Object Notation to Your Types

As we mentioned, one of the most useful aspects of object-oriented programming is the notational convenience of the dot-notation. This extends to other kinds of notation, in particular the *expr*.[*expr*] *indexer* notation, named arguments, optional arguments, operator overloading, and method overloading. In the following sections, we cover how to define and use these notational conveniences.

Working with Indexer Properties

Like methods, properties can also take arguments; these are called *indexer* properties. The most commonly defined indexer property is called Item, and the Item property on a value v is accessed via the special notation v.[i]. As the notation suggests, these are normally used to implement the lookup operation on collection types. In the following example, we implement a sparse vector in terms of an underlying sorted dictionary:

```
open System.Collections.Generic
type SparseVector(items: seq<int * float>)=
    let elems = new SortedDictionary<_,_>()
    do items |> Seq.iter (fun (k,v) -> elems.Add(k,v))

    /// This defines an indexer property
    member t.Item
        with get(idx) =
            if elems.ContainsKey(idx) then elems.[idx]
            else 0.0
```

You can define and use the indexer property as follows:

```
> let v = SparseVector [(3,547.0)];;
val v : SparseVector

> v.[4];;
val it : float = 0.0

> v.[3];;
val it : float = 547.0
```

You can also use indexer properties as mutable "setter" properties with the syntax expr.[expr] <- expr. We cover this in the "Defining Object Types with Mutable State" section. Indexer properties can also take multiple arguments; for example, the indexer property for Microsoft.FSharp.Math.Matrix<'a> takes two arguments. We describe this type in Chapter 10.

Adding Overloaded Operators

Types can also include the definition of overloaded operators. Typically you do this simply by defining static members with the same names as the relevant operator. Here is an example:

```
type Vector2DWithOperators(dx:float,dy:float) =
    member x.DX = dx
    member x.DY = dy

    static member (+) (v1: Vector2DWithOperators ,v2: Vector2DWithOperators) =
        Vector2DWithOperators(v1.DX + v2.DX, v1.DY + v2.DY)

    static member (-) (v1: Vector2DWithOperators ,v2: Vector2DWithOperators) =
        Vector2DWithOperators (v1.DX - v2.DX, v1.DY - v2.DY)
```

```
> let v1 = new Vector2DWithOperators (3.0,4.0);;
val v1 : Vector2DWithOperators

> v1 + v1;;
val it : Vector2DWithOperators = { DX=6.0; DY=8.0 }

> v1 - v1;;
val it : Vector2DWithOperators = { DX=0.0; DY=0.0 }
```

If you add overloaded operators to your type, you may also have to customize how generic equality, hashing, and comparison are performed. In particular, the behavior of generic operators such as hash, <, >, <=, >=, compare, min, and max is not specified by defining new static members with these names, but rather by the techniques described in Chapter 8.

HOW DOES OPERATOR OVERLOADING WORK?

Operator overloading in F# works by having fixed functions that map uses of operators through to particular static members on the static types involved in the operation. These functions are usually defined in the F# library. For example, the F# library includes the following definition for the (+) operator:

```
let inline (+) x y = (^a: (static member (+) : ^a * ^b -> ^c) (x,y))
```

This defines the infix function (+) and is implemented using a special expression that says "implement x + y by calling a static member (+) on the type of the left operand." The function is marked inline to ensure that F# can always check for the existence of this member and call it efficiently. The previous definition for (+) gives a certain asymmetry to this operator; the type of the left operator is more significant than the type of the right. Also, when you name a static member (+), then that is really just shorthand for the name op_Additon, which is the .NET standard "encoded" name for addition operators.

You can also define your own operators if you want, but they will not be overloaded in the same way as the F# library definitions like the one shown previously. For example, the following defines a new infix operator that appends a single element to the end of a list:

```
let (++) x y = List.append x [y]
```

However, this operator is not overloaded; it is a single fixed function. Defining non-overloaded operators can help make some implementation code more succinct, and we use this technique in the symbolic programming examples in Chapter 12.

In principle, you can define new operators that are truly overloaded in the same way as the definition of (+) in the F# library, mapping the operator across to particular static members. However, code is much clearer if you just stick to the standard overloaded operators.

Using Named and Optional Arguments

The F# object-oriented constructs are designed largely for use in APIs for software components. Two useful mechanisms in APIs are to permit callers to name arguments and to let API designers make certain arguments optional.

Named arguments are simple. For example, in Listing 6-2 the implementations of some methods specify arguments by name, as in the expression Vector2D(dx=dx+x, dy=dy). You can use named arguments with all dot-notation method calls. Code written using named arguments is often much more readable and maintainable than code relying on argument position. We will frequently use named arguments throughout the rest of this book.

A member argument is declared optional by prefixing the argument name with ?. Within a function implementation, an optional argument always has an option<_> type; for example, an optional argument of type int will appear as a value of type option<int> within the function body. The value will be None if no argument is supplied by the caller and Some(*arg*) if the argument *arg* is given by the caller. For example:

```
open System.Drawing

type LabelInfo(?text:string, ?font:Font) =
    let text = defaultArg text ""
    let font = match font with
                | None -> new Font(FontFamily.GenericSansSerif,12.0f)
                | Some v -> v
    member x.Text = text
    member x.Font = font
```

The inferred signature for this type shows how the optional arguments have become named arguments accepting option values:

```
type LabelInfo =
    new : text:string option * font:System.Drawing.Font option -> LabelInfo
    member Font : System.Drawing.Font
    member Text : string
```

You can now create LabelInfo values using several different techniques:

```
> LabelInfo (text="Hello World");;
val it : LabelInfo =
    {Font = [Font: Name=Microsoft Sans Serif, Size=12]; Text = "Hello World"}

> LabelInfo("Goodbye Lenin");;
val it : LabelInfo =
    {Font = [Font: Name=Microsoft Sans Serif, Size=12];  Text = "Goodbye Lenin"}

> LabelInfo(font=new Font(FontFamily.GenericMonospace,36.0f),
            text="Imagine");;
val it : LabelInfo =
    {Font = [Font: Name=Courier New, Size=36]; Text = "Imagine"}
```

Optional arguments must always appear last in the set of arguments accepted by a method. They are usually used as named arguments by callers.

The implementation of LabelInfo uses the F# library function defaultArg, which is a useful way to specify simple default values for optional arguments. Its type is as follows:

```
val defaultArg : 'a option -> 'a -> 'a
```

Note The second argument given to the defaultArg function is evaluated *before* the function is called. This means you should take care that this argument is not expensive to compute and doesn't need to be disposed. In the previous example, we used a match expression to specify the default for the font argument for this reason.

Using Optional Property Settings

Throughout this book we have been using a second technique to specify configuration parameters when creating objects, which is using *initial property settings* for objects. For example, in Chapter 2 we used the following code:

```
open System.Windows.Forms
let form = new Form(Visible=true,TopMost=true,Text="Welcome to F#")
```

The constructor for the System.Windows.Forms.Form class takes no arguments, so in this case the named arguments actually indicate post-hoc set operations for the given properties. The code is shorthand for this:

```
open System.Windows.Forms

let form =
    let tmp = new Form()
    tmp.Visible <- true
    tmp.TopMost <- true
    tmp.Text <- "Welcome to F#"
    tmp
```

The F# compiler interprets unused named arguments as calls that set properties of the returned object. This technique is widely used for mutable objects that evolve over time such as graphical components, since it greatly reduces the number of optional arguments that need to be plumbed around. Here's how to define a version of the LabelInfo type used earlier that is configurable by optional property settings:

```
open System.Drawing

type LabelInfoWithPropertySetting() =
    let mutable text = "" // the default
    let mutable font = new Font(FontFamily.GenericSansSerif,12.0f)
    member x.Text with get() = text and set(v) = text <- v
    member x.Font with get() = font and set(v) = font <- v
```

```
> LabelInfoWithPropertySetting(Text="Hello World");;
val it : LabelInfo =
    {Font = [Font: Name=Microsoft Sans Serif, Size=12]; Text = "Hello World"}
```

We use this technique in Chapter 11 when we show how to define a Windows Forms control with configurable properties. We cover mutable objects in more detail in the "Defining Object Types with Mutable State" section later in this chapter.

Adding Method Overloading

.NET APIs and other OO design frameworks frequently use a notational device called *method overloading*. This means a type can support multiple methods with the same name, and uses of methods are distinguished by name, number of arguments, and argument types. For example, the System.Console.WriteLine method of .NET has 19 overloads!

Method overloading is used relatively rarely in F#-authored classes, partly because optional arguments and mutable property setters tend to make it less necessary. However, method overloading is still permitted in F#. First, methods can easily be overloaded by the number of arguments. For example, Listing 6-3 shows a concrete type representing an interval of numbers on the number line. It includes two methods called Span, one taking a pair of intervals and the other taking an arbitrary collection of intervals. The overloading is resolved simply according to argument count.

Listing 6-3. *A Vector2D Type with Length Precomputation*

```
/// Interval(lo,hi) represents the range of numbers from lo to hi,
/// but not including either lo or hi.
type Interval(lo,hi) =
    member r.Lo = lo
    member r.Hi = hi
    member r.IsEmpty = hi <= lo
    member r.Contains(v) = lo < v && v < hi

    static member Empty = Interval(0.0,0.0)

    /// Return the smallest interval that covers both the intervals
    /// This method is overloaded.
    static member Span(r1:Interval,r2:Interval) =
        if r1.IsEmpty then r2 else
        if r2.IsEmpty then r1 else
        Interval(min r1.Lo r2.Lo,max r1.Hi r2.Hi)

    /// Return the smallest interval that covers all the intervals
    /// This method is overloaded.
    static member Span(ranges: #seq<Interval>) =
        Seq.fold (fun r1 r2 -> Interval.Span(r1,r2)) Interval.Empty ranges
```

Second, multiple methods can also have the same number of arguments and be overloaded by type. One of the most common examples is providing multiple implementations of overloaded operators on the same type. The following example shows a Point type that supports two subtraction operations, one subtracting a Point from a Point to give a Vector and one subtracting a Vector from a Point to give a Point:

```
type Vector =
    { DX:float; DY:float }
    member v.Length = sqrt(v.DX*v.DX+v.DY*v.DY)

type Point =
    { X:float; Y:float }

    [<OverloadID("SubtractPointPoint")>]
    static member (-) (p1:Point,p2:Point) = { DX=p1.X-p2.X; DY=p1.Y-p2.Y }

    [<OverloadID("subtractPointVector")>]
    static member (-) (p:Point,v:Vector) = { X=p.X-v.DX; Y=p.Y-v.DY }
```

The version of F# at the time of writing (1.9.2.9) asks for a little help here. You should give a full type signature for each overload (by specifying the types for all arguments) and also annotate each overload with an OverloadID attribute, thus giving a different "name" for each overload. The OverloadID name is used internally by the F# compiler but should match the OverloadID used in the signature of the type should you give one (see Chapter 7 for more details on signatures). The F# designers have indicated that the requirement to use an `OverloadID` may be removed in the future.

Defining Object Types with Mutable State

All the types you've seen so far in this chapter have been immutable. For example, the values of the `Vector2D` types shown in Listing 6-1 and Listing 6-2 cannot be modified once created. Frequently you will want to define mutable objects, particularly since object-oriented programming is a generally useful technique for encapsulating mutable and evolving state. Listing 6-4 shows the definition of a mutable representation of a 2D vector.

Listing 6-4. *A Concrete Object Type with State*

```
type MutableVector2D(dx:float,dy:float) =
    let mutable currDX = dx
    let mutable currDY = dy

    member v.DX with get() = currDX and set(v) = currDX <- v
    member v.DY with get() = currDY and set(v) = currDY <- v

    member v.Length
        with get () = sqrt(currDX*currDX+currDY*currDY)
        and  set len =
            let theta = v.Angle
            currDX <- cos(theta)*len
            currDY <- sin(theta)*len

    member v.Angle
        with get () = atan2 currDY currDX
        and  set theta =
            let len = v.Length
            currDX <- cos(theta)*len
            currDY <- sin(theta)*len
```

The mutable state is held in two mutable local `let` bindings for `currDX` and `currDY`. It also exposes additional settable properties, `Length` and `Angle`, that interpret and adjust the underlying `currDX`/`currDY` values. Here is the inferred signature for the type:

```
type MutableVector2D =
    new : float * float -> MutableVector2D
    member DX : float with get,set
    member DY : float with get,set
    member Angle : float with get,set
    member Length : float with get,set
```

You can use this type as follows:

```
> let v = MutableVector2D(3.0,4.0);;
val v : MutableVector2D

> (v.DX, v.DY);;
val it : float * float = (3.0, 4.0)

> (v.Length, v.Angle);;
val it : float * float = (5.0, 0.927295218)

> v.Angle <- System.Math.PI / 6.0;;      // "30 degrees"
val it : unit = ()

> (v.DX, v.DY);;
val it : float * float = (4.330127019, 2.5)

> (v.Length, v.Angle);;
val it : float * float = (5.0, 0.523598775)
```

Adjusting the Angle property rotates the vector while maintaining its overall length. Here we're using the "long" syntax for properties, where we specify both set and get operations for the property.

Note Constructed types are useful partly because they implicitly *encapsulate* internal functions and mutable state. This is because all the construction arguments and `let` bindings are private to the object instance being constructed. This is just one of the ways of encapsulating information in F# programming. We cover encapsulation more closely in Chapter 7.

OBJECTS AND MUTATION

OO programming is often presented primarily as a technique for controlling the complexity of mutable state. However, many of the concerns of OO programming are orthogonal to this. For example, programming constructs such as object interface types, inheritance, and higher-level design patterns such as publish/subscribe stem from the OO tradition, while techniques such as functions, type abstraction, and aggregate operations such as map and `fold` stem from the functional programming tradition. Many of the OO techniques have no fundamental relationship to object mutation and identity; for example, interfaces and inheritance can be used very effectively with immutable objects. Much of the expressivity of F# lies in the way it brings the techniques of OO programming and functional programming comfortably together.

Getting Started with Object Interface Types

So far in this chapter you've seen only how to define concrete object types and how to use object-oriented notation with these types. One of the key advances in both functional and object-oriented programming has been the move toward using abstract types rather than concrete types for large portions of modern software. These values are typically accessed via *interfaces*, and we'll now look at defining new *object interface types*. Many .NET object interface types begin with the letter I, as in System.IDisposable.

The notion of an object interface type can sound a little daunting at first, but the concept is actually simple; object interface types are just ones whose member implementations can vary from value to value. As it happens, you've already met one important family of types whose implementations also vary from value to value: F# function types!

- In Chapter 3 you saw how functions can be used to model a range of concepts such as comparison functions, aggregation functions, and transformation functions.

- In Chapter 5 you saw how records of function values can be used for the parameters needed to make an algorithm generic.

You've also already met some other important object interface types such as System.Collections.Generic.IEnumerable<'a> and System.IDisposable.

Object interface types are always *implemented*, and the type definition itself doesn't specify how this is done. Listing 6-5 shows an object interface type IShape and a number of implementations of it. We now walk through the definitions in this code piece by piece, because they illustrate the key concepts behind object interface types and how they can be implemented.

Listing 6-5. *An Object Interface Type IShape and Some Implementations*

```
open System.Drawing
type IShape =
    abstract Contains : Point -> bool
    abstract BoundingBox : Rectangle

let circle(center:Point,radius:int) =
    { new IShape with
        member x.Contains(p:Point) =
            let dx = float32 (p.X - center.X)
            let dy = float32 (p.Y - center.Y)
            sqrt(dx*dx+dy*dy) <= float32 radius
        member x.BoundingBox =
            Rectangle(center.X-radius,center.Y-radius,2*radius+1,2*radius+1) }

let square(center:Point,side:int) =
    { new IShape with
        member x.Contains(p:Point) =
            let dx = p.X - center.X
            let dy = p.Y - center.Y
            abs(dx) < side/2 && abs(dy) < side/2
        member x.BoundingBox =
            Rectangle(center.X-side,center.Y-side,side*2,side*2) }
```

```
type MutableCircle() =
    let mutable center = Point(x=0,y=0)
    let mutable radius = 10
    member sq.Center with get() = center and set(v) = center <- v
    member sq.Radius with get() = radius and set(v) = radius <- v
    member c.Perimeter = 2.0 * System.Math.PI * float radius
    interface IShape with
        member x.Contains(p:Point) =
            let dx = float32 (p.X - center.X)
            let dy = float32 (p.Y - center.Y)
            sqrt(dx*dx+dy*dy) <= float32 radius
        member x.BoundingBox =
            Rectangle(center.X-radius,center.Y-radius,2*radius+1,2*radius+1)
```

Defining New Object Interface Types

The key definition in Listing 6-5 is the following (we are also using Rectangle and Point, two types from the System.Drawing namespace):

```
open System.Drawing
type IShape =
    abstract Contains : Point -> bool
    abstract BoundingBox : Rectangle
```

Here we use the keyword abstract to define the member signatures for this type, indicating the implementation of the member may vary from value to value. Also note that IShape is not concrete; it is neither a record nor a discriminated union or constructed object type. It doesn't have any constructors and doesn't accept any arguments. This is how F# infers that it is an object interface type.

Implementing Object Interface Types Using Object Expressions

The following code from Listing 6-5 implements the object interface type IShape using an *object expression*:

```
let circle(center:Point,radius:int) =
    { new IShape with
        member x.Contains(p:Point) =
            let dx = float32 (p.X - center.X)
            let dy = float32 (p.Y - center.Y)
            sqrt(dx*dx+dy*dy) <= float32 radius
        member x.BoundingBox =
            Rectangle(center.X-radius,center.Y-radius,2*radius+1,2*radius+1) }
```

The type of the function circle is as follows:

```
val circle : Point * int -> IShape
```

The construct in the braces, { new IShape with ... }, is the object expression. This is a new expression form that you haven't encountered previously in this book, because it is generally used only when implementing object interface types. An object expression must give implementations for all the members of an object interface type. The general form of this kind of expression is simple:

```
{ new Type optional-arguments with
      member-definitions
  optional-extra-interface-definitions }
```

The member definitions take the same form as members for type definitions described earlier in this chapter. The optional arguments are given only when object expressions inherit from a constructed class type, and the optional interface definitions are used when implementing additional interfaces that are part of a hierarchy of object interface types.

You can use the function circle as follows:

```
> let bigCircle = circle(Point(0,0), 100);;
val bigCircle : IShape

> bigCircle.BoundingBox;;
val it : Rectangle = {X=-100,Y=-100,Width=201,Height=201}

> bigCircle.Contains(Point(70,70));;
val it : bool = true

> bigCircle.Contains(Point(71,71));;
val it : bool = false
```

Listing 6-5 also contains another function square that gives a different implementation for IShape, also using an object expression:

```
> let smallSquare = square(Point(1,1), 1);;
val smallSquare : IShape

> smallSquare.BoundingBox;;
val it : Rectangle = {X=0,Y=0,Width=3,Height=3}

> smallSquare.Contains(Point(0,0));;
val it : bool = false
```

Note In OO languages, implementing types in multiple ways is commonly called *polymorphism*, which we might call *polymorphism of implementation*. Polymorphism of this kind is present throughout F#, and not just with respect to the OO constructs. In functional programming, *polymorphism* is used to mean generic type parameters, which is an orthogonal concept discussed in Chapter 2 and Chapter 5.

Implementing Object Interface Types Using Concrete Types

It is common to have concrete types that both implement one or more object interface types and provide additional services of their own. Collections are one primary example, since they always implement IEnumerable<'a>. To give another example, in Listing 6-5 the type MutableCircle is defined as follows:

```
type MutableCircle() =
    let mutable center = Point(x=0,y=0)
    let mutable radius = 10
    member c.Center with get() = center and set(v) = center <- v
    member c.Radius with get() = radius and set(v) = radius <- v
    member c.Perimeter = 2.0 * System.Math.PI * float radius
    interface IShape with
        member c.Contains(p:Point) =
            let dx = float32 (p.X - center.X)
            let dy = float32 (p.Y - center.Y)
            sqrt(dx*dx+dy*dy) <= float32 radius
        member c.BoundingBox =
            Rectangle(center.X-radius,center.Y-radius,2*radius+1,2*radius+1)
```

This type implements the IShape interface, which means MutableCircle is a subtype of IShape, but it also provides three properties—Center, Radius, and Perimeter—that are specific to the MutableCircle type, two of which are settable. The type has the following signature:

```
type MutableCircle =
    interface IShape
    new : unit -> MutableCircle
    member Perimeter : float
    member Center : Point with get,set
    member Radius : int with get,set
```

We can now "reveal" the interface (through a type cast) and use its members. For example:

```
> let circle2 = MutableCircle();;
val circle2 : MutableCircle

> circle2.Radius;;
val it : int = 10

> (circle2 :> IShape).BoundingBox;;
val it : Rectangle = {X=0,Y=0,Width=3,Height=3}
```

Using Common Object Interface Types from the .NET Libraries

Like other constructs discussed in this chapter, object interface types are often encountered when using .NET libraries. Some object interface types such as IEnumerable<'a> (called seq<'a> in

F# coding) are also used throughout F# programming. It is a .NET convention to prefix the name of all object interface types with I. However, using object interface types is very common in F# OO programming, so this convention is not always followed.

Here's the essence of the definition of the `System.Collections.Generic.IEnumerable<'a>` type and the related type `IEnumerator` using F# notation:

```
type IEnumerator<'a> =
    abstract Current : 'a
    abstract MoveNext : unit -> bool

type IEnumerable<'a> =
    abstract GetEnumerator : unit -> IEnumerator<'a>
```

The `IEnumerable<'a>` type is implemented by most concrete collection types. It can also be implemented by an object expression or by calling a library function such as `Seq.unfold`, which in turn uses an object expression as part of its implementation.

■**Note** The `IEnumerator<'a>` and `IEnumerable<'a>` interfaces are defined in a library component that is implemented using another .NET language. In this section, we have used the corresponding F# syntax. In reality, `IEnumerator<'a>` also inherits from the nongeneric interface `System.Collections.IEnumerator` and the type `System.IDisposable`, and `IEnumerable<'a>` also inherits from the nongeneric interface `System.Collections.IEnumerable`. For clarity we've ignored this here. See the F# library code for full example implementations of these types.

Some other useful predefined F# and .NET object interface types are as follows:

`System.IDisposable`: Represents values that may own explicitly reclaimable resources.

`System.IComparable` and `System.IComparable<'a>`: Represent values that can be compared to other values. F# generic comparison is implemented via these types, as you'll see in Chapter 8.

`Microsoft.FSharp.Control.IEvent`: Represents mutable ports into which you can plug event listeners, or *callbacks*. This technique is described in Chapter 8. Some other entity is typically responsible for raising the event and thus calling all the listener callbacks. In F#, .NET events become values of this type or the related type `Microsoft.FSharp.Control.IDelegateEvent`, and the module `Microsoft.FSharp.Control.IEvent` contains many useful combinators for manipulating these values. This module can be opened simply by using `open IEvent`.

Understanding Hierarchies of Object Interface Types

Object interface types can be arranged in hierarchies using *interface inheritance*. This gives a way to classify types. To create a hierarchy, you simply use the `inherit` keyword in an object interface type definition along with each parent object interface type. For example, the .NET Framework includes a hierarchical classification of collection types: `ICollection<'a>` extends

IEnumerable<'a>. Here are the essential definitions of these types in F# syntax, with some minor details omitted:

```
type IEnumerable<'a> =
    abstract GetEnumerator : unit -> IEnumerator<'a>

type ICollection<'a> =
    inherit IEnumerable<'a>
    abstract Count : int
    abstract IsReadOnly : bool
    abstract Add : 'a -> unit
    abstract Clear : unit -> unit
    abstract Contains  : 'a -> bool
    abstract CopyTo  : 'a[] * int -> unit
    abstract Remove  : 'a -> unit
```

When you implement an interface that inherits from another interface, you must effectively implement both interfaces.

■**Caution** Although hierarchical modeling is useful, it must also be used with care, because poorly designed hierarchies often have to be abandoned late in the software development life cycle, leading to major disruptions. For many applications it is adequate to use existing classification hierarchies in conjunction with new nonhierarchical interface types.

More Techniques to Implement Objects

Objects can be difficult to implement from scratch; for example, a graphical user interface (GUI) component must respond to many different events, often in regular and predictable ways, and it would be tedious to have to recode all this behavior for each component. This makes it essential to support the process of creating *partial implementations* of objects, where the partial implementations can then be completed or customized. In the following sections, we cover techniques to build partial implementations of objects.

Combining Object Expressions and Function Parameters

One of the easiest ways to build a partial implementation of an object is to qualify the implementation of the object by a number of function parameters that complete the implementation. For example, the following code defines an object interface type called ITextOutputSink, a partial implementation of that type called simpleOutputSink, and a function called simpleOutputSink that acts as a partial implementation of that type. The remainder of the implementation is provided by a function parameter called writeCharFunction.

```
type ITextOutputSink =
    abstract WriteChar : char -> unit
    abstract WriteString : string -> unit

let simpleOutputSink(writeCharFunction) =
    { new ITextOutputSink with
          member x.WriteChar(c) = writeCharFunction(c)
          member x.WriteString(s) = s |> String.iter x.WriteChar }
```

This construction function uses function values to build an object of a given shape. Here the inferred type is as follows:

val simpleOutputSink: (char -> unit) -> ITextOutputSink

In the following code, we instantiate the function parameter to output the characters to a particular System.Text.StringBuilder object, an imperative type for accumulating characters in a buffer before converting these to an immutable System.String value:

```
open System.Text
let stringBuilderOuputSink (buf : StringBuilder ) =
    simpleOutputSink (fun c -> buf.Append(c) |> ignore)
```

Here is an example of the use of this function interactively:

```
> let buf = new System.Text.StringBuilder();;
val buf : StringBuilder

> let c = stringBuilderOuputSink(buf);;
val c : ITextOutputSink

> ["Incy"; " "; "Wincy"; " "; "Spider"] |> List.iter c.WriteString;;
val it : unit = ()

> buf.ToString();;
val it : string = "Incy Wincy Spider"
```

Object expressions must still give definitions for all unimplemented abstract members and cannot add other additional members; however, the abstract members can be implemented in terms of function parameters. As you saw in Chapter 3, function parameters can represent a wide range of concepts, so this technique is a powerful one.

You can also use function parameters to qualify concrete types that implement object interface types. For example, here is a type CountingOutputSink that performs effectively the same role as the earlier function simpleOutputSink, except that the number of characters written to the sink is recorded and published as a property:

```
type CountingOutputSink(writeCharFunction: char -> unit) =

    let mutable count = 0

    interface ITextOutputSink with
        member x.WriteChar(c) = count <- count + 1; writeCharFunction(c)
        member x.WriteString(s) = s |> String.iter (x :> ITextOutputSink).WriteChar

    member x.Count = count
```

■**Note** Qualifying object implementations by function parameters can be seen as a simple form of the object-oriented design pattern known as *delegation*, since parts of the implementation are delegated to the function values. Delegation is a powerful and compositional technique for reusing fragments of implementations and is commonly used in F# as a replacement for object-oriented implementation inheritance.

Defining Partially Implemented Class Types

In this chapter, you saw how to define concrete types, such as Vector2D, in Listing 6-2 and Listing 6-3, and you saw how to define object interface types, such as IShape, in Listing 6-5. Sometimes it is useful to define types that are halfway between this, i.e., *partially concrete types*. Partially implemented types are simply constructed class types that also have some abstract members, some of which may be unimplemented and some of which may have default implementations. For example, consider the following class:

```
type TextOutputSink() =
    abstract WriteChar : char -> unit
    abstract WriteString : string -> unit
    default x.WriteString(s) = s |> String.iter x.WriteChar
```

This class defines two abstract members, WriteChar and WriteString, but gives a default implementation for WriteString in terms of WriteChar. Because WriteChar is not yet implemented, you can't create an instance of this type directly; in other words, unlike other concrete types, partially implemented types still need to be implemented. One way to do this is to complete the implementation via an object expression. For example:

```
{ new TextOutputSink() with
      member x.WriteChar(c) = System.Console.Write(c) }
```

Using Partially Implemented Types via Delegation

In this section, we cover how you can use partially implemented types to build complete objects. One approach is to instantiate one or more partially implemented types to put together a complete concrete type. This is often done via delegation to an instantiation of the partially concrete type; for example, in the following example, we create a private, internal TextOutputSink object whose implementation of WriteChar counts the number of characters written through that object. We use this object to build the `HtmlWriter` object that publishes three methods specific to the process of writing a particular format:

```
type HtmlWriter() =
    let mutable count = 0
    let sink =
        { new TextOutputSink() with
                member x.WriteChar(c) =
                    count <- count + 1;
                    System.Console.Write(c) }

    member x.CharCount = count
    member x.WriteHeader() = sink.WriteString("<html>")
    member x.WriteFooter() = sink.WriteString("</html>")
    member x.WriteString(s) = sink.WriteString(s)
```

Using Partially Implemented Types via Implementation Inheritance

Another technique to use partially implemented types is called *implementation inheritance*, which is widely used in OO languages despite being a somewhat awkward technique. Implementation inheritance tends to be much less significant in F# because it comes with major drawbacks:

- Implementation inheritance takes base objects and makes them more complex. This is against the spirit of functional programming, where the aim is to build simple, composable abstractions. Functional programming, object expressions, and delegation tend to provide good alternative techniques for defining, sharing, and combining implementation fragments.

- Implementation hierarchies tend to "leak" across API boundaries, revealing how objects are implemented rather than how they can be used and composed.

- Implementation hierarchies are often fragile to minor changes in program specification.

For example, the `Microsoft.FSharp.Collections.Seq` module (opened using `open Seq`) provides many implementations of the `seq<'a>` interface but uses almost no implementation inheritance. Instead, the techniques described in the previous sections are used.

Nevertheless, hierarchies of classes are important in domains such as GUI programming, and the technique is used heavily by .NET libraries written in other .NET languages. For example, `System.Windows.Forms.Control`, `System.Windows.Forms.UserControl`, and `System.Windows.Forms.RichTextBox` are part of a hierarchy of visual GUI elements. Should you want to write new controls, then you must understand this implementation hierarchy and how to extend it. We show you a complete example of extending `UserControl` in Chapter 11. However, even in this domain, implementation inheritance is often less important than you might think, because these controls can often be configured in powerful and interesting ways by adding function callbacks to events associated with the controls.

Here is a simple example of applying the technique to instantiate and extend the partially implemented type `TextOutputSink`:

```
type CountingOutputSinkByInheritance() =
    inherit TextOutputSink()
    let mutable count = 0
    member sink.Count = count
    default sink.WriteChar(c) = count <- count + 1; System.Console.Write(c)
```

The keywords override and default can be used interchangeably and both indicate that an implementation is being given for an abstract member. By convention override is used when giving implementations for abstract members in inherited types that already had implementations, and default is used for implementations of abstract members that didn't previously have implementations.

Implementations are also free to override and modify default implementations such as the implementation of WriteString provided by TextOutputSink. Here is an example:

```
{ new TextOutputSink() with
      member sink.WriteChar(c) = System.Console.Write(c)
      member sink.WriteString(s) = System.Console.Write(s) }
```

You can also build new partially implemented types by extending existing partially implemented types. In the following example, we take the TextOutputSink type from the previous section and add two abstract members called WriteByte and WriteBytes, add a default implementation for WriteBytes, add an initial implementation for WriteChar, and override the implementation of WriteString to use WriteBytes. The implementations of WriteChar and WriteString use the .NET functionality to convert the Unicode characters and strings to bytes under System.Text.UTF8Encoding, documented in the .NET Framework class libraries.

```
open System.Text
type ByteOutputSink() =
    inherit TextOutputSink()
    abstract WriteByte : byte -> unit
    abstract WriteBytes : byte[] -> unit
    default sink.WriteChar(c) = sink.WriteBytes(Encoding.UTF8.GetBytes([|c|]))
    override sink.WriteString(s) = sink.WriteBytes(Encoding.UTF8.GetBytes(s))
    default sink.WriteBytes(b) = b |> Array.iter (fun c -> sink.WriteByte(c))
```

Using Modules and Static Members

A common OO design technique is to use a class that contains only static items as a way of organizing values, global state, and type definitions. In F# this is called a *module*. A module is a simple container for values, type definitions, and submodules. For example, here is the Vector2D example rewritten to use a module to hold the operations associated with the type:

```
type Vector2D =
    { DX: float; DY: float }

module Vector2DOps =
    let length v = sqrt(v.DX * v.DX + v.DY * v.DY)
    let scale k v = { DX=k*v.DX; DY=k*v.DY }
    let shiftX x v = { v with DX=v.DX+x }
```

```
let shiftY y v = { v with DY=v.DY+y }
let shiftXY (x,y) v = { DX=v.DX+x; DY=v.DY+y }
let zero = { DX=0.0; DY=0.0 }
let constX dx = { DX=dx; DY=0.0 }
let constY dy = { DX=0.0; DY=dy }
```

A module is compiled as a class that contains only static values, types, and additional submodules. Some people prefer to use classes with static members for this purpose, though in practice there is little difference between the two techniques. Modules may also contain type and submodule definitions. Sometimes you want to have a module with the same name as one of your types. You can do this by adding an attribute to your code:

```
type Vector2D =
    { DX: float; DY: float }

[<CompilationRepresentation(CompilationRepresentationFlags.ModuleSuffix)>]
module Vector2D =
    let length v = sqrt(v.DX * v.DX + v.DY * v.DY)
```

Values in a module can be used simply via a long path, e.g., Vector2D.length. Alternatively, you can open the module, which makes all the contents accessible without qualification. For example, open Vector2D makes the identifier length available without qualification.

Note In the non-#light syntax, you delimit modules by begin/end. For compatibility with OCaml modules, this can also be delimited by struct/end. However, the keyword struct has a different meaning in F#, so this declaration form is not recommended except when cross-compiling code with OCaml.

USING MODULES AND TYPES TO ORGANIZE CODE

You will often have to choose whether to use modules or OO dot-notation to organize your code. Here are some of the rules for using these to organize your code effectively and to lay the groundwork for applying good .NET library and framework design principles to your code:

- Use modules when prototyping and to organize scripts, ad hoc algorithms, initialization code, and active patterns.

- Use concrete types (records, discriminated unions, and constructed class types) to implement concrete data structures. In the long term, plan on completely hiding the implementation of these types. We'll see how to do this in Chapter 7. You can provide dot-notation operations to help users access parts of the data structure. Avoid revealing other representation details.

- Use object interface types for types that have several possible implementations.

- Implement object interface types by private concrete types or by object expressions.

- In polished libraries, most concrete types exposed in an implementation should also implement one or more object interface types. For example, collections should implement IEnumerable<'a>, and many types should implement IDisposable (see Chapter 8 for more details on IDisposable).

- Avoid relying on or revealing complex type hierarchies. In particular, avoid relying on implementation inheritance, except as an internal implementation technique or when doing GUI programming or authoring very large objects.

- Avoid nesting modules or types inside other modules or types. Nested modules and types are useful implementation details, but they are rarely made public in APIs. Deep hierarchical organization can be confusing, and when designing a library, you should place nearly all public modules and types immediately inside a well-named namespace.

Extending Existing Types and Modules

The final topic we cover in this chapter is how you can define ad hoc dot-notation extensions to existing library types and modules. This technique is used rarely but can be invaluable in certain circumstances. For example, the following definition adds the member IsPrime. You will see uses of this technique in Chapter 13.

```
module NumberTheoryExtensions =
    let isPrime(i) =
        let lim = int(sqrt(float(i)))
        let rec check j =
            j > lim or (i % j <> 0 && check (j+1))
        check 2

    type System.Int32 with
        member i.IsPrime = isPrime(i)
```

The IsPrime property is then available for use in conjunction with int32 values whenever the NumberTheoryExtensions module has been opened. For example:

```
> open NumberTheoryExtensions;;

> (3).IsPrime;;
val it : bool = true

> (6093711).IsPrime;;
val it : bool = false
```

Type extensions always refer to the type being extended by a fully qualified path System.Int32. Type extensions can be given in any assembly, but priority is always given to the intrinsic members of a type when resolving the dot-notation and then to the most recently opened extension modules.

■**Note** Type extensions are a good technique for equipping simple type definitions with object-oriented functionality. However, don't fall into the trap of adding too much functionality to an existing type via this route. Instead, it is often simpler just to use additional modules and types. For example, the module `Microsoft.FSharp.Collections.List` contains extra functionality associated with the F# list type.

Modules can also be "extended," in a fashion. For example, say you think the `List` module is missing an obvious function such as `List.pairwise` to return a new list of adjacent pairs. You can "extend" the set of values accessed by the path `List` simply by defining a new module `List`:

```
module List =
    let rec pairwise l =
        match l with
        | [] | [_] -> []
        | h1::(h2::_ as t) -> (h1,h2) :: pairwise t
```

```
> List.pairwise [1;2;3;4];;
val it : (int * int) list = [ (1,2); (2,3); (3,4) ]
```

Working with F# Objects and .NET Types

In this chapter, we have de-emphasized the use of .NET terminology for object types, such as `class` and `interface`. However, all F# types are ultimately compiled as .NET types. Here is how they relate:

- Concrete types such as record types, discriminated unions, and constructed class types are compiled as .NET classes.

- Object interface types are by default compiled as .NET interface types.

If you want, you can delimit constructed class types by `class`/`end`. For example:

```
type Vector2D(dx: float, dy: float) =
    class
        let len = sqrt(dx * dx + dy * dy)
        member v.DX = dx
        member v.DY = dy
        member v.Length = len
    end
```

You will see this in F# code samples on the Web and in other books. However, we have found that this tends to make types harder to understand, so we have omitted `class`/`end` throughout. You can also delimit object interface types by `interface`/`end`. For example:

```
open System.Drawing

type IShape =
    interface
        abstract Contains : Point -> bool
        abstract BoundingBox : Rectangle
    end
```

Structs

It is occasionally useful to direct the F# compiler to use a .NET struct (value type) representation for small, generally immutable objects. You can do this by adding a Struct attribute to a class type, here defined with explicit values and an explicit constructor:

```
[<Struct>]
type Vector2DStruct =
    val dx: float
    val dy: float
    new(dx,dy) = {dx=dx; dy=dy}
    member v.DX = v.dx
    member v.DY = v.dy
    member v.Length = sqrt(v.dx * v.dx + v.dy * v.dy)
```

Or you can use a delimited form:

```
type Vector2DStructUsingKeywords =
    struct
        val dx: float
        val dy: float
    end
```

Structs are often more efficient, but you should use them with care because the full contents of struct values are frequently copied. The performance characteristics of structs can also change depending on whether you are running on a 32-bit or 64-bit machine.

Delegates

Occasionally it is necessary to define a new .NET delegate type in F#:

```
type ControlEventHandler = delegate of int -> bool
```

This is usually required only when using C code from F#, because some magic performed by the .NET Common Language Runtime lets you marshal a delegate value as a C function pointer. We'll take a look at interoperating with C and COM in Chapter 17. For example, here's how you add a new handler to the Win32 Ctrl+C handling API:

```
open System.Runtime.InteropServices
let ctrlSignal = ref false
[<DllImport("kernel32.dll")>]
extern void SetConsoleCtrlHandler(ControlEventHandler callback,bool add)

let ctrlEventHandler = new ControlEventHandler(fun i ->  ctrlSignal := true; true)

SetConsoleCtrlHandler(ctrlEventHandler,true)
```

Enums

Occasionally it is necessary to define a new .NET enum type in F#. You do this using a notation similar to discriminated unions:

```
type Vowels =
    | A = 1
    | E = 5
    | I = 9
    | O = 15
    | U = 21
```

This type is compiled as a .NET enum, whose underlying bit representation is a simple integer.

Summary

In this chapter, you looked at the basic constructs of object-oriented programming in F#, including concrete object types, OO notation, and object interface types and their implementations, as well as more advanced techniques to implement object interface types. You also saw how implementation inheritance is less important as an object implementation technique in F# than in other OO languages and then learned how the F# object model relates to the .NET object model. In the next chapter, we'll cover language constructs and practical techniques related to encapsulating, packaging, and deploying your code.

CHAPTER 7

■■■

Encapsulating and Packaging Your Code

Packaging code and making it available for people and programs to use is a key part of making the best use of F#. In this book, you have already seen many of the constructs to help do this: functions, objects, type definitions, modules, namespaces, and assemblies. However, in some cases you have encountered these only peripherally when using the .NET Base Class Library. In this chapter, we'll cover these constructs from the perspective of code organization and packaging.

Packaging code has four distinct but related meanings:

- *Organizing* code into sensible entities using namespaces, types, and modules.

- *Encapsulating* internal data structures and implementation details by making them private.

- *Assembling* code and data as a component, which on .NET is called an *assembly*. An assembly is one or more .dll or .exe packaged together with supporting data as a single logical unit.

- *Deploying* one or more assemblies, such as a web application or framework, often with an installer, for use on client machines, on web servers, or for download over the Web.

The first two of these topics are associated with the F# language itself, and the last is more associated with the pragmatics of deploying, installing, configuring, and maintaining software. The third lies in between, because .NET assemblies can act as both a unit of encapsulation and a unit of deployment.

Knowing these techniques is not the same as knowing how to use them effectively, or indeed when to use them at all. At the end of this chapter, we cover some of the different kinds of .NET software you might write with F# and how you can organize and package your code for these different cases.

Hiding Things Away

In all kinds of software, it is common to hide implementation details of data structures and algorithms behind *encapsulation boundaries*. Encapsulation is a fundamental technique when writing software and is possibly the most important idea associated with OO programming.

For our purposes, *encapsulation* simply means hiding implementation details behind well-defined boundaries. This lets you enforce consistency properties and makes the structure of a program easier to manage. It also lets an implementation evolve over time. A good rule of thumb is that anything you don't want used directly by client code should be hidden.

Later in this chapter, we explain how encapsulation applies when building assemblies, frameworks, and applications. In the extreme, you may even be ensuring that your code is *secure* when used in "partial trust mode," in other words, that it can't be inadvertently or deliberately used to achieve malicious results when used as a library by code that doesn't have full permissions. However, the most important kind of encapsulation is the day-to-day business of hiding the internal implementation details of functions, objects, types, and modules. The primary techniques used to do this are as follows:

- Local definitions

- Accessibility annotations

- Explicit signatures

We cover the first two of these techniques next, and we cover explicit signatures in the "Using Signature Types and Files" section later in this chapter.

Hiding Things with Local Definitions

The easiest way to hide definitions is to make them local to expressions or constructed class definitions using inner `let` bindings. These are not directly accessible from outside their scope. This technique is frequently used to hide state and other computed values inside the implementations of functions and objects. We begin with a simple example. Here is the definition of a function that incorporates a single item of encapsulated state:

```
let generateTicket =
    let count = ref 0
    (fun () -> incr count; !count)
```

If you examine this definition, you'll see that the `generateTicket` function is not defined immediately as a function but instead first declares a local element of state called `count` and then returns a function value that refers to this state. Each time the function value is called, `count` is incremented and dereferenced, but the reference cell itself is never published outside the function implementation and is thus encapsulated.

Encapsulation through local definitions is a particularly powerful technique in F# when used in conjunction with object expressions. For example, Listing 7-1 shows the definition of an object interface type called `IPeekPoke` and a function that implements objects of this type using an object expression.

Listing 7-1. *Implementing Objects with Encapsulated State*

```
type IPeekPoke =
    abstract member Peek: unit -> int
    abstract member Poke: int -> unit

let Counter(initialState) =
    let state = ref initialState
    { new IPeekPoke with
        member x.Poke(n) = state := !state + n
        member x.Peek() = !state  }
```

The type of the function Counter is as follows:

```
val Counter : int -> IPeekPoke
```

As with the earlier generateTicket function, the internal state for each object generated by the Counter function is hidden and accessible only via the published Peek and Poke methods.

The previous examples show how to combine let bindings with anonymous functions and object expressions. You saw in Chapter 6 how let bindings can also be used in constructed class types. For example, Listing 7-2 shows a constructed class type with private mutable state count and that publishes two methods: Next and Reset.

Listing 7-2. *A Type for Objects with Encapsulated State*

```
type TicketGenerator() =
    // Note: let bindings in a type definition are implicitly private to the object
    // being constructed. Members are implicitly public.
    let mutable count = 0

    member x.Next() =
        count <- count + 1;
        count

    member x.Reset () =
        count <- 0
```

The variable count is implicitly private to the object being constructed and is hence hidden from outside consumers. By default, other F# definitions are public, which means they are accessible throughout their scope.

Frequently, more than one item of state is hidden behind an encapsulation boundary. For example, the following code shows a function Averager that uses an object expression and two local elements of state, count and total, to implement an instance of the object interface type IStatistic:

```
type IStatistic<'a,'b> =
    abstract Record : 'a -> unit
    abstract Value : 'b

let Averager(toFloat: 'a -> float) =
    let count = ref 0
    let total = ref 0.0
    { new IStatistic<'a,float> with
            member stat.Record(x) = incr count; total := !total + toFloat x
            member stat.Value = (!total / float !count) }
```

The inferred types here are as follows:

```
type IStatistic<'a,'b> =
    abstract Record : 'a -> unit
    abstract Value: 'b
val Averager : ('a -> float) -> IStatistic<'a,float>
```

The internal state is held in values count and total and is, once again, encapsulated.

Note Most of the examples of encapsulation in this chapter show ways to hide *mutable state* behind encapsulation boundaries. However, encapsulation can be just as important for immutable constructs, especially in larger software components. For example, the implementation of the immutable System.DateTime type in the .NET Base Class Library hides the way the date and time are stored internally but reveals the information via properties. This allows the .NET designers to adjust the implementation of this type between releases of the .NET Framework if necessary.

Hiding Things with Accessibility Annotations

Local definitions are good for hiding most implementation details. However, sometimes you may need definitions that are local to a module, an assembly, or a group of assemblies. You can change the default accessibility of an item by using an *accessibility annotation* to restrict the code locations that can use a construct. These indicate what is private or partially private to a module, file, or assembly. The primary accessibility annotations are private, internal, and public:

- private makes a construct private to the enclosing type definition/module.

- internal makes a construct private to the enclosing assembly (DLL or EXE).

- public makes a construct available globally, which is the default for most constructs.

Accessibility annotations are placed immediately prior to the name of the construct. Listing 7-3 shows how to protect an internal table of data in a module using accessibility annotations.

Listing 7-3. *Protecting a Table Using Accessibility Annotations*

```
open System

module public VisitorCredentials =

    /// The internal table of permitted visitors and the
    /// days they are allowed to visit.
    let private  visitorTable =
        dict [ ("Anna",    set [DayOfWeek.Tuesday; DayOfWeek.Wednesday]);
               ("Carolyn", set [DayOfWeek.Friday]) ]

    /// This is the function to check if a person is a permitted visitor.
    /// Note: this is public and can be used by external code
    let public Check(person) =
        visitorTable.ContainsKey(person) &&
        visitorTable.[person].Contains(DateTime.Today.DayOfWeek)

    /// This is the function to return all known permitted visitors.
    /// Note: this is internal and can only be used by code in this assembly.
    let internal AllKnownVisitors() =
        visitorTable.Keys
```

The private table is visitorTable. Attempting to access this value from another module will give a type-checking error:

```
> VistorCredentials.visitorTable;;
                    ^^^^^^^^^^^^
Error: the value 'visitorTable' is not accessible from this code location.
```

The function Check is marked public and is thus available globally. The function AllKnownVisitors is available only within the same assembly (or the same F# Interactive session) as the definition of the VisitorCredentials module. Note that you could drop the public annotations from Check and VisitorCredentials since these declarations are public by default.

Accessibility annotations are often used to hide state or handles to resources such as files. In Listing 7-4 we protect a single reference cell containing a value that alternates between Tick and Tock. This example uses an internal *event*, a technique covered in more detail in Chapter 8.

Listing 7-4. *Protecting Internal State Using Accessibility Annotations*

```
module public GlobalClock =
    type TickTock = Tick | Tock
    type time = float
    let private clock = ref Tick
```

```
    let (private fireTickEvent,public TickEvent) = IEvent.create<TickTock>()
    let internal oneTick() =
        (clock := match !clock with Tick -> Tock | Tock -> Tick);
        fireTickEvent (!clock)

module internal TickTockDriver =
    open System.Threading
    let timer = new Timer(callback=(fun _ -> GlobalClock.oneTick()),
                          state=null,dueTime=0,period=100)
```

In Listing 7-4, the private state is clock. The assembly-internal module TickTockDriver uses the System.Threading.Timer class to drive the alternation of the state via the internal function oneTick. The GlobalClock module publishes one IEvent value, TickEvent, which any client can use to add handlers to listen for the event. Note that you can give different accessibility annotations for different identifiers bound in the same pattern. The following line from the sample uses the IEvent.create function to return a pair, and the elements of this pair are given different accessibilities. We cover the use of IEvent.create to create events in more detail in Chapter 8.

```
    let (private fireTickEvent,public TickEvent) = IEvent.create<TickTock>()
```

Another assembly can now contain the following code that adds a handler to TickEvent:

```
module TickTockListener =
    do GlobalClock.TickEvent.Add(function
        | GlobalClock.Tick -> printf "tick!"
        | GlobalClock.Tock -> System.Windows.Forms.MessageBox.Show "tock!" |> ignore)
```

You can add accessibility annotations at quite a number of places in F# code:

- In let, module, type, and extern definitions in modules, and in individual identifiers in patterns

- In new(...) object constructor definitions and member definitions associated with types

---

■**Note** You cannot add accessibility annotations to type abbreviations. That is, if you define a type abbreviation such as type label = int and label is a public type, then all users of the type label "know" that it is really just an abbreviation for int and not a distinct type definition of its own. This is because .NET provides no way to hide type abbreviations, and indeed the F# compiler expands type abbreviations in the underlying generated .NET IL code.

Listing 7-5 shows a type where some methods and properties are labeled public but the methods that mutate the underlying collection (Add and the set method associated with the Item property) are labeled internal.

Listing 7-5. *Making Property Setters Internal to a Type Definition*

```
open System.Collections.Generic

type public SparseVector() =

    let elems = new SortedDictionary<int,float>()

    member internal v.Add(k,v) = elems.Add(k,v)

    member public v.Count = elems.Keys.Count
    member v.Item
        with public get i =
            if elems.ContainsKey(i) then elems.[i]
            else 0.0
        and internal set i v =
            elems.[i] <- v
```

■**Note** By default `let` bindings in types are private to the object being constructed, and all `member` bindings are public, that is, have the same accessibility as the type definition. This is a useful default because it corresponds to the common situation where internal implementation details are fully private and published constructs are available widely and because omitting accessibility annotations makes code more readable in the common case. However, when you start to add more specific accessibility annotations, such as by making individual members internal or private, then it is useful to explicitly mark *all* members with accessibility annotations. This will make your code more readable because readers will not have to remember that unmarked members are public. You can leave the remaining `let` bindings unmarked and implicitly private. In short, we recommend that if you mark any members of a type with accessibility annotations, then mark them all.

Using Namespaces and Modules

An important organizational technique is to give sensible qualified names to your types and values. A qualified name is, for example, `Microsoft.FSharp.Collections.List` (for the F# list type) or `System.IO.StreamReader` (for one of the types in the .NET Framework BCL). Qualified names are particularly important when writing frameworks to be used by other people and are also a useful way of organizing your own code.

You give your types and functions qualified names by placing them in namespaces, modules, and type definitions. Table 7-1 shows these three kinds of containers and what they can contain. For completeness, we've included type abbreviations, which are slightly different because you can't use them as a container for other constructs.

Table 7-1. *Namespaces, Modules, Types, and What They Can Contain*

Entity	Description	Examples
Namespace	A namespace can contain further namespaces, modules, and types. Multiple DLLs can contribute to the same namespace.	`System`, `Microsoft.FSharp`
Module	A module can contain nested modules, types, and values.	`Microsoft.FSharp.Collections.Map`, `Microsoft.FSharp.Collections.List`
Concrete type definition	A type definition can contain members and nested type definitions.	`System.String`, `System.Int32`
Type abbreviation	A type abbreviation such as `string` (for `System.String`). These cannot act as a container for additional members, values, or types.	`int`, `string`

Putting Your Code in a Namespace

You saw in Chapter 6 how to define type definitions with members and modules with values, and we'll now look at how to place these in namespaces. Listing 7-6 shows a file that contains two type definitions, both located in the namespace `Acme.Widgets`.

Listing 7-6. *A File Containing Two Type Definitions in a Namespace*

```
#light

namespace Acme.Widgets

    type Wheel    = Square | Round | Triangle

    type Widget   = { id: int; wheels: Wheel list; size: string }
```

Namespaces are *open*, by which we mean that multiple source files and assemblies can contribute to the same namespace. For example, another implementation file or assembly could contain the definitions shown in Listing 7-7.

Listing 7-7. *A File Containing Two Type Definitions in Two Namespaces*

```
#light

namespace Acme.Widgets

    type Lever    = PlasticLever | WoodenLever

namespace Acme.Suppliers

    type LeverSupplier    = { name: string; leverKind: Acme.Widgets.Lever }
```

The file in Listing 7-7 contributes to two namespaces: `Acme.Widgets` and `Acme.Suppliers`. The two files could occur in the same DLL or different DLLs. Either way, when you reference the DLL(s), the namespace `Acme.Widgets` will appear to have at least three type definitions (perhaps more if other DLLs contribute further type definitions), and the namespace `Acme.Suppliers` will have at least one.

Using Files As Modules

We introduced the notion of a module in Chapter 6. In F#, a module is just a simple container for values and type definitions. Modules are also often used to provide outer structure for fragments of F# code, and many of the simple F# programs you've seen so far in this book have actually been in modules without your knowing. In particular:

- Code fragments typed into F# Interactive and delimited by ;; are each implicitly placed in a module of their own.

- Files compiled with the command-line compiler using Visual Studio or loaded into F# Interactive with `#load` have their values and types placed in a namespace or module according to the leading `module` or `namespace` declaration in the file. Declarations in files without a leading `module` or `namespace` declaration are placed in a module whose name is derived from the name of the implementation file.

Let's look at the second case in more detail. You can explicitly declare the name of the namespace/module for a file by using a leading module declaration. For example, Listing 7-8 defines the module `Acme.Widgets.WidgetWheels`, regardless of the name of the file containing the constructs.

Listing 7-8. *An Implementation Module with an Explicit Initial module Declaration*

```
#light
module Acme.Widgets.WidgetWheels

    let wheelCornerCount = Map.of_list [(Wheel.Square,   4);
                                        (Wheel.Triangle, 3);
                                        (Wheel.Round,    0);  ]
```

Here the first line gives the name for the module defined by the file. The namespace is `Acme.Widgets`, the module name is `WidgetWheels`, and the full path to the value is `Acme.Widgets.WidgetWheels.wheelCornerCount`.

If you don't give a `module` or `namespace` declaration, then the module name is determined by capitalizing the name of the file. Listing 7-9 shows an example of the implementation file `transporters.fs` without a leading `module` or `namespace` declaration.

Listing 7-9. *An Implementation File with No Explicit Initial module Declaration*

```
#light

type WheelCount = NoWheels | TwoWheels
let ship = "Ship", NoWheels
let bike = "Bike", TwoWheels
let transporters = [ ship; bike ]
```

The types and values are implicitly placed in a module called Transporters, derived from the file name itself.

Using Signature Types and Files

Every piece of F# code you write has a *signature type*. The inferred signature type for a piece of code is shown for every code fragment you enter into F# Interactive and can also be reported by using the F# command-line compiler, fsc.exe, with the -i option. For example, consider the following code, placed in an implementation file ticktock.fs:

```
module Acme.TickTock

    type TickTock = Tick | Tock

    let ticker x =
        match x with
        | Tick -> Tock
        | Tock -> Tick
```

You can now invoke the command-line compiler from a command-line shell:

```
C:\Users\dsyme\Desktop> fsc -i ticktock.fs

namespace Acme

module TickTock =
    type TickTock = Tick | Tock
    val ticker : TickTock -> TickTock
```

The inferred signature shows the results of type inference and takes into account other information such as accessibility annotations.

Using Explicit Signature Types and Signature Files

If you want, you can make the inferred types explicit by using an *explicit signature type* for each implementation file. The syntax used for explicit signature types is identical to the inferred types reported by F# Interactive or fsc.exe like those shown previously. If you use explicit signatures, they are placed in a *signature file*, and they list the names and types of all values and members that are accessible in some way to the outside world. Signature files should use the same root name as the matching implementation file with the extension .fsi. For example, Listing 7-10 shows the implementation file vector.fs and the explicit signature file vector.fsi.

Listing 7-10. *A Signature File* vector.fsi *with Implementation File* vector.fs

Signature File vector.fsi:

```
#light

namespace Acme.Collections
    type SparseVector with
        new: unit -> SparseVector
        member Add: int * float -> unit
        member Item : int -> float with get
```

Implementation File vector.fs:

```
#light

namespace Acme.Collections
    open System.Collections.Generic
    type SparseVector() =
        let elems = new SortedDictionary<int,float>()
        member v.Add(k,v) = elems.Add(k,v)
        member v.Item
            with get i =
                if elems.ContainsKey(i) then elems.[i]
                else 0.0
            and  set i v =
                elems.[i] <- v
```

You can now invoke the command-line compiler from a command-line shell:

```
C:\Users\dsyme\Desktop> fsc vector.fsi vector.fs
```

Although signature files are optional, many programmers like using them, especially when writing a library framework, because the signature file gives a place to document and maintain the "public" interface to a component. There is, however, a cost to this: signatures duplicate names and some other information found in the implementation.

■**Note** You can use signature types to hide constructs, which can be used as an alternative to giving accessibility annotations on types, values, and members. Neither accessibility annotation nor signatures can hide type abbreviations, for the reasons discussed in the earlier "Hiding Things with Accessibility Annotations" section. Some additional restrictions also apply to both hiding techniques. For example, if a type is revealed to be a constructed class type or interface type, then all its abstract members must be included in the signature. Similarly, a record type must reveal all its fields, and a discriminated union type must reveal all its cases. Also, in some languages such as OCaml, a signature may "restrict" the type of an implementation construct. For example, if a function is inferred to have a generic type 'a -> 'a, then in OCaml the signature may specify a more restricted type such as int -> int. This is not permitted in F#.

When Are Signature Types Checked?

Signature types are checked *after* an implementation has been fully processed. This is unlike type annotations that occur directly in an implementation file, which are applied *before* an implementation fragment is processed. This means the type information in a signature file is not used as part of the type inference process when processing the implementation.

■**Note** Each signature file must appear before its corresponding implementation file in the compilation order for an F# project. In Visual Studio this means the signature file must come before the implementation file in the project listing. This is because the signature is required in order to check the contents of the implementation file after the implementation file is fully processed.

Creating Assemblies, DLLs, and EXEs

In this book we have been using F# Interactive for most of the samples. F# Interactive is excellent when exploring a set of libraries and writing scripts or small applications that use them. However, to understand how to write libraries and organize other kinds of applications, you need to learn how to use the F# command-line compiler, fsc.exe, to compile your code into DLLs and EXEs. A Dynamic Link Library (DLL) is the Windows name for library components, and .exe is the extension used for executable programs.

As you saw at the start of this chapter, all .NET code exists in an *assembly*, which is, roughly speaking, either a DLL or an EXE. Assemblies can also contain some supporting code and data files. Every time you compile a set of files using fsc.exe, you create one assembly: either a DLL or an EXE. Even when you use F# Interactive (fsi.exe), you are dynamically adding code to a dynamically generated DLL. We'll now learn how to use the command-line compiler to create DLLs and EXEs.

Compiling EXEs

To compile code to an EXE, you simply call fsc.exe with the names of your source code files in dependency order. For example, if the file dolphin.fs contains the following code, then you can compile the code using fsc dolphin.fs. You can also use the -o flag to name the generated EXE.

File dolphins.fs

```
#light

let longBeaked = "Delphinus capensis"
let shortBeaked = "Delphinus delphis"
let dolphins = [ longBeaked; shortBeaked ]
printfn "Known Dolphins: %A" dolphins
```

You can now compile this code to an EXE as shown here:

```
C:\fsharp> fsc dolphins.fs
C:\fsharp> dir dolphins.exe
...
05/04/2007  19:21                3,124 dolphins.exe
```

```
C:\fsharp>dolphins.exe
Known Dolphins: ["Delphinus capensis"; "Delphinus delphis"]
```

Compiling DLLs

A DLL is a library containing compiled .NET or F# code (it can also contain "native" code with instructions and data dependent on particular machine architectures such as Intel x86 and AMD x64). To compile F# code into a DLL, you simply take one or more source files and invoke fsc.exe with the -a option. For example, let's assume the file whales.fs contains the code shown in Listing 7-11. (This sample also includes some documentation comments, which we will refer to in the "Generating Documentation" section later in this chapter.)

Listing 7-11. *File* whales.fs

```
module Whales.Fictional

/// The three kinds of whales we cover in this release
type WhaleKind =
    | Blue
    | Killer
    | GreatWhale

/// The main whale
let moby = "Moby Dick, Pacific", GreatWhale

/// The backup whale
let bluey = "Blue, Southern Ocean", Blue

/// This whale is for experimental use only
let orca = "Orca, Pacific", Killer

/// The collected whales
let whales = [| moby; bluey; orca |]
```

You can now compile the code as follows:

```
C:\test> fsc -O3 -g -a whales.fs
C:\test> dir whales.dll
...
05/04/2007  19:18                6,656 whales.dll
```

Here we have also added two other command-line flags: -g to generate debug output and -O3 to turn on maximum optimizations.

When compiling other assemblies, you will need to reference your DLLs. For example, consider the following code that needs to reference whales.dll:

File whaleWatcher.fs

```
open Whales

open System
let idx = Int32.Parse(Environment.GetCommandLineArgs().[1])
let spotted = Fictional.whales.[Int32.of_string idx]

printfn "You spotted %A!" spotted
```

You can compile this file by adding an -r flag to reference the DLLs upon which the code depends. You can also use the -o flag to name the generated EXE or DLL and the -I flag to list search paths.

```
C:\fsharp>fsc -g -O3 -r whales.dll -o watcher.exe whaleWatcher.fs
C:\fsharp>dir watcher.exe
...
05/04/2007  19:25                3,584 watcher.exe

C:\fsharp>watcher.exe 1
You spotted ("Blue, Southern Ocean", Blue)!
```

■**Note** .NET assemblies often contain quite a large amount of code. For example, a single assembly might contain as many as 50 or 100 F# source code files. Having many small assemblies may seem tempting, such as to improve compilation times during development, but can lead to difficulties when managing updates and can be confusing to end users. Large assemblies are easier to version: you have to update only one component, and you can package multiple updates into a single new version of the DLL.

Mixing Scripting and Compiled Code

Small programs are often used as both interactive scripts and as small compiled applications. Here are some useful facts to know about scripting with F# and F# Interactive:

- Small F# scripts use the extension .fsx.

- You can use the scripting directive #load from F# Interactive to load and compile one or more source code files as if they had been compiled using the command-line compiler.

- You can load one script from another script by the F# Interactive directive #use. This is very much like #load except that the file being loaded may contain further scripting directives.

- You can reference DLLs from within scripts by using the #r and #I directives, which act like the -r and -I directives of the F# command-line compiler.

- You can access command-line arguments from within scripts by using the expression fsi.CommandLineArgs. Within compiled code you should use System.Environment. GetCommandLineArgs, and within code used in both modes, you should use conditional compilation to switch between these, as shown in the next coding example.

- You can run a script on start-up by using the --exec command-line option for fsi.exe. You can find other command-line options by using fsi.exe --help.

Conditional compilation is a particularly useful feature for scripts, in particular the predefined conditional compilation symbols COMPILED and INTERACTIVE. The former is set whenever compiling code using the command-line compiler, fsc.exe, and the latter is set whenever loading code interactively using F# Interactive. A common use for these flags is to start the GUI event loop for a Windows Forms or other graphical application, such as using System.Windows.Forms. Application.Run. F# Interactive starts an event loop automatically, so you require a call to this function in the compiled code only:

```
open System.Windows.Forms

let form = new Form(Width=400, Height=300,
                    Visible=true, Text="F# Forms Sample")
#if COMPILED
// Run the main code
do System.Windows.Forms.Application.Run(form)
#endif
```

■**Note** You can specify additional conditional compilation directives by using the --define command-line compiler option.

Choosing Optimization Settings

The F# compiler comes with a simple choice of optimization levels. You will nearly always want to compile your final code using -O3, which applies maximum optimizations to your code.

The F# compiler is a cross-module, cross-assembly optimizing compiler, and it attaches optimization information to each assembly you create when using optimization level -O2 or higher. This information may contain some code fragments of your assembly, which may be inlined into later assemblies by the optimizing compiler. In some situations, you may not want this information included in your assembly. For example, you may expect to independently version assemblies, and in this case you may want to ensure that code is never duplicated from one assembly to another during compilation. In this case, you can use the --no-optimization-data switch to prevent optimization data being recorded with the assemblies you create. You can use this switch even when compiling at the highest optimization levels.

Generating Documentation

In Chapter 2 you saw that comments beginning with /// are XML "documentation" comments, which are used by interactive tools such as Visual Studio. They can also be collected to generate either HTML or XML documentation. HTML documentation is generated using the --generate-html command-line option; by default it creates files in a directory named after the assembly being created, unless the --html-output-directory command-line option is also used. For example:

```
C:\Users\dsyme\Desktop> mkdir whales

C:\Users\dsyme\Desktop> fsc -a --generate-html whales.fs

C:\Users\dsyme\Desktop> dir /s whales
 Volume in drive C has no label.
 Volume Serial Number is 2821-C479

 Directory of C:\Users\dsyme\Desktop\whales

29/07/2007  23:28    <DIR>          .
29/07/2007  23:28    <DIR>          ..
29/07/2007  23:28             2,417 Whales.Fictional.html
29/07/2007  23:28             1,015 Whales.Fictional.type_WhaleKind.html
29/07/2007  23:28               869 Whales.html
               3 File(s)          4,301 bytes
```

By default the generated documentation generates HTML with respect to a Cascading Style Sheets (CSS) file called msdn.css, which is included with the F# distribution.

You can also generate a simple XML documentation file using the -doc command-line option. You must name the output file. For example, using fsc -a -doc whales.xml whales.fs for the code in Listing 7-11 generates the file whales.xml containing the following:

```
<?xml version="1.0" encoding="utf-8"?>
<doc>
    <assembly><name>whales</name></assembly>
    <members>
      <member name="T:Whales.Fictional.WhaleKind">
        <summary> The three kinds of whales we cover in this release</summary>
      </member>
      <member name="P:Whales.Fictional.bluey">
      <summary> The backup whale</summary>
      </member>
      <member name="P:Whales.Fictional.moby">
       <summary>The main whale</summary>
      </member>
```

```
    <member name="P:Whales.Fictional.orca">
     <summary> This whale is for experimental use only</summary>
    </member>
    <member name="P:Whales.Fictional.whales">
     <summary> The collected whales</summary>
    </member>
    <member name="T:Whales.Fictional">
    </member>
   </members>
</doc>
```

Building Shared Libraries and the Using Global Assembly Cache

You will commonly need to share libraries between multiple applications. You can do this by using any of the following techniques:

- Including the same library source file in multiple projects and/or compilations.

- Duplicating the DLL for the library into each application directory.

- Creating a strong name shared library.

In this section, we cover the last option in more detail. A strong name shared library has the following characteristics:

- It is a DLL.

- You install it in the .NET global assembly cache (GAC) on the target machine.

- You give it a "strong name" by using --keyfile.

- You package all of its supporting data files using --link-resource.

- You (optionally) give it a version number using --version.

- You ensure that all of its dependencies are shared libraries.

The usual place to install shared libraries is the .NET GAC. The GAC is a collection of assemblies installed on the machine and available for use by any application that has sufficient privileges. Most libraries used in this book such as System.Windows.Forms.dll are installed in the GAC when you install the .NET Framework on a machine.

The remaining requirements are easy to satisfy and are just conditions that have to hold before you install something in the GAC. For example, assemblies must have strong names. All assemblies have names. For example, the assembly whales.dll (which we compiled in the earlier "Compiling DLLs" section using fsc -a whales.fs) has the name whales. An assembly with a strong name includes a hash using a cryptographic public/private key pair. This means only those people who have access to the private key can create a strong-named assembly that matches the public key. Users of the DLL can verify that the contents of the DLL were generated by someone holding the private key. A strong name looks something like this:

```
mscorlib, Version=2.0.0.0, Culture=neutral, PublicKeyToken=b77a5c561934e089
```

It is easy to create a strong-named assembly: simply generate a public/private key pair using the sn.exe tool that comes with the .NET Framework SDK, and give that as your keyfile argument. You can install libraries into the GAC using the .NET Framework SDK utility gacutil.exe. The following command-line session shows how to do this for the code shown in Listing 7-11:

```
C:\Users\dsyme\Desktop> sn.exe -k whales.snk
Microsoft (R) .NET Framework Strong Name Utility  Version 2.0.50727.42
Copyright (c) Microsoft Corporation. All rights reserved.

Key pair written to whales.snk

C:\Users\dsyme\Desktop> fsc -a --keyfile whales.snk --version 1.0.0.0 whales.fs

C:\Users\dsyme\Desktop> gacutil /i whales.dll
Microsoft (R) .NET Global Assembly Cache Utility. Version 2.0.50727.42
Copyright (c) Microsoft Corporation. All rights reserved.

Assembly successfully added to the cache
```

Installer generators such as WiX also include directives to install libraries into the GAC. We discuss installer generators later in this chapter.

■**Note** If you're planning to write libraries for use by the rest of the world, we recommend you take the time to read the .NET library design guidelines, document them using XML and HTML docs, and learn how to version your libraries. We'll take a deeper look at some guidelines for library design in Chapter 19.

Using Static Linking

Sometimes applications might use a DLL as a library, but when it comes to deploying the application on a website or as installed software, it might be easier to bundle that DLL as part of the application itself. You can do this in two ways: by placing the DLL alongside the EXE for the application or by statically linking the DLL when you create the EXE. You select the DLL by using the --static-link compiler option with the assembly name of the DLL.

You can also bundle the F# libraries into your application to give a zero-dependency application. You statically link all DLLs that depend on the F# libraries by using the --standalone compiler option.

Packaging Applications

In this section, we cover some of the more pragmatic issues in designing applications and choosing how to package both your code and data. First, however, we need to talk about some of the sorts of things you might be building with F#.

Packaging Different Kinds of Code

In Table 7-2 we've listed some of the different kinds of software that are implemented with F#. These tend to be organized in slightly different ways and tend to use encapsulation to varying degrees. For example, encapsulation is used heavily in frameworks, but not when writing 100-line scripts.

Table 7-2. *Some Different Kinds of Software Built Using F#*

Software Entity	Description
Script	A program or set of program fragments, usually in a single file and less than 1,000 lines and usually with an .fsx extension and run through F# Interactive. Sometimes also compiled. Organized using functions and occasional type definitions. Freely uses static global state. Usually has no signature file or accessibility annotations.
Application	An EXE or a web application DLL, perhaps with some supporting DLLs. Organized using namespaces, modules, functions, and some abstract types. Often uses some static global state. Some internal files and data structures may have signatures, but often these aren't needed.
Application extension (plug-in or add-on)	A component that extends an application, often compiled as a DLL containing types along with an accompanying XML file that "describes" the plug-in to the application. The host application loads the DLLs using .NET reflection. Generally has no static state because this lets the application instantiate multiple instances of the plug-in. An example is the DLL plug-ins for Paint.NET, a popular .NET image manipulation program.
Framework	A collection of related type definitions, functions, and algorithms organized according to established .NET and F# library design guidelines. Usually compiled as a DLL, strong-name signed, installed into the GAC on the target machine, and versioned as an independent entity. Generally has no static state except where it mediates essential state on the host computer or operating system.
Framework extension	A component that extends a framework, usually by defining types that implement particular interfaces. Organized in an appropriate namespace as a simple set of classes and functions that generate objects that implement the interfaces defined in a framework. Generally has no static state. For example, the Firebird.NET API provides implementations of the ADO.NET Data Access framework interfaces to enable access to Firebird databases.

Using Data and Configuration Settings

So far in this book the focus has been on code. In reality, almost every program also comes with additional data resources that form an intrinsic part of the application. Common examples of the latter include the resource strings, sounds, fonts, and images for GUI applications. Applications typically select between different data resources based on language or culture settings. Often programs also access additional parameters, such as environment variables derived from the execution context or registry settings recording user configuration options. It can be useful to understand the idioms used by .NET to make managing data and configuration settings a little more uniform. Table 7-3 shows some of the terminology used for data resources.

Table 7-3. *Application Data: Terminology*

Terminology	Meaning	Example
Static application data	A data resource whose name/location is always known, whose value doesn't change during execution, and that your application can generally assume always exists.	The PATH environment variable or a data file distributed with your application.
Strongly typed data	Data accessed as a named, typed .NET value through code written by you or generated by some tool you are using. The code hides away the complexity of locating and decoding the resource.	An icon data resource decoded to a System.Drawing.Icon value. The ResGen.exe tool can generate strongly typed APIs for common Windows resources such as bitmaps and icons.
GUI resource	A string, font, icon, bitmap, image, sound, or other binary resource that is attached to a Windows application or DLL using the Win32 .res format or .NET "managed" .resx format. Often dependent on language/culture settings.	A bitmap added as a resource to a Windows Forms application or an error message from a compiler.

You might need to access many different kinds of data resources and application settings. We've summarized the most common ones in Table 7-4.

Table 7-4. *Some Commonly Used Data and Configuration Settings*

Data Resource	Notes
Source directory	The source directory containing the source file(s) at time of compilation. Often used to access further resources in F# Interactive scripts or for error reporting in compiled applications. Accessed using the __SOURCE_DIRECTORY__ predefined identifier.
Command arguments	Arguments passed to the invocation of the program. Accessed using System.Environment.GetCommandLineArgs and fsi.CommandLineArgs when running in F# Interactive.

Table 7-4. *Some Commonly Used Data and Configuration Settings*

Data Resource	Notes
Installation location	Where a program EXE or DLL is installed. Accessed by using `System.Windows.Forms.Application.StartupPath` or by reading the `Assembly.Location` of any of the types defined in your assembly. For F# Interactive scripts, the installation location is usually the same as the source directory.
User directories	Paths to common logical directories such Program Files, My Documents, and Application Data. Accessed using `System.Environment.GetFolderPath`.
Environment variables	User- or machine-wide settings such as `PATH` and `COMPUTERNAME`. Accessed using `System.Environment.GetEnvironmentVariable`.
Registry settings	User- or machine-wide settings used to hold the vast majority of settings on a Windows machine. Accessed using `Microsoft.Win32.Registry.GetValue` and related types and methods.
Configuration settings	Database connection strings and other configuration settings, often used for web applications. If an application is called `MyApp.exe`, then this is usually stored in a file such as `MyApp.exe.config` alongside the executable, and for web applications a `Web.Config` file is used. Accessed using `System.Configuration.ConfigurationManager`.
Isolated storage	A special storage area accessible only to an installed application and that looks just like disk storage. You can find out more about isolated storage at `http://www.expert-fsharp.com/Topics/IsolatedStorage`.
Fonts, colors, icons, and so on	Specifications of Windows-related resources. Often taken from predefined system fonts and colors using the functions in `System.Drawing`, for example, `Color.MidnightBlue` or new `Font(FontFamily.GenericMonospace, 8.0f)`. Can be added as a binary resource to an assembly and accessed using `System.Resources.ResourceManager`.

You can author GUI data resources such as fonts, images, strings, and colors by creating a `.resx` file using tools such as Visual Studio. These are then compiled to binary resources by using the `resgen.exe` tool that is part of the .NET Framework SDK. Most development environments have tools for designing and creating these resources. Often the .NET Framework will contain one particular canonical type such as `System.Drawing.Color` for any particular kind of resource, and you should avoid writing needless duplicate types to represent them.

Sometimes it's a good idea to make sure a data resource is "officially" part of an assembly. For example, this is required if the assembly will be installed into the GAC. The best way to embed resources in applications (or to associate them with a DLL) is by using the `--resource` or `--link-resource` compiler option. For standard Win32 or .NET resources, you may also just give the `.res` or `.resx` file directly on the command line when invoking the F# compiler.

For example, at the time of writing, the F# distribution included a sample called Samples101. This sample contains the following:

- The source files `samples.fs`, `beginners.fs`, `sampleform.fs`, and `program.fs`.

- The .NET resource file `SampleForm.resx`, created and edited using the Visual Studio tools for designing icons. This file contains 57KB of XML data specifying, among other things, a default icon for the top-left corner image on the Windows operating system and six images used by the application. These are held in an image stream under the XML key `imageList.ImageStream`.

The application is compiled using the following command line:

```
fsc.exe SampleForm.resx sample.fs beginners.fs sampleform.fs program.fs
```

In the application, the resources are accessed from the type `SampleForm` contained in the file `sampleform.fs`. The following code fragments occur in that file. The first creates a `ComponentResourceManager` that is ready to read resources from an assembly. The argument `typeof<SampleForm>` ensures the resource manager reads resources from the assembly that contains the type `SampleForm` (that is, the type being defined). We discuss the `typeof` function in more detail in Chapter 9.

```
open System.ComponentModel
let resources = new ComponentResourceManager(typeof<SampleForm>)
```

The following lines retrieve images from the resource stream:

```
open System.Windows.Forms
let imageList = new System.Windows.Forms.ImageList()
imageList.ImageStream <- (resources.GetObject("imageList.ImageStream")
                            :?> System.Windows.Forms.ImageListStreamer)
imageList.Images.SetKeyName(0, "Help")
imageList.Images.SetKeyName(1, "BookStack")
imageList.Images.SetKeyName(2, "BookClosed")
imageList.Images.SetKeyName(3, "BookOpen")
imageList.Images.SetKeyName(4, "Item")
imageList.Images.SetKeyName(5, "Run")
```

The images from the resource file are associated with graphical components using the `ImageKey` property of various Windows Forms controls. For example, the `Run` button of the application is associated with the `Run` image stored in the resource file using the following lines:

```
let runButton = new Button(ImageAlign = ContentAlignment.MiddleRight,
                            ImageKey = "Run",
                            ImageList = imageList)
```

■Note .NET uses application configuration files (for static application settings) and isolated storage for settings private to an installed application for a particular user, including for applications downloaded from the Web. You can access isolated storage using the `System.IO.IsolatedStorage` namespace and can access the Windows registry using the `Microsoft.Win32.Registry` namespace.

Building Installers

Up until now in this chapter, we have focused on how to encapsulate and package your code as you develop it. However, how do you get your application or libraries to other computers? This section discusses *deployment*, the process by which you make code available and transfer it from your computer to another.

The prerequisite for deployment is that your code is ready to be released. For a web application this means that page debugging is turned off and your database connection strings are updated to point to production databases instead of those used during development. In an unstructured or small-team development project, it is often simplest to package applications as scripts or DLLs and transfer them directly to a target machine. In a structured software development process, a release is preceded by rigorous testing (unit, smoke, functional, performance, and load testing), the creation of various documentation artifacts (release notes, installation guides, and so on), and the finalization and packaging of the transferable resources (help files, images, fonts, and so on). In this and the following section, we briefly discuss two typical scenarios: creating an installer for an application and deploying web applications.

Visual Studio comes with useful tools for building installers and deploying web applications. Whether you have a web application, a library project, a UI application, or any other type of Visual Studio project, you can use the setup project to create an installer application that will install it on another computer. An installer is a special program that can modify the registry on the client machine, execute various scripts and tasks, verify certain conditions, and walk the user through a series of setup steps as the installation proceeds.

You can quickly create the skeleton of your setup project by creating a new project in your solution of the Setup Wizard project type. This walks you through a few simple wizard steps, and you can use it for most typical, simple setup needs. On the other hand, for the fullest control, you should add a setup project to your solution. At core, a setup project is about telling what files are to be included in the installation, and this can be done using the File System Editor. Figure 7-1 shows the various editors you can invoke from Solution Explorer when you select the setup project.

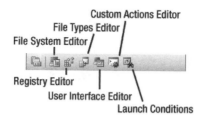

Figure 7-1. *The setup Solution Explorer tools*

The File System Editor shows you the conceptual file system of the client computer. Here you can drop files into the typical installation folders such as the Application folder, the user's Desktop, or the user's Programs menu. You can also add new folders by right-clicking the label for the target computer's file system. You can choose numerous special folders, including the Common Files folder, the Fonts folder, or the user's Favorites or Special Data folder. You can add new folders, files, or assemblies to each, or you can add the output of any of your projects in the current solution.

The Registry Editor lets you add keys and their associated values to any container folder in the client machine's registry. You can use the File Types Editor to register new file types and the User Interface Editor to design the steps of the installer. You can use the Custom Actions Editor to add various tasks that are to be run during the installation process, and the Launch Conditions Editor allows you to define various criteria that must hold for the setup to continue at each step (for instance, the existence of certain files).

When you have configured all aspects of the setup project, you can build it as usual to obtain the installer binary file. This can be copied to the client computer and run to set up the project as defined previously.

Note An alternative solution for creating setup programs is to use WiX, the Windows Installer XML. You can find more information about WiX at `http://wix.sourceforge.net/`. See `http://www.expert-fsharp.com/Topics/InstallationAndPackaging` for more information about packaging and deploying your code.

Deploying Web Applications

Server-side web hosting is an increasingly important way of deploying applications. We discuss how to develop these applications in Chapter 14, and in this section we briefly discuss techniques to deploy ASP.NET web server applications. Here are your typical choices for deploying these applications:

- Copying your source files to the web server using FTP, XCOPY, or any other similar file transfer tool or protocol. Alternatively, you can use the Website/Copy Web Site option in Visual Studio.

- Compiling your web application into a set of DLLs and deploying them using Build/Publish Web Site in Visual Studio. Here you have the option of including source code in the deployment.

- Creating an installer that deploys your web application into the IIS installed on the target computer.

The first option requires you to be able to log on to the web server and place files either via FTP or as a web administrator. Probably the most versatile tool for manual copying of your website is the Copy Web Site dialog box in Visual Studio, which enables you to easily copy or synchronize files between your local copy and the remote web server. For the remote website, you can choose a directory on your local file system, a web folder under your local IIS, an FTP site and directory within, or a remote website configured with the FrontPage Server Extensions.

One problem with manual copying is that each updated page has to be compiled on the server as it is first requested. To remedy this problem, you can precompile your site using the second option. In the Publish Web Site dialog box you can control how your site is precompiled and where it is deployed. The target location can be of any type discussed previously for establishing a connection for manual copy.

For the third option, to create an installer for your web application, Visual Studio provides the Web Setup Project type under Other Project Types/Setup and Deployment in the New Project dialog box. This project type is a customized form of the setup project.

Another option you have besides the web setup project is to install the Web Deployment Project Visual Studio add-in. This add-in adds a new menu item, Build/Add Web Deployment Project, in Visual Studio that you can use to add a deployment project to your web application solution. In the Options dialog box of your deployment project, you can customize the compilation, output, signing, and deployment aspects of your web setup.

Summary

In this chapter, you learned about a number of issues related to encapsulating, organizing, and packaging code, from the raw language devices used for accessibility and encapsulation within code to building assemblies and the related topics of packaging applications, building DLLs, and including data resources as part of your libraries and applications. Finally, we gave some tips on how build installers and deploy web applications.

In the next chapter, we'll look at some of the foundational techniques you will need to master as you progress with learning to program in F#.

■ ■ ■

CHAPTER 8

Mastering F#: Common Techniques

F# is a powerful language with relatively simple constructs. Learning the constructs of the language is easy, but learning how to use the constructs well takes a little more time. In this chapter, we present some of the common F# coding techniques you will need as you work across multiple programming domains. These techniques are either applications of the constructs we've encountered so far or relate to the foundational libraries that ship with F# and .NET.

Equality, Hashing, and Comparison

In Chapter 5 you saw a number of predefined generic operations, including generic comparison, equality, and hashing, accessed via functions such as those shown here:

```
val compare : 'a -> 'a -> int
val (=)    : 'a -> 'a -> bool
val (<)    : 'a -> 'a -> bool
val (<=)   : 'a -> 'a -> bool
val (>)    : 'a -> 'a -> bool
val (>=)   : 'a -> 'a -> bool
val min : 'a -> 'a -> 'a
val max : 'a -> 'a -> 'a
val hash  : 'a -> int
```

In this section, we cover how to customize the behavior of these functions for new type definitions. It's important to note that generic comparison is not implemented using reflection; instead, code is autogenerated for each record and discriminated union type definition. This code implements comparison efficiently and often uses "fast path" comparison techniques. For example, the generated code will use primitive IL/native instructions for integer comparisons. This means in practice generic comparison is fast when used with appropriately sized keys.

You can modify the default implementation of generic comparison for new type definitions by implementing the interface System.IComparable and overriding the method Equals from the .NET type System.Object. Listing 8-1 shows an example, taken from the F# library implementation of the Microsoft.FSharp.Math.BigInt type, which is implemented in terms of an internal library type called BigNat along with a sign field that is 1 or -1. When implementing the BigInt type, it turns out to be convenient to have two different representations of the number zero, one with sign 1 and one with sign -1. Of course, these should be equal as far as generic equality and comparison are concerned. Listing 8-1 shows how to customize generic comparison for the BigInt type so that it respects this desired behavior. The type definition of BigInt includes overrides of Object.Equals and an implementation of the interface System. IComparable.

Listing 8-1. *Customizing Generic Comparison for a New Type Definition*

```
open Microsoft.FSharp.Math.Primitives

type BigInt =
    { sign : int; v : BigNat }
    override x.Equals(yobj:obj) =
        let y = unbox<BigInt>(yobj)
        (x.sign = y.sign) && (x.v = y.v) || BigNat.isZero(x.v) && BigNat.isZero(y.v)

    interface System.IComparable with
        override x.CompareTo(yobj:obj) =
            let y = unbox<BigInt>(yobj)
            match x.sign,y.sign with
            |  1, 1 ->  compare x.v  y.v
            | -1,-1 ->  compare y.v x.v
            | _ when BigNat.isZero(x.v) && BigNat.isZero(y.v) -> 0
            |  1, -1 -> 1
            | -1, 1 -> -1
            | _ -> invalid_arg "BigInt signs should be +/- 1"
```

The System.IComparable interface is defined in the .NET libraries:

```
namespace System

    type IComparable =
        abstract CompareTo : obj -> int
```

An unbox is necessary when implementing both IComparable and Object.Equals; this operation is relatively cheap. Recursive calls to compare subterms should use the following function:

---

val compare : 'a -> 'a -> int

Listing 8-1 defined the implementations of the overrides and interfaces immediately at the point of the type definition. However, it is also common to define the implementations of these as an extension to the type later in the same file. This lets you define a complete set of operations for the type starting with appropriate primitives and building up the set of operations until all are correctly defined. Listing 8-2 shows how to do this for the case of BigInt.

Listing 8-2. *Customizing Generic Hashing and Comparison Using an Extension*

```fsharp
open Microsoft.FSharp.Math.Primitives

type BigInt =
    { sign : int; v : BigNat }
    interface System.IComparable

module BigIntOps =
    let equal x y =
        (x.sign = y.sign) && (x.v = y.v)
        || BigNat.isZero(x.v) && BigNat.isZero(y.v)

    let hashBigInt x = if BigNat.IsZero(x.v) then 0 else hash x.sign + hash x.v

    let compareBigInt x y =
            match x.sign,y.sign with
            |  1, 1 ->  compare x.v  y.v
            | -1,-1 ->  compare y.v x.v
            | _ when BigNat.IsZero(x.v) && BigNat.IsZero(y.v) -> 0
            |  1, -1 -> 1
            | -1, 1 -> -1
            | _ -> invalid_arg "BigInt signs should be +/- 1"

// OK, let's augment the type with generic hash/compare/print behavior
type BigInt with
    override x.GetHashCode() = BigIntOps.hashBigInt(x)
    override x.Equals(y:obj) = BigIntOps.equal x (unbox y)
    override x.ToString() =
        sprintf "%s%A"
            (if x.sign < 0 && not (BigNat.IsZero(x.v))  then "-" else "")
            x.v

    interface System.IComparable with
        member x.CompareTo(y:obj) = BigIntOps.compareBigInt x (unbox y)
```

Listing 8-2 also shows how to implement the System.Object method GetHashCode, the F# technique to implement *generic hashing*, and the method ToString for generic printing. These follow the same pattern as generic comparison. If needed, you can implement more advanced interfaces such as Microsoft.FSharp.Core.IStructuralHash and Microsoft.FSharp.Text. StructuredFormat.IFormattable to give more control over the processing of hashing and formatting large structured terms. (See http://www.expert-fsharp.com/Topics/GenericHashing.)

■**Note** You should be very careful about using generic comparison and hashing on recursive data structures (including ones using pointers) or data you mutate. Changing the value of a field may change the value of the hash or the results of comparison! Floating-point NaN values also have surprising behavior in comparison. When uses of the operators <, >, <=, >=, =, and <> are applied to two floating-point values, the IEEE rules for NaNs apply. In other words, if either argument is a NaN, then the result is false (true for <>).

Efficient Precomputation and Caching

All experienced programmers are familiar with the concept of *precomputation*, where intermediate computations are performed as soon as some of the inputs to a function are known. In the following sections, we cover a number of manifestations of precomputation in F# programming and the related topics of memoization and caching.

Precomputation and Partial Application

Let's say you are given a large input list of words and you want to compute a function that checks whether a word is in this list. You can do this as follows:

```
let isWord (words: string list) =
    let wordTable = Set.Create(words)
    fun w -> wordTable.Contains(w)
```

Here isWord has the following type:

```
val isWord : string list -> (string -> bool)
```

The efficient use of this function depends crucially on the fact that useful intermediary results are computed after only one argument is applied. For example:

```
> let isCapital = isWord ["London";"Paris";"Warsaw";"Tokyo"];;
val isCapital : (string -> bool)

> isCapital "Paris";;
val it : bool = true

> isCapital "Manchester";;
val it : bool = false
```

Here the internal table wordTable is computed as soon as isCapital is applied to one argument. It would be a mistake to write the isCapital as follows:

```
let isCapitalSlow inp = isWord ["London";"Paris";"Warsaw";"Tokyo"] inp
```

This function computes the same results as isCapital. However, it does so inefficiently, because isWord is applied to both its first argument and its second arguments *every time* you use the function isCapitalSlow. This means the internal table would be rebuilt every time the function isCapitalSlow is applied, somewhat defeating the point of having an internal table in the first place! In a similar vein, the definition of isCapital shown previously is more efficient than either isCapitalSlow2 or isCapitalSlow3 in the following:

```
let isWordSlow2 (words: string list) (w:string) =
    List.mem w words

let isCapitalSlow2 inp = isWordSlow2 ["London";"Paris";"Warsaw";"Tokyo"] inp

let isWordSlow3 (words: string list) (w:string) =
    let wordTable = Set.Create(words)
    wordTable.Contains(w)

let isCapitalSlow3 inp = isWordSlow3 ["London";"Paris";"Warsaw";"Tokyo"] inp
```

The first uses an inappropriate data structure for the lookup (an F# list, which has O(*n*) lookup time), and the second attempts to build a better intermediate data structure (an F# set, which has O(log *n*) lookup time) but does so on every invocation.

There are often trade-offs between different intermediate data structures, or indeed whether to use intermediate data structures at all. For example, in the previous example, we could just as well have used an F# HashSet as the internal data structure. This will in general give better lookup times (constant time), but it requires slightly more care to use since a HashSet is a mutable data structure. In this case, we don't mutate the data structure at all after we create it, and we don't reveal it to the outside world, so it is entirely safe:

```
let isWord (words: string list) =
    let wordTable = HashSet.Create(words)
    fun w -> wordTable.Contains(w)
```

Precomputation and Objects

The examples of precomputation given previously are variations on the theme of "computing functions," introduced in Chapter 3. The functions computed capture the precomputed intermediate data structures. However, it is also clear that precomputing via partial applications and functions can be subtle, because it really matters when you apply the first argument of a function (triggering the construction of intermediate data structures) and when you apply the subsequent arguments (triggering the "real" computation that uses the intermediate data structures).

Luckily, functions don't just have to compute functions; they can also return more sophisticated values such as objects. This can help make it clear when precomputation is being performed. It also allows you to build richer services based on precomputed results. For example, Listing 8-3 shows how to use precomputation as part of building a name lookup service. The returned object includes both a Contains method and a ClosestPrefixMatch method.

Listing 8-3. *Precomputing a Word Table Before Creating an Object*

```
open System

type NameLookupService =
    abstract Contains : string -> bool
    abstract ClosestPrefixMatch : string -> string  option
```

```
let buildSimpleNameLookup (words: string list) =
    let wordTable = Set.Create(words)
    let score (w1:string) (w2:string) =
        let lim = (min w1.Length w2.Length)
        let rec loop i acc =
            if i >= lim then acc
            else loop (i+1) (Char.code w1.[i] - Char.code w2.[i] + acc)
        loop 0 0

    { new NameLookupService with
        member t.Contains(w) = wordTable.Contains(w)
        member t.ClosestPrefixMatch(w) =
            if wordTable.Contains(w) then Some(w) else
            let above =
                match wordTable.GetNextElement(w) with
                | Some w2 when w2.StartsWith(w) -> Some w2
                | _ -> None
            let below =
                match wordTable.GetPreviousElement(w) with
                | Some w2 when w2.StartsWith(w) -> Some w2
                | _ -> None
            match above, below with
            | Some w1,Some w2 -> Some(if score w w1 > score w w2 then w2 else w1)
            | Some res,None
            | None,Some res -> Some res
            | None,None -> None }
```

The internal data structure used in Listing 8-3 is the same as before: an F# set of type `Microsoft.FSharp.Collections.Set<string>`. The `ClosestPrefixMatch` method is implemented via the `GetNextElement` and `GetPreviousElement` methods on this data structure, which find the element in the set that is just before/after the given key. These are efficient O(log *n*) operations because F# sets are ultimately implemented via sorted binary trees. The set members before and after the input word w are scored using a simple scoring function `score`. The service can now be instantiated and used as follows:

```
> let capitalLookup = buildSimpleNameLookup ["London";"Paris";"Warsaw";"Tokyo"];;
val capitalLookup : NameLookupService

> capitalLookup.Contains "Paris";;
val it : bool = true

> capitalLookup.ClosestPrefixMatch "Wars";;
val it : string option = Some "Warsaw"

> capitalLookup.ClosestPrefixMatch "We";;
val it : string option = None
```

In passing, we note the following about this implementation:

- The table is built based on the F# default "ordinal" comparison for strings. This is not always an appropriate choice when using natural-language text. You can specify the exact comparison function to use when building sets based on string values by creating a custom key type with a custom comparison function.

- The returned service could be extended to support a richer set of queries of the underlying information by adding further methods to the object returned.

Precomputation of the kind used previously is an essential technique for implementing many services and abstractions, from simple functions to sophisticated computation engines. You will see further examples of these techniques in Chapter 9.

Memoizing Computations

Precomputation is one important way to amortize the costs of computation in F#. Another is called *memoization*. A memoizing function is simply one that avoids recomputing its results by keeping an internal table, often called a *lookaside table*. For example, consider the well-known Fibonacci function, whose naive, unmemoized version is as follows:

```
let rec fib n = if n <= 2 then 1 else fib(n-1) + fib(n-2)
```

Not surprisingly, a version keeping a lookaside table is much faster:

```
let fibFast =
    let t = new System.Collections.Generic.Dictionary<int,int>()
    let rec fibCached n =
        if t.ContainsKey(n) then t.[n]
        else if n <= 2 then 1
        else let res = fibCached(n-1) + fibCached(n-2)
            t.Add(n,res)
            res
    fun n -> fibCached n
```

On one of our laptops, with n = 30, the first runs in 3.65 seconds, and the second runs in 0.015 seconds.

Listing 8-4 shows how to write a generic function that encapsulates the memoization technique.

Listing 8-4. *A Generic Memoization Function*

```
let memoize (f: 'a -> 'b) =
    let t = new System.Collections.Generic.Dictionary<'a,'b>()
    fun n ->
        if t.ContainsKey(n) then t.[n]
        else let res = f n
            t.Add(n,res)
            res
```

```
let rec fibFast =
    memoize (fun n -> if n <= 2 then 1 else fibFast(n-1) + fibFast(n-2))
```

Here the functions have the following types:

```
val memoize : ('a -> 'b) -> ('a -> 'b)
val fibFast : (int -> int)
```

In the definition of fibFast, we use let rec because fibFast is self-referential, that is, used as part of its own definition. You can think of fibFast as a *computed, recursive function*. As with the examples of computed functions from the previous section, it is important that you don't include the extra argument in the application of memoize, since it would lead to a fresh memoization table being allocated each time the function fibNotFast is called:

```
let rec fibNotFast n =
    memoize (fun n -> if n <= 2 then 1 else fibNotFast(n-1) + fibNotFast(n-2)) n
```

Because of this subtlety, it is often a good idea to also define your memoization strategies to generate objects other than functions (note that you can think of functions as very simple kinds of objects). For example, Listing 8-5 shows how to define a new variation on memoize that returns a Table object that supports both a lookup and a Discard method.

Listing 8-5. *A Generic Memoization Service*

```
type Table<'a,'b> =
    abstract Item : 'a -> 'b with get
    abstract Discard : unit -> unit

let memoizeAndPermitDiscard f =
    let lookasideTable = new System.Collections.Generic.Dictionary<_,_>()
    { new Table<_,_> with
          member t.Item
              with get(n) =
                  if lookasideTable.ContainsKey(n)
                  then lookasideTable.[n]
                  else let res = f n
                      lookasideTable.Add(n,res)
                      res
          member t.Discard() =
              lookasideTable.Clear() }


let rec fibFast =
    memoizeAndPermitDiscard
        (fun n ->
            printfn "computing fibFast %d" n
            if n <= 2 then 1 else fibFast.[n-1] + fibFast.[n-2])
```

In Listing 8-5, lookup uses the a.[b] associative Item lookup property syntax, and the Discard method discards any internal partial results. The functions have the following types:

```
val memoizeAndPermitDiscard : ('a -> 'b) -> Table<'a, 'b>
val fibFast : Table<int,int>
```

Here's an example showing how fibFast caches results but recomputes them after a Discard:

```
> fibFast.[3];;
computing fibFast 3
computing fibFast 2
computing fibFast 1
val it : int = 2

> fibFast.[5];;
computing fibFast 5
computing fibFast 4
val it : int = 5

> fibFast.Discard();;
val it : unit = ()

> fibFast.[5];;
computing fibFast 5
computing fibFast 4
computing fibFast 3
computing fibFast 2
computing fibFast 1
val it : int = 5
```

■**Note** Memoization relies on the memoized function being stable and idempotent. In other words, it always returns the same results, and no additional interesting side effects are caused by additional invocations of the function. In addition, memoization strategies rely on mutable internal tables. The implementation of memoize shown in this chapter is not thread safe, because it doesn't lock this table during reading or writing. This is fine if the computed function is used only from at most one thread at a time, but in a multithreaded application you should use memoization strategies that use internal tables protected by locks such as a .NET ReaderWriterLock. We discuss thread synchronization and mutable state further in Chapter 14.

Lazy Values

Memoization is a form of *caching*. Another important variation on caching is a simple *lazy* value. A lazy value is simply a delayed computation of type Microsoft.FSharp.Control.Lazy<'a> for some type 'a. Lazy values are usually formed by using the special keyword lazy (you can also make them explicitly using the functions in the Microsoft.FSharp.Core.Lazy module). For example:

```
> let sixty = lazy (30+30);;
val sixty : Lazy<int>

> sixty.Force();;
val it : int = 60
```

Lazy values of this kind are implemented as thunks holding either a function value that will compute the result or the actual computed result. The lazy value will be computed only once, and thus its effects are executed only once. For example, in the following code fragment, "Hello world" is printed only once:

```
> let sixtyWithSideEffect = lazy (printfn "Hello world"; 30+30);;
val sixtyWithSideEffect: Lazy<int>

> sixtyWithSideEffect.Force();;
Hello world
val it : int = 60

> sixtyWithSideEffect.Force();;
val it : int = 60
```

Lazy values are implemented by a simple data structure containing a mutable reference cell. You can find the definition of this data structure in the F# library source code.

Other Variations on Caching and Memoization

You can apply many different caching and memoization techniques in advanced programming, and we can't hope to cover them all here. Here are some common variations:

- Using an internal data structure that records only the last invocation of a function and basing the lookup on a very cheap test on the input.

- Using an internal data structure that contains both a fixed-size queue of input keys and a dictionary of results. Entries are added to both the table and the queue as they are computed. When the queue is full, the input keys for the oldest computed results are dequeued, and the computed results are discarded from the dictionary.

Cleaning Up Resources

All programming involves the use of real resources on the host machine(s) and operating system. For example:

Stack: Implicitly allocated and deallocated as functions are called

Heap allocated memory: Used by all reference-typed objects

File handles: Such as operating system file handles represented by `System.IO.FileStream` objects and its subtypes

Network connections: Such as operating system I/O completion ports represented by `System.Net.WebResponse` and its subtypes

Threads: Such as operating system threads represented by `System.Threading.Thread` objects and also worker threads in the .NET thread pool

Graphics objects: Such as drawing objects represented by various constructs under the `System.Drawing` namespace

Concurrency objects: Such as operating system synchronization objects represented by `System.Threading.WaitHandle` objects and its subtypes

All resources are necessarily finite. In .NET programming, some resources such as memory are fully *managed*, in the sense that you almost never need to consider when to "clean up" memory. This is done automatically through a process called *garbage collection*. We look at garbage collection in a little more detail in Chapter 17. Other resources must be *reclaimed* and/or *recycled*.

When prototyping, you can generally assume that resources are unbounded, though it is good practice when you are using a resource to be aware of how much of the resource you are using and roughly what your budget for the resource is. For example:

- On a modern 32-bit desktop machine, 10,000 tuple values will occupy only a small fragment of a machine's memory, roughly 160KB of memory. However, 10,000 open file handles is an extreme number and may begin to stress the operating system. 10,000 simultaneous web requests may result in your network administrator complaining!

- In some cases, even memory should be explicitly and carefully reclaimed. For example, on a modern 64-bit machine, the largest single array you can allocate in a .NET 2.0 program is 2GB in size. If your machine has, say, 4GB of real memory, you may be able to have only a handful of these objects and should strongly consider moving to a regime where you explicitly recycle these objects and think carefully before allocating them.

Cleaning Up with use

With the exception of stack and memory, all objects that own resources should be subtypes of the .NET type `System.IDisposable`. This is the primary way you can recognize primitive resources and objects that wrap resources. The `System.IDisposable` interface has a single method; in F# syntax, it could be defined as follows:

```
namespace System
    type IDisposable =
        abstract Dispose: unit -> unit
```

One of the simplest approaches to managing `IDisposable` objects is to give each resource a *lifetime*, that is, some well-defined portion of the program execution for which the object will be active. This is even easier when the lifetime of a resource is lexically scoped, such as when a resource is allocated on entry to a function and deallocated on exit. In this case, the resource can be tied to the scope of a particular variable, and you can protect and dispose of a value that implements IDisposable simply by using a use binding instead of a let binding. For example, in the following code, three values implement IDisposable, all of which are bound using use:

```
let http(url: string) =
    let req = System.Net.WebRequest.Create(url)
    use resp = req.GetResponse()
    use stream = resp.GetResponseStream()
    use reader = new System.IO.StreamReader(stream)
    let html = reader.ReadToEnd()
    html
```

In all three cases, the objects (a WebResponse, a Stream, and a StreamReader) are automatically closed and disposed at the end of an execution of the function. To see what's going on here, just notice that a use binding is simply syntactic sugar. For example, the following:

```
use var = expr in body
```

is shorthand for this:

```
let var = expr
try body
finally
    match var with
    | null -> ()
    | _ -> var.Dispose()
```

A number of important types implement IDisposable; Table 8-1 shows some of them. Indeed, you can use tables such as this to chart the portions of the .NET Framework that reveal operating system functionality to .NET applications.

Table 8-1. *A Selection of the Types That Implement* IDisposable

Namespace	Some Types Implementing IDisposable
System.IO	BinaryReader, BinaryWriter, FileSystemWatcher, IsolatedFileStorage, Stream, TextReader, TextWriter,
System.Drawing	Brush, BufferedGraphics, Font, FontFamily, Graphics, Icon, Image, Pen, Region, TextureBrush, ...
System.Drawing.Text	FontCollection, ...
System.Drawing.Drawing2D	CustomLineCap, GraphicsPath, GraphicsPathIterator, Matrix, ...
System.Drawing.Imaging	EncoderParameter, ImageAttributes, ...
System.Net	WebResponse, ...
System.Net.Sockets	Socket, TcpClient, ...

Table 8-1. *A Selection of the Types That Implement* IDisposable *(Continued)*

Namespace	Some Types Implementing IDisposable
System.Data.SqlClient	SqlBulkCopy, SqlCommand, SqlConnection, SqlTransaction, ...
System.Threading	Timer, WaitHandle, AutoResetEvent, ManualResetEvent, Mutex, Semaphore, ...
System.Web.UI	Control, HttpApplication, ...
System.Web.UI.WebControls	Button, CheckBox, DataGrid, ...
System.Windows.Forms	Button, CheckBox, Cursor, Control, DataGrid, Form, ...
Microsoft.Win32	RegistryKey, ...

■**Tip** A tool such as Visual Studio can help you determine when a type has implemented IDisposable since when you rest your mouse pointer over a value, you will normally see this noted on the information that is displayed for a value.

WHEN WILL THE RUNTIME CLEAN UP FOR ME?

People often ask if the .NET Common Language Runtime will automatically clean up resources such as file handles in the same way it cleans up memory. It is true that when an object gets garbage collected, it may be *finalized*, which, if the object is well-implemented, results in it deallocating any unmanaged resources, closing any outstanding file connections, and releasing any operating system resources. However, although it is appropriate to rely on finalization when prototyping, you should never rely on finalization in code where you are hitting resource limits.

For example, let's say you have a loop where you open files using System.IO.File.OpenRead. If you forget to close the file handles, you may quickly allocate thousands of file handles. If you are lucky, the garbage collector may finalize these before you run out of OS resources, but if not, one of your File.OpenRead calls will fail with an exception, even if the file actually exists on disk.

You should also be aware of the potential for memory leaks. Memory leaks occur when the .NET Common Language Runtime is unable to garbage collect memory even though objects have become "unreachable." This happens especially when long-running computations and inactive callbacks hold on to object handles related to the earlier phases of execution of a program. Memory leaks can also lead to objects never being finalized, reinforcing that you should not rely on finalization to release nonmemory resources. Memory profiling tools such as CLRProfiler are indispensable when tracking down memory leaks in production code or long-running applications.

Managing Resources with More Complex Lifetimes

Sometimes the lifetime of a resource is not simple in the sense that it doesn't follow a stack discipline. In these cases, you should almost always adopt one of two techniques:

- Design objects that can "own" one or more resources and that are responsible for cleaning them up. Make sure these objects implement System.IDisposable.

- Use control constructs that help you capture the kind of computation you're performing. For example, when generating sequences of data (such as from a database connection), you should strongly consider using sequence expressions, discussed in Chapter 3. These may have internal use bindings, and the resources will be disposed when each sequence iteration finishes. Likewise, when using asynchronous I/O, it may be helpful to write your computation as an asynchronous workflow. We give examples in the following sections and in Chapter 13.

You should consider implementing the IDisposable interface on objects and types in the following situations:

- When you build an object that uses one or more IDisposable objects internally.

- When you are writing a wrapper for an operating system resource or some resource allocated and managed in a native (C or C++) DLL. In this case, you should also implement a finalizer by overriding the Object.Finalize method.

- When you implement the System.Collections.Generic.IEnumerable<'a> (that is, sequence) interface on a collection. The IEnumerable interface is not itself IDisposable, but it must generate System.Collection.Generic.IEnumerator<'a> values, and this interface inherits from IDisposable. For nearly all collection types, the disposal action will simply return without doing anything.

We give some examples of these in the following sections.

Cleaning Up Internal Objects

Listing 8-6 shows an example where we implement an object that reads lines from a pair of text files, choosing the file at random. We must implement the type IDisposable because the object owns two internal System.IO.StreamReader objects, which are themselves IDisposable. Note that we explicitly check to see whether the object has already been disposed.

Listing 8-6. *Implementing IDisposable to Clean Up Internal Objects*

```
open System
open System.IO

type LineChooser(fileName1, fileName2) =
    let file1 = File.OpenText(fileName1)
    let file2 = File.OpenText(fileName2)
    let rnd = new System.Random()

    let mutable disposed = false
```

```
    let cleanup() =
        if not disposed then
            disposed <- true;
            file1.Dispose();
            file2.Dispose();

    interface System.IDisposable with
        member x.Dispose() = cleanup()

    member obj.CloseAll() = cleanup()

    member obj.GetLine() =
        if not file1.EndOfStream &&
            (file2.EndOfStream  or rnd.Next() % 2 = 0) then file1.ReadLine()
        elif not file2.EndOfStream then file2.ReadLine()
        else raise (new EndOfStreamException())
```

We can now instantiate, use, and dispose of this object as follows:

```
> open System.IO;;

> File.WriteAllLines("test1.txt", [| "Daisy, Daisy"; "Give me your hand oh do" |]);;
val it : unit = ()

> File.WriteAllLines("test2.txt", [| "I'm a little teapot"; "Short and stout" |]);;
val it : unit = ()

> let chooser = new LineChooser ("test1.txt", "test2.txt");;
val chooser : LineChooser

> chooser.GetLine();;
val it : string = "Daisy, Daisy"

> chooser.GetLine();;
val it : string = "I'm a little teapot"

> (chooser :> IDisposable).Dispose();;
val it : unit = ()

> chooser.GetLine();;
System.ObjectDisposedException: Cannot read from a closed TextReader.
```

Disposal should leave an object in an unusable state, as shown in the last line of the previous example. It is also common for objects to implement a member with a more intuitive name that does precisely the same thing as its implementation of IDisposable.Dispose, which is CloseAll in Listing 8-6.

Cleaning Up Unmanaged Objects

If you are writing a component that explicitly wraps some kind of unmanaged resource, then implementing IDisposable is a little trickier. In Listing 8-7 we show the pattern that is used for this cleanup. Here we mimic an external resource via a data structure that generates fresh, reclaimable integer tickets. The idea is that customers will each be given an integer ticket, but this will be kept internal to the customer, and customers will return their ticket to the pool when they leave (that is, are disposed).

Listing 8-7. *Reclaiming Unmanaged Tickets with IDisposable*

```
open System

type TicketGenerator() =
    let mutable free = []
    let mutable max = 0
    member h.Alloc() =
        match free with
        | [] -> max <- max + 1; max
        | h::t -> free <- t; h
    member h.Dealloc(n:int) =
        printfn "returning ticket %d" n
        free <- n :: free

let ticketGenerator = new TicketGenerator()

type  Customer() =
    let myTicket = ticketGenerator.Alloc()
    let mutable disposed = false
    let cleanup() =
        if not disposed then
            disposed <- true
            ticketGenerator.Dealloc(myTicket)
    member x.Ticket = myTicket
    interface IDisposable with
        member x.Dispose() = cleanup(); GC.SuppressFinalize(x)
    override x.Finalize() = cleanup()
```

Note that we override the Object.Finalize method. This makes sure cleanup occurs if the object is not disposed but is still garbage collected. If the object is explicitly disposed, we call GC.SuppressFinalize() to ensure the object is not later finalized. The finalizer should not call the Dispose() of other managed objects, since they will have their own finalizers if needed. The following example session generates some customers, where tickets used by some of the customers are automatically reclaimed as they exit their scopes:

```
> let bill = new Customer();;
val bill : Customer

> bill.Ticket;;
val it : int = 1

> begin
      use joe = new Customer()
      printfn "joe.Ticket = %d" joe.Ticket
  end;;
joe.Ticket = 2
returning ticket 2

> begin
      use jane = new Customer()
      printfn "jane.Ticket = %d" jane.Ticket
  end;;
jane.Ticket = 2
returning ticket 2
val it : unit = ()
```

In the example, Joe and Jane get the same ticket. Joe's ticket is returned at the end of the scope where the joe variable is declared because of the IDisposable cleanup implicit in the use binding.

Cleaning Up in Sequence Expressions

It is common to implement computations that access external resources such as databases but that return their results on demand. This, however, raises a difficulty: how do we manage the lifetime of the resources for the underlying operating system connections? One solution to this is captured by use bindings in sequence expressions:

- When a use binding occurs in a sequence expression, the resource is initialized each time a client enumerates the sequence.

- The connection is closed when the client disposes of the enumerator.

For example, consider the following function that creates a sequence expression that reads the first two lines of a file on demand:

```
open System.IO

let firstTwoLines(file) =
    { use s = File.OpenText(file)
      yield s.ReadLine()
      yield s.ReadLine() }
```

Let's now create a file and sequence that will read the first two lines of the file on demand:

```
> File.WriteAllLines("test1.txt", [| "Es kommt ein Schiff";
                                      "Hoch soll Sie leben" |]);;
val it : unit = ()

> let seq = firstTwoLines("test1.txt");;
val seq : seq<string>
```

At this point, the file has not yet been opened, and no lines have been read from the file. If we now iterate the sequence expression, then the file is opened, the first two lines are read, and the results are consumed from the sequence and printed. Most important, the file has now also been closed, because the Seq.iter aggregate operator is careful to dispose of the underlying enumerator it uses for the sequence, which in turn disposes of the file handle generated by File.OpenText.

```
> seq |> Seq.iter (printfn "line = '%s'");;
line = 'Es kommt ein Schiff'
line = 'Hoch soll Sie leben'
val it : unit = ()
```

We cover sequence expressions and the more general mechanism of workflows in more detail in Chapter 9.

Using using

In some F# code you will see the function using. For example:

```
using (new Customer()) (fun jane ->
    printfn "jane.Ticket = %d" jane.Ticket
)
```

The definition of using is as follows:

```
let using (ie : #System.IDisposable) f =
    try f(ie)
    finally ie.Dispose()
```

This is more explicit than writing use bindings but can be useful if you like to know what's going on "under the hood."

Stack As a Resource: Tail Calls and Recursion

In the previous section, you saw a range of resources that are best managed explicitly, preferably by automatically cleaning up the construct at the end of its lifetime using constructs such as use x = expr and idioms such as System.IDisposable. We also indicated that two resources are managed automatically, *stack* and *heap-allocated* memory, with the latter allocated on the garbage-collected heap.

Stack space is needed every time you call an F# function and is reclaimed when the function returns or when it performs a *tail call*, which we discuss in a moment. It is perhaps surprising that stack space is more limited than space in the garbage-collected heap. For example, on a 32-bit Windows machine, the default settings are that each thread of a program can use up to 1MB of stack space. Since stack is allocated every time a function call is made, this means a very deep series of nested function calls will cause a StackOverflowException to be raised. For example, on a 32-bit Windows machine, the following program causes a stack overflow when n reaches about 79000:

```
let rec deepRecursion n =
    if n = 1000000 then () else
    if n % 100 = 0 then
        printfn "--> deepRecursion, n = %d" n
    deepRecursion (n+1)
    printfn "<-- deepRecursion, n = %d" n
```

You can see this in F# Interactive:

```
> deepRecursion 0;;
--> deepRecursion, n = 0
...
--> deepRecursion, n = 79100
--> deepRecursion, n = 79200
--> deepRecursion, n = 79300
Process is terminated due to StackOverflowException
Session termination detected. Press Enter to restart.
```

Stack overflows are "extreme" exceptions, because it is often difficult to recover correctly from a stack overflow. For this reason, it is important to ensure that the amount of stack used by your program doesn't grow in an unbounded fashion as your program proceeds, especially as you process large inputs. Furthermore, deep stacks can hurt in other ways; for example, the .NET garbage collector traverses the entire stack on every garbage collection. This can be expensive if your stacks are very deep.

Since recursive functions are quite common in F# functional programming, this might seem to be a major problem. However, there is one important case where a function call recycles stack space eagerly, known as a *tail call*. A tail call is simply *any call that is the last piece of work done by a function*. For example, Listing 8-8 shows the same program where we have deleted the last line.

Listing 8-8. *A Simple Tail-Recursive Function*

```
let rec tailCallRecursion n : unit =
    if n = 1000000 then () else
    if n % 100 = 0 then
        printfn "--> tailCallRecursion, n = %d" n
    tailCallRecursion (n+1)
```

The code now runs to completion without problem:

```
> tailCallRecursion 0;;
...
--> tailCallRecursion, n = 999600
--> tailCallRecursion, n = 999700
--> tailCallRecursion, n = 999800
--> tailCallRecursion, n = 999900
val it : unit = ()
>
```

When a tail call is made, the .NET Common Language Runtime can drop the current stack frame before executing the target function, rather than waiting for the call to complete. Sometimes this optimization is performed by the F# compiler itself. If the n = 1000000 check were removed in the previous program, then the program would run indefinitely. (Note n would cycle around to the negative numbers, since arithmetic is unchecked for overflow unless you open the module Microsoft.FSharp.Core.Operators.Checked.)

Functions such as tailCallRecursion are known as *tail-recursive* functions. When you write recursive functions, you should check either that they are tail recursive or that they will not be used with inputs that cause them to recurse to an arbitrarily large depth. In the following sections, we give some examples of some of the techniques you can use to make your functions tail recursive.

Tail Recursion and List Processing

Tail recursion is particularly important when processing F# lists, because lists can be long and because recursion is the natural way to implement many list-processing functions. For example, here is a function to find the last element of a list (this must traverse the entire list because F# lists are "pointers" to the head of the list):

```
let rec last l =
    match l with
    | [] -> invalid_arg "last"
    | [h] -> h
    | h::t -> last t
```

This function is tail recursive because no "work" happens after the recursive call last t. However, many list functions are written most naturally in non-tail-recursive ways. Although it can be a little annoying to write these functions using tail recursion, it is often better to use tail recursion than to leave the potential for stack overflow lying around your code. For example, the following function creates a list of length n where every entry in the list is the value x:

```
let rec replicateNotTailRecursiveA n x =
    if n <= 0 then []
    else x :: replicateNotTailRecursiveA (n-1) x
```

The problem with this function is that work is done after the recursive call. This becomes obvious when we write the function in the following fashion:

```
let rec replicateNotTailRecursiveB n x =
    if n <= 0 then []
    else
        let recursiveResult = replicateNotTailRecursiveB (n-1) x
        x :: recursiveResult
```

Clearly, a value is being constructed by the expression x :: recursiveResult after the recursive call replicateNotTailRecursiveB (n-1) x. This means the function is not tail recursive. The solution is to write the function using an *accumulating parameter*. This is often done by using an auxiliary function that accepts the accumulating parameter:

```
let rec replicateAux n x acc =
    if n <= 0 then acc
    else replicateAux (n-1) x (x::acc)

let replicate n x = replicateAux n x []
```

Here the recursive call to replicateAux is tail recursive. Sometimes the auxiliary functions are written as inner recursive functions:

```
let replicate n x =
    let rec loop i acc =
        if i >= n then acc
        else loop (i+1) (x::acc)
    loop 0 []
```

The F# compiler will optimize inner recursive functions such as these to produce an efficient pair of functions that pass extra arguments as necessary.

When processing lists, accumulating parameters will often accumulate a list in the "reverse" order. This means a call to List.rev may be required at the end of the recursion. For example, consider the following implementation of List.map, which is not tail recursive:

```
let rec mapNotTailRecursive f inputList =
    match inputList with
    | [] -> []
    | h::t -> (f h) :: mapNotTailRecursive f t
```

Here is an implementation that neglects to reverse the accumulating parameter:

```
let rec mapIncorrectAcc f inputList acc =
    match inputList with
    | [] -> acc              // whoops! Forgot to reverse the accumulator here!
    | h::t -> mapIncorrectAcc f t (f h :: acc)

let mapIncorrect f inputList = mapIncorrectAcc f inputList []
```

```
> mapIncorrect (fun x -> x * x) [1;2;3;4];;
val it : int list = [ 16; 9; 4; 1]
```

Here is a correct implementation:

```
let rec mapAcc f inputList acc =
    match inputList with
    | [] -> List.rev acc
    | h::t -> mapAcc f t (f h :: acc)

let map f inputList = mapAcc f inputList []
```

```
> map (fun x -> x * x) [1;2;3;4];;
val it : int list = [ 1; 4; 9; 16]
```

Tail Recursion and Object-Oriented Programming

You will often need to implement object members with a tail-recursive implementation. For example, consider the following list-like data structure:

```
type Chain =
    | ChainNode of int * string * Chain
    | ChainEnd of string

    member chain.LengthNotTailRecursive =
        match chain with
        | ChainNode(_,_,subChain) -> 1 + subChain.LengthNotTailRecursive
        | ChainEnd _ -> 0
```

The implementation of the LengthNotTailRecursive is *not* tail recursive, simply because the addition 1 + applies to the result of the recursive property invocation. One obvious tail-recursive implementation uses a local recursive function with an accumulating parameter, as shown in Listing 8-9.

Listing 8-9. *Making an Object Member Tail Recursive*

```
type Chain =
    | ChainNode of int * string * Chain
    | ChainEnd of string
    // The implementation of this property is tail recursive.
    member chain.Length =
        let rec loop c acc =
            match c with
            | ChainNode(_,_,subChain) -> loop subChain (acc+1)
            | ChainEnd _ -> acc
        loop chain
```

■**Note** The list-processing functions in the F# library module `Microsoft.FSharp.Collections.List` are tail recursive, except where noted in the documentation, and some of them have implementations that are specially optimized to take advantage of the implementation of the `list` data structure.

Tail Recursion and Processing Unbalanced Trees

In the section, we consider tail-recursion problems that are much less common in practice but where it is important to know what techniques to apply should you require them. The techniques also illustrate some important aspects of functional programming, in particular an advanced technique called *continuation passing*.

Tree-structured data is generally more difficult to process in a tail-recursive way than list-structured data. For example, consider the following tree structure:

```
type Tree =
    | Node of string * Tree * Tree
    | Tip of string

let rec sizeNotTailRecursive tree =
    match tree with
    | Tip _ -> 1
    | Node(_,treeLeft,treeRight) ->
        sizeNotTailRecursive treeLeft + sizeNotTailRecursive treeRight
```

The implementation of this function is not tail recursive. Luckily, this is rarely a problem, especially if you can assume that the trees are *balanced*. A tree is balanced when the depth of each subtree is roughly the same. In that case, a tree of depth 1,000 will have about 2^{1000} entries. Even for a balanced tree of this size, the recursive calls to compute the overall size of the tree will not recurse to a depth greater than 1,000—not deep enough to cause stack overflow except when the routine is being called by some other function already consuming inordinate amounts of stack. Many data structures based on trees are balanced by design; for example, the Set and Map data structures implemented in the F# library are based on balanced binary trees.

However, some trees can be unbalanced; for example, you can explicitly make a highly unbalanced tree:

```
let rec mkBigUnbalancedTree n tree =
    if n = 0 then tree
    else Node("node",Tip("tip"),mkBigUnbalancedTree (n-1) tree)

let tree1 = Tip("tip")
let tree2 = mkBigUnbalancedTree 10000 tree1
let tree3 = mkBigUnbalancedTree 10000 tree2
let tree4 = mkBigUnbalancedTree 10000 tree3
let tree5 = mkBigUnbalancedTree 10000 tree4
let tree6 = mkBigUnbalancedTree 10000 tree5
```

Calling tree6.Size now risks a stack overflow. You can solve this in part by trying to predict whether the tree will be unbalanced to the left or right and by using an accumulating parameter:

```
let rec sizeAcc acc tree =
    match tree with
    | Tip _ -> 1+acc
    | Node(_,treeLeft,treeRight) ->
        let acc = sizeAcc acc treeLeft
        sizeAcc acc treeRight

let size tree = sizeAcc 0 tree
```

This algorithm works for tree6, because it is biased toward accepting trees that are skewed to the right. The recursive call that processes the right branch is a tail call, which the call that processes the left branch is not. This may be OK if you have prior knowledge of the shape of your trees. However, this algorithm still risks a stack overflow, and if necessary, you may have to change techniques. One way to do this is to use a much more general and important technique known as continuation passing.

Using Continuations to Avoid Stack Overflows

A continuation is simply a function that will receive the result of an expression once it has been computed. Listing 8-10 shows an example implementation of the previous algorithm that will handle trees of arbitrary size.

Listing 8-10. *Making a Function Tail Recursive via an Explicit Continuation*

```
let rec sizeCont tree cont =
    match tree with
    | Tip _ -> cont 1
    | Node(_,treeLeft,treeRight) ->
        sizeCont treeLeft (fun leftSize ->
          sizeCont treeRight (fun rightSize ->
            cont (leftSize + rightSize)))

let size tree = sizeCont tree (fun x -> x)
```

What's going on here? Let's look at the type of sizeCont and size:

```
val sizeCont : Tree -> (int -> 'a) -> 'a
val size : Tree -> int
```

The type of sizeCont tree cont can be read as "compute the size of the tree and call cont with that size." If you look at the type of sizeCont, you can see that it will call the second parameter of type int -> 'a at some point—how else could the function produce the final result of type 'a? And indeed when you look at the implementation of sizeCont, you can see that it does indeed call cont on both branches of the match.

Now, if you look at recursive calls in `sizeCont`, you can see that they are both tail calls:

```
sizeCont treeLeft (fun leftSize ->
  sizeCont treeRight (fun rightSize ->
    cont (leftSize + rightSize)))
```

That is, the first call to `sizeCont` is a tail call with a new continuation, as is the second. The first continuation is called with the size of the left tree, and the second is called with the size of the right tree. Finally, we add the results and call the original continuation `cont`. Calling `size` on an unbalanced tree such as `tree6` now succeeds:

```
> size tree6;;
val it : int = 50001
```

How have we been able to turn a tree walk into a tail-recursive algorithm? The answer lies in the fact that continuations are function objects, which are allocated on the garbage-collected heap. Effectively we have generated a work list represented by objects, rather than keeping a work list via a stack of function invocations.

As it happens, using a continuation for both the right and left trees is overkill, and we can use an accumulating parameter for one side. This will lead to a more efficient implementation because each continuation function object is likely to involve one allocation (short-lived allocations such as continuation objects are very cheap but not as cheap as not allocating at all!). For example, Listing 8-11 shows a more efficient implementation.

Listing 8-11. *Combining an Accumulator with an Explicit Continuation*

```
let rec sizeContAcc acc tree cont =
    match tree with
    | Tip _ -> cont (1+acc)
    | Node(_,treeLeft,treeRight) ->
        sizeContAcc acc treeLeft (fun accLeftSize ->
        sizeContAcc accLeftSize treeRight cont)

let size tree = sizeContAcc 0 tree (fun x -> x)
```

The behavior of this version of the algorithm is as follows:

1. We start with an accumulator `acc` of 0.

2. We then traverse the left spine of the tree until a `Tip` is found, building up a continuation for each `Node` along the way.

3. When a `Tip` is encountered, the continuation from the previous `Node` is called with `accLeftSize` increased by 1. The continuation makes a recursive call to `sizeContAcc` for its right tree, passing the continuation for the second-to-last node along the way.

4. When all is done, all the left and right trees will have been explored, and the final result is delivered to the (`fun x -> x`) continuation.

As you can see from this example, continuation passing is a powerful control construct, though it is used only occasionally in F# programming.

Another Example: Processing Syntax Trees

One real-world example where trees might become unbalanced is syntax trees for parsed languages when the inputs are very large and machine generated. In this case, some language constructs may be repeated very large numbers of times in an unbalanced way. For example, consider the following data structure:

```
type Expr =
    | Add  of Expr * Expr
    | Bind of string * Expr * Expr
    | Var  of string
    | Num  of int
```

This data structure would be suitable for representing arithmetic expressions of the forms *var*, *expr + expr*, and *bind var = expr in expr*. Chapter 9 and Chapter 11 are dedicated to techniques for representing and processing languages of this kind. As with all tree structures, most traversal algorithms over this type of abstract syntax trees will not naturally be tail recursive. For example, here is a simple evaluator:

```
type env = Map<string,int>

let rec eval (env: env) expr =
    match expr with
    | Add(e1,e2)        -> eval env e1 + eval env e2
    | Bind(var,rhs,body) -> eval (env.Add(var, eval env rhs)) body
    | Var(var)           -> env.[var]
    | Num(n)             -> n
```

The recursive call eval env rhs is not tail recursive. *For the vast majority of applications, you will never need to worry about making this algorithm tail recursive!* However, stack overflow may be a problem if bindings are nested to very high depth, such as in *bind v1 = (bind v2 = . . . (bind v1000000 = 1. . .)) in v1+v1*. If the syntax trees come from human-written programs, you can safely assume this won't be the case. However, if you ever did need to make the implementation tail recursive, you could use continuations, as shown in Listing 8-12.

Listing 8-12. *A Tail-Recursive Expression Evaluator Using Continuations*

```
let rec evalCont (env: env) expr cont =
    match expr with
    | Add(e1,e2)        ->
        evalCont env e1 (fun v1 ->
        evalCont env e2 (fun v2 ->
        cont (v1+v2)))
    | Bind(var,rhs,body) ->
        evalCont env rhs (fun v1 ->
        evalCont (env.Add(var,v1)) body cont)
```

```
  | Num(n)              ->
      cont(n)
  | Var(var)            ->
      cont(env.[var])

let eval env expr = evalCont env expr (fun x -> x)
```

■**Note** Programming with continuations can be tricky, and you should use them only when necessary. Where possible, abstract the kind of transformation you're doing on your tree structure (for example, a map, fold, or bottom-up reduction) so you can concentrate on getting the traversal right. In the previous examples, the continuations all effectively play the role of a *work list*. You can also reprogram your algorithms to use work lists explicitly and to use accumulating parameters for special cases. Sometimes this is necessary to gain maximum efficiency because an array or a queue can be an optimal representation of a work list. When you make a work list explicit, then the implementation of an algorithm becomes more verbose, but in some cases debugging can become simpler.

Events and Wiring

One recurring idiom in .NET programming is that of *events*. An event is simply something you can "listen to" by registering a callback with the event. For example, here's how you can create a WinForms form and listen to mouse clicks on the form:

```
> open System.Windows.Forms;;
> let form = new Form(Text="Click Form",Visible=true,TopMost=true);;
val form : Form

> form.Click.Add(fun evArgs -> printfn "Clicked!");;
val it : unit = ()
```

When you run this code in F# Interactive, you will see a window appear, and each time you click the window with the mouse, you will see "Clicked!" printed to the console. In .NET terminology, form.Click is an event, and form.Click.Add registers a callback with the event. You can register multiple callbacks with the same event, and many objects publish many events. For example, when you add the following, you will see a stream of output when you move the mouse over the form:

```
> form.MouseMove.Add(fun args -> printfn "Mouse, (X,Y) = (%A,%A)" args.X args.Y);;
val it : unit = ()
```

If necessary, you can also remove event handlers by first adding them by using the AddHandler method and removing them by using RemoveHandler.

The process of clicking the form *triggers* (or fires) the event, which means the callbacks get called in the order they were registered. Events can't be triggered from the outside. In other words, you can't trigger the Click event on a form; you can only handle it. Events also have *event arguments*. In the first example shown previously, the event arguments are called evArgs and are ignored. .NET events usually pass arguments of type System.EventArgs or some related type such as System.Windows.Forms.MouseEventArgs or System.Windows.Forms.PaintEventArgs. These arguments usually carry just pieces of information; for example, a value of type MouseEventArgs has the properties Button, Clicks, Delta, Location, X, and Y.

Events occur throughout the design of the .NET class libraries. Table 8-2 shows some of the more important events.

Table 8-2. *A Selection of Events from the .NET Libraries*

Type	Some Sample Events
System.AppDomain	AssemblyLoad, AssemblyResolve, DomainUnload, ProcessExit, UnhandledException (and others)
System.Diagnostics.Process	ErrorDataReceived, Exited, OutputDataReceived (and others)
System.IO.FileSystemWatcher	Changed, Created, Deleted, Error, Renamed (and others)
System.Windows.Forms.Control	BackgroundImageChanged, Click, Disposed, DragDrop, KeyPress, KeyUp, KeyDown, Layout, LostFocus, MouseClick, MouseDown, MouseEnter, MouseHover, MouseLeave, MouseUp, Paint, Resize, TextChanged, Validated, Validating (and others)
System.Windows.Forms.Timer	Tick
System.Timers.Timer	Elapsed

Events As First-Class Values

In F#, an event such as form.Click is a *first-class value*, which means you can pass it around just like any other value. The main advantage this brings is that you can use the combinators in the F# library module Microsoft.FSharp.Control.IEvent to map, filter, and otherwise transform the event stream in compositional ways. For example, the following code filters the event stream from form.MouseMove so that only events with X > 100 result in output to the console:

```
form.MouseMove
    |> IEvent.filter (fun args -> args.X > 100)
    |> IEvent.listen (fun args -> printfn "Mouse, (X,Y) = (%A,%A)" args.X args.Y)
```

If you work with events a lot, you will find yourself factoring out useful portions of code into functions that preprocess event streams. Table 8-3 shows some of the functions from the F# IEvent module. One interesting combinator is IEvent.partition, which splits an event into two events based on a predicate.

Table 8-3. *Some Functions from the* `IEvent` *Module*

Function	Type
`IEvent.choose`	`: ('a -> 'b option) -> #IEvent<'a> -> IEvent<'b>`
`IEvent.create`	`: unit -> ('a -> unit) * #IEvent<'a>`
`IEvent.filter`	`: ('a -> bool) -> #IEvent<'a> -> IEvent<'a>`
`IEvent.fold`	`: ('b -> 'a -> 'b) -> 'b -> #IEvent<'a> -> IEvent<'b>`
`IEvent.listen`	`: ('a -> unit) -> #IEvent<'a> -> unit`
`IEvent.map`	`: ('a -> 'b) -> #IEvent<'a> -> IEvent<'b>`
`IEvent.partition`	`: ('a -> bool) -> #IEvent<'a> -> IEvent<'a> * IEvent<'a>`

Creating and Publishing Events

As you write code in F#, particularly object-oriented code, you will find yourself needing to implement, publish, and trigger events. The normal idiom for doing this is simply to call `IEvent.create`. Listing 8-13 shows how to define an event object that is triggered at random intervals.

Listing 8-13. *Creating a* `RandomTicker` *That Defines, Publishes, and Triggers an Event*

```
open System
open System.Windows.Forms

type RandomTicker(approxInterval) =
    let timer = new Timer()
    let rnd = new System.Random(99)
    let triggerTickEvent, tickEvent = IEvent.create()

    let chooseInterval() :int =
        approxInterval + approxInterval/4 - rnd.Next(approxInterval/2)

    do timer.Interval <- chooseInterval()

    do timer.Tick.Add(fun args ->
        let interval = chooseInterval()
        triggerTickEvent(interval);
        timer.Interval <- interval)

    member x.RandomTick = tickEvent
    member x.Start() = timer.Start()
    member x.Stop() = timer.Stop()
    interface IDisposable with
        member x.Dispose() = timer.Dispose()
```

Here's how you can instantiate and use this type:

```
> let rt = new RandomTicker(1000);;
val rt : RandomTicker

> rt.RandomTick.Add(fun nextInterval -> printfn "Tick, next = %A" nextInterval);;
val it : unit = ()

> rt.Start();;
Tick, next = 1072
Tick, next = 927
Tick, next = 765
...
val it : unit = ()

> rt.Stop();;
val it : unit = ()
```

Events are an idiom understood by all .NET languages. However, not all F# event values are immediately compiled in the idiomatic .NET form. This is because F# allows you to go one step further and use events as first-class values. If you need to ensure your events can be used by other .NET languages, then you should do both of the following:

- Create the events using IEvent.create_HandlerEvent instead of IEvent.create.

- Publish the event as a property of a type.

Events are used in most of the later chapters of this book, and you can find many examples in the F# samples and manual.

Note Because events allow you to register callbacks, it is sometimes important to be careful about the thread on which an event is being raised. This is particularly the case when programming with multiple threads or the .NET thread pool. Events are usually fired on the GUI thread of an application. See Chapter 13 for more details about concurrent and multithreaded programming.

Summary

In this chapter, we covered some of the techniques that you are likely to use in your day-to-day F# programming, including an in-depth look at hashing, equality, and comparison, resource management, tail calls, caching, memoization, and the basics of how F# reveals the wiring for first-class events. In the next chapter, we introduce a final set of language constructs and techniques related to language-oriented programming tasks.

CHAPTER 9

■■■

Introducing Language-Oriented Programming

In Chapters 3, 4, and 6 we covered three well-known programming paradigms in F#: *functional*, *imperative*, and *object-oriented* programming. In this chapter, we cover techniques and constructs related to what is essentially a fourth programming paradigm, which we call *language-oriented programming*. The word *language* can have a number of meanings in this context. For example, take the simple language of arithmetic expressions and algebra that you learned in high-school mathematics, made up of named variables such as x and y and composite expressions such as $x+y$, xy, $-x$, and x^2. For the purposes of this chapter, this language can have a number of manifestations:

- One or more *concrete representations*, for example, using an ASCII text format or an XML representation of arithmetic expressions.

- One or more *abstract representations*, for example, as F# values representing the normalized form of an arithmetic expression tree.

- One or more *computational representations*, either by functions that compute the values of arithmetic expressions or via other engines that perform analysis, interpretation, compilation, execution, or transformation on language fragments. These can be implemented in F#, in another .NET language, or in external engines.

In this and later chapters, we cover many of the tasks associated with language-oriented programming. The techniques covered in this book are as follows:

- Manipulating formats such as XML, which are often used for concrete representations of languages (Chapters 9 and 11)

- Writing parsers and lexers for other text formats, also often used as concrete representations of languages (Chapter 16)

- Using F# types for abstract representations of languages (Chapters 9 and 11)

- Using three techniques related to computational representations of languages: *active patterns*, *quotations*, and *workflows* (Chapters 9 and 13)

- Interfacing with existing language execution components (SQL via LINQ in Chapter 15)

Language-oriented programming is not a single technique; sometimes you will be working with fully concrete representations (for example, reading bits on a magnetic disk) and sometimes with fully computational representations (for example, defining and using functions that compute the value of arithmetic expressions). Most often you will probably be working somewhere in between (for example, manipulating abstract syntax trees). These tasks require different techniques, and there are trade-offs between choosing to work with different kinds of representations. For example, if you are generating human-readable formulae, then you may need to store more concrete information, but if you're interested just in evaluating arithmetic expressions, then a purely computational encoding may be more effective. You'll see some of those trade-offs in this chapter.

■**Note** The term *language-oriented programming* was originally applied to F# by Robert Pickering in the Apress book *Foundations of F#*, and it really captures a key facet of F# programming. Thanks, Robert!

Using XML As a Concrete Language Format

To get started with language-oriented programming, it is helpful to begin with the standard structured data format Extensible Markup Language (XML), largely because .NET comes with well-engineered libraries for reading and generating XML, so we can initially skirt many of the issues associated with concrete language formats. We also cover XML as a data format in Chapter 15, and we cover techniques to tokenize and parse other textual formats in Chapter 16. We also briefly cover binary formats in Chapter 16.

Using the System.Xml Namespace

XML is a general-purpose markup language and is extensible because it allows its users to define their own tags. Its primary purpose is to facilitate the sharing of data across different information systems, particularly via the Internet. Here is a sample fragment of XML, defined as a string directly in F#:

```
let inp = "<?xml version=\"1.0\" encoding=\"utf-8\" ?>
        <Scene>
          <Composite>
            <Circle radius='2' x='1' y='0'/>
            <Composite>
              <Circle radius='2' x='4' y='0'/>
              <Square side='2' left='-3' top='0'/>
            </Composite>
            <Ellipse top='2' left='-2' width='3' height='4'/>
          </Composite>
        </Scene>"
```

The backbone of an XML document is a hierarchical structure, and each node is decorated with attributes keyed by name. You can parse XML using the types and methods in the

System.Xml namespace provided by the .NET libraries and then examine the structure of the XML interactively:

```
> open System.Xml;;
> let doc = new XmlDocument();;
val doc : XmlDocument

> doc.LoadXml(inp);;
val it : unit = ()

> doc.ChildNodes;;
val it : XmlNodeList
    = seq [seq []; seq [seq [seq []; seq [seq []; seq []]; seq []]]]
```

The default F# Interactive display for the XmlNode type is not particularly useful! Luckily, you can add an interactive printer to the fsi.exe session using the AddPrinter method on the fsi object:

```
> fsi.AddPrinter(fun (x:XmlNode) -> x.OuterXml);;

> doc.ChildNodes;;
val it : XmlNodeList
seq
    [<?xml version="1.0" encoding="utf-8"?>;
     <Scene><Composite><Circle radius="2" x="1" y="0" /><Composite>...</Scene>]

> doc.ChildNodes.Item(1);;
val it : XmlNode
  = <Scene><Composite><Circle radius="2" x="1" y="0" /><Composite>...</Scene>

> doc.ChildNodes.Item(1).ChildNodes.Item(0);;
val it : XmlNode
  = <Composite><Circle radius="2" x="1" y="0" /><Composite>...</Composite>

> doc.ChildNodes.Item(1).ChildNodes.Item(0).ChildNodes.Item(0);;
val it : XmlNode = <Circle radius="2" x="1" y="0" />

> doc.ChildNodes.Item(1).ChildNodes.Item(0).ChildNodes.Item(0).Attributes;;
val it : val it : XmlAttributeCollection = seq [radius="2"; x="1"; y="0"]
```

Table 9-1 shows the most commonly used types and members from the System.Xml namespace.

Table 9-1. *Commonly Used Types and Members from the* `System.Xml` *Namespace*

Type/Member	Description
type `XmlNode`	Represents a single node in an XML document
member `ChildNodes`	Gets all the child nodes of an `XmlNode`
member `Attributes`	Gets all the attributes of an `XmlNode`
member `OuterXml`	Gets the XML text representing the node and all its children
member `InnerText`	Gets the concatenated values of the node and all its children
member `SelectNodes`	Selects child nodes using an XPath query
type `XmlAttribute`	Represents one attribute for an `XmlNode`; also an `XmlNode`
member `Value`	Gets the string value for the attribute
type `XmlDocument`	Represents an entire XML document; also an `XmlNode`
member `Load`	Populates the document from the given `XmlReader`, stream, or file name
member `LoadXml`	Populates the document object from the given XML string
type `XmlReader`	Represents a reader for an XML document or source
type `XmlWriter`	Represents a writer for an XML document

■**Note** .NET provides tools to generate a typed .NET object model view of an XML schema, in particular `xsd.exe` from the .NET Framework SDK. This tool can even be configured to generate F# code through the use of the F# CodeDOM implementation that comes with the F# distribution. However, we don't show how to use these tools in this chapter. An alternative technique for querying XML is the XLinq API that is part of the LINQ framework, covered briefly in Chapter 15. You can also use F# active patterns to define decomposition and query techniques for XML (we cover F# active patterns later in this chapter). You can find more techniques to work with XML at `http://www.expert-fsharp.com/Topics/XML`.

From Concrete XML to Abstract Syntax

Often our first task in processing a concrete language is to bring the language fragments under the type discipline of F#. In this section, we show how to transform the data contained in the XML from the previous section into an instance of the recursive type shown here. This kind of type is usually called an *abstract syntax tree* (AST).

```
open System.Drawing
type Scene =
    | Ellipse   of RectangleF
    | Rect      of RectangleF
    | Composite of Scene list
```

Here we use the types PointF and RectangleF from the System.Drawing namespace, though we could equally define our own types to capture the information carried by the "leaves" of the tree. Listing 9-1 shows a recursive transformation to convert XML documents like the one used in the previous section into the type Scene.

Listing 9-1. *Converting XML into a Typed Format Using the System.Xml Namespace*

```
open System.Xml
open System.Drawing
type Scene =
    | Ellipse of RectangleF
    | Rect    of RectangleF
    | Composite  of Scene list

    /// A derived constructor
    static member Circle(center:PointF,radius) =
        Ellipse(RectangleF(center.X-radius,center.Y-radius,
                           radius*2.0f,radius*2.0f))

    /// A derived constructor
    static member Square(left,top,side) =
        Rect(RectangleF(left,top,side,side))

let extractFloat32 attrName (attribs: XmlAttributeCollection) =
    Float32.of_string(attribs.GetNamedItem(attrName).Value)

let extractPointF (attribs: XmlAttributeCollection) =
    PointF(extractFloat32 "x" attribs,extractFloat32 "y" attribs)

let extractRectangleF (attribs: XmlAttributeCollection) =
    RectangleF(extractFloat32 "left" attribs,extractFloat32 "top" attribs,
               extractFloat32 "width" attribs,extractFloat32 "height" attribs)

let rec extractScene (node: XmlNode) =
    let attribs = node.Attributes
    let childNodes = node.ChildNodes
    match node.Name with
    | "Circle"  ->
        Scene.Circle(extractPointF(attribs), extractFloat32 "radius" attribs)
    | "Ellipse"  ->
        Scene.Ellipse(extractRectangleF(attribs))
    | "Rectangle"  ->
        Scene.Rect(extractRectangleF(attribs))
    | "Square"  ->
        Scene.Square(extractFloat32 "left" attribs,extractFloat32 "top" attribs,
                     extractFloat32 "side" attribs)
```

```
    | "Composite"    ->
        Scene.Composite [ for child in childNodes -> extractScene(child) ]
    | _ -> failwithf "unable to convert XML '%s'" node.OuterXml

let extractScenes (doc: XmlDocument) =
  [ for node in doc.ChildNodes do
      if node.Name = "Scene" then
          yield (Composite
                     [ for child in node.ChildNodes -> extractScene(child) ]) ]
```

The inferred types of these functions are as follows:

```
type Scene =
    | Ellipse of RectangleF
    | Rect of RectangleF
    | Composite of Scene list
    static member Circle : PointF * float32 -> Scene
    static member Square : float32 * float32 * float32 -> Scene

val extractFloat32 : string -> XmlAttributeCollection -> float32
val extractPointF : XmlAttributeCollection -> PointF
val extractRectangleF :  XmlAttributeCollection -> RectangleF
val extractScene : XmlNode -> Scene
val extractScenes : XmlDocument -> Scene list
```

The definition of extractScenes in Listing 9-1 generates lists using sequence expressions, covered in Chapter 3. We can now apply the extractScenes function to our original XML. (We first add a pretty-printer to the F# Interactive session for the RectangleF type using the AddPrinter function on the fsi object, described in Chapter 10.)

```
> fsi.AddPrinter(fun (r:RectangleF) ->
      sprintf "[%A,%A,%A,%A]" r.Left r.Top r.Width r.Height);;
val it : unit = ()

> extractScenes doc;;
val it : Scene list
= [Composite
    [Composite
      [Ellipse [-1.0f,-2.0f,4.0f,4.0f];
       Composite [Ellipse [2.0f,-2.0f,4.0f,4.0f]; Rect [-3.0f,0.0f,2.0f,2.0f]];
       Ellipse [-2.0f,2.0f,3.0f,4.0f]]]]
```

We more closely explain some of the choices we've made in the abstract syntax design for the type Scene in the following sections.

■**Tip** Translating to a typed representation is not always necessary: some manipulations and analyses are better performed directly on heterogeneous, general-purpose formats such as XML or even on strings. For example, XML libraries support XPath, accessed via the SelectNodes method on the XmlNode type. If you need to query a large semistructured document whose schema is frequently changing in minor ways, then XPath is the right way to do it. Likewise, if you need to write significant amounts of code that interprets or analyzes a tree structure, then converting to a typed abstract syntax tree is usually better.

Working with Abstract Syntax Representations

In the previous section, you saw how to move from one particular concrete language format to an abstract syntax format. You'll now learn about some important recurring techniques in designing and working with abstract syntax representations.

Abstract Syntax Representations: "Less Is More"

Let's take a look at the design of the abstract syntax type Scene from Listing 9-1. The type Scene uses fewer kinds of nodes than the concrete XML representation: the concrete XML had node kinds Circle, Square, Composite, and Ellipse, while Scene has just three (Rect, Ellipse, and Composite), with two derived constructors Circle and Square, defined as static members of the Scene:

```
static member Circle(center:PointF,radius) =
    Ellipse(RectangleF(center.X-radius,center.Y-radius,
                       radius*2.0f,radius*2.0f))

/// A derived constructor
static member Square(left,top,side) =
    Rect(RectangleF(left,top,side,side))
```

This is a common step when abstracting from a concrete syntax; details are dropped and unified to make the abstract representation simpler and more general. Extra functions are then added that compute specific instances of the abstract representation. This has pros and cons:

- Transformational and analytical manipulations are almost always easier to program if you have fewer constructs in your abstract syntax representation.

- You must be careful not to eliminate truly valuable information from an abstract representation. For some applications, it might really matter if the user specified a Square or a Rectangle in the original input; for example, an editor for this data may provide different options for editing these objects.

In the AST we have used the types PointF and RectangleF from the System.Drawing namespace. This simplification is also a design decision that should be assessed: PointF and RectangleF use 32-bit low-precision floating-point numbers, which may not be appropriate if you are eventually rendering on high-precision display devices. You should be wary of deciding on abstract representations on the basis of convenience alone, though of course this is useful during prototyping.

The lesson here is that you should look carefully at your abstract syntax representations, trimming out unnecessary nodes and unifying nodes where possible, but only as long as this helps you achieve your ultimate goals.

Processing Abstract Syntax Representations

Common operations on abstract syntax trees include traversals that collect information and transformations that generate new trees from old. For example, the abstract representation from Listing 9-1 has the property that for nearly all purposes the Composite nodes are irrelevant (this would not be the case if you added an extra construct such as an Intersect node). This means you can "flatten" to a sequence of Ellipse and Rectangle nodes as follows:

```
let rec flatten scene =
    match scene with
    | Composite(scenes) -> seq { for x in scenes do yield! flatten x }
    | Ellipse _ | Rect _ -> seq { yield scene }
```

Here flatten is defined using sequence expressions, introduced in Chapter 3. Its type is as follows:

```
val flatten : Scene -> seq<Scene>
```

Let's take a look at this more closely. Recall from Chapter 3 that sequences are on-demand (lazy) computations. Using functions that recursively generate seq<'a> objects can lead to inefficiencies in your code if your abstract syntax trees are deep. It can often be better to traverse the entire tree in an *eager* way (eager traversals are ones that run to completion immediately). For example, it is typically faster to use an accumulating parameter to collect a list of results. Here is an example:

```
let rec flattenAux scene acc =
    match scene with
    | Composite(scenes) -> List.fold_right flattenAux scenes acc
    | Ellipse _
    | Rect _ -> scene :: acc

let flatten2 scene = flattenAux scene [] |> Seq.of_list
```

The following is yet another that does an eager traversal using a local mutable instance of a ResizeArray as the accumulator and then returns the result as a sequence. In this example, we use a local function and ensure the mutable state is locally encapsulated.

```
let flatten3 scene =
    let acc = new ResizeArray<_>()
    let rec flattenAux s =
        match s with
```

```
        | Composite(scenes) -> scenes.Iterate(flattenAux)
        | Ellipse _ | Rect _ -> acc.Add(s)
    flattenAux scene;
    Seq.readonly acc
```

The types of these are as follows:

```
val flatten2 : Scene -> seq<Scene>
val flatten3 : Scene -> seq<Scene>
```

There is no hard and fast rule about which of these is best. For prototyping, the second option—that is, doing an efficient eager traversal with an accumulating parameter—is often the most effective. However, even if you implement an accumulation using an eager traversal, returning the result as an on-demand sequence can still give added flexibility later in the design process.

Transformational Traversals of Abstract Syntax Representations

In the previous section, you saw examples of accumulating traversals of a syntax representation. It is common to traverse abstract syntax in other ways:

Leaf rewriting (mapping): Translating some leaf nodes of the representation but leaving the overall shape of the tree unchanged.

Bottom-up rewriting: Traversing a tree but making local transformations "on the way up."

Top-down rewriting: Traversing a tree but before traversing each subtree, attempting to locally rewrite the tree according to some particular set of rules.

Accumulating and rewriting transformations: For example, transforming the tree left to right but accumulating a parameter along the way.

For example, the following mapping transformation rewrites all leaf ellipses to rectangles:

```
let rec rectanglesOnly scene =
    match scene with
    | Composite(scenes) -> Composite(scenes.Map(rectanglesOnly))
    | Ellipse(rect) | Rect(rect) -> Rect(rect)
```

Often whole classes of transformations are abstracted into aggregate transformation operations taking functions as parameters. For example, here is a function that applies one function to each leaf rectangle:

```
let rec mapRects f scene =
    match scene with
    | Composite(scenes) -> Composite(scenes.Map(mapRects f))
    | Ellipse(rect) -> Ellipse(f rect)
    | Rect(rect) -> Rect(f rect)
```

The types of these functions are as follows:

```
val rectanglesOnly : Scene -> Scene
val mapRects: (RectangleF -> RectangleF) -> Scene -> Scene
```

Here is a use of the mapRects function to adjust the aspect ratio of all the RectangleF values in the scene (RectangleF values support an Inflate method):

```
let adjustAspectRatio scene =
    mapRects (fun r -> RectangleF.Inflate(r,1.1f,1.0f/1.1f)) scene
```

Using On-Demand Computation with Abstract Syntax Trees

Sometimes it is feasible to delay the loading or processing of some portions of an abstract syntax tree. For example, imagine if the XML for the small geometric language from the previous section included a construct such as the following, where the File nodes represent entire subtrees defined in external files:

```
<Composite>
    <File file='spots.xml'/>
    <File file='dots.xml'/>
</Composite>
```

It may be useful to delay the loading of these files. One general way to do this is to add a Delay node to the Scene type:

```
type Scene =
    | Ellipse   of RectangleF
    | Rect      of RectangleF
    | Composite of Scene list
    | Delay     of Lazy<Scene>
```

You can then extend the extractScene function of Listing 9-1 with the following case to handle this node:

```
let rec extractScene (node: XmlNode) =
    let attribs = node.Attributes
    let childNodes = node.ChildNodes
    match node.Name with
    | "Circle"  ->
        ...
    | "File"    ->
        let file = attribs.GetNamedItem("file").Value
        let scene = lazy (let d = XmlDocument()
                          d.Load(file)
                          extractScene(d :> XmlNode))
        Scene.Delay scene
```

Code that analyzes trees (for example, via pattern matching) must typically be adjusted to "force" the computation of delayed values. One way to handle this is to first call a function to eliminate immediately delayed values:

```
let rec getScene scene =
    match scene with
    | Delay d -> getScene (d.Force())
    | _ -> scene
```

Here is the function `flatten2` from the "Processing Abstract Syntax Representations" section but redefined to first eliminate delayed nodes:

```
let rec flattenAux scene acc =
    match getScene(scene) with
    | Composite    scenes -> List.fold_right flattenAux scenes acc
    | Ellipse _  | Rect _  -> scene :: acc
    | Delay _ -> failwith "this lazy value should have been eliminated by getScene"

let flatten2 scene = flattenAux scene []
```

It is generally advisable to have a single representation of laziness within a single syntax tree design. For example, the following abstract syntax design uses laziness in too many ways:

```
type SceneVeryLazy =
    | Ellipse    of Lazy<RectangleF>
    | Rect       of Lazy<RectangleF>
    | Composite of seq<SceneVeryLazy>
    | LoadFile of string
```

The shapes of ellipses and rectangles are lazy computations; each `Composite` node carries a `seq<SceneVeryLazy>` value to compute subnodes on demand, and a `LoadFile` node is used for delayed file loading. This is a bit of a mess, since a single `Delay` node would in practice cover all these cases.

■**Note** The `Lazy<'a>` type is defined in `Microsoft.FSharp.Control` and represents delayed computations. You access a lazy value via the `Force` or `Value` property (they are identical). F# includes the special keyword `lazy` for constructing values of this type. We also covered lazy computations in Chapter 8.

Caching Properties in Abstract Syntax Trees

For high-performance applications of abstract syntax trees, it can occasionally be useful to cache computations of some derived attributes within the syntax tree itself. For example, let's say you want to compute bounding boxes for the geometric language described in Listing 9-1. It is potentially valuable to cache this computation at `Composite` nodes. You can use a type such as the following to hold a cache:

```
type SceneWithCachedBoundingBox =
    | Ellipse of RectangleF
    | Rect    of RectangleF
    | CompositeRepr  of SceneWithCachedBoundingBox list * RectangleF option ref
```

This is useful for prototyping, though you should be careful to encapsulate the code that is responsible for maintaining this information. Listing 9-2 shows the full code for doing this.

Listing 9-2. *Adding the Cached Computation of a Local Attribute to an Abstract Syntax Tree*

```
type SceneWithCachedBoundingBox =
    | Ellipse of RectangleF
    | Rect    of RectangleF
    | CompositeRepr   of SceneWithCachedBoundingBox list * RectangleF option ref

    member x.BoundingBox =
        match x with
        | Ellipse(rect) | Rect(rect) -> rect
        | CompositeRepr(scenes,cache) ->
            match !cache with
            | Some v -> v
            | None ->
                let bbox =
                    scenes
                    |> List.map (fun s -> s.BoundingBox)
                    |> List.fold1_left (fun r1 r2 -> RectangleF.Union(r1,r2))
                cache := Some bbox
                bbox

    // Create a Composite node with an initially empty cache
    static member Composite(scenes)  = CompositeRepr(scenes,ref None)
```

Other attributes that are sometimes cached include the hash values of tree-structured terms and the computation of all the identifiers in a subexpression. The use of caches makes it more awkward to pattern match on terms. This can be largely solved by using active patterns, covered later in this chapter.

Memoizing Construction of Syntax Tree Nodes

In some cases, abstract syntax tree nodes can end up consuming significant portions of the application's memory budget. In this situation, it can be worth memoizing some or all of the nodes constructed in the tree. You can even go as far as memoizing *all* equivalent nodes, ensuring that equivalence between nodes can be implemented by pointer equality, a technique often called *hash-consing*. Listing 9-3 shows an abstract representation of propositional logic terms that ensures that any two nodes that are syntactically identical are shared via a memoizing table. Propositional logic terms are terms constructed using P AND Q, P OR Q, NOT P, and variables a, b, and so on. A non-cached version of the expressions would be as follows:

```fsharp
type Prop =
    | And of Prop * Prop
    | Or  of Prop * Prop
    | Not of Prop
    | Var of string
    | True
```

Listing 9-3. *Memoizing the Construction of Abstract Syntax Tree Nodes*

```fsharp
type Prop =
    | Prop of int
and internal PropRepr =
    | AndRepr of Prop * Prop
    | OrRepr  of Prop * Prop
    | NotRepr of Prop
    | VarRepr of string
    | TrueRepr

open System.Collections.Generic

module PropOps =

    let internal uniqStamp = ref 0
    type internal PropTable() =
        let fwdTable = new Dictionary<PropRepr,Prop>(HashIdentity.Structural)
        let bwdTable = new Dictionary<int,PropRepr>(HashIdentity.Structural)
        member t.ToUnique(repr) =
            if fwdTable.ContainsKey(repr) then fwdTable.[repr]
            else let stamp = incr uniqStamp; !uniqStamp
                 let prop = Prop(stamp)
                 fwdTable.Add(repr,prop)
                 bwdTable.Add(stamp,repr)
                 prop
        member t.FromUnique(Prop(stamp)) =
            bwdTable.[stamp]

    let internal table = PropTable()

    // public construction functions
    let And(p1,p2) = table.ToUnique(AndRepr(p1,p2))
    let Not(p)     = table.ToUnique(NotRepr(p))
    let Or(p1,p2)  = table.ToUnique(OrRepr(p1,p2))
    let Var(p)     = table.ToUnique(VarRepr(p))
    let True       = table.ToUnique(TrueRepr)
    let False = Not(True)

    // deconstruction function
    let getRepr(p) = table.FromUnique(p)
```

You can construct terms using the operations in PropOps much as you would construct terms using the nonmemoized representation:

```
> open PropOps;;
> True;;
val it : Prop = Prop 1

> And(Var("x"),Var("y"));;
val it : Prop = Prop 5

> getRepr(it);;
val it : PropRepr = AndRepr(Prop 3, Prop 4)

> And(Var("x"),Var("y"));;
val it : Prop = Prop 5
```

In this example, when you create two syntax trees using the same specification, And(Var("x"),Var("y")), you get the same Prop object back with the same stamp 5. You can also use memoization techniques to implement interesting algorithms; in Chapter 12 you will see an important representation of propositional logic called a *binary decision diagram* (BDD) based on a memoization table similar to the previous example.

The use of unique integer stamps and a lookaside table in the previous representation also has some drawbacks; it is harder to pattern match on abstract syntax representations, and you may need to reclaim and recycle stamps and remove entries from the lookaside table if a large number of terms is created or if the overall set of stamps must remain compact. You can solve the first problem by using active patterns, covered next in this chapter. If necessary, you can solve the second problem by scoping stamps in an object that encloses the uniqStamp state, the lookaside table, and the construction functions. Alternatively you can explicitly reclaim the stamps by using the IDisposable idiom described in Chapter 8, though this can be quite intrusive to your application.

Introducing Active Patterns

Pattern matching is one of the key techniques provided in F# for decomposing abstract syntax trees and other abstract representations of languages. So far in this book all the examples of pattern matching have been directly over the "core representations" of data structures, for example, directly matching on the structure of lists, options, records, and discriminated unions. However, pattern matching in F# is also *extensible*; that is, you can define new ways of matching over existing types. You do this through a mechanism called *active patterns*.

We'll cover only the basics of active patterns in this book. However, they can be indispensable, since they can let you continue to use pattern matching with your types even after you hide their representations. Active patterns also let you use pattern matching with .NET object types. In the following section, we cover active patterns and how they work.

■**Note** You can find more information on active patterns at `http://www.expert-fsharp.com/` `Topics/ActivePatterns`.

Converting the Same Data to Many Views

In high-school math courses you were probably taught that you can view complex numbers in two ways: as rectangular coordinates $x + yi$ or as polar coordinates of a "phase" r and "magnitude" φ. In most computer systems, complex numbers are stored in the first format, though often the second format is more useful.

Now, wouldn't it be nice if you could look at complex numbers through either lens? You could do this by explicitly converting from one form to another when needed, but it would be better to have your programming language look after the transformations needed to do this for you. Active patterns let you do exactly that. Here is the definition of a pattern that lets you view complex numbers as rectangular coordinates:

```
open Microsoft.FSharp.Math
let (|Rect|) (x:complex) = (x.RealPart, x.ImaginaryPart)
```

And here is an active pattern to help you view complex numbers in polar coordinates:

```
let (|Polar|) (x:complex) = (x.Magnitude, x.Phase)
```

The key thing to note is that these definitions let you use `Rect` and `Polar` as tags in pattern matching. For example, you can now write the following to define addition and multiplication over complex numbers:

```
let addViaRect a b =
    match a, b with
    | Rect(ar,ai), Rect(br,bi) -> Complex.mkRect(ar+br, ai+bi)

let mulViaRect a b =
    match a, b with
    | Rect(ar,ai), Rect(br,bi) -> Complex.mkRect(ar*br - ai*bi, ai*br + bi*ar)
```

As it happens, multiplication on complex numbers is easier to express using polar coordinates, implemented as follows:

```
let mulViaPolar a b =
    match a, b with
    | Polar(m,p), Polar(n,q) -> Complex.mkPolar(m*n, (p+q))
```

Here is an example of using the (|Rect|) and (|Polar|) active patterns directly on some complex numbers via the pattern tags `Rect` and `Polar`. We first make the complex number $3+4i$ using `Complex.mkRect`:

```
> let c = Complex.mkRect(3.0, 4.0);;
val c : complex

> c;;
val it : complex = 3.0r+4.0i

>  match c with
   | Rect(x,y) -> printfn "x = %g, y = %g" x y;;
x = 3, y = 4
val it : unit = ()

>  match c with
   | Polar(x,y) -> printfn "x = %g, y = %g" x y;;
x = 5.0, y = 0.927295
val it : unit = ()

> addViaRect c c;;
val it : complex = 6.0r+8.0i

> mulViaRect c c;;
val it : complex = -7.0r+24.0i

> mulViaPolar c c;;
val it : complex = -7.0r+24.0i
```

As you might expect, you get the same results if you multiply via rectangular or polar coordinates. However, the execution paths are quite different. Let's look closely at the definition of mulViaRect. The important lines are in bold here:

```
let mulViaRect a b =
    match a, b with
    | Rect(ar,ai), Rect(br,bi) ->
        Complex.mkRect(ar*br - ai*bi, ai*br + bi*ar)
```

When F# needs to match the values a and b against the patterns Rect(ar,ai) and Rect(br,bi), it doesn't look at the contents of a and b directly. Instead, *it runs a function as part of pattern matching* (which is why they're called *active* patterns). In this case, the function executed is (|Rect|), which produces a pair as its result. The elements of the pair are then bound to the variables ar and ai. Likewise, in the definition of mulViaPolar, the matching is performed partly by running the function (|Polar|).

The functions (|Rect|) and (|Polar|) are allowed to do anything, as long as they each ultimately produce a pair of results. Indeed, here are the types of (|Rect|) and (|Polar|):

```
val (|Rect|) : complex -> float * float
val (|Polar|) : complex -> float * float
```

These types are identical, but they implement completely different views of the same data.

The definitions of addViaRect and mulViaPolar can also be written using pattern matching in argument position:

```
let add2 (Rect(ar,ai)) (Rect(br,bi))   = Complex.mkRect(ar+br, ai+bi)
let mul2 (Polar(r1,th1)) (Polar(r2,th2)) = Complex.mkPolar(r1*r2, th1+th2)
```

■**Note** The Microsoft.FSharp.Math.Complex type defines addition and multiplication operators accessible via the overloaded operators + and *. The redefinitions in this section are included primarily to show how you can use different active patterns to access the same type in different ways.

Matching on .NET Object Types

One of the useful things about active patterns is that they let you use pattern matching with existing .NET object types. For example, the .NET object type System.Type is a runtime representation of types in .NET and F#. Here are the members found on this type:

```
type System.Type with
    member IsGenericType : bool
    member GetGenericTypeDefinition : unit -> Type
    member GetGenericArguments : unit -> Type[]
    member HasElementType : bool
    member GetElementType : unit -> Type
    member IsByRef : bool
    member IsPointer : bool
    member IsGenericParameter : bool
    member GenericParameterPosition : int
```

This type looks very much like one you'd like to pattern match against. There are clearly three or four distinct cases here, and pattern matching will help you isolate them. You can define an active pattern to achieve this, as shown in Listing 9-4.

Listing 9-4. *Defining an Active Pattern for Matching on System.Type Values*

```
let (|Named|Array|Ptr|Param|) (typ : System.Type) =
    if typ.IsGenericType
    then Named(typ.GetGenericTypeDefinition(),typ.GetGenericArguments())
    elif typ.IsGenericParameter then Param(typ.GenericParameterPosition)
    elif not typ.HasElementType then Named(typ, [| |])
    elif typ.IsArray then Array(typ.GetElementType(),typ.GetArrayRank())
    elif typ.IsByRef then Ptr(true,typ.GetElementType())
    elif typ.IsPointer then Ptr(false,typ.GetElementType())
    else failwith "MSDN says this can't happen"
```

This then lets you use pattern matching against a value of this type:

```
open System

let rec formatType typ =
    match typ with
    | Named (con, [| |]) -> sprintf "%s" con.Name
    | Named (con, args) -> sprintf "%s<%s>" con.Name (formatTypes args)
    | Array (arg, rank) -> sprintf "Array(%d,%s)" rank (formatType arg)
    | Ptr(true,arg) -> sprintf "%s&" (formatType arg)
    | Ptr(false,arg) -> sprintf "%s*" (formatType arg)
    | Param(pos) -> sprintf "!%d" pos
and formatTypes typs =
    String.Join(",", Array.map formatType typs)
```

or collect the free generic type variables:

```
let rec freeVarsAcc typ acc =
    match typ with
    | Array (arg, rank) -> freeVarsAcc arg acc
    | Ptr (_,arg) -> freeVarsAcc arg acc
    | Param _ -> (typ :: acc)
    | Named (con, args) -> Array.fold_right freeVarsAcc args acc
let freeVars typ = freeVarsAcc typ []
```

Defining Partial and Parameterized Active Patterns

Active patterns can also be *partial*. You can recognize a partial pattern by a name such as
(|MulThree|_|) and by the fact that it returns a value of type 'a option for some 'a. For example:

```
let (|MulThree|_|) inp = if inp % 3 = 0 then Some(inp/3) else None
let (|MulSeven|_|) inp = if inp % 7 = 0 then Some(inp/7) else None
```

Finally, active patterns can also be *parameterized*. You can recognize a parameterized
active pattern by the fact that it takes several arguments. For example:

```
let (|MulN|_|) n inp = if inp % n = 0 then Some(inp/n) else None
```

The F# quotation API Microsoft.FSharp.Quotations uses both parameterized and partial
patterns extensively.

Hiding Abstract Syntax Implementations with Active Patterns

Earlier in this chapter you saw the following type that defines an optimized representation of
propositional logic terms using a unique stamp for each syntactically unique term:

```
type Prop = Prop of int
and internal PropRepr =
    | AndRepr of Prop * Prop
    | OrRepr  of Prop * Prop
    | NotRepr of Prop
```

```
| VarRepr of string
| TrueRepr
```

However, what happens if you want to pattern match against values of type Prop? Even if you exposed the representation, then all you would get is an integer, which you would have to look up in an internal table. You can define an active pattern for restoring matching on that data structure, as shown in Listing 9-5.

Listing 9-5. *Extending Listing 9-3 with an Active Pattern for the Optimized Representation*

```
module PropOps =
    ...
    let (|And|Or|Not|Var|True|) prop =
        match table.FromUnique(prop) with
        | AndRepr(x,y) -> And(x,y)
        | OrRepr(x,y) -> Or(x,y)
        | NotRepr(x) -> Not(x)
        | VarRepr(v) -> Var(v)
        | TrueRepr -> True
```

This code defines an active pattern in the auxiliary module PropOps that lets you pattern match against Prop values, despite that they are using optimized unique-integer references "under the hood." For example, you can define a pretty-printer for Prop terms as follows, despite that they are using optimized representations:

```
open PropOps

let rec showProp prec prop =
    let parenIfPrec lim s = if prec < lim then "(" + s + ")" else s
    match prop with
    | Or(p1,p2)  -> parenIfPrec 4 (showProp 4 p1 + " || " + showProp 4 p2)
    | And(p1,p2) -> parenIfPrec 3 (showProp 3 p1 + " && " + showProp 3 p2)
    | Not(p)     -> parenIfPrec 2 ("not "+showProp 1 p)
    | Var(v)     -> v
    | True       -> "T"
```

Likewise, you can define functions to place the representation in various normal forms. For example, the following function computes *negation normal form* (NNF), where all instances of "NOT" nodes have been pushed to the leaves of the representation:

```
let rec nnf sign prop =
    match prop with
    | And(p1,p2) -> if sign then And(nnf sign p1, nnf sign p2)
                    else Or(nnf sign p1, nnf sign p2)
    | Or(p1,p2)  -> if sign then Or(nnf sign p1, nnf sign p2)
                    else And(nnf sign p1, nnf sign p2)
    | Not(p) -> nnf (not sign) p
    | Var(_) | True -> if sign then prop else Not(prop)

let NNF prop = nnf true prop
```

The following demonstrates that two terms have equivalent NNF normal forms:

```
> let t1 = Not(And(Not(Var("x")),Not(Var("y"))));;
val t1 : Prop

> fsi.AddPrinter(showProp);;
> t1;;
val it : Prop = not (not x && not y)

> let t2 = Or(Not(Not(Var("x"))),Var("y"));;
val t2 : Prop

> t2;;
val it : Prop = not (not x) || y

> (t1 = t2);;
val it : bool = false

> NNF t1;;
val it : Prop = x || y

> NNF t2;;
val it : Prop = x || y

> NNF t1 = NNF t2;;
val it : bool = true
```

Embedded Computational Languages with Workflows

In Chapter 3 we introduced a useful notation for generating sequences of data, called *sequence expressions*. For example:

```
> seq { for i in 0 .. 3 -> (i,i*i) };;
val it : seq<int * int> = seq [ (0,0); (1,1); (2,4); (3,9) ]
```

Sequence expressions are used extensively throughout this book. For example, in Chapter 15 we will use sequence expressions for queries that are executed on a database. It turns out that sequence expressions are just one instance of a more general construct called *computation expressions*. These are also called *workflows*, though they bear only a passing similarity to the workflows used to model "business processes." The general form of a computation expression is *builder { comp-expr }*. Table 9-2 shows the primary constructs that can be used within the braces of a computation expression and how these constructs are de-sugared by the F# compiler given a computation expression builder b.

The three most important applications of computation expressions in F# programming are as follows:

- General-purpose programming with sequences, lists, and arrays

- Parallel, asynchronous, and concurrent programming using asynchronous workflows, discussed in detail in Chapter 13

- Database queries, by "quoting" a workflow and translating it to SQL via the .NET LINQ libraries, a technique we'll show how to use in Chapter 15

In this section, we cover briefly how computation expressions work through some simple examples.

Table 9-2. *Constructs in Computation Expressions and Their De-sugaring*

Construct	De-sugared Form
`let! pat = expr in cexpr`	`b.Bind(expr,(fun pat -> «cexpr»))`
`let pat = expr in cexpr`	`b.Let(expr,(fun pat -> «cexpr»))`
`use pat = expr in cexpr`	`b.Using(expr,(fun pat -> «cexpr»))`
`use! pat = expr in cexpr`	`b.Bind(expr,(fun x -> b.Using(x,fun pat -> «cexpr»)))`
`do! expr in cexpr`	`b.Bind(expr,(fun () -> «cexpr»))`
`do expr in cexpr`	`b.Let(expr,(fun () -> «cexpr»))`
`for pat in expr do cexpr`	`b.For(expr,(fun pat -> «cexpr»))`
`while expr do cexpr`	`b.While((fun () -> expr),b.Delay(fun () -> «cexpr»))`
`if expr then cexpr1 else cexpr2`	`if expr then «cexpr1» else «cexpr2»`
`if expr then cexpr`	`if expr then «cexpr» else b.Zero()`
`cexpr1` `cexpr2`	`v.Combine(«cexpr1», b.Delay(fun () -> «cexpr2»))`
`return expr`	`b.Return(expr)`
`return! expr`	`expr`

■Note If you've never seen F# workflows or Haskell monads before, then you may find workflows take a bit of getting used to, since they give you a way to write computations that may behave and execute quite differently than normal programs.

F# WORKFLOWS AND HASKELL MONADS

Computation expressions are the F# equivalent of "monadic syntax" in the programming language Haskell. Monads are a powerful and expressive design pattern and are characterized by a generic type M<'a> combined with at least two operations:

```
bind : M<'a> -> ('a ->  M<'b>) -> M<'b>
return : 'a -> M<'a>
```

These correspond to the primitives let! and return in the F# computation expression syntax. Several other elements of the computation expression syntax can be implemented in terms of these primitives, though the F# de-sugaring process leaves this up to the implementer of the workflow, since sometimes derived operations can have more efficient implementations. Well-behaved monads should satisfy three important rules called the *monad laws*. You can find out more about these at http://www.expert-fsharp.com/Topics/Workflows.

F# uses the terms *computation expression* and *workflow* for three reasons. First, when the designers of F# talked with the designers of Haskell about this, they agreed that the word *monad* is a bit obscure and sounds a little daunting and that using other names might be wise. Second, there are some technical differences: for example, some F# workflows can be combined with imperative programming, utilizing the fact that workflows can have side effects not "tracked" by the F# type system. In Haskell, all side-effecting operations must be "lifted" into the corresponding monad. The Haskell approach has some important advantages: you can know for sure what side effects a function can have by looking at its type. However, it also makes it more difficult to use external libraries from within a computation expression. Third, F# workflows can be reified using F# quotations, giving a way to execute the workflow by alternative means, for example, by translation to SQL. This gives them a different role in practice, since they can be used to model both concrete languages and computational languages.

An Example: Success/Failure Workflows

Perhaps the simplest kind of workflow is one where failure of a computation is made explicit, for example, where each step of the workflow may either *succeed*, by returning a result Some(v), or *fail*, by returning the value None. Such a workflow can be modeled using functions of type unit -> 'a option, that is, functions that might compute a result or might not. In this section, you can assume these functions are pure and terminating, that is, that they have no side effects, raise no exceptions, and always terminate.

Whenever you define a new kind of workflow, it's useful to give a name to the type of values/objects generated by the workflow. In this case let's call them Attempt objects:

```
type Attempt<'a> = (unit -> 'a option)
```

Of course, you can use regular functional programming to start to build Attempt<'a> objects:

```
let succeed x = (fun () -> Some(x)) : Attempt<'a>
let fail     = (fun () -> None) : Attempt<'a>
let runAttempt (a:Attempt<'a>) = a()
```

These conform to the following types:

```
val succeed : 'a -> Attempt<'a>
val fail : Attempt<'a>
val runAttempt : Attempt<'a> -> 'a option
```

However, using only normal F# expressions to build `Attempt` values can be a little tedious and lead to a proliferation of many different functions that stitch together `Attempt` values in straightforward ways. Luckily, as you've seen with sequence expressions, F# comes with predefined syntax for building objects such as `Attempt` values. You can use this syntax with a new type simply by defining a "builder" object that helps stitch together the fragments that make up the computation expression. Here is an example of the kind of object you have to define in order to use workflow syntax with a new type:

```
type AttemptBuilder =
    member Bind : Attempt<'a> * ('a -> Attempt<'b>) -> Attempt<'b>
    member Delay : (unit -> Attempt<'a>) -> Attempt<'a>
    member Let : a * ('a -> Attempt<'a>) -> Attempt<'a>
    member Return : 'a -> Attempt<'a>
```

Typically there is one global instance of each such builder object. For example:

```
let attempt = new AttemptBuilder()
```

```
val attempt : AttemptBuilder
```

We'll show how to define the `AttemptBuilder` type and its members later in the chapter. First we show how you can use the F# syntax for workflows to build `Attempt` objects. You can build `Attempt` values that always succeed:

```
> let alwaysOne = attempt { return 1 };;
val alwaysOne: Attempt<int>

> let alwaysPair = attempt { return (1,"two") };;
val alwaysPair: Attempt<int * string>

> runAttempt alwaysOne;;
val it : int option = Some 1

> runAttempt alwaysPair;;
val it : (int * string) option = Some(1,"two")
```

Note that `Attempt` values such as `alwaysOne` are just functions, so to "run" an `Attempt` value, you just apply it. These correspond to uses of the `succeed` function, as you'll see shortly.

You can also build more interesting Attempt values that check a condition and return different Attempt values on each branch, as shown in the next example:

```
> let failIfBig n = attempt { if n > 1000 then return! fail else return n };;
val failIfBig: int -> Attempt<int>

> runAttempt (failIfBig 999);;
val it : int option = Some 999

> runAttempt (failIfBig 1001);;
val it : int option = None
```

In the previous example, one branch uses return! to return the result of running another Attempt value, and the other uses return to give a single result. These correspond to yield! and yield in sequence expressions.

Next, you can build Attempt values that "sequence together" two Attempt values by running one, getting its result, binding it to a variable, and running the second. This is done by using the syntax form let! *pat* = *expr* that is unique to computation expressions:

```
> let failIfEitherBig (inp1,inp2) =
        attempt { let! n1 = failIfBig inp1
                  let! n2 = failIfBig inp2
                  return (n1,n2) };;
val failIfEitherBig: int * int -> Attempt<int * int>

> runAttempt (failIfEitherBig (999,998));;
val it : (int * int) option = Some(999,998)

> runAttempt (failIfEitherBig (1003,998));;
val it : (int * int) option = None

> runAttempt (failIfEitherBig (999,1001));;
val it : (int * int) option = None
```

Let's take a look at this more closely. First, what does the first let! do? It runs the Attempt value failIfBig inp1, and if this returns None, then the whole computation returns None. If the computation on the right delivers a value (that is, returns Some), then it binds the result to the variable n1 and continues. It is important to note the following for the expression let! n1 = failIfBig inp1:

- The expression on the right (*failIfBig inp1*) has type Attempt<int>.

- The variable on the left (*n1*) is of type int.

This is somewhat similar to a sequence of normal let binding. However, let! also controls whether the rest of the computation will be executed; in the case of the Attempt type, it executes the rest of the computation only when it receives a Some value. Otherwise, it returns None, and the rest of the code is never executed.

You can use normal let bindings in computation expressions. For example:

```
> let sumIfBothSmall (inp1,inp2) =
        attempt { let! n1 = failIfBig inp1
                  let! n2 = failIfBig inp2
                  let sum = n1 + n2
                  return sum };;
```

In this case, the let binding executes exactly as you would expect; it takes the expression n1+n2 and binds its result to the value sum. To summarize, you've seen that computation expressions let you do the following:

- Use an expression-like syntax for building Attempt computations.

- Sequence these computations together using the let! construct.

- Return results from these computations using *return* and *return!*.

- Compute intermediate results using let.

Workflows actually let you do a good deal more than this, as you'll see in the sections that follow.

Defining a Workflow Builder

Listing 9-6 shows the implementation of the workflow builder for Attempt workflows; this is the simplest definition for AttemptBuilder.

Listing 9-6. *Defining a Workflow Builder*

```
let succeed x = (fun () -> Some(x))
let fail      = (fun () -> None)
let runAttempt (a:Attempt<'a>) = a()
let bind p rest = match runAttempt p with None -> fail | Some r -> (rest r)
let delay f = (fun () -> runAttempt (f ()))

type AttemptBuilder() =
    /// Wraps an ordinary value into an Attempt value.
    /// Used to de-sugar uses of 'return' inside computation expressions.
    member b.Return(x) = succeed x

    /// Composes two attempt values. If the first returns Some(x) then the result
    /// is the result of running rest(x).
    /// Used to de-sugar uses of 'let!' inside computation expressions.
    member b.Bind(p,rest) = bind p rest
```

```
    /// Delays the construction of an attempt until just before it is executed
    member b.Delay(f) = delay f

    /// Used to de-sugar uses of 'let' inside computation expressions.
    member b.Let(p,rest) : Attempt<'a> = rest p
let attempt = new AttemptBuilder()
```

The inferred types here are as follows:

```
type AttemptBuilder =
    new : unit -> AttemptBuilder
    member Bind   : Attempt<'a> * ('a -> Attempt<'b>) -> Attempt<'b>
    member Delay  : (unit -> Attempt<'a>) -> Attempt<'a>
    member Let    : 'a * ('a -> Attempt<'b>) -> Attempt<'b>
    member Return : 'a -> Attempt<'a>

val attempt : AttemptBuilder
```

F# implements workflows by "de-sugaring" computation expressions using a builder. For example, given the previous AttemptBuilder, the following workflow:

```
attempt { let! n1 = failIfBig inp1
          let! n2 = failIfBig inp2
          let sum = n1 + n2
          return sum };;
```

de-sugars to this:

```
attempt.Bind( failIfBig inp1,(fun n1 ->
   attempt.Bind(failIfBig inp2,(fun n2 ->
      attempt.Let(n1 + n2,(fun sum ->
         attempt.Return(sum)))))))
```

One purpose of the F# workflow syntax is to make sure you don't have to write this sort of thing by hand.

The de-sugaring of the workflow syntax is implemented by the F# compiler. Table 9-3 shows some of the typical signatures that a workflow builder needs to implement.

Table 9-3. *Some Typical Workflow Builder Members As Required by the F# Compiler*

Member	Description
`member Bind : M<'a> * ('a -> M<'b>) -> M<'b>`	Required member. Used to de-sugar let! and do! within computation expressions.
`member Return : 'a -> M<'a>`	Required member. Used to de-sugar return within computation expressions.

Table 9-3. *Some Typical Workflow Builder Members As Required by the F# Compiler*

Member	Description
`member Let : 'a * ('a -> M<'b>) -> M<'b>`	Required member. Used to de-sugar `let` and `do` within computation expressions.
`member Delay : (unit -> M<'a>) -> M<'a>`	Required member. Used to ensure side effects within a computation expression are performed when expected.
`member For : seq<'a> * ('a -> M<'b>) -> M<'b>`	Optional member. Used to de-sugar `for ... do ...` within computation expressions. `M<'b>` can optionally be `M<unit>`.
`member While : (unit -> bool) * M<'a> -> M<'a>`	Optional member. Used to de-sugar `while ... do ...` within computation expressions. `M<'a>` may optionally be `M<unit>`.
`member Using : 'a * ('a -> M<'a>) -> M<'a> when 'a :> IDisposable`	Optional member. Used to de-sugar `use` bindings within computation expressions.
`member Combine : M<'a> * M<'a> -> M<'a>`	Optional member. Used to de-sugar sequencing within computation expressions. The first `M<'a>` may optionally be `M<unit>`.
`member Zero : unit -> M<'a>`	Optional member. Used to de-sugar empty `else` branches of `if`/`then` constructs within computation expressions.

Most of the elements of a workflow builder are usually implemented in terms of simpler primitives. For example, let's assume you're defining a workflow builder for some type `M<'a>` and you already have implementations of functions `bindM` and `returnM` with the following types:

```
val bindM : M<'a> -> ('a -> M<'b>) -> M<'b>
val returnM : 'a -> M<'a>
```

Then you can implement `Let` and `Delay` using the following functions:

```
let letM v f = bindM (returnM v) f
let delayM f = bindM (returnM ()) f
```

You can now define an overall builder in terms of all four functions:

```
type MBuilder() =
    member b.Return(x)    = returnM x
    member b.Bind(v,f)    = bindM p f
    member b.Delay(f)     = delayM f
    member b.Let(v,f)     = letM v f
```

However, Let and Delay may also have more efficient direct implementations, which is why F# does not insert the previous implementations automatically.

Note You can find out more about implementing workflow builders in terms of simpler primitives at http://www.expert-fsharp.com/Topics/Workflows.

Workflows and "Untamed" Side Effects

It is possible, and in some cases even common, to define workflows that cause side effects. For example, you can use printfn in the middle of an Attempt workflow:

```
let sumIfBothSmall (inp1,inp2) =
    attempt { let! n1 = failIfBig inp1
              do printfn "Hey, n1 was small!"
              let! n2 = failIfBig inp2
              do printfn "n2 was also small!"
              let sum = n1 + n2
              return sum }
```

Here's what happens when you call this function:

```
> runAttempt(sumIfBothSmall (999,999));;
Hey, n1 was small!
n2 was also small!
val it : int option = Some 1998

> runAttempt(sumIfBothSmall (999,1003));;
Hey, n1 was small!
val it : int option = None
```

Side effects in workflows must be used with care, particularly because workflows are typically used to construct "delayed" or "on-demand" computations. In the previous example, printing is a fairly benign side effect. More significant side effects such as mutable state can also be sensibly combined with some kinds of workflows, though take care to ensure you understand how the side effect will interact with the particular kind of workflow you're using. For example, here we allocate a piece of mutable state that is local to the Attempt workflow, and this is used to accumulate the sum:

```
let sumIfBothSmall (inp1,inp2) =
    attempt { let sum = ref 0
              let! n1 = failIfBig inp1
              do sum := sum.Value + n1
              let! n2 = failIfBig inp2
              do sum := sum.Value + n2
              return sum.Value }
```

We leave it as an exercise for you to examine the de-sugaring of this workflow to see that the mutable reference is indeed local, in the sense that it doesn't escape the overall computation, and that different executions of the same workflow will use different reference cells.

As mentioned, workflows are nearly always delayed computations. As you saw in Chapter 4, delayed computations and side effects can interact. For this reason, the de-sugaring of workflow syntax inserts a Delay operation around the entire workflow:

```
let printThenSeven =
      attempt { do printf "starting..."
                return 3 + 4 }
```

de-sugars to:

```
      attempt.Delay(fun () ->
          printf "starting..."
          attempt.Return(3+4))
```

This means that "starting . . ." will be printed each time the printThenSeven attempt object is executed.

Example: Probabilistic Workflows

Workflows provide a fascinating way to embed a range of nontrivial, "nonstandard" computations into F#. To give you a feel for this, in this section we define a *probabilistic* workflow. That is, instead of writing expressions to compute, say, integers, we instead write expressions that compute *distributions* of integers. This case study is based on a paper by Ramsey and Pfeffer from 2002.

For the purposes of this section, we are interested in distributions over discrete domains characterized by three things:

- We want to be able to "sample" from a distribution (for example, sample an integer or a coin flip).

- We want to compute the "support" of a distribution, that is, a set of values where all elements outside the set have zero chance of being sampled.

- We want to compute the "expectation" of a function over the distribution. For example, we can compute the probability of selecting element A by evaluating the expectation of the function (fun x -> if x = A then 1.0 else 0.0).

We can model our notion of a distribution by abstract objects. Listing 9-7 shows the definition of a type of distribution values and an implementation of the basic primitives always and coinFlip, which help build distributions.

Listing 9-7. *Implementing Probabilistic Modeling Using Computation Expressions*

```
type Distribution<'a> =
    abstract Sample : 'a
    abstract Support : Set<'a>
    abstract Expectation: ('a -> float) -> float

let always x =
    { new Distribution<'a> with
        member d.Sample = x
        member d.Support = Set.singleton x
        member d.Expectation(H) = H(x) }

let rnd = System.Random()

let coinFlip (p:float) (d1:Distribution<'a>) (d2:Distribution<'a>) =
    if p < 0.0 || p > 1.0 then failwith "invalid probability in coinFlip"
    { new Distribution<'a> with
        member d.Sample =
            if rnd.NextDouble() < p then d1.Sample else d2.Sample
        member d.Support = Set.Union(d1.Support,d2.Support)
        member d.Expectation(H) =
            p * d1.Expectation(H) + (1.0-p) * d2.Expectation(H) }
```

The types of these primitives are as follows:

```
type Distribution<'a> =
    abstract Expectation: ('a -> float) -> float
    abstract Sample : 'a
    abstract Support : Set<'a>

val always: 'a -> Distribution<'a>
val coinFlip : float -> Distribution<'a> -> Distribution<'a> -> Distribution<'a>
```

The simplest distribution is always x; this is a distribution that always samples to the same value. Its expectation and support are easy to calculate. The expectation of a function H is just H applied to the value, and the support is just a set containing the single value x. The next distribution defined is coinFlip, which is a distribution that models the ability to choose between two outcomes.

Listing 9-8 shows how you can define a workflow builder for distribution objects.

Listing 9-8. *Defining a Builder for Probabilistic Modeling Using Computation Expressions*

```
let bind (dist:Distribution<'a>) (k: 'a -> Distribution<'b>) =
    { new Distribution<'b> with
        member d.Sample = (k(dist.Sample)).Sample
        member d.Support = Set.Union(dist.Support.Map(fun d -> (k d).Support))
        member d.Expectation(H) = dist.Expectation(fun x -> (k x).Expectation(H)) }

type DistributionBuilder() =
    member x.Delay(f) = bind (always ()) f
    member x.Let(v,f) = bind (always v) f
    member x.Bind(d,f) = bind d f
    member x.Return(x) = always x

let dist = new DistributionBuilder()
```

The types of these primitives are as follows:

```
val bind: Distribution<'a> -> ('a -> Distribution<'b>) -> Distribution<'b>
val dist: DistributionBuilder
```

Listing 9-8 shows the all-important bind primitive; this combines two distributions, using the sample from the first to guide the sample from the second. The support and expectation are calculated by taking the support from the first and "splaying" it over the support of the second. The expectation is computed by using the first distribution to compute the expectation of a function derived from the second. These are standard results in probability theory and are the basic machinery you need to get going with some interesting modeling.

Before we begin using workflow syntax, we define two derived functions to compute distributions. Listing 9-9 shows the additional derived operations for distribution objects that we will use later in this example.

Listing 9-9. *Defining the Derived Operations for Probabilistic Modeling Using Computation Expressions*

```
let weightedCases (inp: ('a * float) list) =
    let rec coinFlips w l =
        match l with
        | []         -> failwith "no coinFlips"
        | [(d,_)]    -> always d
        | (d,p)::rest -> coinFlip (p/(1.0-w)) (always d) (coinFlips (w+p) rest)
    coinFlips 0.0 inp

let countedCases inp =
    let total = List.sumByInt (fun (_,v) -> v) inp
    weightedCases (inp.Map (fun (x,v) -> (x,(float v/float total))))
```

The two functions, weightedCases and countedCases, build distributions from the weighted selection of a finite number of cases. The types are as follows:

```
val weightedCases : ('a * float) list -> Distribution<'a>
val countedCases : ('a * int) list -> Distribution<'a>
```

For example, here is the distribution of outcomes on a fair European roulette wheel:

```
type Outcome = Even | Odd | Zero
let roulette = countedCases [ Even,18; Odd,18; Zero,1]
```

We can now use sampling to draw from this distribution:

```
> roulette.Sample;;
val it:  Outcome = Even

> roulette.Sample;;
val it:  Outcome = Odd
```

And we can compute the expected payout of a $5 bet on Even, where we would get a $10 return:

```
> roulette.Expectation (function Even -> 10.0 | Odd -> 0.0 | Zero -> 0.0);;
val it:  float = 4.864864865
```

Now let's model another scenario. Let's say you have a traffic light with the following probability distribution for showing red/yellow/green:

```
type Light =
    | Red
    | Green
    | Yellow

let trafficLightD = weightedCases [ Red,0.50; Yellow,0.10; Green, 0.40 ]
```

A driver is defined by his/her behavior with respect to a traffic light. For example, a cautious driver is highly likely to brake on a yellow light and always stops on a red:

```
type Action = Stop | Drive

let cautiousDriver light =
    dist { match light with
            | Red -> return Stop
            | Yellow -> return! weightedCases [ Stop, 0.9; Drive, 0.1 ]
            | Green -> return Drive }
```

An aggressive driver is unlikely to brake on yellow and may even go through a red light:

```
let aggressiveDriver light =
    dist { match light with
            | Red     -> return! weightedCases [ Stop, 0.9; Drive, 0.1 ]
            | Yellow -> return! weightedCases [ Stop, 0.1; Drive, 0.9 ]
            | Green  -> return Drive }
```

The following gives the value of the light showing in the other direction:

```
let otherLight light =
    match light with
    | Red -> Green
    | Yellow -> Red
    | Green -> Red
```

You can now model the probability of a crash between two drivers given a traffic light. Assume there is a 10 percent chance that two drivers going through the intersection will avoid a crash:

```
type CrashResult = Crash | NoCrash

let crash(driverOneD,driverTwoD,lightD) =
    dist { // Sample from the traffic light
            let! light = lightD

            // Sample the first driver's behavior given the traffic light
            let! driverOne = driverOneD light

            // Sample the second driver's behavior given the traffic light
            let! driverTwo = driverTwoD (otherLight light)

            // Work out the probability of a crash
            match driverOne, driverTwo with
              | Drive,Drive -> return! weightedCases [ Crash, 0.9; NoCrash, 0.1 ]
              | _ -> return NoCrash }
```

You can now instantiate the model to a cautious/aggressive driver pair, sample the overall model, and compute the overall expectation of a crash as approximately 3.7 percent:

```
> let model = crash(cautiousDriver,aggressiveDriver,trafficLightD);;
val model : Distribution<CrashResult>

> model.Sample;;
val it : CrashResult = NoCrash
...
> model.Sample;;
val it : CrashResult = Crash

> model.Expectation(function Crash -> 1.0 | NoCrash -> 0.0);;
val it : float = 0.0369
```

Note In this section, we showed how to define a simplistic embedded *computational probabilistic modeling language*. There are many more efficient and sophisticated techniques to apply to the description, evaluation, and analysis probabilistic models than those shown here, and you can make the implementation of the primitives shown here more efficient by being more careful about the underlying computational representations.

Combining Workflows and Resources

In some situations, workflows can sensibly make use of transient resources such as files. The tricky thing is that you still want to be careful about closing and "disposing" of resources when the workflow is complete or when it is no longer being used. For this reason, the workflow type must be carefully designed to correctly dispose of resources halfway through a computation if necessary. Sequence expressions are a great example where this is useful. For example, the following sequence expression opens a file and reads lines on demand:

```
let linesOfFile(fileName) =
    seq { use textReader = System.IO.File.OpenText(fileName)
          while not textReader.EndOfStream do
              yield textReader.ReadLine() }
```

We discussed the construct use pat = expr in Chapter 8. As shown in Table 9-2, you can also use this construct within workflows. In this case, the use pat = expr construct de-sugars into a call to seq.Using. In the case of sequence expressions, this function is carefully implemented to ensure that textReader is kept open for the duration of the process of reading from the file. Furthermore, the Dispose function on each generated IEnumerator object for a sequence calls the textReader.Dispose() method. This ensures that the file is closed even if we enumerate only half of the lines in the file. Workflows thus allow you to scope the lifetime of a resource over a delayed computation.

Recursive Workflow Expressions

Like functions, workflow expressions can be defined recursively. Many of the best examples are generative sequences. For example:

```
let rnd = System.Random()

let rec randomWalk k =
    seq { yield k
          yield! randomWalk (k + rnd.NextDouble() - 0.5) }
```

```
> randomWalk 10.0;;
val it: seq<float> = seq [10.0; 10.23817784; 9.956430122; 10.18110362; ...]

> randomWalk 10.0;;
val it : seq<float> = seq [10.0; 10.19761089; 10.26774703; 9.888072922; ...]
```

Using F# Reflection

The final topics we cover in this chapter are *F# quotations*, which provide a way to get at a representation of F# expressions as abstract syntax trees, and *reflection*, which lets you get at representations of assemblies, type definitions, and member signatures. Let's look at reflection first.

Reflecting on Types

One of the simplest uses of reflection is to access the representation of types and generic type variables using the `typeof` operator. For example, `typeof<int>` and `typeof<'a>` are both expressions that generate values of type `System.Type`. Given a `System.Type` value, you can use the .NET APIs to access the `System.Reflection.Assembly` value that represents the .NET assembly that contains the definition of the type (.NET assemblies are described in Chapter 7). You can also access other types in the `System.Reflection` namespace such as `MethodInfo`, `PropertyInfo`, `MemberInfo`, and `ConstructorInfo`. For example, here we examine the names associated with some common types:

```
> let intType = typeof<int>;;
val intType : System.Type

> intType.FullName;;
val it : string = "System.Int32"

> intType.AssemblyQualifiedName;;
val it : string = "System.Int32, mscorlib, Version=2.0.0.0, Culture=neutral,
PublicKeyToken=b77a5c561934e089"

> let intListType = typeof<int list>;;
val intListType : System.Type

> intListType.FullName;;
val it : string = "Microsoft.FSharp.Collections.List`1[[System.Int32, mscorlib,
Version=2.0.0.0, Culture=neutral, PublicKeyToken=b77a5c561934e089]]"
```

■Note More information on the functionality provided by .NET Reflection is available at `http://www.expert-fsharp.com/Topics/Reflection`.

Schema Compilation by Reflecting on Types

The F# library includes the namespace `Microsoft.FSharp.Reflection`, which contains types and functions that extend the functionality of the `System.Reflection` namespace of .NET. These types and functions are described in Chapter 10.

You can use the combination of .NET and F# reflection to provide generic implementations of language-related transformations. In this section, we give one example of this powerful technique. Listing 9-10 shows the definition of a *generic schema reader compiler*, where a data schema is described using F# types and the schema compiler helps convert untyped data from text files into this data schema.

Listing 9-10. *Using Types and Attributes to Guide Dynamic Schema Compilation*

```
open System
open System.IO
open Microsoft.FSharp.Reflection

type ColumnAttribute(col:int) =
    inherit Attribute()
    member x.Column = col


/// SchemaReader builds an object that automatically transforms lines of text
/// files in comma-separated form into instances of the given type 'schema.
/// 'schema must be an F# record type where each field is attributed with a
/// ColumnAttribute attribute, indicating which column of the data the record
/// field is drawn from. This simple version of the reader understands
/// integer, string and DateTime values in the CSV format.
type SchemaReader<'schema>() =

    // Grab the object for the type that describes the schema
    let schemaType = typeof<'schema>

    // Grab the fields from that type
    let fields =
        match Type.GetInfo(schemaType) with
        | RecordType(fields) ->  fields
        | _ ->  failwithf "this schema compiler expects a record type"

    // For each field find the ColumnAttribute and compute a function
    // to build a value for the field
    let schema =
        fields |> List.mapi (fun fldIdx (fieldName,fieldType) ->
            let fieldInfo = schemaType.GetProperty(fieldName)
            let fieldConverter =
                match fieldType with
                | ty when ty = typeof<string>   -> (fun (s:string) -> box s)
                | ty when ty = typeof<int>       -> (System.Int32.Parse >> box)
                | ty when ty = typeof<DateTime> -> (System.DateTime.Parse >> box)
                | _ -> failwithf "Unknown primitive type %A" fieldType
```

```fsharp
        let attrib =
            match fieldInfo.GetCustomAttributes(typeof<ColumnAttribute>,
                                        false) with
            | [| (:? ColumnAttribute as attrib) |] ->   attrib
            | _ -> failwithf "No column attribute found on field %s" fieldName
        (fldIdx,fieldName, attrib.Column, fieldConverter))
    |> List.to_array

// Compute the permutation defined by the ColumnAttributes indexes
let columnToFldIdxPermutation =
  Permutation(schema.Length,
            schema |> Array.map (fun (fldIdx,_,colIdx,_) -> (colIdx,fldIdx)))

// Drop the parts of the schema we don't need
let schema =
  schema |> Array.map (fun (_,fldName,_ ,fldConv) -> (fldName,fldConv))

// Compute a function to build instances of the schema type. This uses an
// F# library function.
let objectBuilder = Reflection.Value.GetRecordConstructor(schemaType)

// OK, now we're ready to implement a line reader
member reader.ReadLine(textReader: TextReader) =
    let line = textReader.ReadLine()
    let words = line.Split([|',','|]) |> Array.map(fun s -> s.Trim())
    if words.Length <> schema.Length then
        failwith "unexpected number of columns in line %s" line
    let words = words |> Array.permute columnToFldIdxPermutation

    let convertColumn colText (fieldName, fieldConverter) =
       try fieldConverter colText
       with e ->
           failwithf "error converting '%s' to field '%s'" colText fieldName

    let obj = objectBuilder (Array.map2 convertColumn words schema)

    // OK, now we know we've dynamically built an object of the right type
    unbox<'schema>(obj)

// OK, this read an entire file
member reader.ReadFile(file) =
    seq { use textReader = File.OpenText(file)
        while not textReader.EndOfStream do
            yield reader.ReadLine(textReader) }
```

The type of the SchemaReader is simple:

```
type SchemaReader<'schema> =
    new : unit -> SchemaReader<'schema>
    member ReadFile : string -> seq<'schema>
    member ReadLine : System.IO.TextReader -> 'schema
```

First we show how the SchemaReader is used in practice. Let's say you have a text file containing lines such as this:

```
Steve, 12 March 2007, Cheddar
Sally, 18 Feb 2007, Brie
...
```

Now it's reasonable to want to convert this data to a typed data representation. You can do this simply by defining an appropriate record type along with enough information to indicate how the data in the file maps into this type. This information is expressed using *custom attributes*, which are a way to add extra "meta-information" to assembly, type, member, property, and parameter definitions. Each custom attribute is specified as an instance of a typed object, here ColumnAttribute, defined in Listing 9-10. The suffix Attribute can be dropped when using the custom attribute.

```
type CheeseClub =
    { [<Column(0)>] Name            : string
      [<Column(2)>] FavouriteCheese : string
      [<Column(1)>] LastAttendance  : System.DateTime }
```

You can now instantiate the SchemaReader type and use it to read the data from the file into this typed format:

```
> let reader = new SchemaReader<CheeseClub>();;
val reader : SchemaReader<CheeseClub>

> fsi.AddPrinter(fun (c:System.DateTime) -> c.ToString());;
val it : unit = ()

> System.IO.File.WriteAllLines("data.txt", [| "Steve, 12/03/2007, Cheddar";
                                              "Sally, 18/02/2007, Brie"; |]);;
val it : unit = ()

> reader.ReadFile("data.txt");;
val it : seq<CheeseClub>
 = seq
    [{Name = "Steve";
      FavouriteCheese = "Cheddar";
      LastAttendance = 12/03/2007 00:00:00;};
     {Name = "Sally";
      FavouriteCheese = "Brie";
      LastAttendance = 18/02/2007 00:00:00;}]
```

There is something somewhat magical about this; you have been able to build a layer that has automatically done the "impedance matching" between the untyped world of a text file format into the typed world of F# programming. Amazingly, the SchemaReader type itself is only about 50 lines of code. The comments in Listing 9-10 show the basic steps being performed. The essential features of this technique are as follows:

1. The schema information is passed to the SchemaReader as a type variable. The SchemaReader then uses the typeof operator to extract a System.Type representation of the schema type.

2. The information needed to drive the transformation process comes from custom attributes. Extra information could also be supplied to the constructor of the SchemaReader type if necessary.

3. The let bindings of the SchemaReader type are effectively a form of precomputation (they can also be seen as a form of compilation).They precompute as much information as possible given the schema. For example, the section analyzes the fields of the schema type and computes functions for creating objects of the field types. It also computes the permutation from the text file columns to the record fields, using the type Microsoft. FSharp.Collections.Permutation.

4. The data objects are ultimately constructed using reflection functions, in this case a function computed by Microsoft.FSharp.Reflection.Value.GetRecordConstructor or primitive values parsed using System.Int32.Parse and similar functions. This and other functions for creating F# objects dynamically are in the Microsoft.FSharp.Reflection library. Other functions for creating other .NET objects dynamically are in the System. Reflection library.

5. The member bindings of SchemaReader interpret the residue of the precomputation stage, in this case using the information and computed functions to process the results of splitting the text of a line.

This technique has many potential applications and has been used for CSV file reading and database schema generation.

Using F# Quotations

The other side to reflective meta-programming in F# is *quotations*. These allow you to reflect over expressions in much the same way you've been reflecting over types in the previous section. It's simple to get going with F# quotations; you simply open the appropriate modules and surround an expression with <@ . . . @> symbols:

```
> open Microsoft.FSharp.Quotations;;
> open Microsoft.FSharp.Quotations.Typed;;
> let oneExpr = <@ 1 @>;;
val oneExpr : Expr<int>

> oneExpr;;
val it : Expr<int> = <@ (Int32 1) @>
```

```
> let plusExpr = <@ 1 + 1 @>;;
val plusExpr : Expr<int>

> plusExpr;;
val it : Expr<int>
  = <@ Microsoft.FSharp.Core.Operators.op_Addition (Int32 1) (Int32 1) @>
```

You can see here that the act of quoting an expression gives you the expression back as data. Those familiar with Lisp or Scheme will know a version of this in the form of Lisp quotations, and those familiar with C# 3.0 will find it familiar, since C# uses similar mechanisms for its lambda expressions. F# quotations are distinctive partly because they are *typed* (like C# lambda expressions) and because the functional, expression-based nature of F# means that so much of the language can be quoted and manipulated relatively easily.

We use quotations in only a few places in this book. In Chapter 15, we utilize an F# library that converts F# quotations to SQL via the .NET LINQ library. The essence of the way this converter works is summarized by the following type:

```
val SQL : Expr<'a> -> 'a
```

This function effectively acts as an evaluator for quotations. It will successfully evaluate only a limited range of quotations (a runtime error may occur if the expression can't be converted to SQL).

Another application of quotations is to convert F# code to JavaScript to let you run it in web browsers. This technique is used by the F# Web Tools, described in Chapter 14. This might be implemented by a function with a type such as the following:

```
val CompileToJavaScript : Expr<'a> -> string
```

WHAT ARE F# QUOTATIONS FOR?

The primary rationale for F# quotations is to allow fragments of F# syntax to be executed "by alternative means," for example, as an SQL query via LINQ or by running on another device such as a GPU or as JavaScript in a client-side web browser. F# aims to leverage "heavy-hitting" external components that map subsets of functional programs to other execution machinery. Another example use could be executing a subset of F# array code by dynamic generation of Fortran code and invoking a high-performance vectorizing Fortran compiler. The generated DLL would be loaded and invoked dynamically.

This effectively means you can convert from a *computational* representation of a language (for example, regular F# functions and F# workflow expressions) to an *abstract syntax* representation of the same language. This is a powerful technique, because it lets you prototype using a computational model of the language (for example, sampling from a distribution or running queries against local data) and then switch to a more concrete abstract syntax representation of the same programs in order to analyze, execute, print, or compile those programs in other ways.

Example: Using F# Quotations for Error Estimation

Listing 9-11 shows a prototypical use of quotations, in this case to perform error estimation on F# arithmetic expressions.

Listing 9-11. *Error Analysis on F# Expressions Implemented with F# Quotations*

```
open Microsoft.FSharp.Quotations
open Microsoft.FSharp.Quotations.Typed
open Microsoft.FSharp.Quotations.Raw

type Error = Err of float

let rec errorEstimateAux t (env : Map<_,_>) =

    match t with
    | GenericTopDefnApp <@@ (+) @@> (tyargs,[xt;yt]) ->
        let x,Err(xerr) = errorEstimateAux xt env
        let y,Err(yerr) = errorEstimateAux yt env
        (x+y,Err(xerr+yerr))

    | GenericTopDefnApp <@@ (-) @@> (tyargs,[xt;yt]) ->
        let x,Err(xerr) = errorEstimateAux xt env
        let y,Err(yerr) = errorEstimateAux yt env
        (x-y,Err(xerr+yerr))

    | GenericTopDefnApp <@@ ( * ) @@> (tyargs,[xt;yt]) ->
        let x,Err(xerr) = errorEstimateAux xt env
        let y,Err(yerr) = errorEstimateAux yt env
        (x*y,Err(xerr*abs(x)+yerr*abs(y)+xerr*yerr))

    | GenericTopDefnApp <@@ ( / ) @@> (tyargs,[xt;yt]) ->
        let x,Err(xerr) = errorEstimateAux xt env
        let y,Err(yerr) = errorEstimateAux yt env
        (x/y,Err(xerr*abs(x)+abs(1.0/y)/yerr+xerr/yerr))

    | GenericTopDefnApp <@@ abs @@> (tyargs,[xt]) ->
        let x,Err(xerr) = errorEstimateAux xt env
        (abs(x),Err(xerr))

    | Let((var,vet), bodyt) ->
        let varv,verr = errorEstimateAux vet env
        errorEstimateAux bodyt (env.Add(var.Name,(varv,verr)))

    | App(ResolvedTopDefnUse(info,Lambda(v,body)),arg) ->
        errorEstimateAux  (MkLet((v,arg),body)) env
```

```
    | Var(x) -> env.[x]

    | Double(n) -> (n,Err(0.0))

    | _ -> failwithf "unrecognized term: %A" t

let rec errorEstimateRaw (t : Expr) =
    match t with
    | Lambda(x,t) ->
        (fun xv -> errorEstimateAux t (Map.of_seq [(x.Name,xv)]))
    | ResolvedTopDefnUse(info,body) ->
        errorEstimateRaw body
    | _ -> failwithf "unrecognized term: %A - expected a lambda" t

let errorEstimate (t : Expr<float -> float>) = errorEstimateRaw t.Raw
```

The inferred types of the functions are as follows:

```
val errorEstimateAux : Expr -> Map<ExprVarName,(float * Error)> -> float * Error
val errorEstimateRaw : Expr -> (float * Error -> float * Error)
val errorEstimate : Expr<(float -> float)> -> (float * Error -> float * Error)
```

That is, errorEstimate is a function that takes an expression for a float -> float function and returns a function value of type float * Error -> float * Error. Let's see it in action, though. First we define the prefix function (±) and a pretty-printer for float * Error pairs, here using the Unicode symbol for error bounds on a value:

```
> let (±) x = Err(x);;
val ± : float -> Error

> fsi.AddPrinter (fun (x:float,Err(v)) -> sprintf "%g±%g" x v);;
val it : unit = ()

> errorEstimate <@ fun x -> x+2.0*x+3.0*x*x @> (1.0,±0.1);;
val it : float * Error = 6±0.61

> errorEstimate <@ fun x -> let y = x + x in y*y + 2.0 @> (1.0,±0.1);;
val it : float * Error = 6±0.84
```

The key aspects of the implementation of errorEstimate are as follows:

- The `errorEstimate` function converts the input expression to a raw expression, which is an untyped abstract syntax representation of the expression designed for further processing. It then calls `errorEstimateRaw`. Traversals are generally much easier to perform using raw terms.

- The `errorEstimateRaw` function then checks that the expression given is a lambda expression, using the active pattern `Lambda` provided by the `Microsoft.FSharp.Quotations.Raw` module.

- The `errorEstimateRaw` function then calls the auxiliary function `errorEstimateAux`. This function keeps track of a mapping from variables to value/error estimate pairs. It recursively analyzes the expression looking for +, -, *, /, and `abs` operations. These are all overloaded operators, and hence called *generic functions* in F# terminology, so it uses the active pattern `GenericTopDefnApp` to detect applications of these operators. At each point it performs the appropriate error estimation.

- For variables, the environment map `env` is consulted. For constants, the error is zero.

- Two additional cases are covered in `errorEstimateAux` and `errorEstimateRaw`. The `Let` pattern allows you to include expressions of the form `let x = e1 in e2` in the subset accepted by the quotation analyzer. The `ResolvedTopDefnUse` pattern case allows you to perform analyses on some function calls, as you'll see next.

Resolving Top Definitions

One of the problems with meta-programming with explicit `<@ ... @>` quotation marks alone is that you can't analyze very large programs because the entire expression to be analyzed must be delimited by these markers. This is solved in F# by allowing you to tag top-level `member` and `let` bindings as "reflected." This ensures that their definition is persisted to a table attached to their compiled DLL or EXE. These functions can also be executed as normal F# code. For example, here is a function whose definition will be persisted:

```
[<ReflectedDefinition>]
let poly x = x+2.0*x+3.0/(x*x)
```

The definitions can be retrieved using the `ResolvedTopDefnUse` active pattern, as shown in Listing 9-11. You can now use this function in a regular `<@ ... @>` quotation and thus analyze it for errors:

```
> errorEstimate <@ poly @> (3.0,±0.1);;
val it : float * Error = 9.33333±0.582149

> errorEstimate <@ poly @> (30271.3,±0.0001);;
val it : float * Error = 90813.9±3.02723
```

Note You can find more information on using F# quotations for meta-programming at `http://www.expert-fsharp.com/Topics/Quotations`.

Summary

In this chapter, we covered key topics in a programming paradigm that is central to F#, called *language-oriented programming*. We covered one particular concrete language format, XML, and then looked at abstracted representations of languages using abstract syntax trees. You also saw some techniques to traverse abstract syntax trees. These language representation techniques give powerful ways to manipulate concrete and abstract syntax fragments, which form a key part of modern programming.

You then saw two language representation techniques that are more tightly coupled to F#: the F# workflow syntax, which is useful for embedded computational languages involving sequencing, and quotations, which let you give an "alternative" meaning to existing F# program fragments. Along the way, we also touched on reflection and its use to mediate between typed and untyped representations.

That completes our look at F# as a language and the major programming paradigms it covers. In the following chapters, we look at the libraries that come with F# and the .NET Framework, and then move on to more applied topics, beginning with GUI programming using the .NET Windows Forms library.

CHAPTER 10

Using the F# and .NET Libraries

F# and the .NET Framework offer a rich set of libraries for functional and imperative programming. In this chapter, we step back and give a broader overview of the .NET and F# libraries.

Many of the types and namespaces described here are also covered elsewhere in this book. In these cases, we simply reference the relevant chapter.

A High-Level Overview

One way to get a quick overview of the .NET Framework and the F# library is to simply look at the primary DLLs and namespaces contained in them. Recall from Chapters 2 and 7 that DLLs correspond to the *physical* organization of libraries and that namespaces and types give the *logical* organization of a naming hierarchy. Let's look at the physical organization first. The types and functions we cover in this chapter are drawn from the DLLs in Table 10-1.

Table 10-1. *DLLs Containing the Library Constructs Referred to in This Chapter*

DLL Name	Notes
mscorlib.dll	Minimal system constructs including the types in the System namespace.
System.dll	Additional commonly used constructs in namespaces such as System and System.Text.
System.XML.dll	See the corresponding namespace in Table 10-2.
System.Data.dll	See the corresponding namespace in Table 10-2.
System.Drawing.dll	See the corresponding namespace in Table 10-2.
System.Web.dll	See the corresponding namespace in Table 10-2.
System.Windows.Forms.dll	See the corresponding namespace in Table 10-2.
System.Query.dll	The foundation types for LINQ. From .NET 3.5 onward.

Table 10-1. *DLLs Containing the Library Constructs Referred to in This Chapter (Continued)*

DLL Name	Notes
FSharp.Core.dll	Minimal constructs for F# assemblies. Called fslib.dll in earlier versions of F#.
FSharp.Compatibility.dll	Called mllib.dll in earlier versions of F#.

All of these DLLs except System.Query.dll are referenced automatically from F# projects. To reference additional DLLs, you can embed a reference directly into your source code. For example:

```
#I @"C:\Program Files\Reference Assemblies\Microsoft\Framework\v3.5;;
#r "System.Query.dll";;
```

The first line specifies an include path, the equivalent of the -I command-line option for the F# compiler. The second line specifies a DLL reference, the equivalent of the -r command-line option. We described these in Chapter 7. If you're using Visual Studio, you can adjust the project property settings for your project.

■**Note** Hundreds of high-quality frameworks and libraries are available for .NET, and more are appearing all the time. For space reasons, this chapter covers only the .NET libraries and frameworks listed in Table 10-1. In the "Some Other .NET Libraries" section of this chapter, we list some libraries you might find interesting, and you can see more resources for finding .NET libraries at http://www.expert-fsharp/Topics/Libraries.

Namespaces from the .NET Framework

Table 10-2 shows the primary namespaces in .NET Framework DLLs from Table 10-1. In some cases, parts of these libraries are covered elsewhere in this book. We've noted these cases in the table. For example, Chapter 4 introduced portions of the .NET I/O library from the System.IO namespace.

Table 10-2. *Namespaces in the DLLs from Table 10-1, with MSDN Descriptions*

Namespace	Description
System	Types and methods that define commonly used value and reference data types, events and event handlers, interfaces, attributes, and processing exceptions, supporting data-type conversions, mathematics, application environment management, and runtime supervision of managed and unmanaged applications. See Chapter 3 for many of the basic types in this namespace.
System.CodeDom	Types that can be used to represent the elements and structure of a source code document. Not covered in this book.

Table 10-2. *Namespaces in the DLLs from Table 10-1, with MSDN Descriptions (Continued)*

Namespace	Description
System.Collections	Types that define various nongeneric collections of objects, such as lists, queues, and bit arrays. Partially covered in the section "Using Further F# and .NET Data Structures" later in this chapter.
System.Collections.Generic	Types that define generic collections. See Chapter 4 and the section "Using Further F# and .NET Data Structures" later in this chapter.
System.ComponentModel	Types that are used to implement the runtime and design-time behavior of components and controls. See Chapter 11.
System.Configuration	Types that provide the programming model for handling configuration data. See Chapter 15.
System.Data	Types that represent the ADO.NET database access architecture. See Chapter 15.
System.Diagnostics	Types that allow you to interact with system processes, event logs, and performance counters. See Chapter 18.
System.Drawing	Types that allow access to GDI+ basic graphics functionality. More advanced functionality is provided in the System.Drawing.Drawing2D, System.Drawing.Imaging, and System.Drawing.Text namespaces. See Chapter 11.
System.Globalization	Types that define culture-related information, including the language, the country/region, the calendars in use, the format patterns for dates, the currency, the numbers, and the sort order for strings. Not covered in this book.
System.IO	Types that allow reading and writing files and data streams, as well as types that provide basic file and directory support. See Chapter 4 for a basic overview.
System.Media	Types for playing and accessing sounds and other media formats. Not covered in this book. .NET 3.0 and later.
System.Net	Types to programmatically access many of the protocols used on modern networks. See Chapters 2 and 14 for examples and a basic overview.
System.Reflection	Types that retrieve information about assemblies, modules, members, parameters, and other entities in managed code. See Chapter 9 for a brief overview.
System.Reflection.Emit	Types for generating .NET code dynamically at run time.
System.Resources	Types that allow developers to create, store, and manage various culture-specific resources used in an application. See Chapters 7 and 11 for a brief overview.
System.Security	Types to interface with the underlying structure of the CLR security system, including base classes for permissions. Not covered in this book.

Table 10-2. *Namespaces in the DLLs from Table 10-1, with MSDN Descriptions (Continued)*

Namespace	Description
System.Text	Types representing ASCII, Unicode, UTF-8, and other character encodings. Also abstract types for converting blocks of characters to and from blocks of bytes. See Chapters 3 and the section "Using Regular Expressions and Formatting" later in this chapter.
System.Threading	Types for creating and synchronizing threads. See Chapter 13.
System.Web	Types that enable web applications. See Chapter 14.
System.Windows.Forms	Types for creating windowed applications. See Chapter 11.
System.Xml	Types that implement standards-based support for processing XML. See Chapters 9 and 15.
Microsoft.Win32	Types that wrap Win32 API common dialog boxes and components. Not covered in this book.

Namespaces from the F# Libraries

Table 10-3 shows the primary namespaces in F# library DLLs from Table 10-1. The following are opened by default in F# code:

```
Microsoft.FSharp.Core
Microsoft.FSharp.Collections
Microsoft.FSharp.Control
Microsoft.FSharp.Text
```

Table 10-3. *Namespaces in the DLLs from Table 10-1*

Namespace	Description
Microsoft.FSharp.Core	Provides primitive constructs related to the F# language such as tuples. See Chapter 3.
Microsoft.FSharp.Collections	Provides functional programming collections such as sets and maps implemented using binary trees. See Chapter 3 and the section "Using Further F# and .NET Data Structures" later in this chapter.
Microsoft.FSharp.Control	Provides functional programming control structures including asynchronous and lazy programming. Chapter 8 covers programming with the IEvent<'a> type and the IEvent module, and Chapter 13 covers the Async<'a> type.
Microsoft.FSharp.Text	Provides types for structured and printf-style textual formatting of data. See Chapter 4 for an introduction to printf formatting.
Microsoft.FSharp.Reflection	Provides extensions to the System.Reflection functionality that deal particularly with F# record and discriminated union values. See Chapter 9 for a brief introduction, and see the section "Further Libraries for Reflective Techniques" section later in this chapter for more details.
Microsoft.FSharp.Quotations	Provides access to F# expressions as abstract syntax trees. See Chapter 9.

Using the System Types

Table 10-4 shows some of the most useful core types from the System namespace. These types are particularly useful because they take real care to define correctly.

Table 10-4. *Useful Core Types from the System Namespace*

Function	Description
System.DateTime	A type representing a date and time
System.DayOfWeek	An enumeration type representing a day of the week
System.Decimal	A numeric type suitable for financial calculations requiring large numbers of significant integral and fractional digits and no round-off errors
System.Guid	A type representing a 128-bit globally unique ID
System.Nullable<'a>	A type with an underlying value type 'a but that can be assigned null like a reference type
System.TimeSpan	A type representing a time interval
System.Uri	A type representing a uniform resource identifier (URI), such as an Internet URL

The following session shows some sample uses of the DateTime type:

```
> open System;;
> DateTime.Parse("13 July 1968");;
val it : DateTime = 13/07/1968 00:00:00 {Day = 13;
                                         DayOfWeek = Saturday;
                                         DayOfYear = 195;
                                         Hour = 0;
                                         Millisecond = 0;
                                         Minute = 0;
                                         Month = 7;
                                         Second = 0;
                                         Ticks = 620892000000000000L;
                                         TimeOfDay = 00:00:00;
                                         Year = 1968;}

> let date x = DateTime.Parse(x);;
val date : string -> DateTime

> printfn "date = %A" (date "13 July 1968");;
date = 13/07/1968 00:00:00
val it : unit = ()
```

```
> printfn "birth = %A" (date "18 March 2003, 6:21:01pm");;
birth = 18/03/2003 18:21:01
val it : unit = ()
```

Note that formatting dates depends on the user's localization settings; you can achieve more explicit formatting by using the System.DateTime.ToString overload that accepts explicit format information.

Here we use System.Uri type to parse a URL:

```
> open System;;
> System.Uri.TryCreate("http://www.thebritishmuseum.ac.uk/", UriKind.Absolute);;

val it : bool * System.Uri
= (true,
    http://www.thebritishmuseum.ac.uk/
        { AbsolutePath = "/"; ...
          DnsSafeHost = "www.thebritishmuseum.ac.uk"; ...
          Port = 80; ...
          Scheme = "http"; })

> Uri.TryCreate("e3£%//ww.gibberish.com", UriKind.Absolute);;
val it : bool * Uri = (false, null)
```

Many .NET types are used to hold static functions such as those for converting data from one format to another. Types such as System.Random play a similar role via objects with a small amount of state. Table 10-5 shows some of the most useful of these types.

Table 10-5. *Useful Services from the System Namespace*

Function	Description
System.BitConverter	Contains functions to convert numeric representations to and from bit representations
System.Convert	Contains functions to convert between various numeric representations
System.Math	Contains constants and static methods for trigonometric, logarithmic, and other common mathematical functions
System.Random	Provides objects to act as random number generators
System.StringComparer	Provides objects implementing various types of comparisons on strings (case insensitive, and so on)

Using Regular Expressions and Formatting

In Chapter 3 you saw the different forms of string literals (strings with escape characters, verbatim strings, and byte arrays) and the most typical operations such as concatenation using string builders. You may also remember that string values are *immutable* and that string operations that "change" their input return a new string that represents the result. In the following sections, we cover further ways to work with strings and text.

Matching with System.Text.RegularExpressions

One of the most popular ways of working with strings as data is through the use of *regular expressions*. This is done using the functionality from the .NET System.Text.RegularExpressions namespace. To get started, first note that the F# library includes the following definition:

```
open System.Text.RegularExpressions
let regex s = new Regex(s)
```

To this you can add the following Perl-like operators:

```
let (=~) s (re:Regex) = re.IsMatch(s)
let (<>~) s (re:Regex) = not (s =~ re)
```

Here the inferred types are as follows:

```
val regex : string -> Regex
val ( =~ ) : string -> Regex -> bool
val ( <>~ ) : string -> Regex -> bool
```

The infix operators allow you to test for matches:

```
> let samplestring = "This is a string";;
val samplestring : string

> if samplestring =~ regex "his" then
      printfn "A Match! ";;
A Match!
val it : unit = ()
```

Regular expressions can include *, +, and ? symbols for "zero or more occurrences," "one or more occurrences," and "zero or one occurrences" of the immediately preceding regular expression and can include parentheses to group regular expressions. For example:

```
> "This is a string" =~ regex "(is )+";;
val it : bool = true
```

Regular expressions can also be used to split strings:

```
> (regex " ").Split("This is a string");;
val it : string [] = [|"This"; "is"; "a"; "string"|]
```

Here we have used the regular expression " " for whitespace. In reality, you probably want to use the regular expression " +" to match multiple spaces. Better still, you can match any Unicode whitespace character using \s, including end-of-line markers; however, when using escape characters, you will want to use verbatim strings to specify the regular expression, such as @"\s+". We discussed verbatim strings in Chapter 3. Let's try this:

```
> (regex @"\s+").Split("I'm a little      teapot");;
val it : string [] = [|"I'm"; "a"; "little"; "teapot"|]

> (regex @"\s+").Split("I'm a little  \t\t\n\t\n\t teapot");;
val it : string [] = [|"I'm"; "a"; "little"; "teapot"|]
```

Here's how to match by using the method Match instead of using =~ and IsMatch. This lets you examine the positions of a match.

```
> let m = (regex @"joe").Match("maryjoewashere");;
val m : Match

> if m.Success then
      printfn "Matched at position %d" m.Index;;

Matched at position 4
val it : unit = ()
```

Replacing text is also easy:

```
> let text = "was a dark and stormy night";;
val text: string

> let t2 = (regex @"\w+").Replace(text, "WORD");;
val t2: string

> t2;;
val it : string = "WORD WORD WORD WORD WORD WORD"
```

Here we've used the regular expression "\w+" for a sequence of word characters.

Table 10-6 shows the broad range of specifiers that can be used with .NET regular expressions.

Table 10-6. *Regular Expression Escape Characters*

Characters	Description
Ordinary characters	Characters other than . $ ^ { [(|) * + ? \ match themselves.
.	Matches any character, except \n. If RegexOptions.SingleLine is specified, then it matches every character.
[aeiou0-9]	Matches any of the given characters or character ranges.
[^aeiou0-9]	Any character other than the given characters of character ranges.
\p{name}	Matches any character in the named character class specified by {name}. See the .NET documentation for full details.
\P{name}	Matches text not included in groups and block ranges specified in {name}.
\w	Matches any word character.
\W	Matches any nonword character.
\s	Matches any whitespace character.
\S	Matches any nonwhitespace character.
\d	Matches any decimal digit.
\D	Matches any nondigit.
\a	Matches a bell (alarm) \u0007.
\b	Matches a backspace \u0008 if in a [ ] character class; otherwise, in a regular expression, \b denotes a word boundary (between \w and \W characters). In a replacement pattern, \b always denotes a backspace.
\t	Matches a tab \u0009.
\r	Matches a carriage return \u000D.
\v	Matches a vertical tab \u000B.
\f	Matches a form feed \u000C.
\n	Matches a new line \u000A.
\e	Matches an escape \u001B.
\digit	Matches a back reference.
\040	Matches an ASCII character as octal.
\x20	Matches an ASCII character using hexadecimal representation (exactly two digits).
\cC	Matches an ASCII control character; for example, \cC is Ctrl+C.
\u0020	Matches a Unicode character using hexadecimal representation (exactly four digits).
\	When followed by a character that is not recognized as an escaped character, matches that character. For example, * is the same as \x2A.

You can specify case-insensitive matches by using (?i) at the start of a regular expression:

```
> samplestring =~ regex "(?i)HIS";;
val it : bool = true

> samplestring =~ regex "HIS";;
val it : bool = false
```

Here is a final example, showing the use of "named groups."

```
let entry = @"
Jolly Jethro
13 Kings Parade
Cambridge, Cambs CB2 1TJ
"

let re =
  regex @"(?<=\n)\s*(?<city>[^\n]+)\s*,\s*(?<county>\w+)\s+(?<pcode>.{3}\s*.{3}).*$"
```

You can now use this regular expression to match the text and examine the named elements of the match:

```
> let r = re.Match(entry);;
val r : Match

> r.Groups.Item("city").Value;;
val it : string = "Cambridge"

> r.Groups.Item("county").Value;;
val it : string = "Cambs"

> r.Groups.Item("pcode").Value;;
val it : string = "CB2 1TJ"
```

Note that at the time of writing, F# requires that you use the Item property to examine elements of a match group. The F# designers have indicated that in a future release you will be able to use the shorter notation r.Groups.["city"].Value.

> **Note** .NET regular expressions have many more features than those described here. For example, you can easily compile regular expressions. You can also use regular expressions to define sophisticated text substitutions. With a little more work, you can also define *active patterns* based on functions defined using regular expressions. We discussed active patterns in Chapter 9. This and other more advanced topics are discussed at http://www.expert-fsharp.com/Topics/RegularExpressions.

Formatting Strings Using .NET Formatting

Throughout this book we have used F# printf format strings to format text and output, and we introduced the basic format specifiers for this kind of text formatting in Chapter 4. Functions such as printf and printfn are located in the Microsoft.FSharp.Text.Printf module.

Another way to format strings is to use the System.String.Format static method or the other .NET composite formatting functions such as System.Console.WriteLine and TextWriter. WriteLine. This is a completely distinct set of formatting functions and directives redesigned and implemented from the ground up for the .NET platform. Like printf, these methods take a format specifier and the objects to be formatted. The format specifier is a string with any number of format items acting as placeholders and designating which object is to be formatted and how. Consider the following simple example:

```
> string.Format("{0} {1} {2}", 12, "a", 1.23);;
val it : string = "12 a 1.23"
```

Each format item is enclosed in braces giving the index of the object to be formatted, and each can include an optional alignment specification (always preceded by a comma after the index, giving the width of the region in which the object is to be inserted, as in {0, 10}) and a format type that guides how the given object is formatted (as in {0:C}, where C formats as a system currency). The general syntax of the format item is as follows:

{index[,alignment][:formatType]}

You can use the alignment value to pad the formatted object with spaces, and text alignment is left if its value is negative and right if positive. Table 10-7 summarizes the most often used format types.

Table 10-7. *The .NET Format Specifiers*

Specifier	Type
C	Currency
D	Decimal/long date
E	Scientific
F	Fixed-point
G	General
N	Number
P	Percent
X	Hexadecimal
d/D	Short/long date
t/T	Short/long time
M	Month
Y	Year

You can find more information on .NET composite formatting at http://www.
expert-fsharp.com/Topics/TextFormatting.

Encoding and Decoding Unicode Strings

It is often necessary to convert string data between different formats. For example, files read
using the ReadLine method on the System.IO.StreamReader type are read with respect to a Unicode
encoding; you can specify this when creating the StreamReader; if left unspecified, the .NET
libraries attempt to determine the encoding for you.

One common requirement is to convert strings to and from ASCII representations,
assuming that all the characters in the strings are in the ASCII range 0 to 127. You can do this
using System.Text.Encoding.ASCII.GetString and System.Text.Encoding.ASCII.GetBytes.
Table 10-8 shows the predefined encodings and commonly used members in the System.
Text.Encoding type.

Table 10-8. *Types and Members Related to Unicode Encodings*

Type/Member	Description
System.Text.Encoding	Represents a character encoding
UTF8 : Encoding	The encoding for the UTF-8 Unicode format
ASCII : Encoding	The encoding for the ASCII 7-bit character set
Unicode : Encoding	The encoding for the UTF-16 Unicode format
UTF32 : Encoding	The encoding for the UTF-32 Unicode format
GetEncoding : string -> Encoding	Fetches an encoding by name
member GetBytes : string -> byte[]	Encodes a string to bytes
member GetChars: byte[] -> char[]	Decodes a sequence of bytes
member GetString : byte[] -> string	Decodes a sequence of bytes

Encoding and Decoding Binary Data

Another common requirement is to convert binary data to and from the standard 64-character
string-encoded representation of binary data used in XML, e-mail, and other formats. You can
do this using System.Convert.FromBase64String and System.Convert.ToBase64String.

Using Further F# and .NET Data Structures

As you saw in Chapter 2, F# comes with a useful implementation of some functional programming data structures. Recall that functional data structures are *persistent*: you can't mutate
them, and if you add an element or otherwise "modify" the collection, you are actually generating a new collection value, perhaps sharing some internal nodes but from the outside appearing
as if it is a new value.

Table 10-9 summarizes the most important persistent functional data structures that are
included in FSharp.Core.dll. It is likely that additional functional data structures will also be
added in future F# releases.

Table 10-9. *The F# Functional Data Structures from* `Microsoft.FSharp.Collections`

Type	Description
`List<'a>`	Immutable lists implemented using linked lists
`Set<'a>`	Immutable sets implemented using trees
`Map<'k,'v>`	Immutable maps (dictionaries) implemented using trees
`LazyList<'a>`	Lists generated on demand with each element computed only once

System.Collections.Generic and Other .NET Collections

Table 10-10 summarizes the imperative collections available in the `System.Collections.Generic` namespace.

Table 10-10. *The .NET and F# Imperative Data Structures from* `System.Collections.Generic`

Type	Description
`List<'a>`	Mutable, resizable integer-indexed arrays, usually called `ResizeArray<'a>` in F#.
`SortedList<'a>`	Mutable, resizable lists implemented using sorted arrays.
`Dictionary<'key,'value>`	Mutable, resizable dictionaries implemented using hash tables.
`SortedDictionary<'key,'value>`	Mutable, resizable dictionaries implemented using sorted arrays.
`Queue<'a>`	Mutable, first-in, first-out queues of unbounded size.
`Stack<'a>`	Mutable, first-in, last-out stacks of unbounded size.
`HashSet<'a>`	Mutable, resizable sets implemented using hash tables. New in .NET 3.5. The F# library also defines a `Microsoft.FSharp.Collections.HashSet` type usable in conjunction with earlier versions of .NET.

SOME OTHER COLLECTION LIBRARIES

Two additional libraries of .NET collections deserve particular attention. The first is PowerCollections, currently provided by Wintellect. This provides additional generic types such as `Bag<'a>`, `MultiDictionary<'key,'value>`, `OrderedDictionary<'key,'value>`, `OrderedMultiDictionary<'a>`, and `OrderedSet<'a>`. The second is the C5 collection library, provided by ITU in Denmark. This includes implementations of some persistent/functional data structures such as persistent trees and thus may be of particular interest for use from F#. You can find out more about using these libraries at `http://www.expert-fsharp/Topics/Libraries`.

Introducing Microsoft.FSharp.Math

The F# library includes a namespace `Microsoft.FSharp.Math` that defines a number of mathematical-related constructs including matrix and vector types, double-precision complex numbers (type `Complex`, abbreviated `complex`), arbitrary-precision integers (type `BigInt`, abbreviated `bigint`), and arbitrary-precision rationals (type `BigNum`, abbreviated `bignum`). Over time it is expected that F# will include further functionality in this namespace.

Using Matrices and Vectors

F# includes matrix and column vector types, which are generic and called `Matrix<'a>` and `Vector<'a>`, respectively. For symmetry a type of row vectors, `RowVector<'a>`, is also included. Most commonly, the element types are instantiated to be `double` (that is, `float`), so the following abbreviations are used:

```
type vector = Vector<float>
type matrix = Matrix<float>
type rowvec = RowVector<float>
```

The modules `Matrix`, `Vector`, and `RowVector` in the `Microsoft.FSharp.Math` namespace have many further functions for creating and working with these types. The functions are specialized for use with floating-point matrices, but versions to work with generic types are available at `Microsoft.FSharp.Math.Matrix.Generic` and `Microsoft.FSharp.Math.Vector.Generic`. The functions `vector` and `matrix` are also available for creating literal values. Here are some examples of the uses of these types and functions:

```
> open Microsoft.FSharp.Math;;
> vector [ 1.0; 2.0 ; 3.0 ] + vector [ 1.0; 2.0 ; 3.0 ];;
val it : Vector<float> = vector [2.0; 4.0; 6.0]

> matrix [ [ 1.0; 2.0 ];
           [ 1.0; 3.0 ] ]
  *
  matrix [ [ 1.0; -2.0 ];
           [ 0.5; 3.0 ] ];;
val it : Matrix<float> = matrix [[2.0; 4.0];
                                 [2.5; 7.0];]
```

Table 10-11 summarizes the primary properties of these types.

Table 10-11. *The* `Microsoft.FSharp.Math` *Matrix and Vector Types*

Type/Member	Member Type	Description
type Matrix<'a>		
.[]	: int * int -> 'a with set, get	Gets or sets the item at the given position in the matrix.

Table 10-11. *The* `Microsoft.FSharp.Math` *Matrix and Vector Types (Continued)*

Type/Member	Member Type	Description
`Dimensions`	`: int * int`	Gets the number of (rows, columns) in the matrix.
`NumCols`	`: int`	Gets the number of columns in the matrix.
`NumRows`	`: int`	Gets the number of rows in the matrix.
`GetSlice2D`	`: ?int * ?int * ?int * ?int -> Matrix<'a>`	Gets a submatrix. See the slice syntax for arrays, also usable for matrices, in Chapter 4.
`Transpose`	`: Matrix<'a>`	Gets the transpose of the matrix.
`type Vector<'a>`		
`.[]`	`: int -> 'a with set, get`	Gets or sets the item at the given position in the vector.
`NumRows`	`: int`	Gets the number of rows in the vector.
`GetSlice`	`: ?int * ?int -> Vector<'a>`	Gets a subvector.
`Transpose`	`: RowVector<'a>`	Gets the transpose of the vector.

Using Operator Overloads on Matrices and Vectors

The F# matrix, vector, and row vector types support the use of operators such as +, -, and *. Table 10-12 shows the set of operators supported.

Table 10-12. *Primary Operator Overloads Supported by the F# Matrix and Vector Types*

Operator	Overload	Description
`( $* )`	`: 'a * Matrix<'a> -> Matrix<'a>`	Scalar-matrix multiplication
`( * )`	`: RowVector<'a> * Matrix<'a> -> RowVector<'a>`	Vector-matrix multiplication
`( * )`	`: Matrix<'a> * Vector<'a> -> Vector<'a>`	Matrix-vector multiplication
`( * )`	`: Matrix<'a> * Matrix<'a> -> Matrix<'a>`	Matrix multiplication
`( .* )`	`: Vector<'a> * Vector<'a> -> Vector<'a>`	Pointwise multiplication
`( .* )`	`: Matrix<'a> * Matrix<'a> -> Matrix<'a>`	Pointwise multiplication
`( + )`	`: Vector<'a> * Vector<'a> -> Vector<'a>`	Pointwise addition
`( + )`	`: Matrix<'a> * Matrix<'a> -> Matrix<'a>`	Pointwise addition

> ■**Note** At the time of writing, the F# distribution came with prototype plotting and linear algebra modules for use with libraries that provide plotting and numeric functionality such as Excel, Xceed, and the Intel MKL libraries, as well as the commonly used BLAS and LAPACK libraries. This functionality was not yet fully integrated into the F# libraries at the time of writing. You can find further information at http://www.expert-fsharp.com/Topics/Math.

Supervising and Isolating Execution

The .NET System namespace includes a number of useful types that give functionality related to the execution of running programs in the .NET Common Language Runtime. Table 10-13 summarizes them.

Table 10-13. *Types Related to Runtime Supervision of Applications*

Function	Description
System.Runtime	Contains advanced types that support compilation and native interoperability.
System.Environment	Provides information about, and the means to manipulate, the current environment and platform.
System.GC	Controls the system garbage collector. We discuss garbage collection in more detail in Chapter 17.
System.WeakReference	Represents a weak reference, which references an object while still allowing that object to be reclaimed by garbage collection.
System.AppDomain	Represents an application domain, which is a software-isolated environment where applications execute. Application domains can hold code generated at run time and can be unloaded.

Further Libraries for Reflective Techniques

As discussed in Chapter 9, .NET and F# programming frequently uses reflective techniques to analyze the types of objects, create objects at run time, and use type information to drive generic functions in general ways. For example, in Chapter 9 you saw an example of a technique called *schema compilation*, which was based on .NET attributes, F# data types, and a compiler to take these and use reflective techniques to generate an efficient text file reader and translator. The combination of reflective techniques and .NET generics allows programs to operate at the boundary between statically typed code and dynamically typed data.

Using General Types

There are a number of facets to reflective programming with .NET. One simple kind of reflective programming is when a whole range of data structures are accessed in a "general" way. For example, .NET includes a type System.Array that is a parent type of all array types. The existence of this type allows you to write code that is generic over *all* array types, even one-dimensional and multidimensional arrays. This is occasionally useful, such as when writing a generic array printer.

Table 10-14 summarizes the primary general types defined in the .NET Framework.

Table 10-14. *General Types in the .NET Framework*

Function	Description
System.Array	General type of all array values.
System.Delegate	General type of all delegates.
System.Enum	General type of all enum values.
System.Exception	General type of all exception values.
System.Collections.IEnumerable	General type of all sequence values. This is the nongeneric version of the F# type seq<'a>, and all sequence and collection values are compatible with this type.
System.IComparable	General type of all comparable types.
System.IDisposable	General type of all explicitly reclaimable resources.
System.IFormattable	General type of all types supporting .NET formatting.
System.Object	General type of all values.
System.Type	Runtime representation of .NET types.
System.ValueType	General type of all value types.

Using Microsoft.FSharp.Reflection

In Chapter 9 our schema compiler used some functions from the Microsoft.FSharp. Reflection namespace. This namespace is a relatively thin extension of the System.Reflection namespace. It offers an interesting set of techniques to create and analyze F# values and types in ways that are somewhat simpler than those offered by the System.Reflection namespace. These operations are also designed to be used in precompilation phases to amortize costs associated with reflective programming.

Table 10-15 summarizes the main types in this namespace and some of the more interesting members.

Table 10-15. *Some Operations in the Microsoft.FSharp.Reflection Namespace*

Module and Functions	Description
module Microsoft.FSharp.Reflection.Type	
GetInfo : Type -> TypeInfo	Gets information for a type.
GetTypeOfReprType : Type -> Type	Throws away extraneous compiler-specific information from a runtime type to return a true F# type.
IsOptionType : Type -> bool	Determines whether the given type is an option type.

Table 10-15. *Some Operations in the* `Microsoft.FSharp.Reflection` *Namespace (Continued)*

Module and Functions	Description
`IsUnitType : Type -> bool`	Determines whether the given type is the unit type.
`MaxTupleSize : int`	Gets the maximum size for which the structure of F# tuple types are faithfully reported by reflection.
module Microsoft.FSharp.Reflection.Value	
`GetInfo : 'a -> ValueInfo`	Gets the reflective view of a value.
`GetRecordConstructor : Type -> (obj [] -> obj)`	Precomputes a function for constructing a record value.
`GetRecordFieldReader : Type * string -> (obj -> obj)`	Precomputes a function for reading a particular field from a record.
`GetRecordReader : Type -> (obj -> obj [])`	Precomputes a function for reading all the fields from a record.
`GetSumConstructor : Type * int -> (obj [] -> obj)`	Precomputes a function for constructing a discriminated union value. The integer is the index of a constructor in the discriminated union.
`GetSumRecordReader : Type * int -> (obj -> obj [])`	Precomputes a function for reading all the fields for a particular constructor in the discriminated union.
`GetSumTagConverters : Type -> int * (int -> string) * (string -> int)`	Precomputes a pair of functions for converting between the indexes and names of the constructors in a discriminated union.
`GetSumTagReader : Type -> (obj -> int)`	Precomputes a function for reading the index of the constructor for a discriminated union.
`GetTupleConstructor : Type -> (obj [] -> obj)`	Precomputes a function for creating values of a particular tuple type.
`GetTupleReader : Type -> (obj -> obj [])`	Precomputes a function for reading the values of a particular tuple type.
`GetType : 'a -> Type`	Gets the runtime representation of the F# type of a value. This will often be less specific than `obj.GetType()`.

Some Other .NET Types You May Encounter

When .NET was first designed, the .NET type system did not include "generics" or a general notion of a "function type" as used by F#. Instead of functions, .NET uses delegates, which can be thought of as "named" function types (that is, each different kind of function type is given a different name).

This means you will often encounter delegate types when using .NET libraries from F#. Since .NET 2.0, some of these are even generic, giving an approximation to the simple and unified view of function types used by F#. Every .NET delegate type has a corresponding F# function type. For example, the F# function type for the .NET delegate type System.Windows. Forms.PaintEventHandler is obj -> System.Windows.Forms.PaintEventArgs -> unit. You can figure out this type by looking at the signature for the Invoke method of the given delegate type.

.NET also comes with definitions for some "generic" delegate types. F# tends to use function types instead of these, so you won't see these so often in your coding. However, Table 10-16 shows these delegate types just in case you should meet them.

Table 10-16. *Delegate Types Encountered Occasionally in F# Coding*

Function	F# Function Type	Description
System.Action<'a>	'a -> unit	Used for imperative actions.
System.AsyncCallback	System.IAsyncResult -> unit	Used for callbacks when asynchronous actions complete.
System.Converter<'a,'b>	'a -> 'b	Used to convert between values.
System.Comparison<'a>	'a -> 'a -> int	Used to compare values.
System.EventHandler<'a>	obj -> 'a -> unit	Used as a generic event-handler type.
System.Func<'a,'b>	'a -> 'b	A .NET 3.5 LINQ function delegate. Further arity-overloaded types exist accepting additional arguments, for example, System.Func<'a,'b,'c>, System.Func<'a,'b,'c,'d>.
System.Predicate<'a>	'a -> bool	Used to test a condition.

Some Other .NET Libraries

Any review of the libraries that are usable with F# and .NET is necessarily incomplete; there are just too many high-quality .NET libraries available, and more are appearing all the time. However, people often ask us which libraries we recommend. Table 10-17 shows some of the frameworks and libraries available at the time of writing that we think may be of interest to the readers of this book.

Table 10-17. *Some Frameworks and Libraries Not Covered in This Chapter*

Framework/Library Name	Description
Microsoft Robotics Studio	A .NET environment for creating robotics applications that run across a variety of hardware.
Microsoft XNA	A .NET environment for games for Microsoft gaming platforms such as Xbox 360 and Microsoft Windows.
GTK#	A set of .NET bindings for the GTK+ GUI toolkit, primarily used on Mono to enable windowed applications on Linux and other platforms.

Table 10-17. *Some Frameworks and Libraries Not Covered in This Chapter (Continued)*

Framework/Library Name	Description
Extreme Optimization	A commercial math, vector, statistics, and matrix library for .NET.
Irrlicht	An open-source, high-performance, real-time 3D engine.
LINQ	Language Integrated Queries, contained in .NET 3.5. See Chapter 15.
Windows Presentation Foundation (WPF)	The graphical subsystem of .NET 3.0. Not covered in this book.
Windows Communication Foundation (WCF)	A unified framework for building connected systems. Not covered in this book.

Summary

This chapter gave an overview of the primary libraries available for use with a vanilla installation of F# and .NET. Many, many other libraries are available for .NET, and we couldn't possibly cover them in a single book. Many of the design patterns you've seen here recur in those libraries, so once you get to know the libraries discussed here, you will find that other libraries are easy to use.

In the chapters that follow, we will dig into applications of F# and the .NET Framework more deeply, looking at some of the libraries discussed in this chapter in more detail.

CHAPTER 11

■ ■ ■

Working with Windows Forms and Controls

GUI applications revolve around events, and F# provides a natural way to process events with functions. Graphical interfaces are often developed using visual editors, in particular to build GUIs by assembling *controls*. Applications, however, often need drawing capabilities for displaying and manipulating data, which requires custom programming to augment available controls. In this chapter, we discuss how to develop graphical applications with F# and why the functional traits of the language suit the event-driven programming paradigm typical of GUIs.

To develop our applications, we will use the Windows Forms library, which is a graphical toolkit designed by Microsoft for implementing graphical applications on the .NET platform; this library relies on the GDI+ interface used to develop Windows applications. Other toolkits are also available for programming GUIs with .NET such as GTK#, which is a managed library for writing applications based on the GTK toolkit. These libraries share a similar design with Windows Forms, and you can easily adapt the notions presented in this chapter to these frameworks.

Writing "Hello, World!" in a Click

It's traditional to start with a "Hello, World!" application, so we'll honor that and begin with a simple program that provides a button to display the magic phrase when clicked:

```
open System.Windows.Forms

Application.EnableVisualStyles()

let form = new Form(Text="Hello World WinForms")
let button = new Button(Text="Click Me!", Dock=DockStyle.Fill)

button.Click.Add(fun _ -> MessageBox.Show("Hello, World!", "Hey!") |> ignore)
form.Controls.Add(button)
form.Show()
```

Even in its simplicity, the application captures many traits typical of GUI applications. After opening the namespace associated with Windows Forms, you enable the Windows XP or Vista look of the application through the call to the static method `EnableVisualStyles` of the `Application` class. You create the form `form` that contains the button `button`, set the form and button captions by assigning their `Text` properties, and tell the button that it should fill the entire form.

Most of GUI programming is devoted to handling events through callbacks from the graphical interface. Events themselves were described in Chapter 8. To display a message box containing the `"Hello, World!"` string, you have to configure the button so that when its `Click` event is fired, a function is called. In the previous example, you pass a function to the `Add` method for the button's `Click` event, which adds an event handler to an event source. You then add the button to the form and call the form's `Show` method to display it.

Note that this code should be executed using `fsi.exe`. It will not run as a stand-alone application, unless you add the following line at the end:

```
Application.Run(form)
```

This line relates to the *event loop* of a GUI application, and it is required to handle events such as button clicks. If you use `fsi.exe`, the event loop is handled by F# Interactive.

Understanding the Anatomy of a Graphical Application

Graphical applications are built upon the abstractions provided by the graphical environment hosting them. The application must interact with its environment and process input in an unstructured way. User input is not the only kind of input received from a windowing system. Window management often involves requests to or from the application itself, such as painting or erasing a form.

Windowing systems provide a common and abstract way to interact with a graphical application: the notion of an *event*. When an event occurs, the application receives a message in the *message queue* with information about the event.

The graphical application is responsible for delivering messages from the message queue to the control for which they are meant. A set of functions provided by the API of the windowing system supports this. This activity of reading messages from the message queue and dispatching them is known as the *event loop* of the application. If the loop fails for any reason, the GUI components cease to work, the application hangs, and Windows may eventually inform you that the application is not responding.

It's rare for an application to program the event loop explicitly. Programming toolkits encapsulate this functionality because it's basically always the same. The `Run` method of the `Application` class is responsible for handling the event loop, and it ensures that messages related to events are delivered to targets within the application.

GUI programs often involve multiple *threads* of execution. We discuss threading and concurrency in more detail in Chapter 13, but for this chapter it is important to remember that event dispatching is a single-threaded activity, even if it may seem the opposite. The thread executing the event loop calls the functions and methods registered for handling the various events. In the "Hello, World!" example, for instance, we told the button to call back the function to show the message box when clicked.

AN EXPLICIT EVENT LOOP

A Windows Forms event loop can also be explicitly defined by the application using the `Application.DoEvents` method; in this case, each invocation performs a step in event handling and returns the control to the caller. Some programs can benefit from this control since they can interleave event processing and computation using a single thread. Computer games, for instance, tend to use this approach since event-based timers provided by the framework are not reliable for producing the frames of the game at the required pace. The following loop shows a typical explicit event loop:

```
let form = new Form(Text="Explicit Event Loop")
form.Show()
while form.Created do
    // Perform some task
    Application.DoEvents()
```

When events are handled explicitly, a program must pay attention to call the `DoEvents` method frequently, because if events are not processed, the graphical interface may become unresponsive, which provides the wrong feedback to the user.

Software reuse has always been a priority in the world of graphical applications, because of the many details involved even in realizing simple behaviors. It's not surprising that programming techniques favoring software reuse have always flourished in this context. It's possible to develop a GUI application without writing a single line of code by simply combining existing controls into a new interface.

Articulated frameworks, such as Windows Forms, provide a significant number of reusable controls so that it is possible to develop entire applications without needing to use drawing facilities provided by the interface. For this reason, frameworks have started to support two kinds of customers: those composing interfaces with controls and those that need to develop new controls or explicitly use drawing primitives. In the rest of this chapter, you'll explore the Windows Forms framework, from both perspectives: the functional nature of F# will be very effective in using controls, and the ability to define objects will help you in developing new controls.

Composing User Interfaces

A control is represented by an object inheriting, either directly or indirectly, from the `Control` class in the `System.Windows.Forms` namespace. Building interfaces using controls involves two tasks: placing controls into containers (that are themselves a particular type of control) such as panels or forms and registering controls with event handlers to be notified of relevant events.

As an example, we'll show how to develop a simple web browser based on the Internet Explorer control, which is a control that allows wrapping the HTML renderer (the interior of an Internet Explorer window) into an application. We'll show how to develop the application interactively using `fsi.exe`. Start by opening the libraries required for using Windows Forms:

```
open System
open System.Drawing
open System.Windows.Forms
```

Then you enable the Windows XP/Vista visual styles, declaring through the custom attribute STAThread that the application adopts the *single thread apartment model*, which is a COM legacy often required for Windows Forms applications to interact with COM components:

```
[<STAThread>]
do Application.EnableVisualStyles()
```

We need this in our example because Internet Explorer is a COM component accessible through a .NET wrapped type named WebBrowser in the System.Windows.Forms namespace, as are all the base controls offered by Windows Forms (we will assume that types are from this namespace unless otherwise specified).

Now you have to decide what the browser application should look like (see Figure 11-1). The bare minimum we can think of is a toolbar featuring the address bar and the classic Go button, a status bar with a progress bar shown during page loading, and the browser control in the middle of the form.

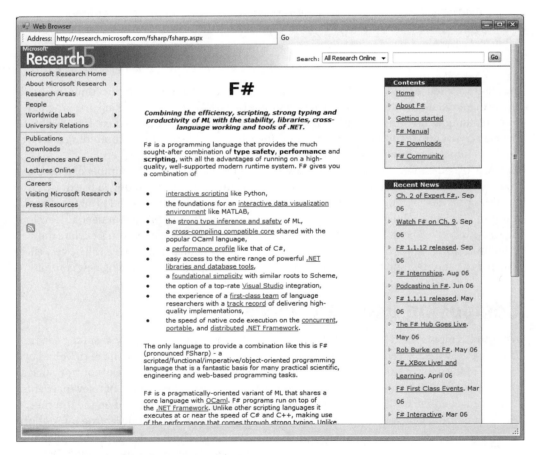

Figure 11-1. *A simple web browser application*

You next configure the elements, starting from the status bar, as shown in the following code. You add the progress bar to the status bar, and you configure both. The Dock property of the status bar is set to Bottom, meaning that the status bar should fill the bottom part of the form. The progress bar is resized, and then its `Style` property is set to `Marquee`, meaning that you do not want to show any specific progress but just something moving during download.

```
let statusProgress =
  new ToolStripProgressBar(Size=new Size(200, 16),
                            Style= ProgressBarStyle.Marquee,
                            Visible=false)
let status = new StatusStrip(Dock=DockStyle.Bottom)
status.Items.Add(statusProgress) |> ignore
```

You can now set up the toolbar of the browser, as shown in the following code. The toolbar should be in the top area of the form, so set its `Dock` property to `Top`. First add a label, the text box for typing the URL, and the button. Then stretch the `address` text box, and an event handler is associated to its `KeyPress` event. In this way, you can catch the Return key and start browsing the typed URL without having to wait for the Go button. Finally, configure the Go button by setting its label and associating an event handler to the `Click` event.

```
let toolbar = new ToolStrip(Dock=DockStyle.Top)
let address = new ToolStripTextBox(Size=new Size(400, 25))
let browser = new WebBrowser(Dock=DockStyle.Fill)
let go = new ToolStripButton(DisplayStyle=ToolStripItemDisplayStyle.Text,
                             Text="Go")
address.KeyPress.Add(fun arg ->
    if (arg.KeyChar = '\r') then browser.Url <- new Uri(address.Text))
go.Click.Add(fun arg -> browser.Url <- new Uri(address.Text))
toolbar.Items.Add(new ToolStripLabel("Address:")) |> ignore
toolbar.Items.Add(address) |> ignore
toolbar.Items.Add(go) |>ignore
```

Both event handlers simply set the `Url` property of the `browser` object, causing the `WebBrowser` control to load the given `Uri`. Notice how nicely and compactly F# lets you specify event handlers. This is possible because F# lets you use functions directly as arguments to `Add`.

You can now take care of the browser control and set its properties. Here you tell the browser to occupy all the area in the form left by the toolbar and the status bar by setting the `Dock` property to `Fill`. You then subscribe two events, `Navigating` and `DocumentCompleted`, in order to be notified by the browser when document loading starts and completes. When the browser starts fetching a URL, you show the progress bar in the status bar, setting its `Visible` property to `true`. Once the document is loaded, you hide the progress bar, and you update the address bar so that if the user has followed a link, the address shown remains consistent with the current document.

```
browser.Navigating.Add(fun args ->
    statusProgress.Visible <- true)
browser.DocumentCompleted.Add(fun args ->
    statusProgress.Visible <- false;
    address.Text <- browser.Url.AbsoluteUri)
```

You're now almost done with the interface. You simply have to tell Windows Forms that the controls are contained in the form `form`. Then you configure the form by setting its caption with the `Text` property and its size with the `Size` property. You call `PerformLayout` to update the current layout of the form, and then you can call `Show` to display the browser.

```
let form = new Form(Text="Web Browser", Size=new Size(800, 600))
form.Controls.Add(toolbar)
form.Controls.Add(status)
form.Controls.Add(browser)
form.PerformLayout()
form.Show()
```

To compile the application rather than execute it interactively, add the following at the end, as mentioned previously:

```
Application.Run(form)
```

WATCH THE APPLICATION GROW

It is possible to see the form growing interactively using `fsi.exe`. Usually applications first configure forms and controls and then call Show to present the user with a form ready to use. It is also useful to set the properties TopMost=true and Visible=true. The properties of a form can also be set after it is visible, allowing you to see the effects of each operation on it. F# Interactive offers a unique opportunity of watching the form growing interactively; you can, for instance, build the interface of the simple web browser by showing the form immediately and then proceed to add controls and set their properties. Thus, you can experiment with the various properties of controls and see how they affect the interface.

What have you learned by developing this application? It's clear that building interfaces based on controls requires a significant amount of code to configure controls by setting their properties. The layout of a form is also set by defining properties of controls, as you did in your browser. Moreover, there is an ever-increasing list of available controls, and each provides a large number of properties.

CONTROL LAYOUT

The layout of controls, either done by hand or through a visual editor, defines how the form looks when opened. Users, however, expect that the layout will gracefully adapt to the form resizing; one simple approach to the problem is to forbid the operation, as is done in many dialog boxes. A better solution is to define how controls must adapt their positions and sizes as the form changes its size.

Windows Forms has two ways to indicate how a control should adapt when the size of its container changes. The control can be *docked* using the property Dock to one of the four edges or to the center of the container (as shown in Figure 11-2). Docking to the edges constrains the control to be always attached to one of them, and either its width or its height should change in order to ensure that the whole edge is filled with it (as shown in Figure 11-2, horizontal edges have precedence over vertical ones). When docked to the middle, a control is resized to fill the area of the container left by the control docked to the edges. Docking is a flexible way to define layouts that adapt to size changes of the interface. If the five areas defined by this strategy are not enough, it is always possible to rely on logical containers such as panels: a panel represents a group of controls with a given layout. Using panels, it is possible to nest layouts and use docking on a panel docked in the surrounding container.

An alternative to docking is *anchoring*. Through the property Anchor, it is possible to impose that the distance between an edge of the control and the corresponding edge of the container should be constant. In this way, it is possible to have finer control over how the component should be resized or simply moved. In fact, when a control is anchored only to a horizontal and vertical edge (for instance Top and Left), its size does not change, and only the position is preserved.

Although docking and anchoring are useful in controlling how the control must be adapted to the interface, sometimes these strategies are not enough to address the needs of a complex layout. The Windows Presentation Framework adopts a more articulated notion of extensible layout management based on the notion of a layout manager (a similar notion has always been present in the Java AWT or in HTML).

Visual designers are graphical applications that allow you to design interfaces using a visual metaphor. Controls are dragged and dropped onto forms and then configured through a property window. Visual Studio 2005 provides a visual designer, though it is not available for all the programming languages. The language must expose a CodeDom provider, and at the time of writing F# does not yet provide one that is sufficiently powerful for this purpose. However, using the Visual Studio designer is still a useful way to explore controls and to play with their properties, and the generated C# fragments can be examined and used in F# code. To understand how the Visual Studio designer works, we've designed the same browser application in C# as shown in Figure 11-2. The Visual Studio designer generates, for the form Browser, a C# file named Browser.Designer.cs containing all the C# code required to set up the interface. If you look at that file, you can see that it contains mainly the assignments of control properties similar to those you manually used to prepare the browser form.

Until the Windows Forms designer or another visual designer is available for F#, there are essentially four options for building graphical interfaces in the language:

- Write the interface code by hand, as you did for the browser sample.

- Develop a visual designer that outputs F# code (though it is a hard job) and use it.

- Use the C# visual designer, and then convert the assignments in *file*.Designer.cs into F#.

- Exploit the interoperability of the .NET platform by designing the interface with the designer, generating C# or another supported language and using the F# code as a library.

You can easily define simple interfaces with F# code, and we show how in the rest of this chapter. We now focus on the more important part in the design of graphical applications: drawing and control development.

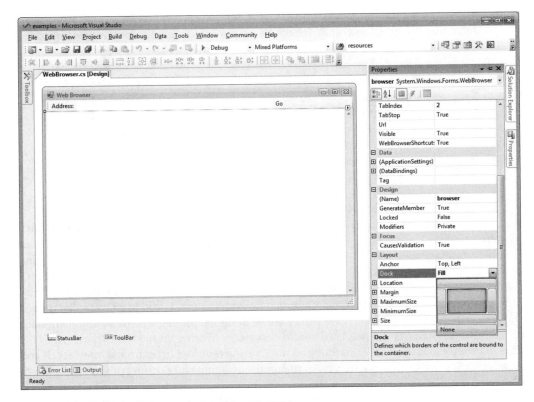

Figure 11-2. *The form designer of Visual Studio 2005*

Drawing Applications

So far you've developed graphical applications based on the composition of predeveloped graphical controls, but what do you do if no graphical control suits your needs? You need to learn how to draw using the drawing primitives provided by the graphical system.

To understand how drawing works, you need to review the model lying behind the rendering process of a graphical application. You know already that the event-driven programming paradigm is the one that best suits graphical applications; so far you have associated event handlers with user actions, but events are used by the graphical system as a general mechanism to communicate with the graphical application.

An application uses resources provided by the graphical system, and these resources are mostly windows. A *window* is simply a rectangular area on the screen, not necessarily a top-level window with buttons, a title bar, and all the amenities you usually associate with it. Windows can be nested and are the unit of traditional windowing systems. Windows can contain other windows, and the windowing system is responsible for ensuring that events are routed to the callbacks registered for handling the events for each window.

Windows are allowed to draw in their own client area, and the drawing is performed through the *device context*, an object provided by the graphical system and used to perform the *graphic primitives* to draw the content. The graphic primitives issued to the graphics system are not retained by it; therefore, when the window is covered for some reason, the portion that becomes hidden must be repainted once uncovered. Since the information required to redraw the hidden portion is held by the application owning the window, the graphical system sends a *paint* message to the window.

To better understand the drawing model, consider a simple graphical application that shows how to draw a curved line using the Bézier curve and canonical splines, given four control points. Start by opening your namespaces and telling Windows Forms that your form can use the XP/Vista look rather than the classic Windows 95 style; also set a global flag to inform standard controls to use the new GDI+ text-rendering primitives rather than those of the traditional GDI (we'll omit this code from now on, but remember to use it later and that these must be before windows are created; otherwise, an exception is thrown):

```
open System
open System.Drawing
open System.Windows.Forms

Application.EnableVisualStyles()
Application.SetCompatibleTextRenderingDefault(false)
```

You next create the form and define the initial values of the control points. The movingPoint variable will be used to keep track of the point the user is dragging to adjust the curve:

```
let form = new Form(Text="Curves")
let cpt = [| Point(20, 60); Point(40, 50); Point(130, 60); Point(200, 200) |]
let mutable movingPoint = -1
```

Let's introduce three menus to configure the application. They will be used to check features to be drawn:

```
let newMenu (s:string) = new ToolStripMenuItem(s,Checked=true,CheckOnClick=true)
let menuBezier = newMenu "Show &Bézier"
let menuCanonical = newMenu "Show &Canonical spline"
let menuControlPoints = newMenu "Show control &points"
```

We'll use a scrollbar to define different values for the tension parameter of the canonical spline curve:

```
let scrollbar = new VScrollBar(Dock=DockStyle.Right, LargeChange=2, Maximum=10)
```

Control points will be drawn if required, and an ellipse will be used to mark them. The function receives the device context in the form of a Graphics object; you draw the ellipse by invoking the DrawEllipse primitive on it. You use a Pen to draw the ellipse, in this case a red pen:

```
let drawPoint (g:Graphics) (p:Point) =
    g.DrawEllipse(Pens.Red, p.X - 2, p.Y - 2, 4, 4)
```

BRUSHES AND PENS

Windows Forms uses two kinds of objects to define colored primitives: brushes and pens. A *brush* is used to fill an area with a given pattern. A number of different patterns are available; solid colors are provided by the SolidBrush class, hatched patterns are provided by the HatchBrush, gradients are provided by the LinearGradientBrush and PathGradientBrush, and textured gradients are provided by the TextureBrush. The Brushes class provides a number of static brush objects describing solid colors.

Pens are brushes with a contour. The line drawn by a pen has a filling (the brush part) but also a width and different styles (dashed or not, with different caps at the beginning and at the end). The Pens class provides a number of static pen objects with the basic solid colors.

Both pen and brush objects contain resources of the graphical system; it is important to dispose of them as soon as they are not required anymore. A use binding or the using function discussed in Chapters 4 and 8 helps ensure you don't forget to call the method Dispose that all these objects provide from the IDisposable interface that otherwise should be called explicitly.

You're now ready to define the function responsible for drawing in your window. You cannot assume anything about the current state of the window; thus, the paint function always draws the visible primitives[1] depending on the state of menu entries.

```
let paint (g:Graphics) =
    if (menuBezier.Checked) then
        g.DrawLine(Pens.Red, cpt.[0], cpt.[1])
        g.DrawLine(Pens.Red, cpt.[2], cpt.[3])
        g.DrawBeziers(Pens.Black, cpt)
    if (menuCanonical.Checked) then
        g.DrawCurve(Pens.Blue, cpt, float32 scrollbar.Value)
    if (menuControlPoints.Checked) then
        for i = 0 to cpt.Length - 1 do
            drawPoint g cpt.[i]
```

Figure 11-3 shows the result of the drawing all the elements.

The Bézier curve, widely used in image-processing and vector applications, uses the four control points to define the start and end points of the curve and the two segments tangent to the curve at its ends. The cubic parametric curve is calculated from these points and produces the red and black lines shown in Figure 11-3. The canonical spline, on the other hand, is a curve that traverses all the control points, and the tension parameter controls how "curvy" the curve is.

You now want to allow users to move control points simply by dragging and dropping. We're interested in mouse events, in particular when the mouse button is pressed, when it moves, and when the button is released. Thanks to the well-defined model for rendering the application, you can simply update the state of your variables and ask the graphical system to issue a *paint* message that will cause the window to receive a paint message and update the current frame.

---

1. If primitives fall out of the area allowed for drawing, they will be clipped, in part or in entirety.

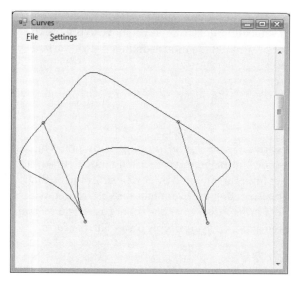

Figure 11-3. *Output of the Curves application*

BACKGROUND PAINTING

In our Curves application, we draw assuming that the window is clean, but who is responsible for clearing the previous drawing in the window? Windows Forms calls the OnPaintBackground method before calling the paint handler, and this method by default clears the area with the color returned by the BackColor property. When the function responsible for painting draws the area entirely, painting the background could be useless and even problematic: the quick repaint may flicker since the eye can perceive the background clear and then the drawing of the current frame. It is possible to use the SetStyle method of the Form class to configure the application to do all the paint operations in the handler of the paint event, and the OnPaintBackground can be overridden to an empty method in order to avoid this effect.

You define a helper function to define a circular area around a point that will be sensible to your interaction. This is required in order to not require the user to pick the exact pixel corresponding to the control point:

```
let isClose (p:Point) (l:Point) =
    let dx = p.X - l.X
    let dy = p.Y - l.Y
    (dx * dx + dy * dy) < 6
```

When the mouse is pressed, you check whether the click is over any control point, and in this case you store its index in the movingPoint variable; otherwise, the event is ignored:

```
let mouseDown (p:Point) =
    for i = 0 to cpt.Length - 1 do
        if (isClose p cpt.[i]) then
            movingPoint <- i
```

When the mouse moves over the client area of the window, the mouse move event gets generated. If the movingPoint member has a value different from –1, you have to update the corresponding control point with the current position of the mouse defined by the variable p:

```
let mouseMove (p:Point) =
    if (movingPoint <> -1) then
        cpt.[movingPoint] <- p
        form.Invalidate()
```

You next define a menu for the window with a File menu and a Settings submenu. The first features the classic Exit option, while the second shows the three checked menu items that control what the method paint should draw. Menus are defined by composing objects that correspond to the various menu entries. You also define the event handlers associated with each menu item. When Exit is clicked, the form is disposed. In all the other cases, you rely on the ability of the menu item changing checked state, and you simply invalidate the form content to force the redraw of the window.

```
let setupMenu () =
    let menu = new MenuStrip()
    let fileMenuItem = new ToolStripMenuItem("&File")
    let settMenuItem = new ToolStripMenuItem("&Settings")
    let exitMenuItem = new ToolStripMenuItem("&Exit")
    menu.Items.Add(fileMenuItem) |> ignore
    menu.Items.Add(settMenuItem) |> ignore
    fileMenuItem.DropDownItems.Add(exitMenuItem) |> ignore
    settMenuItem.DropDownItems.Add(menuBezier) |> ignore
    settMenuItem.DropDownItems.Add(menuCanonical) |> ignore
    settMenuItem.DropDownItems.Add(menuControlPoints) |> ignore
    exitMenuItem.Click.Add(fun _ -> form.Close ())
    menuBezier.Click.Add(fun _ -> form.Invalidate())
    menuCanonical.Click.Add(fun _ -> form.Invalidate())
    menuControlPoints.Click.Add(fun _ -> form.Invalidate())
    menu
```

You're now ready to use the functions you defined to configure the controls. You set up the scrollbar and register the controls in the form and the event handlers for the various events. Finally, you start the event loop of your application and play with it.

```
scrollbar.ValueChanged.Add(fun _ -> form.Invalidate())
form.Controls.Add(scrollbar)
form.MainMenuStrip <- setupMenu()
form.Controls.Add(form.MainMenuStrip)
form.Paint.Add(fun e -> paint(e.Graphics))
form.MouseDown.Add(fun e -> mouseDown(e.Location))
form.MouseMove.Add(fun e -> mouseMove(e.Location))
form.MouseUp.Add(fun e -> movingPoint <- -1)
form.Show()
```

If you're not using F# Interactive, don't forget to add the following:

```
[<STAThread>]
do Application.Run(form)
```

Writing Your Own Controls

The Curves example from the previous section draws inside a form by handling the events, but this is a rare way to draw things in graphical applications, since the resulting code is scarcely reusable and drawing on the surface of a form raises issues when additional controls have to be placed in its client area.

User controls are the abstraction provided by the Windows Forms framework to program custom controls. If delegation is used to handle events generated from controls, inheritance and method overriding are the tools used to handle them in controls.

Developing a Custom Control

To make this discussion concrete, consider a control that implements a simple button. You can use the control from C# inside the Visual Studio designer like the native button, as shown in Figure 11-4.

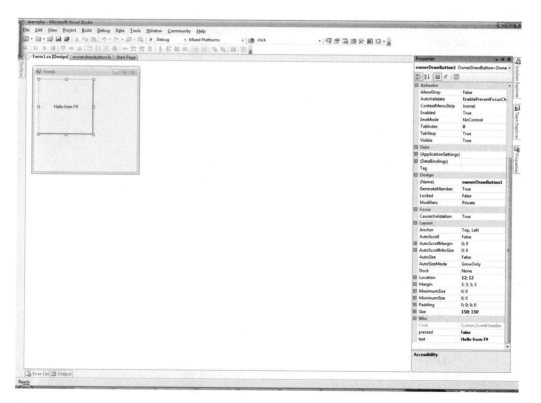

Figure 11-4. *The F# button control used in a C# application and the Visual Studio designer*

You start your control by inheriting from the UserControl class:[2]

```
open System
open System.Drawing
open System.Windows.Forms
open System.ComponentModel

type OwnerDrawButton() =
        inherit UserControl()
```

You then define the state of the control in terms of the fields of the class:

```
let mutable text = ""
let mutable pressed = false
let fireClick,clickEvent = IEvent.create()
```

The text field will contain the label of the button. As you did for the movingPoint variable in the Curves example, the pressed field is responsible for remembering whether the button is currently pressed, allowing the paint handler to behave appropriately. The fireClick and clickEvent fields remember the listeners registered to be notified of the click event of the button by using the F# events described in Chapter 8.

You override the OnPaint method to handle the paint event. You allocate the pens and the brush required to draw and invert the role of the border colors in order to achieve the raised effect when the button is not pressed and the depressed look otherwise. You also measure the size of the label string, since you are interested in drawing the string in the center of your button. You can then draw the lines on the borders, playing with colors to obtain a 3D effect. The pens and brushes are disposed at the end of the function.

```
override x.OnPaint (e:PaintEventArgs) =
    let g = e.Graphics
    use pll = new Pen(SystemColors.ControlLightLight)
    use pl = new Pen(SystemColors.ControlLight)
    use pd = new Pen(SystemColors.ControlDark)
    use pdd = new Pen(SystemColors.ControlDarkDark)
    use bfg = new SolidBrush(x.ForeColor)
    let szf = g.MeasureString(text, x.Font)
    let spt = PointF((float32(x.Width) - szf.Width) / 2.0f,
                     (float32(x.Height) - szf.Height) / 2.0f)
    let ptt = if pressed then pdd else pll
    let pt = if pressed then pd else pl
    let pb = if pressed then pl else pd
    let pbb = if pressed then pll else pdd

    g.Clear(SystemColors.Control)
    g.DrawLine(ptt, 0, 0, x.Width - 1, 0)
    g.DrawLine(ptt, 0, 0, 0, x.Height - 1)
```

---

2. Note that this example has not been designed to be entered using F# Interactive.

```
g.DrawLine(pt, 1, 1, x.Width - 2, 1)
g.DrawLine(pt, 1, 1, 1, x.Height - 2)
g.DrawLine(pbb, 0, x.Height - 1, x.Width - 1, x.Height - 1)
g.DrawLine(pbb, x.Width - 1, 0, x.Width - 1, x.Height - 1)
g.DrawLine(pb, 1, x.Height - 2, x.Width - 2, x.Height - 2)
g.DrawLine(pb, x.Width - 2, 1, x.Width - 2, x.Height - 2)
g.DrawString(text, x.Font, bfg, spt)
```

It is important to note the use of the colors defined in the SystemColors class: you use the system definition of colors so that your button will use the colors set by the user as display settings. Configuration is an important aspect of a user control, since it's normally performed through a visual editor such as Visual Studio. Well-defined controls are those that can be highly customized without having to extend the control programmatically or, even worse, to change its source code.

Now that you've defined the drawing procedure, you can define the behavior of the control by handling mouse events. You restrict the implementation to mouse events, though a key event handler should be provided in order to react to a press of the Enter key.

```
override x.OnMouseUp (e:MouseEventArgs) =
    pressed <- false
    x.Invalidate()
    fireClick()

override x.OnMouseDown (e:MouseEventArgs) =
    pressed <- true
    x.Invalidate()
```

The OnMouseDown event simply sets the pressed member and asks the control to repaint by invalidating its content. When the mouse is released, the OnMouseUp gets called, and you reset the flag, ask for repaint, and notify the event to registered listeners by using fireClick.

Controls are usually configured through the assignment of properties. If you annotate a property with an attribute of type Category, the property will be displayed by Visual Studio in the control property box. To show this, you have defined the Text property that exposes the label of the button to the users of the control.

```
[<Category("Behavior")>]
override x.Text
    with get() = text
    and  set(t:string) = text <- t; x.Invalidate()
```

You're now ready to test your new control by writing a few lines of F# code as follows:

```
let form = new Form(Visible=true)
let c = new OwnerDrawButton(Text="Hello button")

c.Click.Add(fun _ -> MessageBox.Show("Clicked!") |> ignore)
form.Controls.Add(c)
```

Anatomy of a Control

As witnessed by the OwnerDrawButton control example, the structure of a graphic control tends to assume the form of a finite state automaton. Events received by the control make the automaton change its internal state, usually causing an update of its actual display.

A well-known model that describes this structure is the Model-View-Controller design pattern. As shown in Figure 11-5, the model organizes a graphical element (either an application or a single control) into three parts: the model, the view, and the controller.

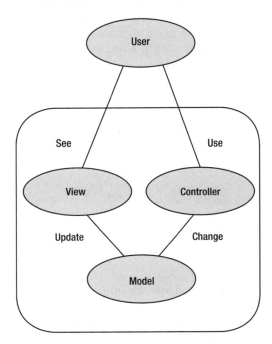

Figure 11-5. *The structure of the Model-View-Controller design pattern*

The model constitutes the internal representation of the information displayed by the control. A word processor, for instance, will store the document in memory as part of the model, even though the whole text does not fit the current visible area. In our simple button, the model is defined by the pressed and text values.

When the model changes, the view must be updated, and a rendering of the information kept in memory should be performed. Usually the paint method corresponds to the view portion of the control. Event handlers triggered by the user form the controller of the control. The controller defines how these elements affect the model.

The Model-View-Controller pattern is not the only model developed to describe graphical interfaces. It captures, however, the intrinsic nature of the problem, providing a good framework for classifying the elements of an interface or a control. In the rest of this chapter, we refer to this pattern to indicate the various elements of the applications we show how to develop.

Displaying Samples from Sensors

Now that you have reviewed the essential concepts behind programming graphical interfaces, we'll now cover some applications. These applications are full of details typical of real graphical applications. In this section, we present a graphic control whose purpose is to plot samples acquired over time, for instance, from a sensor. The control has been designed to be reusable and highly configurable, providing a rich set of properties that can be set even at run time by the application hosting it, as shown in Figure 11-6.

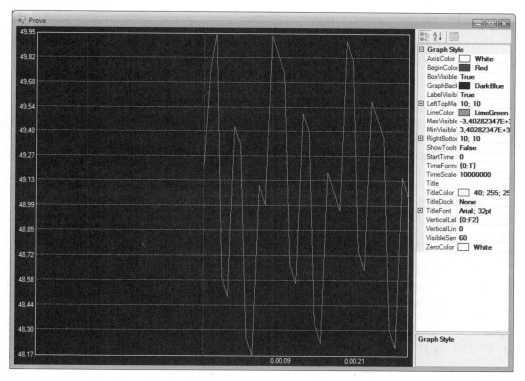

Figure 11-6. *The* GraphControl *used in a test application that lets the user to change its appearance at run time*

The basic function of the control is to receive and store samples labeled with time. If c is the variable that refers to an instance of the control, the application feeds data through an AddSample method that adds a new sample to the data set, causing the control to update the displayed chart:

```
c.AddSample(t, v)
```

We show how to define the control and the AddSample method in the next section.

Despite the simple interface provided by GraphControl to update the data set, the control is not easy to implement, since it must hold a large number of samples and provide a means to navigate through a view that will not fit all the samples. Another area important to controls is *configuration* since users of the control want to customize its appearance to fit the needs of their application. To support these needs, you must adopt the coding conventions required to integrate the control in the Windows Forms framework so that it will integrate with all the tools used to design applications.

Building the GraphControl: The Model

According to the Model-View-Controller paradigm, you first define the model of the control, which should contain all the information needed to draw the control when required. You first define the type of a sample:

```
type Sample = { Time : int64; Value : float32 }
```

Samples are pairs (t, v), with t being the time at which the sample v has been read. Samples are collected in a data structure named DataSamples, whose purpose is to provide a uniform view of data; the class definition is reported in Listing 11-1. We assume that the data set will always be small enough to stay in memory; this limitation could be overcome in the future by changing this class. Samples are collected into a ResizeArray and kept in the field named data. We also use a form of run-length-encoding (RLE) compression to optimize memory usage, and linear interpolation is used to make data appear continuous in order to simplify the implementation of the zoom feature. Since not all the samples are recorded, the count field is used to keep track of the number of added samples.

The AddSample method is used to add a new sample to the data set; it assumes that data comes sorted with respect to time, and if a sample preceding the last added is detected, it is discarded. The Last property returns the last-added sample; since you may have discarded it because it is equal to the previous, you rebuild the sample using the lastTime field that records the time value of the last sample added.

Interpolation is done by the GetValue method, which given a time value calculates the corresponding value. The list of samples is searched using a binary search. If a sample matches the given time, it is returned; otherwise, the interpolation is performed.

The last operation implemented by DataSamples is FindMinMax, which is a method that computes the minimum and maximum values of the data in a given interval. It is possible to initialize the initial values for minimum and maximum, as well as a stride to use to do the search. The stride is useful in conjunction with zoom, because the number of samples that can be displayed is finite and the rendering procedure must subsample when zooming out.

Listing 11-1. *The DataSamples Class Definition*

```
open System

type Sample = { Time : int64; Value : float32 }

type DataSamples() =
    let data = new ResizeArray<Sample>()
    let mutable count = 0
    let mutable lastTime = 0L

    member x.Last = { Time=lastTime; Value=data.[data.Count - 1].Value }
```

```
member x.AddSample(t,v) =
    let s = { Time=t; Value=v }
    let last = if (data.Count = 0) then s else x.Last

    count <- count + 1;
    lastTime <- max last.Time s.Time
    if data.Count = 0 then data.Add(s)

    elif last.Time < s.Time && last.Value <> s.Value then
        if data.[data.Count-1].Time <> last.Time then data.Add(last)
        data.Add(s)

member x.Count = count

// The model is continuous: missing samples are obtained by interpolation
member x.GetValue(time:int64) =

    // Find the relevant point via a binary search
    let rec search (lo, hi) =
        let mid = (lo + hi) / 2
        if hi - lo <= 1 then (lo, hi)
        elif data.[mid].Time = time then (mid, mid)
        elif data.[mid].Time < time then search (mid, hi)
        else search (lo, mid)

    if (data.Count = 0) then failwith "No data samples"

    if (lastTime < time) then failwith "Wrong time!"

    let lo,hi = search (0, data.Count - 1)

    if (data.[lo].Time = time || hi = lo) then data.[lo].Value
    elif (data.[hi].Time = time) then data.[hi].Value
    else
        // interpolate
        let p = if data.[hi].Time < time then hi else lo
        let next = data.[min (p+1) (data.Count-1)]
        let curr = data.[p]
        let spant = next.Time - curr.Time
        let spanv = next.Value - curr.Value
        curr.Value + float32(time-curr.Time) *(spanv/float32(spant))

// This method finds the minimum and the maximum values given
// a sampling frequence and an interval of time
member x.FindMinMax(sampleFreq:int64, start:int64, finish:int64,
                    minval:float32, maxval:float32) =
```

```
            if (data.Count = 0) then (minval, maxval) else
            let start = max start 0L
            let finish = min finish lastTime

            let minv,maxv =
                { start .. sampleFreq .. finish }
                |> Seq.map x.GetValue
                |> Seq.fold (fun (minv,maxv) v -> (min v minv,max v maxv))
                            (minval,maxval)

            if (minv = maxv) then
                let delta = if (minv = 0.0f) then 0.01f else 0.01f * abs minv
                (minv - delta, maxv + delta)
            else (minv, maxv)
```

Building the GraphControl: Style Properties and Controller

Listing 11-2 shows the code for the GraphControl class except the OnPaint drawing method,
shown in the next section. This control exhibits the typical structure of a graphic control; it
features a large number of constants and fields that serve configuration purposes. The class
inherits from UserControl, which is the base class of Windows Forms controls, and it contains
a field named data of type DataSamples that represents the data shown by the control. The
appearance is controlled through properties, fields, and constant values; for instance, the axis
color is controlled by the following pattern:

```
let mutable axisColor:Color = Color.White
[<Category("Graph Style")>]
member x.AxisColor
    with get() = x.axisColor
    and set(v:Color) = x.axisColor <- v; x.Invalidate()
```

The AxisColor property lets the host of the control change the color of the axis color displayed
by the control since properties are part of the controller of the control; thus, when the setter is
invoked, you call the Invalidate method to ensure that a paint message is sent to the control
so that the view gets updated. Note that a fully fledged control might read defaults from a store
of user-specific configuration properties.

Listing 11-2. *The GraphControl Class*

```
open System
open System.Drawing
open System.Drawing.Drawing2D
open System.Windows.Forms
open System.ComponentModel

type GraphControl()  =
    inherit UserControl() as base
```

```
let data = new DataSamples()
let mutable minVisibleValue = Single.MaxValue
let mutable maxVisibleValue = Single.MinValue
let mutable absMax       = Single.MinValue
let mutable absMin       = Single.MaxValue
let mutable lastMin      = minVisibleValue
let mutable lastMax      = maxVisibleValue
let mutable axisColor    = Color.White
let mutable beginColor   = Color.Red
let mutable verticalLabelFormat = "{0:F2}"
let mutable startTime    = 0L
let mutable visibleSamples = 10
let mutable initView = startTime - int64(visibleSamples)
let mutable verticalLines   = 0
let mutable timeScale = 10000000 // In 100-nanoseconds
let mutable timeFormat = "{0:T}"

let rightBottomMargin = Size(10, 10)
let leftTopMargin     = Size(10, 10)

do base.BackColor <- Color.DarkBlue

[<Category("Graph Style")>]
member x.AxisColor
    with get() = axisColor
    and set(v:Color) = axisColor <- v; x.Invalidate()

[<Category("Graph Style")>]
member x.BeginColor
    with get() = beginColor
    and set(v:Color) = beginColor <- v; x.Invalidate()

[<Category("Graph Style")>]
member x.MinVisibleValue
    with get() = minVisibleValue
    and set(v:float32) = minVisibleValue <- v; lastMin <- v; x.Invalidate()

[<Category("Graph Style")>]
member x.MaxVisibleValue
    with get() = maxVisibleValue
    and set(v:float32) = maxVisibleValue <- v; lastMax <- v; x.Invalidate()

[<Category("Graph Style")>]
member x.VerticalLines
    with get() = verticalLines
    and set(v:int) = verticalLines <- v; x.Invalidate()
```

```
[<Category("Graph Style")>]
member x.GraphBackColor
    with get() = x.BackColor
    and set(v:Color) = x.BackColor <- v

[<Category("Graph Style")>]
member x.LineColor
    with get() = x.ForeColor
    and set(v:Color) = x.ForeColor <- v

[<Category("Graph Style")>]
member x.VerticalLabelFormat
    with get() = verticalLabelFormat
    and set(v:string) = verticalLabelFormat <- v; x.Invalidate()

[<Category("Graph Style")>]
member x.StartTime
    with get() = startTime
    and set(v:int64) = startTime <- v; x.Invalidate()

[<Category("Graph Style")>]
member x.Title
    with get() = x.Text
    and set(v:string) = x.Text <- v; x.Invalidate()

[<Category("Graph Style")>]
member x.VisibleSamples
    with get() = visibleSamples
    and set(v:int) =
        visibleSamples <- v;
        initView <- startTime - int64(visibleSamples);
        x.Invalidate()

[<Category("Graph Style")>]
member x.TimeScale
    with get() = timeScale
    and set(v:int) = timeScale <- v; x.Invalidate()

[<Category("Graph Style")>]
member x.TimeFormat
    with get() = timeFormat
    and set(v:string) = timeFormat <- v; x.Invalidate()

// ... Further portions of this class shown further below
```

■**Note** The control shown here is a cut-down version of a larger control available at `http://` `www.expert-fsharp.com/Topics/WindowsFormsControls`. The full control defines tool tips on mouse movements and defines additional style properties, and the style settings can be copied and saved using XML serialization.

Listing 11-3 includes the remaining portions of the `GraphControl` class corresponding to the Controller part of the Model-View-Controller paradigm. Samples are added through the `AddSample` method (the `AddSampleData` simply generates random samples to display inside the control). This method adds the sample to the inner `DataSamples` object and updates the values of two fields meant to store the minimum and maximum values recorded for samples; both of these values will be used in the display process. Since the model of the control changes, you need to update the view, and you invalidate the control as you did for properties.

OVERRIDING VS. DELEGATION

Event handling can be performed by both subscribing delegates and overriding methods. The former approach is more typical of applications; the latter is more common in control development. Method overriding guarantees more control on the event handling because it allows a complete redefinition of the inherited behavior, whereas with delegation it is possible to only add behavior.

When an overridden method starts with a call to the method to be overridden in the base class, then it is functionally equivalent to use delegation rather than method overriding. It is traditional, however, to use method overriding in the case of control development to have a uniform notation for event handling.

It is important to be careful during method overriding since if the call to the overridden method is omitted, the corresponding delegate event is not fired because delegate events are invoked by the event handlers of the base classes.

Let's take a look at how you handle the mouse move events and the use of the mouse wheel. When the wheel of the mouse is scrolled, the control adjusts the scale factor to zoom in or out of the current view. To show how this method works, we must discuss how you decide which portion of the data is made available through the view of the control. You use two fields called `initView` and `visibleSamples`. Since you cannot assume that all the samples fit in the display of the control, the former indicates the time (in the time scale of the samples) corresponding to the leftmost visible value, and the latter indicates the number of time units in the unit scale of samples that should be visible. Zooming is performed by changing the density of time units to be displayed inside the viewport.

The last method of Listing 11-3 is `GetTime`, and it is used to convert the time unit of samples in microseconds using a scale factor that is one of the configuration properties made available by the control.

Listing 11-3. *Extract of the Controller of the GraphControl Class*

```
override x.OnMouseWheel (e:MouseEventArgs) =
    base.OnMouseWheel(e)
    x.Zoom(e.Delta)

override x.OnSizeChanged (e:EventArgs) =
    base.OnSizeChanged(e)
    x.Invalidate()

member x.Zoom (amount:int) =
    let newVisibleSamples = max 5 (visibleSamples + amount)
    if (initView - startTime < 0L) then
        let e = initView + int64(visibleSamples)
        initView <- startTime - int64(newVisibleSamples) + e
        visibleSamples <- newVisibleSamples
        x.Invalidate()

member x.AddSample (time:int64, value:float32) =
    if (value < absMin) then absMin <- value
    if (value > absMax) then absMax <- value
    if (data.Count > 0) then
        initView <- initView + time - data.Last.Time
    data.AddSample(time, value)
    x.Invalidate()

member x.GetTime (time:int64) =
    DateTime(max 0L time * int64(timeScale))
```

Building the GraphControl: The View

The View of the GraphControl is entirely contained within the OnPaint method, which is invoked when the GUI needs to repaint the content of the control or when an invocation of the Invalidate method occurs. Listing 11-4 shows the full code for this method. Programming graphical controls can get complicated, and often the code is factorized further using functions.

The OnPaint method begins computing some information such as the rectangles containing the string with the values to be displayed. The dimension of a string depends on the font used for displaying and from the particular device context used to render it. You rely on the MeasureString method of the Graphics object you received from the GUI. You compute the plotBox rectangle, which represents the area where you will draw the data, and it is obtained by removing from the dimension of the control the margins specified in the configuration and the space required by the labels if visible. You later set an appropriate coordinate system on the device context so that the drawing primitives will render in this new system:

```
g.TranslateTransform(float32(plotBox.Left), float32(x.Height - plotBox.Top))
g.ScaleTransform(1.0f, -1.0f)
```

You translate the origin of the coordinate system in the left-bottom vertex of the margins rectangle. You also flip the *y* axis by setting a scale transform that inverts the direction multiplying *y* coordinates by –1.0f; in this way, you obtain a coordinate system oriented as in mathematics. Coordinate transformation is supported by Windows Forms on the Graphics object: all the coordinates specified in the drawing primitives are affected by a transformation matrix stored in the device context. Once set, a transformation of the library takes care of the calculations necessary to rotate, translate, and scale all the objects.

After clearing the background using the Background color property, you draw the various lines such as the axes and the labels depending on the configuration settings specified by setting the various properties of the control. This is the typical structure of a paint method, where the Model is tested to decide what should be drawn and the style to be used.

The drawing of the data samples is controlled by the timexunit and pixelsPerUnit variables, and then the inner recursive function drawSamples selects the visible samples and uses the DataSamples object to compute results. You rely on the ability of the DataSamples class to interpolate data and not have to deal with discrete samples.

The core business of the paint method is often rather simple (having paid attention when defining the Model and the Controller of the control); it quickly becomes entangled in testing all the configuration properties to determine how the control should be rendered.

Listing 11-4. *Drawing the Control*

```
override x.OnPaint (e:PaintEventArgs) =
    let g = e.Graphics

    // A helper function to size up strings
    let measure s = g.MeasureString(s, x.Font)

    // Work out the size of the box to show the values
    let valBox =
        let minbox = measure (String.Format(verticalLabelFormat, lastMin))
        let maxbox = measure (String.Format(verticalLabelFormat, lastMax))
        let vbw = max minbox.Width maxbox.Width
        let vbh = max minbox.Height maxbox.Height
        SizeF(vbw, vbh)

    // Work out the size of the box to show the times
    let timeBox =
        let lasttime = x.GetTime(initView + int64(visibleSamples))
        let timelbl = String.Format(timeFormat, lasttime)
        measure timelbl

    // Work out the plot area for the graph
    let plotBox =
        let ltm = leftTopMargin
        let rbm = rightBottomMargin
```

```
            let ltm,rbm =
                let ltm = Size(width=max ltm.Width (int(valBox.Width)+5),
                               height=max ltm.Height (int(valBox.Height/2.0f) + 2))
                let rbm = Size(width=rightBottomMargin.Width,
                               height=max rbm.Height (int(timeBox.Height) + 5))
                ltm,rbm

            // Since we invert y axis use Top instead of Bottom and vice versa
            Rectangle(ltm.Width, rbm.Height,
                      x.Width - ltm.Width - rbm.Width,
                      x.Height - ltm.Height - rbm.Height)

        // The time interval per visible sample
        let timePerUnit =
            let samplew = float32(visibleSamples) / float32(plotBox.Width)
            max 1.0f samplew

        // The pixel interval per visible sample
        let pixelsPerUnit =
            let pixelspan = float32(plotBox.Width) / float32(visibleSamples)
            max 1.0f pixelspan

        // Compute the range we need to plot
        let (lo, hi) = data.FindMinMax(int64(timePerUnit),
                                       initView,
                                       initView + int64(visibleSamples),
                                       minVisibleValue,
                                       maxVisibleValue)

        // Save the range to help with computing sizes next time around
        lastMin <- lo; lastMax <- hi

        // We use these graphical resources during plotting
        use linePen  = new Pen(x.ForeColor)
        use axisPen  = new Pen(axisColor)
        use beginPen = new Pen(beginColor)
        use gridPen  = new Pen(Color.FromArgb(127, axisColor),
                               DashStyle=DashStyle.Dash)
        use fontColor = new SolidBrush(axisColor)

        // Draw the title
        if (x.Text <> null && x.Text <> string.Empty) then

            let sz = measure x.Text
            let mw = (float32(plotBox.Width) - sz.Width) / 2.0f
            let tm = float32(plotBox.Bottom - plotBox.Height)
```

```
    let p = PointF(float32(plotBox.Left) + mw, tm)
    g.DrawString(x.Text, x.Font, new SolidBrush(x.ForeColor), p)

// Draw the labels
let nly = int((float32(plotBox.Height) /valBox.Height) / 3.0f)
let nlx = int((float32(plotBox.Width) / timeBox.Width) / 3.0f)
let pxly = plotBox.Height / max nly 1
let pxlx = plotBox.Width / max nlx 1
let dvy = (hi - lo) / float32(nly)
let dvx = float32(visibleSamples) / float32(nlx)
let drawString (s:string) (xp:float32) (yp:float32) =
    g.DrawString(s,x.Font,fontColor,xp,yp)

// Draw the value (y) labels
for i = 0 to nly do
  let liney = i * pxly + int(valBox.Height / 2.0f) + 2
  let lblfmt = verticalLabelFormat
  let posy = float32(x.Height - plotBox.Top - i * pxly)
  let label = String.Format(lblfmt, float32(i) * dvy + lo)
  drawString label (float32(plotBox.Left) - valBox.Width)
                   (posy - valBox.Height / 2.0f)

  if (i = 0 ||((i > 0) && (i < nly))) then
    g.DrawLine(gridPen, plotBox.Left,liney,plotBox.Right, liney)

// Draw the time (x) labels
for i = 0 to nlx do
  let linex = i * pxlx + int(timeBox.Width / 2.0f) + 2
  let time = int64(float32(i) * dvx + float32(initView))
  let label = String.Format(timeFormat, x.GetTime(time))

  if (time > 0L) then
    drawString label
        (float32(plotBox.Left + i * pxlx) + timeBox.Width / 2.0f)
        (float32(x.Height - plotBox.Top + 2))

// Set a transform on the graphics state to make drawing in the
// plotBox simpler
g.TranslateTransform(float32(plotBox.Left),
                     float32(x.Height - plotBox.Top));
g.ScaleTransform(1.0f, -1.0f);

// Draw the plotBox of the plot area
g.DrawLine(axisPen, 0, 0, 0, plotBox.Height)
g.DrawLine(axisPen, 0, 0, plotBox.Width, 0)
g.DrawLine(axisPen, plotBox.Width, 0, plotBox.Width, plotBox.Height)
g.DrawLine(axisPen, 0, plotBox.Height, plotBox.Width, plotBox.Height)
```

```
        // Draw the vertical lines in the plotBox
        let px = plotBox.Width / (verticalLines + 1)
        for i = 1 to verticalLines do
            g.DrawLine(gridPen, i*px, 0, i*px, plotBox.Height)

        // Draw the 'begin' marker that shows where data begins
        if (initView - startTime <= 0L) then
            let off = float32(Math.Abs(x.StartTime - initView))
            let sx = int((off/timePerUnit) * pixelsPerUnit)
            g.DrawLine(beginPen, sx, 0, sx, plotBox.Height)

        // Draw the 'zero' horizontal line if it's visible
        if (hi <> lo && lo < 0.0f) then
            let sy = int((float32(plotBox.Height)/(hi - lo))*(0.0f - lo))
            g.DrawLine(axisPen, 0, sy, plotBox.Width, sy)

        // Draw the visible data samples
        let rec drawSamples i pos =
            if (i < (float32(plotBox.Width) / pixelsPerUnit) &&
                pos <= (initView + int64 visibleSamples - int64 timePerUnit)) then

                if (pos >= 0L) then
                    let dh = float32(plotBox.Height) / (hi - lo)
                    let sx = int(pixelsPerUnit * i)
                    let dx = int(pixelsPerUnit * (i + 1.0f))
                    let sy = int(dh * (data.GetValue(pos) - lo))
                    let dy = int(dh * (data.GetValue(pos + int64 timePerUnit) - lo))
                    g.DrawLine(linePen, sx, sy, dx, dy);

                drawSamples (i + 1.0f) (pos + int64 timePerUnit)

        drawSamples 0.0f initView
```

Putting It Together

Finally, the following is the code that uses the control you aim to develop and that defines the application shown in Figure 11-6.

```
let form = new Form(Text="Chart test",Size=Size(800, 600),Visible=true,TopMost=true)
let graph = new GraphControl(VisibleSamples=60, Dock=DockStyle.Fill)
let properties = new PropertyGrid(Dock=DockStyle.Fill)
let timer = new Timer(Interval=200)
let container = new SplitContainer(Dock=DockStyle.Fill, SplitterDistance=350)

// We use a split container to divide the area into two parts
container.Panel1.Controls.Add(graph)
container.Panel2.Controls.Add(properties)
```

```
// Configure the property grid to display only properties in the
// category "Graph Style"
properties.SelectedObject <- graph
let graphStyleCat = (CategoryAttribute("Graph Style") :> Attribute)
properties.BrowsableAttributes <- AttributeCollection([| graphStyleCat |])
form.Controls.Add(container)
let rnd = new Random()
let time = ref 0
// A timer is used to simulate incoming data
timer.Tick.Add(fun _ ->
    incr time
    let v = 48.0 + 2.0 * rnd.NextDouble()
    graph.AddSample(int64(!time),float32(v)))
timer.Start()
```

The form uses a `SplitContainer` control to define two areas, one for `GraphControl` and the other for a `PropertyGrid` control. A timer object is used to add samples periodically, and you use the `AddSample` method to add random samples to the control.

THE PROPERTYGRID CONTROL

`PropertyGrid` is a graphic control that allows inspecting properties of objects at run time and changing them, as shown in the right side of the window of Figure 11-6. You set the `SelectedObject` property to indicate the control to display, in this case the `GraphControl`.

The `PropertyGrid` uses the reflection abilities of the Common Language Runtime to dynamically inspect the object and generate the visual grid. By default, the control displays the properties of the given object annotated using the `BrowsableAttribute` custom attribute. You set the `BrowsableAttributes` property to indicate you are interested in displaying only the properties annotated as `[<Category("Graph Style")>]`.

Not all types can be edited from the `PropertyGrid`, though the control is able to deal with many. A property of type `Color`, for instance, causes the grid to display the preview of the color and allows defining the value using several methods, including the Color Chooser dialog box.

Creating a Mandelbrot Viewer

Fractals are one of the diamonds of mathematics, and they show the beauty of mathematical structures visually, which allows nonexperts to see something that is often hidden by formulas that few really appreciate. The Mandelbrot set is one of the most famous fractals. In this section, we will show how to develop an application to browse this set. The result is shown in Figure 11-7.

In this application, we adopt the programming style of delegation, subscribing to events rather than using inheritance to override the behavior of a component. This allows you to develop the application interactively using `fsi.exe`. This is a good example of how effectively you can use F# to develop an application interactively while retaining the performance of a compiled language, which is extremely important in such CPU-intensive tasks as computing the points of the Mandelbrot set.

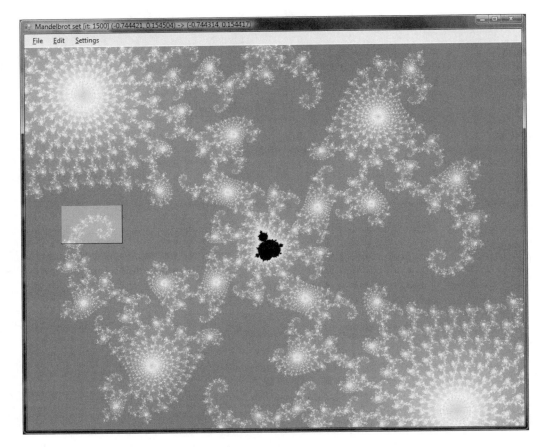

Figure 11-7. *The Mandelbrot viewer in action*

Computing Mandelbrot

First we'll discuss the math required to generate the Mandelbrot set. The set is defined over the set of complex numbers, which is an extension of the real numbers, allowing computation of square roots over negative numbers. A complex number has the following form, where a and b are real numbers and i is the imaginary unit, by definition, $i^2 = -1$:

```
c = a + bi
```

Using standard algebraic calculations, it is possible to define the sum and product of these numbers:

$$c_1 + c_2 = (a_1 + a_2) + i(b_1 + b_2)$$
$$c_1 \cdot c_2 = (a_1 \cdot a_2 - b_1 \cdot b_2) + i(a_1 \cdot b_2 + a_2 \cdot b_1)$$

Since you have two components in the definition of the number, you can graphically represent complex numbers using a plane.

This Mandelbrot viewer shows a portion of the complex plane, where each point in the plane is colored according to a relation that defines the Mandelbrot set. The relation is based on the following iterative definition:

$$M(c) = \begin{cases} z_0 = c \\ z_{i+1} = z_i^2 + c \end{cases}$$

A complex number belongs to the Mandelbrot set if z_n converges for n. You can test each number c in the complex plane and decide whether the number belongs to the Mandelbrot set. Since it's not practical to perform an infinite computation to test each number of the complex plane, there is an approximation of the test based on a theorem that if the distance of z_i from the origin passes 2, then the sequence will diverge and the corresponding z_0 will not belong to the set.

The code to compute membership of the Mandelbrot set is as follows:

```
open Microsoft.FSharp.Math

let sqrMod (x:complex) = x.r * x.r + x.i * x.i

let rec mandel maxit (z:Complex) (c: Complex) count =
    if (sqrMod(z) < 4.0) &&  (count < maxit) then
        mandel maxit ((z * z) + c) c (count + 1)
    else count
```

A simple visual representation of the Mandelbrot set is to simply color all the points belonging to the set. In this way, you obtain the black portion of Figure 11-7. How can you obtain the richness of color? The trick is to color points depending on how fast the sequence reaches the distance of 2 from the origin. You use 250 colors and map the [0, maxit] interval to the [0, 250] discrete color interval.

Setting Colors

We're ready now to discuss the code for the Mandelbrot viewer application. For an appealing coloring, you need to produce some form of continuity in the color variation in the chosen range. You use an array of colors to store these values, but you need some procedure to fill this array so that colors change continuously.

Colors in the Red Green Blue (RGB) space used in the graphics libraries are known to define a color space that is not perceived as continuous by human vision. A color space known to be more effective in this respect is the Hue Saturation Value (HSV), where a color is defined in terms of hue, color saturation, and the value of luminance (see Figure 11-8). This model was inspired by the method used by painters to create colors in oil painting.

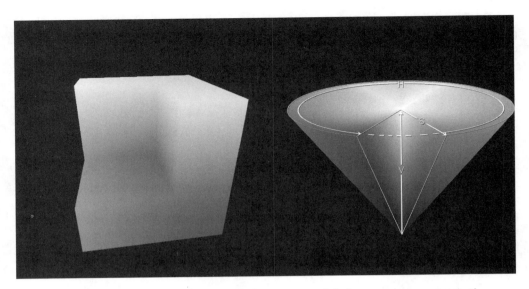

Figure 11-8. *The RGB (left) and HSV (right) color spaces and their geometric representation*

Figure 11-8 shows a typical geometric representation of the two color spaces. In the RGB color model the three axes represent the three base colors varying from black to the full color; in the HSV space, the angle is used to indicate the hue, the distance from the axis of the cone represents the saturation, and the value corresponds to the height of the point inside the cone.

It's possible to define a conversion from RGB color space to HSV, and vice versa. Listing 11-5 shows the F# functions performing the conversions between the two models. These functions assume the three components R, G, and B are in the interval [0, 1] rather than integers between 0 and 255.

Listing 11-5. *Conversion from RGB to HSV, and Vice Versa*

```
let RGBtoHSV (r, g, b) =
    let (m:float) = min r (min g b)
    let (M:float) = max r (max g b)
    let delta = M - m
    let posh (h:float) = if h < 0.0 then h + 360.0 else h
    let deltaf (f:float) (s:float) = (f - s) / delta
    if M = 0.0 then (-1.0, 0.0, M) else
        let s = (M - m) / M
        if r = M then (posh(60.0 * (deltaf g b)), s, M)
        elif g = M then (posh(60.0 * (2.0 + (deltaf b r))), s, M)
        else (posh(60.0 * (4.0 + (deltaf r g))), s, M)

let HSVtoRGB (h, s, v) =
    if s = 0.0 then (v, v, v) else
    let hs = h / 60.0
    let i = floor (hs)
    let f = hs - i
```

```
let p = v * ( 1.0 - s )
let q = v * ( 1.0 - s * f )
let t = v * ( 1.0 - s * ( 1.0 - f ))
match int i with
  | 0 -> (v, t, p)
  | 1 -> (q, v, p)
  | 2 -> (p, v, t)
  | 3 -> (p, q, v)
  | 4 -> (t, p, v)
  | _ -> (v, p, q)
```

To let users choose the coloring of the set, you create an array of 10 functions, given an integer between 0 and 250, for a corresponding color. The default color function is based on the HSV color model, and it simply uses the input parameter to set the hue of the color, leaving the saturation and luminance at the maximum values. The other functions use the RGB color space following directions in the color cube. You use the createPalette function to generate the color palette that will be used while drawing fractal points; the palette mutable variable holds this palette. Listing 11-6 shows the code dealing with colors. The pickColor function is responsible for mapping the iteration, it, at which the computation of the Mandelbrot set has terminated given the maximum number of iterations allowed, maxit.

Listing 11-6. *Color Palette Definition*

```
let makeColor (r, g, b) =
    Color.FromArgb(int32(r * 255.0), int32(g * 255.0), int32(b * 255.0))

let defaultColor i = makeColor(HSVtoRGB(360.0 * (float i / 250.0), 1.0, 1.0))

let coloring =
    [| defaultColor;
       (fun i -> Color.FromArgb(i, i, i));
       (fun i -> Color.FromArgb(i, 0, 0));
       (fun i -> Color.FromArgb(0, i, 0));
       (fun i -> Color.FromArgb(0, 0, i));
       (fun i -> Color.FromArgb(i, i, 0));
       (fun i -> Color.FromArgb(i, 250 - i, 0));
       (fun i -> Color.FromArgb(250 - i, i, i));
       (fun i -> if i % 2 = 0 then Color.White else Color.Black);
       (fun i -> Color.FromArgb(250 - i, 250 - i, 250 - i))
    |]

let createPalette c =
    Array.init 253 (function
            | 250 -> Color.Black
            | 251 -> Color.White
            | 252 -> Color.LightGray
            | i ->   c i)
```

```
let mutable palette = createPalette coloring.[0]

let pickColor maxit it =
    palette.[int(250.0 * float it / float maxit)]
```

Creating the Visualization Application

You're now ready to implement your graphical application. The basic idea is to map a rectangle of the complex plane in the client area of your form. Each point of your window will correspond to a complex number and be colored according to the value computed by the mandel function.

A typical value for maxit is 150 for the initial rendering of the Mandelbrot set, though it should be incremented when zooming into the fractal. The total computation required to compute a whole image is significant; therefore, you cannot rely on the main thread to perform the computation of the various points. It is important to recall that event handlers are invoked by the thread of the graphical interface, and if this thread is used to perform heavy computations, the application windows will not respond to other events.

You introduce a thread responsible for performing the computations required by the Mandelbrot set so that the GUI thread can continue to handle events. (We discuss threads in more detail in Chapter 13.) Here you use shared memory to communicate the results between the threads by using a bitmap image in memory, referenced by the bitmap variable, which is updated by the thread performing the computation task and read by the GUI thread when the form must be painted. The bitmap is convenient because you need a matrix of points to be colored, and the device context is designed to avoid pixel coloring to be device independent (it does not provide a SetColor(x, y) operation). To avoid race conditions, you use the lock function to guarantee exclusive access to the bitmap shared between the two threads. You will look at this in more detail in Chapter 13. The thread responsible for the set computation executes the following function:

```
let run filler (form:#Form) (bitmap:Bitmap) (tlx, tly) (brx, bry) =
    let dx = (brx - tlx) / float bmpw
    let dy = (tly - bry) / float bmph
    let maxit = iterations (tlx, tly) (brx, bry)
    let x = 0
    let y = 0
    let transform x y =
        Complex.Create (tlx + (float x) * dx, tly - (float y) * dy )
    form.Invoke(new MethodInvoker(fun () ->
        form.Text <- sprintf "Mandelbrot set [it: %d] (%f, %f) -> (%f, %f)"
                        maxit tlx tly brx bry
    )) |> ignore
    filler maxit transform
    timer.Enabled <- false
```

You use dx and dy variables to map the x and y coordinates of the bitmap into the complex plane. You then invoke the filler function responsible for performing the calculation. There are different possible filling strategies to compute the colors of the set; the straightforward approach is left to right and top to bottom, implemented by the linearFill function:

```
let linearFill (bw:int) (bh:int) maxit map =
    for y = 0 to bh - 1 do
        for x = 0 to bw - 1 do
            let c = mandel maxit Complex.Zero (map x y) 0
            lock bitmap (fun () -> bitmap.SetPixel(x, y, pickColor maxit c))
```

Another typical filling strategy is to gradually refine the set by computing points in blocks and filling the blocks of the appropriate color; then the missing points are computed by refining the block size. Using this strategy, it is possible to provide a quick preview of the fractal without having to wait for the whole computation. The blockFill function implements this strategy:

```
let blockFill (bw:int) (bh:int) maxit map =
    let rec fillBlock first sz x y =
        if x < bw then
            let c = mandel maxit Complex.Zero (map x y) 0
            lock bitmap (fun () ->
                let g = Graphics.FromImage(bitmap)
                g.FillRectangle(new SolidBrush(pickColor maxit c), x, y, sz, sz)
                g.Dispose()
            )
            fillBlock first sz (if first || ((y / sz) % 2 = 1) then x + sz
                                else x + 2 * sz) y
        elif y < bh then
            fillBlock first sz (if first || ((y / sz) % 2 = 0) then 0 else sz)
                    (y + sz)
        elif sz > 1 then
            fillBlock false (sz / 2) (sz / 2) 0

    fillBlock true 64 0 0
```

The variable fillFun is used to store the current filling function:

```
let mutable fillFun = blockFill
```

You clear the bitmap by obtaining a device context to the bitmap and clear it. The global variable bitmap is used to access the image from the code; this is an effective choice to speed up the development of the application. However, this technique can be a problem from a software engineering standpoint because the program is less modular and the mutable state is not encapsulated.

```
let clearOffScreen (b : Bitmap) =
    use g = Graphics.FromImage(b)
    g.Clear(Color.White)

let mutable bitmap = new Bitmap(form.Width, form.Height)
let mutable bmpw = form.Width
let mutable bmph = form.Height
```

To refresh the application form while the fractal computation is ongoing, you use a timer that triggers a refresh of the form every tenth of a second. The paint function simply draws the bitmap that is updated by the worker thread:

```
let paint (g: Graphics) =
    lock bitmap (fun () -> g.DrawImage(bitmap, 0, 0))
    g.DrawRectangle(Pens.Black, rect)
    g.FillRectangle(new SolidBrush(Color.FromArgb(128, Color.White)), rect)

let timer = new Timer(Interval=100)
timer.Tick.Add(fun _ -> form.Invalidate() )

let stopWorker () =
    if worker <> Thread.CurrentThread then
        worker.Abort()
        worker <- Thread.CurrentThread
```

The drawMandel function is responsible for starting the rendering process:

```
let drawMandel () =
    let bf = fillFun bmpw bmph
    stopWorker();
    timer.Enabled <- true
    worker <- new Thread(fun () -> run bf form bitmap tl br)
    worker.IsBackground <- true
    worker.Priority <- ThreadPriority.Lowest
    worker.Start()
```

Creating the Application Plumbing

Now that you've defined the architecture of the application, you can define all the graphical aspects, the form, and the menus, as well as how users will interact with the application. The code is similar to the previous applications, as shown in Listing 11-7. Note two aspects: the rect variable contains the current selection, and it is drawn as a rectangle filled with transparent white; when the familiar Ctrl+C key sequence is pressed, the current bitmap is copied to the Clipboard.

The selection rectangle is updated by the mouse event handlers. The Copy function defined in the menu simply invokes the SetDataObject method of the Clipboard class. The zoom facility is obtained by setting the bounds of the complex plane defined by the variables tl and br.

Listing 11-7. *Setup of the Application Form and Event Handling*

```
type CanvasForm() as x =
    inherit Form()
    do x.SetStyle(ControlStyles.OptimizedDoubleBuffer, true)
    override x.OnPaintBackground(args) = ()

// Creates the Form
let form = new CanvasForm(Width=800, Height=600,Text="Mandelbrot set")

let mutable worker = Thread.CurrentThread
```

```
let mutable startsel = Point.Empty
let mutable rect = Rectangle.Empty

let mutable tl = (-3.0, 2.0)
let mutable br = (2.0, -2.0)

let mutable menuIterations = 150

let iterations (tlx, tly) (brx, bry) =
    menuIterations

let setCoord (tlx:float, tly:float) (brx:float, bry:float)  =
    let ratio = (float bmpw / float bmph)
    let dx = (brx - tlx) / float bitmap.Width
    let dy = (tly - bry) / float bitmap.Height
    let mapx x = tlx + float x * dx
    let mapy y = tly - float y * dy
    if ratio * float rect.Height > float rect.Width then
        let nw = int (ratio * float rect.Height )
        rect.X <- rect.X - (nw - rect.Width) / 2
        rect.Width <- nw
    else
        let nh = int (float rect.Width / ratio)
        rect.Y <- rect.Y - (nh - rect.Height) / 2
        rect.Height <- nh
    tl <- (mapx rect.Left, mapy rect.Top)
    br <- (mapx rect.Right, mapy rect.Bottom)

let updateView () =
    setCoord tl br
    rect <- Rectangle.Empty
    stopWorker()
    clearOffScreen bitmap
    drawMandel()

let click (arg:MouseEventArgs) =
    if rect.Contains(arg.Location) then
        updateView()
    else
        form.Invalidate()
        rect <- Rectangle.Empty
        startsel <- arg.Location

let mouseMove (arg:MouseEventArgs) =
    if arg.Button = MouseButtons.Left then
        let tlx = min startsel.X arg.X
        let tly = min startsel.Y arg.Y
```

```
            let brx = max startsel.X arg.X
            let bry = max startsel.Y arg.Y
            rect <- new Rectangle(tlx, tly, brx - tlx, bry - tly)
            form.Invalidate()

    let resize () =
        if bmpw <> form.ClientSize.Width ||
           bmph <> form.ClientSize.Height then
             stopWorker()
             rect <- form.ClientRectangle
             bitmap <- new Bitmap(form.ClientSize.Width, form.ClientSize.Height)
             bmpw <- form.ClientSize.Width
             bmph <- form.ClientSize.Height

             updateView()

    let zoom amount =
        let r = form.ClientRectangle
        let nw = int(floor(float r.Width * amount))
        let nh = int(floor(float r.Height * amount))
        rect <- Rectangle(r.X - ((nw - r.Width)/2), r.Y - ((nh-r.Height)/2), nw, nh)
        updateView()

    type Direction = Top | Left | Right | Bottom

    let move (d:Direction) =
        let r = form.ClientRectangle
        match d with
        | Top    -> rect <- Rectangle(r.X, r.Y - (r.Height / 10), r.Width, r.Height)
                    updateView()
        | Left   -> rect <- Rectangle(r.X - (r.Width / 10), r.Y, r.Width, r.Height)
                    updateView()
        | Bottom -> rect <- Rectangle(r.X, r.Y + (r.Height / 10), r.Width, r.Height)
                    updateView()
        | Right  -> rect <- Rectangle(r.X + (r.Width / 10), r.Y, r.Width, r.Height)
                    updateView()

    let selectDropDownItem (l:ToolStripMenuItem) (o:ToolStripMenuItem) =
        l.DropDownItems
        |> Seq.untyped_iter (fun (el:ToolStripMenuItem) -> el.Checked <- ((o = el)))

    let setFillMode (p:ToolStripMenuItem) (m:ToolStripMenuItem) filler _ =
        if (not m.Checked) then
            selectDropDownItem p m
            fillFun <- filler
            drawMandel()
```

```
let setupMenu () =
  let m = new MenuStrip()
  let f = new ToolStripMenuItem("&File")
  let c = new ToolStripMenuItem("&Settings")
  let e = new ToolStripMenuItem("&Edit")
  let ext = new ToolStripMenuItem("E&xit")
  let cols = new ToolStripComboBox("ColorScheme")
  let its = new ToolStripComboBox("Iterations")
  let copy = new ToolStripMenuItem("&Copy")
  let zoomin = new ToolStripMenuItem("Zoom &In")
  let zoomout = new ToolStripMenuItem("Zoom &Out")
  let fillMode = new ToolStripMenuItem("Fill mode")
  let fillModeLinear = new ToolStripMenuItem("Line")
  let fillModeBlock = new ToolStripMenuItem("Block")

  let itchg = fun _ ->
    menuIterations <- System.Int32.Parse(its.Text)
    stopWorker()
    drawMandel()
    c.HideDropDown()
  ext.Click.Add(fun _ -> form.Dispose()) |> ignore

  copy.Click.Add(fun _ -> Clipboard.SetDataObject(bitmap))|> ignore
  copy.ShortcutKeyDisplayString <- "Ctrl+C"
  copy.ShortcutKeys <- Keys.Control ||| Keys.C

  zoomin.Click.Add(fun _ -> zoom 0.9) |> ignore
  zoomin.ShortcutKeyDisplayString <- "Ctrl+T"
  zoomin.ShortcutKeys <- Keys.Control ||| Keys.T
  zoomout.Click.Add(fun _ -> zoom 1.25) |> ignore
  zoomout.ShortcutKeyDisplayString <- "Ctrl+W"
  zoomout.ShortcutKeys <- Keys.Control ||| Keys.W

  for x in [ f;e;c ] do m.Items.Add(x) |> ignore
  f.DropDownItems.Add(ext) |> ignore
  let tsi x = (x :> ToolStripItem)
  for x in [ tsi cols; tsi its; tsi fillMode] do c.DropDownItems.Add(x) |> ignore
  for x in [ tsi copy; tsi zoomin; tsi zoomout ] do e.DropDownItems.Add(x) |> ignore
  for x in ["HSL Color"; "Gray"; "Red"; "Green"] do cols.Items.Add(x) |> ignore
  fillMode.DropDownItems.Add(fillModeLinear) |> ignore
  fillMode.DropDownItems.Add(fillModeBlock) |> ignore
  cols.SelectedIndex <- 0
  cols.DropDownStyle <- ComboBoxStyle.DropDownList
```

```
    cols.SelectedIndexChanged.Add(fun _ ->
      palette <- createPalette coloring.(cols.SelectedIndex)
      stopWorker()
      drawMandel()
      c.HideDropDown()
    )
    its.Text <- string_of_int menuIterations
    its.DropDownStyle <- ComboBoxStyle.DropDown
    for x in [ "150"; "250"; "500"; "1000" ] do its.Items.Add(x) |> ignore
    its.LostFocus.Add(itchg)
    its.SelectedIndexChanged.Add(itchg)
    fillModeBlock.Checked <- true
    fillModeLinear.Click.Add(setFillMode fillMode fillModeLinear linearFill)
    fillModeBlock.Click.Add(setFillMode fillMode fillModeBlock blockFill)
    m

clearOffScreen bitmap
form.MainMenuStrip <- setupMenu()
form.Controls.Add(form.MainMenuStrip)
form.MainMenuStrip.RenderMode <- ToolStripRenderMode.System
form.Paint.Add(fun arg ->  paint arg.Graphics)
form.MouseDown.Add(click)
form.MouseMove.Add(mouseMove)
form.ResizeEnd.Add(fun _ -> resize())
form.Show()

Application.DoEvents()

drawMandel()

[<STAThread>]
do Application.Run(form)
```

The last statement of the program should be used only if the application is compiled; with fsi.exe, it must be omitted. As we already noted, the plumbing code is dominated by setting up menus and configuring the application form; the rest contains the event handlers that are registered with the various controls.

Summary

Event-driven programming is the dominant paradigm of graphical applications. Although object-oriented programming is used to build the infrastructure for graphical frameworks, the event notion is naturally expressed in terms of calling back a given function. F# is effective in GUI programming since it supports both paradigms and it provides access to full-featured frameworks such as Windows Forms.

In this chapter, we covered the basis of GUI programming. We presented controls and applications of a size that could fit an entire book, but we included details typical of real-world applications. Our presentation was based on the Windows Forms framework, but many of the ideas discussed can be easily transposed to other graphical frameworks, since the fundamental structure of this class of applications is mostly unchanged.

CHAPTER 12

■■■

Working with Symbolic Representations

Symbols are everywhere. Numbers are symbols that stand for quantities, and you can add, multiply, or take square roots of numbers that are so small or large that one has a hard time imagining the quantity they represent. You can solve equations, multiply polynomials, approximate functions using series, and differentiate or integrate numerically or symbolically—all of which are a few everyday examples of using symbols in mathematics.

It would be a mistake to think symbols are useful only in mathematics and related fields. General problem solving cannot do without symbols; they provide the ability to abstract away details to make the larger picture clearer and help you understand relationships that may not appear obvious otherwise. Symbols always stand for something and have an attached meaning; they are created to bind this additional content to an existing object. This gives an extraordinary tool to solve problems, describe behavior, make strategic decisions, create new words, and write poetry—the list could go on forever.

F# is well-suited for symbolic computations. In this chapter, we cover in depth two symbolic manipulation problems. First, we present an implementation of a symbolic differentiation application. This includes an implementation of expression rendering using techniques based on Windows Forms programming, discussed in Chapter 11. In our second example, we show how symbolic programming can be used to model hardware circuits, and we present the core of a symbolic hardware verification engine based on binary decision diagrams. We could have chosen other examples of symbolic programming, but these are two that we found particularly enjoyable to code in F#.

We already covered many of the foundational techniques for symbolic programming in Chapter 9. One technique that is particularly important in this chapter is the use of discriminated unions to capture the "shape" of the abstract syntax trees for symbolic languages. Using functions as first-class values and applying recursive problem decomposition also leads to a natural and clean approach to computations on symbolic entities. These and other features of F# combine to make symbolic programming concise and painless, allowing you to focus on the really interesting parts of your application domain.

Symbolic Differentiation and Expression Rendering

You have probably come across the need to perform symbolic differentiation one way or another, and unless you had access to a full-fledged mathematics application such as Matlab or Mathematica, you had to resort to working out the math yourself on paper. Well, this no longer has to be the case, because we will show you how you can develop your own symbolic differentiation tool in almost no time and with surprising brevity and clarity. Figure 12-1 shows the symbolic differentiation application that we implement in this chapter.

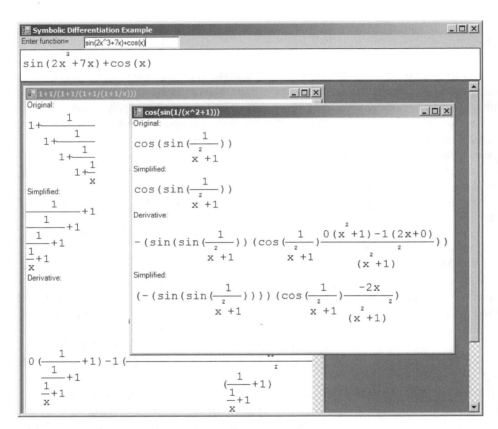

Figure 12-1. *Our visual symbolic differentiation application*

Modeling Simple Algebraic Expressions

We will take it easy at first and assume you are dealing with simple algebraic expressions that can consist only of numbers, a single variable (it doesn't matter what it is, but let's assume it's x), sums, and products. Listing 12-1 shows the implementation of symbolic differentiation over this simple expression type.

Listing 12-1. *Symbolic Differentiation Over a Simple Expression Type*

```
type Expr =
    | Var
    | Num of int
    | Sum of Expr * Expr
    | Prod of Expr * Expr

let rec deriv expr =
    match expr with
    | Var           -> Num 1
    | Num _         -> Num 0
    | Sum (e1, e2)  -> Sum (deriv e1, deriv e2)
    | Prod (e1, e2) -> Sum (Prod (e1, deriv e2), Prod (e2, deriv e1))
```

The type of the deriv function is as follows:

```
val deriv : Expr -> Expr
```

Now let's find the derivative of a simple expression, say 1+2x:

```
> let e1 = Sum (Num 1, Prod (Num 2, Var));;
val e1 : Expr

> deriv e1;;
val it : Expr = Sum (Num 0,Sum (Prod (Num 2,Num 1),Prod (Var,Num 0)))
```

The resulting expression is a symbolic representation of 0+(2*1+X*0), which indeed is 2—so it's right. You'll want to do a couple things next. First, you'll want to install a custom printer so that F# Interactive responds using expressions that you are more used to using. Before you apply brute force and put parentheses around the expressions in each sum and product, let's contemplate it a bit. Parentheses are usually needed to give precedence to operations that would otherwise be applied later in the sequence of calculations. For instance, 2+3*4 is calculated as 2+(3*4) because the product has a higher precedence, so if you were to find (2+3)*4, you would need to use parentheses to designate the new order of calculation. Taking this argument further, you can formulate the rule for using parentheses: they are needed in places where an operator has lower precedence than the one surrounding it. You can apply this reasoning to the expression printer by passing a "context" precedence parameter:

```
let precSum = 10
let precProd = 20

let rec stringOfExpr prec expr =
    match expr with
    | Var    -> "x"
```

```
  | Num i -> Int32.to_string i
  | Sum (e1, e2) ->
     if prec > precSum
     then "(" + stringOfExpr precSum e1 + "+" + stringOfExpr precSum e2 + ")"
     else     stringOfExpr precSum e1 + "+" + stringOfExpr precSum e2
  | Prod (e1, e2) ->
     stringOfExpr precProd e1 + "*" + stringOfExpr precProd e2
```

You can add this as a custom printer for this expression type:

```
> fsi.AddPrinter (fun expr -> stringOfExpr 0 expr);;
val it : unit = ()

> let e3 = Prod (Var, Prod (Var, Num 2));;
val e3 : Expr

> deriv e3;;
val it : Expr = x*(x*0+2*1)+x*2*1
```

Parentheses are omitted only when a sum is participating in an expression that has a higher precedence, which in this simplified example means products. If you did not add precedence to the pretty-printer, you would simply get x*x*0+2*1+x*2*1 for the last expression, which is incorrect.

Implementing Local Simplifications

The next thing you want to do is to get your symbolic manipulator to simplify expressions for you so you don't have to do so. One easy modification is to replace the use of the Sum and Prod constructors in deriv with local functions that perform local simplifications such as removing identity operations, performing arithmetic, bringing forward constants, and simplifying across two operations. Listing 12-2 shows how to do this.

Listing 12-2. *Symbolic Differentiation with Local Simplifications*

```
let simpSum = function
    | Num n, Num m -> Num (n+m)        // constants!
    | Num 0, e | e, Num 0 -> e         // 0+e = e+0 = e
    | e1, e2 -> Sum(e1,e2)

let simpProd = function
    | Num n, Num m -> Num (n*m)        // constants!
    | Num 0, e | e, Num 0 -> Num 0     // 0*e=0
    | Num 1, e | e, Num 1 -> e         // 1*e = e*1 = e
    | e1, e2 -> Prod(e1,e2)

let rec simpDeriv = function
    | Var           -> Num 1
```

```
| Num _          -> Num 0
| Sum (e1, e2)  -> simpSum (simpDeriv e1, simpDeriv e2)
| Prod (e1, e2) -> simpSum (simpProd (e1, simpDeriv e2),
                            simpProd (e2, simpDeriv e1))
```

These measures produce significant improvement over the previous naive approach, but they do not place the result in a normal form, as the following shows:

```
> simpDeriv e3;;
val it : Expr = x*2+x*2
```

However, you cannot implement all simplifications using local rules; for example, collecting like terms across a polynomial involves looking at every term of the polynomial.

Note Listing 12-2 uses the expression form function *pattern-rules* -> *expression*. This is equivalent to (fun x -> match x with *pattern-rules* -> *expression*) and is especially convenient as a way to define functions working directly over discriminated unions.

A Richer Language of Algebraic Expressions

In this section, we go beyond the approach presented and show how to develop a UI application that can accept algebraic expressions as input and simplify, differentiate, and render them graphically. Figure 12-2 shows the project structure. The main Expr type that represents algebraic expressions is contained in Expr.fs. Although you can use the expression constructors defined in this type to create expression values on the fly, the most convenient method for embedding complex expressions into this representation is by parsing them.

Figure 12-2. *The SymbolicDifferentiation project in Visual Studio*

Armed with the ability to encode and parse algebraic expressions, we place the derivation and simplification logic in its own module and file (ExprUtil.fs). The last piece is rendering (in VisualExpr.fs), and finally a simple UI client in Main.fs completes the application.

Listing 12-3 shows the definition of the abstract syntax representation of expressions using a single Expr type. Expressions contain numbers, variables, negation, sums, differences, products, fractions, exponents, basic trigonometric functions (sin x, cos x), and e^x.

Let's take a look at this abstract syntax design more closely. In Chapter 9 you saw that choosing an abstract syntax often involves design choices and that these choices often relate to the roles the abstract syntax representation should serve. In this case, we will use the abstract syntax to compute symbolic derivatives and simplifications (using techniques similar to those earlier in this chapter) and also to graphically visualize the resulting expressions in a way that is pleasant for the human user. For this reason, we don't use an entirely minimalistic abstract syntax (for example, by replacing quotients with an "inverse" node), since it is helpful to maintain some additional structure in the input.

We have chosen to represent sums and differences not as binary terms (as we do for products and quotients), but instead as a list of expression terms. The Sub term also carries the *minuend*, the term that is to be reduced, separately. As a result, we will have to apply different strategies when simplifying them.

Listing 12-3. *The Core Expression Type for the Visual Symbolic Differentiation Application*

```
#light
namespace Symbolic.Expressions

type Expr =
    | Num  of Math.BigNum
    | Var  of string
    | Neg  of Expr
    | Add  of Expr list
    | Sub  of Expr * Expr list
    | Prod of Expr * Expr
    | Frac of Expr * Expr
    | Pow  of Expr * Math.BigNum
    | Sin  of Expr
    | Cos  of Expr
    | Exp  of Expr

    static member StarNeeded e1 e2 =
        match e1, e2 with
        | Num _, Neg _ | _, Num _ -> true
        | _ -> false

    member self.IsNumber =
        match self with
        | Num _ -> true | _ -> false

    member self.NumOf =
        match self with
        | Num num -> num | _ -> failwith "NumOf: Not a Num"
```

```
member self.IsNegative =
    match self with
    | Num num | Prod (Num num, _) -> Math.BigNum.negative num
    | Neg e -> true | _ -> false

member self.Negate =
    match self with
    | Num num -> Num (-num)
    | Neg e -> e
    | exp -> Neg exp
```

Listing 12-3 also shows the definition of some miscellaneous augmentations on the expression type, mostly related to visual layout and presentation. The StarNeeded member is used internally for determining whether the multiplication operator (the star symbol) is needed in the product of two expressions, e1 and e2. Our rule is simple, which you may want to extend: any product where the right side is a number requires the explicit operator, and all other cases don't. Thus, expressions such as 2(x+1) or 2x are rendered without the asterisk.

The IsNumber member returns true if the expression at hand is numeric and is used in conjunction with NumOf, which returns this numeric component. Similarly, the IsNegative and Negate members determine whether you have an expression that starts with a negative sign, and they negate it on demand.

Parsing Algebraic Expressions

This sample uses a lexer and a parser generated by the F# tools fsyacc.exe and fslex.exe. We describe these tools in more detail in Chapter 16, and in this chapter we skip over the details of how these tools work. Listing 12-4 and Listing 12-5 show the code for the lexer and parser. You will need to manually build the lexer (generating ExprLexer.fs) and parser (generating ExprParser.fs) from the command line as follows:

```
C:\samples> fsyacc ExprParser.fsy
C:\samples> fslex ExprLexer.fsl
```

Listing 12-4. *ExprLexer.fsl: Tokenizing the Concrete Syntax for Algebraic Expressions*

```
{
open Lexing
open ExprParser

let special lexbuf = function
    | "+" -> PLUS    | "-" -> MINUS
    | "*" -> TIMES   | "/" -> DIV
    | "(" -> LPAREN  | ")" -> RPAREN  | "^" -> HAT
    | _    -> failwith "Invalid operator"
```

```
let id lexbuf = function
    | "sin" -> SIN  | "cos" -> COS
    | "e"   -> E    | id    -> ID id
}

let digit    = ['0'-'9']
let int      = digit+
let float    = int ('.' int)? (['e' 'E'] int)?
let alpha    = ['a'-'z' 'A'-'Z']
let id       = alpha+ (alpha | digit | ['_' '$'])*
let ws       = ' ' | '\t'
let nl       = '\n' | '\r' '\n'
let special  = '+' | '-' | '*' | '/' | '(' | ')' | '^'

rule main = parse
    | int        { INT     (Int32.of_string (lexeme lexbuf)) }
    | float      { FLOAT   (Float.of_string (lexeme lexbuf)) }
    | id         { id      lexbuf (lexeme lexbuf) }
    | special    { special lexbuf (lexeme lexbuf) }
    | ws | nl    { main    lexbuf }
    | eof        { EOF }
    | _          { failwith (lexeme lexbuf) }
```

The parser has some syntax sugar for polynomial terms, so it can parse 2x, 2x^3, or x^4 without requiring you to add an explicit multiplication after the coefficient.

Listing 12-5. *ExprParser.fsy: Parsing the Concrete Syntax for Algebraic Expressions*

```
%{
open Symbolic.Expressions
open Math
%}

%token <int> INT
%token <float> FLOAT
%token <string> ID

%token EOF LPAREN RPAREN PLUS MINUS TIMES DIV HAT SIN COS E

%left ID
%left prec_negate
%left LPAREN
%left PLUS MINUS
%left TIMES DIV
%left LPAREN
%left HAT
```

```
%start expr
%type <Expr> expr
%%

expr:
    | exp EOF { $1 }

number:
    | INT                         { BigNum.of_int $1 }
    | FLOAT                       { BigNum.of_string (Float.to_string $1) }
    | MINUS INT %prec prec_negate   { BigNum.of_int (-$2) }
    | MINUS FLOAT %prec prec_negate { BigNum.of_string (Float.to_string (-$2)) }

exp:
    | number                { Num $1 }
    | ID                    { Var $1 }
    | exp PLUS exp          { Add [$1; $3] }
    | exp MINUS exp         { Sub ($1, [$3]) }
    | exp TIMES exp         { Prod ($1, $3) }
    | exp DIV exp           { Frac ($1, $3) }
    | SIN LPAREN exp RPAREN { Sin $3 }
    | COS LPAREN exp RPAREN { Cos $3 }
    | E HAT exp             { Exp $3 }
    | term                  { $1 }
    | exp HAT number        { Pow ($1, $3) }
    | LPAREN exp RPAREN     { $2 }
    | MINUS LPAREN exp RPAREN { Neg $3 }

term:
    | number ID             { Prod (Num $1, Var $2) }
    | number ID HAT number  { Prod (Num $1, Pow (Var $2, $4)) }
    | ID HAT number         { Prod (Num 1N, Pow (Var $1, $3)) }
```

Simplifying Algebraic Expressions

At the start of this chapter, you simplified expressions using local techniques, but you also saw the limitations of this approach. Listing 12-6 shows a more complete implementation of a separate function (Simplify) that performs some nonlocal simplifications as well. Both this function and the one for derivation shown in the subsequent section are placed in a separate file (ExprUtil.fs).

Simplify uses two helper functions (collect and negate). The former collects constants from products using a bottom-up strategy that reduces constant subproducts and factors out constants by bringing them outward (to the left). Recall that product terms are binary.

Listing 12-6. *Simplifying Algebraic Expressions*

```
#light
module Symbolic.Expressions.Utils

open Symbolic.Expressions

/// A helper function to map/select across a list while threading state
/// through the computation
let select_fold f l s =
    let l,s' = List.fold_left
                    (fun (l',s') x ->
                        let x',s'' = f x s'
                        (List.rev x') @ l',s'')
                    ([],s) l
    List.rev l,s'

/// Collect constants
let rec collect = function
    | Prod (e1, e2) ->
        match collect e1, collect e2 with
        | Num num1, Num num2      -> Num (num1 * num2)
        | Num n1, Prod (Num n2, e)
        | Prod (Num n2, e), Num n1 -> Prod (Num (n1 * n2), e)
        | Num n, e | e, Num n      -> Prod (Num n, e)
        | Prod (Num n1, e1), Prod (Num n2, e2) ->
            Prod (Num (n1 * n2), Prod (e1, e2))
        | e1', e2'                 -> Prod (e1', e2')
    | Num _ | Var _ as e  -> e
    | Neg e               -> Neg (collect e)
    | Add exprs           -> Add (List.map collect exprs)
    | Sub (e1, exprs)     -> Sub (collect e1, List.map collect exprs)
    | Frac (e1, e2)       -> Frac (collect e1, collect e2)
    | Pow (e1, num)       -> Pow (collect e1, num)
    | Sin e               -> Sin (collect e)
    | Cos e               -> Cos (collect e)
    | Exp _ as e          -> e

/// Push negations through an expression
let rec negate = function
    | Num num         -> Num (-num)
    | Var v as exp    -> Neg exp
    | Neg e           -> e
    | Add exprs       -> Add (List.map negate exprs)
    | Sub _           -> failwith "unexpected Sub"
    | Prod (e1, e2)   -> Prod (negate e1, e2)
    | Frac (e1, e2)   -> Frac (negate e1, e2)
    | exp             -> Neg exp
```

```
/// Simplify an expression
let rec simp = function
    | Num num              -> Num num
    | Var v                -> Var v
    | Neg e                -> negate (simp e)
    | Add exprs ->
        let filterNums (e:Expr) n =
            if e.IsNumber
            then [], n + e.NumOf
            else [e], n
        let summands = function | Add es -> es | e -> [e]
        let exprs', num =
            select_fold (simp >> summands >> select_fold filterNums) exprs ON
        match exprs' with
        | [Num _ as n] when num = ON -> n
        | []                         -> Num num
        | [e] when num = ON          -> e
        | _ when num = ON            -> Add exprs'
        | _                          -> Add (exprs' @ [Num num])
    | Sub (e1, exprs) ->
        simp (Add (e1 :: List.map Neg exprs))
    | Prod (e1, e2) ->
        match simp e1, simp e2 with
        | Num num, _ | _, Num num when num = ON -> Num ON
        | Num num, e | e, Num num when num = 1N -> e
        | Num num1, Num num2                    -> Num (num1 * num2)
        | e1, e2                                -> Prod (e1, e2)
    | Frac (e1, e2) ->
        match simp e1, simp e2 with
        | Num num, _ when num = ON  -> Num num
        | e1, Num num when num = 1N -> e1
        | Num (_ as num), Frac (Num (_ as num2), e) ->
            Prod (Frac (Num num, Num num2), e)
        | Num (_ as num), Frac (e, Num (_ as num2)) ->
            Frac (Prod (Num num, Num num2), e)
        | e1, e2                    -> Frac (e1, e2)
    | Pow (e, n) when n=1N -> simp e
    | Pow (e, n)           -> Pow (simp e, n)
    | Sin e                -> Sin (simp e)
    | Cos e                -> Cos (simp e)
    | Exp e                -> Exp (simp e)

let Simplify e = e |> simp |> simp |> collect
```

The main simplification algorithm works as follows:

- Constants and variables are passed through verbatim. negate is utilized when simplifying a negation, which assumes that the expression at hand no longer contains differences and that sums were "flattened" (see the next item in this list).

- Sums are traversed and nested sums are flattened, at the same time as collecting and adding up all constants. This reduces the complexity of further simplification considerably.

- Differences are converted to sums; for instance, A-B-C is converted to A+(-B)+(-C). Thus, the first element is preserved without negation.

- When simplifying a product, you first simplify its factors, and then you remove identity operations (multiplying by zero or one) and reduce products of constants.

- Fractions are handled similarly. Zero divided by anything is 0, anything divided by 1 is itself, and multiline fractions can be collapsed if you find numeric denominators or numerators.

- The rest of the match cases deal with simplifying subexpressions.

Symbolic Differentiation of Algebraic Expressions

Applying symbolic differentiation is a straightforward translation of the mathematical rules of differentiation into code. We could have used local functions that act as constructors and perform local simplifications, but with the simplification function described earlier this is no longer needed. Listing 12-7 shows the implementation of symbolic differentiation for the Expr type. Note how beautifully and succinctly the code follows the math behind it, and the essence of the symbolic processing is merely 20 lines of code!

Listing 12-7. *Symbolic Differentiation for Algebraic Expressions*

```
let Differentiate v e =
    let rec diff v = function
        | Num num              -> Num 0N
        | Var v' when v'=v      -> Num 1N
        | Var v'                -> Num 0N
        | Neg e                 -> diff v (Prod ((Num -1N), e))
        | Add exprs             -> Add (List.map (diff v) exprs)
        | Sub (e1, exprs)       -> Sub (diff v e1, List.map (diff v) exprs)
        | Prod (e1, e2)         -> Add [Prod (diff v e1, e2); Prod (e1, diff v e2)]
        | Frac (e1, e2) ->
            Frac (Sub (Prod (diff v e1, e2), [Prod (e1, diff v e2)]), Pow (e2, 2N))
        | Pow (e1, num) ->
            Prod (Prod(Num num, Pow (e1, num - 1N)), diff v e1)
        | Sin e                 -> Prod (Cos e, diff v e)
        | Cos e                 -> Neg (Prod (Sin e, diff v e))
        | Exp (Var v') as e when v'=v  -> e
        | Exp (Var v') as e when v'<>v -> Num 0N
        | Exp e                 -> Prod (Exp e, diff v e)
    diff v e
```

Rendering Expressions

Now that you have the basic machinery to easily parse, simplify, and differentiate expressions, you need to be looking at how to visualize them to really enjoy the benefits of the application. The rendering engine (placed in `VisualExpr.fs`) has two main parts: converting expressions to `VisualExpr` values and then rendering them directly. Ideally, you should hide the representation of the `VisualExpr` (and its related `VisualElement`) type by a signature (not shown here) so that it is not possible to construct these values directly.

Before we get to the conversion and rendering functions, there is a bit of setup to do. For controlling how the different parts of an expression are rendered on the screen, we introduce the `RenderOptions` type containing the fonts and pen (which determines the color used to draw) that will be applied during rendering. Listing 12-8 shows the code that defines the rendering options used in the remainder of this sample.

Listing 12-8. *Rendering Options for the Visual Symbolic Differentiation Application*

```
#light
namespace Symbolic.Expressions.Visual

open Symbolic.Expressions
open System.Drawing
open System.Drawing.Imaging
open Math

type RenderOptions =
    { NormalFont: Font;  SmallFont: Font;  IsSuper: bool;  Pen: Pen; }

    static member Default =
        { NormalFont = new Font("Courier New",18.0f,FontStyle.Regular);
          SmallFont = new Font("Courier New", 12.0f, FontStyle.Regular);
          IsSuper = false;
          Pen = new Pen(Color.Black, 1.0f); }

    member self.Brush =
        (new SolidBrush(Color.FromArgb(255, self.Pen.Color)) :> Brush)
```

Each algebraic expression is converted to a `VisualExpr` value as part of the rendering process. This ensures you don't have to deal with the variety of expression forms but only with a small set of simple shapes that can be rendered according to a few simple rules. These more simple building blocks are defined in the `VisualElement` type and shown in Listing 12-9. For instance, there are no sums or products; these and similar expressions are broken down to a sequence of symbols (such as 1, x, or +). The two other visual elements are exponentiation and fractions, which are used to guide the display logic later during the rendering phase. Each visual element carries a size value that is calculated using a given set of rendering options.

Listing 12-9. *Visual Elements and Sizes for the Visual Symbolic Differentiation Application*

```
type VisualElement =
    | Symbol    of string * ExprSize
    | Power     of VisualElement * VisualElement * ExprSize
    | Sequence of VisualElement list * ExprSize
    | Fraction of VisualElement * VisualElement * ExprSize
    member self.Size =
        match self with
        | Symbol (_, size)    | Power (_, _, size)
        | Sequence (_, size) | Fraction (_, _, size) -> size

    member self.Height = self.Size.height
    member self.Width = self.Size.width
    member self.Midline = self.Size.midline

and ExprSize =
    { width: int;  height: int;  midline: int; }

    member self.CenterOnMidline size x y =
        x + (size.width-self.width)/2, y + (size.midline-self.midline)

    member self.Frac size opt =
        { width = max self.width size.width;
          height = self.height + size.height + self.FracSepHeight opt;
          midline = self.height + (self.FracSepHeight opt)/2; }

    member self.FracSepHeight (opt: RenderOptions) =
        max (int (opt.Pen.Width*5.0f)) 4

    member self.AddPower (e: VisualElement) =
        { width = self.width + e.Width;
          height = self.height + e.Height;
          midline = self.midline + e.Height; }

    static member ExpandOne (size: ExprSize) (e: VisualElement) =
        { width   = size.width + e.Width;
          height  = max size.height e.Height;
          midline = max size.midline e.Midline; }

    member self.Expand (exprs: VisualElement list) =
        List.fold_left ExprSize.ExpandOne self exprs

    static member Seq (exprs: VisualElement list) =
        List.fold_left ExprSize.ExpandOne ExprSize.Zero exprs

    static member Zero =
        { width=0; height=0; midline=0; }
```

This size value encodes the dimensions (width and height in pixels) of the related visual expression and is managed through the ExprSize type, which provides various members to compute precise dimensions. Basically, this is the type that handles the gory details of putting small visuals together to compose a large expression and manages how and where these small visuals should be placed. The main guideline is to align these visuals on a line (measured from the top of the expression in pixels and stored in the midline field), as depicted in Figure 12-3.

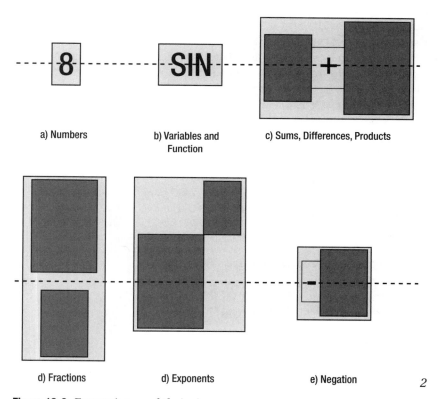

| a) Numbers | b) Variables and Function | c) Sums, Differences, Products |

| d) Fractions | d) Exponents | e) Negation |

Figure 12-3. *Expressions and their sizes*

The darker rectangles in this figure denote arbitrary expressions, whereas the lighter rectangle marks the dimensions of the parent expression aligned on the midline.

Converting to VisualExpr

Listing 12-10 shows the type VisualExpr that carries the main visual element and the rendering options that were used to produce it. This type also provides the method OfExpr to build a VisualExpr from an Expr.

Listing 12-10. *Visual Expressions for the Visual Symbolic Differentiation Application*

```
type VisualExpr =
    { Expression : VisualElement;  RenderOptions: RenderOptions; }

    static member OfExpr (opt: RenderOptions) e =
        use bmp = new Bitmap(100, 100, PixelFormat.Format32bppArgb)
        use gra = Graphics.FromImage(bmp)
        let sizeOf (opt: RenderOptions) s =
            use sFormat = new StringFormat(StringFormat.GenericTypographic)
            let font = if opt.IsSuper then opt.SmallFont else opt.NormalFont
            let size = gra.MeasureString(s, font, PointF(0.0f, 0.0f), sFormat)
            let height = int size.Height
            { width = int size.Width + 2;
              height = height;
              midline = height/2; }
        let precPow = 70
        let precProd1, precProd2 = 30, 40
        let precAdd1, precAdd2 = 10, 11
        let precStart = 5
        let precNeg1, precNeg2 = 1, 20
        let sym opt s = Symbol (s, sizeOf opt s)

        let applyPrec opt pprec prec exprs (size: ExprSize) =
            if pprec > prec then
                sym opt "(" :: exprs @ [sym opt ")"],
                size.Expand [sym opt "("; sym opt ")"]
            else
                exprs, size

        let mkSequence opt pprec prec exprs =
            let size = ExprSize.Seq exprs
            let exprs, size = applyPrec opt pprec prec exprs size
            Sequence (exprs, size)

        let rec expFunc opt f par =
            let f' = sym opt f
            let exprs' = [sym opt "("; exp opt precStart par; sym opt ")"]
            Sequence (f' :: exprs', f'.Size.Expand exprs')

        and exp (opt: RenderOptions) prec = function
            | Num n ->
                let s = BigNum.to_string n in Symbol (s, sizeOf opt s)
            | Var v ->
                Symbol (v, sizeOf opt v)
```

```
| Neg e ->
    let e' = exp opt precNeg1 e
    let exprs, size = applyPrec opt prec precNeg1 [e'] e'.Size
    let exprs' = [sym opt "-"] @ exprs
    mkSequence opt prec precNeg2 exprs'
| Add exprs ->
    let exprs' =
        [ for i,e in Seq.mapi (fun i x -> (i,x)) exprs do
                let first = (i=0)
                let e' = exp opt (if first then precAdd1 else precAdd2) e
                if first or e.IsNegative
                then yield! [e']
                else yield! [sym opt "+"; e'] ]
    mkSequence opt prec precAdd1 exprs'
| Sub (e1, exprs) ->
    let e1' = exp opt prec e1
    let exprs' =
        [ for e in exprs do
                if e.IsNegative then
                    let e' = exp opt precAdd2 e.Negate
                    yield! [sym opt "+"; e']
                else
                    let e' = exp opt precAdd2 e
                    yield! [sym opt "-"; e'] ]

    mkSequence opt prec precAdd1 (e1'::exprs')
| Prod (e1, e2) ->
    let e1' = exp opt precProd1 e1
    let e2' = exp opt precProd2 e2
    let exprs' =
        if Expr.StarNeeded e1 e2
        then [e1'; sym opt "*"; e2']
        else [e1'; e2']
    mkSequence opt prec precProd1 exprs'
| Pow (e1, e2) ->
    let e1' = exp opt precPow e1
    let e2' = exp { opt with IsSuper=true } precPow (Num e2)
    Power (e1', e2', e1'.Size.AddPower e2')
| Sin e ->
    expFunc opt "sin" e
| Cos e ->
    expFunc opt "cos" e
| Exp expo ->
    let e' = sym opt "e"
    let expo' = exp { opt with IsSuper=true } precPow expo
    Power (e', expo', e'.Size.AddPower expo')
```

```
        | Frac (e1, e2) ->
            let e1' = exp opt precStart e1
            let e2' = exp opt precStart e2
            Fraction (e1', e2', e1'.Size.Frac e2'.Size opt)
    let exp = exp opt precStart e
    { Expression=exp; RenderOptions=opt; }
```

The conversion implemented in Listing 12-10 is relatively straightforward. It uses various local helper functions to break each expression into smaller visual elements, carefully keeping track of the bounding box calculation. Furthermore, there are a number of things to consider; for instance, precedence is enforced, and expressions are parenthesized as necessary. For example, consider how you convert a product:

```
| Prod (e1, e2) ->
    let e1' = exp opt precProd1 e1
    let e2' = exp opt precProd2 e2
    let exprs' =
        if Expr.StarNeeded e1 e2
        then [e1'; sym opt "*"; e2']
        else [e1'; e2']
    mkSequence opt prec precProd1 exprs'
```

This code converts the two interior expressions and decides on a list of display symbols by first checking whether a multiplication symbol is required. The function mkSequence then calculates the size of this new list of expressions, applies precedence rules to determine whether parentheses are required, and produces a final visual element as a result.

Other cases are handled similarly; for sums, you iterate through the elements exprs in the sum using sequence expression notation. If you find a negative term, you omit the plus sign (so 1+(-2) is rendered as 1-2). Differences are treated similarly, but here you change negative terms to positive, so 3-2-(-1) becomes 3-2+1. When converting products, you omit the multiplication operator if you can.

Rendering

Listing 12-11 shows the code for rendering visual expressions. You may have noticed in the definition of the VisualElement type that the only directly "drawable" visual element is Symbol. The other constructors carry one or more visual elements that must be drawn recursively and according to a well-defined logic. The key observation in the rendering function in Listing 12-11 is that, when drawing each element, you pass in the *x* and *y* coordinates of the bounding box in which it is to be drawn. You also pass in the size of the parent box in which the element is to be aligned (as guided by the midline property).

Listing 12-11. *Rendering Visual Expressions*

```
type VisualExpr =
    ...
    member self.Render =
        let pt x y = PointF(float32 x, float32 y)
        let rec draw (gra: Graphics) opt x y psize = function
```

```
    | Symbol (s, size) ->
        let font = if opt.IsSuper then opt.SmallFont else opt.NormalFont
        let x', y' = size.CenterOnMidline psize x y
        gra.DrawString(s, font, opt.Brush, pt x' y')
    | Power (e1, e2, size) ->
        let x', y' = size.CenterOnMidline psize x y
        draw gra opt x' (y'+e2.Height) e1.Size e1
        draw gra { opt with IsSuper=true } (x'+e1.Width) y' e2.Size e2
    | Sequence (exps, size) ->
        let x', y' = size.CenterOnMidline psize x y
        List.fold_left (fun (x, y) (e: VisualElement) ->
            let psize' = { width = e.Width; height = psize.height;
                            midline=size.midline; }
            draw gra opt x y psize' e
            x+e.Width, y) (x', y') exps |> ignore
    | Fraction (e1, e2, size) as e ->
        let psize1 = { psize with height=e1.Height; midline=e1.Midline }
        let psize2 = { psize with height=e2.Height; midline=e2.Midline }
        draw gra opt x y psize1 e1
        gra.DrawLine(self.RenderOptions.Pen, x, y+size.midline,
                        x+psize.width, y+size.midline);
        draw gra opt x (y+e1.Height+size.FracSepHeight opt) psize2 e2
let bmp = new Bitmap(self.Expression.Width, self.Expression.Height,
                    PixelFormat.Format32bppArgb)
let gra = Graphics.FromImage(bmp)
gra.FillRectangle(new SolidBrush(Color.White), 0, 0,
                    self.Expression.Width+1, self.Expression.Height+1)
draw gra self.RenderOptions 0 0 self.Expression.Size self.Expression
bmp
```

Building the User Interface

Listing 12-12 is the final piece: the UI client (Main.fs). It is simple yet powerful. The main form contains an input field and a preview panel where the expressions are rendered on the fly as typed in. When the user presses the Enter key, a new MDI child window is created, and the original, simplified, derived, and final expressions are rendered on it. There is a bit of extra work involved in creating the child windows to make them scrollable.

Listing 12-12. *The User Interface Client for the Visual Symbolic Differentiation Application*

```
#light
open Symbolic.Expressions
open Symbolic.Expressions.Visual
open System.Windows.Forms
open System.Drawing
```

```
let createScrollableChildWindow parent =
    let scroll = new ScrollableControl(Dock=DockStyle.Fill, AutoScroll=true)
    let form2 = new Form(MdiParent=parent, BackColor=Color.White)
    form2.Controls.Add scroll
    form2, scroll

let newExpression parent s es =
    let form, scroll = createScrollableChildWindow parent
    let AddLabel (top, maxw) (parent: #Control) s =
        let l = new Label(Text=s, AutoSize=true, Top=top)
        parent.Controls.Add l
        (top+l.Height), max maxw l.Width
    let AddPic (top, maxw) (parent: #Control) (e: Expr) =
        let e' = VisualExpr.OfExpr RenderOptions.Default e
        let bmp = e'.Render
        let pic = new PictureBox(Image=bmp, Height=bmp.Height,
                                 Width=bmp.Width, Top=top)
        parent.Controls.Add pic
        (top+bmp.Height), max maxw bmp.Width
    let height, width = List.fold_left (fun top (lab, e) ->
        AddPic (AddLabel top scroll lab) scroll e) (0, 0) es
    form.Text <- s
    form.Height <- min 640 (height+40)
    form.Width <- min 480 (width+40)
    form.Show()

let updatePreview (scroll :> Control) e =
    let e' = VisualExpr.OfExpr RenderOptions.Default e
    let bmp = e'.Render
    let pic = new PictureBox(Image=bmp, Height=bmp.Height, Width=bmp.Width)
    scroll.Controls.Clear()
    scroll.Controls.Add pic

let newExpressionError form s =
    let cform, scroll = createScrollableChildWindow form
    let label = new Label(Text=s, Font=new Font("Courier New", 10.f), AutoSize=true)
    scroll.Controls.Add label
    cform.Show()

exception SyntaxError

let Parse s =
    let lex = Lexing.from_string s
    try ExprParser.expr ExprLexer.main lex
    with _ -> raise SyntaxError
```

```
let newStringExpression form s =
    try
        let e1 = Parse s
        let e2 = Utils.Simplify e1
        let e3 = Utils.Differentiate "x" e2
        let e4 = Utils.Simplify e3
        newExpression form s ["Original:", e1; "Simplified:", e2;
                              "Derivative:", e3; "Simplified:", e4]
    with
      | SyntaxError ->
          let msg = Printf.sprintf "Syntax error in:\n%s" s
          newExpressionError form msg
      | Failure msg ->
          newExpressionError form msg


let constructMainForm () =
    let form    = new Form(Text="Symbolic Differentiation Example",
                           IsMdiContainer=true,
                           Visible=true, Height=600, Width=700)
    let label   = new Label(Text="Enter function=", Width=100, Height=20)
    let tb      = new TextBox(Width=150, Left=100)
    let panel   = new Panel(Dock=DockStyle.Top, Height=tb.Height+50)
    let preview = new Panel(Dock=DockStyle.Bottom, BackColor=Color.White,
                            Height=50, BorderStyle=BorderStyle.FixedSingle)
    let control c = (c :> Control)
    panel.Controls.AddRange([|control label; control preview; control tb |])
    form.Controls.Add(panel)
    tb.KeyUp.Add (fun arg ->
        if arg.KeyCode = Keys.Enter then
            newStringExpression form tb.Text
            tb.Text <- ""
            tb.Focus() |> ignore
        else
            try
                let e = Parse tb.Text
                updatePreview preview e
            with
            | _ -> ())
    form

let form = constructMainForm ()
newStringExpression form "cos(sin(1/(x^2+1)))"
Application.Run(form)
```

To recap, in this sample you've seen the following:

- Two abstract syntax representations for different classes of algebraic expressions: one simple, and one much more realistic

- How to implement simplification and symbolic differentiation routines on these representations of algebraic expressions

- How to implement parsing and lexing for concrete representations of algebraic expressions

- How to perform size estimation and visual layout for abstract syntax representations of algebraic expressions, here using Windows Forms

- How to put this together into a final application

Verifying Circuits with Propositional Logic

For the next example, we turn to a traditional application area for functional programming: describing digital hardware circuits and symbolically verifying their properties. We assume a passing familiarity with hardware design, but if you haven't looked inside a microprocessor chip for some time, a brief recap is included in the "About Hardware Design" sidebar.

In this example, you will model circuits by *propositional logic*, a simple and familiar symbolic language made up of constructs such as AND, OR, NOT, and TRUE/FALSE values. You then implement an analysis that converts propositional logic formulae into a canonical form called *binary decision diagrams* (BDDs). Converting to a canonical form allows you to check conditions and properties associated with the digital circuits.

ABOUT HARDWARE DESIGN

Digital hardware circuits such as microprocessors almost universally manipulate bits, that is, signals that are either low or high, represented by 0/1 or `false`/`true` values, respectively. The building blocks of interesting hardware circuits are primitives such as *gates* and *registers*. Gates are "logical" components that relate their inputs to their outputs; for example, an AND gate will take two input signals, and if both are "high," it will give a "high" signal on its output. Registers are stateful components associated with a clock. We don't consider registers and stateful circuits in this chapter, though they can be tackled by similar techniques to those described here.

Hardware design is largely about building interesting behavior out of these primitives. For example, you can build arithmetic circuits that compute the sum or product of integers by using logical gates alone. These "combinatorial" circuits can be massive, and a key concern is to both verify their correctness and minimize the overall electrical delay through the circuit.

■**Note** The examples in this section are inspired by the tutorials for the HOL88 system, a symbolic theorem prover implemented using an F#-like language that has been used for many purposes, including hardware verification. The carry/select adder and the BDD implementation follow those given by John Harrison in his HOL Light version of the same system. You can find out more about these and other systems, as well as delve into theorem proving, in *Introduction to Logic and Automated Theorem Proving* by John Harrison (Cambridge University Press, to appear in 2008) and also at `http://www.expert-fsharp.com/ Topics/TheoremProving`.

Representing Propositional Logic

We begin by using language-oriented programming techniques to implement a little logic of Boolean expressions, of the kind that might be used to describe part of a hardware circuit or a constraint. Let's assume these have forms like the following:

```
P1 AND P2
P1 OR P2
P1 IMPLIES P2
NOT(P1)
v                      -- variable, ranging over true/false
TRUE
FALSE
Exists v. P[v]    -- v ranges over true/false, P may use v
Forall v. P[v]    -- v ranges over true/false, P may use v
```

This is known as *quantified Boolean formulae* (QBF) and is an expressive way of modeling many interesting problems and artifacts that work over finite data domains. Listing 12-13 shows how you model this language in F#.

Listing 12-13. *A Minimalistic Representation of Propositional Logic*

```
type Var = string
type Prop =
    | And of Prop * Prop
    | Var of Var
    | Not of Prop
    | Exists of Var * Prop
    | False

let True = Not(False)
let Or(p,q)     = Not(And(Not(p),Not(q)))
let Iff(p,q)    = Or(And(p,q),And(Not(p),Not(q)))
let Implies(p,q) = Or(Not(p),q)
let Forall(v,p) = Not(Exists(v,Not(p)))
```

```
let (&&&) p q = And(p,q)
let (|||) p q = Or(p,q)
let (~~~) p   = Not (p)
let (<=>) p q = Iff(p,q)
let (===) p q = (p <=> q)
let (==>) p q = Implies(p,q)
let (^^^) p q = Not (p <=> q)

let var (nm:Var) = Var(nm)
let fresh =
    let count = ref 0
    fun nm -> incr count; (sprintf "_%s%d" nm !count : Var)
```

Listing 12-13 uses a *minimalistic* encoding of propositional logic terms, where True, Or, Iff, Implies, and Forall are *derived* constructs, defined using their standard classical definitions in terms of the primitives Var, And, Not, Exists, and False. This is adequate for our purposes since we aren't so interested in preserving the original structure of formulae, or if we did need to display a symbolic propositional formula, we are happy to display a form different to the original input.

Variables in formulae of type Prop are *primitive propositions*. A primitive proposition is often used to model some real-world possibility. For example, "it is raining," "it is cold," and "it is snowing" can be represented by Var("raining"), Var("cold"), and Var("snowing"). A Prop formula may be a *tautology*, that is, something that is always true regardless of the interpretation of these primitives. A formula is *satisfiable* if there is at least one interpretation for which it is true. A formula can also be an *axiom*; for example, "if it's snowing, then it's cold" can be represented as the assumption Implies(Var("snowing"), Var("cold")). In our example, variables will be used to represent a wire in a digital circuit that may be low or high.

When dealing directly with the abstract syntax for Prop, it can be convenient to define infix operators to help you build abstract syntax values. Listing 12-13 shows the definition of seven operators (&&&, |||, ~~~, <=>, ===, ==>, and ^^^) that look a little like the notation we expect for propositional logic. We also define the function var for building primitive propositions and fresh for generating fresh variables. The types of these functions are as follows:

```
val var : Var -> Prop
val fresh : (string -> Var)
```

■Note The operators in Listing 12-13 are not overloaded and indeed outscope the default overloaded bitwise operations on integers discussed in Chapter 3. However, that doesn't matter for the purposes of this chapter. If necessary, you could use alternative operator names.

Evaluating Propositional Logic Naively

Before we tackle the problem of representing hardware using propositional logic, we first show you some naive approaches for working with propositional logic formulae. Listing 12-14 shows routines that evaluate formulae given an assignment of variables and that generate the rows of a *truth table* for a Prop formula.

Listing 12-14. *Evaluating Propositional Logic Formulae*

```
let rec eval (env : Map<Var,bool>) inp =
    match inp with
    | Exists(v,p) -> eval (env.Add(v,false)) p || eval (env.Add(v,true)) p
    | And(p1,p2)  -> eval env p1 && eval env p2
    | Var(v)      -> if env.ContainsKey(v) then env.[v]
                        else failwithf "env didn't contain a value for %A" v
    | Not(p)      -> not (eval env p)
    | False       -> false

let rec support f =
    match f with
    | And(x,y)    -> Set.union (support x) (support y)
    | Exists(v,p) -> (support p).Remove(v)
    | Var(p)      -> Set.singleton p
    | Not(x)      -> support x
    | False       -> Set.empty

let rec cases supp =
    seq { match supp with
          | [] ->  yield Map.empty
          | v::rest ->
              yield! rest |> cases |> Seq.map (Map.add v false)
              yield! rest |> cases |> Seq.map (Map.add v true) }

let truthTable  x =
    x |> support |> Set.to_list |> cases |> Seq.map (fun env -> env,eval env x)

let satisfiable x =
    x |> truthTable |> Seq.exists(fun (env,res) -> res)

let tautology x =
    x |> truthTable |> Seq.for_all (fun (env,res) -> res)

let tautologyWithCounterExample x =
    x |> truthTable |> Seq.tryfind (fun (env,res) -> not res) |> Option.map fst

let printCounterExample =
    (function None -> printfn "tautology verified OK"
            | Some env -> printfn "tautology failed on %A" (Seq.to_list env))
```

The types of these functions are as follows:

```
val eval : Map<Var,bool> -> Prop -> bool
val support : Prop -> Set<Var>
val cases : 'a list -> seq<Map<'a,bool>>
val truthTable : Prop -> seq<Map<Var,bool> * bool>
val satisfiable : Prop -> bool
val tautology : Prop -> bool
val tautologyWithCounterExample : Prop -> Map<Var,bool> option
val printCounterExample : #seq<'a> option -> unit
```

The function eval computes the value of a formula given assignments for each of the variables that occurs in the formula. support simply computes the set of variables that occurs in the formula. You can now use these functions to examine truth tables for some simple formulae, though first you may want to define the following functions to display truth tables neatly in F# Interactive:

```
let stringOfBit b = (if b then "T" else "F")
let stringOfEnv env =
    Map.fold(fun k v acc -> sprintf "%s=%s;" k (stringOfBit v)+acc) env ""
let stringOfLine (env,res) = sprintf "%20s %s" (stringOfEnv env) (stringOfBit res)
let stringOfTruthTable tt =
    "\n" + (tt |> Seq.to_list |> List.map stringOfLine |> String.concat "\n")
```

Here are the truth tables for "*x*," "*x* AND *y*," and "*x* OR NOT(*x*)":

```
> fsi.AddPrinter(fun tt -> tt |> Seq.truncate 20 |> stringOfTruthTable);;

> truthTable (var "x");;
> val it : seq<Map<Var,bool> * bool>
=
              x=F; F
              x=T; T

> truthTable (var "x" &&& var "y");;
> val it : seq<Map<Var,bool> * bool>
=
          x=F;y=F; F
          x=F;y=T; F
          x=T;y=F; F
          x=T;y=T; T

> truthTable (var "x" ||| ~~~(var "x"));;
> val it : seq<Map<Var,bool> * bool>
=
              x=F; T
              x=T; T
```

From this you can see that "x OR NOT(x)" is a tautology, since it always evaluates to TRUE regardless of the value of the variable x.

From Circuits to Propositional Logic

Figure 12-4 shows a diagrammatic representation of three hardware circuits: a *half adder*, a *full adder*, and a *2-bit carry ripple adder*. The first of these has two input wires, x and y, and sets the *sum* wire "high" if exactly one of these is "high." If both x and y are "high," then the sum is "low," and the carry wire is "high" instead. Thus, the circuit computes the 2-bit sum of the inputs. Likewise, a full adder computes the sum of three Boolean inputs, which, since it is at most three, can still be represented by 2 bits. A 2-bit carry ripple adder is formed by composing a half adder and a full adder together, wiring the carry from the first adder to one of the inputs of the second adder. The overall circuit has four inputs and three outputs.

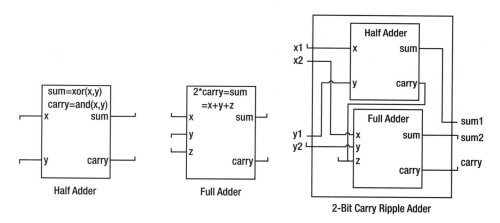

Figure 12-4. *Three simple hardware circuits*

The following code models these circuit components. This uses *relational modeling*, where each circuit is modeled not as a function but as a propositional logic predicate that relates its input wires to its output wires:

```
let sumBit x y = (x ^^^ y)
let carryBit x y = (x &&& y)
let halfAdder x y sum carry =
    (sum === sumBit x y)  &&&
    (carry === carryBit x y)

let fullAdder x y z sum carry =
    let xy = (sumBit x y)
    (sum === sumBit xy z) &&&
    (carry === (carryBit x y ||| carryBit xy z))
```

```
let twoBitAdder (x1,x2) (y1,y2) (sum1,sum2) carryInner carry =
    halfAdder x1 y1 sum1 carryInner &&&
    fullAdder x2 y2 carryInner sum2 carry
```

Note the close relation between the diagram for the 2-bit adder and its representation as code. You can read the implementation as a specification of the diagram, and vice versa. The types of these functions are, however, a little less informative:

```
val sumBit : Prop -> Prop -> Prop
val carryBit : Prop -> Prop -> Prop
val halfAdder : Prop -> Prop -> Prop -> Prop -> Prop
val fullAdder : Prop -> Prop -> Prop -> Prop -> Prop -> Prop
val twoBitAdder : Prop * Prop -> Prop * Prop -> Prop * Prop
                    -> Prop -> Prop -> Prop
```

In practice, circuits are defined largely with respect to vectors of wires, not just individual wires. You can model these using arrays of propositions, and since it's now clear we're modeling bits via propositions, we make an appropriate type abbreviation for them as well:

```
type bit = Prop
type bitvec = bit[]
let Lo : bit = False
let Hi : bit = True
let vec n nm : bitvec = Array.init n (fun i -> var (sprintf "%s%d" nm i))
let bitEq (b1:bit) (b2:bit) = (b1 <=> b2)
let AndL l = Seq.fold1 (fun x y-> And(x,y)) l
let vecEq (v1:bitvec) (v2:bitvec) = AndL (Array.map2 bitEq v1 v2)
```

These functions have types as follows:

```
type bit = Prop
type bitvec = bit []
val Lo : bit
val Hi : bit
val vec : int -> string -> bitvec
val bitEq : bit -> bit -> Prop
val AndL : #seq<Prop> -> Prop
val vecEq : bitvec -> bitvec -> Prop
```

You can now proceed to define larger circuits. For example:

```
let fourBitAdder (x:bitvec) (y:bitvec) (sum:bitvec) (carry:bitvec) =
    halfAdder x.[0] y.[0]            sum.[0] carry.[0] &&&
    fullAdder x.[1] y.[1] carry.[0] sum.[1] carry.[1] &&&
    fullAdder x.[2] y.[2] carry.[1] sum.[2] carry.[2] &&&
    fullAdder x.[3] y.[3] carry.[2] sum.[3] carry.[3]
```

Or, more generally, you can chain an arbitrary series of adders to form an *N*-bit adder. First you define an abbreviation for the AndL function to represent the composition of multiple circuit blocks:

```
let Blocks l = AndL l
```

And here is the definition of an *N*-bit adder with a halfAdder at one end:

```
let nBitCarryRippleAdder (n:int) (x:bitvec) (y:bitvec) (sum:bitvec) (carry:bitvec) =
    Blocks [ for i in 0 .. n-1 ->
               if i = 0
               then halfAdder x.[i] y.[i] sum.[i] carry.[i]
               else fullAdder x.[i] y.[i] carry.[i-1] sum.[i] carry.[i]  ]
```

Using a similar approach, you get the following satisfying specification of a symmetric *N*-bit adder that accepts a carry as input and also gives a carry as output:

```
let rippleAdder (n:int) (x:bitvec) (y:bitvec) (sum:bitvec) (carry:bitvec)  =
    Blocks [ for i in 0 .. n-1 ->
               fullAdder x.[i] y.[i] carry.[i] sum.[i] carry.[i+1] ]
```

Let's now take a look at the propositional formula for a halfAdder with variable inputs and outputs:

```
> halfAdder (var "x") (var "y") (var "sum") (var "carry");;
> val it : Prop
= And(Not
      And
       (Not
         And
          (Var "sum",
            Not
             Not
              And (Not And (Var "x",Var "y"),Not And (Not Var "x",Not Var "y"))),
        Not
         And
          (Not Var "sum",
            Not
             Not
              Not
               And (Not And (Var "x",Var "y"),Not And (Not Var "x",Not Var "y")))),
     Not
      And
       (Not And (Var "carry",And (Var "x",Var "y")),
         Not And (Not Var "carry",Not And (Var "x",Var "y"))))
```

Clearly, you don't want to be doing too much of that! You will see better ways of inspecting circuits and the symbolic values of bit vectors in the section "Representing Propositional Formulae Efficiently Using BDDs."

In passing, we note that the twoBitAdder uses an "internal" wire. You could model this using an existential formula:

```
let twoBitAdderWithHiding (x1,x2) (y1,y2) (sum1,sum2) carry =
    let carryInnerVar = fresh "carry"
    let carryInner = var(carryInnerVar)
    Exists(carryInnerVar, halfAdder x1 y1 sum1 carryInner &&&
                          fullAdder x2 y2 carryInner sum2 carry)
```

However, this brings up issues beyond the scope of this chapter, and instead we take an approach to modeling where there are no boundaries to the circuits and where all internal wires are exposed.

Checking Simple Properties of Circuits

Now that you have modeled the initial hardware circuits, you can check simple properties of these circuits. For example, you can check that if you give a fullAdder all "low" (that is, false) inputs, then the output wires may be "low" as well and, conversely, that you have a contradiction if one of the output wires is high:

```
> tautology (fullAdder Lo Lo Lo Lo Lo);;
val it : bool = true

> satisfiable (fullAdder Lo Lo Lo Hi Lo);;
val it : bool = false
```

It is of course much better to check these results *symbolically* by giving symbolic inputs. For example, you can check that if the same value is given to the two inputs of a halfAdder, then the sum output is low and the carry output is the same as the input:

```
> tautology (halfAdder (var "x") (var "x") Lo (var "x"));;
val it : bool = true
```

Likewise, you can check that a 2-bit adder is commutative, in other words, that it doesn't matter if you swap the *x* and *y* inputs.

```
> tautology
    (nBitCarryRippleAdder 2 (vec 2 "x") (vec 2 "y") (vec 2 "sum") (vec 3 "carry")
 === nBitCarryRippleAdder 2 (vec 2 "y") (vec 2 "x") (vec 2 "sum") (vec 3 "carry"));;
val it : bool = true
```

However, if you repeat the same for sizes of 5 or bigger, things start to slow down a little, and the naive implementation of propositional logic tautology checking based on truth tables begins to break down. Hence, you have to turn to more efficient techniques for processing propositional formulae.

Representing Propositional Formulae Efficiently Using BDDs

In practice, propositional formulae to describe hardware can be enormous, involving hundreds of thousands of nodes. As a result, hardware companies have an interest in smart algorithms to process these formulae and check them for correctness. The circuits in the computers you use from day to day have almost certainly been verified using advanced propositional logic techniques, often using a functional language as the means to drive and control the analysis of the circuits.

A major advance in the application of symbolic techniques to hardware design occurred in the late 1980s with the discovery of *binary decision diagrams*, a representation for propositional logic formulae that is compact for many common circuit designs. BDDs represent a propositional formula via the use of if ... then ... else conditionals alone, which you write as (*variable* => *true-branch* | *false-branch*). Special nodes are used for true and false at the leaves: we'll write these as T and F. Every BDD is constructed with respect to a global variable ordering, so "*x* AND NOT *y*" can be represented as (x => (y => F | T) | F) if *x* comes before *y* in this ordering and as (y => F | (x => T | F)) if *y* comes before *x*. The variable ordering can be critical for performance of the representation.

BDDs are efficient because they use some of the language representation techniques you saw in Chapter 9. In particular, they work by *uniquely memoizing* all BDD nodes that are identical, which works by representing a BDD as an integer index into a lookup table that stores the real information about the node. Furthermore, negative indexes are used to represent the negation of a particular BDD node without creating a separate entry for the negated node. Listing 12-15 shows our implementation of BDDs. Fully polished BDD packages are often implemented in C. It is easy to access those packages from F# using the techniques described in Chapter 19. Here we are content with a clear and simple implementation entirely in F# code.

Listing 12-15. *Implementing Binary Decision Diagrams*

```
open System.Collections.Generic

let memoize f =
    let tab = new Dictionary<_,_>()
    fun x -> if tab.ContainsKey(x) then tab.[x]
             else let res = f x in tab.[x] <- res; res

type BddIndex = int
type Bdd = Bdd of BddIndex
type BddNode = Node of Var * BddIndex * BddIndex
type BddBuilder(order : Var -> Var -> int) =

    // The core data structures that preserve uniqueness
    let uniqueTab = new Dictionary<BddNode,BddIndex>()
    let nodeTab   = new Dictionary<BddIndex,BddNode>()

    // Keep track of the next index
    let mutable nextIdx = 2
    let trueIdx = 1
    let falseIdx = -1
```

```
let trueNode = Node("",trueIdx,trueIdx)
let falseNode = Node("",falseIdx,falseIdx)

// Map indexes to nodes. Negative indexes go to their negation. The special
// indexes -1 and 1 go to special true/false nodes.
let idxToNode(idx) =
    if idx = trueIdx then trueNode
    elif idx = falseIdx then falseNode
    elif idx > 0 then nodeTab.[idx]
    else let (Node(v,l,r)) = nodeTab.[-idx]
        Node(v,-l,-r)

// Map nodes to indexes. Add an entry to the table if needed.
let nodeToUniqueIdx(node) =
    if uniqueTab.ContainsKey(node) then uniqueTab.[node]
    else
        let idx = nextIdx
        uniqueTab.[node] <- idx
        nodeTab.[idx] <- node
        nextIdx <- nextIdx + 1
        idx

// Get the canonical index for a node. Preserve the invariant that the
// left-hand node of a conditional is always a positive node
let mkNode(v:Var,l:BddIndex,r:BddIndex) =
    if l = r then l
    elif l >= 0 then nodeToUniqueIdx(Node(v,l,r) )
    else -nodeToUniqueIdx(Node(v,-l,-r))

// Construct the BDD for a conjunction "m1 AND m2"
let rec mkAnd(m1,m2) =
    if m1 = falseIdx or m2 = falseIdx then falseIdx
    elif m1 = trueIdx then m2 elif m2 = trueIdx then m1
    else
        let Node(x,l1,r1) = idxToNode(m1)
        let Node(y,l2,r2) = idxToNode(m2)
        let v,(la,lb),(ra,rb) =
            match order x y with
            | c when c = 0 -> x,(l1,l2),(r1,r2)
            | c when c < 0 -> x,(l1,m2),(r1,m2)
            | c            -> y,(m1,l2),(m1,r2)
        mkNode(v,mkAnd(la,lb), mkAnd(ra,rb))

// Memoize this function
let mkAnd = memoize mkAnd
```

```
// Publish the construction functions that make BDDs from existing BDDs
member g.False = Bdd falseIdx
member g.And(Bdd m1,Bdd m2) = Bdd(mkAnd(m1,m2))
member g.Not(Bdd m) = Bdd(-m)
member g.Var(nm) = Bdd(mkNode(nm,trueIdx,falseIdx))
member g.NodeCount = nextIdx
```

The types of these functions are as follows:

```
val memoize : ('a -> 'b) -> ('a -> 'b)
type BddIndex = int
type Bdd = Bdd of BddIndex
type BddNode = Node of Var * BddIndex * BddIndex
type BddBuilder = class
                    end
                    with
                      new : order:(Var -> Var -> int) -> BddBuilder
                      member And : _arg1:Bdd * _arg2:Bdd -> Bdd
                      member Not : _arg3:Bdd -> Bdd
                      member Var : nm:Var -> Bdd
                      member False : Bdd
                      member NodeCount : int
                    end
```

Besides the functions that ensure that nodes are unique, the only substantial function in the implementation is mkAnd. This relies on the following logical rules for constructing BDD nodes formed by taking the conjunction of existing nodes. Note how the second rule is used to interleave variables.

- $(x => P \mid Q)$ AND $(x => R \mid S)$ is identical to $(x => P$ AND $R \mid Q$ AND $S)$.

- $(x => P \mid Q)$ AND $(y => R \mid S)$ is identical to $(x => P$ AND $T \mid Q$ AND $T)$ where T is simply $(y => R \mid S)$.

One final important optimization in the implementation is to memoize the application of the mkAnd operation.

Given the previous implementation of BDDs, you can now add the members ToString to convert BDDs to strings, Build to convert a Prop representation of a formula into a BDD, and Equiv to check for equivalence between two BDDs:

```
member g.ToString(Bdd idx) =
    let rec fmt depth idx =
        if depth > 3 then "..." else
        let (Node(p,l,r)) = idxToNode(idx)
        if p = "" then if l = trueIdx then "T" else "F"
        else sprintf "(%s => %s | %s)" p (fmt (depth+1) l) (fmt (depth+1) r)
    fmt 1 idx
```

```
member g.Build(f) =
    match f with
    | And(x,y) -> g.And(g.Build x, g.Build y)
    | Var(p) -> g.Var(p)
    | Not(x) -> g.Not(g.Build x)
    | False -> g.False
    | Exists(v,p) -> failwith "Exists node"

member g.Equiv p1 p2 = (g.Build(p1) = g.Build(p2))
```

You can now install a pretty-printer and inspect the BDDs for some simple formulae:

```
> let bddBuilder = BddBuilder(compare);;
val bddBuilder: BddBuilder

> fsi.AddPrinter(fun bdd -> bddBuilder.ToString(bdd));;
val it: unit = ()

> bddBuilder.Build(var "x");;
val it : Bdd = (x => T | F)

> bddBuilder.Build(var "x" &&& var "x");;
val it : Bdd = (x => T | F)

> bddBuilder.Build(var "x") = bddBuilder.Build(var "x" &&& var "x");;
val it : bool = true

> (var "x") = (var "x" &&& var "x");;
val it : bool = false

> bddBuilder.Build(var "x" &&& var "y");;
val it : Bdd = (x => (y => T | F) | F)

> bddBuilder.Equiv (var "x") (var "x" &&& var "x");;
val it : bool = true
```

Note that the BDD representations of "x" and "x AND x" are identical, while the Prop representations are not. The Prop representation is an *abstract syntax* representation, while the BDD representation is more of a *semantic* or *computational* representation. The BDD representation incorporates all the logic necessary to prove propositional formula equivalent; in other words, this logic is built into the representation itself.

Circuit Verification with BDDs

You can now use BDDs to perform circuit verification. For example, the following verifies that you can swap the *x* and *y* inputs to an 8-bit adder:

```
> bddBuilder.Equiv
    (nBitCarryRippleAdder 8 (vec 8 "x") (vec 8 "y") (vec 8 "sum") (vec 9 "carry"))
    (nBitCarryRippleAdder 8 (vec 8 "y") (vec 8 "x") (vec 8 "sum") (vec 9 "carry"));;
val it : bool = true
```

Thirty-three variables are involved in this circuit. A naive exploration of this space would involve searching a truth table of more than eight billion entries. The BDD implementation takes moments on any modern computer. Efficient symbolic representations pay off!

A more substantial verification problem involves checking the equivalence of circuits that have substantial structural differences. To explore this, let's take a different implementation of addition called a *carry select adder*. This avoids a major problem with ripple adders caused by the fact that the "carry" signal must propagate along the entire length of the chain of internal adders, causing longer delays in the electrical signals and thus reducing the clock rates of a circuit or possibly increasing power consumption. A carry select adder gets around this through a common hardware trick of speculative execution. It divides the inputs into blocks and adds each block twice, once assuming the carry is low and once assuming it is high. The result is then selected *after* the circuit, when the carry for the block has been computed. Listing 12-16 shows the specification of the essence of the hardware layout of a carry select adder using the techniques we've developed so far. The specification uses the slicing syntax for arrays described in Chapter 4.

Listing 12-16. *A Carry Select Adder Modeled Using Propositional Logic*

```
let mux a b c = ((~~~a ==> b) &&& (a ==> c))

let carrySelectAdder
        totalSize maxBlockSize
        (x:bitvec) (y:bitvec)
        (sumLo:bitvec) (sumHi:bitvec)
        (carryLo:bitvec) (carryHi:bitvec)
        (sum:bitvec) (carry:bitvec) =
   Blocks
     [ for i in 0..maxBlockSize..totalSize-1 ->
         let sz = min (totalSize-i) maxBlockSize
         let j = i+sz-1
         let carryLo = Array.append [| False |] carryLo.[i+1..j+1]
         let adderLo = rippleAdder sz x.[i..j] y.[i..j] sumLo.[i..j] carryLo
         let carryHi = Array.append [| True  |] carryHi.[i+1..j+1]
         let adderHi = rippleAdder sz x.[i..j] y.[i..j]  sumHi.[i..j] carryHi
         let carrySelect = (carry.[j+1] === mux carry.[i] carryLo.[sz] carryHi.[sz])
         let sumSelect =
             Blocks [for k in i..j ->
                          sum.[k] === mux carry.[i] sumLo.[k] sumHi.[k]]
         adderLo &&& adderHi &&& carrySelect &&& sumSelect ]
```

You can now check that a carrySelectAdder is equivalent to a rippleAdder. Here's the overall verification condition:

```
let checkAdders n k =
    let x = (vec n "x")
    let y = (vec n "y")
    let sumA    = (vec n "sumA")
    let sumB    = (vec n "sumB")
    let sumLo   = (vec n "sumLo")
    let sumHi   = (vec n "sumHi")
    let carryA = (vec (n+1) "carryA")
    let carryB = (vec (n+1) "carryB")
    let carryLo = (vec (n+1) "carryLo")
    let carryHi = (vec (n+1) "carryHi")
    let adder1 = carrySelectAdder n k x y sumLo sumHi carryLo  carryHi  sumA carryA
    let adder2 = rippleAdder n x y sumB carryB
    (adder1 &&& adder2 &&& (carryA.[0] === carryB.[0]) ==>
        (vecEq sumA sumB &&& bitEq carryA.[n] carryB.[n]))
```

Ignoring the construction of the inputs, the verification condition specifies the following:

- Assume you have the two adder circuits, with the same inputs.

- Assume the input carry bits are the same.

- Then, the output sum vectors are identical, and the final output carry bits are identical.

Here is the verification condition being checked interactively, for 5-bit inputs, in chunks of 2 for the carrySelectAdder:

```
> bddBuilder.Equiv (checkAdders 5 2) True;;
val it : bool = true
```

In practice, BDDs require a good variable ordering, and the default alphabetic ordering is unlikely to be the best. Here is a larger verification using a more random ordering induced by first comparing on the hash codes of the names of the variables:

```
let approxCompareOn f x y =
    let c = compare (f x) (f y)
    if c <> 0 then c else compare x y
let bddBuilder2 = BddBuilder(approxCompareOn hash)
```

```
> bddBuilder2.Equiv (checkAdders 7 2) True;;
val it : bool = true
```

Seventy-four Boolean variables are involved in this last verification problem. You would have to generate up to 2^{74} test cases to explore this systematically via testing; that's 22 thousand billion billion test cases. By using symbolic techniques, you have explored this entire space in a matter of seconds and in only a few hundred lines of code.

■**Note** Hardware and software verification are highly active areas of research and one of the most important applications of symbolic programming techniques in the industrial arena. The verifications performed here aim to give you a taste of how symbolic techniques can prove nontrivial results about circuits in a matter of seconds. We've omitted some simple techniques that can make these verifications scale to very large circuits; for example, we expand "equivalence" nodes in propositional formulae. Preserving them can lead to smaller symbolic descriptions and more efficient processing with BDDs. You can find out more about the applications of F# and functional programming to verification problems at `http://www.expert-fsharp.com/Topics/Verification`.

Summary

In this chapter, you looked at two applications of language-oriented symbolic programming. The first was algebraic symbolic differentiation and visualization, where you learned how to differentiate, simplify, and display algebraic expressions. The second was hardware modeling and verification using propositional logic and binary decision diagrams, where you saw how to use symbolic techniques to describe circuits as propositional logic formulae and then used brute-force and/or "binary decision diagram" techniques to analyze these for correctness.

CHAPTER 13

■ ■ ■

Reactive, Asynchronous, and Concurrent Programming

So far in this book you've seen functions and objects that process their inputs immediately using a single "thread" of execution where the code runs to completion and produces useful results or state changes. In this chapter, you'll turn your attention to *concurrent, parallel, asynchronous,* and *reactive* programs. These each represent substantially different approaches to programming from those you've seen so far. Some of the reasons for turning to these techniques are as follows:

- To achieve better responsiveness in a graphical user interface (GUI)

- To report progress results during a long-running computation and to support cancellation of these computations

- To achieve greater throughput in a reactive application or service

- To achieve faster processing rates on a multiprocessor machine or cluster

- To take advantage of the I/O parallelism available in modern disk drives or network connections

- To sustain processing while network and disk I/O operations are in process

In this chapter, we cover some of the techniques that can help achieve these outcomes:

- Using .NET threads and the BackgroundWorker class for background computations

- Using events and messages to report results back to a GUI

- Using F# asynchronous workflows and the .NET thread pool to handle network requests and other asynchronous I/O operations

- Using F# pattern matching to process message queues

- Using low-level .NET shared-memory primitives to implement new concurrency techniques and control access to mutable data structures

In Chapter 11 we looked at the most common type of reactive program: GUI programs that respond to events raised on the GUI thread. The inner loop of such an application (contained in the Windows Forms library) spends most of its time blocked waiting for the underlying operating system to notify it of a relevant event, such as a click from the user or a timer event from the operating system. This notification is received as an event in a message queue. Many GUI programs have only a single thread of execution, so all computation happens on the GUI thread. This can lead to problems such as nonresponsive user interfaces. This is one of many reasons it is important to master some of the techniques of concurrent and asynchronous programming.

Introducing Some Terminology

Before we begin, let's look more closely at some terminology:

- *Processes* are, in the context of this chapter, standard operating system (OS) processes. Each instance of the .NET CLR runs in its own process, and multiple instances of the .NET CLR will often be running on the same machine.

- *Threads* are, in the context of this chapter, standard .NET threads. On most implementations of .NET these correspond to operating system threads. Each .NET process has many threads running within the one process.

- *Concurrent programs* are ones with multiple threads of execution, each typically executing different code, or are at different execution points within the same code. Simultaneous execution may be simulated by scheduling and descheduling the threads, which is done by the OS. For example, most operating system services and GUI applications are concurrent.

- *Parallel programs* are one or more processes or threads executing simultaneously. For example, many modern microprocessors have two or more physical CPUs capable of executing processes and threads in parallel. Parallel programs can also be *data parallel*. For example, a massively parallel device such as a graphics processor unit (GPU) can process arrays and images in parallel. Parallel programs can also be a cluster of computers on a network, communicating via message passing. Historically, some parallel scientific programs have even used e-mail for communication!

- *Asynchronous programs* perform requests that do not complete immediately but are fulfilled at a later time and where the program issuing the request has to do meaningful work in the meantime. For example, most network I/O is inherently asynchronous. A web crawler is also a highly asynchronous program, managing hundreds or thousands of simultaneous network requests.

- *Reactive programs* are ones whose normal mode of operation is to be in a state waiting for some kind of input, such as waiting for user input or for input from a message queue via a network socket. For example, GUI applications and web servers are reactive programs.

Parallel, asynchronous, concurrent, and reactive programs bring many interesting challenges. For example, these programs are nearly always *nondeterministic*. This makes debugging more challenging since it is difficult to "step" through a program, and even pausing a running program with outstanding asynchronous requests may cause timeouts. Most dramatically, incorrect concurrent programs may *deadlock*, which means all threads are waiting on results from some other thread and no thread can make progress. Programs may also *livelock*, where processing is occurring and messages are being sent between threads but no useful work is being performed.

Using and Designing Background Workers

One of the easiest ways to get going with concurrency and parallelism is to use the System. ComponentModel.BackgroundWorker class of the .NET Framework. A BackgroundWorker class runs on its own dedicated operating system thread. These objects can be used in many situations but are especially useful for "coarse-grained" concurrency and parallelism such as checking the spelling of a document in the background. In this section we show some simple uses of BackgroundWorker and how to build similar objects that use a BackgroundWorker internally.

Listing 13-1 shows a simple use of BackgroundWorker that computes the Fibonacci numbers on the worker thread.

Listing 13-1. *A Simple BackgroundWorker*

```
open System.ComponentModel
open System.Windows.Forms

let worker = new BackgroundWorker()
let numIterations = 1000

worker.DoWork.Add(fun args ->

    let rec computeFibonacci resPrevPrev resPrev i =
        // Compute the next result
        let res = resPrevPrev + resPrev

        // At the end of the computation and write the result into the mutable state
        if i = numIterations then
            args.Result <- box res
        else
            // Compute the next result
            computeFibonacci resPrev res (i+1)

    computeFibonacci 1 1 2)

worker.RunWorkerCompleted.Add(fun args ->
    MessageBox.Show(sprintf "Result = %A" args.Result) |> ignore)

// Execute the worker
worker.RunWorkerAsync()
```

Table 13-1 shows the primary members of a BackgroundWorker object. The execution sequence of the code in Listing 13-1 is as follows:

1. The main application thread creates and configures a BackgroundWorker object.

2. Once configuration is complete, the main application thread calls the RunWorkerAsync method on the BackgroundWorker object. This causes the DoWork event to be raised on the worker thread.

3. The DoWork event handler is executed in the worker thread and computes the 1000th Fibonacci number. At the end of the computation, the result is written into args.Result, a mutable storage location in the event arguments for the DoWork event. The DoWork event handler then completes.

4. At some point after the DoWork event handler completes, the RunWorkerCompleted event is automatically raised on the main application thread. This displays a message box with the result of the computation, retrieved from the args field of the event arguments.

Table 13-1. *Primary Members of the BackgroundWorker Class*

Member and Type	Description
RunWorkerAsync: unit -> unit	Starts the process on a separate thread asynchronously. Called from the main thread.
CancelAsync: unit -> unit	Set the CancellationPending flag of the background task. Called from the main thread.
CancellationPending: bool	Set to true by raising CancelAsync. Used by the worker thread.
WorkerReportsProgress: bool	Set to true if the worker can support progress updates. Used by the main thread.
WorkerSupportsCancellation: bool	Set to true if the worker can support cancellation of the current task in progress. Used by the main thread.
ReportProgress: int -> unit	Indicate the progress of the operation. Used by the worker thread.
DoWork: IEvent<DoWorkEventArgs>	Fires in response to a call to RunWorkerAsync. Invoked on the worker thread.
RunWorkerCompleted: IEvent<RunWorkerCompletedEventArgs>	Fires when the background operation is canceled, when the operation is completed, or when an exception is thrown. Invoked on the main thread.
ProgressChanged: IEvent<ProgressChangedEventArgs>	Fires whenever the ReportProgress property is set. Invoked on the main thread.

■**Note** Objects such as a BackgroundWorker are "two-faced": they have some methods and events that are for use from the main thread and some that are for use on the worker thread. This is common in concurrent programming. In particular, be careful to understand which thread an event is raised on. For BackgroundWorker, the RunWorkerAsync and CancelAsync methods are for use from the GUI thread, and the ProgressChanged and RunWorkerCompleted events are raised on the GUI thread. The DoWork event is raised on the worker thread, and the ReportProgress method and the CancellationPending property are for use from the worker thread when handling this event.

The members in Table 13-1 show two additional facets of BackgroundWorker objects: they can optionally support protocols for cancellation and reporting progress. To report progress percentages, a worker must simply call the ReportProgress method, which raises the ProgressChanged event in the GUI thread. For cancellation, a worker computation need only check the CancellationPending property at regular intervals, exiting the computation as a result.

Building a Simpler Iterative Worker

Capturing common control patterns such as cancellation and progress reporting is an absolutely essential part of mastering concurrent programming. However, one of the problems with .NET classes such as BackgroundWorker is that they are often more imperative than an F# programmer may want, and they force other common patterns to be captured by using mutable data structures shared between threads. This leads to the more difficult topic of shared-memory concurrency, which we discuss later in the chapter. Furthermore, the way BackgroundWorker handles cancellation means that flag-checks and early-exit paths have to be inserted in the executing background process. Finally, BackgroundWorker is not useful for background threads that perform asynchronous operations, since the background thread will exit "too early," before the callbacks for the asynchronous operations have executed.

For this reason, it can often be useful to build abstractions that are similar to BackgroundWorker but that capture richer or different control patterns, preferably in a way that does not rely on the use of mutable state and that interferes less with the structure of the overall computation. Much of the rest of this chapter will look at various techniques to build these control structures.

We start with a case study where we build a type IterativeBackgroundWorker that represents a variation on the BackgroundWorker design pattern. Listing 13-2 shows the code.

Listing 13-2. *A Variation on the BackgroundWorker Design Pattern for Iterative Computations*

```
open System.ComponentModel
open System.Windows.Forms


/// An IterativeBackgroudWorker follows the BackgroundWorker design pattern
/// but instead of running an arbitrary computation it iterates a function
/// a fixed number of times and reports intermediate and final results.
/// The worker is paramaterized by its internal state type.
///
/// Percentage progress is based on the iteration number. Cancellation checks
/// are made at each iteration. Implemented via an internal BackgroundWorker.
type IterativeBackgroundWorker<'a>(oneStep:('a -> 'a),
                                   initialState:'a,
                                   numIterations:int) =

    let worker =
        new BackgroundWorker(WorkerReportsProgress=true,
                             WorkerSupportsCancellation=true)
```

```fsharp
// Create the events that we will later trigger
let triggerCompleted,completed = IEvent.create()
let triggerError    ,error     = IEvent.create()
let triggerCancelled,cancelled = IEvent.create()
let triggerProgress ,progress  = IEvent.create()

do worker.DoWork.Add(fun args ->
    // This recursive function represents the computation loop.
    // It runs at "maximum speed", i.e. is an active rather than
    // a reactive process, and can only be controlled by a
    // cancellation signal.
    let rec iterate state i =
        // At the end of the computation terminate the recursive loop
        if worker.CancellationPending then
            args.Cancel <- true
        elif i < numIterations then
            // Compute the next result
            let state' = oneStep state

            // Report the percentage computation and the internal state
            let percent = int ((float (i+1)/float numIterations) * 100.0)
            do worker.ReportProgress(percent, box state);

            // Compute the next result
            iterate state' (i+1)
        else
            args.Result <- box state

    iterate initialState 0)

do worker.RunWorkerCompleted.Add(fun args ->
    if args.Cancelled        then triggerCancelled()
    elif args.Error <> null then triggerError args.Error
    else triggerCompleted (args.Result :?> 'a))

do worker.ProgressChanged.Add(fun args ->
    triggerProgress (args.ProgressPercentage,(args.UserState :?> 'a)))

member x.WorkerCompleted  = completed
member x.WorkerCancelled  = cancelled
member x.WorkerError       = error
member x.ProgressChanged  = progress

// Delegate the remaining members to the underlying worker
member x.RunWorkerAsync()    = worker.RunWorkerAsync()
member x.CancelAsync()        = worker.CancelAsync()
```

The types inferred for the code in Listing 13-2 are as follows:

```
type IterativeBackgroundWorker<'state> =
    new : ('state -> 'state) * 'state * int -> IterativeBackgroundWorker<'state>
    member RunWorkerAsync : unit -> unit
    member CancelAsync : unit -> unit

    member ProgressChanged : IEvent<int * 'state>
    member WorkerCompleted : IEvent<'state>
    member WorkerCancelled : IEvent<unit>
    member WorkerError     : IEvent<exn>
```

Let's take a look at this signature first, because it represents the design of the type. The worker constructor is given a function of type 'state -> 'state to compute successive iterations of the computation, plus an initial state and the number of iterations to compute. For example, you can compute the Fibonacci numbers using the following iteration function:

```
let fibOneStep (fibPrevPrev:bigint,fibPrev) = (fibPrev, fibPrevPrev+fibPrev);;
```

The type of this function is as follows:

```
val fibOneStep : bigint * bigint -> bigint * bigint
```

The RunWorkerAsync and CancelAsync members follow the BackgroundWorker design pattern, as do the events, except that we have expanded the RunWorkerCompleted event into three events to correspond to the three termination conditions and modified the ProgressChanged to include the state. You can instantiate the type as follows:

```
> let worker = new IterativeBackgroundWorker<_>( fibOneStep,(1I,1I),100);;
val worker : IterativeBackgroundWorker<bigint * bigint>

> worker.WorkerCompleted.Add(fun result ->
      MessageBox.Show(sprintf "Result = %A" result) |> ignore);;
val it : unit = ()

> worker.ProgressChanged.Add(fun (percentage, state) ->
     printfn "%d%% complete, state = %A" percentage state);;
val it : unit = ()

> worker.RunWorkerAsync();;
1% complete, state = (1I, 1I)
2% complete, state = (1I, 2I)
3% complete, state = (2I, 3I)
4% complete, state = (3I, 5I)
...
```

```
98% complete, state = (135301852344706746049I, 218922995834555169026I)
99% complete, state = (218922995834555169026I, 354224848179261915075I)
100% complete, state = (354224848179261915075I, 573147844013817084101I)
val it : unit = ()
```

One difference here is that cancellation and percentage progress reporting are handled automatically based on the iterations of the computation. This is assuming each iteration takes roughly the same amount of time. Other variations on the BackgroundWorker design pattern are possible. For example, reporting percentage completion of fixed tasks such as installation is often performed by timing sample executions of the tasks and adjusting the percentage reports appropriately.

■**Note** We implemented IterativeBackgroundWorker via delegation rather than inheritance. This is because its external members are different from those of BackgroundWorker. The .NET documentation recommends you use implementation inheritance for this, but we disagree. Implementation inheritance can only *add* complexity to the signature of an abstraction and never makes things simpler, whereas an IterativeBackgroundWorker is in many ways simpler than using a BackgroundWorker, despite that it uses an instance of the latter internally. Powerful, compositional, simple abstractions are the primary building blocks of functional programming.

Raising Additional Events from Background Workers

Often you will need to raise additional events from objects that follow the BackgroundWorker design pattern. For example, let's say you want to augment IterativeBackgroundWorker to raise an event when the worker starts its work and for this event to pass the exact time that the worker thread started as an event argument. Listing 13-3 shows the extra code you need to add to the IterativeBackgroundWorker type to make this happen. We use this extra code in the next section.

Listing 13-3. *Code to Raise GUI-Thread Events from an* IterativeBackgroundWorker *Object*

```
open System
open System.Threading

type IterativeBackgroundWorker<'a>(...) =

    let worker = ...

    // The constructor captures the synchronization context. This allows us to post
    // messages back to the GUI thread where the BackgroundWorker was created.
    let syncContext = SynchronizationContext.Current
    do if syncContext = null then failwith "no synchronization context found"

    let triggerStarted,started = IEvent.create()
```

```
    // Raise the event when the worker starts. This is done by posting a message
    // to the captured synchronization context.
    do worker.DoWork.Add(fun args ->
        syncContext.Post(SendOrPostCallback(fun _ -> triggerStarted(DateTime.Now)),
                         state=null)
    ...


    /// The Started event gets raised when the worker starts. It is
    /// raised on the GUI thread (i.e. in the synchronization context of
    /// the thread where the worker object was created).
    // It has type IEvent<DateTime>
    member x.Started             = started
```

The simple way to raise additional events is often wrong. For example, it is tempting to simply create an event, arrange for it to be triggered, and publish it, as you would do for a GUI control. However, if you do that, you will end up triggering the event on the background worker thread, and its event handlers will run on that thread. This is dangerous, because most GUI objects (and many other objects) can be accessed only from the thread they were created on; this is a restriction enforced by most GUI systems.

One of the nice features of the BackgroundWorker class is that it automatically arranges to raise the RunWorkerCompleted and ProgressChanged events on the GUI thread. We have shown how to achieve this in Listing 13-3. Technically speaking, the extended IterativeBackgroundWorker object has captured the *synchronization context* of the thread where it was created and posts an operation back to that synchronization context. A synchronization context is just an object that lets you post operations back to another thread. For threads such as a GUI thread, this means posting an operation will post a message through the GUI event loop.

Connecting a Background Worker to a GUI

To round off this section on the BackgroundWorker design pattern, we show the full code required to build a small application with a background worker task that supports cancellation and reports progress. Listing 13-4 shows the full code.

Listing 13-4. *Connecting an IterativeBackgroundWorker to a GUI*

```
open System.Drawing
open System.Windows.Forms

let form = new Form(Visible=true,TopMost=true)

let panel = new FlowLayoutPanel(Visible=true,
                                Height = 20,
                                Dock=DockStyle.Bottom,
                                BorderStyle=BorderStyle.FixedSingle)

let progress = new ProgressBar(Visible=false,
                               Anchor=(AnchorStyles.Bottom ||| AnchorStyles.Top),
                               Value=0)
```

```fsharp
let text = new Label(Text="Paused",
                     Anchor=AnchorStyles.Left,
                     Height=20,
                     TextAlign= ContentAlignment.MiddleLeft)

panel.Controls.Add(progress)
panel.Controls.Add(text)
form.Controls.Add(panel)

let fibOneStep (fibPrevPrev:bigint,fibPrev) = (fibPrev, fibPrevPrev+fibPrev)

// Run the iterative algorithm 500 times before reporting intermediate results
// Burn some additional cycles to make sure it runs slowly enough
let rec RepeatN n f s = if n <= 0 then s else RepeatN (n-1) f (f s)
let rec BurnN n f s = if n <= 0 then f s else ignore (f s); BurnN (n-1) f s
let step = (RepeatN 500 (BurnN 1000 fibOneStep))

// Create the iterative worker.
let worker = new IterativeBackgroundWorker<_>(step,(1I,1I),100)

worker.ProgressChanged.Add(fun (progressPercentage,state)->
    progress.Value <- progressPercentage)

worker.WorkerCompleted.Add(fun (_,result) ->
    progress.Visible <- false;
    text.Text <- "Paused";
    MessageBox.Show(sprintf "Result = %A" result) |> ignore)

worker.WorkerCancelled.Add(fun () ->
    progress.Visible <- false;
    text.Text <- "Paused";
    MessageBox.Show(sprintf "Cancelled OK!") |> ignore)

worker.WorkerError.Add(fun exn ->
    text.Text <- "Paused";
    MessageBox.Show(sprintf "Error: %A" exn) |> ignore)

form.Menu <- new MainMenu()
let workerMenu = form.Menu.MenuItems.Add("&Worker")

workerMenu.MenuItems.Add(new MenuItem("Run",onClick=(fun _ args ->
    text.Text <- "Running";
    progress.Visible <- true;
    worker.RunWorkerAsync())))
```

```
workerMenu.MenuItems.Add(new MenuItem("Cancel",onClick=(fun _ args ->
    text.Text <- "Cancelling";
    worker.CancelAsync())))

form.Closed.Add(fun _ -> worker.CancelAsync())
```

When run in F# Interactive, a window appears as in Figure 13-1.

Figure 13-1. *A GUI window with a* BackgroundWorker *reporting progress percentage*

■Note Forcibly aborting computations uncooperatively is not recommended in .NET programming. You can attempt to do this using System.Threading.Thread.Abort(), but the use of this method may have many unintended consequences, discussed later in this chapter.

Introducing Asynchronous Computations

The two background worker samples we've shown so far run at "full throttle." In other words, the computations run on the background threads as active loops, and their reactive behavior is limited to flags that check for cancellation. In reality, background threads often have to do different kinds of work, either by responding to completing asynchronous I/O requests, by processing messages, by sleeping, or by waiting to acquire shared resources. Fortunately, F# comes with a powerful set of techniques for structuring asynchronous programs in a natural way. These are called *asynchronous workflows*. In the next three sections, we cover how to use asynchronous workflows to structure asynchronous and message-processing tasks in ways that preserve the essential logical structure of your code.

Fetching Multiple Web Pages Asynchronously

One of the most intuitive asynchronous tasks is fetching a web page; we all use web browsers that can fetch multiple pages simultaneously. In the samples in Chapter 2 we showed how to fetch pages synchronously. This is useful for many purposes, but browsers and high-performance web crawlers will have tens or thousands of connections "in flight" at once.

The type `Microsoft.FSharp.Control.Async<'a>` lies at the heart of F# asynchronous workflows. A value of type `Async<'a>` represents a program fragment that will generate a value of type `'a` "at some point in the future." Listing 13-5 shows how to use asynchronous workflows to fetch several web pages simultaneously.

Listing 13-5. *Fetching Three Web Pages Simultaneously*

```
open System.Net
open System.IO
open Microsoft.FSharp.Control.CommonExtensions

let museums = ["MOMA",              "http://moma.org/";
               "British Museum", "http://www.thebritishmuseum.ac.uk/";
               "Prado",            "http://museoprado.mcu.es"]

let fetchAsync(nm,url:string) =
    async { do printfn "Creating request for %s..." nm
            let req  = WebRequest.Create(url)

            let! resp  = req.GetResponseAsync()

            do printfn "Getting response stream for %s..." nm
            let stream = resp.GetResponseStream()

            do printfn "Reading response for %s..." nm
            let reader = new StreamReader(stream)
            let! html = reader.ReadToEndAsync()

            do printfn "Read %d characters for %s..." html.Length nm }
for nm,url in museums do
    Async.Spawn (fetchAsync(nm,url))
```

The types of these functions and values are as follows:

```
val museums : (string * string) list
val fetchAsync : string * string -> Async<unit>
```

When run on one of our machines via F# Interactive, the output of the code from Listing 13-5 is as follows:

```
Creating request for MOMA...
Creating request for British Museum...
Creating request for Prado...
Getting response for MOMA...
Reading response for MOMA...
```

```
Getting response for Prado...
Reading response for Prado...
Read 188 characters for Prado...
Read 41635 characters for MOMA...
Getting response for British Museum...
Reading response for British Museum...
Read 24341 characters for British Museum...
```

The heart of the code in Listing 13-5 is the construct introduced by async { ... }. This is an application of the workflow syntax introduced in Chapter 9. Now let's take a closer look at Listing 13-5. The key operations are the two let! operations within the workflow expression:

```
async { do ...
        let! resp  = req.GetResponseAsync()
        do ...
        ...
        let! html = reader.ReadToEndAsync()
        do ... }
```

Within asynchronous workflow expressions, the language construct let! *var* = *expr* in *body* simply means "perform the asynchronous operation *expr* and bind the result to *var* when the operation completes. Then continue by executing the rest of the computation *body*."

With this in mind, you can now see what fetchAsync does:

- It synchronously requests a web page.

- It asynchronously awaits a response to the request.

- It gets the response Stream and StreamReader synchronously after the asynchronous request completes.

- It reads to the end of the stream asynchronously.

- After the read completes, it prints the total number of characters read synchronously.

Finally, the method Async.Spawn is used to initiate the execution of a number of asynchronous computations. This works by queuing the computations in the .NET thread pool. The .NET thread pool is explained in more detail in the following section.

Understanding Thread Hopping

Asynchronous computations are different from normal, synchronous computations: an asynchronous computation tends to "hop" between different underlying .NET threads. To see this, let's augment the asynchronous computation with diagnostics that show the ID of the underlying .NET thread at each point of active execution. You can do this by replacing uses of printfn in the function fetchAsync with uses of the following function:

```
let tprintfn fmt =
    printf "[.NET Thread %d]" System.Threading.Thread.CurrentThread.ManagedThreadId;
    printfn fmt
```

After doing this, the output changes to the following:

```
[.NET Thread 12]Creating request for MOMA...
[.NET Thread 13]Creating request for British Museum...
[.NET Thread 12]Creating request for Prado...
[.NET Thread 8]Getting response for MOMA...
[.NET Thread 8]Reading response for MOMA...
[.NET Thread 9]Getting response for Prado...
[.NET Thread 9]Reading response for Prado...
[.NET Thread 9]Read 188 characters for Prado...
[.NET Thread 8]Read 41635 characters for MOMA...
[.NET Thread 8]Getting response for British Museum...
[.NET Thread 8]Reading response for British Museum...
[.NET Thread 8]Read 24341 characters for British Museum...
```

Note how each individual Async program "hops" between threads; the MOMA request started on .NET thread 12 and finished life on .NET thread 8. Each asynchronous computation in Listing 13-5 executes in the following way:

- Each asynchronous computation starts life as a work item in the .NET thread pool. (The .NET thread pool is explained in the "What Is the .NET Thread Pool?" sidebar.) These are processed by a number of .NET threads.

- When the asynchronous computations reach the GetResponseAsync and ReadToEndAsync calls, the requests are made and the continuations are registered as "I/O completion actions" in the .NET thread pool. No thread is used while the request is in progress.

- When the requests complete, they trigger a callback in the .NET thread pool. These may be serviced by different threads than those that originated the calls.

WHAT IS THE .NET THREAD POOL?

.NET objects such as BackgroundWorker use a single .NET background thread, which corresponds to a single Windows or other OS thread. OS threads have supporting resources such as an execution stack that consume memory and are relatively expensive resources to create and run.

However, many concurrent processing tasks require only the ability to schedule short-lived tasks that then suspend, waiting for further input. To simplify the process of creating and managing these tasks, the .NET Framework provides the System.Threading.ThreadPool class. The thread pool consists of two main sets of suspended tasks: a queue containing user work items and a pool of "I/O completion" callbacks, each waiting for a signal from the operating system. The number of threads in the thread pool is automatically tuned, and items can be either queued asynchronously or registered against a .NET WaitHandle synchronization object (for example, a lock, a semaphore, or an I/O request). This is how to queue a work item in the .NET thread pool:

```
open System.Threading

ThreadPool.QueueUserWorkItem(fun _ -> printf "Hello!") |> ignore
```

Under the Hood: What Are Asynchronous Computations?

Async<'a> values are essentially a way of writing "continuation-passing" or "callback" programs explicitly. Continuations themselves were described in Chapter 8 along with techniques to pass them explicitly. Async<'a> are computations that call a *success continuation* when the asynchronous computation completes and an *exception continuation* if it fails. They provide a form of *managed asynchronous computation*, where "managed" means that several aspects of asynchronous programming are handled automatically:

- *Exception propagation is added "for free"*: If an exception is raised during an asynchronous step, then the exception terminates the entire asynchronous computation and cleans up any resources declared using use, and the exception value is then handed to a continuation. Exceptions may also be caught and managed within the asynchronous workflow by using try/with/finally.

- *Cancellation checking is added "for free"*: The execution of an Async<'a> workflow automatically checks a cancellation flag at each asynchronous operation. Cancellation is controlled through the use of asynchronous groups, a topic covered at http://www.expert-fsharp.com/Topics/Cancellation.

- *Resource lifetime management is fairly simple*: You can protect resources across parts of an asynchronous computation by using use inside the workflow syntax.

If we put aside the question of cancellation, values of type Async<'a> are effectively identical to the following type:

```
type Async<'a> = Async of ('a -> unit) * (exn -> unit) -> unit
```

Here the functions are the success continuation and exception continuations, respectively. Each value of type Async<'a> should eventually call one of these two continuations. The async object is of type AsyncBuilder and supports the following methods, among others:

```
type AsyncBuilder with
    member Return : 'a -> Async<'a>
    member Delay : (unit -> Async<'a>) -> Async<'a>
    member Using: 'a * ('a -> Async<'b>) -> Async<'b> when 'a :> System.IDisposable
    member Let: 'a * ('a -> Async<'b>) -> Async<'b>
    member Bind: Async<'a> * ('a -> Async<'b>) -> Async<'b>
```

The full definition of Async<'a> values and the implementations of these methods for the async object are given in the F# library source code. As you saw in Chapter 9, builder objects such as async containing methods like those shown previously mean that the syntax async { ... } can be used as a way of building Async<'a> values.

Table 13-2 shows the common constructs used in asynchronous workflow expressions. For example, the following asynchronous workflow:

```
async { let req  = WebRequest.Create("http://moma.org/")
        let! resp = req.GetResponseAsync()
        let stream = resp.GetResponseStream()
        let reader = new StreamReader(stream)
        let! html = reader.ReadToEndAsync()
        html }
```

is shorthand for the following code:

```
async.Delay(fun () ->
    async.Let(WebRequest.Async("http://moma.org/"), (fun req ->
        async.Bind(req.GetResponseAsync(), (fun resp ->
            async.Let(resp.GetResponseStream(), (fun stream ->
                async.Let(new StreamReader(stream), (fun reader ->
                    async.Bind(reader.ReadToEndAsync(), (fun html ->
                        async.Return(html)))))))))))
```

As you saw in Chapter 9, the key to understanding the F# workflow syntax is always to understand the meaning of let!. In the case of async workflows, let! executes one asynchronous computation and schedules the next computation for execution once the first asynchronous computation completes. This is syntactic sugar for the Bind operation on the async object.

Table 13-2. *Common Constructs Used in async { ... } Workflow Expressions*

Construct	Description
let! *pat* = *expr*	Execute the asynchronous computation expr and bind its result to *pat* when it completes. If *expr* has type Async<'a>, then *pat* has type 'a. Equivalent to async.Bind(expr,(fun pat -> ...)).
let pat = expr	Execute an expression synchronously and bind its result to *pat* immediately. If *expr* has type 'a, then *pat* has type 'a. Equivalent to async.Let(expr,(fun pat -> ...)).
do! *expr*	Equivalent to let! () = expr.
do *expr*	Equivalent to let () = expr.
return *expr*	Evaluate the expression, and return its value as the result of the containing asynchronous workflow. Equivalent to async.Return(expr).
return! *expr*	Execute the expression as an asynchronous computation, and return its result as the overall result of the containing asynchronous workflow. Equivalent to expr.
use *pat* = *expr*	Execute the expression immediately, and bind its result immediately. Call the Dispose method on each variable bound in the pattern when the subsequent asynchronous workflow terminates, regardless of whether it terminates normally or by an exception. Equivalent to async.Using(expr,(fun pat -> ...)).

File Processing Using Asynchronous Workflows

We now show a slightly longer sample of asynchronous I/O processing. Our running sample is an application that must read a large number of image files and perform some processing on them. This kind of application may be *compute bound* (if the processing takes a long time and the file system is fast) or *I/O bound* (if the processing is quick and the file system is slow). Using asynchronous techniques tends to give good overall performance gains when an application is I/O bound and can also give performance improvements for compute-bound applications if asynchronous operations are executed in parallel on multicore machines.

Listing 13-6 shows a synchronous implementation of our image transformation program.

Listing 13-6. *A Synchronous Image Processor*

```
open System.IO
let numImages = 200
let size = 512
let numPixels = size * size

let MakeImageFiles() =
    printfn "making %d %dx%d images... " numImages size size
    let pixels = Array.init numPixels (fun i -> byte i)
    for i = 1 to numImages  do
        System.IO.File.WriteAllBytes(sprintf "Image%d.tmp" i, pixels)
    printfn "done."

let processImageRepeats = 20

let TransformImage(pixels, imageNum) =
    printfn "TransformImage %d" imageNum;
    // Perform a CPU-intensive operation on the image.
    pixels |> Func.repeatN processImageRepeats (Array.map (fun b -> b + 1uy))

let ProcessImageSync(i) =
    use inStream =  File.OpenRead(sprintf "Image%d.tmp" i)
    let pixels = Array.zero_create numPixels
    let nPixels = inStream.Read(pixels,0,numPixels);
    let pixels' = TransformImage(pixels,i)
    use outStream =  File.OpenWrite(sprintf "Image%d.done" i)
    outStream.Write(pixels',0,numPixels)

let ProcessImagesSync() =
    printfn "ProcessImagesSync...";
    for i in 1 .. numImages do
        ProcessImageSync(i)
```

We assume the image files are already created using the following code:

```
> System.Environment.CurrentDirectory <- __SOURCE_DIRECTORY__;;
val it : unit = ()

> MakeImageFiles();;
val it : unit = ()
```

We have left the transformation on the image largely unspecified, such as the function TransformImage. By changing the value of processImageRepeats, you can adjust the computation from compute bound to I/O bound.

The problem with this implementation is that each image is read and processed sequentially, when in practice multiple images can be read and transformed simultaneously, giving much greater throughput. Listing 13-7 shows the implementation of the image processor using an asynchronous workflow.

Listing 13-7. *The Asynchronous Image Processor*

```
open Microsoft.FSharp.Control
open Microsoft.FSharp.Control.CommonExtensions

let ProcessImageAsync(i) =
    async { use inStream = File.OpenRead(sprintf "Image%d.tmp" i)
            let! pixels = inStream.ReadAsync(numPixels)
            let  pixels' = TransformImage(pixels,i)
            use outStream = File.OpenWrite(sprintf "Image%d.done" i)
            do! outStream.WriteAsync(pixels')  }

let ProcessImagesAsync() =
    printfn "ProcessImagesAsync...";
    let tasks = [ for i in 1 .. numImages -> ProcessImageAsync(i) ]
    Async.Run (Async.Parallel tasks)  |> ignore
    printfn "ProcessImagesAsync finished!";
```

On the one of our machines, the asynchronous version of the code ran up to three times as fast as the synchronous version (in total elapsed time), when processImageRepeats is 20 and numImages is 200. A factor of 2 was achieved consistently for any number of processImageRepeats since this machine had two CPUs.

Let's take a closer look at this code. The call Async.Run (Async.Parallel ...) executes a set of asynchronous operations in the thread pool, collects their results (or their exceptions), and returns the overall array of results to the original code. The core asynchronous workflow is introduced by the async { ... } construct. Let's look at the inner workflow line by line:

```
async { use inStream = File.OpenRead(sprintf "Image%d.tmp" i)
        ... }
```

This line opened the input stream synchronously using File.OpenRead. Although this is a synchronous operation, the use of use indicates that the lifetime of the stream is managed over the remainder of the workflow. The stream will be closed when the variable is no longer in scope, that is, at the end of the workflow, even if asynchronous activations occur in between. If any step in the workflow raises an uncaught exception, then the stream will also be closed while handling the exception.

The next line reads the input stream asynchronously using `inStream.ReadAsync`:

```
async { use inStream = File.OpenRead(sprintf "Image%d.tmp" i)
        let! pixels = inStream.ReadAsync(numPixels)
        ... }
```

`Stream.ReadAsync` is an extension method added to the .NET `System.IO.Stream` class by opening the F# namespace `Microsoft.FSharp.Control.CommonExtensions`, and it generates a value of type `Async<byte[]>`. The use of `let!` executes this operation asynchronously and registers a callback. When the callback is invoked, the value `pixels` is bound to the result of the operation, and the remainder of the asynchronous workflow is executed. The next line transforms the image synchronously using `TransformImage`:

```
async { use inStream = File.OpenRead(sprintf "Image%d.tmp" i)
        let! pixels = inStream.ReadAsync(numPixels)
        let  pixels' = TransformImage(pixels,i)
        ... }
```

Like the first line, the next line opens the output stream. Using `use` guarantees that the stream is closed by the end of the workflow regardless of whether exceptions are thrown in the remainder of the workflow.

```
async { use inStream = File.OpenRead(sprintf "Image%d.tmp" i)
        let! pixels = inStream.ReadAsync(numPixels)
        let  pixels' = TransformImage(pixels,i)
        use outStream = File.OpenWrite(sprintf "Image%d.done" i)
        ... }
```

The final line of the workflow performs an asynchronous write of the image. Once again, `WriteAsync` is an extension method added to the .NET `System.IO.Stream` class by opening the F# namespace `Microsoft.FSharp.Control.CommonExtensions`.

```
async { use inStream = File.OpenRead(sprintf "Image%d.tmp" i)
        let! pixels = inStream.ReadAsync(numPixels)
        let  pixels' = TransformImage(pixels,i)
        use outStream = File.OpenWrite(sprintf "Image%d.done" i)
        do! outStream.WriteAsync(pixels')  }
```

If you now return to the first part of the function, you can see that the overall operation of the function is to create `numImages` individual asynchronous operations, using a sequence expression that generates a list:

```
let tasks = [ for i in 1 .. numImages -> ProcessImageAsync(i) ]
```

You can then compose these tasks in parallel using `Async.Parallel` and then run the resulting process using `Async.Run`. This waits for the overall operation to complete and returns the result.

```
Async.Run (Async.Parallel tasks)
```

Table 13-3 shows some of the primitives and combinators commonly used to build asynchronous workflows. Take the time to compare Listings 13-7 and 13-6. Notice the following:

- The overall structure and flow of the core of Listing 13-7 is quite similar to Listing 13-6, that is, the synchronous algorithm, even though it includes steps executed asynchronously.

- The performance characteristics of Listing 13-7 are the same as those of Listing 13-6. Any overhead involved in executing the asynchronous workflow is easily dominated by the overall cost of I/O and image processing. It is also much easier to experiment with modifications such as making the write operation synchronous.

Table 13-3. *Some Common Primitives Used to Build* Async<'a> *Values*

Member/Type	Description
Async.Catch: Async<'a> -> Async<Choice<'a,exn>>	Catches any errors from an asynchronous computation and returns a Choice result indicating success or failure.
Async.Primitive: ('a -> unit) * (exn -> unit) -> Async<'a>	Builds a single primitive asynchronous step of an asynchronous computation. The function that implements the step is passed continuations to call once the step is complete or if the step fails.
Async.Parallel: Async<#seq<'a>> -> Async<'a[]>	Builds a single asynchronous computation that runs the given asynchronous computations in parallel and waits for results from all to be returned. Each may either terminate with a value or return an exception. If any raise an exception, then the others are cancelled, and the overall asynchronous computation also raises the same exception.

Running Asynchronous Computations

Values of type Async<'a> are usually run using the functions listed in Table 13-4. Async<'a> values can be built by using functions and members in the F# libraries.

Table 13-4. *Common Methods in the* Async *Type Used to Run* Async<'a> *Values*

Member/Type	Description
Async.Run: Async<'a> -> 'a	Runs an operation in the thread pool and waits for its result.
Async.Spawn: Async<unit> -> unit	Queues the asynchronous computation as an operation in the thread pool.
Async.SpawnChild: Async<unit> -> Async<unit>	Queues the asynchronous computation, initially as a work item in the thread pool, but inherits the cancellation handle from the current asynchronous computation.

Table 13-4. *Common Methods in the Async Type Used to Run Async<'a> Values*

Member/Type	Description
Async.SpawnThenPostBack: Async<'a> * ('a -> unit) -> unit	Queues the asynchronous computation, initially as a work item in the thread pool. When its result is available, executes the given callback by posting a message to the synchronization context of the thread that called SpawnThenPostBack. Useful for returning the results of asynchronous computations to a GUI application.
Async.Future: Async<'a> -> Future<'a>	Queues the asynchronous computation as an operation in the thread pool and returns an object that can be used to later rendezvous with its result.

Common I/O Operations in Asynchronous Workflows

Asynchronous programming is becoming more widespread because of the use of multicore machines and networks in applications, and many .NET APIs now come with both synchronous and asynchronous versions of their functionality. For example, all web service.APIs generated by .NET tools have asynchronous versions of their requests. A quick scan of the .NET API documentation on the Microsoft website reveals the asynchronous operations listed in Table 13-5. These all have equivalent Async<'a> operations defined in the F# libraries as extensions to the corresponding .NET types.

Table 13-5. *Some Asynchronous Operations in the .NET Libraries and Corresponding F# Extensions*

.NET Asynchronous Operation	F# Extension	Description
Stream.Begin/EndRead	ReadAsync	Read a stream of bytes asynchronously. See also FileStream, NetworkStream, DeflateStream, IsolatedStorageFileStream, and SslStream.
Stream.Begin/EndWrite	WriteAsync	Write a stream of bytes asynchronously. See also FileStream.
Socket.BeginAccept/EndAccept	AcceptAsync	Accept an incoming network socket request asynchronously.
Socket.BeginReceive/EndRecevie	ReceiveAsync	Receive data on a network socket asynchronously.
Socket.BeginSend/EndSend	SendAsync	Send data on a network socket asynchronously.
WebRequest.Begin/EndGetResponse	GetResponseAsync	Make an asynchronous web request. See also FtpWebRequest, SoapWebRequest, and HttpWebRequest.

Table 13-5. *Some Asynchronous Operations in the .NET Libraries and Corresponding F# Extensions*

.NET Asynchronous Operation	F# Extension	Description
SqlCommand.Begin/EndExecuteReader	ExecuteReaderAsync	Execute an SqlCommand asynchronously.
SqlCommand.Begin/EndExecuteXmlReader	ExecuteXmlReaderAsync	Execute a read of XML asynchronously.
SqlCommand.Begin/EndExecuteNonQuery	ExecuteNonQueryAsync	Execute a nonreading SqlCommand asynchronously.

Sometimes you may need to write a few primitives to map .NET asynchronous operations into the F# asynchronous framework. We give some examples later in this section and in Chapter 14.

Under the Hood: Implementing a Primitive Asynchronous Step

Let's take a moment to look at how to implement one of the primitive Async<'a> actions we've been using earlier in the chapter. Listing 13-8 shows the essence of the implementation of Stream.ReadAsync, which is a primitive asynchronous action that wraps a pair of Stream.BeginRead and Stream.EndRead calls using Async.Primitive. We implement this as an extension to the System.IO.Stream type to ensure it is easy to find the asynchronous version of this functionality alongside existing functions (extension members were described in Chapter 6).

Listing 13-8. *An Implementation of an Async.Primitive*

```
open System

let trylet f x = (try Choice2_1 (f x) with exn -> Choice2_2(exn))

let protect cont econt f x =
    match trylet f x with
    | Choice2_1 v -> cont v
    | Choice2_2 exn -> econt exn

type System.IO.Stream with
    member stream.ReadAsync (buffer,offset,count) =
        Async.Primitive (fun (cont,econt) ->
            stream.BeginRead
                (buffer=buffer,
                 offset=offset,
                 count=count,
                 state=null,
                 callback=AsyncCallback(protect cont econt stream.EndRead))
            |> ignore)
```

The type of Async.Primitive is as follows:

```
val Async.Primitive : (('a -> unit) * (exn -> unit) -> unit) -> Async<'a>
```

The inferred type of the extension to the System.IO.Stream type in Listing 13-8 is as follows:

```
type System.IO.Stream with
    member ReadAsync: buffer:byte[] * offset:int * count:int -> Async<int>
```

In Listing 13-8, Async.Primitive builds an Async<int> value, where the integer result indicates the number of bytes read from the stream. But what are all these function values? As you saw earlier, asynchronous computations work via *continuations*. This means a primitive step is given two continuation functions, cont and econt, which must be called upon success and/or exceptional failure of the operation. The previous implementation calls BeginRead and passes it a callback that will be invoked when the asynchronous operation returns. Note that the call to BeginRead uses named arguments, covered in Chapter 6. The callback calls EndRead to retrieve the result and passes this result to the success continuation cont; the call to EndRead is protected by an exception handler that calls the exception continuation econt should something go wrong.

The simple wrapper shown in Listing 13-8 now allows us to use ReadAsync in workflows, such as in the following line of our asynchronous image processor:

```
async { use inStream =  File.OpenRead(sprintf "Image%d.tmp" i)
        let! pixels = inStream.ReadAsync(numPixels)
        ... }
```

Note that the econt continuation of a primitive step should be called if an exception occurs. The example includes the try/catch handlers required to catch exceptions from EndRead. For more details, see the full implementation of ReadAsync and other similar wrappers in the F# library source code.

Under the Hood: Implementing Async.Parallel

Async.Parallel can appear magical. Computation tasks are created, executed, and resynchronized almost without effort. However, Listing 13-9 shows that a basic implementation of this operator is simple and again helps you see how Async<'a> values work "under the hood."

Listing 13-9. *A Basic Implementation of Async.Parallel*

```
let Parallel(taskSeq) =
    Async.Primitive (fun (cont,econt) ->
        let tasks = Seq.to_array taskSeq
        let count = ref tasks.Length
        let results = Array.zero_create tasks.Length
        tasks |> Array.iteri (fun i p ->
            Async.Spawn
                (async { let! res = p
                         do results.[i] <- res;
                         let n = System.Threading.Interlocked.Decrement(count)
                         do if n=0 then cont results })))
```

This basic implementation `Parallel` first converts the input task sequence to an array and then creates mutable state `count` and `results` to record the progress of the parallel computations. It then iterates through the tasks and queues each for execution in the .NET thread pool. Upon completion, each writes its result and decrements the counter using an atomic `Interlocked.Decrement` operator, discussed further in the section "Understanding Shared-Memory Concurrency" at the end of this chapter. The last process to finish calls the continuation with the collected results.

In practice, `Parallel` is implemented slightly differently to take into account exceptions and cancellation; once again, see the F# library code for full details.

Understanding Exceptions and Cancellation

Two recurring topics in asynchronous programming are exceptions and cancellation. Let's first explore some of the behavior of asynchronous programs with regard to exceptions.

```
> let failingTask = async { do failwith "fail" };;
val failingTask: Async<unit>

> Async.Run failingTask;;
Microsoft.FSharp.Core.FailureException: fail
stopped due to error

> let failingTasks = [ async { do failwith "fail A" };
                       async { do failwith "fail B" }; ];;
val failingTasks: Async<unit>

> Async.Run (Async.Parallel failingTasks);;
Microsoft.FSharp.Core.FailureException: fail A
stopped due to error

> Async.Run (Async.Parallel failingTasks);;
Microsoft.FSharp.Core.FailureException: fail B
stopped due to error
```

From this you can see the following:

- Tasks fail only when they are actually executed. The construction of a task using the `async { ... }` syntax will never fail.

- Tasks run using `Async.Run` report any failure back to the controlling thread as an exception.

- It is nondeterministic which task will fail first.

- Tasks composed using `Async.Parallel` report the first failure from amongst the collected set of tasks. An attempt is made to cancel other tasks by setting the cancellation flag for the group of tasks, and any further failures are ignored.

You can wrap a task using the `Async.Catch` combinator. This has the following type:

```
static member Catch : Async<'a> -> Async<Choice<'a,exn>>
```

For example:

```
> Async.Run (Async.Catch failingTask);;
val it : Choice<unit,exn> = Choice2_2 (FailureException ())
```

You can also handle errors by using try/finally in an async { ... } workflow.

> ■**Note** You can find further information and examples of asynchronous workflows at http://www.
> expert-fsharp.net/topics/AsyncWorkflows.

Passing and Processing Messages

A distinction is often made between *shared-memory* concurrency and *message passing* concurrency. The former is often more efficient on local machines and is covered in the section "Using Shared-Memory Concurrency" later in this chapter. The latter scales to systems where there is no shared memory, for example, distributed systems, and can also be used to avoid performance problems associated with shared memory. Asynchronous message passing and processing is a common foundation for concurrent programming, and in this section we look at some simple examples of message-passing programs.

Introducing Message Processing

In a sense you have already seen a good deal of message passing in this chapter. For example:

- In the BackgroundWorker design pattern, the CancelAsync method is a simple kind of message.

- Whenever you raise events on a GUI thread from a background thread, you are, under the hood, posting a message to the GUI's event queue. On Windows this event queue is managed by the operating system, and the processing of the events on the GUI thread is called the Windows Event Loop.

In this section we cover a simple kind of message processing called *mailbox processing*. This is popular in languages such as Erlang. A *mailbox* is a message queue that you can scan for a message particularly relevant to the message-processing agent you are defining. Listing 13-10 shows a concurrent agent that implements a simple counter by processing a mailbox as messages arrive. The type MailboxProcessor is defined in the F# library module Microsoft.FSharp.Control.Mailboxes.

Listing 13-10. *Implementing a Counter Using a* MailboxProcessor

```
open Microsoft.FSharp.Control.Mailboxes

let counter =
    MailboxProcessor.Create(fun inbox ->
        let rec loop(n) =
            async { do printfn "n = %d, waiting..." n
                    let! msg = inbox.Receive()
                    return! loop(n+msg) }
        loop(0))
```

The type of counter is MailboxProcessor<int>, where the type argument indicates that this object expects to be sent messages of type int.

```
val counter : MailboxProcessor<int>
```

The "The Message Processing and State Machines" sidebar describes the general pattern of Listing 13-10 and the other MailboxProcessor examples in this chapter, all of which can be thought of as *state machines*. With this in mind, let's take a closer look at Listing 13-10. First let's use counter on some simple inputs:

```
> counter.Start();;
n = 0, waiting...

> counter.Post(1);;
n = 1, waiting...

> counter.Post(2);;
n = 3, waiting...

> counter.Post(1);;
n = 4, waiting...
```

Looking at Listing 13-10, note calling the MailboxProcessor.Start method causes the processing agent to enter loop with n = 0. The agent then performs an asynchronous Receive request on the inbox for the MailboxProcessor; that is, the agent waits asynchronously until a message has been received. When the message msg is received, the program calls loop(n+msg). As additional messages are received, the internal "counter" (actually an argument) is incremented further.

We post messages to the agent using mailbox.Post. The type of mailbox.Receive is as follows:

```
member Mailbox<'msg>.Receive: unit -> Async<'msg>
```

Using an asynchronous receive ensures no "real" threads are blocked for the duration of the wait. This means the previous techniques scale to many thousands of concurrent agents.

MESSAGE PROCESSING AND STATE MACHINES

Listing 13-10 shares a common structure with many of the other message-processing components you'll be looking at in this chapter, all of which are *state machines*. This general structure is as follows:

```
let agent =
    MailboxProcessor.Start(fun inbox ->

        // The states of the state machine
        let rec state1(args) =  async { ... }
        and     state2(args) =  async { ... }
        ...
        and     stateN(args) =  async { ... }

        // Enter the initial state
        state1(initialArgs))
```

That is, message-processing components typically use sets of recursive functions, each defining an asynchronous computation. Each of these functions can be thought of as a state, and one of these states is identified as the initial state. Arguments may be passed between these states just as you pass them between any other set of recursive functions.

Creating Objects That React to Messages

Often it is wise to hide the internals of an asynchronous computation behind an object, since the use of message passing can be seen as an implementation detail. Furthermore, Listing 13-10 hasn't shown you how to retrieve information from the counter, except by printing it to the standard output. Furthermore, it hasn't shown how to ask the processing agent to exit. Listing 13-11 shows how to implement an object wrapping an agent that supports Increment, Stop, and Fetch messages.

Listing 13-11. *Hiding a Mailbox and Supporting a Fetch Method*

```
open Microsoft.FSharp.Control.Mailboxes

/// The internal type of messages for the agent
type internal msg = Increment of int | Fetch of IChannel<int> | Stop
```

```
type CountingAgent() =
    let counter = MailboxProcessor.Start(fun inbox ->
            // The states of the message-processing state machine...
            let rec loop(n) =
                async { let! msg = inbox.Receive()
                        match msg with
                        | Increment m ->
                            // increment and continue...
                            return! loop(n+m)
                        | Stop ->
                            // exit
                            return ()
                        | Fetch  replyChannel  ->
                            // post response to reply channel and continue
                            do replyChannel.Post(n)
                            return! loop(n) }

            // The initial state of the message-processing state machine...
            loop(0))

    member a.Increment(n) = counter.Post(Increment(n))
    member a.Stop() = counter.Post(Stop)
    member a.Fetch() = counter.PostSync(fun replyChannel -> Fetch(replyChannel))
```

The inferred public types indicate how the presence of a concurrent agent is successfully hidden by the use of an object:

```
type CountingAgent =
    new : unit -> CountingAgent
    member Fetch : unit -> int
    member Increment : n:int -> unit
    member Stop : unit -> unit
```

Here you can see an instance of this object in action:

```
> let counter = new CountingAgent();;
val counter : CountingAgent

> counter.Increment(1);;
val it : unit = ()

> counter.Fetch();;
val it : int = 1
```

```
> counter.Increment(2);;
val it : unit = ()

> counter.Fetch();;
val it : int = 3

> counter.Stop();;
val it : unit = ()
```

Listing 13-11 shows several important aspects of message passing and processing using the mailbox-processing model:

- Internal messages protocols are often represented using discriminated unions. Here the type msg has cases Increment, Fetch, and Stop corresponding to the three methods accepted by the object that wraps the overall agent implementation.

- Pattern matching over discriminated unions gives a succinct way to process messages. A common pattern is a call to inbox.Receive() or inbox.TryReceive() followed by a match on the message contents.

- The PostSync on the MailboxProcessor type gives a way to post a message and wait for a reply. A temporary *reply channel* is created and should form part of the message. A reply channel is simply an object of type Microsoft.FSharp.Control.IChannel<'reply>, which in turn simply supports a Post method. This can be used by the MailboxProcessor to post a reply to the waiting caller. In Listing 13-11 the channel is sent to the underlying message-processing agent counter as part of the Fetch message.

Table 13-6 summarizes the most important members available on the MailboxProcessor type.

Table 13-6. *Some Members of the MailboxProcessor<'msg> Type*

Member/Type	Description
Post: 'msg -> unit	Posts a message to a mailbox queue.
Receive: ?timeout:int -> Async<'msg>	Returns the next message in the mailbox queue. If no messages are present, performs an asynchronous wait until the message arrives. If a timeout occurs, then raises a TimeoutException.
Scan: ('msg -> Async<'a> option) * ?timeout:int -> Async<'a>	Scans the mailbox for a message where the function returns a Some(_) value. Returns the chosen result. If no messages are present, performs an asynchronous wait until more messages arrive. If a timeout occurs, then raises a TimeoutException.
TryReceive : ?timeout:int -> Async<'msg option>	Like Receive, but if a timeout occurs, then returns None.
TryScan : ('msg -> Async<'a> option) * ?timeout:int -> Async<'a option>	Like Scan, but if a timeout occurs, then returns None.

Scanning Mailboxes for Relevant Messages

It is common for a message-processing agent to end up in a state where it's not interested in all messages that might appear in a mailbox but only a subset of them. For example, you may be awaiting a reply from another agent and aren't interested in serving new requests. In this case, it is essential you use `MailboxProcessor.Scan` rather than `MailboxProcessor.Receive`. Table 13-6 shows the signatures of both of these. The former lets you choose between available messages by processing them in order, while the latter forces you to process every message. Listing 13-12 shows an example of using `Mailbox.Scan`.

Listing 13-12. *Scanning a Mailbox for Relevant Messages*

```
open Microsoft.FSharp.Control.Mailboxes

type msg =
    | Message1
    | Message2 of int
    | Message3 of string

let agent =
    MailboxProcessor.Start(fun inbox ->
        let rec loop() =
            inbox.Scan(function
                | Message1 ->
                    Some (async { do printfn "message 1!"
                                  return! loop() })
                | Message2 n ->
                    Some (async { do printfn "message 2!"
                                  return! loop() })
                | Message3 _ ->
                    None)
        loop())
```

We can now post these agent messages, including messages of the ignored kind `Message3`:

```
> agent.Post(Message1) ;;
message 1!
val it : unit = ()

> agent.Post(Message2(100));;
message 2!
val it : unit = ()

> agent.Post(Message3("abc"));;
val it : unit = ()
```

```
> agent.Post(Message2(100));;
message 2!
val it : unit = ()

> agent.UnsafeMessageQueueContents;;
val it : seq<msg> = seq [Message3("abc")]
```

When we sent `Message3` to the message processor, the message was ignored. However, the last line shows that the unprocessed `Message3` is still in the message queue, which we have examined by using the "backdoor" property `UnsafeMessageQueueContents`.

■**Note** You can find further examples of asynchronous message processing with F# at `http://www.expert-fsharp.net/topics/MessageProcessing`.

Example: Asynchronous Web Crawling

At the start of this chapter we mentioned that the rise of the Web and other forms of networks is a major reason for the increasing importance of concurrent and asynchronous programming. Listing 13-13 shows an implementation of a web crawler using asynchronous programming and mailbox-processing techniques.

Listing 13-13. *A Scalable, Controlled Asynchronous Web Crawler*

```
open System.Collections.Generic
open System.Net
open System.IO
open System.Threading
open System.Text.RegularExpressions
open Microsoft.FSharp.Control
open Microsoft.FSharp.Control.Mailboxes
open Microsoft.FSharp.Control.CommonExtensions

let limit = 50
let linkPat = "href=\s*\"[^\"h]*(http://[^&\"]*)\""
let getLinks (txt:string) =
    [ for m in Regex.Matches(txt,linkPat)  -> m.Groups.Item(1).Value ]

let (<--) (mp: #IChannel<_>) x = mp.Post(x)

// A type that helps limit the number of active web requests
type RequestGate(n:int) =
    let semaphore = new Semaphore(initialCount=n,maximumCount=n)
    member x.AcquireAsync(?timeout) =
        async { let! ok = semaphore.WaitOneAsync(?millisecondsTimeout=timeout)
```

```
                if ok then
                    return
                      { new System.IDisposable with
                          member x.Dispose() =
                              semaphore.Release() |> ignore }
                else
                    return! failwith "couldn't acquire a semaphore" }


// Gate the number of active web requests
let webRequestGate = RequestGate(5)

// Fetch the URL, and post the results to the urlCollector.
let collectLinks (url:string) =
    async { // An Async web request with a global gate
           let! html =
               async { // Acquire an entry in the webRequestGate. Release
                       // it when 'holder' goes out of scope
                       use! holder = webRequestGate.AcquireAsync()

                       let req = WebRequest.Create(url,Timeout=5)

                       // Wait for the WebResponse
                       use! response = req.GetResponseAsync()

                       // Get the response stream
                       use reader = new StreamReader(response.GetResponseStream())

                       // Read the response stream
                       return! reader.ReadToEndAsync()   }

           // Compute the links, synchronously
           let links = getLinks html

           // Report, synchronously
           do printfn "finished reading %s, got %d links" url (List.length links)

           // We're done
           return links }

/// 'urlCollector' is a single agent that receives URLs as messages. It creates new
/// asynchronous tasks that post messages back to this object.
let urlCollector =
    MailboxProcessor.Start(fun self ->

        // This is the main state of the urlCollector
        let rec waitForUrl (visited : Set<string>) =
```

```
async { // Check the limit
        if visited.Count < limit then

             // Wait for a URL...
             let! url = self.Receive()
             if not (visited.Contains(url)) then
                 // Spawn off a new task for the new url. Each collects
                 // links and posts them back to the urlCollector.
                 do! Async.SpawnChild
                          (async { let! links = collectLinks url
                                   for link in links do
                                   do self <-- link })

             // Recurse into the waiting state
             return! waitForUrl(visited.Add(url)) }

    // This is the initial state.
    waitForUrl(Set.empty))
```

We can initiate a web crawl from a particular URL as follows:

```
> urlCollector <-- "http://news.google.com";;
finished reading http://news.google.com, got 191 links
finished reading http://news.google.com/?output=rss, got 0 links
finished reading http://www.ktvu.com/politics/13732578/detail.html, got 14 links
finished reading http://www.washingtonpost.com/wp-dyn/content/art..., got 218 links
finished reading http://www.newsobserver.com/politics/story/646..., got 56 links
finished reading http://www.foxnews.com/story/0,2933,290307,0...1, got 22 links
...
```

The key techniques shown in Listing 13-13 are as follows:

- The type RequestGate encapsulates the logic needed to ensure that we place a global limit on the number of active web requests occurring at any one point in time. This is instantiated to the particular instance webRequestGate with limit 5. This uses a System. Threading.Semaphore object to coordinate access to this "shared resource." Semaphores are discussed in more detail in the section "Using Shared-Memory Concurrency."

- The RequestGate type ensures that web requests sitting in the request queue do not block threads but rather wait asynchronously as callback items in the thread pool until a slot in the webRequestGate becomes available.

- The collectLinks function is a regular asynchronous computation. It first enters the RequestGate (that is, acquires one of the available entries in the Semaphore). Once a response has been received, it reads off the HTML from the resulting reader, scrapes the HTML for links using regular expressions, and returns the generated set of links.

- The `urlCollector` is the only message-processing program. It is written using a `MailboxProcessor`. In its main state it waits for a fresh URL and spawns a new asynchronous computation to call `collectLinks` once one is received. For each collected link a new message is sent back to the `urlCollector`'s mailbox. Finally, we recurse to the waiting state, having added the fresh URL to the overall set of URLs we have traversed so far.

- The operator `<--` is used as shorthand for posting a message to an agent. This is a recommended abbreviation in F# asynchronous programming.

- The `AcquireAsync` method of the `RequestGate` type uses a design pattern called a *holder*. The object returned by this method is an `IDisposable` object that represents the acquisition of a resource. This "holder" object is bound using `use`, and this ensures the resource is released when the computation completes or when the computation ends with an exception.

Listing 13-13 shows that it is relatively easy to create sophisticated, scalable asynchronous programs using a mix of message passing and asynchronous I/O techniques. Modern web crawlers have thousands of outstanding open connections, indicating the importance of using asynchronous techniques in modern scalable web-based programming.

Using Shared-Memory Concurrency

The final topics we cover in this chapter are the various "primitive" mechanisms used for threads, shared-memory concurrency, and signaling. In many ways, these are the "assembly language" of concurrency.

In this chapter we've concentrated mostly on techniques that work well with immutable data structures. That is not to say you should *always* use immutable data structures. It is, for example, perfectly valid to use mutable data structures as long as they are accessed from only one particular thread. Furthermore, private mutable data structures can often be safely passed through an asynchronous workflow, because at each point the mutable data structure will be accessed by only one thread, even if different parts of the asynchronous workflow are executed by different threads. This does not apply to workflows that use operators such as `Async.Parallel` or `Async.SpawnChild` that start additional threads of computation.

This means that we've largely avoided covering shared-memory primitives so far, because F# provides powerful declarative constructs such as asynchronous workflows and message passing that often subsume the need to resort to shared-memory concurrency. However, a working knowledge of thread primitives and shared-memory concurrency is still very useful, especially if you want to implement your own basic constructs or highly efficient concurrent algorithms on shared-memory hardware.

Creating Threads Explicitly

In this chapter we've avoided showing how to work with threads directly, instead relying on abstractions such as `BackgroundWorker` and the .NET thread pool. If you do want to create threads directly, here is a short sample:

```
open System.Threading
let t = new Thread(ThreadStart(fun _ ->
                printfn "Thread %d: Hello" Thread.CurrentThread.ManagedThreadId));
t.Start();
printfn "Thread %d: Waiting!" Thread.CurrentThread.ManagedThreadId
t.Join();
printfn "Done!"
```

When run, this gives the following:

```
val t : Thread

Thread 1: Waiting!
Thread 10: Hello
Done!
```

■**Caution** Always avoid using `Thread.Suspend`, `Thread.Resume`, and `Thread.Abort`. These are a guaranteed way to put obscure concurrency bugs in your program! The MSDN website has a good description of why `Thread.Abort` may not even succeed. One of the only compelling uses for `Thread.Abort` is to implement Ctrl+C in an interactive development environment for a general-purpose language such as F# Interactive.

Shared Memory, Race Conditions, and the .NET Memory Model

Many multithreaded applications use mutable data structures shared between multiple threads. Without synchronization, these data structures will almost certainly become corrupt, because threads may read data that has been only partially updated (because not all mutations are *atomic*), or two threads may write to the same data simultaneously (a *race condition*). Mutable data structures are usually protected by *locks*, though lock-free mutable data structures are also possible.

Shared-memory concurrency is a difficult and complicated topic, and a considerable amount of good material on .NET shared-memory concurrency is available on the Web. All this material applies to F# when programming with mutable data structures such as reference cells, arrays, and hash tables when the data structures can be accessed from multiple threads simultaneously. F# mutable data structures map to .NET memory in fairly predictable ways; for example, mutable references become mutable fields in a .NET class, and mutable fields of word size can be assigned atomically.

On modern microprocessors multiple threads can see views of memory that are not consistent; that is, not all writes are propagated to all threads immediately. The guarantees given are called a *memory model* and are usually expressed in terms of the ordering dependencies between instructions that read/write memory locations. This is, of course, deeply troubling, because you have to think about a huge number of possible reorderings of your code, and it is one of the main reasons why shared mutable data structures are difficult to work with. You can find further details on the .NET memory model at http://www.expert-fsharp.net/topics/MemoryModel.

Using Locks to Avoid Race Conditions

Locks are the simplest way to enforce mutual exclusion between two threads attempting to read or write the same mutable memory location. Listing 13-14 shows an example of code with a race condition.

Listing 13-14. *Shared-Memory Code with a Race Condition*

```
type MutablePair<'a,'b>(x:'a,y:'b) =
    let mutable currentX = x
    let mutable currentY = y
    member p.Value = (currentX,currentY)
    member p.Update(x,y) =
        // Race condition: This pair of updates is not atomic
        currentX <- x;
        currentY <- y

let p = new MutablePair<_,_>(1,2)
do Async.Spawn (async { do (while true do p.Update(10,10)) })
do Async.Spawn (async { do (while true do p.Update(20,20)) })
```

Here is the definition of the F# lock function:

```
open System.Threading
let lock (lockobj :> obj) f  =
    Monitor.Enter(lockobj);
    try
        f()
    finally
        Monitor.Exit(lockobj)
```

The pair of mutations in the Update method is not atomic; that is, one thread may have written to currentX, another then writes to both currentX and currentY, and the final thread then writes to currentY, leaving the pair holding the value (10, 20) or (20, 10). Mutable data structures are inherently prone to this kind of problem if shared between multiple threads. Luckily, of course, F# code tends to have fewer mutations than imperative languages, because functions normally take immutable values and return a calculated value. However, when you do use mutable data structures, they should not be shared between threads, or you should design them carefully and document their properties with respect to multithreaded access.

Here is one way to use the F# lock function to ensure that updates to the data structure are atomic. Locks would also be required on uses of the property p.Value.

```
do Async.Spawn (async { do (while true do lock p (fun () -> p.Update(10,10))) })
do Async.Spawn (async { do (while true do lock p (fun () -> p.Update(20,20))) })
```

> ■**Caution** If you use locks inside data structures, then do so only in a simple way that uses them to enforce just the concurrency properties you have documented. Don't lock "just for the sake of it," and don't hold locks longer than necessary. In particular, beware of making indirect calls to externally supplied function values, interfaces, or abstract members while a lock is held. The code providing the implementation may not be expecting to be called when a lock is held and may attempt to acquire further locks in an inconsistent fashion.

Using ReaderWriterLock

It is common that mutable data structures get read more than they are written. Indeed, mutation is often used only to initialize a mutable data structure. In this case, you can use a .NET ReaderWriterLock to protect access to a resource. The following two functions are provided in the F# library module Microsoft.FSharp.Control.SharedMemory.Helpers:

```
open System.Threading

let readLock (rwlock : ReaderWriterLock) f  =
  rwlock.AcquireReaderLock(Timeout.Infinite)
  try
      f()
  finally
      rwlock.ReleaseReaderLock()

let writeLock (rwlock : ReaderWriterLock) f  =
  rwlock.AcquireWriterLock(Timeout.Infinite)
  try
      f();
      Thread.MemoryBarrier()
  finally
      rwlock.ReleaseWriterLock()
```

Listing 13-15 shows how to use these functions to protect the MutablePair class.

Listing 13-15. *Shared-Memory Code with a Race Condition*

```
type MutablePair<'a,'b>(x:'a,y:'b) =
    let mutable currentX = x
    let mutable currentY = y
    let rwlock = new ReaderWriterLock()
    member p.Value =
        readLock rwlock (fun () ->
            (currentX,currentY))
    member p.Update(x,y) =
        writeLock rwlock (fun () ->
            currentX <- x;
            currentY <- y)
```

Some Other Concurrency Primitives

Table 13-7 shows some of the other shared-memory concurrency primitives available in the .NET Framework.

Table 13-7. *.NET Shared-Memory Concurrency Primitives*

Type	Description
System.Threading.WaitHandle	A synchronization object for signaling the control of threads.
System.Threading.AutoResetEvent	A two-state (on/off) WaitHandle that resets itself to "off" automatically after the signal is read. Similar to a two-state traffic light.
System.Threading.ManualResetEvent	A two-state (on/off) WaitHandle that requires a call to ManualResetEvent.Reset() to set it "off."
System.Threading.Mutex	A lock-like object that can be shared between operating system processes.
System.Threading.Semaphore	Used to limit the number of threads simultaneously accessing a resource. However, use a mutex or lock if at most one thread can access a resource at a time.
System.Threading.Interlocked	Atomic operations on memory locations. Especially useful for atomic operations on F# reference cells.

Summary

In this chapter, we covered concurrent, reactive, and asynchronous programming, which is a set of topics of growing importance in modern programming because of the widespread adoption of multicore microprocessors, network-aware applications, and asynchronous I/O channels. We've covered in depth background processing and a powerful F# construct called asynchronous workflows. Finally, we covered applications of asynchronous workflows to message-processing agents and web crawling, and we covered some of the shared-memory primitives for concurrent programming on the .NET platform. In the next chapter, we'll look at web programming, from serving web pages to delivering applications via web browsers.

■ ■ ■

CHAPTER 14

Building Web Applications

Delivering content and applications via web browsers is one of the most important aspects of modern software development. In this chapter, we examine how you can build web applications using F#. The topics we cover are as follows:

- Serving static files and dynamic content by directly responding to HTTP requests

- Using the ASP.NET framework to develop page-based, server-side web applications that use input controls and read data from a database using F# Linq

- A walk-through of the ASP.NET essentials: web forms and site organization, a discussion of the various types of server controls (web and HTML), user control creation, and web application configuration and debugging

- The fundamentals of the ASP.NET event model: page and control events, page life cycle, posting information from a page (postback and cross-page posting), and maintaining state

- A look at techniques to build client-side web applications, including the use of the F# Web Tools open source project

- Consuming web services to deliver programmatic services via web connections

Serving Static Web Content

When you point your browser at a web page or call a web service from your application, you are effectively issuing one or more requests (commands) to a web (HTTP) server. HTTP commands are simple text-based instructions that are automatically generated by your web browser. For instance, when your browser goes to a particular URL, it does the following:

1. Requests the page from the web server and waits for the response

2. Analyzes it for further content to be fetched (images, for example) and issues the appropriate requests if necessary

3. Displays the results and executes any dynamic scripts and content contained in the page

Responses can be a verbatim copy of a resource found on the web server (most often a static file such as an image, a style sheet, or a media file) or can be generated on the fly. In this section, we show how you can use F# to serve content directly.

Listing 14-1 shows a simple web server written directly in F#.

Listing 14-1. *A Simple Web Server*

```
#light

open System.Net
open System.Net.Sockets
open System.IO
open System.Text.RegularExpressions
open Microsoft.FSharp.Text.Printf
open System.Text

/// A table of MIME content types
let mimeTypes =
    dict [".html", "text/html";
          ".htm",  "text/html";
          ".txt",  "text/plain";
          ".gif",  "image/gif";
          ".jpg",  "image/jpeg";
          ".png",  "image/png"]

/// Compute a MIME type from a file extension
let getMimeType(ext) =
    if mimeTypes.ContainsKey(ext) then mimeTypes.[ext]
    else "binary/octet"

/// The pattern Regex1 uses a regular expression to match
/// one element
let (|Regex1|_|) (patt: string) (inp: string) =
    try Some(Regex.Match(inp, patt).Groups.Item(1).Captures.Item(0).Value)
    with _ -> None

/// The root for the data we serve
let root = @"c:\inetpub\wwwroot"

/// Handle a TCP connection for an HTTP GET
let handleClient(client: TcpClient) =
    use stream = client.GetStream()
    let out = new StreamWriter(stream)
    let inp = new StreamReader(stream)
    match inp.ReadLine() with
```

```
    | Regex1 "GET (.*?) HTTP/1\\.[01]$" fileName ->
        let fname = root + @"\" + fileName.Replace("/", @"\")
        let mimeType = getMimeType(Path.GetExtension(fname))
        let content = File.ReadAllBytes(fname)
        twprintfn out "HTTP/1.0 200 OK"
        twprintfn out "Content-Length: %d" content.Length
        twprintfn out "Content-Type: %s" mimeType
        twprintfn out ""
        out.Flush()
        stream.Write(content, 0, content.Length)
    | line ->
        ()

/// The server as an asynchronous process. We handle requests
/// sequentially.
let server =
    async { let socket = new TcpListener(IPAddress.Parse("127.0.0.1"), 8090)
            do socket.Start()
            while true do
                use client = socket.AcceptTcpClient()
                do try handleClient(client) with _ -> ()
          }
```

You can use this code as follows, where `http` is the function defined in Chapter 2 for requesting web pages and where we assume the directory `c:\inetpub\wwwroot` contains the file `iisstart.htm`:

```
> Async.Spawn server;;
val it : unit = ()

> http "http://127.0.0.1:8090/iisstart.htm";;
val it : string = "..."    // the text of the iisstart.htm file will be shown here
```

This HTTP request (or you can also open the previous URL in a browser) ultimately sends the following text down the TCP socket connection:

```
GET iisstart.htm HTTP/1.1
```

When started, the server in Listing 14-1 attaches itself to a given port (8090) on the local machine (which has IP 127.0.0.1) and listens for incoming requests. These requests are line-based, so when one comes in, we read the full input line and attempt to parse a valid GET request using regular expression matching. Other commands and error recovery are not dealt with.

The server's actions in response are simple: it locates the requested file relative to a "root" web directory, determines the MIME type from a fixed table, and sends the necessary response header and the content of the file through the client TCP connection. When all this is done, the connection is disposed, and the session ends. The main "loop" of the server task is a busy waiting loop—we simply wait for requests indefinitely and handle them one by one.

Listing 14-1 uses two techniques not directly related to web programming:

- `Regex1` as a very simple and common *active pattern* for regular expression pattern matching. You learned about active patterns in Chapter 9. Our example is particularly interesting because it also shows how to use a parameterized active pattern.

- The value `server` as an *asynchronous task*. You learned about asynchronous tasks in Chapter 13. Many web servers handle multiple requests simultaneously, and high-performance web servers use asynchronous techniques extensively. In our example, the server task serves requests sequentially using a single thread, but we could just as well have started a dedicated thread for the server using more explicit threading techniques from `System.Threading`.

Serving Dynamic Web Content with ASP.NET

In practice, it is rare to develop and implement a web server manually as we did in the previous section. Instead, most web development adds an extension to an existing web server via a web development framework such as ASP.NET, PHP, or JavaServer Pages (JSP). In this section, we cover how F# can be used to write server-side applications using ASP.NET.

ASP.NET is a fully compiled dynamic server technology that allows developers to write web applications as a set of dynamic pages and to describe how the pages should interact via a rich object model and an abundance of server-side controls. The resulting web applications are easy to deploy—they are independent of the hosting environment and the system registry—and can be configured through an integrated web application configuration tool or via XML-based configuration files. ASP.NET was originally designed by Microsoft and is often used with Microsoft's Internet Information Services (IIS) web server but can also be used with Apache and others via the Mono implementation of ASP.NET and the CLI.

■**Note** Modern web development frameworks allow you to put together sophisticated websites with many useful features with almost no coding at all. Code is often used as "glue" between the incoming requests and back-end databases. For this reason, web programmers often need a variety of design, security, database, and system skills in addition to mastery of one or more programming languages. Some resources for these additional topics are discussed at `http://www.expert-fsharp.com/Topics/WebDevelopment`.

ABOUT DYNAMIC PAGE-BASED WEB DEVELOPMENT FRAMEWORKS

You may already be familiar with various web scripting languages and technologies that allow you to embed bits of code (usually in certain meta-tags or inside special markers) in your pages. When a request is made to such pages (which typically have a different file extension, such as `.asp`, `.aspx`, `.php`, `.jsp`, and so on), the web server invokes a preprocessor that consumes the page script and outputs the resulting HTML after "evaluating" each dynamic block. Depending on your web server architecture, such processors can be plugged in on demand (as with Apache's modules) or tied directly to the server technology (as with the Java-based web server Tomcat or as with ASP.NET).

Roughly speaking, there are two main types of dynamic content generation. In the first, the "scripting" type, requests for the same scripted resource produce the same actions: the source page is pumped through the preprocessor every time, and each dynamic construct is distilled to HTML. Typically, this type of content generation is limited to using special tags and local code expressions that may refer only to a set of built-in features and occasionally a set of global "state" variables such as the server response. The problem with this approach is inherent: the dynamic functionality is often too limited, although it is simple to use. Most important, no caching or compilation is done, and as such it is much slower than the compiled alternatives. Furthermore, as dynamic functionality is added to a page, it becomes progressively more complex and more difficult to maintain, often leading to "spaghetti" code. Tying the dynamic content to the presentation layer in this way is well recognized as a significant drawback.

The second approach is the one taken by ASP.NET and JSP. Here a page scripting model is combined with an underlying compiled language (Java for JSP, and any .NET language for ASP.NET) and the speed of serving static content. In this model, pages are composed of objects with complex life cycles and are generated/maintained by compiled programs, so a scripted page is translated to a program that generates the final HTML page and as a result can contain arbitrary logic expressed in the source language. These programs are produced on the fly and maintained by the web container. A change to a web page results in updating the server-side resource responsible for creating that web page. This compilation causes a one-time penalty, but subsequent requests will be served without any processing by simply sending the result of the new "page-behind" code.

Understanding the Languages Used in ASP.NET

Web development frameworks such as ASP.NET can be a little bewildering at first. One reason for this is the number of languages involved in even simple websites. For example, developing a minimal website using ASP.NET involves using at least five different languages to represent the necessary information:

- ASP.NET page markup (ASPX), used for the declarative construction and configuration of server controls that form the page

- HTML, used for the basic presentation content embedded in the ASP.NET markup

- Cascading Style Sheets (CSS), used for declarative control over visual characteristics of the presentation content

- XML, used for the configuration files of the website

- F# and/or another .NET language, used for expressing the website logic

In contrast, the programs you've seen so far in this book have used only one language (F#) with only one kind of file (source code files with the suffix .fs). Furthermore, a fully fledged website can involve further additional languages and schemas:

- SQL, for the queries and commands used for database access and management

- JavaScript, for dynamic client-side behavior, a topic we discuss later in this chapter

- Further XML schemas, for files specifying additional website data or security and configuration information

- Database connection strings, for configuring access to underlying databases

This has the effect of making simple website projects seem quite complex. To help you through this, Table 14-1 shows the most common file types used when writing web applications using F# and ASP.NET. Table 14-2 shows some additional file types that are useful to be aware of.

Table 14-1. *The Most Common File Types for F# and ASP.NET*

Extension	Type	Language	Characteristics
.aspx	Web form (web page)	ASPX	The presentation layer, often authored using visual editing tools. These files include ASP.NET control declarations and embedded HTML tags. They may also include fragments of other languages such as CSS and scripts written in F#.
.ascx	User control	ASPX	Similar to the .aspx file but is used for writing elementary building blocks that can be reused on multiple pages in the application.
.fs	Server-side code	F#	The programmatic portion of the website logic. Typically makes extensive use of the System.Data and System.Web namespaces.
.dll	Precompiled server-side code	Binary	Compiled DLLs referenced by your server-side code.
web.config	Configuration	XML	Configuration files that may be located in every application directory and are used to specify aspects such as security or compilation options.

Table 14-2. *Additional File Types Used with ASP.NET*

Extension	Type	Language	Characteristics
.resx	Resource	XML	Resources such as bitmaps and error strings, often used for localizing websites to multiple languages. Resources were described in passing in Chapter 7. These files use the .NET resource schema.
.sql	Database scripts and stored procedures	T-SQL	Many websites use relational databases heavily. Operations on these databases are typically described using scripts written in database scripting languages such as T-SQL.
.css	Style	CSS	Cascading Style Sheets, a W3C standard for declarative configuration of the HTML presentation layer. CSS fragments can also appear in HTML and ASPX documents.
.master	Master page	ASPX	Similar to the .aspx file but used as a template for other pages in the website. When used with a page, the content page must fill the placeholders declared in the master page.

Table 14-2. *Additional File Types Used with ASP.NET*

Extension	Type	Language	Characteristics
.sitemap	Site map	XML	Defines the structure of the website and can be used with ASP.NET navigation controls to generate content like a menu bar, a breadcrumb, or a site map.
.mdf	Database file	Binary	Many websites use databases accessed via SQL Server Express 2005. The .mdf format is a detached, file-based database used by SQL Server Express.

■**Caution** Although this book is primarily about programming in F#, be aware that typically only a small portion of a website's content is ultimately represented in F# itself. Indeed, one valid model for using F# on the server side is to simply use it to author custom controls and static DLLs that are referenced by server-side components authored using more standard web programming languages such as C# or Visual Basic. This is easy to do since C# and Visual Basic code can access compiled F# code directly, as discussed in Chapter 19. You can find out more about this option at http://www.expert-fsharp.com/Topics/WebDevelopment.

UNDERSTANDING THE STRUCTURE OF AN ASP.NET WEBSITE

ASP.NET files of the types shown in Tables 14-1 and 14-2 are located in the web application's *web root directory* and the various subfolders within. The standard ASP.NET folders are as follows:

- App_Code: Utility, application, and data access layer code—basically, all source files that are not code-behind files

- App_Data: Database and XML files

- App_GlobalResources: Global resource files, such as those related to localization

- App_LocalResources: Resource files associated with specific controls or pages

- App_WebReferences: Web reference discovery files and service descriptions (wsdl)

- Bin: Third-party binaries, libraries—these are automatically referenced in the web application

A Simple ASP.NET Web Application

The simplest websites use only HTML static content. We do not consider these in this book, though we assume you are familiar with authoring HTML. Beyond this, the building blocks of the *dynamic* content on ASP.NET websites are .aspx web forms (web pages). These are essentially HTML files that contain ASPX markup for server-side controls, although they are not processed as embedded scripts; instead, the page should be viewed as an object type that produces the final HTML based on the declarative markup and the behavior expressed as code inside standard HTML `<script>` blocks or in code-behind files. Listing 14-2 shows a simple web form that uses the server to compute the current time and allows the user to refresh the page. Listing 14-3 (later in this chapter) shows an ASP.NET `web.config` website configuration file suitable for use with all the examples in this chapter.

Listing 14-2. *Time.aspx: A Simple ASP.NET Web Form with an Embedded F# Server-Side Script*

```
<%@ Page Language="F#" %>

<!DOCTYPE html PUBLIC "-//W3C//DTD XHTML 1.0 Transitional//EN"
                      "http://www.w3.org/TR/xhtml1/DTD/xhtml1-transitional.dtd">

<script language="F#" runat="server">
    /// F# scripts embedded in ASPX pages must be a set of 'member' declarations.
    /// ASP.NET inserts these into the code generated for the page object type.

    /// This member is invoked on the server when the page is loaded. It tests
    /// whether the page was loaded for the first time and updates the content of
    /// this.Time control.
    member this.Form1_Load(sender: obj, e: EventArgs) =
        if not this.Page.IsPostBack then
            this.Time.Text <- DateTime.Now.ToString()

    /// This member is invoked on the server when the Reload button is clicked.
    member this.Reload_Click(sender: obj, e: EventArgs) =
        this.Time.Text <- "(R) " + DateTime.Now.ToString()
</script>

<html xmlns="http://www.w3.org/1999/xhtml">
<head runat="server">
   <title>Current time</title>
   <style type="text/css">
      body { font-family:calibri,verdana,sans-serif; }
   </style>
</head>
<body>
   <form id="Form1" runat="server" OnLoad="Form1_Load">
      The current time is:
      <asp:Label  runat="server" id="Time" />
      <asp:Button runat="server" id="Reload" text="Reload" OnClick="Reload_Click" />
   </form>
</body>
</html>
```

■**Note** You will need to make sure that the F# compiler is referenced in `web.config`, as shown in
Listing 14-3. You should check that the version number (we used 1.9.2.9 in the listing) matches the one
reported by F# Interactive and that the other information matches what is used in the ASP.NET samples in
your F# distribution.

Let's take a closer look at Listing 14-2. ASP.NET files can initially look like a sea of strange
symbols. Table 14-3 shows the meanings of some of the symbolic forms you'll see in ASP.NET files.

Table 14-3. *The Primary Symbolic and HTML Directives in ASP.NET* `.aspx` *Files*

Example Directive	What It Means
`<%@ ... %>`	ASP.NET directives. See Table 14-4 for a list of commonly used ASP.NET directives.
`<!-- ... -->`	HTML comment.
`<!DOCTYPE ... >`	HTML meta-information. Usually generated when the file is first created and can be ignored.
`<script language="F#" runat="server">...</script>`	Inserts F# or other scripting code as part of the generated code for the page. The F# code should be a portion of an object type definition.
`<form id="Form1" runat="server">`	Indicates that the given HTML element is treated as an ASP.NET control and generated dynamically on the server as part of the page object (with the ID as its name).
`<%= ... %>`	Inserts F# or other scripting code into a rendering of the page as an expression. For example, `<%= let a = 40+2 in a.ToString() %>`.
`<%# ... %>`	Data-binding expression: inserts F# code as the current item of an ASP.NET data control. A convenient shortcut for referring to a given data field is via the `Eval` method. For example, `<%# this.Eval("Rgb") %>`.

Beyond the HTML and ASP.NET controls, the key code in Listing 14-2 is the embedded F#
script beginning with `<script language="F#" runat="server">`. F# scripts embedded in `.aspx`
pages must be a set of "member" declarations, in other words, fragments of an F# type definition. ASP.NET inserts these into the code generated for the page object.

The embedded F# script contains two members. The first is as follows:

```
member this.Form1_Load(sender: obj, e: EventArgs) =
    if not this.Page.IsPostBack then
        this.Time.Text <- DateTime.Now.ToString()
```

This member is associated with the `Form1` control and is invoked on the server when the
page is loaded, in other words, as part of the process of generating the final HTML for the page.
We can see this because the event callback for the control mentions this event handler:

```
<form id="Form1" runat="server" onload="Form1_Load">
```

The implementation of Form1_Load uses the IsPostBack property of the page object to detect whether the page is loaded for the first time or whether it is loaded in reaction to some event invoked by a control. The reaction to an event that involves executing server-side code is called a *postback*, and it is triggered by sending data from the client back to the current page. When the page is loaded for the first time, this event handler sets the content of this.Time. This is the label element of the page being presented to the user (note the close correspondence between ASP.NET elements and HTML elements).

The second part of the script is the following member:

```
member this.Reload_Click(sender: obj, e: EventArgs) =
    this.Time.Text <- "(R) " + DateTime.Now.ToString()
```

This member is associated with the Reload button control and is invoked when the button is clicked. Because the event handler associated with the button has to be executed on the server, the page will be reloaded, and the event will be triggered. Note that the entire page is reloaded, so the Form1_Load handler will be called as well, but for this and subsequent reloads, the IsPostBack property is set to true and the label will not be updated by that event handler.

■**Note** When ASP.NET serves the page, it generates F# code using the F# CodeDom dynamic code generator. The text of embedded script fragments are added verbatim to the generated code, indented to an appropriate position. The generated code may appear in error messages including syntax errors, so you may occasionally need to look at the details of the generated ASP.NET code.

Deploying and Running the Application

Figure 14-1 shows the simple web application from Listing 14-2 accessed via a web browser on the local machine. You can deploy and run simple web application like this in three ways.

- You can simply create an ASP.NET project inside Visual Studio, add the Time.aspx file to the project, and adjust the web.config file in the project to contain the given compiler entry. Visual Studio comes with its own built-in web server so that when you run the web application using F5 from inside Visual Studio, a browser is automatically opened with a reference to this web server.

- You can also deploy the application to your local web server. For example, simply copy Time.aspx and web.config to an application directory in an ASP.NET-enabled web server. When using IIS, you can copy them to a directory c:\inetpub\wwwroot\Time and reference the website via http://localhost/Time/Time.aspx. Ensure your web server is ASP.NET-enabled as described later in the sidebar "Serving ASP.NET Pages Locally."

- Finally, you can deploy the files to a live web server. Again, copy Time.aspx and web.config to an application directory in an ASP.NET-enabled web server. Ensure the F# compiler has been installed on the web server, or deploy the F# compiler as part of the bin directory of your web application.

Figure 14-1 shows the results of launching the application via the second technique.

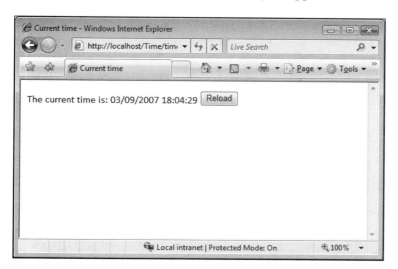

Figure 14-1. *The simple web application from Listing 14-1*

SERVING ASP.NET PAGES LOCALLY

You need to enable a number of configuration settings in order to ensure you can use your local machine as an experimental development web server.

When using Visual Studio, by far the easiest way to get going with developing web applications is to use the local web server built into Visual Studio itself, which is invoked when you "run" ASP.NET projects using F5. This starts the built-in web server using a random port and opens the default page by constructing a URL such as `http://localhost:59120/Time/time.aspx`.

Another option is using Microsoft's IIS web server; here you can deploy web applications under separate folders in the main web root folder, for instance, `c:\inetpub\wwwroot\Time`, and these can then be accessed via URLs such as `http://localhost/Time/time.aspx`. Here are some tips for doing this:

- Ensure that ASP.NET support is enabled in IIS. On Windows Vista this is done using Control Panel ➤ Programs ➤ Programs and Features ➤ Turn Windows features on or off. Ensure the checkbox at Internet Information Services ➤ World Wide Web Services ➤ Application Development Features ➤ ASP.NET is checked.

- Ensure that the default web root folder `c:\inetpub\wwwroot` exists and that you have copied your `.aspx` and `web.config` files to that directory.

- Ensure the `web.config` file contains an entry for the F# compiler. If not, ASP.NET will not be able to invoke the compiler dynamically. This is automatically done if you have used the F# Website project type.

- Check that you can access other local URLs such as `http://localhost/iisstart.htm`, the default starting page for IIS. If not, check the settings for IIS under Control Panel ➤ Administrative Tools ➤ Internet Information Services (IIS) Manager.

- Add a debug entry to your `web.config` file as shown in Listing 14-3 to ensure that verbose debugging information is generated for your F# code. Otherwise, errors reported by ASP.NET will be difficult to diagnose.

A number of application settings are relevant to web applications, but most of these are beyond the scope of this book. The easiest way to get some guidance is by looking at the `web.config.comments` file. For Microsoft .NET, you can find this file in your Windows directory and the `Microsoft.Net\Framework\ {your .NET version}\CONFIG` folder within. This same directory also contains another configuration file called `machine.config`, which has settings that apply to all web applications on the host machine. Many of the common, default settings are stored in this file.

Listing 14-3. *`web.config`: An ASP.NET Website Configuration File for Listing 14-2*

```
<?xml version="1.0"?>
<configuration>
  <system.web>
    <compilation debug="true" />
  </system.web>

  <system.codedom>
    <compilers>
      <compiler language="F#;f#;fs;fsharp"
                extension=".fs"
                type="Microsoft.FSharp.Compiler.CodeDom.FSharpAspNetCodeProvider,
                      FSharp.Compiler.CodeDom,
                      Version=1.9.2.9,
                      Culture=neutral,
                      PublicKeyToken=a19089b1c74d0809"/>
    </compilers>
  </system.codedom>
</configuration>
```

Using Code-Behind Files

Embedded scripts in web applications tend to create spaghetti code that confuses details of the presentation layer with the underlying logic of the application. However, embedding scripts is a useful way of trying new features.

The normal practice for ASP.NET website development is for each `Page.aspx` file to have backing code in a particular language, such as `Page.aspx.fs` for F# code. Listing 14-4 shows the code from Listing 14-2 but without the embedded script and with ASP.NET directives at the top of the file indicating that a code-behind file is being used.

Listing 14-4. *`Time2.aspx`: A Simple ASP.NET Web Form with F# Code-Behind*

```
<%@ Page Language="F#"
        AutoEventWireup="true"
        CodeFile="Time2.aspx.fs"
        Inherits="FSharpWeb.Time2" %>
```

```
<!DOCTYPE html PUBLIC "-//W3C//DTD XHTML 1.0 Transitional//EN"
                      "http://www.w3.org/TR/xhtml1/DTD/xhtml1-transitional.dtd">

<html xmlns="http://www.w3.org/1999/xhtml">
<head runat="server">
    <title>Current time</title>
    <style type="text/css">
        body { font-family:calibri,verdana,sans-serif; }
    </style>
</head>
<body>
    <form runat="server">
      The current time is:
      <asp:Label  runat="server" id="Time" />
      <asp:Button runat="server" id="Reload" text="Reload" OnClick="Reload_Click" />
    </form>
</body>
</html>
```

In turn, Listing 14-5 shows the accompanying F# code placed in a code-behind file. To place F# code in the code-behind file, we have done the following:

- Placed the code in a namespace.

- Defined a page type with the same base name as the .aspx page. The code generated from the .aspx file will use implementation inheritance to merge with the type defined here (see Chapter 6 for a description of implementation inheritance). This is standard practice for ASP.NET and matches the Inherits directive in Listing 14-4.

- Placed the implementation of the callback members into the page.

Listing 14-5. *Time2.aspx.fs: The F# Code-Behind for Time2.aspx*

```
#light
namespace FSharpWeb

open System
open System.Web
open System.Web.UI
open System.Web.UI.WebControls

type Time2() =
    inherit Page()

    [<DefaultValue>]
    val mutable Time : Label
    [<DefaultValue>]
    val mutable Reload : Button
```

```
    member this.Page_Load(sender: obj, e: EventArgs) =
        if not this.Page.IsPostBack then
            this.Time.Text <- DateTime.Now.ToString()

    member this.Reload_Click(sender: obj, e: EventArgs) =
        this.Time.Text <- "(R) " + DateTime.Now.ToString()
```

Using ASP.NET Input Controls

The minimalist application shown in Listing 14-2 and Figure 14-1 does nothing but use the
server to compute the time, something easily done on the local machine. Listing 14-6 shows the
.aspx code for a web application shown in Figure 14-2 that computes a list of prime numbers for a
selected range. The web.config file for this application remains the same.

Listing 14-6. *Computing and Displaying a Range of Prime Numbers Using the Web Server*

```
<%@ Page Language="F#" %>

<!DOCTYPE html PUBLIC "-//W3C//DTD XHTML 1.0 Transitional//EN"
                      "http://www.w3.org/TR/xhtml1/DTD/xhtml1-transitional.dtd">

<script language="F#" runat="server">
    member page.GenerateData_Click(sender: obj, e: EventArgs) =
        let isPrime(i: bigint) =
            let lim = Math.BigInt.FromInt64(int64(sqrt(float(i))))
            let rec check j =
                j > lim or (i % j <> 0I && check (j+1I))
            check 2I

        let lowerLimit = Math.BigInt.Parse(page.LowerLimit.Text)
        let upperLimit = Math.BigInt.Parse(page.UpperLimit.Text)
        let data =
            [ let previousTime = ref System.DateTime.Now
              for i in lowerLimit..upperLimit do
                  if isPrime(i) then
                      let time = System.DateTime.Now
                      yield (i, time-previousTime.Value)
                      do previousTime := time ]
        page.Repeater.DataSource <- data
        page.Repeater.DataBind()
</script>

<html xmlns="http://www.w3.org/1999/xhtml">
<head id="Head1" runat="server">
    <title>Current time</title>
    <style type="text/css">
        body { font-family:calibri,verdana,sans-serif; }
    </style>
```

```
</head>
<body>
    <form id="Form1" runat="server">
        <h2>Displaying data</h2>
        <p>
            Compute primes
            from <asp:TextBox runat="server" id="LowerLimit" />
            to   <asp:TextBox runat="server" id="UpperLimit" />.
        </p>
        <asp:Button runat="server"
                    id="GenerateData"
                    text="Generate" OnClick="GenerateData_Click" />
        <p>
        Results:

        <ul>
        <asp:Repeater id="Repeater" runat="server">
            <ItemTemplate>
                <li style="color:blue">
                    n = <%# this.Eval("Item1") %>,
                    time since previous: <%# this.Eval("Item2") %></li>
            </ItemTemplate>
            <AlternatingItemTemplate>
                <li style="color:green">
                    n = <%# this.Eval("Item1") %>,
                    time since previous: <%# this.Eval("Item2") %></li>
            </AlternatingItemTemplate>
        </asp:Repeater>
        </ul>

        </p>
    </form>
</body>
</html>
```

The application in Listing 14-6 consists of two input controls with the ASP.NET names LowerLimit and UpperLimit and an ASP.NET data-listing control called Repeater. The rest of the code is HTML markup and the F# embedded script to naively compute a sequence of prime numbers in the given range using the F# bigint type.

- The function isPrime implements the basic naive primality test.

- The computed value data is a list of tuples containing the prime numbers found in the given range. The type of each entry of this data list is (bigint * System.TimeSpan).

This code demonstrates how to acquire input data from forms filled in by the client and how to display data grids back to the client. The input data is acquired simply by using page.LowerLimit.Text and page.UpperLimit.Text in the server-side event handlers.

The data grid is generated by using the `Repeater` control to iteratively generate HTML; conceptually this is somewhat like a `for` loop that prints HTML at each step. Here is the relevant snippet:

```
<asp:Repeater id="Repeater" runat="server">
    <ItemTemplate>
        <li style="color:blue">
            n = <%# this.Eval("Item1") %>,
            time since previous: <%# this.Eval("Item2") %></li>
    </ItemTemplate>
    <AlternatingItemTemplate> ... </AlternatingItemTemplate>
</asp:Repeater>
```

The repeater control contains two templates that define the HTML code that is generated during the iteration. It is common that subsequent lines use different formatting, and `Repeater` automatically switches between `ItemTemplate` and `AlternatingItemTemplate`. The body of the template uses somewhat cryptic ASP.NET constructs such as `<%# this.Eval("Item1") %>`. These are instances of one of the ASP.NET-embedded F# expression forms from Table 14-3. ASP.NET textually evaluates this element at each step of the repeated iteration.

The repeater iterates over a data source. The data source can be specified either declaratively as we will see later or programmatically as in this example using the following lines:

```
page.Repeater.DataSource <- data
page.Repeater.DataBind()
```

Figure 14-2. *Computing a data table using Listing 14-4*

Displaying Data from Databases

After introducing the ASP.NET framework and the usual organization of the code in ASP.NET web applications, we're ready for a more complicated example. On the next few pages we will present a web application that displays data from the sample Northwind database.

As a first step, we will implement an F# module, DataSource.fs, as shown in Listing 14-7, that contains functions for accessing the database. To do this we use F# Linq, which will be described in more detail in Chapter 15. In short, F# Linq makes it possible to use F# sequence expressions for writing database queries and thus reduces the number of languages you need to master when writing data-aware web applications.

Listing 14-7. *App_Code/DataSource.fs: The F# Module for Accessing the Northwind Database*

```
#light
namespace FSharpWeb

open System.Web.Configuration
open Microsoft.FSharp.Quotations.Typed
open Microsoft.FSharp.Data.Linq
open nwind

type CategoryInfo = { CategoryID: int;  Name: string; }
type ProductInfo  = { ProductName: string;  Price: System.Decimal; }

module DataSource =
    let db = new Northwind(WebConfigurationManager.ConnectionStrings.
                            Item("NorthwindData").ConnectionString)
    let GetCategories () =
        SQL <@ seq { for c in §db.Categories
                        -> { CategoryID = c.CategoryID
                             Name       = c.CategoryName } } @>

    let GetProducts (categoryId) =
        SQL <@ seq { for p in §db.Products
                        when p.CategoryID = §categoryId
                        -> { ProductName = p.ProductName
                             Price       = p.UnitPrice.Value } } @>
```

The code in Listing 14-7 first declares two simple record types that are used in the database queries for returning results. You could use tuples for these results, but record types are easier to work with when accessing the information stored using ASP.NET markup. The code in the DataSource module first creates a value of the Northwind type, which is a class representing the Northwind database and was generated by the LINQ tool SqlMetal, described in Chapter 15. The constructor of the generated type takes the connection string as an argument, so we use WebConfigurationManager provided by ASP.NET to read it from the web.config file, which we will look at shortly. Finally, the module contains two functions, both implemented using F# Linq. As you can see, the database query is written as a sequence expression and is wrapped in F# quotations that were discussed in Chapter 9. The query is executed using the SQL function, which is discussed in more detail in Chapter 15. The first function for querying the database is called GetCategories and simply returns the IDs and names of all the categories in the database; the second one is called GetProducts and it returns information about products in a specified category passed as a parameter. Note that when referring to a concrete variable in the F# Linq query, you must use the paragraph symbol (§) to splice it as such into the query representation.

Now, let's look at the Category.aspx file, shown in Listing 14-8, which contains the ASP.NET markup for viewing products in a specified category. You can specify the category that will be displayed as an argument in the URL, for example, Category.aspx?id=3.

Listing 14-8. *Category.aspx: The ASP.NET Page for Displaying Products in a Category*

```
<%@ Page Language="F#" %>
<html>
<head runat="server">
    <title>Category Listing</title>
</head>
<body>
    <form runat="server">
        <!-- Unordered list of products using ASP.NET Repeater -->
        <ul>
        <asp:Repeater runat="server" id="rptProducts"
                    DataSourceID="nwindProducts">
            <ItemTemplate>
                <li><%# this.Eval("ProductName") %>
                    (price: <%# this.Eval("Price") %>)</li>
            </ItemTemplate>
        </asp:Repeater>
        </ul>

        <!-- ASP.NET DataSource control for loading the data -->
        <asp:ObjectDataSource id="nwindProducts" runat="server"
            TypeName="FSharpWeb.DataSource" SelectMethod="GetProducts">
            <SelectParameters>
                <asp:QueryStringParameter Name="categoryId" Type="Int32"
                    QueryStringField="id" DefaultValue="0"/>
            </SelectParameters>
        </asp:ObjectDataSource>
    </form>
</body>
</html>
```

The ASP.NET markup in Listing 14-8 is not using any code-behind code, because all we need for accessing the data is already available in the module we wrote in Listing 14-7. The first part of the markup declares the ASP.NET Repeater control including an ItemTemplate that will be used for rendering a single product. Similarly to the earlier examples, we use the Eval construct for accessing the data, but in this example the product is represented using the ProductInfo record declared earlier, so we can use the appropriate labels as an argument to the Eval function.

The second part of the markup is far more interesting; it declares an ASP.NET ObjectDataSource control, which is a nonvisual control, meaning it will not generate any HTML code. It serves simply as a source of data for the Repeater control in the first part, and as you can see, these two are linked together using the DataSourceID attribute of the Repeater control, which is set to the ID of the data source control. The ObjectDataSource is configured using the TypeName attribute, which specifies the .NET type that implements the functionality (in our case we're using an F# module instead of an object type). The attribute SelectMethod sets a name of the method (or a function in our case) that should be called when the data is required. Since the method has one argument, we also need to use SelectParameters to specify what value should be passed as an argument to our function. We want to take the argument from the URL query string so we can use QueryStringParameter provided by ASP.NET. It has several attributes; the most important are QueryStringField, which sets the name of the argument in the URL address (id in our example), and Name, which has to match the parameter name of the GetProducts function in our F# module.

We looked only at the ASP.NET page for displaying the products in a specified category, but to make the application complete, we also need a page that will list all the categories using the GetCategories function. To do this, you simply need to create a page similar to Category.aspx and modify a few details, so we do not show it here. As the last step, Listing 14-9 shows the web configuration file.

Listing 14-9. *web.config: Configuration of the Sample Database Viewing Application*

```
<?xml version="1.0"?>
<configuration>
  <connectionStrings>
    <!-- Connection string for the Northwind database -->
    <add name="NorthwindData" providerName="System.Data.SqlClient"
         connectionString=".. database connection string .." />
  </connectionStrings>

  <system.web>
  <compilation><assemblies>
    <!-- Referenced .NET 3.5 assemblies required by F# Linq -->
    <add assembly="System.Core, Version=3.5.0.0, Culture=neutral,
                PublicKeyToken=b77a5c561934e089" />
    <add assembly="System.Data.Linq, Version=3.5.0.0, Culture=neutral,
                PublicKeyToken=b77a5c561934e089" />
    <add assembly="System.Xml.Linq, Version=3.5.0.0, Culture=neutral,
                PublicKeyToken=b77a5c561934e089" />
  </assemblies></compilation>
  </system.web>

  <system.codedom>
    <compilers>
      <compiler language="F#;f#;fs;fsharp"
                extension=".fs"
                type="Microsoft.FSharp.Compiler.CodeDom.FSharpAspNetCodeProvider,
```

```
                              FSharp.Compiler.CodeDom,
                              Version=1.9.2.9,
                              Culture=neutral,
                              PublicKeyToken=a19089b1c74d0809"/>
        </compilers>
      </system.codedom>
    </configuration>
```

In the configuration file, you first configure the connection string referenced by name as `NorthwindData`, which you used earlier in the module that contains the data-access functionality. Connection strings describe the connection details to the database and are discussed in Chapter 15. In the second section, you need to reference the additional .NET and F# Linq assemblies that we are using in the project. These assemblies are installed in the GAC, so you can just add a reference to them. The additional assemblies, namely, the `FSharp.Linq.dll` file, which includes the F# Linq implementation, and `northwind.dll`, which includes the generated `Northwind` type, can simply be copied to the `Bin` directory of the application, and ASP.NET will discover them automatically. Finally, the `web.config` file also has to include a configuration of the F# CodeDom provider.

Going Further with ASP.NET

So far you've seen some very simple kinds of web applications with ASP.NET and F#. In practice, ASP.NET offers an enormously powerful framework for all aspects of server-side web development. In the following sections we'll explore some additional aspects, though for full details we recommend you consult some of the excellent books dedicated to the topic of ASP.NET. Some of these books are listed at `http://www.expert-fsharp.com/Topics/WebProgramming`.

ASP.NET Directives

The first line of an `.aspx` file usually contains special markup embedded inside <%@ ... %> ... %> containing a number of ASP.NET directives, which are instructions given to the processing environment, indicating, among other things, which scripting language is used. Table 14-4 explains the most important directives and some of their attributes.

Table 14-4. *Some ASP.NET Directives and Their Attributes*

Directive/Attribute	Description
Page or Control	
AutoEventWireup	Wires page events that follow the Page_ naming convention automatically if true (default). If false, event handlers need to be wired explicitly.
CodeFile	Specifies the path to the code-behind file.
Inherits	Specifies the name of the class that goes together with the page.
Language	Specifies the language used for writing inline code in the page.
Import	Opens a namespace specified by the Namespace attribute and makes it available to all code in the page.

Table 14-4. *Some ASP.NET Directives and Their Attributes*

Directive/Attribute	Description
Register	Registers a user control for use with the page. See the section "Creating Custom ASP.NET Server Controls" later in this chapter.
OutputCache	Declaratively controls caching; if present, ASP.NET keeps the rendered output of a page or a control in a cache for a specified amount of time.
Assembly	References an external assembly. The Name attribute can be used to specify the name of the assembly (without the extension).
Implements	Specifies that the page implements the interface specified in the Interface attribute.
Reference	Associates another page or user control with the current one. The Control, Page, or VirtualPath attribute can be used to identify the component to be referenced, causing it to be compiled together.

Server Controls

Ordinary HTML markup in web forms such as <strong>, <ul>, and <h2> is treated as text and is passed to the browser verbatim (via the LiteralControl server control class). On the other hand, explicit server controls (those with the runat="server" attribute) are processed on the server and translated to HTML markup (just to illustrate, there are server controls that equate to hundreds of HTML tags, and many can be mapped nearly one to one). All server controls can be programmatically managed, which typically means you customize the way they respond to various events or how they appear or behave visually. Categorically speaking, there are two main types of server controls: HTML server controls that directly correspond to an HTML element and web server controls. The second type can be divided into several groups depending on the use of the control. There are, for example, validation controls that ensure that entered values fulfill some criteria, data source controls similar to the ObjectDataSource mentioned earlier, membership controls for handling user login and registration, and many others.

In Listing 14-2 you saw server controls such as labels and buttons, both of which are web server controls. It is beyond the scope of this book to discuss the great number of web server controls available in ASP.NET 2.0 and above. As a reference, Table 14-5 shows some of the ones most commonly used.

Table 14-5. *Common ASP.NET Server Controls*

Type	Controls
Basic	Button, TextBox, Label, Panel, CheckBox, ListBox, RadioButton, PlaceHolder, DropDownList
Data viewing/editing	Repeater, DataList, GridView, DetailsView
Data sources	ObjectDataSource, SqlDataSource
Membership	Login, LoginView
Validation	RequiredFieldValidator, CompareValidator, RegularExpressionValidator

HTML server controls correspond to a given HTML tag and are simply applied by adding the runat="server" attribute. This turns the standard HTML tag into a server control, allowing you to change its appearance or behavior programmatically. Since web server controls offer a more robust object model, they are almost always preferable to HTML server controls.

Validation controls are a special type of web controls that perform typical validation patterns on your web form input fields and display error messages where appropriate. The Validation section of your Visual Studio Toolbox contains the available validation controls, as summarized in Table 14-6.

Table 14-6. *Common ASP.NET Validation Controls*

Control Name	Description
RequiredFieldValidator	Ensures that the associated input control is not empty.
RangeValidator	Validates that the user input is in a given range.
RegularExpressionValidator	Checks whether the user input matches a regular expression pattern. See Chapter 10 for a description of using .NET regular expressions.
CompareValidator	Compares the user input against a given value or another control.
CustomValidator	Validates the user input based on a custom, user-specified logic.
ValidationSummary	Lists all validation error messages.

Each validator has an ErrorMessage and a Text property that you can set in conjunction with displaying an error message. When the validator fails, it displays the content of the Text property at the place where it is inserted in your page markup. A typical scenario is ensuring that a given user input control has a value entered. Here, all you need to do is add your input control and a RequiredFieldValidator next to it, set its ControlToValidate property to the ID of the associated input control, and set the Text property to say *. This will show an asterisk when no value is entered in the input control at the time of submitting the page. Using another validator is just as easy, except you need to customize different properties. Table 14-7 summarizes these main properties for each validator.

Table 14-7. *The Main Customizable Validator Properties*

Control Name	Main Properties
RequiredFieldValidator	InitialValue
RangeValidator	MinimumValue, MaximumValue, Type
RegularExpressionValidator	ValidationExpression
CompareValidator	ControlToCompare, Operator, ValueToCompare, Type
CustomValidator	ClientValidationFunction, ServerValidate (event)
ValidationSummary	DisplayMode, HeaderText, ValidationGroup

You may end up working with complex web pages that have many, even dozens, of input controls that belong to different forms on the page (for instance, a web page with a search form, a user registration form, and a contact form). By default, all validators defined on the page would be run and most likely prohibit your end user from moving onto the next page because of validation errors that are seemingly unrelated to the chosen action of the user. To solve this problem, you can turn to using validation groups, which specify a set of related controls and their validators. A validation group is formed by specifying a common group name (as a string) for the ValidationGroup property of each validator and the input control that triggers a page submission. This will ensure that only the validators that are related to the control initiating the page submission will be run. Finally, you can disable any validation by setting the CausesValidation property of a postback control to false.

Debugging, Profiling, and Tracing

Debugging ASP.NET applications is easy when using a tool such as Visual Studio. You can set breakpoints in your F# code, and these will allow you to break into the middle of code executing when server requests are performed. We discuss debugging techniques for regular F# code in Chapter 18.

During development, it is often necessary to trace what happens on a page, as well as during the process of serving that page. You can enable page tracing by adding the Trace="true" page attribute to your web form. This will append information shown in Table 14-8 to the page displayed. Figure 14-3 shows an example of this information for the application from Listing 14-4.

Table 14-8. *Information Generated by Tracing an ASP.NET Page*

Section	Information Collected
Request Details	Shows the session ID, request type, time of request, status code, and request/response encoding for the request
Trace Information	Shows the various page life cycle events and the time spent on processing each
Control Tree	Shows each server control, its type, render size, view state size, and control state size in a parent-children tree
Session State	Shows the various keys, their associated values, and their types defined in the page's session state
Application State	Shows the various keys, their associated values, and their types defined in the server's application state
Request/Response Cookies Collection	Shows the name/value/size of each cookie
Headers Collection	Shows the name and value of each page header
Response Headers Collection	Shows the name and value for the server response
Server Variables	Shows the various server variables and their values at the time of processing

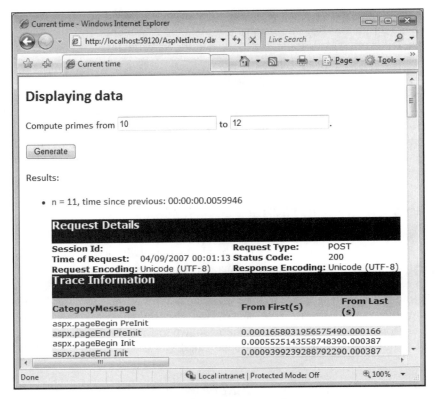

Figure 14-3. *Debugging and tracing an ASP.NET web page*

Understanding the ASP.NET Event Model

In the previous sections, you saw various server controls triggering events, submitting pages with form data, validating input controls, and so on. These all involve events. ASP.NET has an event-driven architecture: each web form and server control supports a number of events that it can respond to, and these events can be attached to various event handlers. As you would expect, these events fall in two different categories: page and control events, respectively. Consider what happens as we interact with a simple SayHello.aspx page that has a text box for a name, an empty label, and a submit button:

1. First, an HTTP GET request is made for SayHello.aspx to the server.

2. On receiving this request, the server processes the page (doing compilation if necessary), calls the appropriate page event handlers (Page_Load, and so on), and ultimately returns an HTML response.

3. This HTML response, along with the state/content of the HTML controls (the view state: an empty text box and label), is sent back to the browser, and the page is displayed.

4. We now fill in our name and click the submit button. This causes the form containing the text box and button controls to post back to the server, passing the view state with it.

5. The server executes the appropriate page handlers and the control event handler(s) for the button click, and an HTML response is generated (the same page with the label now greeting you by name).

6. This HTML response is sent back to the browser and displayed.

As this simple but representative example shows, the server controls on a given page are in constant contact with the server: they catch events and pass them onto the server where they are handled and responded to accordingly.

Page events occur when a page is requested from the server, either via the GET (the first time) or POST (when data is posted to the page) HTTP methods. For instance, there are events for page initialization (PreInit, Init), page loading (Load), rendering (Render), and so on. These page events are always handled in a given order as defined by the ASP.NET page life cycle (see "The ASP.NET Page Life Cycle" sidebar). Although you can programmatically bind a delegate to a given page event, ASP.NET makes it even easier. As you saw it in Listing 14-5, you can add page event handlers by simply declaring members of the form Page_XXX, where XXX is the name of the page event. This works because by default, the AutoEventWireup page attribute is true, and this causes wiring the intended event handler (using this naming convention) to the appropriate event automatically.

Control events are triggered by the end user: clicking a button, selecting an item in a list box, and so on. Contrary to page events, control events cannot be automatically wired, and thus you need to establish the link between the handler and the event manually. This is quite easy to do: simply set the OnXXX attribute of the server control to the event handler, as we did with the Reload button in the first example.

Not all control events are immediately posted back to the server; in fact, only a few are, such as button clicks. All other control events are so-called *change events* (because they are triggered as a control undergoes some changes: the selected item in a drop-down list has changed or a check box or radio button has been selected) and as such are not posted to the server automatically for efficiency reasons. You can, on the other hand, enable postback in such situations by overriding the control's AutoPostBack property to true. This can be quite useful; for instance, a page can respond directly to a change in a drop-down list without the end user having to click a submit button, thus saving valuable clicks and time in the appropriate situations.

THE ASP.NET PAGE LIFE CYCLE

The ASP.NET page life cycle consists of a few dozen steps and as such is beyond the scope of this book to discuss in detail. However, it is important to understand the main steps involved in this life cycle. For a complete reference, you can refer to books devoted to ASP.NET. Here we give a brief and simplified description, sufficient enough for most situations.

Given a request for a page and assuming that the appropriate page class exists in a compiled form on the server (if not, the ASP.NET runtime kicks in and performs a number of code compilation steps), a page instance is created with all server controls declared but not yet initialized. At this point there are three main life cycle phases (initialization, loading, and rendering). Initialization starts with determining whether the page requested is in postback mode (in which case the view state is encoded in the page request) or for the first time. At this point, the PreInit handler is executed, and the page theme and master page are applied. Next, the Init handler is called, initializing all server controls and the page itself, and then the InitCompleted event is triggered.

> The loading phase involves loading any view state (in case of a postback request) from the page request and loading it in into the server controls. When the view state is restored, the PreLoad event is triggered, followed by the Load event. This is where you normally put your page processing logic that runs on every page request. Following this event, loading the view state is executed again to catch any dynamically added controls (for instance, those created in the Load event handler). Then any control change events and postback events are handled, and finally the LoadComplete event is raised.
>
> The rendering phase starts with performing all data binding (which involves the DataBinding and DataBound events for each data-bound control), and then the PreRender event is triggered. Next, any asynchronous tasks (registered via RegisterAsyncTask) are fired off, and the PreRenderComplete event is called. Before the actual rendering takes place, the view state is saved back to the page (by default to the default hidden input field). Finally, the page's Render method is called that produces HTML by recursively invoking the same method on each server control. Before this HTML is passed to the client, the Unload event is triggered and every object involved in the page creation is disposed.

Both page and control events are executed on the server, so when they are triggered, the parent page along with its view state is posted to the server, where the event is handled and a response (the same or another page) is sent back to the client. A so-called *postback* occurs if a page posts information to the server requesting the same page back. This round-trip scenario is quite common: the Reload button in Listing 14-2 or the Generate button from Listing 14-4 are both examples of triggering a postback.

In both of these cases, we have a postback because we "remain" on the same page; for example, the originating page handles the data submission by updating the content of a label (an HTML <span> element) in the button click handler. More often, though, data is posted to another page, in which case it is referred to as *cross-page posting*. You can easily enable cross-page posting by setting the PostBackUrl property of the submitting control. For instance, a SayHello button could be declared as follows:

```
<asp:Button ID="btnSayHello" runat="server" Text="Greet" PostBackUrl="SayIt.aspx" />
```

There is a significant difference between how data submissions are handled via postback and cross-page posting: whereas the former is done in the submitting control's click event handler (for example, Reload_Click in the timer example), with cross-page posting the submission event is handled in the Load event handler of the page to which the postback URL points. What slightly complicates matters is that the form data submitted is not available directly on the receiving page, but instead you have to reference it through the PreviousPage property of the page.

Because oftentimes you place initialization or cross-page posting code in a page event (typically for the Load event), you need to make sure that this code is executed only for initialization or when data is being posted to the page. You can do so by checking the IsPostBack property of the Page object, which returns false if the page is requested the first time.

Maintaining the View State

HTTP is a stateless protocol, so special care must be taken to preserve the state of a given page. For instance, your visitor may have just filled out a long form and, as it sometimes happens, he or she made an error. After posting the page, this visitor expects to see all entered data preserved with an indication of where the missing or incorrect entry is. Recovering form values after a postback is possible because ASP.NET maintains the so-called *view state*, that is, the state of all server controls on the page. These values are passed as HTTP form variables on a post and returned as hard-wired HTML.

View state is automatically encoded as a hidden `<input>` element in your pages, and no special handling is needed to enable it. You can, on the other hand, disable it altogether by adding `EnableViewState="false"` to your `Page` directive or partially on the control level by setting the same control property for any control for which no view state is to be maintained. This may be necessary if your page displays large amounts of data but with no possibility of a postback or the data on the page cannot be modified, thus making the page source considerably smaller and quicker to download to your clients.

Understanding the Provider Model

ASP.NET comes with a number of built-in application services that you can use and customize as you build your web applications. These encapsulate much of the core functionality common to most websites, such as membership and role management, profiles and personalization, and site navigation, and you can easily plug them into your website logic right out of the box.

These services interact with service-specific data (the users registered, the different user roles your site is programmed for, various data associated with the authenticated users, and so on) via *providers*, which are classes that implement the appropriate interfaces to fulfill contracts for various services. ASP.NET comes with a number of built-in providers; for instance, it has a SQL and an Active Directory membership provider. The provider model allows you to plug in your own providers (simply by specifying them in the appropriate section of your `web.config`), so you may write an Oracle or a custom membership provider to your existing user/membership database or a role service provider based on simple XML files.

Table 14-9 shows some common provider-based services in ASP.NET.

Table 14-9. *ASP.NET Provider-Based Services*

Service	Description
Encryption	Handles the encryption and decryption of ASP.NET configuration files and sections within
Membership	Manages users and their accounts
Profile	Adds user information (for instance, user preferences) that is to be collected and stored for each user
Role Management	Manages roles and their associated access rights
Session Management	Manages session state for a user visit
Site Map	Stores information about each page and its place in the site's structure
Web Events	Allows the monitoring of an application for control purposes
Web Parts	Manages a set of controls and their content and appearance that make up a portal

Configuring the Provider Database

By default (as guided by the server's machine.config file), the data-aware services use SQL providers that work against a SQL Express database (by default aspnetdb.mdf in the App_Data folder). The relevant part of the machine.config containing the default connection strings is as follows:

```
<connectionStrings>
    <clear />
    <add name="LocalSqlServer"
        connectionString="data source=.\SQLEXPRESS;Integrated Security=SSPI;
AttachDBFilename=|DataDirectory|aspnetdb.mdf;User Instance=true"
        providerName="System.Data.SqlClient" />
</connectionStrings>
```

This defines a LocalSqlServer connection string that all data-centric providers use by default, which points to the aspnetdb.mdf SQL Express database in the web data directory. (Note how the database server is set to be running as a SQL Express named instance.) This database file is automatically created upon first use or by triggering the website administration console. It is important to remember that these default settings will work only with SQL Express, but on a typical development machine with a standard SQL Express installation, everything works like a charm out of the box.

Even if you are using SQL Express and all the default providers, you should (re)define your connection string settings in your site web.config file, mostly because it is more portable that way and because this simply becomes necessary if you use a different database server, say SQL Server. At the time of writing, SQL Server does not allow attaching database files to the server using the AttachDBFilename property, so you will need to use a regular database and refer to it using the Initial Catalog or the Database keywords in your connection string.

If for some reason you cannot automatically generate the default database when using SQL Server, you can simply build it by hand by first creating an empty database (for instance, by right-clicking Server Explorer/Data Connections and selecting Create New SQL Server Database) and running aspnet_regsql.exe (found in your .NET installation folder) in wizard mode with the information on your newly created database. This tool generates all the data tables and stored procedures needed by the default providers. You can then change your web.config file to include a reference to this new database:

```
<connectionStrings>
    <remove name="LocalSqlServer" />
    <add name="LocalSqlServer"
        connectionString="Data Source=localhost;Integrated Security=SSPI;
Initial Catalog=YourDatabase"
        providerName="System.Data.SqlClient" />
</connectionStrings>
```

Here we used localhost for SQL Server and the YourDatabase database within. You may need to change the host when you deploy your application to point to the right database server. Furthermore, you should be aware that SQL Server does not support detached databases (.mdf files); therefore, if you are migrating from a SQL Express instance (for example when your hosting provider supports only SQL Server), you will need to "manually" import the contents of the detached database file into a SQL Server database (either by attaching it from the hosting provider's administrative console or creating a backup from the Express database and importing it); in other words, there is no way to use the .mdf database with SQL Server directly.

Creating Custom ASP.NET Server Controls

You can create new server controls for ASP.NET on two conceptual levels: user controls and custom (web) server controls. User controls are similar to web forms: they are a collection of server control and/or HTML markup, which is named (declared) and then used via reference. They can also expose public properties that can be set to control various aspects of the user control. In this chapter we consider only user controls.

User controls are contained in .ascx files. You can create a new user control in Visual Studio by selecting the Web User Control template from the New/File menu option. The new user control is empty except for a Control directive that acts similarly to the Page directive of a web form. You can add any additional markup as needed. As an example, consider a user control that repeats a given text fragment a specified number of times.

Our user control (RepeatText.ascx in Listing 14-10) contains a single control, a placeholder label. The code-behind file is located in RepeatText.ascx.fs, shown in Listing 14-11.

Listing 14-10. *RepeatText.ascx: A Simple User Control Implemented in F#*

```
<%@ Control Language="F#"
            AutoEventWireup="true"
            CodeFile="RepeatText.ascx.fs"
            Inherits="MyUserControl.RepeatText" %>


<asp:Label ID="Place" runat="server"/>
```

Listing 14-11. *RepeatText.ascx.fs: The Implementation of an ASP.NET User Control*

```
#light
namespace MyUserControl

open System
open System.Web.UI.WebControls

type RepeatText() =
    inherit System.Web.UI.UserControl()

    /// This is the internal state and parameters of the control
    let mutable text = ""
    let mutable count = 0

    /// This internal control is initialized by ASP.NET
    [<DefaultValue>]
    val mutable Place : Label
```

```
/// These properties allow the state to be used from the page
member self.Text       with get() = text  and set(v) = text <- v
member self.RepeatCount with get() = count and set(v) = count <- v

/// This event is automatically wired up through the use of the
/// AutoEventWireup ASP.NET directive (true by default)
member self.Page_Load (sender: obj, e: EventArgs) =
    let acc = new Text.StringBuilder()
    for i in 1..count do
        acc.Append(self.Text) |> ignore
    self.Place.Text <- acc.ToString()
```

The state and parameters of the control are ultimately held in the variables text and count. Note how we defined public properties (Text and RepeatCount) that will be available when we use the control from a page. All we need to use this user control from a page is to register it using the Register directive, giving a tag prefix and a tag name by which we can refer to it. For example, the code in Listing 14-12 results in an HTML label element containing the text "Monkey!" 10 times.

Listing 14-12. *TestRepeat.aspx: Using the Control from Listing 14-4*

```
<%@ Page AutoEventWireup="true" %>
<%@ Register Src="RepeatText.ascx" TagName="Repeater" TagPrefix="text" %>
<!DOCTYPE html PUBLIC "-//W3C//DTD XHTML 1.0 Transitional//EN"
                      "http://www.w3.org/TR/xhtml1/DTD/xhtml1-transitional.dtd">
<html xmlns="http://www.w3.org/1999/xhtml">
<head runat="server">
    <title>My User Control Test</title>
</head>
<body>
    <form runat="server">
        <text:Repeater id="chart" runat="server" RepeatCount="10" Text="Monkey!" />
    </form>
</body>
</html>
```

You can find more details on implementing user controls in the books on ASP.NET referenced at http://www.expert-fsharp.com/Topics/WebProgramming.

Building Ajax Rich Client Applications

So far in this chapter we have looked at server-side web applications. In recent years a new class of rich-client web applications has emerged, leading to what is commonly called the Ajax development paradigm. This is a general term for any web application that incorporates substantial amounts of code executed on the client side of the application by running JavaScript in the web browser.

Developing Ajax applications can be done in two ways when using F#:

- You can manually write and serve additional JavaScript files as part of your web application.

- You can use the F# Web Tools to write both client and server code purely in F#.

Developing Ajax applications by the first technique follows a fairly standard path mostly independent of F#. You can find more details on this technique at http://www.expert-fsharp.com/Topics/WebProgramming.

More on F# Web Tools

F# Web Tools is an open source project at http://www.codeplex.com/fswebtools. These tools represent an extremely powerful way of writing robust, efficient, integrated client/server applications in a single, type-checked framework. In particular, they draw on several advanced features of F#, the combination of which offers a unique programming experience for web applications:

- Client-side and server-side code is authored in one project, and code to handle client-side events can be written in the same way as server-side event handlers that we used in many places in this chapter.

- The program runs initially as a server-side application.

- The client-side code is written as an F# workflow and is automatically translated to JavaScript using F# quotations and reflection and is served to the client. (See Chapter 9 for details on F# quotations and workflows.)

- The client side can also use some .NET and F# libraries. The calls are mapped to a corresponding JavaScript functionality through fairly straightforward techniques.

- The client side may make asynchronous calls to the server using variations on the techniques described in Chapter 13. Some type safety is guaranteed by making modal distinctions using F# workflows.

These tools were under development at the time the book was written, and some details of their use are likely to change. For this reason we don't give detailed code using these tools in this book, though this chapter gives a good grounding in the ASP.NET techniques on which the tools are based.

Figure 14-4 shows part of one sample web application written using F# Web Tools. In this sample, which is authored entirely in F#, all symbolic computation is executed as JavaScript on the client side. The image displaying the curve is generated on the server side, since JavaScript has relatively weak abilities for image generation in a portable fashion.

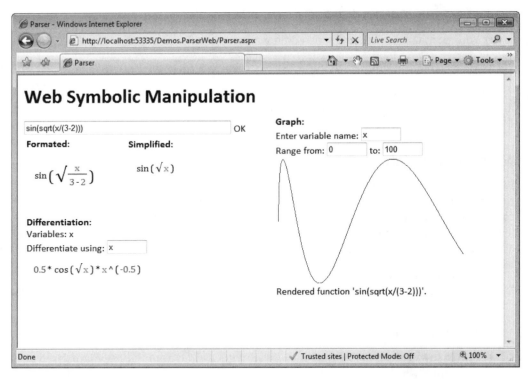

Figure 14-4. *An example rich client web application written using F# Web Tools*

Using Web Services

Web services can be used to implement *service-oriented architectures,* a popular application integration strategy where the interacting software components and services are loosely coupled in a distributed environment. The benefits of such integration include allowing offering services as independent entities that can be used and reused from different systems within an organization or even the entire world. Consuming web services thus is a great way to expand the functionality of your application.

A web service is a set of functionality that is offered through a platform-independent interface. Applications can explore the pieces of functionality offered by a web service by examining its Web Services Description Language (WSDL) signature. This WSDL definition uses XML to describe the signature of each operation by declaring the data types of the parameters and optional return values. Communicating with a web service occurs via the Simple Object Access Protocol (SOAP), which encodes service invocations and return values in an XML envelope over HTTP. Because web services are invoked over HTTP, they can be used by any application with Internet connectivity.

Communicating with web services is usually performed via so-called *proxy classes.* A proxy performs all the grunge work involved in calling the service and deciphering the results, freeing you from a lot work. A typical workflow when calling a web service is the following:

1. The client instantiates the proxy and calls the desired operation on it.

2. The proxy creates a SOAP XML request and sends it to the web service via HTTP.

3. The web service receives the request and performs the requested operation.

4. The web service packages the return value from the operation (or any exception that occurred within) into a SOAP XML response and returns it to the proxy via HTTP.

5. The proxy deserializes the response into a .NET data type and returns it to the calling class.

Consuming Web Services

Many great web services are available on the Internet. For instance, Microsoft's TerraService is a free web service at `http://terraservice.net` that enables you to integrate USGS images and data into your applications. Also, `http://webservicex.net` is another great source for web services; for instance, its WeatherForecast web service can supply weather information for any given U.S. location. Calling these and other web services in your .NET applications is quite painless using F# web references.

All web services are called via generated proxy code. The easiest way to generate this code is by adding a web reference to Visual Studio, which automatically generates a .NET proxy class for the given web service. Figure 14-5 shows the available operations for the web service from `http://webservicex.net/WeatherForecast.asmx`.

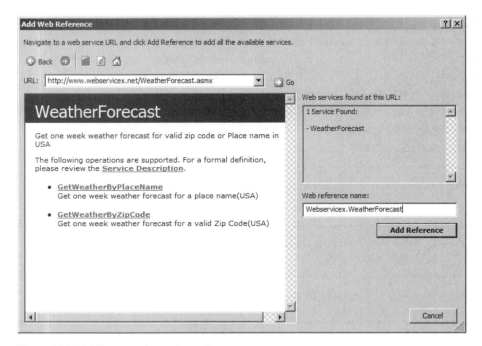

Figure 14-5. *Adding a web service reference*

You can also generate code using the .NET command-line tool wsdl.exe. Here is an example where you generate C# code for TerraService and WeatherForecast and compile it explicitly:

```
C:\fsharp> wsdl /namespace:WebReferences http://webservicex.net/WeatherForecast.asmx
Microsoft (R) Web Services Description Language Utility
Writing file 'C:\fsharp\WeatherForecast.cs'.

C:\fsharp> csc /target:library WeatherForecast.cs

C:\fsharp> wsdl /namespace:WebReferences http://terraservice.net/terraservice.asmx
Microsoft (R) Web Services Description Language Utility
Writing file 'C:\fsharp\TerraService.cs'.

C:\fsharp> csc /target:library TerraService.cs

C:\fsharp> dir *.dll
...
04/09/2007  00:18              10,752 WeatherForecast.dll
04/09/2007  00:18              57,344 TerraService.dll
```

Note You can also use wsdl.exe to generate F# code by adding a command-line option that gives an explicit reference to the F# CodeDom dynamic code generator. For example, an option such as /language: "Microsoft.FSharp.Compiler.CodeDom.FSharpCodeProvider, Microsoft.FSharp.Compiler. CodeDom, Version=1.9.2.9, Culture=neutral, PublicKeyToken=a19089b1c74d0809" can be used. Note the similarity with the CodeDom reference used in the web.config file in Listing 14-2. The generated file can then be compiled as normal, though the authors have found that small adjustments sometimes need to be made to the generated code.

You can reference these two generated DLLs from F# Interactive using the following references:

```
> #r @"C:\fsharp\WeatherForecast.dll";;
> #r @"C:\fsharp\TerraService.dll";;
```

You can now use these web services directly from F# Interactive:

```
> open System;;
> open WebReferences;;

> let ws = new WeatherForecast();;
val ws : WeatherForecast
```

```
> let weather = ws.GetWeatherByPlaceName("Los Angeles");;
val weather : WeatherForecasts

> let today = weather.Details.[0];;
val today : WeatherData

> printf "Temperature: %sF/%sC\n" today.MaxTemperatureF today.MaxTemperatureC;;
Temperature: 100F/38C
val it : unit = ()

> let ts = new TerraService();;
val ts : TerraService

> let place = new Place(City="Los Angeles", State="CA", Country="USA");;
val place : Place

> let facts = ts.GetPlaceFacts(place);;
val facts : PlaceFacts

> printfn "Lat/Lon: %f/%f" facts.Center.Lat facts.Center.Lon;;
Lat/Lon: 33.833000/-118.217003
```

Calling Web Services Asynchronously

If you put a timer on these web service calls, you would see that they take significant time to execute, even seconds depending on your network connection, and this can be a serious idle time for your application. To remedy this problem, you can either minimize the number of web service calls through some sort of caching (for instance, in a web application you can store web service data in the session or even the application state and reuse it instead of making new calls) or make these calls in parallel, *asynchronously*. For example, it makes sense to connect to two webs services simultaneously and wait for both responses to come back before proceeding with the rest of an operation.

The easiest and most compositional way to access a web service asynchronously is to use the *asynchronous workflows* discussed in Chapter 13. The proxy code generated for the web service includes methods such as BeginGetWeatherByPlaceName and EndGetWeatherByPlaceName that follow the style for .NET library asynchronous invocations described in Chapter 13. We first map these pairs of operations into methods that construct asynchronous tasks. As in Chapter 13, we do this by defining extension members to the types in the generated code.

```
type WebReferences.WeatherForecast with
    member ws.GetWeatherByPlaceNameAsyncr(placeName) =
        Async.BuildPrimitive(placeName,
                            ws.BeginGetWeatherByPlaceName,
                            ws.EndGetWeatherByPlaceName)
```

```
type WebReferences.TerraService with
    member ws.GetPlaceFactsAsyncr(place) =
        Async.BuildPrimitive(place,
                                ws.BeginGetPlaceFacts,
                                ws.EndGetPlaceFacts)
```

These have the following types:

```
member ws.GetWeatherByPlaceNameAsyncr : placeName:string -> Async<WeatherForecast>
member ws.GetPlaceFactsAsyncr: place:string -> Async<PlaceFacts>
```

We can now define various asynchronous tasks using these primitives. For example, we can define a function getWeather that collects both the weather and position data for a given location but executes the two calls simultaneously.

```
let getWeather(city,state,country) =
    async { let ws = new WeatherForecast()
            let ts = new TerraService()
            let place = new Place(City=city, State=state, Country=country)
            let! weather,facts =
                Async.Parallel2
                    (ws.GetWeatherByPlaceNameAsyncr(city),
                     ts.GetPlaceFactsAsyncr(place))
            let today = weather.Details.[0]
            return (today.MinTemperatureF,today.MaxTemperatureC,
                    facts.Center.Lat,facts.Center.Lon) }
```

The type of this function is as follows:

```
val getWeather : string * string * string -> Async<string * string * float * float>
```

One simple use of this task is to run it and print the results when the operation completes:

```
Async.Run (async { let! (maxF,maxC,lat,lon) = getWeather("Los Angeles","CA","USA")
                   do printfn "Temperature: %sF/%sC" maxF maxC
                   do printfn "Lat/Lon: %f/%f" lat lon })
```

With an active web connection, this results in output such as the following (after a short delay while the connections are resolved):

```
Temperature: 100F/38C
Lat/Lon: 33.833000/-118.217003
```

Summary

In this chapter, you saw how you can use F# to perform a range of web programming tasks. You started by using sockets and TCP/IP to implement a web server directly, an example of a system network programming task. We then described how ASP.NET can be used to implement web applications involving HTML and input server controls and how to use embedded scripts and code-behind files. We also showed how you can access a database using F# Linq and display data coming from this database. You then looked briefly at web applications that incorporate significant client-side scripting using F# Web Tools and finally took a quick look at how to use web services from F#, including making compositional asynchronous invocations of web services.

Data access is a topic that complements web programming and often forms a major part of server-based web applications. In the next chapter, you will look at how to access relational databases from F# programs and also at other aspects of working with data from F#.

CHAPTER 15

■ ■ ■

Working with Data

Software applications deal with data in a wide array of forms: single values such as integers or strings; composite values paired together as tuples, records, or objects; collections of smaller pieces of data represented as lists, sets, arrays, or sequences; XML strings with tags describing the shape and kind of data; or data coming from relational or object-oriented databases, just to name a few.

In this chapter, we look at ways of working with some common data sources:

- In Chapter 3 you saw that sequences, similar to other enumerable data types such as lists, arrays, maps, and sets, have various aggregate iteration, query, and transform operators. We first look at how these operators can be used in a straightforward manner to form SQL-like operations over in-memory collections. This mechanism can be further tuned and applied to other data sources where the original data source is mapped to a sequence.

- We cover how you can work with relational databases from F# programs using the ADO.NET libraries. We discuss how you can connect to a database; create, update, and delete tables and records using simple SQL statements; access database data sequentially; and work with parts of tables using disconnected in-memory representations. You will also learn how to manage database connections and data sources; create databases; add new tables; and work with relationships, constraints, and stored procedures using Visual Studio.

- We cover how the Language Integrated Query (LINQ) infrastructure can be used in combination with F# meta-programming to bring relational data query logic into reach without explicit use of SQL. The essential goal here is to write database queries in F# itself using the same techniques you use to query in-memory data structures.

- Finally, we look at the use of XML as a generic data format. You already saw in Chapter 9 how to work with the XML Document Object Model (DOM), and we briefly survey how to desugar XML into sequences using LinqToXml.

Querying In-Memory Data Structures

Query languages are often made up of building blocks that transform and filter data. Functional programming gives you the basic tools that allow you to apply standard query logic on all F# types that are compatible with the F# sequence type, such as F# lists, arrays, sequences, and anything else that implements the `IEnumerable<'a>`/`seq<'a>` interface.

Select/Where/From Queries Using Aggregate Operators

Consider the following aggregate operators described in Chapter 3:

```
let select = Seq.map
let where  = Seq.filter
```

Here we have renamed the operations in the F# Seq module to correspond to more standard database query terminology: the select operator is defined as a transform operation, since in a selection we are taking sequence elements and mapping (often narrowing) them to new values. Similarly, the where operator is defined as a filter applied on a sequence that takes an 'a -> bool predicate to filter out the desired elements. You can use these aggregate operators in a straightforward manner to query and transform in-memory data. The only other piece you need is the glue that will make the query and transform operators work together: the standard pipe operator (|>). Recall that this operator simply "flips" the order of its arguments; being an infix operator, it feeds the left-side argument into the function on the right. This is useful, because the argument to the function is seen before the function itself, propagating important typing information into the function.

For instance, given a string * int * string array, representing the name, age, and department of various employees, you can select those names that start with letter *R* as follows:

```
let people = [| ("Joe", 27, "Sales");  ("Rick", 35, "Marketing");
                ("Mark", 40, "Sales"); ("Rob", 31, "Administration");
                ("Bob", 34, "Marketing") |]

let namesR =
    people |> select (fun (name, age, dept) -> name)
           |> where  (fun name -> name.StartsWith "R")
```

Note that the types of name, age, and dept have been inferred from people, and no type annotation is necessary. Finding those people who work in sales and are older than 30 years old is also straightforward:

```
> let namesSalesOver30 =
    people |> where  (fun (_, age, _)  -> age >= 30)
           |> where  (fun (_, _, dept) -> dept = "Sales")
           |> select (fun (name, _, _) -> name);;
val namesSalesOver30 : seq<string>

> namesSalesOver30;;
val it : seq<string> = seq ["Mark"]
```

Using Aggregate Operators in Queries

In the previous section, we used alternative names such as `select` and `where` for some standard F# operations such as `Seq.map` and `Seq.filter`. This is for illustrative purposes to show the connection between these operators and SQL-like querying. In most F# code, you should just continue to use the standard F# operators from the `Seq` module.

Besides the restriction (`filter`/`where`) and projection (`map`/`select`) operators, the `Seq` module contains many other useful functions, many of which were described in Chapter 3, and you can easily define further operators. For instance, you can define sorting over sequences by using sorting over a more concrete data structure:

```
let sortBy comp seq = seq |> Seq.to_list |> List.sort comp |> Seq.of_list
let revOrder i j = -(compare i j)
```

Here the inferred types are as follows:

```
val sortBy : ('a -> 'a -> int) -> #seq<'a> -> seq<'a>
val revOrder : 'a -> 'a -> int
```

The function `sortBy` takes a comparison function `comp` as an argument and converts its enumerable argument to a list and back as it performs the sorting. `revOrder` provides a comparison function that reverses the default ordering for a type by negating the result of the generic comparison function `compare` discussed in Chapter 5 and Chapter 8. Note that `sortBy` will evaluate all elements in the sequence as it converts it to a list, so you should use it with care when the source sequence is large or potentially infinite.

Another useful query-like function is `Seq.truncate`, which takes the first n elements and truncates the rest. Using these new operators—given, for example, an unbounded stream of random numbers—you can extract the first three even numbers and return a pair of those numbers and their square in reverse order, as the following example shows:

```
let rand = System.Random()
let numbers = seq { while true do yield rand.Next(1000) }

numbers |> Seq.filter (fun i -> i % 2 = 0)  // "where"
        |> Seq.truncate 3
        |> sortBy revOrder
        |> Seq.map (fun i -> i, i*i)         // "select"
```

```
// random - results will vary!
val it : seq<int * int> = seq [(814, 662596); (686, 470596); (242, 58564)]
```

Accumulating Using "Folding" Operators

Some of the most general operators supported by most F# data structures are the fold, fold_left, and fold_right operators. These apply a function to each element of a collection and accumulate a result. For fold_left and fold_right, the function is applied in left-to-right or right-to-left order, respectively. If the name fold is used, then typically the ordering is left to right. Both functions also take an initial value for the accumulator. For example:

```
> List.fold_left (fun acc x -> acc + x) 0 [4; 5; 6];;
val it : int = 15

> Seq.fold (fun acc x -> acc + x) 0.0 [4.0; 5.0; 6.0];;
val it : float = 15.0

> List.fold_right (fun x acc -> min x acc) [4; 5; 6; 3; 5] System.Int32.MaxValue;;
val it : int = 3
```

The following are equivalent, but no explicit anonymous function values have been used:

```
> List.fold_left (+) 0 [4; 5; 6];;
val it : int = 15

> Seq.fold (+) 0.0 [4.0; 5.0; 6.0];;
val it : float = 15.0

> List.fold_right min [4; 5; 6; 3; 5] System.Int32.MaxValue;;
val it : int = 3
```

If used carefully, the various fold_right operators are pleasantly compositional, because they let you apply a selection function as part of the accumulating function:

```
> List.fold_right (fst >> min) [(3, "three"); (5, "five")] System.Int32.MaxValue;;
val it : int = 3
```

At the time of writing, the F# library also includes more direct accumulation functions such as Seq.sumByFloat and Seq.sumByInt. These use a fixed accumulation function (addition) with a fixed initial value (zero).

■**Caution** Folding operators are very powerful and can help you avoid many explicit uses of recursion or loops in your code. However, they are sometimes overused in functional programming and can be hard for novice users to read and understand. Take the time to document uses of these operators, or consider using them to build simpler operators that apply a particular accumulation function.

Expressing Some Queries Using Sequence Expressions

Using aggregate operators to form queries is closely related to the sequence expression notation described in Chapter 3 and is used frequently in this book. For example, namesSalesOver30 defined previously can also be defined as follows:

```
seq { for (name, age, dept) in people do
        if (age >= 30 && dept = "Sales") then
            yield name }
```

This is simply a different notation for the same computation. For very simple queries, F# sequence expressions also support an even more compact form where if/then clauses are replaced by when, the final do is dropped from the for statement, and yield is replaced by ->:

```
seq { for (name, age, dept) in people
      when (age >= 30 && dept = "Sales")
      -> name }
```

There is no difference between these two sequence expressions—it's just a matter of syntax. You can use sequence expressions in conjunction with the |> operator. For example:

```
seq { for i in numbers do
        if i % 2 = 0 then
            yield (i, i*i) }
|> Seq.truncate 3
|> sortBy revOrder
```

There are pros and cons to using sequence expression syntax for some parts of queries:

- Sequence expressions are very good for the subset of queries expressed using iteration (for), mapping (select/yield), and filtering (if/then/when/where). They are particularly good for queries containing multiple nested for statements.

- Other query constructs such as ordering, truncating, grouping, and aggregating must be expressed directly using aggregate operators such as Seq.orderBy and Seq.groupBy.

- Some queries depend on the index position of an item within a stream. These are best expressed directly using aggregate operators such as Seq.mapi.

- Many queries are often part of a longer series of transformations chained by |> operators. Often the type of the data being transformed at each step varies substantially through the chain of operators. These queries are best expressed using aggregate operator chains.

■**Note** It is likely that in the future the F# sequence expression syntax will include support for specifying grouping and aggregation operations within the expression syntax. However, at the time of writing, it was necessary to explicitly use operators such as Seq.orderBy and Seq.groupBy for these operations.

IN-MEMORY QUERIES AND LINQ

In this section you saw how you can use aggregate sequence operators and sequence expressions to query and manipulate in-memory data structures using a SQL-like syntax. This is essentially the idea behind Microsoft's LINQ technology. We apply the same techniques to queries over relational data (LINQ to SQL) later in this chapter.

In Chapter 3 you saw that sequences can be used to wrap collections and that a number of collection data types implement the sequence interface. It is possible to provide parallel implementations for the iteration, aggregation, and transformation operations of these data types—for instance, a parallel list implementation that uses worker threads—and assume independence between the transformation steps. This idea forms the basis of PLINQ, a parallel version of LINQ. PLINQ also covers LINQ to SQL where parallelism is introduced in the SQL code that is generated behind the scenes.

Using Databases to Manage Data

Storing data in various files, reading them into memory, and querying and manipulating the resulting in-memory data collection is a sufficient approach for many applications working with data, but there comes a point where a more persistent data handling is required.

For example, consider a business that has two applications that need to access the same set of data about employees. One way to do this is to store data in a text file and work with this data file from both applications. But this approach is quite vulnerable; you would quickly realize how redundant text files can get when adding new pieces of data (say you wanted to add an address next to the name, department, and age of each employee) or if you wanted to group your employee data by introducing various relationships (say, multiple addresses per employee). Even if you did manage to find a good storage alternative, you would still have to modify both applications to read and write this new data format. Databases make scenarios like these much easier to cope with by enforcing centralized control of persistent data (data that is more persistent than what appears in a single application) and by giving you the freedom to define, manipulate, and query this data in an application-neutral way.

Databases give you many benefits; some of the more important ones are listed here:

- *Data security:* Having a centralized control of data, it becomes possible to erect a full security system around your data, giving specific access rules for each type of access or parts of the database.

- *Sharing of data*: Any number of applications with the appropriate access rights can "connect" to your database and read the data stored within—all without the need to worry about containing the logic to extract this data. As you will see shortly, applications use various query languages (most notably SQL) to communicate with databases.

- *A logical organization of data*: You can write new applications that work with the same data without having to worry about how the data is physically represented and stored. On the basic level, this logical structure is given by a set of entities (data tables) and their relationships.

- *Avoiding data redundancy*: Having all requirements from each consuming application up front helps to identify a logical organization for your data that minimizes possible redundancy. For instance, you can use foreign keys instead of duplicating pieces of data. *Data normalization* is the process of systematically eliminating data redundancy, a large but essential topic that we don't consider in this book.

- *Transactions*: Reading from and writing to databases occurs atomically, and as a result two concurrent transactions can never leave data in an inconsistent, inaccurate state. *Isolation levels* refer to the specific measures taken to ensure transaction isolation by locking various parts of the database (fields, records, tables). Higher isolation levels increase locking overhead and can lead to a loss of parallelism by rendering concurrent transactions sequential; on the other hand, no isolation can lead to inconsistent data.

- *Maintaining data integrity*: In other words, databases make sure that the data stored within is accurate. Having no redundancy is one way to maintain data integrity (if a piece of data is changed, it is changed in the only place it occurs; thus, it remains accurate); on the other hand, data security and transaction isolation are needed to ensure that the data stored is modified in a controlled manner.

THE RELATIONAL MODEL: DATA RELATIONS

A relational database table is essentially a two-dimensional matrix with rows (records) and columns (fields). A *primary key* is a column that uniquely identifies each row, and that means you cannot store the same value in a primary key column of any two records (so it is also a *unique key*). The primary key is usually a single numeric column, but it can also be composed as a set of columns, in which case it is called a *composite primary key*.

Tables can be linked or related to one another using relationships. To set up a relationship, you need *foreign keys*, which are columns that store primary key values in a "host" table. For instance, in a *one-to-one relationship*, a record in table A can be associated with a record in table B by A containing a foreign key to B's primary key column, or vice versa, or both, depending on the *navigability* of the relationship. A one-to-one relationship is rare because it makes more sense to merge the two tables, unless the foreign key is allowed to be null. On the other hand, *one-to-many* (1..*) relationships are ubiquitous, allowing records in table A to be associated with multiple records in table B. For instance, a Customers table is likely to be associated with an Orders table this way, allowing each customer to have multiple orders. This can be modeled by storing a foreign key in Orders that refers to a Customers primary key. By moving two (or more) foreign keys in a separate so-called *association table*, we obtain a *many-to-many* relationship between those tables.

Referential integrity refers to the fact that only valid primary key values are allowed in a foreign key column.

Choosing Your Database Engine

Table 16-1 shows some of the most common database engines, all of which can be used from F# and .NET.

Table 16-1. *Common Databases*

Name	Type	Description	Available from
PostgreSQL	Open source	Open source database engine	http://postgresql.org/
SQLite	Open source	Small, embeddable, zero-configuration SQL database engine	http://www.sqlite.org/
Firebird	Open source	Based on Borland Interbase	http://www.firebirdsql.org/
MySQL	Open source	Reliable and popular database	http://www.mysql.com/
Mimer SQL	Commercial	Reliable database engine	http://www.mimer.com/
Oracle	Commercial	One of the most popular enterprise database engines	http://www.oracle.com/
SQL Server	Commercial	Microsoft's main database engine	http://www.microsoft.com/sql/default.mspx
SQL Server Express	Commercial	Free and easy-to-use version of SQL Server	http://www.microsoft.com/sql/editions/express/default.mspx
Sybase iAnywhere	Commercial	Mobile database engine	http://www.ianywhere.com/

Applications communicate with relational databases using Structured Query Language (SQL). Each time you create tables, create relationships, insert new records, or update or delete existing ones, you are explicitly or implicitly issuing SQL statements to the database. The examples in this chapter use a dialect of Standard SQL, called Transact-SQL (T-SQL), used by SQL Server and SQL Server Express. SQL has syntax to define the structure of a database schema (loosely speaking, a collection of data tables and their relations) and also syntax to manage the data within. These subsets of SQL are called *Data Definition Language* (DDL) and *Data Manipulation Language* (DML), respectively. The most important DDL statements are the following:

```
CREATE/ALTER/DROP TABLE
CREATE/DROP VIEW
```

Understanding ADO.NET

ADO.NET is the central database access machinery in the .NET Framework, and it provides full XML support, disconnected and typed datasets, scalability, and high performance. In this section, we give a brief overview of the ADO.NET fundamentals.

With ADO.NET, data is acquired through a *connection* to the database via a provider. This connection serves as a medium to execute a *command* against; this can be used to fetch, update, insert, or delete data from the data store. Statements and queries are articulated as SQL text (CREATE, SELECT, UPDATE, INSERT, and DELETE statements) and are passed to the command object's constructor. When you execute these statements, you obtain data (in the case of queries) or the number of affected rows (in the case of UPDATE, INSERT, or DELETE statements). The data returned can be processed via two main mechanisms: sequentially in a read-only fashion using a DataReader object or by loading it into an in-memory representation (a DataSet object) for further disconnected processing. DataSet objects store data in a set of table objects and along with them metadata that describes their relationships and constraints in a fully contained model.

ADO.NET 2.0 comes with four data providers: SQLClient, OleDb, Oracle, and Odbc. Table 16-2 describes them and a couple of more commonly used providers. These providers act as the main gateway to the database.

Table 16-2. *Common Data Providers*

Name	Namespace	Available From
SQLClient	System.Data.SqlClient	.NET 2.0
OleDb	System.Data.OleDb	.NET 2.0
Oracle	System.Data.OracleClient	.NET 2.0
ODBC	System.Data.Odbc	.NET 2.0
PostgreSQL	Npgsql	http://npgsql.projects.postgresql.org/
MySql	MySql.Data.MySqlClient	http://dev.mysql.com/downloads/

The OleDb and ODBC data providers are provided for compatibility with earlier database access technologies. All ADO.NET connection and command classes have the data provider name as the prefix to their class name, as in OdbcConnection and OdbcCommand or OleDbConnection and OleDbCommand.

Establishing Connections to a Database Engine

Before you can do any work with a database, you need to establish a connection to it. For instance, you can connect to a locally running instance of SQL Server 2005 Express using the following code:

```
open System.Data
open System.Data.SqlClient

let connString = @"Server='.\SQLEXPRESS';Integrated Security=SSPI"
let conn = new SqlConnection(connString)
```

The value connString is a connection string. Regardless of how you created your connection object, to execute any updates or queries on it you need to open it first:

```
> conn.Open();;
val it : unit = ()
```

If this command fails, then you may need to do one of the following:

- Install SQL Server 2005 Express or a newer version of the same.

- Consult the latest SQL Server Express samples for alternative connection strings.

- Add `UserInstance='true'` to the connection string. This starts the database engine as a user-level process.

- Change the connection string if you have a different database engine installed and running (for instance, if you are using SQL Server instead of SQL Server Express).

Connections established using the same connection string are pooled and reused depending on your database engine. Connections are often a limited resource and should generally be closed as soon as possible within your application.

■**Tip** The "More on Connection Strings" sidebar contains more details on creating and managing connection strings. A useful website for complete connection strings is `http://www.connectionstrings.com`.

Creating a Database

Now that we have established a connection to the database engine, we can explicitly create a database from F# code by executing a SQL statement directly. For example, you can create a database called company as follows:

```
open System.Data
open System.Data.SqlClient

let execNonQuery conn s =
    let comm = new SqlCommand(s, conn, CommandTimeout = 10)
    comm.ExecuteNonQuery() |> ignore

execNonQuery conn "CREATE DATABASE company"
```

You will be using execNonQuery in the subsequent sections. This method takes a connection object and a SQL string and executes it as a SQL command, ignoring its result.

■**Note** If you try to create the same database twice, you will receive a runtime exception. However, if you do intend to drop an existing database, you can do so by issuing a DROP DATABASE company SQL command. The DROP command can also be used for other database artifacts, including tables, views, and stored procedures.

MORE ON CONNECTION STRINGS

Before a connection can be opened, its ConnectionString property has to be initialized, typically by passing it to the connection constructor. Although you can assemble this connection string by hand, it is error prone because it is subject to various insertion traps, and the exact keys that various providers accept are many and hard to remember.

For these reasons, it is common to either externalize entire connection strings in configuration files (discussed next) or use a ConnectionStringBuilder object from the appropriate provider namespace. This object contains all the known connection keys as properties that can be safely set, avoiding passing values of incorrect type or misspelling the key names. Consider the following example (this time, using SQL Server running on localhost and referencing the company database; initially, before that database is created, you should remove the InitialCatalog reference from your connection string):

```
open System.Data
open System.Data.SqlClient

let connStr = new SqlConnectionStringBuilder(DataSource="localhost",
                                             IntegratedSecurity=true,
                                             InitialCatalog="company")
```

On the other hand, not all keys accepted by the various providers are contained in these builder objects, and it is sometimes necessary to add custom key/value pairs. You can do this by using the Add method. For instance, for an OleDb provider, user credentials can be given as follows:

```
connStr.Add("User Id",  "your_user_id")
connStr.Add("Password", "your_password")
```

This naturally requires extra care to ensure that the proper keys are assigned. You can now access the resulting connection string by reading the ConnectionString property and use it to create a connection object:

```
let conn = new SqlConnection(connStr.ConnectionString)
```

You can also store your connection strings in configuration files (web.config for web applications or YourProgram.exe.config for regular applications). The main advantage here is that connection details can be configured without affecting the application. Consider the following configuration file:

```
<?xml version='1.0' encoding='utf-8'?>
<configuration>
  <connectionStrings>
    <add name="MyCS"
         connectionString="Data Source='localhost';Initial Catalog='company'" />
  </connectionStrings>
</configuration>
```

This defines a new connection string called MyCS. From within your application, you can read the value of this connection string using the ConfigurationManager class:

```
#r "System.Configuration.dll"
open System.Configuration
open System.Data.SqlClient

let cs = ConfigurationManager.ConnectionStrings.Item("MyCS")
let conn = new SqlConnection(cs.ConnectionString)
```

For this to work, make sure you reference `System.Configuration.dll` in your project properties using the `-r` option, or use the `#r` directive in your code as above, because this DLL is not automatically included at compile time.

Creating Tables, Inserting, and Fetching Records

You can execute a simple SQL command to create a table; all you need is to specify its data fields and their types and whether null values are allowed. In the following example, we create an Employees table with a primary key EmpID and FirstName, LastName, and Birthday fields.

```
execNonQuery conn "CREATE TABLE Employees (
    EmpID int NOT NULL,
    FirstName varchar(50) NOT NULL,
    LastName varchar(50) NOT NULL,
    Birthday datetime,
    PRIMARY KEY (EmpID))"
```

We can now insert two new records as follows:

```
execNonQuery conn "INSERT INTO Employees (EmpId, FirstName, LastName, Birthday)
    VALUES (1001, 'Joe', 'Smith', '02/14/1965')"
```

```
execNonQuery conn "INSERT INTO Employees (EmpId, FirstName, LastName, Birthday)
    VALUES (1002, 'Mary', 'Jones', '09/15/1985')"
```

and retrieve two columns of what was inserted using a fresh connection and a data reader:

```
let query() =
    seq { use conn = new SqlConnection(connString)
          do conn.Open()
          use comm = new SqlCommand("SELECT FirstName, Birthday FROM Employees",
                                    conn)
          use reader = comm.ExecuteReader()
          while reader.Read() do
              yield (reader.GetString 0, reader.GetDateTime 1)  }
```

When we evaluate the query expression in F# Interactive, a connection to the database is created and opened, the command is built, and the reader is used to read successive elements:

```
> fsi.AddPrinter(fun (d: System.DateTime) -> d.ToString());;
val it : unit = ()

> query();;
val it : seq<string * System.DateTime> =
    seq [("Joe", 14/02/1965 00:00:00); ("Mary", 15/09/1985 00:00:00)]
```

The definition of query uses sequence expressions that locally define new IDisposable objects such as conn, comm, and reader using declarations of the form use *var* = *expr*. These ensure that the locally defined connection, command, and reader objects are disposed after exhausting the entire sequence. See Chapters 4, 8, and 9 for more details on sequence expressions of this kind.

F# sequences are on-demand (that is, lazy), and the definition of query does not itself open a connection to the database. This is done when the sequence is first iterated, and indeed a connection is maintained until the sequence is exhausted.

Note that the command object's ExecuteReader method returns a DataReader instance that is used to extract the typed data returned from the query. You can read from the resulting sequence in a straightforward manner using a sequence iterator. For instance, we can use a simple anonymous function to print data on the screen:

```
> query() |> Seq.iter (fun (fn, bday) -> printfn "%s has birthday %O" fn bday);;
Joe has birthday 14/02/1965 00:00:00
Mary has birthday 15/09/1985 00:00:00
val it : unit = ()
```

The query brings the data from the database "in-memory," though still as a lazy sequence. You can then use standard F# in-memory data transformations on the result:

```
> query()
  |> Seq.filter (fun (nm, bday) -> bday < System.DateTime.Parse("01/01/1985"))
  |> Seq.length;;
val it : int = 1
```

However, be aware that these additional transformations are happening in-memory and not on the database.

The command object has different methods for executing different queries. For instance, if you have a nonselect query, you need to use the ExecuteNonQuery method (for UPDATE, INSERT, or DELETE statements, like previously in execNonQuery), which returns the number of rows affected (updated, inserted, or deleted), or the ExecuteScalar method, which returns the first column of the first row of the result providing a fast and efficient way to extract a single value, such as the number of rows in a table or a result set.

In the previous command, we extracted fields from the result rows using GetXXX methods on the reader object. The particular methods have to match the types of the fields selected in the SQL query, and a mismatch will result in a runtime InvalidCastException. For these and other reasons, DataReader tends to be suitable only in situations when the following items are true:

- You need to read data only in a sequential order (as returned from the database). DataReader provides forward-only data access.

- The field types of the result are known, and the query is not configurable.

- You are reading only and not writing data. DataReader provides read-only access.

- Your use of the DataReader is localized. The data connection is open throughout the reader loop.

COMMAND BEHAVIORS

Database connections are precious resources, and you should always release them as soon as possible. In the previous case, we did this by using a locally defined connection. It is also sufficient to implicitly close the reader by constructing it with the CloseConnection option that causes it to release and close the data connection upon closing the reader instance.

Further, common options include SchemaOnly that you can use to extract field information only (without any data returned), SingleResult to extract a single value only (the same as using the ExecuteScalar method discussed earlier), SingleRow to extract a single row, and KeyInfo to extract additional columns (appended to the end of the selected ones) automatically that uniquely identify the rows returned.

Using Untyped Datasets

Datasets allow applications to work in a so-called disconnected mode, which means the application connects to the database, loads relevant data to an in-memory representation, and processes the data locally. When the processing is completed, the data in the in-memory dataset can be synchronized with the database.

ADO.NET datasets are compact in-memory databases and provide similar functionality to real databases; however, they are designed to work with a limited amount of data. A DataSet contains a collection of tables, the relationships between those tables, and various constraints. Tables are represented by the DataTable type. And like in a SQL server, tables are defined by their columns (DataColumn objects), and the data is stored in rows (DataRow objects).

In ADO.NET, the loading of data to the dataset and the synchronization to the database are coordinated by *data adapters*, for instance, SqlDataAdapter objects. Consider the following example in which we define a buildDataSet function that takes a connection and a SQL SELECT query and returns the resulting DataSet object:

```
let dataAdapter = new SqlDataAdapter()

let buildDataSet conn queryString =
    dataAdapter.SelectCommand <- new SqlCommand(queryString, conn)
    let dataSet = new DataSet()
    // This line is needed to configure the command
    let _ = new SqlCommandBuilder(dataAdapter)
    dataAdapter.Fill(dataSet) |> ignore  // ignore the number of records returned
    dataSet
```

The inferred types are as follows:

```
val dataAdapter : SqlDataAdapter
val buildDataSet : SqlConnection -> string -> DataSet
```

When setting up the data adapter, we initialize its SelectCommand property to the query string that was passed as an argument. This SQL query will be used to populate the DataSet when the Fill method is called. The somewhat mysterious line let _ = new SqlCommandBuilder(dataAdapter) creates a command builder object, which has the side effect of building the INSERT, UPDATE, and DELETE commands automatically from the query in SelectCommand, making the dataset capable of persisting changes. Also, note that we do not have to worry about opening or closing connections, because this is all taken care of with the data adapter; all we need is the connection object itself.

```
let dataSet =
    buildDataSet conn "SELECT EmpID, FirstName, LastName, Birthday from Employees"
```

The resulting DataSet will contain a single table that we obtain by index and print its content. This table is assembled based on the query and contains the columns that were part of the SELECT statement.

```
let table = dataSet.Tables.Item(0)
for row in table.Rows do
    printfn "%O, %O - %O"
        (row.Item "LastName")
        (row.Item "FirstName")
        (row.Item "Birthday")
```

When run in F# Interactive, this produces the following output:

```
Smith, Joe - 14/02/1965 00:00:00
Jones, Mary - 15/09/1985 00:00:00
```

You can refer to each column of a row by the same field name that was used in the SELECT query. Adding a new row to table is treated similarly:

```
let row = table.NewRow()
row.Item("EmpID") <- 1003
row.Item("FirstName") <- "Eve"
row.Item("LastName") <- "Smith"
row.Item("Birthday") <- System.DateTime.Today
table.Rows.Add row
dataAdapter.Update(dataSet) |> ignore  // ignore the number of affected rows
```

Repeating the SQL query from the previous section reveals the addition of the new entry to the database table:

```
> query();;
val it : seq<string * System.DateTime> =
    seq [("Joe", 14/02/1965 00:00:00);
         ("Mary", 15/09/1985 00:00:00);
         ("Eve", 27/09/2007 00:00:00)]
```

Note that we utilize the INSERT statement that was built by the command builder object based on the selection query. Using untyped datasets is a great way to execute dynamic queries and to provide ad hoc access to your data. On the other hand, the lack of strong typing means that it suffers from possible type mismatches or incorrect field names.

Generating Typed Datasets Using xsd.exe

Typed datasets are derived from ordinary datasets and allow you to work with data in a type-safe manner. This means that instead of (row.Item "FirstName" :?> string), you can simply write row.FirstName. Typed datasets can be created using the xsd.exe command-line tool included in the .NET SDK. This tool generates source code from XML schema documents, so to use it you must obtain an XSD document for the tables you want data objects for. (You can quickly generate an XML schema document using Visual Studio; select File ➤ New ➤ File ➤ XML Schema, and drag the needed data tables onto the design canvas.)

Alternatively, we can extract this schema definition using code:

```
open System.IO

let dataSet2 = buildDataSet conn "SELECT * FROM Employees"
let file name = Path.Combine(@"c:\fsharp", name)

do File.WriteAllText(file "employees.xsd", dataSet2.GetXmlSchema())
```

Using this extracted XSD document, we can now fire up xsd.exe from the command-line shell:

```
C:\fsharp> xsd.exe employees.xsd /d /l:CS /n:Employees.Data
Writing file 'C:\fsharp\Employees.cs'.
C:\fsharp> csc /target:library Employees.cs
```

This generates a C# file Employees.cs in the Employees.Data namespace containing a typed dataset for the Employees table, which we then compile to Employees.dll. We can now reference this DLL and create an instance of a typed dataset:

```
> #r @"employees.dll";;
Binding session to 'C:\fsharp\Employees.dll'...

> let employeesTable = new Employees.Data.NewDataSet();;
val employeesTable : Employees.Data.NewDataSet

> dataAdapter.Fill(employeesTable) |> ignore;;   // ignore the number of records
val it : unit = ()

> for emp in employeesTable._Table do
    printfn "%s, %s - %O" emp.LastName emp.FirstName emp.Birthday;;
Smith, Joe - 14/02/1965 00:00:00
Jones, Mary - 15/09/1985 00:00:00
Smith, Eve - 27/09/2007 00:00:00
```

Note that in the iteration emp is known to have a strong type that allows us to access fields LastName, FirstName, and Birthday.

Finally, it is very easy to dump out XML for our data:

```
> printf "%s" (employeesTable.GetXml());;
<NewDataSet>
  <Table>
    <EmpID>1001</EmpID>
    <FirstName>Joe</FirstName>
    <LastName>Smith</LastName>
    <Birthday>1965-02-14T00:00:00+00:00</Birthday>
  </Table>
  <Table>
    <EmpID>1002</EmpID>
    <FirstName>Mary</FirstName>
    <LastName>Jones</LastName>
    <Birthday>1985-09-15T00:00:00+01:00</Birthday>
  </Table>
```

```
<Table>
  <EmpID>1003</EmpID>
  <FirstName>Eve</FirstName>
  <LastName>Smith</LastName>
  <Birthday>2007-09-27T00:00:00+01:00</Birthday>
</Table>
</NewDataSet>
```

or to write it to a file:

```
> System.IO.File.WriteAllText(file "employees.xml", employeesTable.GetXml());;
val it : unit = ()
```

Using Stored Procedures

Stored procedures are defined and stored in your relational database and provide a number of benefits over literal SQL. First, they are external to the application and thus provide a clear division of the data logic from the rest of the application. This enables you to make data-related modifications without having to change application code or having to redeploy the application. Second, they are stored in the database in a prepared or compiled form and thus are executed more efficiently than literal SQL statements (although those can be "prepared" as well at a one-time cost, but they are still contained in application space, which is undesirable). Supplying arguments to stored procedures simply instantiates the compiled formula.

In Visual Studio, you can add stored procedures just like any other database artifacts using the Server Explorer window by right-clicking the Stored Procedures item in the appropriate database and selecting Add New Stored Procedure. This creates a stored procedure template that can be easily customized. Alternatively, you can add stored procedures programmatically using the CREATE PROCEDURE SQL command. Consider the following stored procedure that returns the first and last names of all employees whose last name matches the given pattern:

```
execNonQuery conn "
CREATE PROCEDURE dbo.GetEmployeesByLastName
        (
        @Name nvarchar(50)
        )
AS
    SELECT
        Employees.FirstName, Employees.LastName
    FROM Employees
    WHERE Employees.LastName LIKE @Name"
```

We can wrap this stored procedure in a function as follows:

```
let GetEmployeesByLastName (name: string) =
    use comm = new SqlCommand("GetEmployeesByLastName", conn,
                        CommandType=CommandType.StoredProcedure)
```

```
comm.Parameters.AddWithValue("@Name", name) |> ignore
use adapter = new SqlDataAdapter(comm)
let table = new DataTable()
adapter.Fill(table) |> ignore
table
```

We can execute the stored procedure as follows to find the employees with the last name Smith:

```
> for row in (GetEmployeesByLastName "Smith").Rows do
    printfn "row = %O, %O" (row.Item("FirstName")) (row.Item("LastName"));;
row = Joe, Smith
row = Eve, Smith
val it : unit = ()
```

Using Data Grids

You saw in Chapter 14 how data tables can be visualized in web applications. The return value of GetEmployeesByLastName from the previous section is a DataTable. These objects can also be directly bound to a Windows Forms data grid, a visual data control that supports the DataSource property and that can display data in a tabular format. Windows Forms controls were discussed in Chapter 11.

```
open System.Windows.Forms

let emps = GetEmployeesByLastName "Smith"
let grid = new DataGrid(Width=300, Height=200, DataSource=emps)
let form = new Form(Visible=true, TopMost=true)
form.Controls.Add(grid)
```

Figure 15-1 shows what you will see when you run this code.

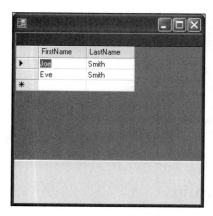

Figure 15-1. *Calling the GetEmployeesByLastName stored procedure*

Stored procedures can also perform deletions or updates (executed via the `ExecuteNonQuery()` method of the command object) or return data through "out" parameters. These can be defined using the `OUTPUT` keyword after a single parameter definition in the stored procedure. When calling the stored procedure, the out parameter has to have its direction set to `ParameterDirection.Output`, and after executing the stored procedure, its return value can be read using the `Value` property of the given parameter.

Working with Databases in Visual Studio

Many of the database tasks you saw earlier in this chapter can be easily performed using the built-in capabilities of Visual Studio. It also gives you good tools for working with stored procedures and views, building SQL queries, or designing entity models.

Creating a Database

Assuming you have a version of SQL Server installed, you can create a new SQL Server database in Visual Studio's Server Explorer (Ctrl+Alt+S, or View ➤ Server Explorer) by right-clicking Data Connections and selecting the Create New SQL Server Database menu item. In the screen shown in Figure 15-2, you can configure your connection details and specify the name of the new SQL Server database.

Figure 15-2. *Creating a new Microsoft SQL Server database*

Besides creating a new database, this also creates a Server Explorer connection to the new database, which you can use in Visual Studio to browse, create, manipulate, or delete tables, triggers, views, stored procedures, functions, and other database artifacts.

Visual Data Modeling: Adding Relationships

Various tools exist to assist application architects in designing their data layer. On a logical level, entity-relationship (ER) models provide a visual representation of data tables and their relationships, showing table fields, primary and foreign keys, and various constraints. Visual

Studio simplifies the design process and supports visual modeling, so let's take a brief look at how you can exploit its capabilities.

In the previous section, you used Visual Studio to create an SQL Server database called company, and earlier you saw how to create a table to store data about employees. We now want to extend this database with a new table that stores addresses and link the existing Employees table to it to enable us to store an optional address record for each employee. This means we allow multiple employees to live at the same address, but not multiple addresses for a given employee.

You can start by creating the Addresses table by right-clicking Add New Table from the Tables list item in Server Explorer ➤ Data Connections under the company database. You should add the columns shown in Figure 15-3.

	Column Name	Data Type	Allow Nulls
▶🔑	AddID	int	☐
	Street	varchar(50)	☑
	City	varchar(50)	☑
	State	varchar(50)	☑
	Zip	varchar(10)	☑
			☐

Figure 15-3. *The Addresses table in the designer mode*

Note that we designated AddID as a non-null primary key (right-click, select Set Primary Key, and clear the Allow Nulls flag). Also, under the Column Properties you should set the Is Identity property to Yes; this will take care of automatically incrementing the primary key value when inserting new records. Next, create a new database diagram and add/drag your existing two tables, Employees and Addresses, onto it. Before you can add a relationship between these two tables, you must create a new nullable field in the Employees table to store the address foreign key; you should call it AddressID.

Now you are ready to link the two tables. First, right-click the Employees table, and select Relationships. Next, click Add to add a new foreign key relationship, name it FK_Employee_Address under Identity, and then click the ellipsis icon next to Tables and Columns Specification under General to configure the relationship. The foreign key table (the table that stores references to rows in another table) is Employees, and this is grayed out since you started by adding a relationship to the Employees table, but you can select the foreign key field to be AddressID. Then select the primary key table to be Addresses, with the field AddID. This will link the two tables by storing unique address IDs in the AddressID field of the Employees table records, giving you a one-to-many relationship between addresses and employees. Figure 15-4 shows our table design canvas after we are done. Similarly, linking two primary keys will yield a one-to-one relationship.

■Note Linking tables via explicit relationships and controlling the nullability of the foreign key columns gives you fine control of referential integrity. For instance, you will run into a foreign key violation if you try to remove a record that is linked to another by a foreign key constraint. On the other hand, storing raw primary key values without an explicit constraint in related tables will lose these benefits.

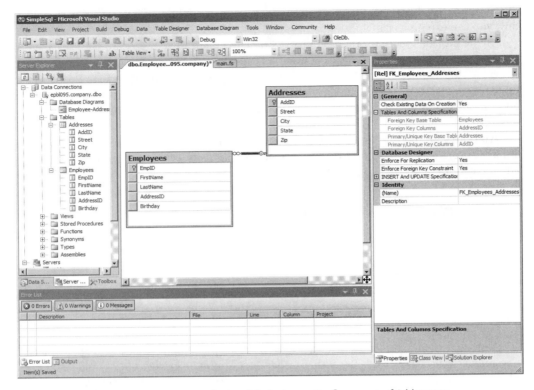

Figure 15-4. *Adding a one-to-many relationship between* `Employees` *and* `Addresses`

In the previous example, you had made the `AddressID` field nullable, meaning that it is possible that not every employee will have an address. You can also control what happens if employees or addresses are removed or updated. (However, as a design decision you need to carefully consider one-to-many relationships such as those shown earlier: should the change in the address of one employee cause the same change in the addresses of all other employees with the same address? Probably, if indeed it is the same address; otherwise, a particular employee should be updated with a different address record.) Placing a cascade on deletes will remove all records that are linked to a record that is deleted; naturally you should treat this option with care.

Accessing Relational Data with F# LinqToSql

In the following sections, we show how to perform relational database queries using F# LinqToSql. F# LinqToSql uses F# quotation meta-programming to represent SQL queries. These are then translated across to SQL and executed using the Microsoft LINQ libraries that are part of the .NET Framework 3.5. At the time of writing, you can work with F# LinqToSql as part of the Beta 2 release of this framework, but check the latest samples in the F# distribution for full details and updates. In the following sections, we will assume we are working with the `Northwnd.mdf` database, a common database used in many LINQ samples. You can find instructions on downloading this sample database at `http://www.expert-fsharp.com/Topics/Linq`.

Generating the Object/Relational Mapping

The first step in using LINQ with F# is to generate the code that implements the *object/relational* (O/R) mapping for the database tables to which you are connecting. Let's first look at why you want to do this. You learned previously how you can create simple tables and store and retrieve data using SQL code. However, this approach doesn't work well for large data schemas with multiple related tables and constraints. For instance, creating a hierarchy of records in a number of related tables connected by foreign keys involves issuing multiple SQL statements to create the base data and to connect them in ways that obey the foreign key and other constraints that may be in place. Instead, it can often be much better to view records in tables as if they were objects. This is part of what an O/R mapping provides.

You already saw that datasets can be used to fetch and manipulate data in a disconnected way. These datasets are managed by data adapters that handle the gory details of producing and issuing the appropriate SQL statements to the underlying database when fetching records or synchronizing the changes made to the dataset back to the database. The main goal of a separate Data Access Layer (DAL) is to bridge the gap between two disparate domains: the database and your application logic. Practically speaking, this means freeing you from having to write SQL code and mingling it with your application code.

O/R mappings use "smart" data objects that can load and persist record-level data, and underneath they use objects such as ADO.NET datasets that are filled and flushed on demand.

The tool we focus on in this section is SqlMetal, which computes the O/R mapping for LINQ, part of the .NET Framework 3.5. For example, to use SqlMetal to generate bindings for the `Northwnd.mdf` database, you can use this:

```
sqlmetal /code:northwind.cs /namespace:Nwind /server:.\SQLExpress Northwnd.mdf
```

This assumes you are running SQL Server Express on your machine as a named instance. Further options are available when you run SqlMetal without parameters. You may want to use the `/code` and `/xml` flags to specify a different output file of the object bindings and to create a schema definition, respectively. The resulting code by default uses C#, which can be changed using the `/language` option. You can easily add the generated mappings under a separate DLL project in your F# solution and reference it from your F# project.

For the remainder of this section, we will be using the generated data object layer for the classic Northwind database, as used by the F# LINQ samples in the F# distribution. This C# source file contains classes for each data table in the Northwind database, and the relationships between those tables are strongly typed.

■**Tip** Regardless of your choice to work with SQL explicitly or implicitly, in applied database scenarios you will frequently want to separate data definitions entirely from application code. DDL scripts that create schemas, tables, triggers, and views and scripts that create seed data should be managed as separate artifacts that are executed prior to application deployment.

Building the DataContext Instance

One of the classes (with the same name as your database) generated by SqlMetal represents the entire database. This class inherits from the `DataContext` class and carries with it all the connection details that are used when accessing the data contained in the database through the mapped objects. You can supply a connection string when you instantiate this main database object, as the following code snippet shows (to run this, you will need the Northwnd.mdf file in your source directory):

```
#light
#I @"c:\Program Files\Reference Assemblies\Microsoft\Framework\v3.5"
#r "System.Core.dll"
#r "System.Data.Linq.dll"
#r "FSharp.Linq.dll"
#r "Northwind.dll"

open System
open System.Data.SqlClient
open Nwind

let db =
    let connB = new SqlConnectionStringBuilder()
    connB.AttachDBFilename <- __YOUR_SOURCE_DIRECTORY__ + @"\Northwnd.mdf"
    connB.IntegratedSecurity <- true
    connB.Enlist <- false
    connB.DataSource <- @".\SQLExpress"
    new Northwind(connB.ConnectionString)
```

Using LinqToSql from F#

So far you have seen how you can perform LINQ-style queries using a set of aggregate operators that work on enumerable objects, and you will see these very same operators query and manipulate XML data in the coming section. Performing querying and manipulation on relational data is done almost the same way, except that these are implemented under the hood by calling LINQ. Assuming that you have mapped your employees database with SqlMetal and created the main database object as db, here is an example similar to those in earlier sections using F# LinqToSql syntax:

```
open Microsoft.FSharp.Quotations.Typed
open Microsoft.FSharp.Data.Linq
open Microsoft.FSharp.Linq.SequenceOps

let res =
    SQL <@ { for emp in ($db.Employees)
                 when emp.BirthDate.Value.Year > 1960
                     && emp.LastName.StartsWith "S"
                 -> (emp.FirstName, emp.LastName) }
             |> take 5 @>

for (first, last) in res do
  printfn "%s %s" first last
```

One notable difference between this and previous queries is the use of F# quotations inside `<@` and `@>`. As shown in Chapter 9, quotations are reified syntax trees that can be read and manipulated by F# programs. Quoted expressions (provided by the `Microsoft.FSharp.Quotations.Typed` namespace) are of type `Expr<'a>`, where `'a` is the type of the unquoted expression. You can read more on meta-programming via F# quotations in depth in Chapter 9.

Note that in F# quotation literals, the § "splice" symbol indicates that a value is being inserted into the quotation expression tree. This allows quotations to reference defined objects and values such as those representing the database.

The type of the previous SQL function is as follows:

```
val SQL: Expr<'a> -> 'a
```

This function works on F# quotations. These are converted to LINQ `Expression` objects and passed to the underlying LINQ mechanism to produce SQL that is then executed on demand.

Note When writing embedded queries using F# LinqToSql, you can use only a limited subset of operators to express your queries, in particular those defined in the F# LinqToSql library. Check the latest F# LINQ documentation for more details.

HOW LINQ APPEARS FROM F#

You can make LINQ-style queries on two types of objects: those implementing the `IEnumerable<'a>` / `seq<'a>"` and `IQueryable<'a>` interfaces. The former is used for in-memory objects or those that can be iterated one by one to provide a uniform way to query and transform, while the latter provides more customization in terms of the deriving object's identity and enables you to control how those operations are actually carried out.

Much of the LINQ architecture relies on representing query expressions using reified expression trees through the `System.Expressions.Expression` type. This type is used to encode lambda expressions in C#, thus giving a straightforward syntax embedding for LINQ-style queries. In F#, meta-programming is built around a similar mechanism—F# quotations, discussed in Chapter 9. A bridge is used to convert between F# quotations and LINQ expression trees. LINQ queries on queryable objects are encoded as expression trees and translated to the underlying LINQ machinery at run time.

Working with XML As a Generic Data Format

XML provides a platform-, operating system–, and application-independent way to represent data in a plain-text format. In fact, nowadays XML is ubiquitous; it is widely used to describe application configuration data, as output format for applications such as Microsoft Word and Excel, to wrap data that is sent across networks or as a way to interact with the new generation of database servers, including Oracle 8*i* and newer or Microsoft SQL Server 2000 and 2005. These database servers can work with XML data directly, allowing you to update the database from XML documents or extract data in XML. Data represented as XML carries various tags and meta-information that helps to identify what sort of data is contained within. This also amounts to a larger size, but typically this can be compensated for by applying compression on the XML text.

As an example, consider the following classic XML example (contacts.xml):

```
<contacts>
  <contact>
    <name>John Smith</name>
    <phone type="home">+1 626-123-4321</phone>
  </contact>
</contacts>
```

One way to represent and work with XML documents is via the XML Document Object Model (DOM) contained in the System.Xml namespace, and you saw how to work with this model in Chapter 9. Using the XML DOM constructors and methods, you can create the previous XML as follows:

```
open System.Xml

let doc = new XmlDocument()
let rootNode = doc.CreateElement "contacts"
doc.AppendChild rootNode |> ignore
let contactNode = doc.CreateElement "contact"
let nameNode = doc.CreateElement "name"
let nameText = doc.CreateTextNode "John Smith"
let phoneNode = doc.CreateElement "phone"
phoneNode.SetAttribute("type", "home")
let phoneText = doc.CreateTextNode "+1 626-123-4321"
nameNode.AppendChild nameText |> ignore
contactNode.AppendChild nameNode |> ignore
contactNode.AppendChild phoneNode |> ignore
phoneNode.AppendChild phoneText |> ignore
rootNode.AppendChild contactNode |> ignore
```

Here you are building up an XML document in a bottom-up fashion via a series of method calls that mutate the main XML document object. This means various XML elements cannot be constructed without this document container object and also construction by mutation makes the shape of the XML hard to read. Using XmlWriter is a bit more readable:

```
let doc = new XmlDocument()
let writer = doc.CreateNavigator().AppendChild()
writer.WriteStartElement "contacts"
writer.WriteStartElement "contact"
writer.WriteElementString ("name", "John Smith")
writer.WriteStartElement "phone"
writer.WriteAttributeString ("type", "home")
writer.WriteString "+1 626-123-4321"
writer.WriteEndElement()
writer.Close()
```

Here you don't have to worry about creating the structure of the document; instead, you simply output each element in a sequence. XmlWriter will also take care of the closing tags, even if you forget them before closing the writer.

Constructing XML via LINQ

LINQ to XML (LinqToXml) offers a new and easier way to work with XML than using the traditional XML DOM. The System.Xml.Linq namespace contains everything you need to construct, load and save, manipulate, and query over XML documents. You can reference the DLL containing this namespace using this:

```
#I @"c:\Program Files\Reference Assemblies\Microsoft\Framework\v3.5"
#r "System.Xml.Linq.dll"
```

Being a data format for tree-like structures, the XML trees are made up by a collection of XNode objects. Structurally, there are two XNode descendants that can contain other nodes (and thus inherit from XContainer, a subclass of XNode): XDocument and XElement. Therefore, all XML documents are represented either as an XDocument with nested XElement objects or simply as a collection of nested XElements.

A fully qualified XML document (an instance of XDocument) contains meta-information such as declarations (added as a child XDeclaration object) and a DTD (added as a XDocumentType) and may contain various XML processing instructions (instances of XProcessingInstruction). Typically, you need an XDocument only if the XML you produce is exchanged with the external world (such as information passed through a web service, for instance); in any other case, you will be working with a collection of nested XElement objects. These can have other XNode objects such as XText for storing text, which often represents binary data encoded using Base64 encoding mentioned in Chapter 10, or XComment for embedding comments. On the other hand, XElements typically have attributes (XAttribute)—key/value pairs, which are non-XNode objects. Both the XElement names (the tag itself) and the XAttribute keys are XName objects.

The easiest way to construct an XML document is to simply call the Parse method of the XDocument or XElement class on a string:

```
open System.Xml.Linq

let xml =
    "<contacts>
       <contact>
          <name>John Smith</name>
          <phone type=\"home\">+1 626-123-4321</phone>
       </contact>
    </contacts>"
let doc = XDocument.Parse xml
```

LinqToXml makes *functional construction* of XML possible. This is done by making all XML constituents first-class values that can be created and embedded in each other. The functional construction also requires that we treat these values uniformly. Let's assume we create a few shorthand functions for various XML constructors:

```
open System.Xml.Linq

let xname n                       = XName.op_Implicit(n)
let xdoc (el : #seq<XElement>)  = new XDocument(Array.map box (Array.of_seq el))
let xelem s el                    = new XElement(xname s, box el)
let xatt  a b                     = new XAttribute(xname a, b) |> box
let xstr  s                       = box s
```

Using these functions, we can construct the XML from the beginning of this section as follows:

```
let doc =
    xdoc
        [ xelem "contacts"
            [ xelem "contact"
                [ (xelem "name" (xstr "John Smith"))
                  (xelem "phone"
                      [ xatt "type" "home"
                        xstr "+1 626-123-4321" ])
                ]
            ]
        ]
```

This also includes the default document header (`<?xml version="1.0" encoding="utf-8"?>`). If this header is not needed, you can simply omit the top-level call to xdoc.

Storing, Loading, and Traversing LinqToXml Documents

Loading an existing XML document is straightforward; you can call the Load static method on either an XDocument or an XElement:

```
let file name = Path.Combine(__YOUR_SOURCE_DIRECTORY__, name)

XElement.Load (file "contacts.xml")
```

Saving is just as easy, reusing doc from earlier:

```
doc.Save (file "contacts2.xml")
```

LinqToXML considers an XML document as a collection of XElement objects, each in a parent/child relationship. The root XElement's Parent property is null, even if it is embedded in an XDocument, which can simply be ignored as far as the data in the XML is concerned. XElement children can be obtained using the Elements() method, or its override, which expects an XName argument and returns all elements with a given name.

```
let contacts = doc.Element(xname "contacts")  // Get the first contact
for elem in contacts.Elements() do
    printfn "Tag=%s, Value=%A" elem.Name.LocalName elem.Value
```

Querying XML

Queries on XML are often expressed using the XPath query language, which we don't cover in detail in this book but which is supported by the types in the System.Xml namespace. As a good alternative to XPath, you can use the standard sequence operators to perform queries over XML data. The following example uses the helper functions and the file contacts2.xml created in the previous section:

```
open System
open System.Xml.Linq

let elem (e: XElement) s        = e.Element(xname s)
let elemv e s                   = (elem e s).Value

let contactsXml = XElement.Load(file "contacts2.xml")
let contacts = contactsXml.Elements ()
```

```
> contacts |> Seq.filter (fun e -> (elemv e "name").StartsWith "J")
           |> Seq.map (fun e -> (elemv e "name"), (elemv e "phone"));;
val it : seq<string * string> = seq [("John Smith", "+1 626-123-4321")]
```

In this example, we also defined some helper functions: elem to extract from an XElement object the first child element with a given name and elemv to convert that to a string value.

You can also use the query operators in building new XML:

```
xelem "results"
  [ contacts |> Seq.filter  (fun e -> (elemv e "name").StartsWith "J")  ]
```

This creates a <results> tag and inserts all employees whose last name starts with the letter *J*. You can also use sequence expressions to achieve the same:

```
xelem "results"
  [ for e in contacts do
        if (elemv e "name").StartsWith "J" then
           yield e ]
```

Summary

In this chapter, you saw how the functional programming techniques from Chapter 3 are often used to implement in-memory queries similar to those used to access databases. You also saw how to use sequence expressions as an alternative notation for these query expressions. We then turned to databases themselves and covered how to use ADO.NET to access relational databases. You also saw how to perform a variety of database-related tasks from Visual Studio. You next saw how to perform simple, typed queries using F# LinqToSql, taking particular advantage of the object/relational data objects generated by the LINQ tool SqlMetal.exe. Finally, you saw how to use XML as a generic data format, partly by using functionality from the LINQ libraries.

In the next chapter, we'll cover parsing techniques, including using the lexer and parser generator tools that come with the F# distribution.

CHAPTER 16

Lexing and Parsing

In this chapter, you'll take a closer look at lexing and parsing, topics introduced briefly in Chapters 9 and 11. In particular we introduce the lexer and parser generators, fslex and fsyacc, that come with the F# distribution. A typical scenario when these techniques and tools can come in handy is the following:

- You want to read "user-readable" input that has a well-defined syntax.

- You have a type (often an *abstract syntax tree* [AST] type) to represent this input.

The typical task is to parse the user input into your internal representation by breaking down the input string into a sequence of tokens (a process called *lexical analysis*) and then constructing an instance of your internal representation based on a grammar (via *syntactic analysis*). Lexing and parsing do not have to be separated, and there are often convenient .NET methods for extracting information from text in particular formats, as we show in this chapter. Nevertheless, it is often best to treat the two processes separately.

Our goal in this chapter is to give the background needed to use the built-in lexing and parsing facilities of .NET and F# effectively and to understand the options for lexing and parsing other input formats.

- For lexing, we cover simple line-based techniques to "crack" data formats using the .NET libraries directly. We then show how to use fslex to break text into simple tokens, strings with escape characters, and nested comments, and we show table-based token generation and stateful lexing (passing state as a parameter as opposed to using mutable state).

- For parsing, we cover the core parsing topics of languages, grammar formalisms, and various parser types. We then explain the typical problems for recursive-descent parsing and introduce fsyacc by giving a parser for Kitty, a small BASIC-like language. This highlights how to parse lists of symbols, how to assign precedence and associativity to your tokens and production rules, and how you can recover from parsing errors. We also look at conflicts that can arise in the fsyacc specifications and how to resolve them.

Finally, we cover combinator-based techniques, which are particularly useful for writing parsers for binary formats, without relying on fslex and fsyacc.

> ### SYNTAX VS. SEMANTIC ANALYSIS
>
> *Lexical analysis* is concerned with identifying those tokens that make up a given input. A *token* is simply a piece of the input text that constitutes a word from the lexer's perspective. This can be a number, an identifier, a special word, or any sequence of characters deemed to make a unit.
>
> During syntax analysis you check whether the input (a series of tokens) is structured according to a set of grammar rules that makes up your language. For instance, the F# construct `let a = b*2 in ..` is syntactically correct, but it is a semantically valid expression only if the variable b is bound in the preceding scope. The notion of scope and binding depends on the semantics of your language, and these are the topics of interest for *semantic* analysis. In a typical compiler, for instance, source programs go through the following stages:
>
> Lexing ➤ Parsing ➤ Semantic Analysis ➤ Optimization(s)/Transformations ➤ Code Generation
>
> We cover examples of semantic analysis and optimization/transformation in Chapters 9 and 11.

Processing Line-Based Input

A common simple case of parsing and lexing is when you are working with an existing line-based text-file format. In this case, parsing is often as easy as splitting each line of input at a particular separator character and trimming whitespace off the resulting partial strings:

```
> let line = "Smith, John, 20 January 1986, Software Developer";;
val line : string

> line.Split [| ',' |];;
val it : string [] = [|"Smith"; " John"; " 20 January 1986"; " Software Developer"|]

> line.Split [| ',' |] |> Array.map (fun s -> s.Trim());;
val it : string [] = [|"Smith"; "John"; "20 January 1986"; "Software Developer"|]
```

You can then process each column in the data format:

```
let splitLine (line: string) =
    line.Split [| ',' |] |> Array.map (fun s -> s.Trim())

let parseEmployee (line: string) =
    match splitLine line with
    | [| last; first; startDate; title |] ->
        last, first, System.DateTime.Parse(startDate), title
    | _ ->
        failwithf "invalid employee format: '%s'" line
```

The type of this function is as follows:

```
val parseEmployee : string -> string * string * System.DateTime * string
```

Here is an example use:

```
> parseEmployee line;;
val it : string * string * System.DateTime * string
     = ("Smith", "John", 20/01/1986 00:00:00, "Software Developer")
```

On-Demand Reading of Files

You can turn a file into an on-demand sequence of results using Seq.generate_using:

```
open System.IO

let readEmployees (fileName : string) =
    Seq.generate_using
        (fun () -> File.OpenText(fileName))
        (fun reader ->
            if reader.EndOfStream then None
            else Some(parseEmployee(reader.ReadLine())) )
```

The following example takes the first three entries from an artificially generated file containing 10,000 copies of the same employee:

```
> File.WriteAllLines("employees.txt", Array.create 10000 line);;
val it : unit

> let firstThree = readEmployees("employees.txt") |> Seq.take 3;;
val firstThree : (string * string * System.DateTime * string) list

> for (last,first,startDate,title) in firstThree do
      printfn "%s %s started on %A" first last startDate;;
John Smith started on 20/01/1986 00:00:00
John Smith started on 20/01/1986 00:00:00
John Smith started on 20/01/1986 00:00:00
```

This technique is often used to do exploratory analysis of large data files. Once the algorithm is refined using a prefix of the data, the analysis can then easily be run directly over the full data file.

Using Regular Expressions

Another technique frequently used to extract information from strings is to use regular expressions. The System.Text.RegularExpressions namespace provides convenient string matching and replacement functions. For example, let's say you have a log file containing a record of HTML GET requests. Here is a sample request:

```
GET /favicon.ico HTTP/1.1
```

The following code captures the name of the requested resource (favicon.ico) and the lower version number of the HTML protocol (1) used:

```
open System.Text.RegularExpressions

let parseHttpRequest line =
    let result = Regex.Match(line, @"GET (.*?) HTTP/1\.([01])$")
    let file = result.Groups.Item(1).Value
    let version = result.Groups.Item(2).Value
    file, version
```

The relevant fields are extracted by using the Groups attribute of the regular expression match to access the matched strings for each parenthesized group in the regular expression.

Tokenizing with FsLex

Although it is possible to hand-code lexers by using a range of ad hoc techniques such as those discussed in the previous section or by writing functions that explicitly manipulate lists of characters, doing so can be boring and time consuming. Instead, it is often easier to rely on a *lexer generator* to do this job for you. In this section, you will look at how to use the fslex tool that comes with the F# distribution to perform lexical analysis.

We'll start with a simple example. Listing 16-1 shows a lexer that replaces all < and > characters in an input stream with their HTML equivalents, < and >. Listing 16-2 shows a small program that uses this generated lexer.

Listing 16-1. *Replacing Characters with Their HTML Equivalents: text2htmllex.fsl*

```
{ (* You can add your helper functions here *) }

rule convertHtml chan = parse
  | '<'    { fprintf chan "&lt;";
             convertHtml chan lexbuf }
  | '>'    { fprintf chan "&gt;";
             convertHtml chan lexbuf }
  | eof    { () }
  | _      { fprintf chan "%s" (Lexing.lexeme lexbuf);
             convertHtml chan lexbuf }
```

Listing 16-2. *Replacing Characters with Their HTML Equivalents: text2html.fs*

```
#light
open System.IO
open System.Text

let main() =
  let args = System.Environment.GetCommandLineArgs()
    if args.Length <= 2 then
        let base = Path.GetFileName(args[0])
        eprintfn "Usage: %s dir pattern" base
```

```
        exit 1
let directory = args[1]
let pattern = args[2]

for fileName in Directory.GetFiles(directory, pattern) do

    // Open a file stream for the file name
    use inputReader = File.OpenText(fileName)

    // Create a lex buffer for use with the generated lexer. The lex buffer
    // reads the inputReader stream.
    let lexBuffer = Lexing.from_text_reader Encoding.ASCII inputReader

    // Open an output channel
    let outputFile = Path.ChangeExtension(fileName,"html")
    use outputWriter = (new StreamWriter(outputFile) :> TextWriter)

    // Write the header
    fprintfn outputWriter "<html>\n<head></head>\n<pre>"

    // Run the generated lexer
    Text2htmllex.convertHtml outputWriter lexBuffer

    // Write the footer
    fprintfn outputWriter "</pre>\n</html>\n"

do main()
```

You can produce an F# source file from the previous lexer definition by running this:

```
fslex text2htmllex.fsl
```

This produces text2htmllex.fs, which contains the implementation of the lexer convertHtml. This lexer is *imperative*, in that it prints to an output stream instead of returning tokens. The signature of the entry point to the generated lexer is as follows:

```
val Text2htmllex.convertHtml: System.IO.TextWriter -> Lexing.lexbuf -> unit
```

You can now compile the driver and the lexer together:

```
fsc text2htmllex.fs text2html.fs
```

You can run the resulting program as follows, giving a source directory and a file pattern and producing an .html version of each file that matches by applying the HTML conversion:

```
text2html . *.txt
```

Let's take a look at the previous example more closely. The rule section of text2htmllex.fsl defines the lexer, which takes the output channel as an argument before the lexing buffer. It says that if you encounter the < or > character, you should output its HTML equivalent and recursively call your lexer to process the remaining input. If you find the end of the file, you simply stop, and for any other character you print it to the output channel. In each rule, you can refer to a predefined variable (visible only inside the rule) named lexbuf that has the type Lexing.lexbuf, an instantiation of the Microsoft.FSharp.Tools.FsLex.LexBuffer type. You can access various bits of information through this variable about the lexing state; some of these are collected in Table 16-1.

The driver is all F# code. You check the input arguments and then iterate through files in the directory given by the first argument whose name matches the pattern given by the second argument. You then open each file and instantiate your generated lexer with the following lines:

```
use inputReader = File.OpenText(fileName)
let lexBuffer = Lexing.from_text_reader Encoding.ASCII inputReader
...
Text2htmllex.convertHtml outputWriter lexBuffer
```

This code uses some important functions from the Lexing module. Table 16-1 shows the important functions in this module, along with some of the properties of the LexBuffer (lexbuf) type.

Table 16-1. *Some Functions from the Lexing Module and Properties of the LexBuffer Type*

Function	Type	Description
Lexing.from_string	string -> lexbuf	Makes a lexbuf for the given string
Lexing.from_text_reader	#Encoding -> #TextReader -> lexbuf	Makes a lexbuf for the given text reader
Lexing.from_binary_reader	#BinaryReader -> lexbuf	Makes a lexbuf for the given binary reader
Lexing.lexeme	Lexing.lexbuf -> string	Returns the matched string
LexBuffer.EndPos	Lexing.position	Gets/sets the current position associated with the end of the matched token
LexBuffer.IsPastEndOfStream	bool	True if the lex buffer has exhausted the available input
LexBuffer.StartPos	Lexing.position	Gets/sets the current position associated with the start of the matched token

> **■Note** FsLex works by constructing a table-driven finite automaton that is executed to consume the input character sequence one by one until a full token can be returned. The automaton blocks until further input is received. The states of this machine are derived from the regular expressions defined by each rule. Single-character literals advance the machine to a new state, and repetitions cause it to remain in the same state. These states form a graph, and the edges between the states are those symbols that advance between the states.

The fslex Input in More Detail

You saw the basic structure of lexer files in the preceding example, which contained a handful of rules only. In general, `fslex` input files have the following simple structure:

```
// Preamble - any user code you need for the lexer, such as opening modules, etc.
{ [Code] }

// Definitions - named patterns that you can use in the rules or other definitions
let [Ident_1] = [Pattern]
let ...

// Rules - text patterns that trigger certain actions
rule [Rule_1] [arg1... argn] = parse
    | [Pattern] { [Action] }
    | ...
    | [Pattern] { [Action] }
and [Rule_2] [arg1... argn] = parse
    ...
rule [Rule_3] ...

// Epilogue - code that can call the lexer rules defined above
{ [Code] }
```

Each rule defined in the lexer will become an F# function that can be accessed from other modules and the lexer itself. Comments can be placed between (* and *), and you can also use // comments in the actions just like in any other F# code. Patterns can be any of the forms listed in Table 16-2.

Lexical actions are pieces of F# code enclosed in braces that are executed when a lexer match is made. You can put any logic here that you like; typically you construct a token. Tokens are specified in the parser definition using the %token directive (you will see this later in this chapter), or if you do not have a parser, any user-defined type will do. If your lexer rules do not construct tokens or if your lexer is simple enough, often you may simply want to put all driver code in the epilogue section to create a stand-alone lexer.

Table 16-2. *Patterns in Lexer Rules*

Pattern Form	Description
`'c'`	Character constants; in single quotes such as `'+'` and `'.'`
`['a' 'b' 'c']`	Character sets; matches any character in the given set
`['a'-'z']`	Character ranges; matches any character in the given range, in ASCII ordering
`[^'a' 'b' 'c']`	Complementary character sets; matches any character except those in the given character set
`"abc"`	Matches the given string of characters
`_`	Matches any character
`eof`	Matches the end of the stream
identifier	A predefined named regular expression (named earlier in the file using a `let` binding)
pattern?	Zero or one occurrences of *pattern*
pattern+	One of more occurrences of *pattern*
pattern*	Zero or more occurrences of *pattern*
pattern1 | *pattern2*	Either *pattern1* or *pattern*
pattern1 pattern2	Concatenation; *pattern1* followed by *pattern2*

Generating a Simple Token Stream

Listing 16-3 shows a lexer that constructs a list of tokens that then is printed. It can recognize integers, floats, identifiers, and the symbols ^, *, -, and +. Any other character will cause a runtime exception.

Listing 16-3. `simpleTokensLex.fsl`: *Lexing Simple Tokens: Integers, Floats, and Identifiers*

```
{
type token =
    | INT    of int
    | FLOAT  of float
    | ID     of string
    | STRING of string
    | PLUS | MINUS | TIMES | HAT
    | EOF
}

let num        = ['0'-'9']+
let intNum     = '-'? num
let floatNum   = '-'? num ('.' num)? (['e' 'E'] num)?
let ident      = ['a'-'z']+
let whitespace = ' ' | '\t'
```

```
let newline    = '\n' | '\r' '\n'

rule token = parse
    | intNum      { INT (Int32.of_string (Lexing.lexeme lexbuf)) }
    | floatNum    { FLOAT (Float.of_string (Lexing.lexeme lexbuf))  }
    | ident       { ID (Lexing.lexeme lexbuf)  }
    | '+'         { PLUS }
    | '-'         { MINUS }
    | '*'         { TIMES }
    | '^'         { HAT }
    | whitespace { token lexbuf }
    | newline    { token lexbuf }
    | eof        { EOF }
    | _           { failwithf "unrecognized input: '%s'" (Lexing.lexeme lexbuf) }
```

You can generate the lexer using this:

```
fslex simpleTokensLex.fsl
```

The generated lexer contains a single module SimpleTokensLex (named after the input file) with one entry-point function for each rule. In this case, the type of this function will be as follows:

```
val token: Lexing.lexbuf -> SimpleTokensLex.token
```

The following indicates how you can imperatively generate a simple token stream from a string and print the results in F# Interactive:

```
> #load "simpleTokensLex.fs";;
...
> let lexbuf = Lexing.from_string "3.4 x 34 xyx";;
val lexbuf : Lexing.lexbuf

> SimpleTokensLex.token lexbuf;;
val it : SimpleTokensLex.token = FLOAT 3.4

> SimpleTokensLex.token lexbuf;;
val it : SimpleTokensLex.token = ID "x"

> SimpleTokensLex.token lexbuf;;
val it : SimpleTokensLex.token = INT 34

> SimpleTokensLex.token lexbuf;;
val it : SimpleTokensLex.token = ID "xyx"
```

```
> SimpleTokensLex.token lexbuf;;
val it : SimpleTokensLex.token = EOF

> SimpleTokensLex.token lexbuf;;
Microsoft.FSharp.Core.FailureException: End of file on lexing stream
```

Tracking Position Information Correctly

Lexers generated by fslex keep track of partial information about the position of the most recently accepted token within the source stream of characters. In particular, the StartPos and EndPos properties on the LexBuffer type return Lexing.Position values. A partial signature of this position type is as follows:

```
type Position with
        // The file name associated with the input stream.
        member FileName : string

        // The line number in the input stream, assuming fresh
        // positions have been updated by modifying the EndPos
        // property of the LexBuffer as each newline is lexed.
        member Line : int

        // The character number in the input stream
        member AbsoluteOffset : int

        // The column number marked by the position.
        member Column : int

        // Convert a position just beyond the end of a line to a
        // position at the start of the next line.
        member NextLine : position
        ...
end
```

In some cases, certain lexer actions must perform extra bookkeeping. In particular, the lexer should update the EndPos property of the LexBuffer each time a newline marker is processed (this is left up to the lexer since the interpretation of newline characters can differ between various lexers). In particular, you can change the endOfLine rule in the lexer in Listing 16-3 to make this update:

```
| newline    { lexbuf.EndPos <- lexbuf.EndPos.NextLine;
                 token lexbuf }
```

You can now experiment with this updated lexer in F# Interactive and examine the StartPos and EndPos properties after fetching each token:

```
> let lexbuf = Lexing.from_string "3.4 \n 34 xyx";;
val lexbuf : Lexing.lexbuf

> SimpleTokensLex.token lexbuf;;
val it : SimpleTokensLex.token = FLOAT 3.4

> (lexbuf.StartPos.Line, lexbuf.StartPos.Column);;
val it : int * int = (0,0)

> (lexbuf.EndPos.Line, lexbuf.EndPos.Column);;
val it : int * int = (0,3)

> SimpleTokensLex.token lexbuf;;
val it : SimpleTokensLex.token = INT 34

> (lexbuf.StartPos.Line, lexbuf.StartPos.Column);;
val it : int * int = (1,1)
```

Often you may need to attach position information to each lexer token. However, when using lexers in conjunction with fsyacc parser generators, the position information is automatically read after each token is processed and then stored in the parser's state. We return to this topic later in this chapter.

Handling Comments and Strings

So far you have seen examples with one lexing rule only. This is because the main lexer rule was sufficient for all tokens and you have not yet come across the need to lex input that cannot be described by a regular expression. To illustrate this point, for instance, say you want to lex comments enclosed by (* and *). Formally, you have an opening delimiter, followed by the body of the comment, and finally enclosed by the closing delimiter. The first attempt, shown here:

```
"(*" _* "*)"
```

fails because the middle pattern matches everything and you will never reach the closing *). So, the best compromise could be follows:

```
"(*" [^ '*']* "*)"
```

where you match the inside of the comment as long as you do not see a star symbol and then you try to match the closing *). This of course will fail on any comment that contains a star symbol inside. You can play with this regular expression a little more. The inside of the comment is either anything but a star or all those stars that are not followed by another star or right parenthesis:

```
"(*" ([^ '*'] | ('*'+ ([^ '*' ')']))* '*'+ ')'
```

This is about as close as you can get, and yet even this pattern has a problem: it cannot match nested comments; it will always stop at the first closing delimiter, ignoring all nested comment openers.

You can handle this problem by using a multirule lexer. The following rules show the additions you can make to the simpleTokensLex.fsl lexer from Listing 16-3 in order to properly handle comments and strings:

```
rule token =
    ...
    | "(*"         { comment lexbuf; token lexbuf }
    | "\""         { STRING (string lexbuf.StartPos "" lexbuf) }

and comment = parse
    | "(*"         { comment lexbuf; comment lexbuf  }
    | "*)"         { () }
    | "\n"         { lexbuf.EndPos <- lexbuf.EndPos.NextLine;
                     comment lexbuf }
    | eof          { failwith "Unterminated comment" }
    | _            { comment lexbuf }

and string pos s = parse
    | "\\" ('"' | 'n' | 'r' | 't')
                   { let s' = s + (match Lexing.lexeme lexbuf with
                             | "\\\"" -> "\""
                             | "\\n" ->  "\n"
                             | "\\r" ->  "\r"
                             | "\\t" ->  "\t"
                             | "\\\\" -> "\\"
                             | _ ->      "") in
                     string pos s' lexbuf }
    | "\""         { s }
    | "\n"         { lexbuf.EndPos <- lexbuf.EndPos.NextLine;
                     string pos (s + "\n") lexbuf }
    | eof          { failwithf "end of file in string started at or near %A" pos }
    | _            { string pos (s + (Lexing.lexeme lexbuf)) lexbuf }
```

Comment processing begins when you encounter (* in the token rule. When the closing *) is encountered, you exit one invocation of the comment rule. The idea is that you deal with nested comments by recursively applying the lexer when a nested comment is reached. Note the double invocation of comment lexbuf for nested comment delimiters: once to tokenize the comment that belongs to the opener and again to tokenize the rest of the enclosing comment. There are also two further matches within the comment rule. If you hit the end of the source stream, you have an unterminated comment and you raise an exception, and in every other case you move forward inside the comment.

In the example, strings are also handled by a separate lexer rule string that is invoked by the token lexer when you encounter the double-quote character. This rule takes two parameters: the string consumed so far and the start position of the string. The latter is used to report a nicer error for an unterminated string (note you could also use this technique for the matching case for comments). You can also check whether you have an escaped character in the input.

If so, you append the appropriate escape sequence to the string already accumulated and advance the current position. Upon encountering the closing character, you return the overall string. An imperative System.Text.StringBuffer object could also have been used to accumulate the string, which is more efficient if strings get very long.

■**Note** Because lexer rules can pass arguments, there is little need to use mutable state in a lexer—simply pass additional arguments.

Recursive-Descent Parsing

You can now turn your attention to parsing. Let's assume for the moment you are writing an application that performs simple symbolic differentiation, say on polynomials only. Let's say you want to read polynomials such as x^5-2x^3+20 as input from your users, which in turn will be converted to your internal polynomial representation so that you can perform symbolic differentiation and pretty-print the result to the screen. One way to represent polynomials is as a list of terms that are added or subtracted to form the polynomial:

```
type term =
    | Term  of int * string * int
    | Const of int

type polynomial = term list
```

For instance, the polynomial in this example is as follows:

```
[Term (1,"x",5); Term (-2,"x",3); Const 20]
```

In Listing 16-3 we built a lexer and a token type suitable for generating a token stream for the input text (shown as a list of tokens here):

```
[ID "x"; HAT; INT 5; MINUS; INT 2; ID "x"; HAT; INT 3; PLUS; INT 20]
```

Listing 16-4 shows a *recursive-decent parser* that consumes this token stream and converts it into the internal representation of polynomials. The parser works by generating a lazy list for the token stream. Lazy lists are a data structure in the F# library module Microsoft.FSharp. Collections.LazyList, and they are a lot like sequences with one major addition—lazy lists effectively allow you to pattern match on a sequence and return a residue lazy list for the tail of the sequence.

Listing 16-4. *Recursive-Descent Parser for Polynomials*

```
#light
open SimpleTokensLex
open Lexing
```

```
type term =
    | Term  of int * string * int
    | Const of int

type polynomial = term list
type tokenStream = LazyList<token * position * position>

let tryToken (src: tokenStream) =
    match src with
    | LazyList.Cons ((tok, startPos, endPos), rest) -> Some(tok, rest)
    | _ -> None

let parseIndex src =
    match tryToken src with
    | Some (HAT, src) ->
        match tryToken src with
        | Some (INT num2, src) ->
            num2, src
        | _ -> failwith "expected an integer after '^'"
    | _ -> 1, src

let parseTerm src =
    match tryToken src with
    | Some (INT num, src) ->
        match tryToken src with
        | Some (ID id, src) ->
            let idx, src = parseIndex src
            Term (num, id, idx), src
        | _ -> Const num, src
    | Some (ID id, src) ->
            let idx, src = parseIndex src
            Term(1, id, idx), src
    | _ -> failwith "end of token stream in term"

let rec parsePolynomial src =
    let t1, src = parseTerm src
    match tryToken src with
    | Some (PLUS, src) ->
        let p2, src = parsePolynomial src
        (t1 :: p2), src
    | _ -> [t1], src
```

The functions here have the following types:

```
val tryToken          : tokenStream -> (token * tokenStream) option
val parseIndex        : tokenStream -> int * tokenStream
val parseTerm         : tokenStream -> term * tokenStream
val parsePolynomial : tokenStream -> polynomial * tokenStream
```

You can turn the fslex-generated lexer for the lexer specification in Listing 16-3 into a tokenStream using the following code:

```
let tokenStream inp : tokenStream =
    // Generate the token stream as a seq<token>
    seq { let lexbuf = Lexing.from_string inp
          while not lexbuf.IsPastEndOfStream do
              match SimpleTokensLex.token lexbuf with
              | EOF -> yield! []
              | token -> yield (token, lexbuf.StartPos, lexbuf.EndPos) }

    // Convert to a lazy list
    |> LazyList.of_seq

let parse input =
    let src = tokenStream input
    let result, src = parsePolynomial src
    match tryToken src with
    | Some _ -> failwith "unexpected input at end of token stream!"
    | None -> result
```

These functions have the following types:

```
val tokenStream: string -> tokenStream
val parse: string -> polynomial
```

Note in the previous examples that you can successfully parse either constants or complete terms, but once you locate a HAT symbol you insist on having a number following. This sort of parsing, when you look only at the next token to guide the parsing process is referred to as LL(1), which stands for Left-to-right, Leftmost derivation parsing, where 1 means that only one look-ahead symbol is used. The parser approach we used earlier is called *recursive-descent*. This has various advantages and disadvantages, and we will be discussing those in a bit. To conclude here, you can look at the parse function in action:

```
> parse "1+3";;
val it : polynomial = [Const 1; Const 3]

> parse "2x^2+3x+5";;
val it : polynomial = [Term (2,"x",2); Term (3,"x",1); Const 5]
```

MORE ON GRAMMARS AND THEIR NOTATIONS

LL parsers such as the recursive-descent parser in the previous example are based on a subset of the so-called *context-free grammars* (CFGs). These can be defined by giving their corresponding grammar as a set of *production rules*. For context-free languages each rule has a single nonterminal symbol (the head) on the left side, defining a substitution of the nonterminal and/or terminal symbols on the right side. A terminal symbol is simply part of the concrete string that is parsed. A convenient notation for describing context-free languages is the Backus-Naur Form (BNF). Here, nonterminals are inside brackets (<>), and terminal symbols are either named (such as ID) or quoted. The Extended BNF (EBNF) notation provides further convenient operators to express optionality (inside brackets) and repetition (using the +, ?, and * symbols with the same meaning as in regular expressions), thus providing a more succinct and readable description.

The recursive-descent parser from this section parses each nonterminal in the following simple grammar expressed in EBNF:

```
<polynomial> ::= <term> ['+' <polynomial>]
<idxterm> ::=  ID '^' NUM | ID
<term> ::=  NUM [ <idxterm> ] | <idxterm>
```

Grammars give rise to corresponding derivations; for instance, consider how 2x^3+1 is derived:

```
<polynomial> ➤ <term> '+' <polynomial>
             ➤ NUM <idxterm> '+' <polynomial>
             ➤ NUM ID '^' NUM '+' <polynomial>
             ➤ NUM ID '^' NUM '+' <term>
             ➤ NUM ID '^' NUM '+' NUM
             ➤ 2x^3 + 1
```

You could produce different derivations depending on what nonterminal you expand at each step. In the previous derivation, we chose to always expand the leftmost nonterminals, but you could just as easily expand from the right or even mix the two strategies. Usually, we stick to either left or rightmost derivation using LL or LR parsers, respectively, and if your grammar is written in a well-defined way, you will get the same parse tree. On the other hand, if given a particular derivation strategy you get more than one parse tree for a given input, the grammar is said to be *ambiguous*.

As we mentioned in the example, recursive-descent parsers are LL(n) parsers; in other words, they perform leftmost derivation. Typically only a single look-ahead symbol is used to drive parsing—these are LL(1) parsers—but our example can be extended to LL(n) for some n>1, since inside a given parsing function you can retrieve several look-ahead symbols and make the appropriate parsing decisions. This is possible because our look-ahead calculation is nondestructive; in other words, there is no global parsing state. Instead, we pass around the particular input string (the remaining token stream) instance on which we want to base our parsing.

LR parsers are a special subset of bottom-up parsers; they read their input from left to right and produce a rightmost derivation (that is, always the rightmost nonterminal is expanded during parsing). Special subsets include Simple LR (SLR) and Look-Ahead LR (LALR; as generated by the yacc family of parser generators, including fsyacc, as you will see in the coming sections), and extensions include LR(1) (where the parse tables are typically larger because of the one symbol look-ahead), and Generalized LR (GLR), which can handle nondeterminism and ambiguous grammars.

Limitations of Recursive-Descent Parsers

There are various limitations you cannot handle with recursive-descent parsers. For instance, if you translate a left-recursive production into code, you get an infinite recursion, like so:

```
<polynomial> ::= <polynomial> '+' <term> | <term>
```

which would correspond to the following:

```
let rec parsePolynomial src =
    let poly, src = parsePolynomial src
    ...
```

Another common problem with LL(k) parsing for some k>=1 is that the grammar rules for a given nonterminal cannot start with the same symbols, or else there is no easy way to decide which rule to apply (because each is decided to be applicable upon checking k number of symbols). In such cases, *left-factoring* can be applied. For example, moving the symbols after the common part into another production, as shown here:

```
<polynomial> ::= <term> | <term> '+' <polynomial>
```

can be refactored as

```
<polynomial> ::= <term> <polymomialTail>
<polynomialTail> ::= EPSILON | '+' <polynomial>
```

Here EPSILON is the empty symbol, so the function that parses polynomialTail would both check for a plus symbol and then issue a call to parse a polynomial or exit in the absence of an initial plus symbol leaving the input unchanged. Although this case is relatively simple (you can parse terms until they are followed by a plus sign iteratively), coding such grammar rules in the general case is quite cumbersome.

Problems such as these arise because you have to make parsing decisions early on (such as deciding which grammar rule you are pursuing if there are multiple for a given nonterminal), because they aim to construct the parse tree from the top and proceed downward. LR parsers, on the other hand, aim to postpone these decisions as much as possible and construct the parse tree bottom-up, resulting in much more flexibility both in terms of how naturally grammar rules can be expressed and how they can be mapped into code.

Parsing with FsYacc

The tool fsyacc generates LALR(1) parsers, which are a special subset of LR(1) parsers where the state table is compressed by merging similar states. This in practice does not limit the languages that can be parsed, but it does result in significant savings over the parse table size. The generated parser automaton performs one of four distinct operations in any state based on the look-ahead token, and these are important to understand if you have various grammar conflicts to fix. It can *shift* the look-ahead (always a terminal symbol) to its stack, *reduce* a number of stack entries by a grammar rule leaving the head symbol in their place, *accept* the input as syntactically correct, or *reject* in the opposite case. Parsing proceeds until an accept or a reject state is reached.

We'll first show how to develop a parser for a simple programming language. A sample fragment of the BASIC-like language we want to parse is shown here:

```
a := 1;
b := 0;
if a then d := 20 + 20;
if b then d := 40 * 20 + 20;
print d;
while d do
    begin
        d := d + 1;
        print d
    end;
print d
```

For simplicity we will call this language Kitty. As the previous example shows, Kitty supports naming values, printing values, basic arithmetic operators, and a while and conditional construct. The Ast module (shown in Listing 16-5) defines the internal representation for Kitty programs.

Listing 16-5. *kittyAst.fs: Defining the AST for Kitty Programs*

```
type expr =
    | Val   of string
    | Int   of int
    | Plus  of expr * expr
    | Minus of expr * expr
    | Times of expr * expr

type stmt =
    | Assign     of string * expr
    | While      of expr * stmt
    | Seq        of stmt list
    | IfThen     of expr * stmt
    | IfThenElse of expr * stmt * stmt
    | Print      of expr

type prog = Prog of stmt list
```

The Lexer for Kitty

Listing 16-6 shows a lexer for the language in the file kittyLexer.fsl. It is similar to lexers developed earlier in this chapter. The one exception is that we use a *keyword table*. Matching against lexemes to identify tokens is a sensible solution only if there are relatively few cases. Tokenizing a large set of keywords and operators using explicit rules can lead to large lexers. This situation is often handled using tables that contain the possible lexeme matches and the tokens to be returned. Listing 16-6 uses simple dictionaries (maps).

Listing 16-6. *kittyLexer.fsl: Lexer for Kitty*

```
{
open System
open KittyParser
open Lexing
let ids = [ ("while",   WHILE);
            ("begin",   BEGIN);
            ("end",     END);
            ("do",      DO);
            ("if",      IF);
            ("then",    THEN);
            ("else",    ELSE);
            ("print",   PRINT);]

let idsMap = Map.of_list ids

let ident lexbuf tokenText =
    if Map.mem tokenText idsMap then Map.find tokenText idsMap
    else ID tokenText
}

let num        = ['0'-'9']+
let alpha      = ['a'-'z' 'A'-'Z']
let ident      = alpha+ (alpha | ['_' '$'])*
let integer    = '-'? num
let whitespace = ' ' | '\t'
let newline    = '\n' | '\r' '\n'

rule token = parse
    | whitespace { token lexbuf }
    | newline    { (lexbuf: lexbuf).EndPos <- lexbuf.EndPos.NextLine; token lexbuf }
    | "("        { LPAREN }
    | ")"        { RPAREN }
    | "+"        { PLUS }
    | "-"        { MINUS }
    | "*"        { TIMES }
    | ";"        { SEMI }
    | ":="       { ASSIGN }
    | ident      { ident lexbuf (lexeme lexbuf) }
    | integer    { INT (Int32.Parse(lexeme lexbuf)) }
    | eof        { EOF }
```

Note that at compilation time the lexer depends on the parser we define later in Listing 16-7. This is because the lexer must return the type of tokens required by the parser.

You can generate the lexer by calling `fslex`:

```
fslex kittyLexer.fsl
```

This produces `kittyLexer.fs`, which contains the implementation of the lexer.

The Parser for Kitty

Listing 16-7 shows the parser specification for the Kitty language in the file `kittyParser.fsy`.

Listing 16-7. *kittyParser.fsy: Parser for Kitty*

```
%{
open KittyAst
%}

// The start token becomes a parser function in the compiled code.
%start start

// These are the terminal tokens of the grammar along with the types of
// the data carried by each token:
%token <string> ID
%token <int> INT
%token PLUS MINUS TIMES LPAREN RPAREN IF THEN ELSE
%token WHILE DO BEGIN END PRINT SEMI ASSIGN EOF

// Associativity and Precedences - Lowest precedence comes first
%left PLUS MINUS
%left TIMES

// This is the type of the data produced by a successful reduction
// of the 'start' symbol:
%type <prog> start

%%

start: Prog                  { $1 }

Prog: StmtList               { Prog (List.rev $1) }

Expr: ID                     { Val $1 }
    | INT                    { Int $1 }
    | Expr PLUS Expr         { Plus ($1, $3) }
    | Expr MINUS Expr        { Minus ($1, $3) }
    | Expr TIMES Expr        { Times ($1, $3) }
    | LPAREN Expr RPAREN     { $2 }
```

```
Stmt: ID ASSIGN Expr              { Assign ($1, $3) }
    | WHILE Expr DO Stmt          { While ($2, $4) }
    | BEGIN StmtList END          { Seq (List.rev $2) }
    | IF Expr THEN Stmt           { IfThen ($2, $4) }
    | IF Expr THEN Stmt ELSE Stmt { IfThenElse ($2, $4, $6) }
    | PRINT Expr                  { Print $2 }

StmtList:
    | Stmt                  { [$1] }
    | StmtList SEMI Stmt { $3 :: $1  }
```

You can generate the parser by calling fsyacc:

```
fsyacc kittyParser.fsy
```

This produces kittyParser.fs, which contains the implementations of the parser, along with a signature file kittyParser.fsi. The generated parser has one entry point for each %start symbol (here there is only one). The type of this entry point is as follows:

```
val start : (LexBuffer<'pos,'c> -> token) -> LexBuffer<'pos,'c> -> KittyAst.prog
```

You'll see how to use this function a little later in this chapter. In a roundabout way the type says, "If you give me a lexing function that generates tokens and give me a LexBuffer to supply to that lexing function, then I'll generate you a KittyAst.prog." The generic type variables indicate that the parser is independent of the kind of position marks or characters (ASCII or Unicode) manipulated by the LexBuffer.

We now cover in more detail the different aspects of fsyacc parsing illustrated by this example.

THE FSYACC INPUT IN MORE DETAIL

The general structure of fsyacc input files is as follows:

```
// Preamble - any code you need for the parser, such as opening modules, etc.
%{ [Code] %}


// Tokens and their types - each line may contain several tokens
%token <[Type]> [TokenName] ... [TokenName]
...
// Associativity and precedences - where tokens associate (left, right,
// nonassoc) and how strongly they bind (in the order of their declaration)
%left     [TokenName]
%right    [TokenName]
%nonassoc [TokenName]
...
```

```
// Start symbols and their types
%start [StartSymbol]
%type <[Type]> [StartSymbol]
%%


// Productions - defining how non-terminals are derived
[Symbol] : [Symbols_1] { [Code_1] }
         | [Symbols_2] { [Code_2] }
...
```

The preamble can contain F# code, typically opening various modules and defining helper functions. The tokens (terminal symbols) of the grammar are defined with the `%token` directive, giving the name of the token(s) preceded by its type enclosed in `<>`. The type can be omitted if a token carries no data. There must be at least one start symbol defined using the `%start` and its type given with the `%type` directive. The resulting parser will expose only those parsing functions that were designated as start symbols. The productions for the same nonterminal can be merged into the same rule separated by an `|` character.

Parsing Lists

In Kitty, statements can be separated by semicolons. This is handled in the `StmtList` grammar production whose semantic extract is a list of statements. Note that you could have written this rule in a head-recursive way:

```
StmtList:
    | Stmt                { [$1] }
    | Stmt SEMI StmtList { $1 @ [ $3 ] }
```

Unlike in recursive-descent or any other LL parsing technique, the previous rule does not pose a problem for `fsyacc`, and thus no left-factoring is needed. However, it does create a copy of the statement list each time a new expression is appended to it. We have eliminated this by using the following productions:

```
StmtList:
    | Stmt                { [$1] }
    | StmtList SEMI Stmt { $3 :: $1 }
```

combined with a `List.rev` where the rule is used. This rule consumes all statements and inserts each one by one to the singleton list that contains the first statement. As a result, the return list will be in reverse order, which is why you need to apply `List.rev`. You may want to define a separate rule to perform this operation. Another feature that is often needed is the ability to parse empty or optional lists. This can be easily accomplished using an empty (epsilon) symbol as in the following example:

```
StmtListOpt:
                { [] }
    | StmtList { $1 }
```

This rule matches an optional list of statements and returns an empty list if no statements can be parsed.

Resolving Conflicts, Operator Precedence, and Associativity

As usual with arithmetic operators, division and multiplication should take precedence over addition and subtraction, so 1+2*3 should be parsed as 1+(2*3). With fsyacc this can be expressed easily using the associativity directives or, to be more precise, their ordering:

```
// Associativity and Precedences - Lowest precedence comes first
%left PLUS MINUS
%left TIMES
```

By specifying what tokens associate and where (how strongly they bind), you can control how parse derivations are performed. For instance, giving left-associativity to the addition operator (PLUS), given an input 1+2+3, the parser will automatically generate a nonambiguous derivation in the form of (1+2)+3. The basic arithmetic operators are left-associative and should be listed from the lowest precedence to the highest; in our example, the addition and subtraction operators have lower precedence than multiplication—the way it should be. Other associativity specifications include %nonassoc and %right, which are used to denote that a given symbol does not associate or associates to the right, respectively. The former is useful for relational and equality operators such as <, >, or !=, where the operator is not applicable if applied multiple times, so 1 > 2 > 3 would yield a syntax error.

You can also give precedence to a rule by using %prec at the end of the rule and giving a token whose precedence is to be applied. You can list arbitrary tokens in the associativity and precedence declarations, even if they have not been declared as tokens, and use them in such situations. You can find more details on specifying precedence at http://www.expert-fsharp.com/Topics/FsYacc.

■**Tip** One useful option for fsyacc.exe is -v, which causes fsyacc to produce a readable extract of the parser's states. This is useful when there are various conflicts to resolve.

Each state in this extract corresponds to one or more *items*, which are productions that indicate what has been seen while parsing them. This "current" position with respect to a rule is marked with a period (.). Furthermore, to each state belongs various actions that are triggered by certain look-ahead symbols. For instance, the action in some state as follows:

```
action 'ID' (noprec):    shift 7
```

indicates that if the ID token, which has no defined precedence, is encountered as look-ahead, the parser will push this token to the parsing stack and shift to state 7. For reduce actions, the rule that is reduced is shown. An error (reject) and accept action is shown for tokens that trigger a syntax error or acceptance, respectively.

The parser state extract also provides useful information on conflicts in your grammar. Conflicts arise when your grammar is ambiguous (which translates to having more than one choice for a parser action at any time), ultimately meaning there can be more than one derivation that accepts a given input. You can do a number of things to disambiguate your grammar. You can apply precedence to various tokens or rules or rewrite your rules to be consistent and unambiguous. There are two main sources of grammar conflicts: reduce-reduce and shift-reduce conflicts. Reduce-reduce conflicts are considered really bad because there are multiple rules to reduce by at a given situation. Although fsyacc applies a disambiguation strategy (reducing by the grammar rule that was defined earlier), you should really avoid reduce-reduce conflicts as much as possible.

Shift-reduce conflicts arise when the parser has the choice to shift a token or reduce by a rule. Unless you fix this conflict, fsyacc favors the shift action and defers the reduction to a later point, which in some situations (for instance, the dangling-else problem) yields the expected behavior, but in general any such conflict is also considered a serious problem.

Putting It Together

You can generate the parsers and lexers by calling fslex and fsyacc:

```
fslex kittyLexer.fsl
fsyacc kittyParser.fsy
```

This produces kittyLexer.fs and kittyParser.fs, which contain the implementations of the parser and lexer. You can test these using F# Interactive by loading the files directly using the #load directive. The following code creates a LexBuffer called lexbuf. It then calls the KittyParser.start entry point for the parser, passing KittyLexer.token as the lexical analysis engine and lexbuf as the LexBuffer. This connects the parser and the lexer.

```
open KittyAst
open KittyParser
open KittyLexer

let parseText text =
    let lexbuf = Lexing.from_string text
    try
        KittyParser.start KittyLexer.token lexbuf
    with e ->
        let pos = lexbuf.EndPos
        failwithf "Error near line %d, character %d\n" pos.Line pos.Column
```

You can now test this function interactively:

```
> let sample = "counter := 100; accum := 0; \n\
                while counter do \n\
                begin \n\
                    counter := counter - 1; \n\
                    accum := accum + counter \n\
                end; \n\
                print accum";;
val sample : string

> parseText sample;;
val it : KittyAst.prog
= Prog
```

```
[Assign ("counter",Int 100); Assign ("accum",Int 0);
 While
  (Val "counter",
   Seq
    [Assign ("counter",Minus (Val "counter",Int 1));
     Assign ("accum",Plus (Val "accum",Val "counter"))]); Print Val "accum"]
```

Writing an evaluator for Kitty is straightforward. Here we utilize an environment that maps variable names to the integer values they "store." As you expect, assignments in the source language add a binding for a given variable, and evaluating variables reads a value from this environment. Because of the lack of other types in Kitty, we use a nonzero value for the Boolean true and zero for false and wire the logic of the conditional and looping construct accordingly:

```
let rec evalE (env: Map<string, int>) = function
    | Val v           -> if env.ContainsKey v then env.[v]
                            else failwith ("unbound variable: " + v)
    | Int i           -> i
    | Plus  (e1, e2) -> evalE env e1 + evalE env e2
    | Minus (e1, e2) -> evalE env e1 - evalE env e2
    | Times (e1, e2) -> evalE env e1 * evalE env e2

and eval (env: Map<string, int>) = function
    | Assign (v, e) ->
        env.Add(v, evalE env e)
    | While (e, body) ->
        let rec loop env e body =
            if evalE env e <> 0 then
                loop (eval env body) e body
            else env
        loop env e body
    | Seq stmts ->
        List.fold_left eval env stmts
    | IfThen (e, stmt) ->
        if evalE env e <> 0 then eval env stmt else env
    | IfThenElse (e, stmt1, stmt2) ->
        if evalE env e <> 0 then eval env stmt1 else eval env stmt2
    | Print e ->
        print_int (evalE env e); env
```

With these at hand, continuing the same interactive session, you can now evaluate the sample Kitty program:

```
> match parseText sample with
    | Prog stmts ->
        eval Map.empty (Seq stmts) |> ignore;;
4950
val it : unit = ()
```

If necessary, you can also compile the AST, the lexer, and the parser together into a DLL or as part of an EXE:

```
fsc -a -o KittySyntax.dll  kittyAst.fs kittyParser.fs kittyLexer.fs
```

Binary Parsing and Pickling Using Combinators

There is one final case of parsing that is common when working with binary data. That is, say you want to work with a format that is conceptually relatively easy to parse and generate (such as a binary format) but where the process of actually writing the code to "crack" and "encode" the format is somewhat tedious. In this section, we cover a useful set of techniques to write readers and writers for binary data quickly and reliably.

As the running example, we will show a set of *pickling* (also called *marshalling*) and *unpickling* combinators to generate and read a binary format of our own design. The combinators can easily be adapted to work with existing binary formats such as those used for network packets. Picklers and unpicklers for different data types will be function values that have signatures as follows:

```
type outstate = System.IO.BinaryWriter
type instate  = System.IO.BinaryReader

type pickler<'a> = 'a -> outstate -> unit
type unpickler<'a> = instate -> 'a
```

Here instate and outstate are types that will record information during the pickling or parsing process. In this section, these are just binary readers and writers, but more generally they can be any type that can collect information and help compact the data during the writing process, such as by ensuring that repeated strings are given unique identifiers during the pickling process.

At the heart of every such library lies a set of primitive leaf functions for the "base" cases of aggregate data structures. For example, when working with binary streams, this is the usual set of primitive read/write functions:

```
let byteP (b: byte) (st: outstate) = st.Write(b)
let byteU (st: instate) = st.ReadByte()
```

You can now begin to define additional pickler/unpickler pairs:

```
let boolP b st = byteP (if b then 1uy else 0uy) st
let boolU st = let b = byteU st in (b = 1uy)

let int32P i st =
    byteP (byte (i &&& 0xFF)) st
    byteP (byte ((i >>> 8) &&& 0xFF)) st
    byteP (byte ((i >>> 16) &&& 0xFF)) st
    byteP (byte ((i >>> 24) &&& 0xFF)) st
```

```
let int32U st =
    let b0 = int (byteU st)
    let b1 = int (byteU st)
    let b2 = int (byteU st)
    let b3 = int (byteU st)
    b0 ||| (b1 <<< 8) ||| (b2 <<< 16) ||| (b3 <<< 24)
```

These functions have the following types:

```
val byteP  : byte pickler
val byteU  : byte unpickler
val boolP  : bool pickler
val boolU  : bool unpickler
val int32P : int pickler
val int32U : int unpickler
```

So far, so simple. One real advantage of this approach comes as you write combinators that put these together in useful ways. For example for tuples:

```
let tup2P p1 p2 (a, b) (st: outstate) =
    (p1 a st : unit)
    (p2 b st : unit)

let tup3P p1 p2 p3 (a, b, c) (st: outstate) =
    (p1 a st : unit)
    (p2 b st : unit)
    (p3 c st : unit)

let tup2U p1 p2 (st: instate) =
    let a = p1 st
    let b = p2 st
    (a, b)

let tup3U p1 p2 p3 (st: instate) =
    let a = p1 st
    let b = p2 st
    let c = p3 st
    (a, b, c)
```

and for lists:

```
// Outputs a list into the given output stream by pickling each element via f.
let rec listP f lst st =
    match lst with
    | [] ->      byteP 0uy st
    | h :: t -> byteP 1uy st; f h st; listP f t st
```

```
// Reads a list from a given input stream by unpickling each element via f.
let listU f st =
    let rec ulist_aux acc =
        let tag = byteU st
        match tag with
        | 0uy -> List.rev acc
        | 1uy -> let a = f st in ulist_aux (a::acc)
        | n ->   failwithf "listU: found number %d" n
    ulist_aux []
```

These functions conform to the types:

```
val tup2P  : 'a pickler -> 'b pickler -> ('a * 'b) pickler
val tup3P  : 'a pickler -> 'b pickler -> 'c pickler -> ('a * 'b * 'c) pickler
val listP  : 'a pickler -> 'a list pickler
val tup2U  : 'a unpickler -> 'b unpickler -> ('a * 'b) unpickler
val tup3U  : 'a unpickler -> 'b unpickler -> 'c unpickler -> ('a* 'b* 'c) unpickler
val listU  : 'a unpickler -> 'a list unpickler
```

It is now beginning to be easy to pickle and unpickle aggregate data structures using a consistent format. For example, imagine the internal data structure is a list of integers and Booleans:

```
type format = list<int32 * bool>
let formatP = listP (tup2P int32P boolP)
let formatU = listU (tup2U int32U boolU)

open System.IO

let writeData file data =
    use outStream = new BinaryWriter(File.OpenWrite(file))
    formatP data outStream

let readData file  =
    use inStream = new BinaryReader(File.OpenRead(file))
    formatU inStream
```

You can now invoke the pickle/unpickle process as follows:

```
> writeData "out.bin" [(102, true); (108, false)] ;;
val it : unit

> readData "out.bin";;
val it : (int * bool) list = [(102, true); (108, false)]
```

Combinator-based pickling is a powerful technique and can be taken well beyond what has been shown here. For example, it is possible to do the following:

- Ensure data is compressed and shared during the pickling process by keeping tables in the input and output states. Sometimes this requires two or more phases in the pickling and unpickling process.

- Build in extra-efficient primitives that compress leaf nodes, such as writing out all integers using `BinaryWriter.Write7BitEncodedInt` and `BinaryReader.Read7BitEncodedInt`.

- Build extra combinators for arrays, sequences, and lazy values and for lists stored in other binary formats than the 0/1 tag scheme used here.

- Build combinators that allow "dangling references" to be written to the pickled data, usually written as a symbolic identifier. When the data is read, the identifiers must be resolved and relinked, usually by providing a function parameter that performs the resolution. This can be a useful technique when processing independent compilation units.

Combinator-based pickling is used mainly because it allows data formats to be created and read in a relatively bug-free manner. It is not always possible to build a "single" pickling library suitable for all purposes, and you should be willing to customize and extend code samples such as those listed previously in order to build a set of pickling functions suitable for your needs.

■**Note** Combinator-based parsing borders on a set of techniques that we don't cover in this book called *parser combinators*. The idea is very much the same as the combinators presented here; parsing is described using a compositional set of functions. You also can write parser combinators using the workflow notation described in Chapter 9.

Summary

In this chapter, we covered *lexing* and *parsing*, which are tasks that can be tiresome if you don't use the right tools and techniques for the job. You learned about working with simple line-oriented formats, including on-demand reading of large data files, and then with the `fslex` and `fsyacc` tools, which are particularly suited for parsing programming languages and other languages with structured, rather than line-oriented, formats. Finally, we covered some combinator-based approaches for generating and reading binary data, which is also a form of parsing. In the next chapter, we'll switch to a different area of programming and look at how to write F# code that interoperates with native code.

■ ■ ■

CHAPTER 17

Interoperating with C and COM

Software integration and reuse is becoming one of the most relevant activities of software development nowadays. In this chapter, we discuss how F# programs can interoperate with the outside world, accessing code available in the form of DLLs and COM components.

Common Language Runtime

Libraries and binary components provide a common way to reuse software; even the simplest C program is linked to the standard C runtime to benefit from core functions such as memory management and I/O. Modern programs depend on a large number of libraries that are shipped in binary form, and only some of them are written in the same language of the program. Libraries can be linked statically during compilation into the executable or can be loaded dynamically during program execution. Dynamic linking has become significantly common to help share code (dynamic libraries can be linked by different programs and shared among them) and adapt program behavior while executing.

Interoperability among binaries compiled by different compilers, even of the same language, can be a nightmare. One of the goals of the .NET initiative was to ease this issue by introducing the Common Language Runtime (CLR), which is targeted by different compilers and different languages to help interoperability among software developed in those languages.

The CLR is a runtime designed to run programs compiled for the .NET platform. The binary format of these programs differs from the traditional one adopted by executables; according to the Microsoft terminology, we will use the term *managed* for the first class of programs and *unmanaged* otherwise (see Figure 17-1).

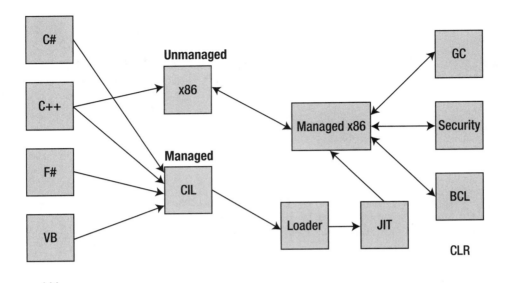

Figure 17-1. *Compilation scheme for managed and unmanaged code*

A DEEPER LOOK INSIDE .NET EXECUTABLES

Programs for the .NET platform are distributed in a form that is executed by the CLR. Binaries are expressed in an intermediate language that is compiled incrementally by the Just-In-Time (JIT) compiler during program execution. A .NET assembly, in the form of a .dll or an .exe file, contains the definition of a set of types and the definition of the method bodies, and the additional data describing the structure of the code in the intermediate language form is known as *metadata*. The intermediate language is used to define method bodies based on a stack-based machine, where operations are performed by loading values on a stack of operands and then invoking methods or operators.

Consider the following simple F# program:

```
open System
let i = 2
Console.WriteLine("Input a number:")
let v = Int32.Parse(Console.ReadLine())
Console.WriteLine(i * v)
```

The F# compiler generates an executable that can be disassembled using the ildasm.exe tool distributed with the .NET Framework. The following screenshot shows the structure of the generated assembly. Since everything in the CLR is defined in terms of types, the F# compiler must introduce the class Hw (named after the file name Hw.fs) in the <StartupCode> namespace. In this class, there is the definition of the _main static method that is the entry point for the execution of the program. This is the method that will contain the intermediate language corresponding to the example F# program. The F# compiler generates several elements that are not defined in the program, whose goal is to preserve the semantics of the F# program in the intermediate language.

If you open the _main method, you'll find the following code that we have annotated with the corresponding F# statements:

```
.method public static void _main() cil managed
{
  .entrypoint
  // Code size       56 (0x38)
  .maxstack  4

  // let i = 2;;
  IL_0000:  ldc.i4.2
  IL_0001:  stsfld     int32 '<StartupCode>'.Hw::i@3

  // do Console.WriteLine("Input a number:");;
  IL_0006:  ldstr      "Input a number:"
  IL_000b:  call       void [mscorlib]System.Console::WriteLine(string)
  IL_0010:  ldnull

  // let v = Int32.Parse(Console.ReadLine());;
  IL_0011:  stsfld
     class [fslib]Microsoft.FSharp.Core.Unit '<StartupCode>'.Hw::_doval@6@6
  IL_0016:  call       string [mscorlib]System.Console::ReadLine()
  IL_001b:  call       int32 [mscorlib]System.Int32::Parse(string)
  IL_0020:  stsfld     int32 '<StartupCode>'.Hw::v@8

  // do Console.WriteLine(i * v);;
  IL_0025:  ldc.i4.2
  IL_0026:  call       int32 Hw::get_v()
  IL_002b:  mul
  IL_002c:  call       void [mscorlib]System.Console::WriteLine(int32)
```

```
    IL_0031:  ldnull
    IL_0032:  stsfld
          class [fslib]Microsoft.FSharp.Core.Unit '<StartupCode>'.Hw::_doval@11@11
    IL_0037:  ret
} // end of method Hw::_main
```

The `ldxxx` instructions are used to load values onto the operand's stack of the abstract machine, and the `stxxx` instructions store values from that stack in locations (locals, arguments, or class fields). In this example, variables are declared as top level, and the compiler introduces static fields into the `Hw` class. The first assignment requires the value 2 to be loaded onto the stack using the `ldc` instruction, and the `stfld` instruction stores the value in the static variable that represents `i` in the compiled program. For method invocations, arguments are loaded on the stack, and a `call` operation is used to invoke the method.

The JIT compiler is responsible for generating the binary code that will run on the actual processor. The code generated by the JIT interacts with all the elements of the runtime, including external code loaded dynamically in the form of DLLs or COM components.

Since the F# compiler targets the CLR, its output will be managed code, allowing compiled programs to interact directly with other programming languages targeting the .NET platform. We already showed how to exploit this form of interoperability in Chapter 10, when we showed how to develop a graphic control in F# and use it in a C# application.

Memory Management at Run Time

Interoperability of F# programs with unmanaged code requires an understanding of the structure of the most important elements of a programming language's runtime. In particular, you must consider how program memory is organized at run time. Memory used by a program is generally classified in three classes depending on the way it is handled:

- *Static* memory, allocated for the entire lifetime of the program

- *Automatic* memory, allocated and freed automatically when functions or methods are executed

- *Dynamic* memory, explicitly allocated by the program and freed explicitly or by an automatic program called the *garbage collector*

As a rule of thumb, top-level variables and static fields belong to the first class, function arguments and local variables belong to the second class, and memory explicitly allocated using the `new` operator belongs to the last class. The code generated by the JIT compiler uses different data structures to manage memory and automatically interacts with the operating system to request and release memory during program execution.

Each execution thread has a stack where local variables and arguments are allocated when a function or method is invoked (see Figure 17-2). A stack is used because it naturally follows the execution flow of method and function calls. The topmost record contains data about the currently executing function; below that is the record of the caller of the function, which sits on top of another record of its caller, and so on. These *activation records* are memory blocks used to hold the memory required during the execution of the function and are naturally freed at the end of its execution by popping the record out of the stack. The stack data structure is used to implement the automatic memory of the program, and since different threads execute different functions at the same time, a separate stack is assigned to each of them.

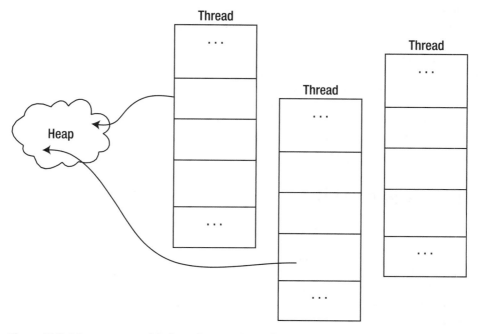

Figure 17-2. *Memory organization of a running CLR program*

Dynamic memory is allocated in the *heap*, which is a data structure where data resides for an amount of time not directly related to the events of program execution. The memory is explicitly allocated by the program, and it is deallocated either explicitly or automatically depending on the strategy adopted by the run time to manage the heap. In the CLR, the heap is managed by a *garbage collector*, which is a program that tracks memory usage and reclaims memory that is no longer used by the program. Data in the heap is always referenced from the stack—or other known areas such as static memory—either directly or indirectly. The garbage collector can deduce the memory potentially reachable by program execution in the future, and the remaining memory can be collected. During garbage collection, the running program may be suspended since the collector may need to manipulate objects needed by its execution. In particular, a garbage collector may adopt a strategy named *copy collection* that can move objects in memory, and during this process, the references may be inconsistent. To avoid dangling references, the memory model adopted by the CLR requires that methods access the heap through object references stored on the stack, and objects in the heap are forbidden to reference data on the stack.

Data structures are the essential tool provided by programming languages to group values. A data structure is rendered as a contiguous area of memory in which the constituents are available at a given offset from the beginning of the memory. The actual layout of an object is determined by the compiler (or by the interpreter for interpreted languages) and is usually irrelevant to the program since the programming language provides operators to access fields without having to explicitly access the memory. System programming, however, often requires explicit manipulation of memory, and programming languages such as C allow controlling the in-memory layout of data structures. The C specification, for instance, defines that fields of a structure are laid out sequentially, though the compiler is allowed to insert extra space between them. Padding is used to align fields at word boundaries of the particular architecture in order to optimize the access to the fields of the structure. Thus, the same data structure in a program may lead to different memory layout depending on the strategy of the compiler or the runtime, even in a language such as C where field ordering is well-defined. By default, the CLR lays out structures in memory without any constraint, which gives the freedom of optimizing memory usage on a particular architecture, though it may introduce interoperability issues if a portion of memory must be shared among the runtimes of different languages.[1]

Interoperability among different programming languages revolves mostly around memory layouts, since the execution of a compiled routine is a jump to a memory address. But routines access memory explicitly, expecting that data is organized in a certain way. In the rest of this chapter, we discuss the mechanisms used by the CLR to interoperate with external code in the form of DLLs or COM components.

COM Interoperability

Component Object Model (COM) is a technology that Microsoft introduced in the 1990s to support interoperability among different programs possibly developed by different vendors. The Object Linking and Embedding (OLE) technology that allows embedding arbitrary content in a Microsoft Word document, for instance, relies on this infrastructure. COM is a binary standard that allows code written in different languages to interoperate, assuming that the programming language supports this infrastructure. Most of the Windows operating system and its applications are based on COM components.

The CLR was initially conceived as an essential tool to develop COM components, being that COM was the key technology at the end of 1990s. It is no surprise that the Microsoft implementation of CLR interoperates easily and efficiently with the COM infrastructure.

In this section, we briefly review the main concepts of the COM infrastructure and its goals in order to show you how COM components can be consumed from F# (and vice versa) and how F# components can be exposed as COM components.

A COM component is a binary module with a well-defined interface that can be dynamically loaded at run time by a running program. The COM design was influenced by CORBA and the Interface Definition Language (IDL) to describe a component as a set of interfaces. In the case of COM, however, components are always loaded inside the process using the dynamic loading of DLLs. Even when a component runs in a different process, a stub is loaded as a DLL, and it is responsible for interprocess communication.

When you create an instance of a COM component, you obtain a pointer to an IUnknown interface that acts as the entry point to all interfaces implemented by the component. The QueryInterface method of this interface allows you to get pointers to additional interfaces.

Interface pointers in COM are pointers to tables of pointers defining the method's location. The program must know the layout of the table in order to read the desired pointer and invoke the corresponding method. This knowledge can be compiled into the program (interfaces

---

1. Languages targeting .NET are not affected by these interoperability issues since they share the same CLR runtime.

must be known at compile time) or acquired at run time by accessing component metadata in the form of an interface named IDispatch or a database called *type library.*

Since COM components can be compiled by any compiler supporting the generation of memory layouts compatible with the standard, it is necessary that the client shares the same layout for data structures that must be passed or returned by the component methods. The standard type system for COM, defined in ole.dll, defines a simple and restricted set of types. COM types correspond to the Variant type of Visual Basic and provide only basic types and arrays. For structured types, COM requires a custom marshaller to be developed, but this has been rarely used in components that are widely available.

The COM infrastructure provides a memory manager that uses reference counting to automatically free components when they are not used anymore. Whenever a copy of a pointer to an interface is copied, the programmer is required to invoke the AddRef method of the IUnknown interface (every interface inherits from IUnknown), and when the pointer is no longer required, the Release method should be called to decrement the counter inside the component. When the counter reaches zero, the component is automatically freed. This strategy of memory management, though more automatic than the traditional malloc/free handling of the heap, has proven to be error prone, because programmers often forget to increment the counter when pointers are copied (risk of dangling pointers) or decrement when a pointer is no longer needed (risk of memory wasted in garbage).

When Microsoft started developing the runtime that has become the CLR, which was doomed to replace the COM infrastructure, several design goals addressed common issues of COM development:

Memory management: Reference counting has proven to be error prone; so a fully automated memory manager was needed to address this issue.

Pervasive metadata: The COM type system was incomplete, and the custom marshaller was too restrictive. A more complete and general type system whose description was available at run time would have eased interoperability.

Data and metadata separation: The separation between data and metadata has proven to be fragile because components without their description are useless, and vice versa. A binary format containing both components and their descriptions avoids these issues.

Distributed components: DCOM, the distributed COM infrastructure, has proven to be inefficient. The CLR has been designed with a distributed memory management approach to reduce the network overhead required to keep remote components alive.

The need for better component infrastructure led Microsoft to create the CLR, but the following concepts from COM proved so successful that they motivated several aspects of the CLR:

Binary interoperability: The ability to interoperate at the binary level gives you the freedom to develop components from any language supporting the component infrastructure, allowing, for instance, Visual Basic developers to benefit from C++ components, and vice versa.

Dynamic loading: The interactive dynamic loading of components is an essential element to allow scripting engines such as Visual Basic for Applications to access the component model.

Reflection: The component description available at run time allows programs to deal with unknown components; this is especially important for programs featuring scripting environments as witnessed by the widespread use of IDispatch and type libraries in COM.

COM METADATA AND WINDOWS REGISTRY

COM components are compiled modules that conform to well-defined protocols designed to allow binary interoperability among different languages. An essential trait of component architectures is the ability to dynamically create components at run time. It is necessary for an infrastructure to locate and inspect components in order to find and load them. The Windows registry holds this information, which is why it is such an important structure in the operating system.

The HKEY_CLASSES_ROOT registry key holds the definition of all the components installed on the local computer. It is helpful to understand the basic layout of the registry in this respect when dealing with COM components. The following is a simple script in Jscript executed by the Windows Scripting Host, which is an interpreter used to execute Visual Basic and Jscript scripts on Windows:

```
w = WScript.CreateObject("Word.Application");
w.Visible = true;
WScript.Echo("Press OK to close Word");
w.Quit();
```

This simple script creates an instance of a Microsoft Word application and shows programmatically its window by setting the Visible property to true. Assuming that the script is executed using the wscript command (the default), its execution is stopped until the message box displayed by the Echo method is closed, and then Word is closed.

How can the COM infrastructure dynamically locate the Word component and load without prior knowledge about it? The COM infrastructure is accessed through the ubiquitous CreateObject method that accepts a string as input that contains the *program ID* of the COM component to be loaded. This is the human-readable name of the component, but the COM infrastructure was conceived as a foundation of a potentially large number of components and therefore adopted the global unique identifier (GUID) strings to define components. GUIDs are often displayed during software installation and are familiar for their mysterious syntax of a sequence of hexadecimal digits enclosed in curly braces. These GUIDs are also used to identify COM classes; these IDs are known as CLSIDs and are stored in the Windows registry as subkeys containing further metadata about the COM object. When CreateObject is invoked, the code infrastructure looks for the key:

```
HKEY_CLASSES_ROOT\Word.Application\CLSID
```

The default value for the key in this example (on one of our computers) is as follows:

```
{000209FF-0000-0000-C000-000000000046}
```

Now you can access the registry key defining the COM component and find all the information relative to the component. The following screenshot shows the content of the LocalServer32 subkey, where it says that winword.exe is the container of the Word.Application component. If a COM component should be executed in a process different from that of the creator, LocalServer32 contains the location of the executable. Components are often loaded in-process in the form of a DLL, and in this case it is the InprocServer32 key that indicates the location of the library.

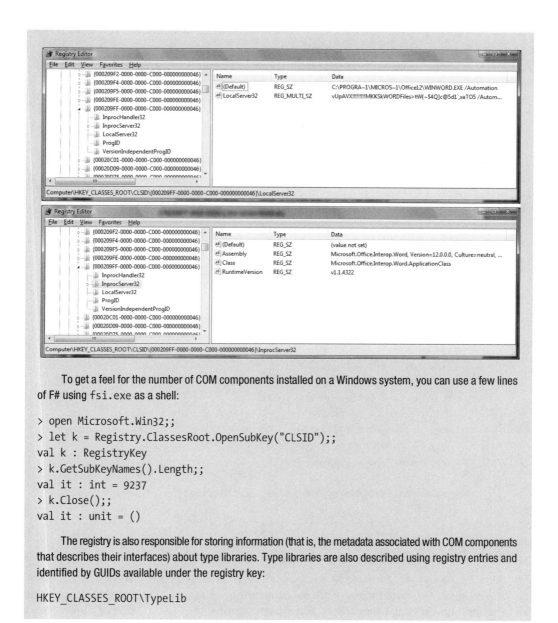

To get a feel for the number of COM components installed on a Windows system, you can use a few lines of F# using `fsi.exe` as a shell:

```
> open Microsoft.Win32;;
> let k = Registry.ClassesRoot.OpenSubKey("CLSID");;
val k : RegistryKey
> k.GetSubKeyNames().Length;;
val it : int = 9237
> k.Close();;
val it : unit = ()
```

The registry is also responsible for storing information (that is, the metadata associated with COM components that describes their interfaces) about type libraries. Type libraries are also described using registry entries and identified by GUIDs available under the registry key:

```
HKEY_CLASSES_ROOT\TypeLib
```

COM components can be easily consumed from F# programs, and the opposite is also possible by exposing .NET objects as COM components. The following example is similar to the one discussed in the "COM Metadata and Windows Registry" sidebar; it is based on the Windows Scripting Host but uses F# and `fsi.exe`:

```
> open System;;
> let o = Activator.CreateInstance(Type.GetTypeFromProgID("Word.Application"));;
val o : obj
> let t = o.GetType();;
val t : Type
> t.GetProperty("Visible").SetValue(o, (true :> Object), null);;
val it : unit  = ()
> let m = t.GetMethod("Quit");;
val m : Reflection.MethodInfo
> m.GetParameters().Length;;
val it : int = 3
> m.GetParameters();;
val it : ParameterInfo []
      = [|System.Object& SaveChanges
            {Attributes = In, Optional, HasFieldMarshal;
             DefaultValue = System.Reflection.Missing;
             IsIn = true;
             IsLcid = false;
             IsOptional = true;
             IsOut = false;
             IsRetval = false;
             Member =
               Void Quit(System.Object ByRef,
                         System.Object ByRef, System.Object ByRef);
             MetadataToken = 134223449;
             Name = "SaveChanges";
             ParameterType = System.Object&;
             Position = 0;
             RawDefaultValue = System.Reflection.Missing;};
          ... more ... |]
> m.Invoke(o, [| null; null; null |]);;
val it : obj = null
```

Since F# imposes type inference, you cannot use the simple syntax provided by an interpreter. The compiler should know in advance the number and type of arguments of a method and the methods exposed by an object. You must remember that even if fsi.exe allows you to interactively execute F# statements, it still is subjected to the constraints of a compiled language. Since you are creating an instance of a COM component dynamically in this example, the compiler does not know anything about this component. Thus, it can be typed as just System.Object. To obtain the same behavior of an interpreted language, you must resort to the reflection support of the .NET runtime. Using the GetType method, you can obtain an object describing the type of the object o. Then you can obtain a PropertyInfo object describing the Visible property, and you can invoke the SetValue method on it to show the Word main window. The SetValue method is generic; therefore, you have to cast the Boolean value to System.Object to comply with the method signature.

In a similar way, you can obtain an instance of the MethodInfo class describing the Quit method. Since a method has a signature, you ask for the parameters; there are three of them, and they are optional. Therefore, you can invoke the Quit method by calling the Invoke method and passing the object target of the invocation and an array of arguments that you set to null because arguments are optional.

How can the runtime interact with COM components? The basic approach is based on the so-called COM callable wrapper (CCW) and the runtime callable wrapper (RCW), as shown in Figure 17-3. The former is a chunk of memory dynamically generated with a layout compatible with the one expected from COM components so that external programs, even legacy Visual Basic 6 applications, can access services implemented as managed components. The latter is more common and creates a .NET type dealing with the COM component, taking care of all the interoperability issues. It is worth noting that although the CCW can always be generated because the .NET runtime has full knowledge about assemblies, the opposite is not always possible. Without IDispatch or type libraries, there is no description of a COM component at run time. Moreover, if a component uses custom marshalling, it cannot be wrapped by an RCW. Fortunately, for the majority of COM components, it is possible to generate the RCW.

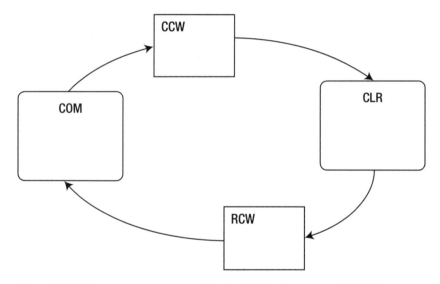

Figure 17-3. *The wrappers generated by the CLR to interact with COM components*

Programming patterns based on event-driven programming are widely adopted, and COM components have a programming pattern to implement callbacks based on the notion of *sink*. The programming pattern is based on the delegate event model, and the sink is where a listener can register a COM interface that should be invoked by a component to notify an event. The Internet Explorer Web Browser COM component (implemented by shdocvw.dll), for instance, provides a number of events to notify its host about the various events such as loading a page or clicking a hyperlink. The RCW generated by the runtime exposes these events in the form of delegates and takes care of handling all the details required to perform the communication between managed and unmanaged code.

Although COM components can be accessed dynamically using .NET reflection, explicitly relying on the ability of the CLR to generate CCW and RCW, it is desirable to use a less verbose approach to COM interoperability. The .NET runtime ships with tools that allow you to generate RCW and CCW wrappers offline, which allows you to use COM components as .NET classes, and vice versa. These tools are as follows:

tlbimp.exe: This is a tool for generating an RCW of a COM component given its type library.

aximp.exe: This is similar to tlbimp.exe and supports the generation of ActiveX components[2] that have graphical interfaces (and that need to be integrated with Windows Forms).

tlbexp.exe: This generates a COM type library describing a .NET assembly. The CLR will be loaded as a COM component and will generate the appropriate CCW to make .NET types accessible as COM components.

regasm.exe: This is similar to tlbexp.exe. It also performs the registration of the assembly as a COM component.

To better understand how COM components can be accessed from your F# programs, and vice versa, consider two examples: in the first one, you will wrap the widely used Flash Player into a form interactively, and in the second one, you will see how an F# object type can be consumed as if it were a COM component.

The Flash Player that you are accustomed to using in your everyday browsing is an ActiveX control that is loaded by Internet Explorer using an OBJECT element in the HTML page (it is also a plug-in for other browsers, but here we are interested in the COM component). By using a search engine, you can easily find that an HTML element similar to the following is used to embed the player in Internet Explorer:

```
<OBJECT
      classid ="clsid:D27CDB6E-AE6D-11cf-96B8-444553540000"
      codebase="http://download.macromedia.com/pub/shockwave/cabs/flash/swflash.cab"
      width   ="640" height="480"
      title   ="My movie">
   <param name="movie"   value="MyMovie.swf" />
   <param name="quality" value="high" />
</OBJECT>
```

From this tag, you know that the CLSID of the Flash Player ActiveX component is the one specified with the classid parameter of the OBJECT element. You can now look in the Windows registry under HKEY_CLASSES_ROOT\CLSID for the subkey corresponding to the CLSID of the Flash ActiveX control. If you look at the subkeys, you notice that the ProgID of the component is ShockwaveFlash.ShockwaveFlash, and InprocServer32 indicates that its location is C:\Windows\system32\Macromed\Flash\Flash9b.ocx. You can also find the GUID relative to the component type library that, when investigated, shows that the type library is contained in the same OCX file.

Since Flash Player is an ActiveX control with a GUI, you can rely on aximp.exe rather than just tlbimp.exe to generate the RCW for the COM component:

---

2. ActiveX components are COM components implementing a well-defined set of interfaces, and they have a graphical interface. Internet Explorer is well known for loading these components, but ActiveX can be loaded by any application using the COM infrastructure.

```
C:\> aximp c:\Windows\System32\Macromed\Flash\Flash9b.ocx
Generated Assembly: C:\ShockwaveFlashObjects.dll
Generated Assembly: C:\AxShockwaveFlashObjects.dll
```

If you use `ildasm.exe` to analyze the structure of the generated assemblies, you'll notice that the wrapper of the COM component is contained in `ShockwaveFlashObjects.dll` and is generated by the `tlbimp.exe` tool; the second assembly simply contains a Windows Forms host for ActiveX components and is configured to host the COM component, exposing the GUI features in terms of the elements of the Windows Forms framework.

You can test the Flash Player embedded in an interactive F# session:

```
> #I "c:\\"
--> Added 'c:\ ' to library include path
> #r "AxShockwaveFlashObjects.dll";;
--> Referenced 'c:\AxShockwaveFlashObjects.dll'
> open AxShockwaveFlashObjects;;
> open System.Windows.Forms;;
> let f = new Form();;
val f : Form
> let flash = new AxShockwaveFlash();;
val flash : AxShockwaveFlash
Binding session to 'c:\AxShockwaveFlashObjects.dll'...
> f.Show();;
val it : unit = ()
> flash.Dock <- DockStyle.Fill;;
val it : unit = ()
> f.Controls.Add(flash);;
val it : unit = ()
> flash.LoadMovie(0, "http://laptop.org/img/meshDemo18.swf");;
val it : unit = ()
```

Here you first add to the include path of the `fsi.exe` directory containing the assemblies generated by `aximp.exe` using the #I directive, and then you reference the `AxShockwaveFlashObjects.dll` assembly using the #r directive. The namespace `AxShockwaveFlashObjects` containing the `AxShockwaveFlash` class is opened; this is the managed class wrapping the ActiveX control. You create an instance of the Flash Player that is now exposed as a Windows Forms control; then you set the `Dock` property to `DockStyle.Fill` to let the control occupy the entire area of the form, and finally you add the control to the form. When typing the commands into F# Interactive, it is possible to test the content of the form. When it first appears, a right-click on the client area is ignored. After the ActiveX control is added to the form, the right-click displays the context menu of the Flash Player. You can now programmatically control the player by setting the properties and invoking its methods; the generated wrapper will take care of all the communications with the ActiveX component.

Now we'll show an example of exposing an F# object type as a COM component. There are several reasons it can be useful to expose a managed class as a COM component, but perhaps the most important is interoperability with legacy systems. COM has been around for a decade and has permeated every aspect of Windows development. Systems have largely used COM infrastructures, and they can also be extended using this technology. COM components are heavily used by applications based on the Active Scripting architecture such as ASP or VBA in Microsoft Office. The ability of exposing F# code to existing applications is useful because it allows you to immediately start using this new language and integrating it seamlessly into existing systems.

In this example, suppose you are exposing a simple F# object type as a COM component and invoke a method of this object type from a JScript script. You define the following type in the hwfs.fs file:

```
open System

type FSCOMComponent =
    new() as x = {}
    member x.HelloWorld() = "Hello world from F#!"
```

The assembly that must be exposed as a COM component should be added to the global assembly cache (GAC), which is where shared .NET assemblies are stored. Assemblies present in the GAC must be strongly named, which means a public key cryptographic signature must be used to certify the assembly. To perform the test, you generate a key pair to be used to sign the assembly using the sn.exe command available with the .NET SDK:

```
C:> sn -k testkey.snk

Microsoft (R) .NET Framework Strong Name Utility  Version 2.0.50727.42
Copyright (c) Microsoft Corporation.  All rights reserved.

Key pair written to testkey.snk
```

Now you can compile the program in a DLL called hwfs.dll:

```
C:\> fsc -a -keyfile testkey.snk hwfs.fs
```

Note that you use the -keyfile switch to indicate to the compiler that the output should be signed using the specified key pair. Now you can add the assembly to the GAC (note that under Windows Vista the shell used should run with administrator privileges):

```
C:\ > gacutil /i hwfs.dll
Microsoft (R) .NET Global Assembly Cache Utility.  Version 2.0.50727.42
Copyright (c) Microsoft Corporation.  All rights reserved.

Assembly successfully added to the cache
```

Now you can use the regasm.exe tool to register the hwfs.dll assembly as a COM component:

```
C:\ > regasm hwfs.dll
Microsoft (R) .NET Framework Assembly Registration Utility 2.0.50727.312
Copyright (C) Microsoft Corporation 1998-2004.  All rights reserved.

Types registered successfully
```

Now you have to write the script using the Jscript language to test the component; the script will use the CreateObject method to create an instance of the F# object type, with the CCW generated by the CLR taking care of all the interoperability issues. But what is the ProgID of the COM component? You use regasm.exe with the /regfile switch to generate a registry file containing the keys corresponding to the registration of the COM component instead of performing it. The generated registry file contains the following component registration (we've included only the most relevant entries):

```
[HKEY_CLASSES_ROOT\Hwfs+FSCOMComponent]
@="Hwfs+FSCOMComponent"

[HKEY_CLASSES_ROOT\Hwfs+FSCOMComponent\CLSID]
@="{41BFA014-8389-3855-BD34-81D8933045BF}"

[HKEY_CLASSES_ROOT\CLSID\{41BFA014-8389-3855-BD34-81D8933045BF}]
@="Hwfs+FSCOMComponent"

[HKEY_CLASSES_ROOT\CLSID\{41BFA014-8389-3855-BD34-81D8933045BF}\InprocServer32]
@="mscoree.dll"
"ThreadingModel"="Both"
"Class"="Hwfs+FSCOMComponent"
"Assembly"="hwfs, Version=0.0.0.0, Culture=neutral, PublicKeyToken=97db6c0b1207bed4"
"RuntimeVersion"="v2.0.50727"
```

The InprocServer32 subkey indicates that the COM component is implemented by mscoree.dll, which is the CLR, and the additional attributes indicate the assembly that should be run by the runtime.

Note that the ProgID and the class name of the component is Hwfs+FSCOMComponent, which is partly derived from the namespace Hwfs generated by the F# compiler. You can now try to write the following script in the hwfs.js file:

```
o = WScript.CreateObject("Hwfs+FSCOMComponent");
WScript.Echo(o.HelloWorld());
```

If you execute the script (here using the command-based host cscript), you obtain the expected output:

```
C:\ > cscript foo.js
Microsoft (R) Windows Script Host Version 5.7
Copyright (C) Microsoft Corporation. All rights reserved.

Hello world from F#!
```

But how can you obtain a ProgID with dot-notation instead of the ugly plus sign? So far, you have used only the basic features of the COM interoperability, but a number of custom attributes can give you finer control over the CCW generation. These attributes are defined in the System.Runtime.InteropServices namespace; and among these classes you'll find the ProgIdAttribute class whose name hints that it is somewhat related to the ProgID. In fact, you can annotate your F# object type using this attribute:

```
open System
open System.Runtime.InteropServices

[<ProgId("Hwfs.FSComponent")>]
type FSCOMComponent =
    new() as x = {}
    member x.HelloWorld() = "Hello world from F#!"
```

First unregister the previous component:

```
C:\> regasm hwfs.dll /unregister
Microsoft (R) .NET Framework Assembly Registration Utility 2.0.50727.312
Copyright (C) Microsoft Corporation 1998-2004.  All rights reserved.

Types un-registered successfully
C:\> gacutil /u hwfs
Microsoft (R) .NET Global Assembly Cache Utility.  Version 2.0.50727.42
Copyright (c) Microsoft Corporation.  All rights reserved.

Assembly: hwfs, Version=0.0.0.0, Culture=neutral,
    PublicKeyToken=8c1f06f522fc70f8, processorArchitecture=MSIL
Uninstalled: hwfs, Version=0.0.0.0, Culture=neutral,
    PublicKeyToken=8c1f06f522fc70f8, processorArchitecture=MSIL
Number of assemblies uninstalled = 1
Number of failures = 0
```

Now you can update the script as follows and register everything again after recompiling the F# file:

```
o = WScript.CreateObject("Hwfs.FSComponent");
WScript.Echo(o.HelloWorld());
```

Using other attributes, it is possible to specify the GUIDs to be used and several other aspects that are important in some situations. When a system expects a component implementing a given COM interface, it is expected that the COM component returns the pointer to the interface with the appropriate GUID; in this case, the ability to explicitly indicate a GUID is essential to defining a .NET interface that should be marshalled as the intended COM interface.

Complex COM components can be tricky to wrap using these tools, and official wrappers are maintained by component developers. Microsoft provides the managed version of the Office components, the managed DirectX library, and the Web Browser control to spare programmers from having to build their own wrappers.

In conclusion, it is possible to use COM components from F#, and vice versa. You can expose F# libraries as COM components, which allows you to extend existing systems using F#, or use legacy code in F# programs

Platform Invoke

COM interoperability is an important area of interoperability in F#, but it is limited to Windows and to the Microsoft implementation of the ECMA and ISO standards of the Common Language Infrastructure (CLI). The CLI standard, however, devises a standard mechanism for interoperability that is called Platform Invoke (PInvoke to friends), and it is a core feature of the standard available on all CLI implementations, including Mono.

The basic model underlying PInvoke is based on loading dynamic linking libraries into the program, which allows managed code to invoke exported functions. Dynamic linking libraries do not provide information other than the entry point location of a function; this is not enough to perform the invocation unless additional information is made available to the runtime.

The invocation of a function requires the following:

- The address of the code in memory

- The calling convention, which is how parameters, return values, and other information is passed through the stack to the function

- Marshalling of values and pointers so that the different runtime support can operate consistently on the same values

The address of the entry point is obtained using a system call that returns the pointer to the function given a string. The remaining information must be provided by the programmer to instruct the CLR about how the function pointer should be used.

CALLING CONVENTIONS

Function and method calls (a method call is similar to a function call but with an additional pointer referring to the object passed to the method) are performed by using a shared stack between the caller and the callee. An activation record is pushed onto the stack when the function is called, and memory is allocated for arguments, the return value, and local variables. Additional information is also stored in the activation record, such as information about exception handling and the return address when the execution of the function terminates.

The physical structure of the activation record is established by the compiler (or by the JIT in the case of the CLR), and this knowledge must be shared between the caller and the called function. When the binary code is generated by a compiler, this is not an issue, but when code generated by different compilers must interact, it may become a significant issue. Although each compiler may adopt a different convention, the need to perform system calls requires that the calling convention adopted by the operating system is implemented, and it is often used to interact with different runtimes. Another popular approach is to support the calling convention adopted by C compilers because it is widely used and has become a fairly universal language for interoperability. Note that although many operating systems are implemented in C, the libraries providing system calls may adopt different calling conventions. This is the case of Microsoft Windows where the operating system adopts the so-called *stdcall* calling convention rather than the C calling convention.

A significant dimension in the arena of possible calling conventions is the responsibility for removing the activation record from the thread stack. At first glance, it may seem obvious that it is the called function that before returning resets the stack pointer to the previous state. This is not the case for programming languages such as C that allow functions with a variable number of arguments such as `printf`. When variable arguments are allowed, it is the caller that knows exactly the size of the activation record; therefore, it is its responsibility to free the stack at the end of the function call. Apart from being consistent with the chosen convention, it may seem that there is little difference between the two choices, but if the caller is responsible for cleaning the stack, each function invocation requires more instructions, which leads to larger executables; for this reason, Windows uses the stdcall calling convention instead of the C calling convention. It is important to notice that the CLR uses an array of objects to pass a variable number of arguments, which is very different from the variable arguments of C because the method receives a single pointer to the array that resides in the heap.

It is important to note that if the memory layout of the activation record is compatible, as it is in Windows, the use of the cdecl convention instead of the stdcall convention leads to a subtle memory leak. If the runtime assumes the stdcall convention (that is the default) and the callee assumes the cdecl convention, the arguments pushed on the stack are not freed, and at each invocation the height of the stack grows until a stack overflow happens.

The CLR supports a number of calling conventions. The two most important are stdcall, which is the convention used by Windows APIs (and many others DLLs), and *cdecl*, which is the convention used by the C language. Other implementations of the runtime may provide additional conventions to the user. In the PInvoke design, there is nothing restricting the supported conventions to these two (and in fact the runtime uses the *fcall* convention for invoking services provided by the runtime from managed code).

The additional information required to perform the function call is provided by custom attributes that are used to decorate a function prototype and inform the runtime about the signature of the exported function.

Getting Started with PInvoke

This section starts with a simple example of a DLL developed using C++ to which you will add code during your experiments using PInvoke. The CInteropDLL.h header file declares a macro defining the decorations associated with each exported function:

```
#define CINTEROPDLL_API __declspec(dllexport)
extern "C" {
void CINTEROPDLL_API HelloWorld();
}
```

The __declspec directive is specific to the Microsoft Visual C++ compiler, and other compilers may provide different ways to indicate the functions that must be exported when compiling a DLL.

The first function is the HelloWorld function; its definition is as expected:

```
void CINTEROPDLL_API HelloWorld()
{
    printf("Hello C world invoked by F#!\n");
}
```

Say you now want to invoke the HelloWorld function from an F# program. You simply have to define the prototype of the function and inform the runtime how to access the DLL and the other information needed to perform the invocation. The program performing the invocation is the following:

```
open System.Runtime.InteropServices

module CInterop =
    [<DllImport("CInteropDLL", CallingConvention=CallingConvention.Cdecl)>]
    extern void HelloWorld()


CInterop.HelloWorld()
```

The extern keyword informs the compiler that the function definition is external to the program and must be accessed through the PInvoke interface. A C-style prototype definition follows the keyword, and the whole declaration is annotated with a custom attribute defined in the System.Runtime.InteropServices namespace. The F# compiler adopts C-style syntax for extern prototypes, including argument types (as you'll see later), because C headers and prototypes are widely used, and this choice helps in the PInvoke definition. The DllImport custom attribute provides the information needed to perform the invocation. The first argument is the name of the DLL containing the function; the remaining option specifies the calling convention chosen to make the call. Since not specified otherwise, the runtime assumes that the name of the F# function is the same as the name of the entry point in the DLL. It is possible to override this behavior using the EntryPoint parameter in the DllImport attribute.

It is important to note the declarative approach of the PInvoke interface. There is no code involved in accessing external functions. The runtime interprets metadata in order to automatically interoperate with native code contained in a DLL. This is a different approach from the one adopted by different virtual machines such as, for example, the Java virtual machine. The Java Native Interface (JNI) requires that the programmer defines a layer of code using types of the virtual machine and invokes the native code.

Platform Invoke requires high privileges in order to execute native code, because the activation record of the native function is allocated on the same stack containing the activation records of managed functions and methods. Moreover, as we will discuss shortly, it is also possible to have the native code invoking a delegate marshalled as a function pointer, allowing stacks with native and managed activation records to be interleaved.

The HelloWorld function is a simple case since the function does not have input arguments and does not return any value. Consider this function with input arguments and a return value:

```
int CINTEROPDLL_API Sum(int i, int j)
{
    return i + j;
}
```

Invoking the Sum function requires integer values to be marshalled to the native code and the value returned to managed code. Simple types such as integers are easy to marshal since they usually are passed by value and use types of the underlying architecture. The F# program using the Sum function is as follows:

```
module CInterop =
    [<DllImport("CInteropDLL", CallingConvention=CallingConvention.Cdecl)>]
    extern int Sum(int i, int j)

printf "Sum(1, 1) = %d\n" (CInterop.Sum(1, 1));
```

Parameter passing assumes the same semantics of the CLR, and parameters are passed by value for value types and by the value of the reference for reference types. Again, you use the custom attribute to specify the calling convention for the invocation.

Data Structures

We first cover what happens when structured data gets marshalled by the CLR in the case of nontrivial argument types. Here we show the SumC function responsible for adding two complex numbers defined by the Complex C data structure:

```
typedef struct _Complex {
    double re;
    double im;
} Complex;

Complex CINTEROPDLL_API SumC(Complex c1, Complex c2)
{
    Complex ret;
    ret.re = c1.re + c2.re;
    ret.im = c1.im + c2.im;
    return ret;
}
```

To invoke this function from F#, you must define a data structure in F# corresponding to the Complex C structure. If the memory layout of an instance of the F# structure is the same as that of the corresponding C structure, then values can be shared between the two languages. But how can you control the memory layout of a managed data structure? Fortunately, the PInvoke specification helps with custom attributes that allow specifying memory layout of data structures. The StructLayout custom attribute consents to indicate the strategy adopted by the runtime to lay out fields of the data structure. By default, the runtime adopts its own strategy in the attempt to optimize the size of the structure, keeping fields aligned to the machine world in order to ensure fast access to the fields of the structure. The C standard ensures that fields are laid out in memory sequentially in the order they appear in the structure definition; other languages may use different strategies. Using an appropriate argument, you can indicate that a C-like sequential layout strategy should be adopted. Moreover, it is also possible to provide an explicit layout for the structure indicating the offset in memory for each field of the structure. For this example, here we use the sequential layout for the Complex value type:

```
module CInterop =
    [<Struct; StructLayout(LayoutKind.Sequential)>]
    type Complex =
        val mutable re:double
        val mutable im:double

        new(r,i) = { re = r; im = i; }

    [<DllImport("CInteropDLL")>]
    extern Complex SumC(Complex c1, Complex c2)

let c1 = CInterop.Complex(1.0, 0.0)
let c2 = CInterop.Complex(0.0, 1.0)

let mutable c3 = CInterop.SumC(c1, c2)
printf "c3 = SumC(c1, c2) = %f + %fi\n" c3.re c3.im;
```

The SumC prototype refers to the F# Complex value type, but since the layout in memory of the structure is the same as the corresponding C structure, the runtime passes the bits that are consistent with those expected by the C code.

MARSHALLING PARAMETERS

A critical aspect in dealing with PInvoke is to ensure that values are marshalled correctly between managed and native code, and vice versa. The memory layout of a structure does not depend on the order of the fields only. Compilers often introduce padding to align fields to memory addresses so that access to fields requires fewer memory operations since CPUs load data into registers with the same strategy. Padding may speed up access to the data structure, though it introduces inefficiencies in memory usage since there may be gaps in the structures leading to allocated but unused memory.

Consider, for instance, the following C structure:

```
struct Foo {
    int i;
    char c;
    short s;
};
```

Depending on compiler decision, it may occupy from 8 up to 12 bytes on a 32-bit architecture. The most compact version of the structure uses the first four bytes for i, a single byte for c, and two more bytes for s. If the compiler aligns fields to addresses that are multiples of four, then the integer i occupies the first slot, four more bytes are allocated for c (though only one is used), and the same happens for s.

Padding is a common practice in C programs, and since it may affect performance and memory usage, compilers provide directives to instruct the compiler about padding. It is possible to have data structures with different padding strategies running within the same program.

The first step to be faced when using PInvoke to access native code is to find the definition of data structures, including information about padding. Then it is possible to annotate F# structures to have the same layout as the native ones, and the CLR can automate the marshalling of data. It is important to note that it is possible to pass parameters by reference; thus, the C code may access the memory managed by the runtime, and errors in memory layout may result in corrupted memory. For this reason, PInvoke code should be kept to the minimum and verified accurately to ensure that the execution state of the virtual machine is preserved. The declarative nature of the interface is of great help in this respect since the programmer has to check simply declarations and not interop code.

Not all the values are marshalled as-is to native code; some values may require additional work from the runtime. Strings, for instance, have different memory representations between native and managed code. C strings are arrays of bytes that are null terminated, while runtime strings are .NET objects with a different layout. Also, function pointers are mediated by the runtime: the calling convention adopted by the CLR is not compatible with external conventions, so code stubs are generated that can be called by native code from managed code, and vice versa.

In the SumC example, arguments are passed by value, but native code often requires data structures to be passed by reference to avoid the cost of copying the entire structure and passing only a pointer to the native data. The ZeroC function resets a complex number whose pointer is passed as an argument:

```
void CINTEROPDLL_API ZeroC(Complex* c)
{
    c->re = 0;
    c->im = 0;
}
```

The F# declaration for the function is the same as the C prototype:

```
[<DllImport("CInteropDLL")>]
extern void ZeroC(Complex* c)
```

Now you need a way to obtain a pointer given a value of type Complex in F#. You can use the && operator that is used to indicate a pass by reference and that results in passing the pointer to the structure expected by the C function:

```
let mutable c4 = CInterop.SumC(c1, c2)
printf "c4 = SumC(c1, c2) = %f + %fi\n" c4.re c4.im

CInterop.ZeroC(&&c4)
printf "c4 = %f + %fi\n" c4.re c4.im
```

In C and C++, the notion of objects (or struct instances) and the classes of memory are orthogonal: an object can be allocated on the stack or on the heap and share the same declaration. In .NET, this is not the case; objects are instances of classes and are allocated on the heap, and value types are stored in the stack or wrapped into objects in the heap.

Is it possible to pass objects to native functions through PInvoke? The main issue with objects is that the heap is managed by the garbage collector, and one possible strategy for garbage collection is copy collection, which is a technique that moves objects in the heap when a collection occurs. Thus, the base address in memory of an object may change over time, which can be a serious problem if the pointer to the object has been marshalled to a native function through a PInvoke invocation. The CLR provides an operation called *pinning* that allows pinning an object and preventing it from moving during a garbage collection. Pinned pointers are assigned to local variables, and pinning is released when the function performing the pinning exits. It is important to understand the scope of pinning, since if the native code stores the pointer somewhere before returning, the pointer may become invalid but still usable from native code.

Now let's define an object type for `Complex` and marshal F# objects to a C function. The goal is to marshal the F# object to the `ZeroC` function. In this case, you cannot use the pass-by-reference operator, and you must define everything so that the type checker is happy with it. You can define another function that refers to `ZeroC` but with a different signature involving `ObjComplex`, which is an object type similar to the `Complex` value type. The `EntryPoint` parameter maps the F# function onto the same `ZeroC` C function, though in this case the argument is of type `ObjComplex` rather than `Complex`:

```
module CInterop =
    [<StructLayout(LayoutKind.Sequential)>]
    type ObjComplex =
        val mutable re:double
        val mutable im:double

        new() as x = { re = 0.0; im = 0.0 }
        new(r:double, i:double) as x = { re = r; im = i }

    [<DllImport("CInteropDLL", EntryPoint="ZeroC")>]
    extern void ObjZeroC(ObjComplex c)

let oc = CInterop.ObjComplex(2.0, 1.0)
printf "oc = %f + %fi\n" oc.re oc.im
CInterop.ObjZeroC(oc)
printf "oc = %f + %fi\n" oc.re oc.im
```

In this case, the object reference is marshalled as a pointer to the C code, and you don't need the && operator in order to call the function; the object is pinned to ensure that it does not move during the function call.

Marshalling Strings

Platform Invoke defines default behavior for mapping common types used by the Win32 API; Table 17-1 shows the default conversions. Most of the mappings are natural, but it is important to note that there are several entries for strings. This is because strings are represented in different ways in programming language runtimes.

To show how strings are marshalled, we start with a simple C function that echoes a string on the console:

```
void CINTEROPDLL_API echo(char* str)
{
    puts(str);
}
```

Table 17-1. *Default Mapping for Types of Win32 API and Listed in* Wtypes.h

Unmanaged Types in Wtypes.h	Unmanaged C Type	Managed Class	Description
HANDLE	void*	System.IntPtr	32 bits on 32-bit Windows operating systems, 64 bits on 64-bit Windows operating systems
BYTE	unsigned char	System.Byte	8 bits
SHORT	short	System.Int16	16 bits
WORD	unsigned short	System.UInt16	16 bits
INT	int	System.Int32	32 bits
UINT	unsigned int	System.UInt32	32 bits
LONG	long	System.Int32	32 bits
BOOL	long	System.Int32	32 bits
DWORD	unsigned long	System.UInt32	32 bits
ULONG	unsigned long	System.UInt32	32 bits
CHAR	char	System.Char	Decorate with ANSI
LPSTR	char*	System.String or System.Text.StringBuilder	Decorate with ANSI
LPCSTR	const char*	System.String or System.Text.StringBuilder	Decorate with ANSI
LPWSTR	wchar_t*	System.String or System.Text.StringBuilder	Decorate with Unicode
LPCWSTR	const wchar_t*	System.String or System.Text.StringBuilder	Decorate with Unicode
FLOAT	Float	System.Single	32 bits
DOUBLE	Double	System.Double	64 bits

The corresponding F# PInvoke prototype is as follows:

```
[<DllImport("CInteropDLL", CallingConvention=CallingConvention.Cdecl)>]
extern void echo(string s);
```

What happens when the F# function echo is invoked? The managed string is represented by an array of Unicode characters described by an object in the heap; the C function expects a pointer to an array of single-byte ANSI characters that are null terminated. The runtime is responsible for performing the conversion between the two formats, and it is performed by default when mapping a .NET string to an ANSI C string.

It is common to pass strings that are modified by C functions, yet .NET strings are immutable. For this reason, it is also possible to use a System.Text.StringBuilder object instead of a string. Instances of this class represent mutable strings and have an associated buffer containing the characters of the string. You can write a C function in the DLL that fills a string buffer given the size of the buffer:

```
void CINTEROPDLL_API sayhello(char* str, int sz)
{
    static char* data = "Hello from C code!";
    int len = min(sz, strlen(data));
    strncpy(str, data, len);
    str[len] = 0;
}
```

Since the function writes into the string buffer passed as an argument, you must take care and use a StringBuilder rather than a string to ensure that the buffer has the appropriate room for the function to write. You can use the following F# PInvoke prototype:

```
[<DllImport("CInteropDLL", CallingConvention=CallingConvention.Cdecl)>]
extern void sayhello(StringBuilder sb, int sz);
```

Since you have to indicate the size of the buffer, you can use a constructor of the StringBuilder class that allows you to specify the initial size of the buffer:

```
let sb = new StringBuilder(50)

CInterop.sayhello(sb, 50)
printf "%s\n" (sb.ToString())
```

You have used ANSI C strings so far, but this is not the only type of string. Wide-character strings are becoming widely adopted and use two bytes to represent a single character; and following the C tradition, the string is terminated by a null character. Consider a wide-character version of the sayhello function:

```
void CINTEROPDLL_API sayhellow(wchar_t* str, int sz)
{
    static wchar_t* data = L"Hello from C code Wide!";
    int len = min(sz, wcslen(data));
    wcsncpy(str, data, len);
    str[len] = 0;
}
```

How can you instruct the runtime that the StringBuilder should be marshalled as a wide-character string rather than an ANSI string? The declarative nature of PInvoke helps by providing a custom attribute to annotate function parameters of the prototype and to inform the CLR about the marshalling strategy to be adopted. The sayhellow function is declared in F# as follows:

```
[<DllImport("CInteropDLL", CallingConvention=CallingConvention.Cdecl)>]
extern void sayhellow([<MarshalAs(UnmanagedType.LPWStr)>]StringBuilder sb, int sz);
```

In this case, the MarshalAs attribute indicates that the string should be marshalled as LPWSTR rather than LPSTR.

Function Pointers

Another important data type that often should be passed to native code is a function pointer. Function pointers are widely used to implement callbacks and provide a simple form of functional programming; think for instance of a sort function that receives as input the pointer to the comparison function. Graphical toolkits have widely used this data type to implement event-driven programming, and they often have to pass a function that will be invoked by another one.

PInvoke is able to marshal delegates as function pointers, and again the runtime is responsible for generating a suitable function pointer callable from native code. When the marshalled function pointer is invoked, a stub is called, and the activation record on the stack is rearranged to be compatible with the calling convention of the runtime. Then the delegate function is invoked.

Although in principle the generated stub is responsible for implementing the calling convention adopted by the native code receiving the function pointer, the CLR supports only the stdcall calling convention for marshalling function pointers. Thus, the native code should adopt this calling convention when invoking the pointer; this is a restriction that may cause problems, but in general on the Windows platform the stdcall calling convention is widely used.

The following C function uses a function pointer to apply a function to an array of integers:

```
typedef int (CALLBACK *TRANSFORM_CALLBACK)(int);

void CINTEROPDLL_API transformArray(int* data, int count, TRANSFORM_CALLBACK fn)
{
    int i;
    for (i = 0; i < count; i++)
        data[i] = fn(data[i]);
}
```

The TRANSFORM_CALLBACK type definition defines the prototype of the function pointer we are interested in here: a function taking an integer as the input argument and returning an integer as a result. The CALLBACK macro is specific to the Microsoft Visual C++ compiler and expands to __stdcall in order to indicate that the function pointer, when invoked, should adopt the stdcall calling convention instead of the cdecl calling convention.

The transformArray function simply takes as input an array of integers with its length and the function to apply to its elements. You now have to define the F# prototype for this function by introducing a delegate type with the same signature as TRANSFORM_CALLBACK:

```
type Callback = delegate of int -> int

[<DllImport("CInteropDLL", CallingConvention=CallingConvention.Cdecl)>]
extern void transformArray(int[] data, int count, Callback transform);
```

Now you can increment all the elements of an array by one using the C function:

```
let data = [| 1; 2; 3 |]
printf "%s\n" (string.Join("; ", (Array.map any_to_string data)))

CInterop.transformArray(data, data.Length, new CInterop.Callback(fun x -> x + 1))
printf "%s\n" (string.Join("; ", (Array.map any_to_string data)))
```

PInvoke declarations are concise, but you must pay attention that for data types such as function pointers, parameter passing can be expensive. In general, libraries assume that crossing the language boundary causes a loss of efficiency and callbacks are invoked at a price different from ordinary functions. In this respect, the example represents a situation where the overhead of PInvoke is significant since a single call to transformArray causes a number of callbacks without performing any real computation into the native code.

PInvoke Memory Mapping

As a more complicated example of PInvoke usage, in this section we show how to benefit from memory mapping into F# programs. Memory mapping is a popular technique that allows a program to see a file (or a portion of a file) as if it was in memory, providing an efficient way to access files because the operating system uses the machinery of virtual memory for accessing files and significantly speeding up data access on files. After proper initialization, which we will cover in a moment, the program obtains a pointer into the memory, and access to that portion of memory appears the same as accessing data stored in or into the file. Memory mapping can be used both for reading and writing files, and every access performed into the memory is reflected into the corresponding position into the file.

This is a typical sequence of system calls in order to map a file in memory:

1. A call to the CreateFile system call to open the file and obtain a handle to the file.

2. A call to the CreateFileMapping system call to create a mapped file object.

3. One or more calls to MapViewOfFile and UnmapViewOfFile to map and release portions of a file into memory. In a typical usage, the whole file is mapped at once in memory.

4. A call to CloseHandle to release the file.

The PInvoke interface to the required functions involves simple type mappings as is usual for Win32 API functions. All the functions are in kernel32.dll, and the signature can be found in the Windows SDK. Listing 17-1 contains the definition of the F# wrapper for memory mapping.

The SetLastError parameter informs the runtime that the called function uses the Windows mechanism for error reporting and that the GetLastError function can be read in case of error; otherwise, the CLR ignores such a value. The CharSet parameter indicates the character set assumed, and it is used to distinguish between ANSI and Unicode characters; with Auto, you delegate the runtime to decide the appropriate version.

You can define the generic class MemMap that uses the functions to map a given file into memory. The goal of the class is to provide access to memory mapping in a system where memory is not directly accessible because the runtime is responsible for its management. A natural programming abstraction to expose the memory to F# code is to provide an array-like interface where the memory is seen as a homogeneous array of values.

Listing 17-1. *Exposing Memory Mapping in F#*

```
#light

module MMap =
```

```fsharp
open System
open System.IO
open System.Runtime.InteropServices
open Microsoft.FSharp.NativeInterop
open Printf

type HANDLE = nativeint
type ADDR   = nativeint

[<DllImport("kernel32", SetLastError=true)>]
extern bool CloseHandle(HANDLE handler)

[<DllImport("kernel32", SetLastError=true, CharSet=CharSet.Auto)>]
extern HANDLE CreateFile(string lpFileName,
                         int dwDesiredAccess,
                         int dwShareMode,
                         HANDLE lpSecurityAttributes,
                         int dwCreationDisposition,
                         int dwFlagsAndAttributes,
                         HANDLE hTemplateFile)

[<DllImport("kernel32", SetLastError=true, CharSet=CharSet.Auto)>]
extern HANDLE CreateFileMapping(HANDLE hFile,
                                HANDLE lpAttributes,
                                int flProtect,
                                int dwMaximumSizeLow,
                                int dwMaximumSizeHigh,
                                string lpName)

[<DllImport("kernel32", SetLastError=true)>]
extern ADDR MapViewOfFile(HANDLE hFileMappingObject,
                          int dwDesiredAccess,
                          int dwFileOffsetHigh,
                          int dwFileOffsetLow,
                          int dwNumBytesToMap)

[<DllImport("kernel32", SetLastError=true, CharSet=CharSet.Auto)>]
extern HANDLE OpenFileMapping(int dwDesiredAccess,
                              bool bInheritHandle,
                              string lpName)

[<DllImport("kernel32", SetLastError=true)>]
extern bool UnmapViewOfFile(ADDR lpBaseAddress)

let INVALID_HANDLE = new IntPtr(-1)
let MAP_READ     = 0x0004
let GENERIC_READ = 0x80000000
```

```
let NULL_HANDLE = IntPtr.Zero
let FILE_SHARE_NONE = 0x0000
let FILE_SHARE_READ = 0x0001
let FILE_SHARE_WRITE = 0x0002
let FILE_SHARE_READ_WRITE = 0x0003
let CREATE_ALWAYS  = 0x0002
let OPEN_EXISTING   = 0x0003
let OPEN_ALWAYS  = 0x0004
let READONLY = 0x00000002


type MemMap<'a> (fileName) =

    let ok =
        match (type 'a) with
        | ty when ty = (type int)     -> true
        | ty when ty = (type int32)   -> true
        | ty when ty = (type byte)    -> true
        | ty when ty = (type sbyte)   -> true
        | ty when ty = (type int16)   -> true
        | ty when ty = (type uint16)  -> true
        | ty when ty = (type int64)   -> true
        | ty when ty = (type uint64)  -> true
        | _ -> false

    do if not ok then failwithf
        "the type %s is not a basic blittable type" ((type 'a).ToString())
    let hFile =
        CreateFile (fileName,
                    GENERIC_READ,
                    FILE_SHARE_READ_WRITE,
                    IntPtr.Zero, OPEN_EXISTING, 0, IntPtr.Zero  )
    do if ( hFile.Equals(INVALID_HANDLE) ) then
        Marshal.ThrowExceptionForHR(Marshal.GetHRForLastWin32Error());
    let hMap = CreateFileMapping (hFile, IntPtr.Zero, READONLY, 0,0, null )
    do CloseHandle(hFile) |> ignore
    do if hMap.Equals(NULL_HANDLE) then
        Marshal.ThrowExceptionForHR(Marshal.GetHRForLastWin32Error());

    let start = MapViewOfFile (hMap, MAP_READ,0,0,0)

    do  if ( start.Equals(IntPtr.Zero) ) then
        Marshal.ThrowExceptionForHR(
            Marshal.GetHRForLastWin32Error())


    member m.AddressOf(i: int) : 'a nativeptr =
        NativePtr.of_nativeint(start + Int32.to_nativeint i)
```

```
member m.GetBaseAddress (i:int) : int -> 'a =
    NativePtr.get (m.AddressOf(i))

member m.Item
    with get(i : int) : 'a = m.GetBaseAddress 0 i

member m.Close() =
    UnmapViewOfFile(start) |> ignore;
    CloseHandle(hMap) |> ignore

interface IDisposable with
    member m.Dispose() =
        m.Close()
```

The class exposes two properties, `Item` and `Element`. The former returns a function that allows access to data in the mapped file at a given offset using a function; the latter allows access to the mapped file at a given offset from the origin.

The following example uses the `MemMap` class to read the first byte of a file:

```
let mm = new MMap.MemMap<byte>("somefile.txt")

printf "%A\n" (mm.[0])

mm.Close()
```

Memory mapping provides good examples of how easy it can be to expose native functionalities into the .NET runtime and how F# can be effective in this task. It is also a good example of the right way to use PInvoke to avoid calling PInvoked functions directly and build wrappers that encapsulate them. Verifiable code is one of the greatest benefits provided by virtual machines, and PInvoke signatures often lead to nonverifiable code that requires high execution privileges and are under the risk of corrupting the whole memory of the runtime.

A good approach to reduce the amount of potentially unsafe code is to define assemblies that are responsible for accessing native code with PInvoke and that expose functionalities in a .NET verifiable approach. In this way, the code that should be trusted by the user is smaller, and programs can have all the benefits provided by verified code.

Wrapper Generation and Limits of PInvoke

Platform Invoke is a flexible and customizable interface, and it is expressive enough to define prototypes for most libraries available. There are, however, pathological situations where it can be difficult to map directly the native interface into the corresponding signature. A significant example is given by function pointers embedded into structures, which are typical C programming patterns that approximate object-oriented programming. Here the structure contains a number of pointers to functions that can be used as methods, having care to pass the pointer to the structure as the first argument to simulate the `this` parameter. Sleepycat's Berkeley Database (BDB) is a popular database library that adopts this programming pattern. The core structure describing an open database has the following structure:

```
struct __db {
     /* ... */
     DB_ENV *dbenv;              /* Backing environment. */
     DBTYPE type;                /* DB access method type. */
     /* ... */
     int  (*close) __P((DB *, u_int32_t));
     int  (*cursor) __P((DB *, DB_TXN *, DBC **, u_int32_t));
     int  (*del) __P((DB *, DB_TXN *, DBT *, u_int32_t));
     // ...
}
```

It was impossible to access directly from the PInvoke interface until .NET 2.0 because function pointers in managed structures were impossible to describe. With version 2 of the runtime, the System.Runtime.InteropServices.Marshal class features the GetFunctionPointerForDelegate for obtaining a pointer to a function that invokes a given delegate. The caller of the function has to guarantee that the delegate object will remain alive for the lifetime of the structure, since stubs generated by the runtime are not moved by the garbage collector but can still be collected. Furthermore, there is the problem that callbacks must adopt the stdcall calling convention in order, and if this is not the case, the PInvoke interface cannot interact with the library.

When the expressivity of PInvoke is not enough for wrapping a function call, it is still possible to write an adapter library in a native language such as C. This was the approach followed by the BDB# library where an intermediate layer of code has been developed to make the interface to the library compatible with PInvoke. The trick has been, in this case, to define a function for each database function, taking as input the pointer to the structure and performing the appropriate call:

```
DB *db;
// BDB call
db->close(db, 0);
// Wrapper call
db_close(db, 0);
```

The problem with wrappers is that they have to be maintained manually, when the signatures of the original library change. The intermediate adapter makes it more difficult to maintain the overall interoperability of code.

Many libraries have a linear interface that can be easily wrapped using PInvoke, and of course wrapper generators have been developed. At the moment there are no wrapper generators for F#, but the C-like syntax for PInvoke declarations makes it easy enough to translate C# wrappers into F# code. An example of such a tool is SWIG, which is a multilanguage wrapper generator that reads C header files and generates interop code for a large number of programming languages such as C#.

Summary

In this chapter, you saw how F# can interoperate with native code in the form of COM components and the standard Platform Invoke interface defined by the ECMA and ISO standards. Neither mechanism is dependent on F#, but the language exposes the appropriate abstractions built into the runtime. You studied how to consume COM components from F# programs, and vice versa, and how DLLs can be accessed through PInvoke.

■ ■ ■

CHAPTER 18

Debugging and Testing F# Programs

Anecdotal evidence indicates that functional programming frequently leads to a substantially reduced bug rate for good programmers. This is primarily because programs built using functional techniques tend to be highly compositional, building correct programs out of correct building blocks. Functional programming style, moreover, avoids or substantially reduces the use of side effects in the program, one property that makes programs more compositional. However, debugging and testing are still essential activities to ensure that a program is as close as possible to its specifications. Bugs and misbehaviors are facts of life, and F# programmers must learn techniques to find and remove them.

As a result, software testing is an important activity when developing large systems. Tests are initially carried out by simply writing small programs and interactively running them, but then a larger infrastructure quickly becomes necessary as a system grows and as new functionalities must preserve the existing ones. In this chapter, we will discuss how you can perform testing with F# using F# Interactive, using the debugging facilities provided by Visual Studio and the .NET infrastructure, and using the NUnit framework for unit testing.

A widely adopted debugging technique is the "do-it-yourself-by-augmenting-your-program-with-`printf`" approach. However, this is a technique that suffers from several problems and, although still useful, should not be the only technique you are prepared to apply to the complexities associated with program testing and debugging.

For testing, there are several strategies to test programs and ensure that they behave as expected, and the testing theory developed by software engineering has introduced several techniques used every day in software development. In this chapter, we focus on three aspects of program debugging and testing with F#:

- Using the Visual Studio debugger and the .NET debugging framework

- Using F# Interactive for testing and debugging

- Doing unit testing using NUnit, a freely available framework for unit testing

Alternative tools for debugging and unit testing are available, such as the .NET debugger that ships with the .NET Framework and the testing framework included in the Team Edition of Visual Studio. The concepts behind these tools are similar to those presented here, and the techniques discussed in this chapter can be easily adapted when using them. All these techniques and tools are very helpful, but it is important to remember that these are just tools and you must use them in the appropriate way.

Debugging F# Programs

Programming systems such as .NET support debugging as a primary activity through tools to help programmers inspect the program for possible errors. The debugger is one of the most important of these tools, and it allows you to inspect the program state during the execution. It is possible to execute the program stepwise and analyze its state during execution.

DEBUGGABLE PROGRAMS

The debugger requires support from debugged programs in order to work properly; for interpreted languages, it is the interpreter that supervises the program execution, and the debugger must interact with it. Compiled languages, on the other hand, must include this support during compilation so that the debugger can properly interact with the running program.

The CLR provides support for program debugging, and compiled programs provide information to the debugger via a file with a .pdb file extension, which is the program debugging database. Since the compilation process maps high-level programming constructs into equivalent ones in a less expressive language (in this case the intermediate language), some information gets lost during this process even if the semantics of the program are preserved. An example is the name of local variables that in the intermediate language are referred to use indexes into an array rather than names. A database is used to preserve the information on the correspondence between the program instructions and the intermediate language instructions, and it is used by the debugging infrastructure to create the illusion that the program is interpreted at the language level showing the current line of execution in the source code rather than the one in the compiled and actually running program. The database retains correspondence among intermediate language instructions (and those that have been used to generate them) and other important information, such as local variable names, that is lost during compilation. The program database is language independent so that the debugger tool can be shared among different programming languages and the programmer can analyze the program execution even when a program has been developed with different languages. It is also possible to step through unmanaged code from managed code, and vice versa.

Debugging without the .pdb file is still possible, though the debugger is incapable of showing the source code, and the intermediate code or the machine code is shown to the user.

We'll start with the following simple function that is, in principle, meant to return true if the input string is a palindrome and false otherwise:

```
let isPalindrome (str:string) =
    let rec check(s:int, e:int) =
        if s = e then true
        elif str.[s] <> str.[e] then false
        else check(s + 1, e - 1)

    check(0, str.Length - 1)
```

The function appears correct at first sight. However, it works only for strings with an odd number of characters and strings with an even length that are not palindromes. In particular, the program raises an exception with the "abba" string as input.

We'll show how to use the Visual Studio debugger to figure out the problem with this simple function. The algorithm recursively tests the characters of the string pair-wise at the beginning and at the end of the string because a string is a palindrome if the first and last characters are equal and the substring obtained by removing them is a palindrome too. The s and e variables define the boundaries of the string to be tested and initially refer to the first and last characters of the input string. Recursion terminates when the outermost characters of the string to be tested differ or when you have tested the whole string and the indexes collide.

Figure 18-1 shows the debugging session of the simple program. You set a breakpoint at the instruction that prints the result of the isPalindrome function for the "abba" string by clicking where the red circle is shown, which indicates the location of the breakpoint. When the program is started in debug mode, its execution stops at the breakpoint, and you can step through the statements. The current instruction is indicated by the yellow arrow, and the current statement is highlighted, as shown in Figure 18-1.

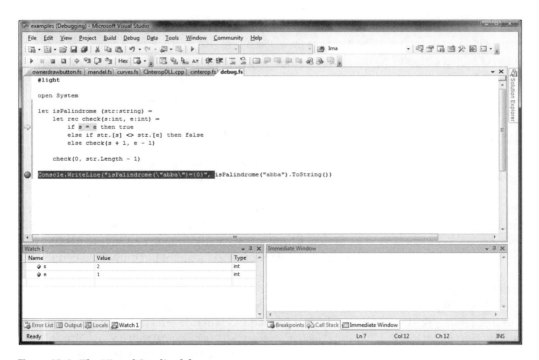

Figure 18-1. *The Visual Studio debugger*

The state of the program is accessible through a number of windows showing different aspects of the running program, usually docked at the bottom of the debugging window. It is possible, for instance, to inspect the state of the local variables of the current method (the Locals window showing the local variables and arguments, e and s in this example) or the state of the call stack to see the sequence of method calls (the Call Stack window). An important window is the Watch view, which can be used to write variable names and simple expressions and watch them change during the execution. It is also possible to evaluate expressions in the Immediate window and invoke methods, as shown in Figure 18-1, where the simple expressions e and s are used. More views are available through the Debug menu, including the state of executing threads and the memory.

In this simple example, you are examining why isPalindrome misbehaves for an input string of even length. As shown in Figure 18-1, the Watch window has been used to monitor the s and e variables intended to define the bounds of the substring that has still to be checked; in this case, the two indexes cross without ever becoming equal, which is the criteria used to successfully stop the recursion. This happens when s has value 2 and e has value 1 in the example. The symptom of the misbehavior of the function is that an exception is thrown; this is frequently where debugging starts. In this example, the exception would have been thrown a few steps forward when e gets value -1, which is an invalid index for accessing a character in a string. If we used str[e] as the watch expression or in the Immediate window, the problem would appear rather evident. Now that we have found the bug, we can fix it by extending the test from s = e to s >= e to ensure that even if the end index becomes smaller than the starting one, we deal the situation appropriately.

■**Note** In Visual Studio and other Microsoft .NET debugging tools, the debugger expressions follow the C# syntax, and arrays do not require the dot before the square braces. The most noticeable differences between C# and F# expression syntax are that access to arrays uses [ ] rather than . [ ] and the equality operator is == rather than =.

Using Advanced Features of the Visual Studio Debugger

We'll now focus on relevant aspects of the debugging facilities that the CLR provides to managed applications and via tools such as the Visual Studio debugger.

Consider the notion of breakpoint, an essential tool to mark a statement in the program where you want to suspend its execution and inspect the program state. Often a bug appears only under very specific conditions. Trivial bugs such as the one we have discussed are the easiest to track and the first to be fixed in a program. It can be difficult or even impossible to suspend program execution not at the first execution of a statement but only when certain conditions are satisfied. Many programmers introduce an if statement with a dummy statement for the body and set the breakpoint to the statement to suspend the program under the defined condition; this requires a recompilation of the program and a change to the source code, which may lead to further problems, particularly when several points of the program must be kept under control. A more effective strategy is to use *conditional breakpoints*, a powerful tool offered by the debugger. With a right-click on a breakpoint in the editor window or in the Breakpoints window (accessible through the Debug menu), a number of additional options become available.

For each breakpoint it is possible to indicate the following:

- *A condition*: An expression indicates a condition that must be satisfied by the program state in order to suspend the program execution.

- *A hit count*: The number of times that the breakpoint should be hit before suspending the execution.

- *A filter*: A mechanism to filter the machine, process, and thread to select the set of threads that will be suspended when the breakpoint is hit.

- *An action*: This is to be executed when the breakpoint is hit, causing the execution of a given action.

Breakpoint conditions and hit counts are the most frequently used options. Hit count is useful when a bug appears only after a significant period of execution; for instance, when debugging a search engine, a bug may occur only after indexing gigabytes of data and the number of hits of the breakpoint can be determined. Conditional expressions are more useful when it is difficult to reproduce exactly the execution and when the number of times that the breakpoint is hit is variable. As for expressions typed in the Immediate window, conditional expressions are expressed as in C#, and this is for all languages, since the debugger infrastructure within the CLR is designed to deal with compiled programs and ignores the source language.

Sometimes it is necessary to debug a running program that has been started without the debugger; a typical situation is when debugging a service started through the Service snap-in of the Management Console or when debugging a Web application live that is executed by IIS rather than by the web server used for development by Visual Studio 2005. In these situations, it is possible to attach the debugger to a running process by selecting the Attach to Process item of the Debug menu and selecting the process to debug. There are standard processes that are generally known to programmers, such as w3p.exe, which is used by IIS to run application pools where ASP.NET applications run, or the svchost.exe process, which generally hosts Windows services. However, sometimes it can be difficult to find out which process is running the code to debug, since there are several of these generic process hosts for running applications.

Debugging a program slows down significantly its speed since the debugger infrastructure injects code to monitor program execution. Conditional breakpoints tend to make the situation worse because every time the breakpoint is hit, the condition must be tested before resuming the standard execution.

The CLR debugging infrastructure operates at the level of compiled assemblies; this has several implications. The objects and types that are visible to the debugger are those generated by the compiler and not always explicitly defined by the programmer in the source code; the program database information tends to preserve the mapping between the source and the compiled program, but sometimes the underlying structure surfaces to the user. On the other hand, it is possible to debug programs written in different programming languages, even when managed and unmanaged code must interoperate.

■**Note** One tricky problem with F# programs can be debugging *tail calls*. We described tail calls in Chapter 8. In particular, when a tail call is executed, the calling stack frame will be removed prior to the call. This means the calls shown in the Visual Studio call stack window may not be complete. It may be missing entries that should, logically speaking, be present, according to the strict call sequence that caused a program to arrive at a particular point. Likewise, the debugger commands step-into and step-out can behave a little unusually when stepping into a tail call.

Figure 18-2 shows a debugging session of the program discussed in Chapter 17; we have stepped into the HelloWorld method, which is a C function accessed through the PInvoke interface as witnessed by the Call Stack window. To enable the cross-language debugging, we indicated in the project options, specifically in the Debug section, that the debugging scope is the whole program rather than the current project.

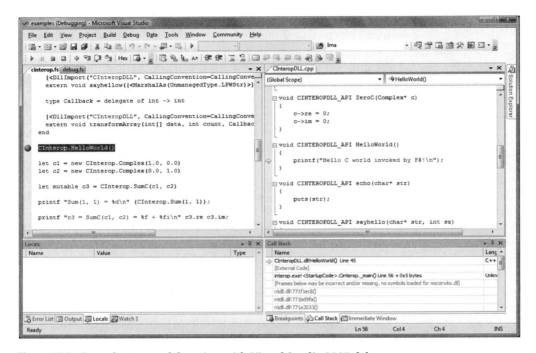

Figure 18-2. *Cross-language debugging with Visual Studio 2005 debugger*

Instrumenting Your Program with the System.Diagnostics Namespace

A managed application can programmatically access the debugging services of the CLR through the types contained in the System.Diagnostics namespace. There are several types in the namespace encompassing several aspects of the runtime, including stack tracing, communications with the debugger, performance counter access for reading statistics about the computer state (memory and CPU usage are typically available using them), and operating system processes handling.

We'll focus on the classes related to debugging and the debugger. There are mainly three ways to interact with the debugging infrastructure:

- The Debug class is used to programmatically assert conditions in the program and output debugging and tracing information to debuggers and other listeners.

- The Debugger class is used to interact with the debugger, check whether it is attached, and trigger breaks explicitly from the program.

- The debugging attributes are a set of custom attributes that can be used to annotate the program to control its behavior (see Chapters 9 and 10 for more information about custom attributes).

The Debug class provides a mean to output diagnostics messages without assuming that the program has been compiled as a console application, and all the debug output is collected by one or more *listeners* that receive the output notifications and do something with them. Each listener is an instance of a class inherited from the TraceListener class and typically sends the output to the console, or to a file, or notifies the user with a dialog box (you can find more information about how to write a listener in the class library documentation). In the following example, we have instrumented the isPalindrome function with tracing statements:

```
let isPalindrome (str:string) =
    let rec check(s:int, e:int) =
        Debug.WriteLine("check call")
        Debug.WriteLineIf((s = 0), "check: First call")
        Debug.Assert((s >= 0 || s < str.Length), sprintf "s is out of bounds: %d" s)
        Debug.Assert((e >= 0 || e < str.Length), sprintf "e is out of bounds: %d" e)
        if s = e || s = e + 1 then true
        else if str.[s] <> str.[e] then false
        else check(s + 1, e - 1)
```

The Write*XXX* methods of the Debug class are used to output data of a running program and are a sophisticated version of the printf debugging approach, where the program is enriched with print statements that output useful information about its current state. In this case, however, it is possible to redirect all the messages to different media rather than just print them to the console. It is also possible to conditionally output messages to reduce the number of messages sent to the debug output. In the example, we output a message each time the check method is invoked and use the conditional output to mark the first invocation.

Assertions are a well-known mechanism to assert conditions about the state of a running program, ensuring that at a given point in the program certain preconditions must hold; for instance, assertions are often used to ensure that the content of an option-valued variable is not None at some point in the program. During testing we want to ensure that if this precondition is not satisfied, the program execution will be suspended as soon as possible. This avoids a tracing back from the point where the undefined value of the variable would lead to an exception. The Assert method allows specifying a Boolean condition that must hold; otherwise, the given message is displayed, prompting the user with the failed assertion.

Both debug output and assertions are statements that typically are useful during the program development, though when a release is made, these calls introduce unnecessary overhead. Often the program compiled with these extra checks is indicated as the checked version of the program. The .NET Framework designers devised a general mechanism to strip out the calls to methods under a particular condition with the help of the compiler. The ConditionalAttribute custom attribute is used to label methods whose calls are included in the program only if a given compilation symbol is defined; for the methods in the Debug type, it is the DEBUG symbol. The F# compiler supports this mechanism, making it is possible to leverage these tools to instrument the F# program in a way that is supported by the .NET infrastructure.

The Debugger type lets you check whether the program is attached to a debugger and to trigger a break if required. It is also possible to programmatically launch the debugger using this type and send log messages to it. This type is used less often than the Debug type, but it may be useful if a bug arises only without an attached debugger. In this case, it is possible to programmatically start the debugging process when needed.

Another mechanism that allows controlling the interaction between a program and the debugger is based on a set of custom attributes in the System.Diagnostics namespace. Table 18-1 shows the attributes that control in part the behavior of the debugger.

Table 18-1. *Attributes Controlling Program Behavior Under Debug*

Attribute	Description
DebuggerBrowsableAttribute	Determines whether and how a member is displayed in the debug window.
DebuggerDisplayAttribute	Indicates how a type or field should be displayed in the debug window.
DebuggerHiddenAttribute	The debugger may interpret this attribute and forbid interaction with the member annotated with it.
DebuggerNonUserCodeAttribute	Marks code that is not user written (for instance, designer-generated code) and that can be skipped to not complicate the debugging experience.
DebuggerStepperBoundaryAttribute	Used to locally override the usage of DebuggerNonUserCodeAttribute.
DebuggerStepThroughAttribute	The debugger may interpret this attribute and disallow stepping into the target method.
DebuggerTypeProxyAttribute	Indicates a type that is responsible for defining how a type is displayed in the debug window; it may affect debugging performance and should be used only when it is really necessary to radically change how a type is displayed.
DebuggerVisualizerAttribute	Indicates for a type the type that defines how to render it while debugging.

These attributes allow you to control essentially two aspects of the debugging: how data is visualized by the debugger and how the debugger should behave with respect to the visibility of members.

The ability to control how types are displayed by the debugger can be helpful to produce customized views of data that may significantly help inspect the program state into an aggregate view. The easiest way is to use the DebuggerDisplayAttribute attribute, which supports the customization of the text associated with a value in the debugger window; an object of that type can still be inspected in every field. Consider the following simple example:

```
[<DebuggerDisplay("{re}+{im}i")>]
type MyComplex=
    { re : double
      im : double }
let c = { re = 0.0; im = 0.0 }
Console.WriteLine("{0}+{1}i", c.re, c.im)
```

Here we're introducing a record named MyComplex with the classic definition of a complex number. The DebuggerDisplayAttribute attribute is used to annotate the type so that the debugger will display its instances using the mathematical notation rather than just displaying the type name. The syntax allowed assumes that curly braces are used to indicate the name of a property whose value should be inserted in the format string. Figure 18-3 shows the result in the Visual Studio 2005 debugger: on the left side is how the debugger window appears when `MyComplex` is without the `DebuggerDisplay` annotation; on the right side the custom string appears, and the properties in the string appear in curly braces. As you can see, the difference is in the value field, and the structure can still be inspected. You can use a custom visualizer to fully customize the appearance of the data within the debugger, but it may affect debugging performance.

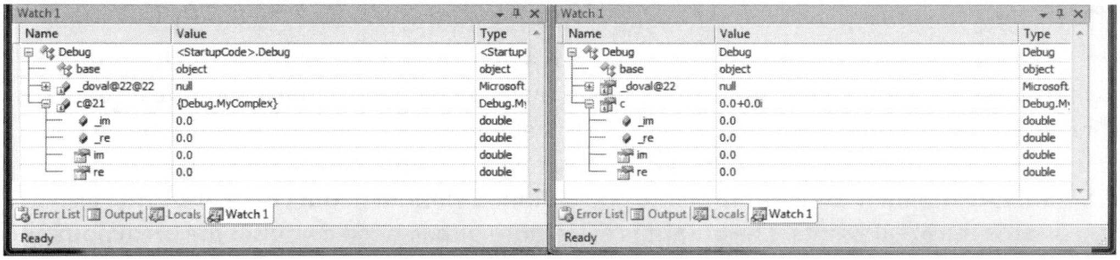

Figure 18-3. *The* `MyComplex` *type shown by the debugger without and with* `DebuggerDisplay`

Figure 18-3 is also interesting because it shows how the debugger displays information from the compiled program. In this case, the association between the name c and the runtime local variable has been lost, and the record appears because it has been compiled by the compiler as a pair of fields and public properties.

The rest of the namespace contains classes to interact with the runtime: the event logging infrastructure, processes and threads management, and the representation of the stack of a thread. Stack manipulation can be useful if it is necessary to know the call sequence that leads to executing a particular method. The `StackTrace` type exposes a list of `StackFrame` objects that provide information about each method call on the stack.

Debugging Concurrent and Graphical Applications

Although a debugger is a fundamental tool for inspecting applications, it is not the Holy Grail, and it must be used carefully, being aware of the fact that the process will interfere with the normal execution of the application. The most relevant impact that the debugging process has over a running program is the influence over the execution timing, which is a critical aspect of concurrent and graphical applications, which are becoming common nowadays. Sometimes a bug even disappears while using the debugger because of these changes to execution timings.

Debugging and testing concurrent applications can be particularly difficult because the use of a debugger is guaranteed to alter execution timings. There is no general rule for debugging concurrent applications, but here we briefly discuss how the debugger can be used in these cases. Consider this simple example of a multithreaded application:

```
#light
open System
open System.Threading
```

```
let t1 = Thread(fun () ->
    while true do
        printf "Thread 1\n"
)
let t2 = Thread(fun () ->
    while true do
        printf "Thread 2\n"
)
t1.Start()
t2.Start()
```

Threads t1 and t2 access the console, which is a shared resource; when we run the program without a debugger attached, the string printed by the two threads appears interleaved on the console. If you set a breakpoint on the two printf statements and you start a debugging session, you see that stepping automatically moves from one thread to the other and the output of the program is completely different from the one obtained without debugging; this is true also if you disable the breakpoints. The output is even more unbalanced if you set the breakpoint in only one of the two threads.

We discussed shared memory multithreaded applications in Chapter 13. In these applications, shared objects accessed by different threads are critical resources that may be viewed in the debugger. If the debug of a single thread fails, setting breakpoints in different threads may help to study the dynamic of the application, even if the full interaction of the threads cannot be fully simulated. If this approach fails, it may be useful to introduce tests inside the application and use the Debugger type only when a given condition occurs. Channel-based message-passing applications are generally easier to debug than those that rely on shared memory, because it is possible to monitor the communication end points using breakpoints or logging messages. Although the careful use of the debugger may help in debugging concurrent applications, sometimes external observation is enough to influence a running program. In these cases, tracing through debug output becomes a viable alternative, and in fact, large systems have different levels of traces to monitor program execution while running.

Graphical applications also present issues when debugging. As discussed in Chapter 11, the event loop of a GUI application is handled by a single thread, and if this is blocked, the GUI of the application will cease working until it is suspended in the debugger. Consider the following simple application:

```
open System
open System.Windows.Forms

let f = new Form(Text="Hello world")
let b = new Button(Text="Click me!", Dock=DockStyle.Fill)
b.Click.Add(fun _ ->
    b.Text <- "Click me again"
    MessageBox.Show("Hello world") |> ignore
)
f.Controls.Add(b)

f.Show()

Application.Run(f)
```

If you set a breakpoint at the MessageBox statement and debug the application, then when the button is clicked, the debugger suspends execution, and the form stops responding. Moreover, the text of the button does not change until the execution is resumed. This effect is because the thread suspended by the debugger is responsible for handling GUI events, including the paint event that will refresh the content of the button updating the button label.

More specifically, event handlers can affect the appearance of a form in two ways: by setting properties of graphical controls and by explicitly drawing using a Graphics object. In the first case, the change will not be noticed until the execution is resumed; this is because the property change usually asks for a refresh of the control appearance, which will eventually result in a paint event that must be processed by the thread that is suspended in the debugger. In the second case, updates are immediately visible when a statement involving drawing primitives is executed (unless double buffering has been enabled on the particular window).

For example, consider the following program displaying a window with a number of vertical lines:

```
open System
open System.Windows.Forms
open System.Drawing

let f = new Form(Text="Hello world")
f.Paint.Add(fun args ->
    let g = args.Graphics

    for i = 0 to f.Width / 10 do
        g.DrawLine(Pens.Black, i*10, 0, i*10, f.Height)

)
f.Show()
Application.Run(f)
```

You can set the breakpoint at the DrawLine statement and start debugging the application, paying attention to move the debugger window in order to make the application form visible. If you continue the execution one statement at a time, you can see the lines appearing in the form. In this case, the interaction with the graphical system does not trigger an event but interacts directly with the Graphics object by emitting graphic primitives that are rendered immediately.

We have discussed the issues of debugging graphical applications by showing examples based on Windows Forms. The same considerations apply to all event systems where a thread is responsible for event notification. For graphical systems such as WPF based on the retention of graphic primitives, things work slightly differently, though analogous considerations can be made.

Debugging and Testing with F# Interactive

Functional programming languages have traditionally addressed many debugging and testing issues through the ability to interactively evaluate statements of the program and print the value of variables, inspecting the program state interactively. F# Interactive allows you to execute code fragments and quickly test them; moreover, the state of the FSI script can be inspected by querying values from the top level.

Development and testing using F# Interactive can effectively reduce development time, because code fragments can be evaluated more than once without having to recompile the entire system. The Visual Studio add-in makes this process even more productive because code is edited in the development environment with type checking and IntelliSense, and code can be sent to F# Interactive simply by selecting and pressing the Alt+Enter shortcut. In this scenario, the isPalindrome function from the previous section could have been developed incrementally and tested by simply invoking it with a test input argument. Once found and fixed, the function definition could have been evaluated again and tested for further bugs.

During software development it is common practice to write simple programs to test specific features of software (we will discuss this topic more extensively in the "Unit Testing" section). With F# Interactive, tests can be defined as functions stored into a file and selectively evaluated in Visual Studio. This approach can be useful in developing and defining new tests, but more specific tools can be used to run tests in a more organic way.

Controlling F# Interactive

As you saw in Chapter 9, programs run within F# Interactive have access to an object called fsi that lets you control some aspects of the interactive execution. This is contained in the assembly FSharp.Interactive.Settings.dll, which is automatically referenced in files ending .fsx and within F# Interactive sessions.

Table 18-2 shows some of the methods supported by this object.

Table 18-2. *Members on the fsi Object*

Member	Type	Description
fsi.FloatingPointFormat	string	Gets or sets the format used for floating-point numbers, based on .NET Formatting specifications
fsi.FormatProvider	System.IFormatProvider	Gets or sets the cultural format used for numbers, based on .NET Formatting specifications
fsi.PrintWidth	int	Gets or sets the print width used for formatted text output
fsi.PrintDepth	int	Gets or sets the depth of output for tree-structured data
fsi.PrintLength	int	Gets or sets the length of output for lists and other linear data structures
fsi.ShowProperties	bool	Gets or sets a flag indicating if properties should be printed for displayed values
fsi.AddPrinter	('a -> string) -> unit	Adds a printer for values compatible with the specific type 'a

Table 18-2. *Members on the* fsi *Object*

Member	Type	Description
fsi.AddPrintTransformer	('a -> obj) -> unit	Adds a printer that shows any values compatible with the specific type 'a as if they were values returned by the given function
fsi.CommandLineArgs	string[]	Gets the command-line arguments after ignoring the arguments relevant to the interactive environment and replacing the first argument with the name of the last script file

Some Common F# Interactive Directives

Table 18-3 shows some common directives accepted by F# Interactive, some of which correspond to options for the F# command-line compiler.

Table 18-3. *Some Commonly Used F# Interactive Directives*

Directive	Description
#r *path*	References a DLL. The DLL will be loaded dynamically when first required.
#I *path*	Adds the given search path to that used to resolve referenced DLLs.
#use *file*	Accepts input from the given file.
#load *file* ... *file*	Loads the given file(s) as if it had been compiled by the F# command-line compiler.
#time	Toggles timing information on/off.
#quit	Exits F# Interactive.

Understanding How F# Interactive Compiles Code

Although the F# Interactive is reminiscent of the read-eval-print loops of interpreted languages, it is substantially different because it compiles code rather than interprets it. Whenever a code fragment is typed on the top level, it gets compiled on the fly as part of a dynamic assembly, and it gets evaluated for side effects. This is particularly important for types because it is possible to create new ones at the top level and their dependencies may be tricky to fully understand. We start with an example of nontrivial use of F# Interactive that shows these intricacies, and we define the class APoint representing points using an angle and a radius:

```
type APoint(angle,radius) =
    member x.Angle = angle
    member x.Radius = radius
    new() = APoint(angle=0.0, radius=0.0)
```

If you create an instance of the class using F# Interactive, you can inspect the actual type by using the GetType method, and you get the following output:

```
> let p = APoint();;
val p : APoint

> p.GetType();;
val it : System.Type
= FSI_0002+APoint
    {Assembly = FSI-ASSEMBLY, Version=0.0.0.0, Culture=neutral, PublicKeyToken=null;
     AssemblyQualifiedName = "FSI_0002+APoint, FSI-ASSEMBLY, Version=0.0.0.0, ... }
```

Now suppose you want to extend the APoint class with an additional member that stretches the point radius of a given amount; it is natural to type the new definition of the class into the top level and evaluate it. And in fact F# Interactive does not complain about the redefinition of the type with the following:

```
type APoint(angle,radius) =
    member x.Angle = angle
    member x.Radius = radius
    member x.Stretch (k:double) = APoint(angle=x.Angle, radius=x.Radius + k)
    new() = APoint(angle=0.0, radius=0.0)
```

Since we have redefined the structure of APoint, we may be tempted to invoke the stretch method on it, but we get an error:

```
> p.Stretch(22.0);;
  p.Stretch(22.0);;
  --^^^^^^^^

stdin(2,2): error: FS0039: The field, constructor or member 'Stretch' is not defined.
```

To really understand what is happening, we create a new instance p2 of the class APoint and ask for the type:

```
> let p2 = APoint();;
val p2 : APoint

> p2.GetType();;
val it : System.Type
= FSI_0005+APoint
    {Assembly = FSI-ASSEMBLY, Version=0.0.0.0, Culture=neutral, PublicKeyToken=null;
     AssemblyQualifiedName = "FSI_0005+APoint, FSI-ASSEMBLY, Version=0.0.0.0, ... }
```

As you can see, the name of the type of p2 is FSI_0005+APoint, whereas the type of p is FSI_0002+APoint and is different. Under the hood, F# Interactive compiles types into different modules to ensure that types can be redefined and ensures that the most recent definition of a type is used. Besides, the older definitions are still available, and their instances are not affected by the type redefinition.

Understanding the inner mechanisms of F# Interactive is useful when using it to test F# programs because interactive evaluation is not always equivalent to running code compiled using the command-line compiler. On the other hand, the compiled nature of the system guarantees that the code executed by F# Interactive performs as well as compiled code.

Unit Testing

Software testing is an important task in software development; its goal is to ensure that a program or a library behaves according to the system specifications. It is a relevant area of software engineering research, and tools have been developed to support the increasing effort of software verification. Among a large number of testing strategies, unit testing has become rapidly popular because of software tools used to support this strategy. The core idea behind this approach is that programmers often write small programs to test single features of a system during development. When bugs are found, new unit tests are added to ensure that a particular bug does not occur again. Recently it has been proposed that testing should drive software development, because tests can be used while developing programs to check new code and later to conduct regression tests, ensuring that new features do not affect existing ones.

In this section, we will discuss how test units can be developed in F# using the NUnit tool from http://www.nunit.org, a freely available tool supporting this testing strategy. The tool was inspired from JUnit, a unit testing suite for the Java programming language, but the interface has been redesigned to take advantage of the extensible metadata provided by the CLR by means of custom attributes.

To make the experience more concrete, we'll start with an example and develop a very simple test suite for the isPalindrome function. The first choice you have to face is whether tests should be embedded into the application. If tests are created as a separated application, you can invoke only the public interface of your software, and features internal to the software cannot be tested directly; on the other hand, if you embed unit tests within the program, you introduce a dependency from the nunit.framework.dll assembly, and unit tests are available at runtime even where unneeded. Because the NUnit approach is based on custom attributes, performance is not affected in both cases. If tests are used during program development, it is more convenient to define them inside the program; in this case, conditional compilation may help to include them only in checked builds.

Listing 18-1 shows a test fixture for the isPalindrome function, which is a set of unit tests. Test fixtures are represented by a class annotated with the TestFixture custom attribute, and tests are instance methods with the signature unit -> unit and annotated with the Test custom attribute. Inside a test case, methods of the Assert class are used for testing conditions that have to be satisfied during the test. If one of these fails, the test is considered failed, and it is reported to the user by the tool that coordinates test execution.

Listing 18-1. *A Test Fixture for the* isPalindrome *Function*

```
#light

open System
open NUnit.Framework
open IsPalindrome

[<TestFixture>]
type Test() =

    let posTests(strings) =
        for s in strings do
            Assert.IsTrue(isPalindrome s,
                          sprintf "isPalindrome(\"%s\") must return true" s)

    let negTests(strings) =
        for s in strings do
            Assert.IsFalse(isPalindrome s,
                           sprintf "isPalindrome(\"%s\") must return false" s)

    [<Test>]
    member x.EmptyString () =
        Assert.IsTrue(isPalindrome(""),
                      "isPalindrome must return true on an empty string")

    [<Test>]
    member x.SingleChar () = posTests ["a"]

    [<Test>]
    member x.EvenPalindrome () = posTests [ "aa"; "abba"; "abaaba" ]

    [<Test>]
    member x.OddPalindrome () = posTests [ "aba"; "abbba"; "abababa" ]

    [<Test>]
    member x.WrongString () = negTests [ "as"; "F# is wonderful"; "Nice" ]
```

Test units are simply methods that invoke objects of the program and test return values to check that its behavior conforms to the specification. As you can see, we also introduced the posTests and negTests functions used in several tests. Developing unit tests is simply a matter of defining types containing the tests. Although it is possible to write a single test for a program, it is a good idea to have many small tests checking various features and different inputs. In this case, we have been able to introduce five tests for a simple function; of course, we did it to show the main idea, but nevertheless we have developed a test for each significant input to the function. We could have developed a single test with all the code used for the single tests together, but as you will see shortly, this would have reduced the ability of the test suite to spot problems in the program. In general, the choice of the granularity of a test suite for a program is up to the developer, and it is a matter of finding a reasonable trade-off between having a large number of unit tests checking very specific conditions and having a small number of unit tests checking broader areas of the program.

To compile the project, you must reference the `nunit.framework.dll` assembly; usually the `-R` compiler switch is used to ensure that the assembly is copied in the output directory of the program. Once the program has been compiled, you can start NUnit and open the executable.

As shown in Figure 18-4, the assembly containing the unit tests has been inspected using the reflection capabilities of the CLR, the classes annotated with the `TestFixture` attribute are identified by NUnit, and searched-for methods are annotated with the `Test` attribute. Initially, all the fixtures and the tests are marked with gray dots. When tests are run, the dot is colored green or red depending on the outcome of the particular test.

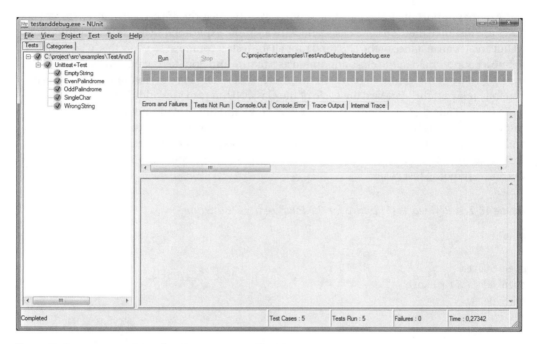

Figure 18-4. *Test unit of* `isPalindrome` *executed in NUnit*

If we reintroduce the original bug in the `isPalindrome` function and run NUnit again, `EmptyString` and `EvenPalindrome` will fail, the corresponding dots will be marked as red, and the Errors and Failures tab will contain details about the test failure. This is the main benefit of having a large number of small unit tests: tools may run them automatically and help identify problems in a program as well as the area potentially involved in the problem. Even in this simple example, a single test for the whole function would have indicated the problem with the function but failed to spot the kind of input responsible for the problem.

As every other piece of software, unit tests have to be maintained, documented, and updated to follow the evolution of the software for which they are designed. The number of test cases, organized in fixtures, tends to grow with the system during development, and in a large system it is possible to have thousands of these tests. Tools such as NUnit have features to control tests and allow you to run subsets of the whole set of test cases for a system. The notion of test fixtures that you have already encountered is a form of grouping: a test suite may contain different test fixtures that may group test cases for different aspects to be tested.

NUnit features a number of additional attributes to support the documentation and classification of test cases and test fixtures. The Description attribute allows associating a description with annotated test fixtures and test cases. Category and Culture attributes can be used to associate a category and a culture string with test fixtures and test cases; in addition, to provide more information about tests, NUnit allows filtering tests to be run using the content of the attributes. The ability to select the tests that must be run is important because running all tests for a system may require a significant amount of time. Other mechanisms to control the execution of tests are offered by the Ignore and Explicit attributes; the former can be used to disable a test fixture for a period without having to remove all the annotations, and the latter indicates that a test case or a fixture should be run only explicitly.

Another important area for testing nontrivial software is the life cycle of a test fixture. Test cases are instance methods of a class, and with a simple experiment, you can easily find that NUnit creates an instance of the class and runs all the tests it contains. To verify this, it is enough to define a counter field in the class annotated as a fixture and update its value every time a test is run; the value of the counter is consistently incremented for each test in the suite. Although you may relay on the standard life cycle of the class, NUnit provides additional annotations to indicate the code that must be run to set up a fixture and the corresponding code to free the resources at the end of the test; it is also possible to define a pair of methods that are run before and after each test case. The attributes controlling these aspects are TestFixtureSetUp and TestFixtureTearDown for annotating methods to set up and free a fixture and SetUp and TearDown for the corresponding test cases.

Listing 18-2. *A Refined Test Fixture for the isPalindrome Function*

```
#light

open System
open NUnit.Framework
open Debug

[<TestFixture;
  Description("Test fixture for the isPalindrome function")>]
type Test() =
    [<TestFixtureSetUp>]
    member x.InitTestFixture () =
        printfn "Before running Fixture"

    [<TestFixtureTearDown>]
    member x.DoneTestFixture () =
        printfn "After running Fixture"

    [<SetUp>]
    member x.InitTest () =
        printfn "Before running test"
```

```
[<TearDown>]
member x.DoneTest () =
    Console.WriteLine("After running test")

[<Test;
  Category("Special case");
  Description("An empty string is palindrome")>]
member x.EmptyString () =
    Assert.IsTrue(isPalindrome(""),
                    "isPalindrome must return true on an empty string")
```

Listing 18-2 shows a test fixture for the isPalindrome function that includes most of the attributes we have discussed and one test case. We mark the category of this test case as a "Special case." We also include a description for each test case and the methods invoked before and after the fixture and single test cases are run. The graphical interface of NUnit provides a tab reporting the output sent to the console, and when tests run, the output shows the invocation sequence of the setup and teardown methods.

The ability to set up resources for test cases may introduce problems in the unit testing; in particular, the setup and teardown methods of test fixtures must be treated carefully because the state shared by different test cases may affect the way they execute. Suppose, for instance, that a file is open during the setup of a fixture. This may save time because the file is opened only once and not for each test case. If a test case fails and the file is closed, the subsequent tests may fail because they assume that the file has been opened during the setup of the fixture. Nevertheless, there may be situations where the ability of preloading resources only once for a fixture can save a significant amount of time.

NUnit comes with two versions of the tool: one displaying the graphical interface shown in Figure 18-4 and a console version of the tool printing the results to the console. Both versions are useful; the windowed application is handy to produce reports about tests and interactively control the test processing, and the console version can be used to include the test process into a chain of commands invoked via scripts. Also, the output of the tool can be read by other programs to automate tasks after unit tests. A large number of command-line arguments are available in the console version to specify all the options available, including test filtering based on categories.

When a unit test fails, there is the problem of setting up a debugging session to check the application state and the reason of the failure. It is possible to debug tests using the Visual Studio debugger by simply configuring the Debug tab in the project properties in a similar way, as shown in Figure 18-5. Once configured, it is possible to set breakpoints in the code and start the debugging session as usual. This is important when code development is driven by tests, since new features can be implemented alongside test cases. This is a good way to capitalize on the small test programs that developers frequently write. These small programs become the test cases and can be collected without having to develop a new test program each time.

In the example shown in Figure 18-5, we pass a single argument to nunit-console.exe, the assembly containing the tests to be executed. It is also possible to specify an additional argument to filter the tests that must be run. In this example, if you set a breakpoint in one of the test cases annotated explicitly, the debugger will not stop, because by default these tests are skipped.

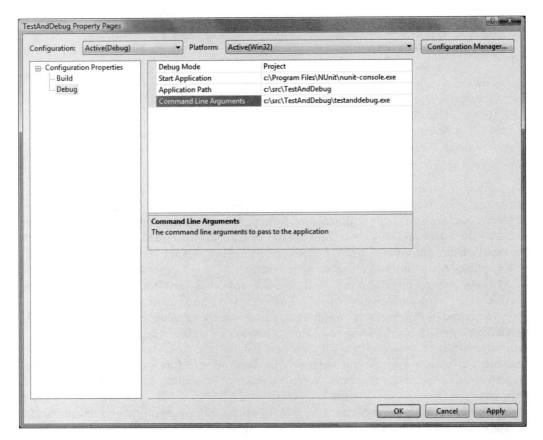

Figure 18-5. *Configuring an F# project for debugging NUnit test fixtures*

■**Note** In this section we have shown how you can use NUnit to define test cases using F#. NUnit is not the only tool for unit testing available for .NET. For example, Visual Studio 2005 includes powerful unit testing tools. NUnit also integrates with other software development tools such as NCover, a coverage testing tool capable of conducting coverage tests driven by test fixtures and test cases.

Summary

In this chapter, we introduced techniques and tools that you can employ to debug F# programs and automate the execution of unit tests. Since testing and debugging activities relate to the execution of programs, these tools tend to work on the compiled version of the program, relying on additional information such as metadata exposed through the reflection API or program debug database information files generated by compilers. Programming languages such as F# featuring programming abstractions don't map directly to the CLR intermediate language and type system, and as a result, the details of the compilation may surface when using these tools that operate on compiled assemblies. Nevertheless, these are valuable tools for developing large systems.

In the next chapter, we'll cover another set of software engineering issues for F# code: library design in the context of F# and .NET.

CHAPTER 19

Designing F# Libraries

This book deals with F#, a language situated in the context of .NET-based software construction and engineering. As an expert F# programmer, you will need more than a knowledge of the F# language; you will also need to use a range of software engineering tools and methodologies wisely to let you build software that is truly valuable for the situation where it is deployed. We touched on some important tools in the previous chapter. In this final chapter, we look at some of the methodological issues related to F# library design. In particular:

- We take a look at designing "vanilla" .NET libraries according to existing .NET design conventions and that minimize the use of F#-specific constructs.

- We briefly consider some of the elements of "functional programming design methodology," which offers important and deep insights into programming but doesn't address several important aspects of the library or component design problems.

- We give some specific suggestions on designing .NET and F# libraries, including naming conventions, how to design types and modules, and guidelines for using exceptions.

F# is often seen as a functional language, but, as we have emphasized in this book, it is in reality a multiparadigm language; the OO, functional, imperative, and language-manipulation paradigms are all well supported. That is, F# is a *function-oriented* language—many of the defaults are set up to encourage functional programming, but programming in the other paradigms is effective and efficient, and a combination is often best of all. A multiparadigm language brings challenges for library designs and coding conventions.

It is a common misconception that the functional and object-oriented programming methodologies are competing; it fact, they are largely orthogonal. However, it is important to note that functional programming does not directly solve many of the practical and prosaic issues associated with practical library design—for solutions to these problems, we must turn elsewhere. In the context of .NET programming, this means turning first to the *.NET Library Design Guidelines*, published online by Microsoft and as a book by Addison-Wesley.

In the official documents, the .NET library design is described in terms of conventions and guidelines for the use of the following constructs in public framework libraries:

- Assemblies, namespaces, and types (see Chapters 6 and 7 in this book)

- Classes and objects, containing properties, methods, and events (see Chapter 6)

- Interfaces (in other words, object interface types; see Chapter 6)

- .NET delegate types (mentioned briefly in Chapters 5 and 6)

- Enumerations (that is, enums from languages such as C#; mentioned briefly in Chapter 6)

- Constants (that is, constant literals from languages such as C#)

- Type parameters (that is, generic parameters; see Chapter 5)

From the perspective of F# programming, you must also consider the following constructs:

- Discriminated union types and their tags (Chapters 3 and 9)

- Record types and their fields (Chapter 3)

- Type abbreviations (Chapter 3)

- Values and functions declared using `let` and `let rec` (Chapter 3)

- Modules (Chapter 6)

- Named arguments (Chapter 6)

- Optional arguments (Chapter 6)

Framework library design is always nontrivial and often underestimated. F# framework and library design methodology is inevitably strongly rooted in the context of .NET object-oriented programming. In this chapter, we give our opinions on how you can go about approaching library design in the context of F# programming. The opinions are neither proscriptive nor "official." More official guidelines may be developed by the F# team and community at some future point, though ultimately the final choices lie with F# programmers and software architects.

■**Note** Some F# programmers choose to use library and coding conventions much more closely associated with OCaml, with Python, or with a particular application domain such as hardware verification. For example, OCaml coding uses underscores in names extensively, a practice avoided by the .NET Framework guidelines but used in places by the F# library itself. Some also choose to adjust coding conventions to their personal or team tastes.

Designing Vanilla .NET Libraries

One way to approach library design with F# is to simply design libraries according to the .NET Library Design Guidelines. This implicitly can mean avoiding or minimizing the use of F#-specific or F#-related constructs in the public API. We will call these libraries *vanilla .NET libraries*, as opposed to libraries that use F# constructs without restriction and are mostly intended for use by F# applications.

Designing vanilla .NET libraries means adopting the following rules:

- Apply the .NET Library Design Guidelines to the public API of your code. Your internal implementation can use any techniques you want.

- Restrict the constructs you use in your public APIs to those that are most easily used and recognized by .NET programmers. This means avoiding the use of some F# idioms in the public API.

- Use the .NET quality assurance tool FxCop to check the public interface of your assembly for compliance. Use FxCop exemptions where you deem necessary.

At the time of writing, here are some specific recommendations from the authors of this book:

- Avoid using F# list types 'a list in vanilla .NET APIs. Use seq<'a> or arrays instead of lists.

- Avoid using F# function types in vanilla .NET APIs. F# function values tend to be a little difficult to create from other .NET languages. Instead consider using .NET delegate types such as the overloaded System.Func<...> types available from .NET 3.5 onward.

- Avoid using F#-specific language constructs such as discriminated unions and optional arguments in vanilla .NET APIs.

For example, consider the code in Listing 19-1, which shows some F# code that we intend to adjust to be suitable for use as part of a .NET API.

Listing 19-1. *An F# Type Prior to Adjustment for Use as Part of a Vanilla .NET API*

```
open System
type APoint(angle,radius) =
    member x.Angle = angle
    member x.Radius = radius
    member x.Stretch(l) = APoint(angle=x.Angle, radius=x.Radius * l)
    member x.Warp(f) = APoint(angle=f(x.Angle), radius=x.Radius)
    static member Circle(n) =
        [ for i in 1..n -> APoint(angle=2.0*Math.PI/float(n), radius=1.0) ]
    new() = APoint(angle=0.0, radius=0.0)
```

The inferred F# type of this class is as follows:

```
type APoint =
    new : unit -> APoint
    new : angle:double * radius:double -> APoint
    static member Circle : n:int -> APoint list
    member Stretch : l:double -> APoint
    member Warp : f:(double -> double) -> APoint
    member Angle : double
    member Radius : double
```

Let's take a look at how this F# type will appear to a programmer using C# or another .NET library. The approximate C# "signature" is as follows:

```
// C# signature for the unadjusted APoint class of Listing 19-1

public class APoint {
    public APoint();
    public APoint(double angle, double radius);
    public static Microsoft.FSharp.Collections.List<APoint> Circle(int count);
    public APoint Stretch(double factor);
    public APoint Warp(Microsoft.FSharp.Core.FastFunc<double,double> transform);
    public double Angle { get; }
    public double Radius  { get; }
}
```

There are some important points to notice about how F# has chosen to represent constructs here. For example:

- Metadata such as argument names has been preserved.

- F# methods that take two arguments become C# methods that take two arguments.

- Functions and lists become references to corresponding types in the F# library.

The full rules for how F# types, modules, and members are represented in the .NET Common Intermediary Language are explained in the F# language reference on the F# website.

To make a .NET component, we place it in a file component.fs and compile this code into a strong-name signed DLL using the techniques from Chapter 7:

```
C:\fsharp> sn -k component.snk
C:\fsharp> fsc -a component.fs --version 1.0.0.0 --keyfile component.snk
```

Figure 19-1 shows the results of applying the Microsoft FxCop tool to check this assembly for compliance with the .NET Framework Design Guidelines.

Figure 19-1 reveals a number of problems with the assembly. For example, the .NET Framework Design Guidelines require the following:

- Types must be placed in namespaces.

- Public identifiers must be spelled correctly.

- Additional attributes must be added to assemblies related to .NET Security and Common Language Specification (CLS) compliance.

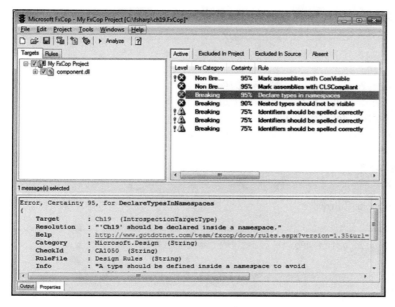

Figure 19-1. *Running FxCop on the code from Listing 19-1*

Listing 19-2 shows how to adjust this code to take these things into account.

Listing 19-2. *An F# Type After Adjustment for Use As Part of a Vanilla .NET API*

```fsharp
#light

namespace ExpertFSharp.Types

open System
open System.Security.Permissions

[<assembly: SecurityPermission(SecurityAction.RequestMinimum, Execution = true);
  assembly: System.Runtime.InteropServices.ComVisible(false);
  assembly: System.CLSCompliant(true);
  assembly: PermissionSet(SecurityAction.RequestOptional, Name = "Nothing")>]
type RadialPoint(angle,radius) =
    member x.Angle = angle
    member x.Radius = radius
    member x.Stretch(factor) = RadialPoint(angle=x.Angle, radius=x.Radius * factor)
    member x.Warp(transform:Converter<_,_>) =
        RadialPoint(angle=transform.Invoke(x.Angle), radius=x.Radius)
    static member Circle(count) =
        seq { for i in 1..count ->
                    RadialPoint(angle=2.0*Math.PI/float(count), radius=1.0) }
    new() = RadialPoint(angle=0.0, radius=0.0)
```

The inferred F# type of the code in Listing 19-2 is as follows:

```
type RadialPoint =
    new : unit -> RadialPoint
    new : angle:double * radius:double -> RadialPoint
    static member Circle : count:int -> seq<RadialPoint>
    member Stretch : factor:double -> RadialPoint
    member Warp : transform:System.Converter<double,double> -> RadialPoint
    member Angle : double
    member Radius : double
```

The C# signature is now as follows:

```
// C# signature for the unadjusted APoint class of Listing 19-2

public class RadialPoint {
    public RadialPoint();
    public RadialPoint(double angle, double radius);
    public static System.Collections.Generic.IEnumerable<RadialPoint> Circle(int count);
    public RadialPoint Stretch(double factor);
    public RadialPoint Warp(System.Converter<double,double> transform);
    public double Angle { get; }
    public double Radius  { get; }
}
```

The fixes we have made to prepare this type for use as part of a vanilla .NET library are as follows:

- We added several attributes as directed by the FxCop tool. You can find the meaning of these attributes in the MSDN documentation referenced by the FxCop warning messages.

- We adjusted several names; APoint , n, l, and f became RadialPoint, count, factor, and transform, respectively.

- We used a return type of seq<RadialPoint> instead of RadialPoint list by changing a list construction using [...] to a sequence construction using seq { ... }. An alternative option would be to use an explicit upcast ([...] :> seq<_>).

- We used the .NET delegate type System.Converter instead of an F# function type.

After applying these, the last remaining FxCop warning is simply telling us that namespaces with two to three types are not recommended.

The last two previous points are not essential, but, as mentioned, delegate types and sequence types tend to be easier for C# programmers to use than F# function and list types (F# function types are not compiled to .NET delegate types, partly for performance reasons). Note you can use FxCop exemptions to opt out of any of the FxCop rules, either by adding an exemption entry to FxCop itself or by attaching attributes to your source code.

■**Tip** If you're designing libraries for use from any .NET language, then there's no substitute for actually doing some experimental C# and Visual Basic programming to ensure that uses of your libraries look good from these languages. You can also use tools such as .NET Reflector and the Visual Studio Object Browser to ensure that libraries and their documentation appear as expected to developers. If necessary, enroll the help of a C# programmer and ask them what they think.

Understanding Functional Design Methodology

So far in this chapter you have looked at how to do "vanilla" .NET library design with F#. However, frequently F# programmers are designing libraries that are free to make more sophisticated use of F# and more or less assume that client users are using F# as well. To make the best use of F# in this situation, it is helpful to use functional programming design techniques as part of the library design process. For this reason, we'll next cover what functional programming brings to the table with regard to design methodology.

Understanding Where Functional Programming Comes From

Let's recap the origins of the major programming paradigms from a design perspective:

- Procedural programming arises from the fundamentally imperative nature of processing devices: microprocessors are state machines that manipulate data using side effects.

- Object-oriented programming arises from the need to encapsulate and reuse large objects such as those used for GUI applications.

- Functional programming differs in that it arises from one view of the *mathematics* of computation. That is, functional programming, in its purest form, is a way of describing computations using constructs that have useful mathematical properties, independent of their implementations.

For example, functional programming design methodology places great importance on constructs that are *compositional*. Let's take a simple example: in F#, we can map a function over a list of lists as follows:

```
open List
```

```
let map2 f inp = map (map f) inp
```

This is a simple example of the inherent compositionality of generic functions: the expression map f has produced a new function that can in turn be used as the argument to map. Understanding compositionality is the key to understanding much of what goes by the name of functional programming. For example, functional programmers aren't interested in a lack of side effects "just for the sake of it"—instead, they like programs that don't use side effects simply because they tend to be more compositional than those that do.

Functional programming often goes further by emphasizing *transformations that preserve behavior*. For example, we expect to be able to make the following refactorings to our code regardless of the function f or of the values inp, x, or rest:

```
open List
```

```
hd (x :: rest) replaced by x
```

```
concat (map (filter f) inp) replaced by filter f (concat inp)
```

Equations like these can be a source of useful documentation and test cases, and in some situations they can even be used to specify whole programs. Furthermore, good programmers routinely manipulate and optimize programs in ways that effectively assume these transformations are valid. Indeed, if these transformations are *not* valid, then it is easy to accidentally insert bugs when working with code. That said, many important transformation equations aren't guaranteed to *always* be valid—they typically hold only if additional assumptions are made—for example, in the first example the expression `rest` should not have side effects.

Transformational reasoning works well for some kinds of code and badly for others. Table 19-1 lists some of the F# and .NET constructs that are highly compositional and for which transformational reasoning tends to work well in practice.

Table 19-1. *Some Compositional F# Library Constructs Amenable to Equational Reasoning*

Constructs	Examples	Explanation
Base types	int, float	Code using immutable basic types is often relatively easy to reason about. There are some exceptions to the rule: the presence of NaN values and approximations in floating-point operations can make it difficult to reason about floating-point code.
Collections	Set<'a>, Map<'k,'v>	Immutable collection types are highly amenable to equational reasoning. For example, we expect equations such as Set.union Set.empty x = x to hold.
Control types	Lazy<'a>, Async<'a>	Control constructs are often highly compositional and have operators that allow you to combine them in interesting ways. For example, we expect equations such as (lazy x).Force() = x to hold.
Data abstractions	seq<'a>	F# sequences are not "pure" values, because they may access data stores using major side effects such as network I/O. However, in practice, uses of sequences tend to be very amenable to equational reasoning. This assumes that the side effects for each iteration of the sequence are isolated and independent.

Understanding Functional Design Methodology

Functional design methodology itself is thus rooted in compositionality and reasoning. In practice, it is largely about the following steps:

1. Deciding what values you're interested in representing. These values may range from simple integers to more sophisticated objects such expression trees from Chapter 9 or the asynchronous tasks from Chapter 13.

2. Deciding what operations are required to build these values, extracting information from them, and combining them and transforming them.

3. Deciding what equations and other algebraic properties should hold between these values and assessing whether these properties hold the implementation.

Steps 1 and 2 explain why functional programmers often prefer to define operations separately from types. As a result, functional programmers often find object-oriented programming strange because it emphasizes operations on *single* values, while functional programming emphasizes operations that *combine* values. This carries over to library implementation in functional programming, where you will often see types defined first and then modules containing operations on those types.

Because of this, one pattern that is quite common in the F# library is the following:

- The type is defined first.

- Then there is a module that defines the functions to work over the type.

- Finally, there is a with augmentation that adds the most common functions as members. We described augmentations in Chapter 6.

One simple example of functional programming methodology in this book is in Chapter 12, where you saw how a representation for propositional logic is defined using a type:

```
type Var =  string
type Prop =
    | And of Prop * Prop
    | Var of Var
    | Not of Prop
    | Exists of Var * Prop
    | False
```

Operations were then defined to combine and analyze values of type Prop. It would not make sense to define all of these operations as intrinsic to the Prop type, an approach often taken in OO design. In that same chapter, you saw another representation of propositional logic formulae where two logically identical formulae were normalized to the same representations. This is an example of step 3 of functional design methodology: the process of designing a type involves specifying the equations that should hold for values of that type.

You've seen many examples in this book of how object-oriented programming and functional programming can work very well together. For example, F# objects are often immutable but use OO features to group together some functionality working on the same data. Also, F# object interface types are often used as a convenient notation for collections of functions.

However, there are some tensions between functional programming and object-oriented design methodology. For example, when you define operations independently of data (that is, the functional style), it is simple to add a new operation, but modifying the type is more difficult.

In object-oriented programming using abstract and virtual methods, it is easy to add a new inherited type, but adding new operations (that is, new virtual methods) is difficult.

Similarly, functional programming emphasizes *simple but compositional* types, for example, functions and tuples. Object-oriented programming tends to involve creating many (often large and complex) types with considerable amounts of additional metadata. These are often less compositional but sometimes more self-documenting.

Finally, we mention that although functional programming does not provide a complete software design methodology, it is beautiful and powerful when it works, creating constructs that can be wielded with amazing expressivity and a very low bug rate. However, not all constructs in software design are amenable to compositional descriptions and implementations, and an over-reliance on "pure" programming can leave the programmer bewildered and abandoned when the paradigm doesn't offer useful solutions that scale in practice. This is the primary reason why F# is a multiparadigm language: to ensure that functional techniques can be combined with other techniques where appropriate.

■**Note** Some functional languages such as Haskell place strong emphasis on the equational reasoning principles. In F#, equational reasoning is slightly less important; however, it still forms an essential part of understanding what functional programming brings to the arena of design methodology.

Applying the .NET Design Guidelines to F#

In this section, we will present some additional recommendations for applying the .NET Library Design Guidelines to F# programming. We do this by making a series of recommendations that can be read as extensions to these guidelines.

Recommendation: Use the .NET naming and capitalization conventions where possible.

Table 19-2 summarizes the .NET guidelines for naming and capitalization in code. We have added our own recommendations for how these should be adjusted for some F# constructs. This table refers to the following categories of names:

- *PascalCase*: LeftButton and TopRight, for example

- *camelCase*: leftButton and topRight, for example

- *Verb*: A verb or verb phrase; performAction or SetValue, for example

- *Noun*: A noun or noun phrase; cost or ValueAfterDepreciation, for example

- *Adjective*: An adjective or adjectival phrase; Comparable or Disposable, for example

In general, the .NET guidelines strongly discourage the use of abbreviations (for example, "use OnButtonClick rather than OnBtnClick"). Common abbreviations such as Async for Asynchronous are tolerated. This guideline has historically been broken by functional programming; for example, List.iter uses an abbreviation for iterate. For this reason, using abbreviations tends to be tolerated to a greater degree in F# programming, though we discourage using additional abbreviations beyond those already found in existing F# libraries.

Acronyms such as XML are not abbreviations and are widely used in .NET libraries, though in uncapitalized form (Xml). Only well-known, widely recognized acronyms should be used.

The .NET guidelines say that casing cannot be used to avoid name collisions and that you must assume that some client languages are case insensitive. For example, Visual Basic is case insensitive.

Table 19-2. *Conventions Associated with Public Constructs in .NET Frameworks and Author-Recommended Extensions for F# Constructs*

Construct	Case	Part	Examples	Notes
Concrete types	PascalCase	Noun/ adjective	`List`, `DoubleComplex`	Concrete types are structs, classes, enumerations, delegates, records, and unions. Type names are traditionally lowercase in OCaml, and F# code has generally followed this pattern. However, as F# matures as a language, it is moving much more to follow standardized .NET idioms.
DLLs	PascalCase		`Microsoft.FSharp.Core.dll` `<Company>.<Component>.dll`	
Union tags	PascalCase	Noun	`Some`, `Add`, `Success`	Do not use a prefix in public APIs. Optionally use a prefix when internal, such as `type Teams = TAlpha | TBeta | TDelta`.
Event	PascalCase	Verb	`ValueChanged`	
Exceptions	PascalCase		`WebException`	
Field	PascalCase	Noun	`CurrentName`	
Interface types	PascalCase	Noun/ adjective	`IDisposable`	
Method	PascalCase	Verb	`ToString`	
Namespace	PascalCase		`Microsoft.FSharp.Core`	Generally use `<Organization>.<Technology>[.<Subnamespace>]`, though drop the organization if the technology is independent of organization.
Parameters	camelCase	Noun	`typeName`, `transform`, `range`	
let values (internal)	camelCase	Noun/verb	`getValue`, `myTable`	

Table 19-2. *Conventions Associated with Public Constructs in .NET Frameworks and Author-Recommended Extensions for F# Constructs (Continued)*

Construct	Case	Part	Examples	Notes
`let` values (external)	camelCase or PascalCase	Noun	`List.map`, `Dates.Today`	let-bound values are often public when following traditional functional design patterns. However, generally use PascalCase when the identifier can be used from other .NET languages.
Property	PascalCase	Noun/ adjective	`IsEndOfFile`, `BackColor`	Boolean properties generally use `Is` and `Can` and should be affirmative, as in `IsEndOfFile`, not `IsNotEndOfFile`.
Type parameters	Any	Noun/ adjective	`'a`, `'t`, `'Key`, `'Value`	

We generally recommend using lowercase for variable names, unless you're designing a library:

✓ `let x = 1`
✓ `let now = System.DateTime.Now`

We recommend using lowercase for all variable names bound in pattern matches, functions definitions, and anonymous inner functions. Functions may also use uppercase:

✗ `let add I J = I+J`
✓ `let add i j = i + j`

Use uppercase when the natural convention is to do so, as in the case of matrices, proper nouns, and common abbreviations such as I for the "identity" function:

✓ `let f (A:matrix) (B:matrix) = A+B`
✓ `let Monday = 1`
✓ `let I x = x`

We recommend using camelCase for other values, including the following:

- Ad hoc functions in scripts

- Values making up the internal implementation of a module

- Locally bound values in functions

✓ `let emailMyBossTheLatestResults = ...`
✓ `let doSomething () =`
       `let firstResult = ...`
       `let secondResult = ...`

Recommendation: Avoid using underscores in names.

The F# library uses underscore naming conventions to qualify some names. For example:

- Suffixes such as _left and _right

- Prefix verbs such as add_, remove_, try_, and is_, do_

- Prefix connectives such as to_, of_, from_, and for_

This is to ensure compatibility with OCaml. However, we recommend limiting the use of this style to the previous situations or avoiding it altogether, partly because it clashes with .NET naming conventions. Over time we expect the use of this style will be minimized in the F# libraries. We recommend you avoid using two underscores in a value name and always avoid three or more underscores.

Note No rules are "hard and fast," and some F# programmers ignore this advice and use underscores heavily, partly because functional programmers often dislike extensive capitalization. Furthermore, OCaml code uses underscores everywhere. However, beware that the style is often disliked by others who have a choice about whether to use it. It has the advantage that abbreviations can be used in identifiers without them being run together.

Recommendation: Follow the .NET guidelines for exceptions.

The .NET Framework Design Guidelines give good advice on the use of exceptions in the context of all .NET programming. Some of these guidelines are as follows:

- Do not return error codes. Exceptions are the main way of reporting errors in frameworks.

- Do not use exceptions for normal flow of control. Although this technique is often used in languages such as OCaml, it is bug-prone and furthermore slow on .NET. Instead consider returning a None option value to indicate failure.

- Do document all exceptions thrown by your code when a function is used incorrectly.

- Where possible throw existing exceptions in the System namespaces.

- Do not throw System.Exception or System.SystemException.

- Use failwith, failwithf, raise System.ArgumentException, and raise System.InvalidOperationException as your main techniques to throw exceptions.

Note Other exception-related topics covered by the .NET guidelines include advice on designing custom exceptions, wrapping exceptions, choosing exception messages, and special exceptions to avoid throwing (that is, OutOfMemoryException, ExecutionEngineException, COMException, SEHException, StackOverflowException, NullReferenceException, AccessViolationException, or InvalidCastException).

Recommendation: Consider using option values for return types instead of raising exceptions.

The .NET approach to exceptions is that they should be "exceptional"; that is, they should occur relatively infrequently. However, some operations (for example, searching a table) may fail frequently. F# option values are an excellent way to represent the return types of these operations.

Recommendation: Follow the .NET guidelines for value types.

The .NET guidelines give good guidance about when to use .NET value types (that is, structs, which you saw introduced in Chapter 6). In particular, they recommend using a struct only when the following are all true:

- A type logically represents a single value similar to a primitive type.

- It has an instance size smaller than 16 bytes.

- It is immutable.

- It will not have to be boxed frequently (that is, converted to/from the type System.Object).

Recommendation: Consider using explicit signature files for your framework.

Explicit signature files were described in Chapter 7. Using explicit signatures files for framework code ensures that you know the full public surface of your API and can cleanly separate public documentation from internal implementation details.

Recommendation: Consider avoiding the use of implementation inheritance for extensibility.

Implementation inheritance is described in Chapter 6. In general, the .NET guidelines are quite agnostic with regard to the use of implementation inheritance. In F#, implementation inheritance is used more rarely than in other .NET languages. The main rationale for this has been given in Chapter 6, where you also saw many alternative techniques for designing and implementing object-oriented types using F#. However, implementation inheritance is used heavily in GUI frameworks.

■**Note** Other object-oriented extensibility topics discussed in the .NET guidelines include events and call-backs, virtual members, abstract types and inheritance, and limiting extensibility by sealing classes.

Recommendation: Use properties and methods for attributes and operations essential to a type.

For example:

```
✓ type HardwareDevice with
    ...
    member ID: string
    member SupportedProtocols: seq<Protocol>
```

Consider supporting using methods for the intrinsic operations essential to a type:

```
✓ type HashTable<'k,'v> with
    ...
    member Add           : 'k * 'v -> unit
    member ContainsKey  : 'k -> bool
    member ContainsValue : 'v -> bool
```

Consider using static methods to hold a Create function instead of revealing object constructors:

```
✓ type HashTable<'k,'v> with
       static member Create : IHashProvider<'k> -> HashTable<'k,'v>
```

Recommendation: Avoid revealing concrete data representations such as records.

Where possible, avoid revealing concrete representations such as records, fields, and implementation inheritance hierarchies in framework APIs.

The rationale for this is that one of the overriding aims of library design is to avoid revealing concrete representations of objects. For example, the concrete representation of System. DateTime values is not revealed by the external, public API of the .NET library design. At runtime the Common Language Runtime knows the committed implementation that will be used throughout execution. However, compiled code does not itself pick up dependencies on the concrete representation.

Recommendation: Use active patterns to hide the implementations of discriminated unions.

Where possible, avoid using large discriminated unions in framework APIs, especially if you expect there is a chance that the representation of information in the discriminated union will undergo revision and change. For frameworks, you should typically hide the type altogether or use active patterns to reveal the ability to pattern match over language constructs. We described active patterns in Chapter 9.

This does not apply to the use of discriminated unions internal to an assembly or to an application. Likewise, it doesn't apply if the only likely future change is the addition of further cases and you are willing to require that client code be revised for these cases. Finally, active patterns can incur a performance overhead, and this should be measured and tested, though their benefits will frequently outweigh this cost.

■**Note** The rationale for this is that using large, volatile discriminated unions freely in APIs will encourage people to use pattern matching against these discriminated union values. This is appropriate for unions that do not change. However, if you reveal discriminated unions indiscriminately, you may find it very hard to version your library without breaking user code.

Recommendation: Use object interface types instead of tuples or records of functions.

In Chapter 5 you saw various ways to represent a dictionary of operations explicitly, such as using tuples of functions or records of functions. In general, we recommend you use object interface types for this purpose, because the syntax associated with implementing them is generally more convenient.

Recommendation: Understand when currying is useful in functional programming APIs.

Currying is the name used when functions take arguments in the "iterated" form, that is, when the functions can be partially applied. For example, the following function is curried:

```
let f x y z = x + y + z
```

This is not:

```
let f (x,y,z) = x + y + z
```

Here are some of our guidelines for when to use currying and when not to use it:

- Use currying freely for rapid prototyping and scripting. Saving keystrokes can be very useful in these situations.

- Use currying when partial application of the function is highly likely to give a useful residual function (see Chapter 3).

- Use currying when partial application of the function is necessary to permit useful precomputation (see Chapter 8).

- Avoid using currying in vanilla .NET APIs or APIs to be used from other .NET languages.

When using currying, place arguments in order from the least varying to the most varying. This will make partial application of the function more useful and lead to more compact code. For example, List.map is curried with the function argument first because a typical program usually applies List.map to a handful of known function values but many different concrete list values. Likewise, you saw in Chapters 8 and 9 how recursive functions can be used to traverse tree structures. These traversals often carry an environment. The environment changes relatively rarely—only when you traverse the subtrees of structures that bind variables. For this reason, the environment is the first argument.

When using currying, consider the importance of the pipelining operator; for example, place function arguments first and object arguments last.

F# also uses currying for let-bound binary operators and combinators:

✓ let divmod n m = ...
✓ let map f x = ...
✓ let fold f z x = ...

However, see Chapters 6 and 8 for how to define operators as static members in types, which are not curried.

Recommendation: Use tuples for return values, arguments, and intermediate values.

Here is an example of using a tuple in a return type:

✓ val divmod : int -> int -> int * int

Some Recommended Coding Idioms

In this section, we look at a small number of recommendations when writing implementation code, as opposed to library designs.

We don't give many recommendations on formatting, because formatting code is relatively simple for #light indentation-aware code. We do give a couple of formatting recommendations that early readers of this book asked about.

Recommendation: Use the standard operators.

The following operators are defined in the F# standard library and should be used wherever possible instead of defining equivalents. Using these operators tends to make code much easier to read, so we strongly recommend it. This is spelled out explicitly because OCaml doesn't support all of these operators, and thus F# users who have first learned OCaml are often not aware of this.

```
f >> g    -- forward composition
g << f    -- reverse composition
x |> f    -- forward pipeline
f <| x    -- reverse pipeline

x |> ignore    -- throwing away a value

x + y     -- overloaded addition (including string concatenation)
x - y     -- overloaded subtraction
x * y     -- overloaded multiplication
x / y     -- overloaded division
x % y     -- overloaded modulus

x <<< y  -- bitwise left shift
x >>> y  -- bitwise right shift
x ||| y  -- bitwise left shift, also for working with enumeration flags
x &&& y  -- bitwise right shift, also for working with enumeration flags
x ^^^ y  -- bitwise left shift, also for working with enumeration flags

x && y   -- lazy/short-cut "and"
x || y   -- lazy/short-cut "or"
```

Recommendation: Place pipeline operator |> at the start of a line.

People often ask how to format pipelines. We recommend this style:

```
let methods =
    System.AppDomain.CurrentDomain.GetAssemblies
    |> List.of_array
    |> List.map (fun assem -> assem.GetTypes())
    |> Array.concat
```

Recommendation: Format object expressions using the member syntax.

People often ask how to format object expressions. We recommend this style:

```
let thePlayers =
      { new Organization() with
            member x.Chief = "Peter Quince"
            member x.Underlings =
                [ "Francis Flute"; "Robin Starveling";
                  "Tom Snout"; "Snug"; "Nick Bottom"]
        interface IDisposable with
            member x.Dispose() = ()  }
```

■**Note** The discussion of F# design and engineering issues in Chapters 18 and 19 has necessarily been limited. In particular, we haven't covered topics such as aspect-oriented programming, design and modeling methodologies, software quality assurance, or software metrics, all of which are outside the scope of this book.

Summary

In this chapter, we covered some of the rules you might apply to library design in F#, particularly taking into account the idioms and traditions of .NET. We also considered some of the elements of "functional programming" design methodology, which offers many important and deep insights. Finally, we gave some specific suggestions on designing .NET and F# libraries. That concludes our tour of F#, and we hope you enjoy a long and productive career coding in the language.

F# Brief Language Guide

This appendix describes the essential constructs of the F# language in a compact form. You can find a full guide to the F# language in the F# Language Specification on the F# website.

Comments and Attributes

Comments (Chapter 2)

```
// comment

(* comment *)

/// XML doc comment
let x = 1
```

Attaching Attributes (Chapter 9)

```
[<Obsolete("Deprecated at 1.2")>]
type Type =
    ...

[<Conditional("DEBUG")>]
let Function(x) =

[<assembly: Note("argument")>]
do ()
```

Basic Types and Literals

Basic Types and Literals (Chapter 3)

```
sbyte       = System.SByte        76y
byte        = System.Byte         76uy
int16       = System.Int16        76s
uint16      = System.UInt16       76us
int32       = System.Int32        76
uint32      = System.UInt32       76u
int64       = System.Int64        76L
uint64      = System.UInt64       76UL
string      = System.String       "abc", @"c:\etc"
single      = System.Single       3.14f
double      = System.Double       3.14, 3.2e5
char        = System.Char         '7'
nativeint   = System.IntPtr       76n
unativeint  = System.UIntPtr      76un
bool        = System.Boolean      true, false
unit        = Microsoft.FSharp.Core.Unit  ()
```

Basic Type Abbreviations

```
int8     = sbyte
uint8    = byte
int      = int32
float32  = single
float    = double
```

Types

Types (Chapters 3 and 5)

ident	Named type
ident<type,...,type>	Type instantiation
type * ... * *type*	Tuple type
type[]	Array type
#*type*	Flexible type (accepts any subtype)
'*ident*	Variable type
type -> *type*	Function type

Type instantiations can be postfix:`int list`

Patterns and Matching

Patterns (Chapters 3 and 9)

_	Wildcard pattern
literal	Constant pattern
ident	Variable pattern
(*pat*, …, *pat*)	Tuple pattern
[*pat*; …; *pat*]	List pattern
[| *pat*; …; *pat* |]	Array pattern
{ *id=pat*; …; *id=pat* }	Record pattern
id(*pat*, …, *pat*)	Union case pattern
id expr … expr (*pat*, …, *pat*)	Active pattern
pat | *pat*	"Or" pattern
pat & *pat*	"Both" pattern
pat as *id*	Named pattern
:? *type*	Type test pattern
:? *type* as *id*	Type cast pattern
`null`	Null pattern

Matching (Chapter 3)

```
match expr with
| pat -> expr
...
| pat -> expr
```

Note: Rules of a match may use
```
| pat when expr -> expr
```

Active Patterns (Chapter 9)

```
let (|Tag1|Tag2|) inp = …
let (|Tag1|_|)    inp = …
let (|Tag1|)      inp = …
```

Functions, Composition, and Pipelining

Function values (Chapter 3)

`fun` *pat … pat* -> *expr*	Function
`function` | *pat* -> *expr* … | *pat* -> *expr*	Match function

Application and Pipelining (Chapter 3)

`f x`	Application
`x |> g`	Forward pipe
`f >> g`	Function composition

Binding and Control Flow

Control Flow (Chapters 3 and 4)	
expr *expr*	Sequencing
do *expr* *expr*	Sequencing
for *id* = *expr* to *expr* do *expr*	Simple loop
for *pat* in *expr* do *expr*	Sequence loop
while *expr* do *expr*	While loop

Binding and Scoping (Chapter 3)	
let *pat* = *expr* *expr*	Value binding
let *id args* = *expr* *expr*	Function binding
let rec *id args* = *expr* *expr*	Recursive binding
use *pat* = *expr* *expr*	Auto dispose binding

Syntax Forms Without Indentation

```
let pat = expr in expr
while expr do expr done
for pat in expr do expr done
expr ; expr
do expr in expr
```

Exceptions

Exception Handling	

try
    expr
with
    | *pat* -> *expr*
    | *pat* -> *expr*
	Handling

try
    expr
finally
    expr
	Compensation

use *id* = *expr*	Automatic Dispose

Some Exceptions (Chapter 4)

```
Microsoft.FSharp.Core.FailureException
System.MatchFailureException
System.InvalidArgumentException
System.StackOverflowException
```

Raising Exceptions (Common Forms)	
raise *expr*	Throw exception
failwith *expr*	Throw FailureException

Catch and Rethrow

```
try expr
with
    | :? ThreadAbortException ->
    printfn "thrown!"
    rethrow ()
```

Tuples, Arrays, Lists, and Collections

Tuples (Chapter 3)

`(expr, …, expr)`	Tuple
`fst expr`	First of pair
`snd expr`	Second of pair

F# Lists (Chapter 3)

`[ expr; …; expr ]`	List
`[ expr..expr ]`	Range list
`[ comp-expr ]`	Generated list
`expr :: expr`	List cons
`expr @ expr`	List append

F# Options (Chapter 3)

`None`	No value
`Some(expr)`	With value

Arrays (Chapter 4)

`[| expr; …; expr |]`	Array literal
`[| expr..expr |]`	Range array
`[| comp-expr |]`	Generated array
`Array.create size expr`	Array creation
`Array.init size expr`	Array init
`arr.[expr]`	Lookup
`arr.[expr] <- expr`	Assignment
`arr.[expr..expr]`	Slice
`arr.[expr..]`	Right slice
`arr.[..expr]`	Left slice

See Chapter 4 for multi-dimensional operators.

Some Other Collection Types

```
System.Collections.Generic.Dictionary
System.Collections.Generic.List
System.Collections.Generic.SortedList
System.Collections.Generic.SortedDictionary
System.Collections.Generic.Stack
System.Collections.Generic.Queue
Microsoft.FSharp.Collections.Set
Microsoft.FSharp.Collections.Map
```

Operators

Overloaded Arithmetic (Chapter 3)

x + y	Addition
x - y	Subtraction
x * y	Multiplication
x / y	Division
x % y	Remainder/modulus
-x	Unary negation

Overloaded Math Operators

abs, acos, atan, atan2,
ceil, cos, cosh, exp,
floor, log, log10, pow,
pown, sqrt, sin, sinh,
tan, tanh

Overloaded Conversion Operators

byte, sbyte, int16, uint16,
int, int32, uint32, int64,
uint64, float32, float, single,
double, nativeint,
unativeint

Mutable Locals (Chapter 4)

let mutable *var* = *expr*	Declare
var	Read
var <- *expr*	Update

Mutable Reference Cells (Chapter 4)

ref *expr*	Allocate
!*expr*	Read
expr.Value	Read
expr := *expr*	Assign

Booleans

not *expr*	Boolean negation
expr && *expr*	Boolean "and"
expr || *expr*	Boolean "or"

Overloaded Bitwise Operators (Chapter 3)

x >>> y	Shift right
x <<< y	Shift left
x &&& y	Bitwise logical and
x ||| y	Bitwise logical or
x ^^^ y	Bitwise exclusive or
~~ x	Bitwise logical not

Generic Comparison and Hashing

hash x	Generic hashing
x = y	Generic equality
x <> y	Generic inequality
compare x y	Generic comparison
x >= y, x <= y,	
x > y, x < y,	
min x y, max x y	

Note: Records, tuples, arrays and unions automatically implement structural equality and hashing (see Chapters 5 and 8)

Indexed Lookup and Assignment (Chapter 4)

expr.[*idx*]	Lookup
expr.[*idx*] <- *expr*	Assignment
expr.[*idx*..*idx*]	Slice
expr.[*idx*..]	Right slice
expr.[..*idx*]	Left slice

See Chapter 4 for multidimensional operators

Object-Related Operators and Types

type obj = System.Object

box(x)	Convert to type obj
unbox<*type*>(x)	Extract from type obj
typeof<*type*>	Extract System.Type
x :> *type*	Static cast to supertype
x :?> *type*	Dynamic cast to subtype

Type Definitions and Objects

Union Types (Chapters 3 and 6)

```
type UnionType =
  | TagA of type * … * type
  | TagB of type * … * type
```

Record Types (Chapters 3 and 6)

```
type Record =
  { Field1: type
    Field2: type }
```

Object Expressions (Chapter 6)

```
{ new IObject with
    member x.Prop1 = expr
    member x.Meth1 args = expr }

{ new Object() with
    member x.Prop1 = expr
    interface IObject with
      member x.Meth1 args = expr
    interface IWidget with
      member x.Meth1 args = expr }
```

Implementation Inheritance

```
type ObjectType(args) as x =
  inherit BaseType(expr) as base
  …
```

Constructed Class Types (Chapter 6)

```
type ObjectType(args) =
    let internalValue = expr
    let internalFunction args = expr
    let mutable internalState = expr
    member x.Prop1 = expr
    member x.Meth2 args = expr
```

Object Interface Types (Chapter 6)

```
type IObject =
    interface ISimpleObject
    abstract Prop1 : type
    abstract Meth2 : type -> type
```

Some Special Members

```
member x.Prop                setter property
  with get() = expr
  and  set(v) = expr

member x.Item                indexer property
  with get(idx) = expr
  and  set(idx,v) = expr

static member (+) (x,y) = expr  operator
```

Named and Optional Arguments for Members

```
member obj.Method(?optArgA)          Declaring optional arg

new ObjectType(x=expr, y=expr)       Object construction with properties
obj.Method(optArgA=expr, PropB=expr) Call with optional args and properties
```

Namespaces and Modules

<table>
<tr><td>

Namespaces (Chapter 7)

```
namespace Org.Product.Feature

type TypeOne =
    ...

module ModuleTwo =
    ...
```

</td><td>

Files As Modules (Chapter 7)

```
module Org.Product.Feature.Module

type TypeOne =
    ...

module ModuleTwo =
    ...
```

</td></tr>
</table>

Sequence Expressions and Workflows

Sequence Expressions and Workflows (Chapters 3, 9, and 13)

`[ comp-expr ]`	Generated list
`[| comp-expr |]`	Generated array
`seq { comp-expr }`	Generated sequence
`async { comp-expr }`	Asynchronous workflow
`ident { comp-expr }`	Arbitrary workflow

Syntax for Workflows

`let! pat = expr` `comp-expr`	Execute and bind computation
`let pat = expr` `comp-expr`	Execute and bind expression
`do! expr` `comp-expr`	Execute computation
`do expr` `comp-expr`	Execute expression
`if expr then comp-expr else comp-expr`	Conditional workflow
`if expr then comp-expr`	Conditional workflow
`while expr do comp-expr`	Repeated workflow
`for pat in expr do comp-expr`	Enumeration loop
`try comp-expr with pat -> expr`	Workflow with catch
`try comp-expr finally expr`	Workflow with compensation
`use pat = expr in comp-expr`	Workflow with auto dispose
`return expr`	Return expression
`return! expr`	Return computation
`yield expr` (or `-> expr`)	Yield expression (for sequences only)
`yield! expr` (or `->> expr`)	Yield sequence (for sequences only)

Index

You Need the Companion eBook

Your purchase of this book entitles you to buy the companion PDF-version eBook for only $10. Take the weightless companion with you anywhere.

We believe this Apress title will prove so indispensable that you'll want to carry it with you everywhere, which is why we are offering the companion eBook (in PDF format) for $10 to customers who purchase this book now. Convenient and fully searchable, the PDF version of any content-rich, page-heavy Apress book makes a valuable addition to your programming library. You can easily find and copy code—or perform examples by quickly toggling between instructions and the application. Even simultaneously tackling a donut, diet soda, and complex code becomes simplified with hands-free eBooks!

Once you purchase your book, getting the $10 companion eBook is simple:

❶ Visit **www.apress.com/promo/tendollars/**.

❷ Complete a basic registration form to receive a randomly generated question about this title.

❸ Answer the question correctly in 60 seconds, and you will receive a promotional code to redeem for the $10.00 eBook.